Music, Theater, and Cultural Transfer

Music, Theater, and Cultural Transfer

PARIS, 1830–1914

*Edited by Annegret Fauser
and Mark Everist*

THE UNIVERSITY OF CHICAGO PRESS   *Chicago and London*

ANNEGRET FAUSER is professor of music at the University of North Carolina, Chapel Hill, and the author of *Musical Encounters at the 1889 Paris World's Fair.* MARK EVERIST is professor of music at the University of Southampton and the author of *Giacomo Meyerbeer and Music Drama in Nineteenth-Century Paris.*

The University of Chicago Press, Chicago 60637
The University of Chicago Press, Ltd., London
©2009 by The University of Chicago
All rights reserved. Published 2009
Printed in the United States of America

18 17 16 15 14 13 12 11 10 09   1 2 3 4 5

ISBN-13: 978-0-226-23926-2
ISBN-13: 978-0-226-23927-9
ISBN-10: 0-226-23926-8
ISBN-10: 0-226-23927-6

Library of Congress Cataloging-in-Publication Data

Music, theater, and cultural transfer : Paris, 1830–1914 / edited by
Annegret Fauser and Mark Everist.
p. cm.
Rev. papers from the international symposium "The Institutions
of Opera in Paris from the July Revolution to the Dreyfus Affair,"
held in Chapel Hill and Durham, N.C., Sept. 24–26, 2004.
Includes bibliographical references and index.
ISBN-13: 978-0-226-23926-2 (cloth : alk. paper)
ISBN-13: 978-0-226-23927-9 (pbk. : alk. paper)
ISBN-10: 0-226-23926-8 (cloth : alk. paper)
ISBN-10: 0-226-23927-6 (pbk. : alk. paper)
1. Opera—France—Paris—19th century—Congresses. 2. Opera—France—Paris—20th
century—Congresses. 3. Musical theater—France—Paris—History—19th century—
Congresses. 4. Musical theater—France—Paris—History—20th century—Congresses.
I. Fauser, Annegret. II. Everist, Mark. III. International symposium "The Institutions
of Opera in Paris from the July Revolution to the Dreyfus Affair" (2004 : Chapel Hill
and Durham, N.C.). IV. Title: Music, theater, and cultural transfer.
ML1727.8.P2M85 2009
782.10944′36109034—dc22
2008045154

In memory of

M. ELIZABETH C. BARTLET

our inspiration, friend,
teacher, colleague

CONTENTS

ACKNOWLEDGMENTS

The present volume is based largely on revised contributions to "The Institutions of Opera in Paris from the July Revolution to the Dreyfus Affair," an international symposium co-organized by M. Elizabeth C. Bartlet and Annegret Fauser and held jointly in Chapel Hill and Durham by the University of North Carolina at Chapel Hill and Duke University, 24–26 September 2004. We are grateful to the National Endowment for the Humanities, Duke University, and the University of North Carolina at Chapel Hill for their generous support for this event. The National Endowment for the Humanities also supported the preparation of this volume. We would like to thank Elizabeth Arndt in particular for making our work with this venerable federal institution a pleasure. We are also grateful to Duke University for supporting financially the publication of this volume, thus honoring the memory of one of that university's finest scholars.

The editors are grateful for the generosity we experienced from colleagues in the preparation of this volume. Philip Gossett warmly encouraged publication of the essay volume and suggested to us that we should work with the press of Beth Bartlet's alma mater. Kathleen Hansell, editor extraordinaire of the University of Chicago Press, has overseen the genesis of the present volume with wise advice and great enthusiasm, from the first discussions with Beth and Annegret to the final stages of publication. The two readers for this volume went into great detail in their reports, sharing their rich expertise, which only increased the quality of the book. Alicia Levin contributed significantly to the development of the iconographic program in addition to writing the chronology, volunteering her time and expertise to make this book so much more attractive. Joyce Kurpiers assisted with the scanning of the illustrations. William Gibbons very kindly volunteered his time to set the music examples in such professional manner. All of our authors went to great lengths to respond to our suggestions; it was a pleasure working with them. We would like to thank Barbara Norton for her fine and thoughtful work during the copy-editing process, and the team of the University of Chicago Press for putting together a beautiful book. Last but not least, our spouses, Tim Carter and Jeanice Brooks, who were both friends of Beth, did what they could to ease the inevitable stress during the publication of this volume. To all of you, heartfelt thanks. We hope that this volume would have made Beth proud.

A. F. and M. E.
21 April 2008

FIGURE O.I. M. Elizabeth C. Bartlet (1948–2005). This photograph from 1990 shows Bartlet surrounded by posters reflecting two key areas of her research. Those from La Scala (Milan) and the Royal Opera House Covent Garden (London) announce performances of her *Guillaume Tell* edition; the third poster publicizes an international bicentennial conference on music of the French Revolution of 1789. © Kate Bartlet.

INTRODUCTION

Nothing was more central to cultural life in nineteenth-century Paris than the lyric stage. The capital's theaters and opera houses served as a showcase not only for the artworks themselves but for France as a nation. Works and their performances were the focus of aesthetic discussion in both the general press and specialized music journals, and Walter Benjamin's much-cited characterization of Paris as the "capital of the nineteenth century" points to the wider impact of Parisian stage music in Europe, the United States, and Australia.[1] French stage music was ever-present in the Parisian and international press when political incidents, social affairs, and artistic achievement were reported on. Novels—from Honoré de Balzac's *Gambara* (1837) to Gaston Leroux's *Phantom of the Opera* (1912)—and paintings and sculptures (especially by Edgar Degas) captured the nineteenth century's fascination with the opera house, its performers, and its audience. And even in the late twentieth century, films such as Jean-Jacques Beinex's *Diva* (1981) related the magic of opera to Paris.

From its beginnings, however, French opera developed within a tightly controlled institutional field. Since its foundation in 1672, the Paris Opéra had been beholden to the state, whether in the form of the absolutist monarch Louis XIV or in that of the government of the Third Republic. Other Parisian opera houses—the Opéra-Comique, the Théâtre-Italien, and the Théâtre-Lyrique—were similarly subject to government regulation, while still other forms of music theater offered various attempts at breaking the mold of institutionalized opera. Each institution was defined not only as and for itself, but also in relationship to its rivals. Both written and unwritten laws distinguished the houses from each other and affected choice of repertoire, performance forces, the composition of their audience, and the reception of works they promoted.

But the acknowledgment of this institutional context has also created a problematic approach to the understanding of lyric theater in France. Too often, institutions such as the Opéra were read as the cause rather than an effect of artistic production and consumption. Whether in studies of the Opéra in the nineteenth century, for ex-

---

1. Walter Benjamin coined this phrase in his 1935 essays "Paris, die Hauptstadt des XIX. Jahrhunderts" and "Paris, capitale du XIXe siècle," in which he outlines the issues to be discussed in his Arcades project. See Walter Benjamin, *Das Passagenwerk,* ed. Rolf Tiedemann (Frankfurt am Main: Edition Suhrkamp, 1983), 1:45–77.

ample by Castil-Blaze in 1855, or in more recent monographs by Jane Fulcher and Anselm Gerhard, or in the 2003 *Cambridge Companion to Grand Opera,* not composers but Parisian institutions of lyric theater—especially the Académie (Royale, Impériale, or Nationale) de Musique—were cast in the role of agents of artistic creation.[2] In contrast to scholars such as Joseph Kerman, whose dictum that "in opera, the dramatist is the composer" embodies the composer-centered approach to this complex art form, such institutional biographies replaced the individual creator with the opera house as the "hero" of the historical or biographical narrative.[3]

However, this act of superimposition brought about two concerns that proved tricky. On the one hand, the institution in question often was seen in isolation from the culture that spawned it. Thus studies of the Opéra reflect its character as the nation's "first house." Indeed both its prestige and its funding reflected this centrality. *Grand opéra* became synonymous with the spectacular realities of Parisian music theater during the nineteenth century and even afterward. The most thoroughly researched institution of French operatic life, it is nonetheless too often seen as separate from the complex network of musical institutions in Paris. On the other hand, the attribution of creative agency to the Parisian institutions replicates (often inadvertently) notions of nineteenth-century value judgments: although Wagner's operas or Beethoven's symphonies have been and are read as artistic, cultural, social, or political artifacts and celebrated for their transcendental qualities, French opera was and is often seen as first and foremost a product of the conventions of this institutional matrix. Rare are studies such as Steven Huebner's *French Opera at the* fin de siècle: *Wagnerism, Nationalism, and Style,* in which musical composition—though seen in the context of the institution—is accorded agency of its own, with aesthetic concerns considered just as important as institutional ones.[4] The tension between institutional convention and artistic creation often remained unspoken in musicological accounts of the reception of French lyric production, yet operas by Mozart, Tchaikovsky, Wagner or even (ironically) Debussy were seen as transcending their historical and institutional context; indeed, their intrinsic aesthetic value was celebrated because of their ability to shed the burden of history (in existing simultaneously in past and present), while French operas (especially *grands opéras* of the nineteenth century) were cast as

2. See Castil-Blaze [François-Henri-Joseph Blaze], *L'Académie Impériale de Musique: Histoire littéraire, musicale, choréographique, pittoresque, morale, critique, facétieuse, politique et galante de ce théâtre,* Théâtres lyriques de Paris [1] (Paris: The author, 1855); Jane F. Fulcher, *The Nation's Image: French Grand Opera as Politics and Politicized Art* (Cambridge: Cambridge University Press, 1987); Anselm Gerhard, *The Urbanization of Opera: Music Theater in Paris in the Nineteenth Century,* trans. Mary Whittall (Chicago: University of Chicago Press, 1998); and David Charlton, ed., *The Cambridge Companion to Grand Opera* (Cambridge: Cambridge University Press, 2003).

3. See Joseph Kerman, *Opera as Drama,* new and revised ed. (Berkeley and Los Angeles: University of California Press, 1988), 91.

4. See Steven Huebner, *French Opera at the* fin de siècle: *Wagnerism, Nationalism, and Style* (Oxford: Oxford University Press, 1999).

artistic productions imprisoned by the conventions of their institutional context.[5] Like other repertoire (such as Italian madrigals and early opera) whose aesthetic presence was marginal during the mid- to late twentieth century, the music of the French lyric stage came to be validated on the basis of its historical place, especially when it could be interpreted, rightly or wrongly, as a metaphor for the state.[6]

By diverting the musicological discourse away from formalist, transcendentalist, or biographical methodologies and toward cultural and institutional contextualizations, this extrinsic approach to musical artifacts has opened up a new field of studies that has challenged readings of the works which for over a century were seen as absolute music in the broadest sense of the term. What started out as a scholarly project to understand and historically locate music that was no longer part of the Western canon, even though it had dominated cultural production and consumption for almost a century, became a methodological opportunity that relocated Mozart and Beethoven in Vienna and Stravinsky in imperialist Russia.[7] With the publication of Susan McClary's *Conventional Wisdom,* the word "convention"—so long a problematic term for mainstream musicology—finally entered the musicological canon.[8] "Convention" as understood by McClary remains limited, however, to the time-honored musicological inquiry into form and style and has little to do with the complex cultural field of the music, protagonists, and institutions of the lyric stage in Paris in the nineteenth century.

During the past three decades, the intricate interfaces of institution, musical production, and reception have been explored in studies of individual Parisian opera houses, selected repertoires, or limited time periods. Interest in these aspects of French opera reached a new height in recent work by scholars, many of whom are represented in this book, who have shown that institutional history can be pushed beyond the boundaries of the institution as a fixed context for cultural production and consumption.[9] Instead, what becomes increasingly clear is the fluidity and complexity of artistic and administrative agency, aesthetic meaning, and legal frameworks.

5. See, in particular, Carl Dahlhaus, *Grundlagen der Musikgeschichte* (Cologne: Musikverlag Hans Gerig, 1977), especially his discussion of aesthetic presentism in chapter 1 ("Verlust der Geschichte," 12–33) and of "Gleichzeitigkeit des Ungleichzeitigen" ("Geschichtlichkeit und Kunstcharakter," 35–55).

6. Key studies which locate Italian madrigals within its institutional context include, for example, Anthony Newcomb, *The Madrigal at Ferrara, 1579–1597* (Princeton, NJ: Princeton University Press, 1978), and Iain Fenlon, *Music and Patronage in Sixteenth-Century Mantua,* vol. 1 (Cambridge and New York: Cambridge University Press, 1980).

7. See, for example, Volkmar Braunbehrens, *Mozart in Vienna, 1781–1791,* trans. Timothy Bell (New York: Grove Weidenfeld, 1990); Konrad Küster, *Beethoven* (Stuttgart: Deutsche Verlagsanstalt, 1994); and Richard Taruskin, *Stravinsky and the Russian Traditions: A Biography of the Works through "Mavra"* (Berkeley and Los Angeles: University of California Press, 1996).

8. See Susan McClary, *Conventional Wisdom: The Content of Musical Form* (Berkeley and Los Angeles: University of California Press, 2000).

9. See, for example, Olivier Bara, *Le Théâtre de l'Opéra Comique sous la Restauration: Enquête autour d'un genre moyen* (Hildesheim and New York: Georg Olms Verlag, 2001); Mark Everist,

The essays in this book take these issues further and in a range of directions, widening the scale of historical investigation in terms both of historical and institutional scope and of methodologies. The July Revolution lends itself as a starting point, particularly because of the enduring myth of Daniel-François-Esprit Auber's *La muette de Portici* (1828)—which, as Jane Fulcher has shown, embodied the new institutional horizon of *grand opéra* as the "nation's image"—as a catalyst for the revolution.[10] Furthermore, the Opéra was significantly recast as an institution under the directorship of Louis Véron (1831–35), while other theaters changed owing to shifts either in location (the Opéra-Comique moved to the Salle Ventadour in 1829) or in repertoire (the Théâtre-Italien premiered *Anna Bolena,* its first Donizetti opera, in 1831). In addition, the economic and social changes brought about by Louis-Philippe's July Monarchy were reflected in broader public access to the Paris opera houses—both literally, because of the increasing number of middle-class music consumers, and virtually, because freedom of the press laws increased newspaper circulation, including detailed reports from the opera houses. The beginning of World War I brought significant economic, social, and cultural changes that reflected on shifts within the institutional context of the lyric stage in Paris. These included, among other things, changes in programming owing to the removal of an increasing number of German operas—in particular Wagner—from France's musical institutions.

Although both the starting point and the endpoint of this essay collection are marked by historical change, they can also be seen as arbitrary markers. The Napoleonic legislation of Parisian theaters, for example, in 1806 had already introduced a licensing system that defined the characters of Paris's three main lyric stages: the Opéra, the Opéra-Comique, and the Théâtre-Italien.[11] One major change in Parisian lyric theater occurred in 1864, when Napoléon III revoked the licensing system yet left financial support intact for France's two main opera houses: the Opéra and the Opéra-Comique. The effect of the 1864 legislation was mitigated by Haussmann's removal of most of the boulevard theaters during the previous five years. Indeed, World War I brought no change in that respect: the Paris Opéra, as the premier lyric stage of France, is still today financed largely by a hefty national subvention.

The institutional scope of this volume examines, for the first time, a wide variety of theaters and their interplay over a significant span of the "long" nineteenth century. Although the Opéra and the Opéra-Comique are well-known features in the panorama of Parisian institutions, other stages are equally important: the Théâtre-Lyrique, the Bouffes-Parisiens, the Théâtre-Italien, the Théâtre de la Gaîté, and a host

---

Music Drama at the Paris Odéon, 1824–1828 (Berkeley and Los Angeles: University of California Press, 2002); Hervé Lacombe, *The Keys to French Opera,* trans. Edward Schneider (Berkeley and Los Angeles: University of California Press, 2001); and Marian Smith, *Ballet and Opera in the Age of "Giselle"* (Princeton, NJ: Princeton University Press, 2000).

10. See Fulcher: *Nation's Image,* 11–46.

11. For additional information on a selection of lyric stages, see Alicia Levin's contribution to this volume.

of alternative stages such as the Théâtre de l'Œuvre. In addition to this broadened view of the theatrical landscape in Paris, this volume emphasizes the complexities and reciprocal relationships of institutions and agents. Whether treating individuals (such as Halévy, Wagner, Offenbach, and Carvalho) or professional groups (stage designers, choreographers, singers, and critics), the essays in this volume illuminate the repertoire of the Parisian lyric institutions from a number of angles. Rather than a linear, institutional history, this volume offers studies that bring to life the cultural activities of performers, creators, administrators, critics, and audiences and shows that notions of national identity, genre, and institution are indeed complex—often competitive, and sometimes contradictory.

By resisting an isolationist view of Parisian institutions, the essays in this volume challenge the view that specific French and foreign repertoires were restricted to specific performance spaces. When Rebecca Harris-Warrick traces the itinerary of a work such as *Lucie de Lammermoor* from one Parisian institution to another, she shows not only shifts in musical and scenic production but also in the work's reception, which was dependent on the cultural and social specificity of each of the three performance contexts. The case of *Tannhäuser* raises the question of how the "premier lyric stage of France" could serve as "the nation's image" when a disputed foreign work was staged with all possible pomp. Reading of the reception of Wagner's *Tannhäuser* says more about the institution of French music criticism and its notions of French opera than about Wagner's work. Offenbach's revival of eighteenth-century scores at the Bouffes-Parisiens and his self-reflexive reference to *opéra comique* of the period shift discussions about these "eminently French" works and genres from the state-funded theaters to the world of operetta.

One key aspect of this book lies in its integration of reading and interpreting performance on the stages of Paris. The essays discuss the performance of the various lyric genres in the Parisian theaters as an integral part of the institutions themselves and as a key to the meaning of lyric theater in Paris. Thus Sarah Hibberd maintains that we can understand a staging such as that of Auber's *Gustave III* by tracing its historical and political resonances through close examination of the pertinent documents. But even those documents may pose challenges to the scholar, as Arnold Jacobshagen shows in his study of Halévy's *La juive* at the Salle Le Peletier. His careful reading of the surviving documents reveals that the oft-used mise-en-scènes of Parisian premieres prove much less trustworthy than previously thought.[12] Indeed, as M. Elizabeth C. Bartlet has demonstrated in her published and unpublished work, the spectacle is as much a part of French opera as music and libretto, if not more.[13]

12. See H. Robert Cohen, ed., *The Original Staging Manuals for Ten Parisian Operatic Premières, 1824–1843/Dix livrets de mise en scène lyrique datant des créations parisiennes, 1824–1843* (Stuyvesant, NY: Pendragon Press, 1998).

13. See M. Elizabeth C. Bartlet, "Staging French Grand Opera: Rossini's *Guillaume Tell* (1829)," in *Gioachino Rossini, 1792–1992: Il testo e la scena; Convegno internazionale di studi, Pesaro, 24–28*

One important case in point is the 1855 staging of Verdi's *Les vêpres siciliennes* at the Académie Impériale de Musique.

None of the chapters in this collection of essays strays far from the issue of cultural transfer. A critical category for scholarly fields as wide-ranging as translation studies, the critique of the slave trade, and the history of tourism, cultural transfer deals with the transport of cultural materials from one domain to another.[14] In most contemporary usages, the term "culture" is rooted in nation, region, or some other ethnography, but cultural transfer seeks to explain the migration of sets of practices from one geographical position to another. A number of key themes emerge: the focus on individuals rather than texts; the concept of *métissage* (cross-breeding) rather than confrontation; the disassociation of cultural-historical events from traditional political or military ones; and the idea that identity and difference are not contradictory but complementary.[15]

Music, Theater, and Cultural Transfer represents an attempt to bring these ideas within the domain of musicology.[16] Fauser's and Harris-Warrick's chapters explain some of the conditions under which German- and Italian-language cultural artifacts were able to be relocated from one environment to another (in the case of *Lucie de Lammermoor*, two others). Both Italian and German works also appear in Ellis's and Everist's accounts of two institutions in the 1850s, a circumstance complicated by the fact that cultural transfer involved not only place (from Italian and German states to France) but also time (the transfer of eighteenth-century works to the mid-nineteenth century). And the third section of the book looks at two other geographical spots, the Midi and Spain, and the way in which their cultural materials were transferred to metropolitan Paris via the mediation of works and performances themselves.

It could be argued that the now orthodox view of cultural transfer, which applies

---

giugno 1992, ed. Paolo Fabbri (Pesaro: Fondazione Rossini, 1994), 623–48; and Bartlet, *Guillaume Tell di Gioachino Rossini: Fonti Iconografiche* (Pesaro: Fondazione Rossini, 1996).

14. See Ute M. Röschenthaler, "Translocal Cultures: The Slave Trade and Cultural Transfer in the Cross River Reason," *Social Anthropology* 14 (2006): 71–91; John O. Ogbor and Johnnie Williams, "The Cross-Cultural Transfer of Management Practices: The Case for Creative Synthesis," *Cross-Cultural Management: An International Journal* 10 (2003): 3–23; "European Cultural Transfer in the Eighteenth-Century Cultures in Europe," proceedings of the Eleventh Quadrennial Congress of the International Society of Eighteenth-Century Studies, University of California, Los Angeles, 3–10 August 2003; and Michael Werner and Michel Espagne, eds., *Transferts: Les relations interculturelles dans l'espace franco-allemand (XVIIIe et XIXe siècle)* (Paris: Éditions Recherche sur les Civilisations, 1988).

15. For a useful introduction that self-consciously reviews much work of the 1990s, see Michel Espagne, *Les transferts culturels franco-allemands* (Paris: Presses Universitaires de France, 1999), especially the two chapters entitled "Les limites d'une notion" and "Au-delà du comparatisme" (17–49).

16. Other attempts to relate the concept of cultural transfer to musicology were part of the European Science Foundation project Musical Life in Europe, 1600–1900: Circulation, Institutions, Representation, which ran from 1998 to 2001.

only to regional culture, does not do justice to the understanding of culture as a critical concept in the last half century, most obviously in the works of Clifford Geertz and Raymond Williams. In the context of stage music in nineteenth-century France, there is a good case to be made for conceptualizing cultural transfer in terms of both discipline and institution. When Hibberd speaks of opera, spectacle, politics, and history in Auber's *Gustave III*, she is pointing to a range of disciplinary transfers, the best-known of which clearly connects history and opera. Although *Gustave III* is a complex case, more straightforward examples of operas on historical librettos transfer actual history to the stage and in so doing undertake all the work of decontextualization, extraction, and insertion that characterizes orthodox accounts of cultural transfer in history or literature. It is a truism that opera itself and the cohabiting genres of *opéra comique* and *grand opéra* in particular represent a cultural transfer from one artistic domain (play, novel, historical text) to another (stage music). Again, in a world where scenic elements are so important to the complex culture of Parisian music drama, costume and mise-en-scène emerge as important correlatives to history and politics.

Institutions are cultures too, and one of the most striking features of the chapters in the first part of this book is the level of interchange that may be witnessed among them. Management models (state subsidy, private enterprise, the system of *sociétaires*) are transferred from one institution to another. Works move from institution to institution, and the chapters on the Théâtre-Lyrique, Offenbach, and *Lucie de Lammermoor* show how works thereby lose and gain contexts, audiences, and meanings. And perhaps the most potent means of reading cultural transfer within Parisian musical life concerns individuals: singers, audiences, librettists, and composers. Some composers and librettists had particular institutional preferences, and when these were compromised the results could be disastrous;[17] but others—Scribe and Halévy, for example—moved apparently without effort from Opéra-Comique to Opéra. This aspect of both men's careers remains to be explained; a reading against the backdrop of the scholarly study of cultural transfer could help address this gap in our understanding.

This book has its origins in a conference held jointly at the music departments of the University of North Carolina at Chapel Hill and Duke University in September 2004,

---

17. A good example of just such a compromise was Adolphe Adam's *Richard en Palestine*, a three-act opera to a libretto by Paul Foucher that was premiered at the Académie Royale de Musique on 7 October 1844. Adam's operatic career had focused on the Théâtre des Nouveautés, the Opéra-Comique, and the Théâtre-Lyrique, and *Richard en Palestine*—his first work for the Académie Royale de Musique—was completely unsuccessful. The two further works for the same institution, *La bouquétiaire* and *Le fanal*, were in one and two acts, respectively, and were designed to accompany ballets. Adam's nine ballet scores for the Académie Royale de Musique and its successors tell a very different, and successful, story.

organized by Annegret Fauser and M. Elizabeth C. Bartlet (shown in fig. 0.1). Working with the materials in circulation at that event as the basis for this book occupied its current editors for over a year, but their efforts were troubled by the absence of the conference's co-organizer. When Beth Bartlet died on 11 September 2005, it was as if the lights had gone out in the exquisitely furnished *salon* we know as nineteenth-century French opera. The omission of her name—she should have been one of the book's co-editors, of course—from this book is all the more marked by the absence of the paper on the costumes for Verdi's *Les vêpres siciliennes* that she read at the original event, a year almost to the day before her death. What she left behind was the torso of a clearly brilliant essay, and one of the editors' principal regrets is that it was insufficiently complete to allow its being brought to publication. As we walked around Paris three months after her death, trying unsuccessfully to think of ways of incorporating Beth's paper into the book, we could only be struck by the places—so many of them—where we had worked, talked, and mused with Beth. They will never be quite the same again.

Annegret Fauser
Mark Everist

PART I

Institutions

The Company at the Heart of the Operatic Institution

CHOLLET AND THE CHANGING NATURE OF COMIC-OPERA
ROLE TYPES DURING THE JULY MONARCHY

Olivier Bara

A study of the singers who worked at the Opéra-Comique constitutes of necessity an analysis of vocal profiles, acting types, and performance traditions, as opposed to a study of the institution itself, the "house"—its administration, artistic policies, internal organization, political ties, and level of public support. As a subject, singers tend to channel scholarly attention toward essentially aesthetic, postproduction concerns such as performance and reception, whereas essays on the institution—the subject of the present conference—presuppose a preproduction point of view that highlights external forces and effectively casts factors affecting the germination of works into the shadows. But how may our knowledge of performers be integrated in a sociological, economic, and political study of the Parisian operatic institution as an agent of creativity?

We must consider the company of actor-singers to be a central element that shapes musical composition and, more generally, programming. Political legislation, theater directors, and composers aside, the Opéra-Comique may be understood from the point of view of its singers—subjects revealed in a powerful light when other factors impinging on musical production fade momentarily into the shadows. The central question is this: how do the institution's singers affect the composition of works at the preproduction stage? Two fundamental aspects of Parisian theaters appear particularly germane for the Opéra-Comique: the company (*troupe*), and its established role types (*emplois*), which strongly predetermine many aspects of the libretto and score, and even appear prima facie as conservative agents against radical aesthetic in-

FIGURE I.I. Jean-Baptiste Chollet in the costume for his starring role of Chapelou in Adophe Adam's *Le postillon de Lonjumeau*, act I. From *Petite galerie dramatique* (1836), plate 1079. Bibliothèque nationale de France.

novation.[1] How do librettists and composers use the stock role types and dramatic characters that result from an almost immutable ensemble of main characters and theatrical functions reproduced in work after work? What facilitates the doubtless fertile cross-pollination of the company's preexistent vocal role types and the librettists' and composers' own artistic impulses? How are the singers' social circumstances, economic conditions, and administrative organization ultimately transmuted in the works? Clearly, the Opéra-Comique's uniqueness among Parisian opera houses, its status as a venue for standard repertoire as well as new works, and its programming

I. The Opéra-Comique's system of role types (*emplois*) during the nineteenth century was, of course, not unique. It has been used from the earliest times of opera up to the present day in a wide range of institutions and repertoires. The following discussion and its conclusion may well be relevant beyond the specific case of the Opéra-Comique, which serves as a particularly revealing example.

of two to three different works per evening (unlike the Opéra or the Théâtre-Italien) channeled to the actor-singers decisive power over the creative process.[2] This incredible degree of influence notwithstanding, individual comic opera singers of the July Monarchy also appear to have been caught up in a drive away from the collective creativity of the company and toward personal stardom.

Limited bodies of works and short periods of transformation often prove highly revealing. Hence the locus of my study in the first decade of the July Monarchy, during a time of reform within the company, and against the background of an institutional crisis at the Opéra-Comique. (Such crucial moments in history inevitably appeal to scholars.) The argument will be centered on one legendary comic opera singer, Jean-Baptiste Chollet (see fig. 1.1), whose career began in the final years of the Restoration with a debut in 1825 and ended only one year before the end of the July Monarchy. Chollet retired from the Opéra-Comique in 1847, leaving behind a legacy of principal roles in major works of the period such as *Fra Diavolo, Zampa, L'éclair,* and *Le postillon de Lonjumeau.* A successor to the vocal and dramatic heritage of Jean-Blaise Martin, Chollet greatly surpassed the tenor Louis-Antoine Ponchard in popularity, only to be eclipsed by Gustave Roger. As an artistic "ferryman," Chollet preserved long-standing traditions even as he invented new characters in a pathbreaking career as one of the first comic opera singers to rise to international stardom. Studying Chollet also reveals the personal and family ties that existed among singers at the Opéra-Comique. Prior to his personal alliance with the celebrated Jenny Colon, Chollet enjoyed a notorious relationship with the singer Zoé Prévost. Their affair resulted in a daughter, Caroline Prévost, who also sang at the Opéra-Comique, like her husband, Achille Montaubry, Chollet's successor. Clearly theater companies—and not just that company at the Opéra-Comique—were often family affairs. These eminent reigning families profoundly influenced the evolution of staged musical events and ensured stability and continuity in the face of institutional and administrative chaos within the theater.[3]

A Crucial Point in Time? From Society Members to Directors

From an institutional, physical, and financial point of view, the early years of the July Monarchy coincided with a period of great instability at the Opéra-Comique. The institution's troubles stemmed not only from social and political factors ranging from

2. This study builds chronologically on earlier work: a section devoted to the company at the Opéra-Comique between 1815 and 1830 in Olivier Bara, *Le Théâtre de l'Opéra-Comique sous la Restauration: Enquête autour d'un genre moyen* (Hildesheim and New York: Georg Olms Verlag, 2001); and an article devoted to the Consulate and the Empire: Bara, "Influence des emplois sur la dramaturgie d'opéra-comique: Elleviou, Martin et l'âge d'or de la comédie," in *L'Opéra-comique à l'époque de Boieldieu (1775–1834): Actes du Colloque international de Rouen, mars 2001,* ed. Patrick Taïeb (Paris: CNRS Éditions, forthcoming).

3. See Arthur Pougin, *Figures d'Opéra-Comique, Madame Dugazon, Elleviou, les Gavaudan* (Paris: Tresse, 1875; reprint, Geneva: Minkoff, 1973).

the July Revolution to the uprisings of 1831 and the cholera epidemic of 1832, but also from internal issues.[4] In a radical organizational overhaul, the actor-singers dissolved their company in August 1828.[5] Succeeding them at the head of the Opéra-Comique was the director Paul-Auguste Ducis, described as the "concessionaire of the privilege of exploitation of the royal theater of the Opéra-Comique for thirty years."[6] Further change followed in April 1829, when the Opéra-Comique abandoned the older Salle Feydeau for Salle Ventadour, for the new hall's exorbitant rent plunged the institution into a cycle of recurring bankruptcies. In the months that followed the July Revolution, directors came and went in quick succession: Ducis ceded to Jules-Henri Vernoy de Saint-Georges, who was replaced in August 1830 by Alexandre Singier, former director of theaters in Lyon, who was forced to close the theater with little notice. Émile Lubbert replaced Singier in October 1831 but had no more success than his predecessor. In 1832, after yet another closing, Émile Laurent, former director of the Théâtre des Italiens, attempted to revive the theater and build up a new company—efforts quashed by the cholera epidemic, which followed the reopening on January 14 of the same year. In a bid to save the Opéra-Comique, the singers reconstituted their former association, thereby reclaiming their status as association members, and appointed Paul Dutreih as manager. They also deserted the ruinously expensive Salle Ventadour for a smaller hall, the Théâtre des Nouveautés, at the place de la Bourse. Opening night, 24 September 1832, marked the end of two agitated years that nonetheless bore witness to the premiere of Hérold's *Zampa* in May 1831, with Chollet in the title role.

Between 1832 and 1834 Opéra-Comique singers regained in part the power they had renounced in August 1828. The period resembled a return to the Restoration and the Salle Feydeau, with the premiering of works such as *Le pré aux clercs,* given 19 January 1833.[7] But the reincorporation of the singers' association proved provisional, and it was dissolved in May 1834. The shrewd manager-entrepreneur François-Louis Crosnier took over the Opéra-Comique and reopened the hall the same month

4. I have based this preliminary historical synthesis in part on Nicole Wild, "Opéra-Comique," in *Dictionnaire des théâtres parisiens: Les théâtres et la musique* (Paris: Aux Amateurs de Livres, 1989), as well as Raphaëlle Legrand and Nicole Wild, *Regards sur l'opéra-comique: Trois siècles de vie théâtrale* (Paris: Éditions du CNRS, 2002).

5. The declaration dissolving the association bears the signatures of Huet, Ponchard, Lemonnier, Lafeuillade, Valère Faubault, Chollet, Marie Desbrosses, Mme Paul Dutreh, Marie-Julie Boulanger, Antoinette-Eugénie Rigault, Félicité Pradher, Marie-Sophie Ponchard, and Zoé Prévost, all of whom were members of the society (*F-Pan,* AJ[13] 1051).

6. "Concessionaire du privilège pour l'exploitation du théâtre royal de l'Opéra-Comique pendant trente ans." Ibid.

7. Summarized by the press, however, as a "resurrection of worked-up larynxes" (résurrection de larynx énervés) in a ferocious review: "These are throat-searing screams, isolated head and chest tones, wailing cries that rend the ear and heart" (Ce sont des déchirements de gosier, des sons de tête ou de ventre, des cris lamentables à fendre l'oreille et le cœur); L'Opéra-Comique, *Le Figaro,* 1 October 1832. The effort to revive a bygone era appears to have been a futile one.

with a performance of *Lestocq*. As director, he steered the Opéra-Comique into an era of stability that was to last nine years, which were marked in particular by the inauguration of Salle Favart on 16 May 1840. With the return of a director, first Crosnier and later Alexandre Basset from 1845 to 1848, the Opéra-Comique entered a minor golden age that saw the premieres of many fine works, including Auber's *Le cheval de bronze* (23 March 1835), with Ponchard and Marie-Virginie Casimir; Adam's *Le postillon de Lonjumeau* (13 October 1836), with Chollet and Zoé Prévost; Eugène Scribe and Auber's *Le domino noir* (2 December 1837), with Laure Cinti-Damoreau and Théodore François Moreau-Sainti; and Saint-Georges, Jean-François Bayard, and Donizetti's *La fille du régiment* (11 February 1840), with Marie-Julie Boulanger.

This list of works reveals the names of several major stars cast in leading roles at the Opéra-Comique. Naturally Chollet figures among the tenors, but so do Gustave Roger and Théodore François Moreau-Sainti, along with Ponchard, whose career actually peaked during the Restoration. Performers who were better actors than singers also deserve mention, in particular Louis Second, known as Féréol (Dickson in *La dame blanche*). A comic tenor in the tradition of Antoine Trial, Féréol could not have had a career in an operatic theater other than the Opéra-Comique, where, during the July Monarchy, he created the roles of Daniel Capuzzi in *Zampa*, Cantarelli in *Le pré aux clercs,* and Tsing-Tsing in *Le cheval de bronze*. With a move to the Théâtre de la Renaissance, he shifted to mainly spoken roles, notably Don Guritan for the premiere of Victor Hugo's *Ruy Blas* in 1838. Félicité Pradher, Marie-Julie Boulanger, Marie-Virginie Casimir, and Zoé Prévost stand out as artists who dominated the stage in the early years of the July Monarchy. This far-from-exhaustive list should also include Jenny Colon, who was active from 1836 to 1840, and Laure Cinti-Damoreau, who enthralled audiences of the Opéra-Comique between 1837 and 1843. The presence of Cinti-Damoreau, formerly of the Théâtre-Italien and the Opéra, attests to higher levels of vocal prowess at the Opéra-Comique—an increase in technical ability and musical interest that is clearly apparent in Auber's *Le domino noir*.

Brief historical overviews such as this of the Opéra-Comique during the July Monarchy inevitably bring to light only the titles of major productions, framed by the names of managers and singers. This warps the history of the institution, reducing it to its most obvious activities. Further discussion necessitates entering into more obscure, though perhaps more significant, zones of theater life, including the administrative regulation of performers' careers, which strongly shaped the choice of repertoire. Moreover, the makeup of the company of actor-singers and the structure of its role types (*emplois*) would effectively guide the dramatic and musical course of comic opera in any given period. Role types are often designated by archetypal names (i.e., names used as nouns) derived from characters or artists—for example, Jean Elleviou, Jean-Blaise Martin, and Trial, as well as Louise-Rosalie Dugazon, to name only four of the most famous. These artists directed dramatic and musical creativity by inscribing it in a historical context unique to comic opera: each new role has a lineage and refers to a preexistent typology. A company's degree of stability, the transfer of a role type from creator to successor, and the significant transformation of a role type by an exceptional performer all constitute fundamental institutional factors that could sway the direction of the genre.

Granted, theater companies driven by a role-type system were no more unique to the Opéra-Comique than they were to the July Monarchy. They characterized all repertoire and contemporary theaters that had companies bound by performance contracts. But at the Opéra-Comique, provincial tours necessitated the easy identification of dramatic and vocal profiles. Originality would have rendered performances outside Paris impossible; it was adherence to a creative template that assured the rapid dissemination of works. Moreover, the Opéra-Comique resorted to its established repertoire every day to fill a bill that changed nightly. Thus the demand that singers learn a great number of pieces imposed a degree of continuity among characters. This in turn allowed individual artists effortlessly to resume former roles, as they were contractually obligated to do. Rooted in these circumstances are obvious recurrences of dramatic situations, comic devices, and aria structures, in particular easily learned strophic forms. The creative process is part of the mix: new dramatic situations and musical materials blend with preexistent elements.

Company and Role Type:
Administrative Constraints and Artistic Influences

In her recent work devoted to actresses, Anne Martin-Fugier points out that "it is difficult to imagine the pace that actors were required to maintain for the better part of the nineteenth century. Today, an actor performs in one work at a time, and not every night. During the nineteenth century, actors performed simultaneously in several, and almost every night."[8] Artist contracts preserved at the Archives nationales de France, notably those signed by the director Émile Laurent in January 1832, reveal some of the specific demands made on the singers at the Opéra-Comique and also indicate a strikingly heavy workload. In Pradher's contract, for example, the director agrees to limit the singer's performances to a maximum of fifteen events per month, four of which may be "doubled," meaning she would be playing roles in two single-act works.[9] Pradher's contract is actually fairly advantageous compared to Chollet's from the same period, which stipulates performances at eighteen events per month and fines for absences.[10] As many as six of these events (or one-third) could include

---

8. "On imagine mal le rythme de travail que devaient soutenir les comédiens pendant une grande partie du XIXe siècle. Aujourd'hui, un acteur joue une seule pièce à la fois et il ne joue pas tous les soirs. Au XIXe siècle, il jouait dans plusieurs pièces simultanément, et quasiment tous les soirs." Anne Martin-Fugier, *Comédienne: De Melle Mars à Sarah Bernhardt* (Paris: Éditions du Seuil, 2001), 52.

9. Contract dated 16 January 1832 between Mme Pradher and Émile Laurent (*F-Pan*, AJ[13] 1059).

10. Contract dated 14 January 1832 between Jean-Baptiste Chollet and Émile Laurent (*F-Pan*, AJ[13] 1059).

two distinct roles. A previous contract records the amount of notice that had to be given Chollet to prepare for a role: three days for a role performed in the same year, virtually none for one already performed in the same month, and in general, eight days for any character in his repertoire.[11] This compulsory frenzy of activity appears to have resulted in a certain amount of routine in performances of comic opera. Singers responsible for secondary parts faced even greater demands, a circumstance clearly revealed in Féréol's contract: he was required to assume comic tenor roles at twenty events each month, half of which were to include two separate roles.[12] The further down in the hierarchy an actor went, the more stage time was required of him or her. These contracts also reveal the scarcity of leave, reserved for the very best singers who frequently performed in the provinces or in other countries. For example, Chollet received one month of vacation, "to exercise his talent in the provinces as well as other countries as he saw fit," but was allowed to take this time only during the theater's off-season, between June and September.[13] Zoé Prévost, also a principal singer (and Chollet's lover), signed a contract at the same time that also stipulated one month of vacation.[14] Additional clauses indicate that she was obliged to perform at eighteen events per month and to provide attestation of any illness she claimed from a physician attached to the theater or chosen by the manager. The contract further required the singer to obtain reports from three different physicians in the event of litigation. A performer's entire life fell under scrutiny, including pregnancies: contracts normally allowed for only one month of leave following childbirth.

Conditions such as these literally bound the comic opera singer to the theater and further encumbered the artist with a number of weighty roles that were, of necessity, similar in aesthetic. In 1830, a singer such as Pradher had thirty-six roles in her active repertoire, while Ponchard maintained thirty-four, six of which were either leading or double-cast in order to ensure the frequent return of the more popular works even in his absence. These included *La dame blanche, Jean de Paris, Les visitandines, Adolphe et Clara, Maison à vendre,* and *Le prisonnier.*[15] Several long manuscript lists of individual performers' roles are preserved at the archives of the Opéra-Comique. Annotations such as "knows" or "to be learned" indicate the singer's degree of preparedness. There are also printed documents called "warning notices" (*billets d'avertissement*) used to apprise singers of an evening's programming (the two or three works they had to know for the night) and the rehearsal schedule. Whether or not a role was exclusive to one singer or double cast was obviously as decisive in terms of programming as it

11. Contract dated 10 August 1830 between Jean-Baptiste Chollet and Alexandre Singier (*F-Pan,* AJ[13] 1059).

12. Contract dated 6 January 1832 between Féréol and Émile Laurent (*F-Pan,* AJ[13] 1059).

13. "Pour exercer son talent en province ou à l'étranger comme il l'entendra." Contract dated 14 January 1832; see also n. 10.

14. Contract dated 11 January 1832 between Zoé Prévost and Émile Laurent (*F-Pan,* AJ[13] 1059).

15. Repertoire list for Ponchard, c. 1830 (*F-Pan,* AJ[13] 1060).

was for the future of a work: roles were retained by the singer who created them and could not be assumed by another performer except in the particular case of a new singer's debut. In some instances the singer who created a role became in a sense its proprietor, and that ownership could not be relinquished without the director's approval. At the same time, a singer could be called upon to perform only in works listed on his or her "repertoire list" (*tableau de répertoire*), as was the case in Pradher's contract.[16] This meant that roles in newly composed works were predetermined, for both the librettist and the composer, by a singer's acting technique, performance style, vocal qualities, and learning abilities. Individual performance styles and learning curves weighed heavily on a composition at the precompositional stage. These same factors also guided a character's dramatic and vocal depiction in such practical matters as the length of the role and the number of arias. Formulas in contracts dating from 1830 provide ample proof of this, including one in a document signed by Chollet on 10 August 1830:

> Monsieur Chollet shall not refuse to fill the roles in new pieces that are analogous to the ones he plays, which shall be attributed to him by the authors or by the Director. He further commits himself to learn said roles or any other new ones to a limit of twenty-five poetic lines or two pages of music per day in total, excluding repeats, and without allowing his study to delay or interrupt the course of ordinary service.[17]

The actor-singer's learning abilities thus influenced in part the degree of difficulty in librettos and scores.

This insistence on preservation of role types and performance models had one final, concrete reality that worked to the detriment of renewed creativity. In contracts drawn up in the early years of the July Monarchy, responsibility for costumes was placed in the singer's hands. Indeed, in printed contracts dating from the end of the Restoration (1830), a recurring formula stipulated that a singer was required to supply "at his own expense all of the clothing suited to his functions and role types (town dress and formal attire), except character costumes, which will be furnished

16. A note from her husband, the composer Louis Barthélémy Pradher, stipulates that Pradher's roles could not be played by another actor-singer without her consent. He adds that "the first condition of agreement is that she may not be called to perform in any work other than those here designated" (la première condition de l'engagement est de ne jamais l'appeler à jouer dans aucune pièce autre que celles désignées, rôle créé ou non). Note dated 17 September 1830 (*F-Pan*, AJ[13] 1053).

17. "M. Chollet ne pourra se refuser à remplir dans les pièces nouvelles les rôles *analogues à ceux qu'il joue* qui lui seront attribués par les auteurs ou par le Directeur, et il s'engage à apprendre les dits rôles ou tous autres nouveaux à raison de 25 lignes de poème ou deux pages de musique par jour, le tout sans les répliques, et sans que les études puissent retarder ou interrompre le cours du service ordinaire." *F-Pan*, AJ[13] 1059.

by the Administration, and to be satisfied with those presented to him."[18] Despite the reforms envisioned early in the century by François-Joseph Talma at the Théâtre-Français, a degree of freedom survived here in the individual choice of costume. Anxious to make an impression with their attire, actors persisted in their resistance, motivating Théophile Gautier to remark as late as the 1851 revival of Méhul's *Joseph* at the Opéra-Comique that "we know that all actors refuse to be dressed; there is no possible influence except on the choirs, who are forced to endure the historical costumes imposed on them."[19] Still, pecuniary considerations appear to have motivated some performers to yield to the director or stage manager's wishes, concerns that were probably at the root of the director Émile Laurent's commitment to furnish singer Eugénie Martinet with all of her costumes.[20] Arrangements differed for Pradher, a more celebrated artist on the Parisian scene, who was free "to have all of said character costumes designed and sewn by the workers, and at the expense of the administration."[21] The contract also stipulated that she retain full ownership of her costumes. Yet another variant applied to the comic actor Féréol, who was allotted 1500 francs per year to furnish all of the clothing and paraphernalia required for his roles.[22] Control over costuming reinforced the idea of the actor-singer as proprietors of their theatrical roles and keepers of their characters' actions and appearances. The "town dress" costume meshed with the performance panoply of the actor-singer, who was prone to trade on his stage clothing in the very formulas he had established. Once more, the influence of the company generated institutional habits, and it was this inertia, above and beyond the direct influence of the librettists or composers, that determined the staged event.

These examples underscore a conservative tendency that arose from a company structured by role types, an inclination also linked to the productivity of this particular theater as a custodian of French comic opera. But these preliminary conclusions deserve greater nuance: the role-type system could also be artistically fertile.

The theatrical identity of the performer may be read in each role type: the artist's vocal and dramatic classification, physical characteristics, and specific theatrical abilities, as well as the performer's name, which a kind of brand for all of his or her roles. The contract set the role type as well as the degree of possession, with qualifications

---

18. "De se fournir à ses frais tous les habits convenables à ses rôles et emplois (habits de ville et français) excepté les costumes de caractère, qui lui seront fournis par l'Administration, et de se contenter de ceux qui lui seront présentés de sa part." Ibid.

19. "Nous savons que tout acteur se refuse à se laisser habiller; il n'y a d'influence possible que sur les chœurs, qui sont forcés de subir les costumes historiques qu'on leur impose." Cited in Martin-Fugier, *Comédienne*, 69.

20. Contract dated 6 January 1832 (*F-Pan*, AJ[13] 1059).

21. "De faire confectionner tous les costumes dits à caractère par les ouvriers et au compte de l'administration." Contract dated 16 January 1832 (*F-Pan*, AJ[13] 1059).

22. Contract dated 6 January 1832 (*F-Pan*, AJ[13] 1059).

such as "exclusive principal" (*en chef et sans partage*), "principal and double cast" (*en chef et en partage*), understudy, and replacement. This is how the main members of the Opéra-Comique's company appear in a list dating from 1830:[23]

M. Ponchard (Louis-Antoine-Eléonore): principal *haute contre,* Elleviou
M. Lemonnier (Louis-Augustin): principal *haute contre,* Elleviou, lovers
M. Moreau-Sainti (Théodore-François): principal tenor, Elleviou, Ponchard
M. Thianni (Louis-Charles): tenor roles and Colins
M. Huet (Louis-Auguste): uncles, fathers, and Philippes
M. Chollet (Jean-Baptiste-Marie): Martins and others
M. Tilly (Nicolas-Auguste-Didier): Martins and principal comic roles
M. Féréol (Louis Second): Trials, Lesages, Moreaus, Laruettes
Mme Lemonnier: Mother Dugazon, Mother Noblets
Mme Rigault: lovers and principal roles
Mme Pradher: principal lovers without bravura, Gavaudan, country women,
　　breeches roles
Mme Casimir (Marie-Virginie): principal singer, principal Dugazon, Mme
　　Boulanger's principal singer roles
Mme Colon mère: chaperone-companions

This list reveals the complex identification of role types in the intersection of character and actor, where the two were often confounded. Comic-opera role types invariably resulted from the articulation of the following simultaneously heterogeneous and complementary criteria:

- the social quality of the character ("country folk")
- the dramatic function as subject or object, opponent or supporter ("male lover," "female lover," "father," "chaperone")
- the characteristics of the costume ("breeches")
- the physical characteristics ("male lover" versus "father"; "female lover" versus "chaperone")
- the type of character, identified by his generic name ("Colins," or comic-opera male lover)
- the name of the performer who established a specific role type, around which the original characteristics settled ("Trials," "Philippes," "Martins," "Ellevious," "Ponchards")
- the age of this referential performer ("principal Dugazon," "Mother Dugazon")
- vocal characteristics and tessituras ("*haute contre,*" "tenor," "bravura singer," "without bravura")
- ranking within the company ("principal tenor," "principal comic actor")

23. Undated list (*F-Pan,* AJ[13] 1053).

Adherence to a role type depended on the interaction of elements on a syntagmatic axis: an artist suited to the functions of a lover, who showed to advantage in military costume, and who possessed an excellent high tessitura could be a principal Elleviou or Ponchard. A tenor with a weak or nasal voice and lacking in physical beauty might ably fill naive countryfolk roles. If endowed with a comic streak, he might also become an excellent Trial. This was reflected in the contract for Féréol, who was assigned the "Trial" or "Lesage" role type specified as "comic" and "written in tenor clef."[24] Thus Féréol's roles were determined by a combination of three fundamental criteria: performance history, theatrical genre (e.g., comic), and vocal tessitura.

Yet these conditions opened the door to a play of combinations that could be as flexible as they were fertile. In each new work, the boundaries of a given role type might be pushed back, the stultifying habits of an actor-singer changed. An example of this is Féréol's creation of the dramatic role of Grégorio in Halévy's *Ludovic* (1834)—a substantial break with the conventions of his role type. Moreover, each work was born from the dialectic relationship between systematization and ingenuity: role types affected the creation of comic operas and were affected by this creativity in turn, thereby displacing the dramatic and musical boundaries of the roles. The system was not entirely rigid. It existed and evolved alongside new works and performers, leaving room for the latter to develop new theatrical and vocal models.

From the Company to the Star System: The Emancipation of Chollet

The dialectic of new and old may be understood more clearly in the particular example of Chollet. His case provides insight into the way new role types developed out of older models, how these developments were reflected in the repertoire, and how dramatic templates and performance traditions eventually stagnated into mere convention. Chollet's story also illustrates the emancipation of artists from the company's artistic straitjacket. During the July Monarchy, the submission of artists to the power of directors and their career path to stardom led the conservative Opéra-Comique into a uniquely modern era.

Chollet entered the Opéra-Comique when it was still controlled by the singers' association, when the institutional regime ranked society members (who were legally, administratively, and financially committed to the theater) above boarders, apprentice singers, and artists on tryout. After a triumphant debut in the role of Rodolphe for Boieldieu's *Le petit chaperon rouge*, Chollet was engaged on 26 April 1825 in "Martin role types suitable to the range of his voice and physical qualities, as exclusive lead or double cast, and aside from this, all the roles analogous to his physique and talents."[25]

24. Contract dated 6 January 1832 (*F-Pan*, AJ[13] 1059).

25. "Les rôles de l'emploi dit de Martin qui seront convenables à l'étendue de sa voix et à son physique, soit en chef, soit en partage, et en outre tous les rôles analogues à son physique et à ses

Focusing on the terms of this 1825 contract reveals a subtle blend of intractability and lenience, constraint and flexibility.

Chollet's contract confined him to the "Martin" role type, a series of roles amassed by his illustrious predecessor Jean-Blaise Martin that included Frontin in Boieldieu's *Le nouveau seigneur de village.* At the time the term "Baryton Martin" indicated a high baritone voice.[26] But during the nineteenth century at the Opéra-Comique, the Martin role type simultaneously denoted the *concordant* voice, a blend of tenor and baritone (*basse-taille*) registers that extended into higher ranges through the use of pure head voice. It was associated with a performance style rooted in a particular kind of vocal exhibitionism, including a fairly pronounced taste for cadenzas and ornamentation. This type of character included mainly cunning valets, Frontins, and humorous artisans, and it necessitated a cheerful stage attitude—even though Martin was never considered a comic actor.

Chollet's assumption of this legacy and his furthering of the tradition coincided with the distancing of the actor-singer Martin from the Opéra-Comique. Martin retired in 1823 but returned in February 1826 for a few performances and again in 1833 for Halévy's pastiche *Les souvenirs de Lafleur,* a retrospective of his career, roles, and favorite arias. His retirement created a void at the Opéra-Comique, and a whole series of roles in new and repertoire works alike might have died without had there been no successor. Chollet was first engaged to fill this void, less for his talent than for his ability to fill Martin's dramatic and vocal shoes and other castoffs. Chollet thus appeared in the role of Picaros in Dalayrac's *Picaros et Diégo,* one of Martin's fetish roles. He came to the role type as a baritone with a range that could be stretched to encompass the required tessitura and was obliged to walk in his predecessor's shoes even in new works, where he appeared more as an imitator than a creator. As a successor to the role type, he was reproached by the *Revue Musicale* in January 1827 for "playing the Martin" in Halévy's *L'artisan,* for throwing himself into cadenzas without forethought, and for misusing his head voice. Yet it was Halévy who wrote this consummately Martin role for young Chollet, complete with a barrage of trills and other vocal devices. Moreover, in *Les deux nuits,* Boieldieu cast Chollet in the role of

talents." Jean-Baptiste Chollet's first contract (*F-Pan,* AJ[13] 1060). The contract stipulates that he enter the association as a "partial member after two years" (sociétaire à demi-part après deux ans). In his previous engagement with the Théâtre du Havre, Chollet was assigned Martin, Laïs, and Solié roles. See François-Joseph Fétis, "Chollet," in *Biographie universelle des musiciens,* vol. 2 (Paris: Firmin-Didot, 1860–81).

26. "The 'Baryton Martin' (from the name of the singer Jean-Blaise Martin), a light voice more nearly approaching the tenor than the bass, was developed in French opera and comic opera. A characteristic example is Pelléas in Debussy's *Pelléas et Mélisande*" (L'école française d'opéra et d'opéra-comique a développé pour sa part la tradition du "baryton-Martin" [du nom du chanteur Jean-Blaise Martin], à la voix légère, plus proche du ténor que de la basse: le rôle de Pelléas dans l'opéra de Debussy *Pelléas et Mélisande* en fournit un exemple caractéristique). Pierre Saby, *Vocabulaire de l'opéra* (Paris: Éditions Minerve, 1999), 30.

the cunning manservant Victor, extending the tradition of liveried heroes created by Martin—for whom Boieldieu initially intended the role.[27] The threat to this young member of the Opéra-Comique's company was clear: typecasting put a break on career development and begat imitation, to the point of snuffing out individual talent. As such, the largely autodidactic Chollet was quickly accused of imitating Martin's faults more than his merits: overuse of cadenzas, jerky delivery, lack of continuity between the head and chest registers, and artificial high notes sung in *falsetto*. Chollet, paralyzed by his role type, risked devolving into a pale imitation:

> If this singer ever accepts that he is a tenor and not a baritone in the least, if he works on his head voice, to make it more equal, flexible, and well-placed, above all, more easily blended with his chest voice, if in the end he becomes more certain of what he wants to do when he begins a cadenza, we will be able to promise him that he will be counted among our best singers.[28]

Fortunately, the artist's contract provided the singer with a degree of leeway. On the one hand, Chollet assumed responsibility not for all Martin roles, but only those appropriate to his physique. On the other hand, he could opt to revive or create non-Martin roles on the condition that they were suited to him. There resided the creative role left to the new arrival. As such, in addition to clever manservant roles, Chollet could be cast as a lover in tenor ranges more comfortable for him, such as Henri in Hérold's *Marie* (1826) and Fritz in Auber's *La fiancée* (1829).[29] Still, these roles failed to enable Chollet to become Chollet, that is, to break free of the limits of his role

27. The announcement that Martin would fortunately be replaced by Chollet reads: "Martin was to sing a role in it. I will not say play, because it is well known that this particular virtuoso acts very little" (Martin devait y chanter un rôle; nous ne disons pas jouer, car on sait que le dit virtuose jouait fort peu). *Le courrier des théâtres*, 21 May 1829. Berlioz reports that the "full-length opening act aria for the clever servant, sung and played to perfection by Monsieur Chollet was roundly applauded" (Au premier acte, le grand air du serviteur rusé, chanté et joué à la perfection par M. Chollet, a été beaucoup applaudi). *Berliner Allgemeine Musikalische Zeitung*, 6 June 1829; reproduced in Hector Berlioz, *Critique musicale*, vol. 1, ed. H. Robert Cohen and Yves Gérard (Paris: Buchet/Chastel, 1996), 19–20.

28. "Si ce chanteur acquérait enfin la conscience qu'il est un ténor et non point un baryton, s'il se mettait à travailler sa voix de tête, à la faire devenir plus égale, plus souple, plus posée, surtout à rendre plus facile son mélange avec la voix de poitrine, si enfin il devenait plus sûr de ce qu'il veut faire quand il commence un point d'orgue, on pourrait d'avance lui promettre d'être compté parmi nos meilleurs chanteurs." Review of the premiere of Louise Bertin's *Le loup-garou*, *Le globe*, 17 March 1827.

29. In the role of Fritz, the carpet layer, Chollet "was naive without doing silly things, natural without excess. His contribution to making the work a success was great, for he almost always sings, and completes this task well" (a été naïf sans sottise, naturel sans excès. La part qui lui revient dans le succès de la partition est grande, car il chante presque toujours, et s'acquitte au mieux de cette tâche). *Le courrier des théâtres*, 12 January 1829.

type, to generate a new comic opera figure. As an amorous tenor he strayed into the territory of Ponchard, and it was in fact one of the latter's former roles (Rodolphe in *Le petit chaperon rouge*) that had launched Chollet's career. The true metamorphosis of Chollet—a rare and subtle moment in which a new role type emerged from the combination of a role, a score, and a performer in full bloom—dates from 1830, with his performances in the title role of *Fra Diavolo* and then in Hérold's *Zampa* (1831).[30] These roles relieved the constraints of the company and the repertoire, freed him from the necessity of accommodating roles for which he was more or less unsuited, and further crystallized the moment in which librettist and composer adapted roles to suit the individual talent of the performer. At this point repertorial conventions and institutional routines ceased to be considered. With the Calabrian outlaw and would-be gentleman Fra Diavolo, and the Sicilian bandit and gentleman seducer Zampa, together Scribe, Auber, Hérold, and Chollet created new character roles that enabled the singer to distance himself from the liveried valet characters *à la Martin*, as well as the sentimental Ponchard and Moreau-Sainti types of lovers. He became an outlaw figure, at once disquieting and familiar, dramatic and powerful. One might ask, moreover, whether these figures did not bear some resemblance to those of Robert Macaire in contemporary melodrama. With the creation of these two roles Chollet broke free of his identity as nothing more than Martin's successor and distinguished himself from his two rival tenors in the company, Ponchard and Moreau-Sainti. Composers took his vocal abilities into account and adapted their music to Chollet's limitations, including his discomfort with *spianato* singing for sentimental, melodic outpourings.[31] Hérold reserved *Zampa*'s middle tessitura for Chollet—part baritone, part tenor—while allowing extensions into the upper register. In terms of physical presence and in contrast to Ponchard, Chollet's great height served these striking new creations for the stage well: he was compared to Féréol, the company's comic tenor and a specialist in *rôles marqués* (elderly characters).[32] The disadvantage of these colorful, powerfully energetic roles was that they were difficult to recreate in the absence of their originator: Chollet's departure in April 1832 for Brussels and The Hague, where he stayed until April 1834, compromised *Zampa*'s stage life at the Opéra-Comique.[33]

30. *Le corsaire,* 29 January 1830, noted that "Chollet acted and sang with such energy that he amazed the public" (Chollet a joué et chanté avec une verve qui a enlevé tous les suffrages).

31. According to Auguste Laget, *Chollet, premier sujet du Théâtre de l'Opéra-Comique* (Toulouse: A. Chauvin et fils, 1880).

32. Adolphe Adam makes a notable comparison between the two and credits Chollet with two stages of development ("A Provincial Debut" [Un début en province] and "A Conspiracy Under Louis XVIII" [Une conspiration sous Louis XVIII]). Adam, *Souvenirs d'un musicien* (Paris: Michel Lévy frères, 1857).

33. Chollet made his reentry into the Opéra-Comique with Zoé Prévost in June 1835 in Gomis's *Le portefaix*. In his monograph on Hérold, Arthur Pougin writes that "without Chollet, *Zampa* was impossible. We know that this artist's voice, in some ways similar to Martin's, had an exceptional

The composition of Adolphe Adam's *Le postillon de Lonjumeau* marks a second stage in the evolution of Chollet's career. Like Auber and Hérold before him, Adam exploited Chollet's individual talents, particularly his ease onstage and his predilection for character roles. With the role of Chapelou, the popularity of sentimental and somewhat insipid lover role types created by Ponchard during the Restoration died a definitive death. French gaiety, previously brought to life in Elleviou roles and snuffed out by Restoration sentimentality and melodrama, returned to the Opéra-Comique. Chollet's head register fueled Adam's success, notably in the celebrated aria "Mes amis écoutez l'histoire," and with the role of Chapelou Chollet reestablished a degree of continuity between his new roles and the Martin role type. But Adam's work also ushered in a new stage in Chollet's artistic development: in this story of a horseman turned opera singer, the performer was invited to sing his own role in some way, to play or construct a play *about* tenors. From this point onward Chollet played himself, and he fully indulged in stage and vocal exhibitionism. The space between Chapelou and Chollet was narrow and gray, the more so because Chapelou leaves his wife Madeleine in order to become a singer. This appears to reflect Chollet's own matrimonial situation at the time of the premiere: he had abandoned Zoé Prévost, who played Madeleine, for the sweet gaze of Jenny Colon. In the minds of the spectators, the person and the performer, life and art, are confounded.

With this role Chollet discovered his own style, built up his own individual repertoire, and made his own name. Breaking free of the company and asserting his freedom in the face of the Opéra-Comique's administration, he avoided contractual engagements, except for short periods averaging two years, in order to tour the provinces, Belgium, Holland, and England. This arrangement appears to have been much more financially rewarding for Chollet.[34] The disbanding of the actor-singer association at the Opéra-Comique ushered in yet another new phase in comic opera production: the star system and the triumph of individualism over collectivity and artistic solidarity.[35] A figure such as Chollet so disrupted conventions that the ripple effect

range and character, at once a tenor and baritone. Martin was a baritone with tenor tendencies, but Chollet was a tenor with baritone leanings. No artist would dare take on the role after him, which he imbued with an extraordinary character as much as a singer as an actor" (*Zampa* sans Chollet était alors impossible. On sait que la voix de cet artiste, à peu près analogue à celle de Martin, était d'une étendue et d'un caractère exceptionnels, et tenait à la fois du ténor et du baryton. Martin était un baryton ténorisant, et Chollet était un ténor barytonant. Aucun artiste n'aurait osé se charger après lui de ce rôle, auquel il avait donné d'ailleurs, tant comme chanteur que comme comédien, un relief extraordinaire). See Pougin, *Hérold* (Paris: H. Laurens, 1906), 91.

34. *La revue et gazette musicale de Paris* followed the tribulations of Chollet and Prévost, reporting in November 1840 that they would not renew their contract with the Opéra-Comique when it expired on 12 May 1841, at which point they would be in Metz and Nancy. Officially in Brussels in 1842, the couple returned to the Opéra-Comique in May of the same year for a revival of Nicolo's *Jeannot et Colin*. The individual star system clearly superseded the order of the company.

35. See Dominique Leroy, "Personnel artistique et formation du star system," in *Histoire des arts du spectacle en France* (Paris: Éditions L'Harmattan, 1990), 254–56.

reached even into the workings of a "family" theater such as the Opéra-Comique. By 1838, the critic for the *Revue et gazette musicale de Paris* was able to report that Chollet was not "pigeonholed" (*classé*) in a role type, which he interpreted as "progress in the art of the actor" (un progrès dans l'art du comédien) who was obliged to take on a great variety of roles.[36]

Did total freedom for the performer necessarily result from breaking free of the stifling yet protective system of the company? The singer risked relinquishing his function as the artist of a single character, replicated over and over within the role type of his own creation. Of course, it was the singer who created the individual performance model, but doing so created detrimental restrictions. Chollet's own role type, developed mainly in operas by Adam that were premiered before 1853,[37] emerged through an increase in the number of stock comic episodes (*lazzi*), a marshaling of his comic or vocal effects, and, in particular, recourse to and misuse of *portamenti*, *falsetto* passages, and even nasal intonations that certain critics considered the height of tastelessness.[38] In short, Chollet secured a degree of freedom of which he took full advantage in tours of the provinces and abroad in the company of Zoé Prévost. But he imprisoned himself in his own performance automatisms, repeated on stage after stage, and became bogged down in his narcissistic and sterilizing self-representation. One critic described the highly visible Chollet's aesthetic "signature" in a review of a performance of *Le postillon* at the Théâtre-Lyrique in 1852:

> Chollet has lost nothing of his previous talent. He still has his original figure, comic gestures, clean and energetic pronunciation, wit, finesse, passion, verve, clownish inflections, and prodigious portamenti that have made him, if not an artist of irreproachable taste, at least one of the most amusing singers there ever was on earth.[39]

This praise is a double-edged sword: while the aging singer is said to have maintained his performance qualities, they have failed to evolve. They have in fact devolved into

36. Henri Blanchard, "Physiologie musicale: Chollet," *La revue et gazette musicale de Paris,* 19 August 1838.

37. The last role he created was Beaufort in Adam's *Le roi des halles.* He created roles in four other works by the same composer, including *Le fidèle berger* and *Le brasseur de Preston,* both in 1838; *Le roi d'Yvetot* in 1842; and *Cagliostro* in 1844.

38. In 1844 an illness altered Chollet's already nasal timbre, which was already considered nasal, among other flaws. Nonetheless, he continued his career at the Opéra-Comique with a new three-year contract before assuming directorship of the Théâtre de Bordeaux in 1847 and 1848 and the Royal Theater in The Hague in 1851.

39. "Chollet n'a rien perdu de son talent d'autrefois. Il a toujours sa figure originale, ses gestes comiques, sa prononciation nette et énergique, son esprit, sa finesse, son ardeur, sa verve, et ces inflexions bouffonnes, ces ports de voix prodigieux, qui faisaient de lui, sinon un artiste d'un goût irréprochable, du moins l'un des chanteurs les plus amusants qu'il y eût au monde." *Revue et gazette musicale de Paris,* 7 November 1852.

mannerisms—performance "tics" that derive more from grand spectacle than from vocal art.

Chollet's artistic stagnation, which could bring nothing new to the repertoire at the Opéra-Comique and failed to inspire new vocal and dramatic figures, emerges in two letters from Scribe to Auber dating from as early as 1843. Written while Scribe was working on the libretto for *La sirène,* in which the role of Scopetto was initially intended for Chollet, the letters show the librettist to have been mollified that the role was eventually offered to Gustave Roger. Two passages from these letters reveal the creative process and clarify the manner in which performers conditioned roles. They reveal the singer to be as much a hindrance as a fertile artistic inspiration or collaborator. In Scribe's letter of 25 August 1843, Chollet appears very much as a burden:

> In the end, and not without difficulty, my dear friend, I believe I have our affair even more in hand than I told you, for I have been able to secure the lead role for Roger. This will entail a lot of work for me, but none for you, given that, and it was this that made the problem so difficult to resolve that I did not change a note of music except in the finale to Act 1, which you have not completed.
>
> When I wrote the role for Chollet there was no way to do [it] differently, though it depressed me. Because Chollet, who may still be good in *rôles de charge* and *hors nature,* is detestable once it is necessary to have truth, verve, and above all, interest. Interest is not possible with him, and now with Roger I will have verve, interest, and comedy.[40]

In a second letter, dated September 4, Scribe criticizes Chollet even more severely and in greater detail:

> I was desperate, I must tell you, about writing such a role for Chollet, who can still be very good in *rôles de charges, hors nature,* and *rôles de blague;* but who understands nothing of nature and truth, even less of true comedy and interest. There was no way to do otherwise, and I resigned myself. But from the moment I had the means to rework this character for Roger, I paid no regard to my time or my work, because with Chollet we would have had a *Chaperons blancs*–type success,

---

40. "Enfin et non sans peine, mon cher ami, je crois que je tiens notre affaire mieux encore que je ne vous l'avais dit, car je suis parvenu à arranger le principal rôle pour Roger. Cela me donnera à moi beaucoup de travail, mais à vous aucun, attendu et c'était là ce qui rendait le problème difficile à résoudre que je n'ai pas changé une note à la musique sauf au final du 1er acte que vous n'aviez pas fait.

"Lorsque j'ai écrit le rôle pour Chollet il n'y avait pas moyen de faire autrement, mais cela me désolait. Car Chollet qui peut encore être bon dans des rôles de charge et hors nature est détestable dès qu'il faut de la vérité, de la verve et surtout de l'intérêt. L'intérêt n'est pas possible avec lui et maintenant j'aurai avec Roger de la verve, de l'intérêt et du comique." Eugène Scribe and Daniel-François-Esprit Auber, *Correspondance d'Eugène Scribe et Daniel-François-Esprit Auber,* ed. Herbert Schneider (Liège: Éditions Mardaga, 1998), 32.

and with Roger, we will have, I hope, a *part of the Devil* [*part du Diable*]. His role is charming, and he will play it with gaiety, energy, and feeling.[41]

These two letters draw attention to an important quality expected of the comic-opera artist, a quality from which Chollet distanced himself in the course of his career: the "natural," born, of course, from convention, but capable of prompting spectators to overlook the artifice, business, and weight of determinations and habit in comic opera. It is precisely a quest for "true comedy," "interest," and the "natural" that fueled comic opera under the July Monarchy—the revitalizing energy that sprang from comic opera's capacity regularly to transform the stagnating elements of the institution and the company into fertile qualities. Chollet's ability to secure a fair degree of artistic freedom in spite of the strictures of the Opéra-Comique's administrative structure demonstrates that the star system was not necessarily the most productive avenue for the lyric theater.

41. "J'étais désolé, il faut vous le dire, d'écrire un rôle pareil pour Chollet qui peut être très bon encore dans des charges ou dans des rôles hors nature ou dans des rôles de blague; mais qui ne comprend rien à la nature et à la vérité, encore moins au vrai comique et à l'intérêt. Il n'y avait pas moyen de faire autrement et je me résignais, mais du moment où j'ai vu moyen de tourner ce personnage pour Roger, je n'ai regardé ni à mon temps ni à mon travail, parce qu'avec Chollet nous aurions eu un succès des *Chaperons blancs* et avec Roger, nous aurons je l'espère une *part du Diable*. Son rôle est charmant et il le jouera avec gaîté, entrain et sentiment." *Les chaperons blancs* (1836) received only twelve performances in Paris, compared to the fifty-two stagings of *La part du diable* in 1843 and thirty-nine more in 1844 and 1845, among others. Ibid., 35.

Fromental Halévy within the Paris Opéra

COMPOSITION AND CONTROL

Diana R. Hallman

For young French composers in the second quarter of the nineteenth century, no loftier goal existed than writing for the stage of the Paris Opéra (Académie Royale de Musique). Although aspirants eagerly sought opportunities at the Opéra-Comique and Théâtre-Italien, the truly enterprising knew that lasting reputations could be built at this exceedingly prestigious Parisian lyric theater. Certainly two of the most ambitious contemporaries were Fromental Halévy (1799–1862; see fig. 2.1) and Hector Berlioz (1803–1869), who shared the sanction of the Conservatoire and the Prix de Rome and who both achieved the goal of writing for the Opéra—albeit through strikingly different professional paths and with varied results. Berlioz's story, which he colorfully, and bitterly, relates in his memoirs, is undoubtedly the more familiar one: after only four performances at the Opéra in 1838–39, his two-act opera *Benvenuto Cellini* was pulled, and despite his many efforts and artistic connections, his five-act *Les Troyens* was never performed on its stage in his lifetime.[1] By contrast, Halévy, with the staging of six *grands opéras,* one three-act and one two-act opera, a ballet, and a

---

1. See Hector Berlioz, *The Memoirs of Hector Berlioz,* trans. and ed. David Cairns (London: Victor Gollancz, 1969), 243–45. Performances of *Benvenuto Cellini* took place on 10, 12, and 14 September 1838, with a fourth on 11 January 1839. In the 1840s Berlioz worked on, but did not complete, the five-act *La nonne sanglante* to a libretto by Eugène Scribe and commissioned by Léon Pillet (ibid., 444–47). Acts 3–5 of *Les Troyens* were premiered as *Les Troyens à Carthage* on 4 November 1863 at the Théâtre-Lyrique; for a good discussion of the performance history of this work and its posthumous resurrection, see Lesley Wright, "Berlioz in the *Fin-de-siècle* Press," in

FIGURE 2.1. Portrait of Fromental Halévy by P. S. Germain. *L'illustration*, 25 March 1843. Courtesy of Fordham University Library.

ballet-opéra, would become a leading figure at the Opéra, in part by working within the institution itself.

In 1829, at the age of thirty, Halévy began to forge a role of practical behind-the-scenes musician with that of Opéra composer when he accepted the position as assistant (*troisième*) *chef de chant*, essentially retracing the steps he had recently taken at the Théâtre-Italien. In the years leading up to his employment with the Opéra, he had accompanied rehearsals at the Italien while teaching at the Conservatoire and working to have his first operas performed.[2] In 1827 and 1829 he succeeded with the

Berlioz: Past, Present, Future; Bicentenary Essays, ed. Peter Bloom (Rochester, NY: University of Rochester Press, 2003), 160–66.

2. Halévy had attempted to have his work performed at the Opéra-Comique as early as 1819,

production of three one-act *opéras comiques*—*L'artisan, Le roi et le batelier,* and *Le dilettante d'Avignon*—at the Opéra-Comique, as well as an *opera semiseria, Clari,* at the Théâtre-Italien in 1828.[3] Not long after he joined the Opéra staff, Halévy's ballet-pantomime *Manon Lescaut* had its premiere in that theater on 3 May 1830;[4] it was followed by his ballet-opéra *La tentation* on 20 June 1832.

Halévy's subsequent success in getting his works performed at the Opéra undoubtedly depended on a range of forces, perhaps most important among them his consistent realization of the theater's musical-dramatic expectations, his ability to work diplomatically within the theatrical bureaucracy, and his building of solid though at moments contentious relationships with Opéra directors, performers, and administrative and musical staff. But also significant was the reputation that he established, first as a promising talent at the Conservatoire and later as a skilled composer of powerful and poignant music for the stage. Halévy's golden moment came relatively early, with the brilliant, career-marking success of *La juive* of 1835. Yet it was a moment that could have easily slipped out of his hands, had it not been for Meyerbeer's return of the libretto to Eugène Scribe, or for Louis Véron's backing of Halévy.[5] The opera's consistent revenues ensured that Halévy's future endeavors would be looked upon favorably within the Opéra, but his work as institutional "insider" would soon prove to be a mixed blessing, leading to a more problematic creative environment than he enjoyed under Louis Véron's leadership. Although he would not struggle with the same types of frustrations either within or outside the musical establishment as did Berlioz, his behind-the-scenes work might be viewed as both productive and counterproductive to his compositional efforts and achievements. In this chapter I shall turn my attention to Halévy's first decade at the Opéra in search of insights into his varied responsibilities and the possible impact that his employment may have had on his composition, the Opéra's willingness to stage his works, and his artistic standing. I shall center the discussion in particular on the years under Edmond Duponchel, from 1835 to 1840—shortly after the explosive success of *La juive* and Véron's departure—

---

as reflected in his appeal to Baron d'Est for a hearing of *Les deux pavillons* (*F-Pn*, Mus., *Lettres autographes,* vol. 50, no. 17, 20 December 1819).

3. *Le dilettante d'Avignon* and *Clari,* both of which were critically acclaimed, especially helped to strengthen Halévy's reputation as an opera composer. Mark Everist writes that the composer's status rose more significantly in the early 1830s with his completion of Ferdinand Hérold's two-act opéra comique, *Ludovic,* in 1833. See Everist, "Fromental Halévy: From *opéra comique* to *grand opéra,*" in *Giacomo Meyerbeer and Music Drama in Nineteenth-Century Paris* (Aldershot: Ashgate, 2005), 221–22.

4. An annotated tabular index to the Opéra correspondence of Rochefoucauld, *F-Po,* AD 54, No. 795, 11 9bre [November], records that "Mr. Halévy was given the task of composing the music of *Manon Lescaut*" (Mr. Halevy etait chargé de faire la musique de *Manon Lescaut*).

5. See Diana R. Hallman, *Opera, Liberalism, and Antisemitism in Nineteenth-Century France: The Politics of Halévy's "La Juive"* (Cambridge: Cambridge University Press, 2002), 26–29.

when Halévy began to take on administrative duties himself in addition to those of *chef de chant*. This period would prove to be a time of artistic crisis for the composer, one that appears to have been bound up in problems within the administration itself and in intensified public attacks on the Opéra's director.

When Halévy began his work under the director Émile Lubbert, his central responsibility was to help oversee and prepare the chorus, beginning with rehearsals for the premiere of *Guillaume Tell*,[6] but he also worked directly with composers and helped coordinate forces in rehearsal, as suggested in Meyerbeer's diaries. In the preparation of *Robert le diable* in 1831, Meyerbeer worked out details with Halévy on 24 June in company with the *deuxième chef de chant*, Jean Schneitzhoeffer, and the *chef d'orchestre*, François Habeneck; on 15 July he sought out Halévy to ask whether Conservatoire students could study the choral parts as back-up to Opéra regulars; in orchestral rehearsals in October and November he consulted with Halévy about the bells in act 5, a cut in the organ piece, a request to simplify a chorus, the replacement of cymbals with the gong, and the need to test the thunder effect.[7]

Under Véron, the former doctor, medical marketer, and founder of *La revue de Paris* who became the Opéra's highly regarded director from 1831 to 1835, Halévy took on added responsibility and status when he was appointed *premier chef de chant* in January 1833, shortly after the death of Ferdinand Hérold. As leading *chef de chant* under Véron and, from September 1835, Duponchel, he oversaw the budget for the *chant*, scheduled and judged auditions, recommended the hiring and firing of singers, supported requests for vacation and pay increases (as well as complaints about hardships suffered by chorus members and soloists), worked closely with and set rehearsal schedules for both soloists and choruses, and continued to aid composers and other *chefs* in rehearsals.[8] As *Les huguenots* was being prepared in late 1835 and early 1836, Meyerbeer's correspondence and diary notes offer snapshots of backstage interactions during this period and highlight Halévy's role in scheduling and coordinating rehearsals. In one letter Meyerbeer carefully dictates to Halévy the schedule he desires for the following day: at 11:30 A.M., the rehearsal of Mme Gras's aria of act 2 and the women's chorus in act 3; at 12:30, the rehearsal of all roles and chorus of act 1.[9] In his diary notes Meyerbeer cites meetings with Halévy concerning "Falcon, the women's chorus, [and] rehearsal time"; "the chorus in Damoreau's aria" of [act 2]; the assignments of the

6. Léon Halévy, *F. Halévy: Sa vie et ses œuvres,* 2nd ed. (Paris: Heugel, 1863), 32.

7. Giacomo Meyerbeer, *The Diaries of Giacomo Meyerbeer,* vol. 1, *1791–1839,* trans., ed., and annotated Robert Ignatius Letellier (Madison, NJ: Fairleigh Dickinson University Press; London: Associated University Presses, 1999), 416–20.

8. Fromental Halévy, letter to Louis Véron, 24 April 1835, in Halévy, *Lettres,* ed. Marthe Galland (Heilbronn: Musik-Edition Lucie Galland, 1999), 8–9; Halévy to Meyerbeer [July 1835] and "mardi 3" [November 1835], in ibid., 11; Meyerbeer to Halévy, "ce lundi soir" [end of 1835], in ibid., 12.

9. Meyerbeer, letter to Halévy, "ce lundi soir" [end of 1835], in ibid., 12.

second *coryphée* part and four soldiers; the rehearsal of the litanies "Vierge Marie"; and the use of the *cor anglais* and *cors à pistons* in the rehearsal of act 4.[10]

Halévy's balancing of his roles as *chef de chant* and composer was not unprecedented. Hérold, although he wrote primarily for the Opéra-Comique, also contributed two works to the Opéra in the early 1820s.[11] Schneitzhoeffer, who worked alongside Halévy as *deuxième chef de chant* from 1824 to 1839, wrote or co-wrote the music for two ballet-pantomimes of 1826 and 1827 and for the popular ballet-pantomime *La sylphide* of 1832.[12] Following in Halévy's footsteps, François Benoist, *troisième chef de chant* from 1835 to 1840 and the leading *chef de chant* from 1840 to 1850, wrote four ballets as well as the two-act opera *L'apparition;* and Pierre-Louis Dietsch, *chef de chœur* from 1840 to 1860, composed the two-act *Le vaisseau fantôme* for the Opéra.

Although various directors seemed to encourage and at times solicit compositions by Opéra employees, administrative documents also reveal efforts to limit their contributions and imply a preference for composers with proven successes outside the Opéra. Under Véron, the restrictions were not clearly spelled out in his *Cahier des charges* of 28 February 1831, the official document defining the expectations and limitations of the "Entrepreneur-Directeur" in his dual capacity as financial and artistic director of this grand enterprise and in relation to the oversight of the Commission de Surveillance, the government-appointed, non-censorship body of Opéra administrators, and the minister of the interior.[13] A mild constraint appears in the supplement to the *Cahier* dated 30 May 1831—article 8 stipulates that only two works of the same composer or librettist can be performed in the same year without administrative approval—but it does not mention a restriction on Opéra employees per se:

10. Meyerbeer, *Diaries,* 462–64, 471.

11. Among Hérold's *opéras comiques* was *Ludovic,* the work that he left unfinished at his death and that was completed by Halévy. Hérold's one-act *Lasthénie,* with libretto by de Chaillou, had its premiere at the Opéra on 8 September 1823, and the three-act *Vendôme en Espagne,* co-written with Auber to a libretto by E. Mennechet and A.-J.-S. D'Empis, first appeared at the theater on 5 December 1823.

12. Schneitzhoeffer's four-act *Mars et Venus, ou les filets de Vulcain* appeared at the Opéra on 29 May 1826; the one-act *Le Sicilien, ou l'amour peintre,* co-written with Sor, was first performed on 11 June 1827; and the two-act *La sylphide,* with libretto by Adolphe Nourrit, had its premiere on 12 March 1832. Marian Smith, *Ballet and Opera in the Age of "Giselle"* (Princeton, NJ: Princeton University Press, 2000), 212 n. 9, attributes the overture and several dance airs of *Le Sicilien* to Schneitzhoeffer.

13. See Jane F. Fulcher, *The Nation's Image: French Grand Opera as Politics and Politicized Art* (Cambridge: Cambridge University Press, 1987), 55–58, 60–62. Fulcher discusses certain stipulations in Véron's *Cahier,* including one requesting that the director maintain grandeur in the Opéra's productions and another "mandating scrupulous accuracy in all historical designs and details" (60); she also refers to Véron's frustrations over having to consult with the commission for approval of plans and productions (61–62).

ARTICLE 8.

Beginning 1 January 1832, the Entrepreneur will not be allowed to put on more than two works, regardless of genre, by the same composers or authors. However, this restriction could be lifted by a deliberation of the Commission [of Surveillance] approved by the minister [of the interior] if the situation might warrant it.[14]

Because no language appears restricting the compositions of Opéra employees, Véron apparently did not need permission to choose Halévy to write *La juive* (even though he became known for skirting *Cahier* stipulations and was fined for disregarding some of them).[15] Halévy's name was not included in the contract with the librettist, Eugène Scribe, on 25 August 1833, although Véron was already considering the *chef de chant* by the time he signed it—perhaps because the director was still awaiting Meyerbeer's final decision about setting the libretto or Scribe's approval of Halévy's collaboration.[16] But the omission of Halévy's name may simply have followed an earlier tradition of not designating names of Opéra employees in contracts, as Elizabeth Bartlet observed.[17]

When the Opéra designer and *metteur en scène* Edmond Duponchel was chosen to succeed Véron, he had to work within the confines not only of newly reinstated theatrical censorship, but also of a more restrictive *Cahier* and tougher fines for infringements of certain conditions.[18] In regard to employee-composers, one pointed qualification of Duponchel's *Cahier des charges* of 15 August 1835 suggests the desire for greater control. Article 23 repeats the clause mentioned above in Véron's *Cahier* supplement but adds: "No artist, *chef de chant*, [or] *chef d'Orchestre* employed by the Académie Royale de Musique will be allowed to perform his composition without our authorization."[19] The appearance of this language may reflect the commission's or minister's fears that an Opéra insider would gain too much influence and in essence turn the theater into a vehicle for his own works, or, at the least, the fear of

---

14. "L'Entrepreneur ne pourra faire jouer par an à partir du 1 Janvier 1832 plus de deux ouvrages n'importe le genre, des mêmes compositeurs ou auteurs. Toutefois cette prohibition pourroit être levée, si quelque circonstance pouvoit y donner lieu, par une délibération de la Commission [de Surveillance] approuvée du Ministre [de l'Intérieur]." *F-Pan*, AJ[13] 187, *Cahier des charges,* 28 February 1831; first *supplément* to the *Cahier des charges* ("Appendice au Cahier des charges de la direction de l'Opéra en régie intéressée, contenant les éclaircissemens et additions jugés nécessaires à l'exécution du traité et consentis par M. Véron, Directeur Entrepreneur"), 30 May 1831; second *supplément,* 31 May 1833.

15. Fulcher, *Nation's Image,* 62, 87.

16. See the discussion and transcription of the contract in Hallman, *Opera, Liberalism, and Antisemitism,* 26–28; appendix C, 314–16.

17. Private communication, c. November 1993.

18. Fulcher, *Nation's Image,* 87–88.

19. "Aucun artiste, chef de chant, chef d'Orchestre, employé à l'Académie Royale de Musique ne pourra faire représenter d'Opéra de sa composition, sans notre autorisation." *F-Pan*, AJ[13] 180, *Cahier des charges,* 15 August 1835, Direction Duponchel.

public criticism such a situation would bring. Coming on the heels of the undeniable success of *La juive,* which had had its premiere only seven months prior to the signing of Duponchel's *Cahier,* this clause may have been directed most pointedly at Halévy.

Yet the stipulation did not make Duponchel hesitate too long. The director wrote to the comte de Montivalet, the minister of the interior, on 5 March 1836—only months into his tenure—for authorization to prepare a contract with Halévy, arguing that the *chef de chant* merited an exception to the rule because of his past service to the Opéra as well as his success with *La juive* (see fig. 2.2).[20] The minister must have granted permission, because Duponchel signed a contract the next day with Halévy and Scribe for a four-act opera entitled *Le duc d'Albe.* Although the contract calls for Halévy to complete the score by the end of July 1837, it also places several works in the queue before it. Article 4 of the contract states that Duponchel was to produce Halévy's opera not only after a number of ballets, but also after (1) *Notre Dame de Paris,* by Louise Bertin; (2) *Stradella,* by Louis Niedermeyer; (3) *Le comte Julien,* by José-Melchor Gomis, (4) an opera by Daniel-François-Esprit Auber (no title given); and, finally, a work by Gioachino Rossini.[21] This last seems to have been wishful thinking, for a work by Rossini was not to be, but *Notre Dame* was produced under the title *La Esmeralda* on 14 November 1836 and *Stradella* on 3 March 1837; the work by Auber—the five-act *Le lac des fées*—did not appear until 1 April 1839. Gomis, a Spanish émigré composer, would never complete *Le comte Julien,* nor would Halévy ever realize *Le duc d'Albe* (Scribe's libretto was later turned over to Donizetti, who left the score incomplete after composing just two acts in 1839).[22] At some point, the minister sent Halévy's contract back.[23] If it is indeed true that the contract for *Le duc d'Albe* was rescinded, it seems surprising that Duponchel would ask for another exception to article 23 so soon. But, as explained in the new contract, Duponchel feared that *Le comte Julien* would not be ready owing to Gomis's illness, and he would need *Guido et Ginevra* to take its place. (Gomis in fact died in August 1836.) And certain qualifications in the contract suggest that Duponchel is treading carefully around article 23, perhaps obscuring his support for Halévy but, on the other hand, reflecting a halfhearted commitment: other than

20. *F-Pan,* AJ[13] 182, Dossier I, "Representations/correspondance général," letter from Duponchel, director, to the minister of the interior, 5 March 1836.

21. *F-Pn,* MS, n.a.fr. 22839, papers of Eugène Scribe, *Traités* I, fol. 281.

22. See the contract dated 13 January 1839 between Donizetti, Duponchel, and Scribe citing conditions for both *Le duc d'Albe* and *Polyeucte. F-Pn,* MS, n.a.fr. 22839, fol. 290. The libretto for *Le duc d'Albe* was later reworked for Giuseppe Verdi's *Les vêpres siciliennes* (Académie Impériale de Musique, 13 June 1855).

23. This seems to be the case, at least, if I have correctly read a marginal note in yet another *traité* with Halévy and Scribe signed two months later on 26 May 1836 for the five-act *Guido et Ginevra. F-Pn,* MS, n.a.fr. 22839, fol. 282. The marginal insert on fol. 282r refers to the contract for *Le duc d'Albe,* "shelved by a ministerial decision" (ajourné par une decision ministérielle).

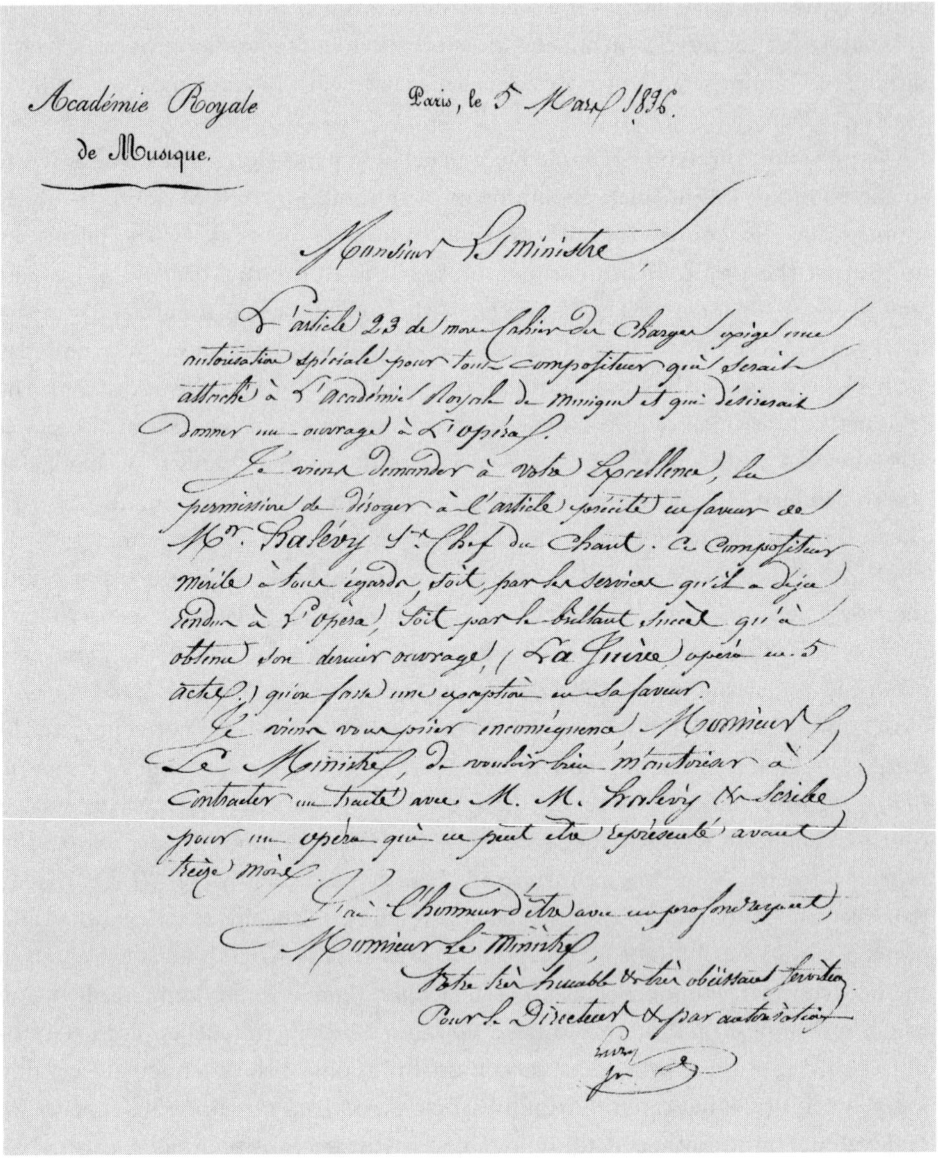

FIGURE 2.2. Letter of 5 March 1836 from Edmond Duponchel, director of the Académie Royale de Musique, to the comte de Montivalet, minister of the interior, requesting authorization for the contract with Fromental Halévy and Eugène Scribe for *Le duc d'Albe* (*F-Pan*, AJ[13] 182). Photograph by the author.

the clause on the state of Gomis's health, the same conditions given in the earlier *Le duc d'Albe* contract are referred to here—that is, *Guido et Ginevra* should appear only *after* works by Bertin, Niedermeyer, Auber, and Rossini. These qualifications may also suggest that the director views Halévy above all as a dependable back-up rather than as a front-runner, in spite of the continuing revenues brought in by *La juive*. The rules were bent for Halévy, but not to the same extent as for Rossini and, later, Donizetti, whose *La favorite* was pushed ahead of other scheduled operas in 1840.[24]

Close to the time of the 1836 contracts, Halévy began to take on an expanded role at the Opéra, and with it came increasing tensions. Although he remained *chef de chant*, he also became, in essence, assistant or even at times acting director. The composer's close friend Édouard Monnais, who himself would serve as co-director from December 1839 to May 1840, and later as royal or imperial commissioner at the Opéra, wrote that when Duponchel took over in 1835, he asked Halévy to become his "viceroy." The intimacy between composer and director, reflected in their use of *tu* in correspondence with each other, undoubtedly affected Duponchel's decision and colored their working relationship.[25] To what degree the director would depend on Halévy is difficult to assess fully, but various accounts and documents suggest that the composer shouldered substantial responsibilities. For over three years, a time that Monnais would define as "the administrative period" of Halévy's life, he portrays the composer as Duponchel's alter ego, who spent much of his time as a mediator and built on his *chef de chant* duties as he tried to resolve conflicts between librettists, composers, and artists and to convince recalcitrant singers and dancers to perform.[26] Halévy's correspondence supports Monnais's description.

In a brief note of early 1836, the composer writes to Adolphe Nourrit to request that he perform on a Friday night instead of Saturday, adding with a twist of humor that he is writing "on behalf of director Duponchel, [who is] in his bed and in a predicament."[27] Two other letters to Nourrit show Halévy not only trying to work out alternate casting, but also selecting and scheduling repertoire. In one letter of 1836, the composer-administrator explains that he will not be able to substitute Rossini's *Moïse et Pharaon* for the scheduled performance of *Guillaume Tell* because of the illness of Pauline Laurent, the soprano who was to have sung the role of Sinaïde, but he plans to go forward with his casting of Marcelin Lafont as Arnold if Nourrit's hoarseness did not respond to treatment. He then explains to Nourrit that Duponchel cannot come to see him because "he is busy all day with contentious matters."[28] In the second

24. See M. Elizabeth C. Bartlet, "From Rossini to Verdi," in *The Cambridge Companion to Grand Opera*, ed. David Charlton (Cambridge: Cambridge University Press, 2003), 259.

25. Fromental Halévy, letter to Edmond Duponchel, n.d. *F-Pn*, MSS, acq. nouv. fr. 1304. By comparison, Halévy used the formal *vous* in letters to Véron, as well as to the tenors Nourrit and Duprez, with whom he had warm artistic friendships.

26. Édouard Monnais, *F. Halévy: Souvenirs d'un ami pour joindre à ceux d'un frère* (Paris: Imprimerie Centrale des Chemins de Fer, 1863), 18, 20.

27. "De la part du directeur Duponchel, dans son lit et dans l'embarras." Fromental Halévy, letter to Adolphe Nourrit, [early 1836], in Halévy, *Lettres*, 14.

28. "Il est occupé toute la journée par des affaires contentieuses." Fromental Halévy, letter to Adolphe Nourrit, [1836], in ibid., 14. Marthe Galland suggests 6 April 1836 as the date of this letter, but this seems unlikely because it refers to *Guillaume Tell* as the opera which had been announced

letter, this one concerning a performance of Meyerbeer's *Les huguenots,* he writes asking for the tenor's final decision about singing before canceling the evening's performance. Despite Nourrit's illness, Halévy clearly presses him to sing while underscoring the awkwardness and burden of his position; were he the director, he insists, he would not trouble the singer so, and he certainly would not put ticket sales before his welfare:

My dear friend,

It appears that it is practically impossible to give some spectacle or other this evening: I have clear proof of that. I come to ask you again, before advertising the fatal closure, if it is not possible for you, with an announcement, to sing *Les huguenots.* Forgive me, my dear friend; if I had received your first letter, I would have informed the machinist. Do you see my enormous responsibility? If I were director (God forbid!), personally, I would not torment you in this way; but I do the business of another, and, before deciding to give up box-office receipts, which are not mine, I must use all the means in my power to save them.

My dear friend, you tell me that the *avertisseur* didn't come to see you this morning. You know that you told him definitely that he must never come to ask you if you are singing; in saying that, when you are ill, you should let him know. Remember, my good friend, that I received your letter only two hours ago. I only say all this to you because of the moral and *potential* responsibility that weighs on me.

I tell you again, if it were a matter of my own affairs, I would have gladly made the voluntary sacrifice of a performance rather than annoy you in this way.

I await your final decision. Knowing your devotion and your supreme loyalty, I am convinced in advance that, if you refuse me, it will distress you as much as me.

Your friend,
F. Halévy

Please answer me in writing.[29]

---

for that evening, while a second letter that she dates to 6 April 1836 speaks of *Les huguenots* as the advertised piece for the same evening.

29. Mon cher ami,

Il est démontré qu'il est matériellement impossible de faire un spectacle quelconque pour ce soir: j'en ai les preuves évidentes. Je viens vous demander encore, avant d'afficher le fatal *relâche,* s'il ne vous est pas possible, avec une annonce, de chanter *les Huguenots.* Pardonnez-moi, mon cher ami; si j'avais reçu votre première lettre, j'aurais prévenu le machiniste. Voyez mon énorme responsabilité. Si j'étais directeur pour mon compte, ce qu'à Dieu ne plaise! Je ne vous tourmenterais pas ainsi; mais je fais les affaires d'un autre, et, avant de me decider à sacrifier une recette qui ne m'appartient pas, je dois user de tous les moyens qui sont en mon pouvoir pour la sauver.

Mon cher ami, vous me dites que l'avertisseur n'est pas venu chez vous ce matin. Vous savez que vous lui avez formellement dit qu'il ne devait jamais venir vous demander si vous chantiez, en disant que, quand vous seriez malade, vous le feriez dire. Rappelez-vous, mon bon ami, que je n'ai reçu votre

After receiving a response in the early afternoon that Nourrit could not sing, Halévy went to check on his condition. The next day he confirmed to the commissioner that Nourrit had indeed been too ill to perform, then enumerated his failed efforts to put another work in its place: first Auber's *Le philtre,* but the ballet masters would not be able to supply the dance; then *La muette de Portici,* but *machiniste en chef* Constant did not have the necessary time to exchange the scenery. Finally he said that Lafont could not sing in Nourrit's place because he did not know the changes that had been made to the role of Raoul during his time away on an approved *congé.*[30] Halévy makes clear that he is handling matters in lieu of Duponchel, for he signs off with the phrase, "for the absent Director" ("Pour le Directeur absent").

Opéra correspondence also confirms that when Duponchel went away on *congés—*for example, in August of 1837, 1838, and 1839; eight days in September after the premiere of *Benvenuto Cellini;* eight days the following September; and for an extended time in February 1839—Halévy was officially entrusted with the Opéra's direction, including the duties that he seems to have overseen during other parts of the season, that is, "announcing the spectacle and putting on the current repertoire."[31] Moreover, in his capacity either as *chef,* assistant director, or composer, Halévy influenced initial casting decisions, as reflected in his direct, confident appeal to Duponchel to give the young soprano Maria Nau a role opposite Gilbert Duprez.[32] He also helped to coordinate gratifications for good service as well as singers' requests for their own *congés* or performances outside the Opéra: in a letter of 1838, for example, Duponchel writes to the tenor Eugène Massol that he has learned "by means of Mr. Halévy" that the tenor desires an eight-day vacation in order to rest.[33]

Inevitably, Halévy's administrative power under Duponchel, as Monnais relates,

---

lettre qu'à deux heures. Je ne vous dis tout cela qu'à cause de la responsabilité morale et *virtuelle* qui pèse sur moi.

Je vous répète que, s'il s'agissait de mes propres affaires, j'aurais fait volontiers le sacrifice volontaire d'une réprésentation, plutôt que de vous fatiguer ainsi.

J'attends votre dernière décision. Connaissant votre dévouement et votre haute loyauté, je suis convaincu d'avance que, si vous me refusez, cela vous affligera autant que moi.

Votre ami,
F. Halévy.

Répondez-moi par écrit, s'il vous plait.

Fromental Halévy, letter to Adolphe Nourrit, [6 April 1836], in ibid., 15.

30. Fromental Halévy, letter to the royal commissioner, 7 April 1836, in ibid., 15–17. For other examples of Halévy's management of schedules and singers, see his letters to Louis Alizard and Gilbert Duprez (15 July 1837, [June 1838], and undated), in ibid., 20, 22, 24, and 235.

31. *F-Po,* AD 59, Correspondence (29 June 1837–18 July 1838), No. 35, 11 August 1837; *F-Pan,* AJ[13] 180, Dossier 3, Sept. 1838.

32. *F-Pn,* MSS, acq. nouv. fr. 1304, n.d.

33. *F-Po,* AD 59, no. 163, 5 April 1838. See his letter to "Monsieur le Directeur," 20 December 1839, and his "Gratification extraordinaire" for the chorus member M. Duclon, 5 February 1840,

led to jealousies and personal difficulties often bound up in angry castigations of the director, whom many viewed as grossly incompetent.[34] A writer in the *Courrier des théâtres,* for example, found his administration "detestable."[35] Monnais may have had a number of public attacks on Duponchel in mind when he spoke of the atmosphere of suspicion that surrounded Halévy at the Opéra, but he was also likely aware of the attitudes of Jean-Pierre-Louis Gentil, controller of the theater's immense *matériel.* In the now well-known source *Les cancans de l'Opéra,* written under the disguise of an *habilleuse,* Gentil caricatures Halévy both as a controlling force and a "chien" to Duponchel rather than an alter ego, one who exacerbated rather than made up for Duponchel's incompetence. Gentil's descriptions seem fueled by bitterness, and he apparently did not keep his feelings about Halévy to himself or confine them to the pages of his hidden writings: Meyerbeer jots in his diary in September 1837, "Why is Gentil angry with Halévy?"[36] The administrator's commentary is tinged with anti-Semitic shadings: in his portrayal of the Monday committee meetings of Duponchel, division chiefs, and inspectors, Gentil writes: "It is to this Sanhédrin (because Halévy himself controls completely) that important questions relating to pantomime, drama, and music are submitted."[37] In another entry he presents an image of the scheming Jew who takes advantage of Duponchel's affection, and he hopes that "the disruptive and shady dealings" of Halévy's "Judaic race" will become clear to the director as well as the Opéra's financial supporter Alexandre-Marie Aguado.[38]

Matching Gentil's remarks were complaints in *Le Figaro* of 8 March 1838 that accused Halévy of conflict of interest and of having too much influence in casting and repertoire choice, and even blamed him for the heavy expenditures at the Opéra. As the author highlights the preferential treatment it assumes the composer enjoys and

---

in Halévy, *Lettres,* 26–27; see also his letter to Duponchel, n.d., *F-Pn,* MSS, acq. nouv. fr. 1304, in which he asks for a release of several singers for a Conservatoire concert.

34. Monnais, *F. Halévy,* 18.

35. "Nouvelles de Paris," *Courrier des théâtres,* 5 September 1838. Léon Escudier later wrote in retrospect: "M. Duponchel was a director of indisputable incapacity. No director . . . drew to himself more gibes and antipathies" (M. Duponchel était un directeur d'une incapacité incontestable. Aucun directeur . . . n'a attiré sur sa tête plus de quolibets et plus d'antipathies). Escudier, "La vérité sur l'Opéra," *La France musicale,* 3 January 1841.

36. 23 September 1837, in Meyerbeer, *Diaries,* 499.

37. "C'est à ce *sanhédrin,* car Halévy le domine entièrement, que les questions importantes de l'exploitation mimo-dramatico-lyrique sont soumises." Louis Gentil, "Composition du spectacle," in Jean-Louis Tamvaco, ed., *Les cancans de l'Opéra: Le journal d'une habilleuse, 1836–1848* (Paris: Éditions du CNRS, 2000), 1:357–58. Also see Hallman, *Opera, Liberalism, and Antisemitism,* 277–78. The Sanhédrin may refer to the council of Jewish rabbis who debated the Torah in the Temple in Jerusalem, but it more likely alludes to the Jewish leaders assembled by Napoléon for the purposes of coordinating Jewish law with French civil law and customs.

38. "Les menées ténébreuses, désorganisatrices, de la race judaïque." Louis Gentil, "L'alter-ego de M. Duponchel," in Tamvaco, *Les cancans,* 1:294–95. See also Hallman, *Opera, Liberalism, and Antisemitism,* 277–78.

affords certain artists, it warns against the breaking of the Opéra's contract restrictions against employee-composers and calls for Halévy's resignation:

> In effect, it is humanly impossible that a composer, *maître* of singing and the direction of the repertoire, does not give preference to his own works over all others, and also to the artists who perform his works over all the other artists. . . .
>
> Vacations and favors are granted by M. Halévy, master of singing, exclusively to singers and dancers who sing and dance for M. Halévy, author of *La juive* and *Guido et Ginevra.*
>
> This infraction of the contract which was passed between the competent authority and Duponchel only serves to demonstrate, right up to the most recent evidence, the wisdom of the broken clause; one is assured that this state of things aroused attention and that M. Halévy will be invited to give his resignation.[39]

Following on the heels of this straightforward attack on the composer's Opéra positions came a series of edgy conversational parodies in *Le Figaro* that alluded to Duponchel's verbal wit and portrayed Halévy as a sycophantic sidekick. Although the subtle allusions may be lost on today's readers, among those with less esoteric references, one imagined conversation of 22 March 1838 plays with the name of Assuérus, or the Wandering Jew, as it hints of sexual indiscretions, most likely those of Halévy, who was rumored to have had a long-running affair with an Opéra chorister in the 1830s.[40] Another of 5 April 1838, which points to the intimacy between Duponchel and Halévy in its use of *tu,* sounds a pun on the words "les relais," whose double meaning of "l'air laid" could be interpreted as Halévy's "unattractive look" or "ugly expression," or perhaps even his "unattractive aria":

> M. Duponchel asked M. Halévy yesterday:—Do you know who is the most discreet lover?—I don't know, answered M. Halévy. Well, M. Duponchel continued, it's *Assuérus,* because he knew how to love and keep quiet (Esther).

* * *

> M. Duponchel said to M. Halévy yesterday:—Halévy, my friend, tell me something: do you know why you resemble a postmaster?—I don't know, answered

---

39. "En effet, il est humainement impossible qu'un compositeur, maître du chant et de la direction du répertoire, ne donne pas à ses ouvrages le pas sur tous les autres; et aussi aux artistes qui jouent dans ses ouvrages sur tous les autres artistes. . . . Les congés, les faveurs, sont accordés par M. Halévy, maître du chant, exclusivement aux chanteurs et aux danseurs qui chantent et qui dansent pour M. Halévy, auteur de la *Juive* et de *Guido et Ginevra.* . . . Cette infraction au contrat passé entre l'autorité compétente et M. Duponchel ne sert qu'à montrer jusqu'à la dernière évidence la sagesse de la clause enfreinte; on assure que cet état de choses a éveillé l'attention et que M. Halévy va être invité à donner sa démission." "Chronique," *Le Figaro,* 8 March 1838.

40. For a discussion of this relationship, see Hallman, *Opera, Liberalism, and Antisemitism,* 85–88.

Halévy.—Well, M. Duponchel continued, it's because you have relays (an unattractive look).[41]

In sharp contrast to such parodies, accounts friendlier to Halévy describe the composer as amiable, warm, and sincere, traits that appear to have made him a natural diplomat. In Nourrit's eyes, he was a modest man who "did not shout out loud" that he was the best composer at the Opéra and who because of his modesty was treated as a "petit garçon."[42]

Some depictions of Halévy in the late 1830s accuse the composer of foiling opportunities for other composers at the Opéra. Berlioz complained mildly to his father on 8 March 1837 that Halévy, as well as Auber, "refus[ed] to yield their rightful position and make way for [*Benvenuto Cellini*]," despite the fact that he had completed his score and they had not (for *Guido et Ginevra* and *Le lac des fées*, respectively).[43] Gentil's accusations are sharper, as are the strikingly parallel statements in *Le Figaro*.[44] Among the composers against whom Halévy allegedly schemed, Gentil cites Donizetti specifically: he implies that Halévy could "undo" Duponchel's commitments to Donizetti and other composers if he did not approve of them and notes that "sooner or later" Halévy would find the means to take over what was promised to the Italian composer.[45] Because the Opéra wanted to maintain the hegemony of Meyerbeer, Auber, Halévy, and Scribe, Gentil concludes, it went along with the actions of its *chef de chant*. Undermining Gentil's claims, other than the venomous, irrational tone that recurs throughout his critique, are the clauses in Halévy's contracts discussed above, the transferring of the libretto of *Le duc d'Albe* from Halévy to Donizetti, and Duponchel's agreements and contracts with Donizetti for *Les martyrs* and *La favorite*. William Ashbrook's descriptions resonate with Gentil's conclusions when he reports that Halévy's three-act opera *Le drapier* stalled the appearance of *Les martyrs*, which he claims was ready for rehearsal while Halévy was still refining his score. According to Ashbrook, Donizetti appealed to Halévy the day after he signed his contract (on 13 January 1839), requesting that he allow *Les martyrs* to be staged before *Le drapier*

41. "M. Duponchel demandait hier à M. Halévy:—Sais-tu quel est l'amant le plus discret?—Je ne sais pas, répondit M. Halévy.—Eh bien! Reprit M. Duponchel, c'est *Assuérus*, parce qu'il sut aimer *et se taire* (Esther)"; "Bon mots de la journée," *Le Figaro*, 22 March 1838. "M. Duponchel disait hier à M. Halévy:—Halévy, mon ami, dis-moi z'un [*sic*] peu: sais-tu pourquoi tu ressembles à un maître de poste?—Je ne sais pas, répondit Halévy.—Eh bien, reprit M. Duponchel, c'est que tu as *les relais* (l'air laid);" ibid., 5 April 1838. This series of "bons mots," which all concern Duponchel and Halévy, appeared daily from 11 March to 1 May 1838. Their author is unknown at present.

42. Adolphe Nourrit, letter to Monsieur Éd. P., 27 March 1835, in Louis Quicherat, *Adolphe Nourrit: Sa vie, son talent, son caractère, sa correspondance* (Paris: L. Hachette, 1867), 3:9.

43. *Selected Letters of Berlioz*, ed. Hugh Macdonald, trans. Roger Nichols (New York: W. W. Norton, 1997), 141.

44. Tamvaco, *Les cancans*, 1:400–401, 522, as cited in Bartlet, "From Rossini to Verdi," in *Cambridge Companion*, 448 n. 6.

45. Tamvaco, *Les cancans*, 1:401.

and explaining that he did not want his work to come directly after Auber's *Le lac des fées*. Ashbrook adopts a Gentilian (or perhaps Berliozian) tone as he complains that the "dilatory" practices of the Opéra, as well as the actions of the "irresolute" Halévy, hindered Donizetti unreasonably, though without faulting the Italian composer for withdrawing *Les martyrs* from the rehearsal schedule that conductor Habeneck had mapped out (i.e., the alternation of rehearsals for *Le drapier* and *Les martyrs*). He also neglects to mention that Halévy had signed his contract for *Le drapier* on 17 November 1838, three months before Donizetti's for *Les martyrs*.[46]

Whether Halévy consciously put obstacles in Donizetti's way in particular is difficult to conclude, given the undocumented claims and lack of other evidence, but one might question whether a certain French territorialism lay beneath the surface of Opéra tensions. Perhaps the composer was concerned about a Donizettian threat in a manner similar to Berlioz, who—undoubtedly still reeling from the failure of *Benvenuto Cellini*—complained of the excessive number of Donizetti's works on the stage in a *Journal des débats* review of 16 February 1840. After listing seven works planned for the Opéra and other theaters, Berlioz quipped, "M. Donizetti seems to treat us like a conquered country; it is a veritable invasion."[47] In such a world, Berlioz reasoned, the French artists were on their own; it was they who were forced to "cherish their ambitions," since the French government abandoned them after educating them.[48] Whether Halévy at least partially agreed with him we can only speculate, but the letters of recommendation that he wrote for young French composers as well as his endorsement of plans for a new theater that would bring greater compositional opportunities for them suggest that he was a less self-serving artist than Gentil and others portray.[49]

The threat that Halévy seemed to pose touched some of the journalistic critiques of his works in the late 1830s. Perhaps sharpest among them was Henri Blaze's withering denigration of Halévy's new opera *Guido et Ginevra*, and of his talent as a whole, in the *Revue des deux mondes* in March 1838. Blaze arrogantly pronounces the limits of the composer's talent as he draws attention to his personal power at the Opéra and the wasting of its vast resources on him:

46. William Ashbrook, *Donizetti and His Operas* (Cambridge: Cambridge University Press, 1982), 144–45. Ashbrook does acknowledge in a note (141 n. 15) that Halévy allowed other works to intervene: Casimir Gide's ballet *La tarentule* (24 June 1839), Henri de Ruolz's *La vendetta* (11 September 1839), and Mario Aurelio Marliani's *La xacarilla* (28 October 1839). The first performances of *Le drapier* and *Les martyrs* were 6 January 1840 and 10 April 1840, respectively. For the contract for *Le drapier,* see *F-Pn*, MS, n.a.fr. 22839, I, fol. 288.

47. Cited in translation in Ashbrook, *Donizetti*, 146.

48. Ashbrook, *Donizetti*, 146–47.

49. See, e.g., his recommendation of the Prix de Rome winner Antoine Elwart to François Crosnier, director of the Opéra-Comique, 12 October [1836], and his proposal to the Institut de France to open a new theater devoted to new works and opportunities for young composers, 26 October 1844; in Halévy, *Lettres*, 18, 46–48.

La juive, L'éclair, Ginevra—here is the work of M. Halévy; it would be childish to want to bother with the rest. To my mind, these three scores suffice to give the measure of a man. M. Halévy will not be able to go lower than *Ginevra*, but he definitely will never rise higher than *La juive*. That is the limit that he imposed on himself and that he will not go beyond. . . .

It seems that the time had come for M. Halévy to gather all his forces in a serious work, and to justify, at least by its merit, the rank to which the anguished French school permitted him to rise: no occasion was more ideal to seize upon. *Thanks to the personal influence that he acquired in the administration of the Opera,* M. Halévy had at hand the most vast resources that a musician could have: an immense orchestra, numerous choruses, and above all, the voice of Duprez, this treasure that would make Rossini envious. Furthermore, M. Halévy found himself, with regard to the public, in a favorable position already secured through his success. But, with all that, the author of *La juive* knew how to create only *Ginevra,* that is, the most deplorable score that he had yet to produce.[50] (Emphasis added)

Elsewhere in the article, Blaze portrays Halévy as a false, unnatural, and uninspired composer hampered by his Conservatoire training and "scientific" approach.[51]

In its many-pronged attack on Halévy, also in the spring of 1838, *Le Figaro* included a few positive remarks on *Guido et Ginevra* but dismissed much of its music:

The first two acts of the opera are noteworthy for their two inferior sets—and by the complete absence of all that could resemble music, with the exception of a romance sung by Duprez.

50. "*La Juive, l'Éclair, Ginevra,* voilà l'oeuvre de M. Halévy; il serait puéril de vouloir s'occuper du reste. A mon sens, ces trois partitions suffisent à donner la mesure d'un homme. M. Halévy pourra descendre plus bas que *Ginevra,* mais à coup sûr il ne s'élèvera jamais plus haut que *la Juive.* C'est là une limite qu'il s'est posée lui-même et qu'il ne franchira point. . . . Il semble que le temps était venu pour M. Halévy de rassembler toutes ses forces dans une oeuvre sérieuse, et de justifier, au moins par son mérite, le rang où la détresse de l'école française lui a permis de s'élever: jamais occasion ne fut plus belle à saisir. *Grâce à l'influence personnelle qu'il s'est acquise sur l'administration de l'Opéra,* M. Halévy avait sous sa main les plus vastes ressources dont un musicien puisse disposer: un orchestre immense, des choeurs nombreux, et par-dessus tout, la voix de Duprez, ce trésor qui ferait envie à Rossini. En outre, M. Halévy se trouvait, vis-à-vis du public, dans la position favorable d'un homme que le succès a déjà consacré. Or, avec tout cela, l'auteur de *la Juive* n'a su faire que *Ginevra,* c'est-à-dire la plus triste partition qu'il ait produite encore" (emphasis added). Henri Blaze, "Lettres sur les musiciens français," part 1, "M. Halévy: *Guido et Ginevra,*" *Revue des deux mondes* 13 (15 March 1838): 773–74, 777.

51. Kerry Murphy reports on similar characterizations of Meyerbeer's composition by music journalists in her essay "Berlioz, Meyerbeer, and the Place of Jewishness in Criticism," in *Berlioz: Past, Present, Future,* ed. Peter Bloom (Rochester, NY: University of Rochester Press, 2003), 93–96.

The third act contains some very beautiful parts. . . . The last two are nearly as insignificant as the first and second.[52]

Among other negative reviews of the opera, one in the *Courrier des théâtres* of 6 March called it a "half-failure" ("demi-chute"), whose "score was among the weakest" ("la partition a été des plus faibles"); the writer also puns that the real plague was not the one that played a minor role in the plot, but that which Duponchel had brought to the Opéra.[53]

Such onslaughts from within the Opéra as well as from the press undoubtedly unsettled Halévy, although their effects may have been mitigated by the endorsements that *Guido et Ginevra* did receive. In *La revue et gazette musicale de Paris*, the journal edited by Halévy's publisher, Maurice Schlesinger, Berlioz praises the composer for his "great and beautiful score" ("[cette] grande et belle partition"), even going so far as to say that it is "already classed among the masterpieces of the modern school" ("déjà classée parmi les chefs-d'œuvre de l'école moderne").[54] He points out, among many other details, Halévy's new, brilliant, and "piquant" instrumentation, his adept writing for his soloists (particularly Duprez as Guido and Massol as Forte-Braccio), and his effective use of rhythm, local color, and recurring music.[55] Other critics seemed to agree with the judgment of Monnais: that the opera was less uniformly well-written than *La juive*.[56] The writer "A." of *Le constitutionnel* reminded audiences not to make a hasty judgment of this large, intricate work of "continually tragic and solemn" character ("un caractère continuellement tragique et solennel"), suggesting that they should go beyond the immediate appreciation of only a few numbers such as Guido's romance, "Pendant la fête inconnue."[57] Despite Berlioz's laudatory critiques, he also

52. "Les deux premiers actes de l'opéra sont remarquables par deux mauvaises décorations—et par l'absence complète de tout ce qui pourrait ressembler à de la musique, à l'exception d'une romance chantée par Duprez. . . . Le troisième acte renferme de fort belles parties. . . . Les deux derniers ont à peu près l'insignifiance du premier et du second." "Académie Royale de Musique," *Le Figaro,* 7 March 1838.

53. "Académie Royale de Musique," *Courrier des théâtres,* 6 March 1838.

54. Hector Berlioz, "Académie Royale de Musique: Première représentation de *Guido et Ginevra,* paroles de M. Scribe, musique de M. Halévy, ballets de M. Mazilier, décors de MM. Feuchieres et Cambon," *La revue et gazette musicale de Paris,* 11 March 1838; and Berlioz, "Académie Royale de Musique: Première représentation de *Guido et Ginevra,* paroles de M. Scribe, musique de M. Halévy, ballets de M. Mazilier, décors de MM. Feuchieres et Cambon," *La revue et gazette musicale de Paris,* 18 March 1838.

55. These assessments are drawn from all three of Berlioz's articles dealing with this work: ibid., 11 March 1838; ibid., 18 March 1838; and "Académie Royale de Musique: Première représentation de *Guido et Ginevra,* paroles de M. Scribe, musique de M. Halévy, ballets de M. Mazilier, décors de MM. Feuchieres et Cambon," *La revue et gazette musicale de Paris,* 1 April 1838.

56. Monnais, *F. Halévy,* 19.

57. A., "Académie Royale de Musique: *Guido et Ginevra;* La musique, les décors, les chanteurs," *Le constitutionnel,* 17 March 1838.

implied—in a generally positive review in the *Journal des débats*—that Halévy had not had or had not taken the time to let the work cohere. After chastising the composer (somewhat hypocritically) for scarcely having begun the score thirteen months prior, he added: "A *grand opéra* in five acts is not a work that is prepared in several weeks; much time, much work, much reflection are needed, and the task that the composer imposed on himself this time, to compose and rehearse simultaneously, is certainly as difficult as it is dangerous."[58]

Monnais acknowledged the fits and starts in the opera's creation and rehearsals, and he suggests that the tedious, continuous administrative tasks that had interrupted its progress had weighed heavily on the composer. "If I were given three years to write a work," Halévy queried his friend sometime after the opera's production, "would I really know if I could manage to satisfy myself?"[59] Although Monnais chided him that he would still most likely follow his habit of waiting for the pressure of "la dernière moment," Halévy was undoubtedly concerned that his myriad administrative duties had indeed distracted him from composing. In his reflective words to Monnais, he perhaps realized in hindsight that he had in fact juggled dangerously with *Guido et Ginevra,* as he revealed a yearning to write a *grand opéra* not only more fully gratifying to his critics and public than *Guido et Ginevra,* but to himself—and undoubtedly one that would bring back the initial glories of *La juive.*

But also affecting Halévy at this turning point in his artistic life was the new pressure brought to bear within the Opéra that went well beyond Gentil's grumblings and journalists' complaints, although their commentary may have hit their mark within the administration. A draft of a letter of 5 December 1839 from the minister of the interior to the president of the Commission des Théâtres Royaux, which authorizes the rehearsals for *Le drapier,* also warns that the exceptions to article 23 so continuously made for Halévy must end—the Opéra could not continue to condone such favoritism or allow such influence:

> Article 23, in its second disposition, has as its objective to give composers a guarantee against rival influences that they could encounter in the administration or the establishment for which they work and at the same time to shelter this administration from all suspicion of partiality and interference in aid of its members. In the spirit and the letter of this article, its principle is prohibition; the ministerial authorization, which tempers the severity of the regulation, is only the exception.

58. "Un grand opéra en cinq actes n'est pas de ces oeuvres qui se confectionnent en quelques semaines; il faut beaucoup de temps, beaucoup de travail, beaucoup de réflexion, et la tâche que le compositeur s'était imposée cette fois, de composer et de faire répéter en même temps, est certes aussi pénible que dangereuse." Hector Berlioz, "Théâtre de l'Opéra," feuilleton, *Journal des débats,* 7 March 1838. In his memoirs, Berlioz also spoke of the extended, uninterrupted time needed to compose an opera and his own difficulty in finding it (*Memoirs,* 246).

59. "Si l'on me donnait trois ans pour faire un ouvrage, . . . je voudrais bien savoir si je parviendrais à me satisfaire?" Monnais, *F. Halévy,* 19.

M. Halévy, whom public opinion ranks among three or four principal composers whose works form the standard repertory of the Opéra, and who, with only two scores over the course of the last year, has filled one performance out of seven—a proportion that, given the youth and fecundity of the author, can only increase from day to day. M. Halévy is not in a position to remain the constant object of an exception of this nature. The exception, as contained and practiced in this manner, would have the effect of making the regulation completely illusory.[60]

The author reminds the president of another manner of skirting the restrictions of article 23, noting that when it is in fact necessary to call for the minister's authorization, it should be done *before* works are commissioned or written, and not "on the eve of their first performance" (à la veille de leur représentation).[61]

Perhaps sensing the end of rule bending in his favor and the loss of Duponchel's power, as well as, certainly, the intensifying vehemence of his detractors, Halévy left the Opéra, first stepping down as assistant director sometime in 1839, and then resigning as *chef de chant* by June 1840 when Léon Pillet became director. As Monnais tells us, he resigned with great relief and "no regrets," happy to sit in the theater with fewer cares and, as announced in various articles and *Nouvelles,* to devote himself exclusively to composition.[62] The composer had gained much during his decade-long rise to prominence under Véron and Duponchel, having strengthened his understanding of the dramaturgy of historical *grand opéra* even as he contributed to its development. He had deepened his knowledge of the musical and technical abilities of soloists, chorus, and orchestra, refined his negotiating and collaborating skills, and solidified

60. Charles Marie Tanneguy Duchâtel, "L'article 23, dans sa seconde disposition a pour objet d'assurer aux compositeurs une garantie contre les influences rivales qu'ils pourraient rencontrer dans l'administration même de l'Etablissement pour lequel ils trouaillent et en même temps de mettre cette administration a l'abri de tout soupçon de partialité et d'envaissement au profit de ses membres. Dans l'espoir et dans le les lettres de cet article, le principe, c'est la prohibition; l'autorisation ministérielle, qui tempere la rigueur de la règle, n'est que l'exception. . . . M. Halévy, que l'opinion place au rang des trois ou quatre principaux compositeurs dans les ouvrages fameux de répertoire ordinaire de l'opéra, qui avec deux partitions seulement a pendant le course de l'année dernière rempli une représentation sur sept—proportion qui la jeunesse et le fécondité de cet auteur, ne peut qu'accroître de jour en jour, M. Halévy n'est pas en position de demeurer l'objet constant d'une exception de cette nature. Ainsi comprise et pratiquée, l'exception aurait pour effet de rendre la règle complément illusoire." *F-Pan,* AJ[13] 183, "Ouvrages: *Le drapier.*" See Berlioz's narrative about Roqueplan's use of this regulation as a way of manipulating the composer to give back the libretto of *La nonne sanglante:* the director reminded Berlioz that he could not compose the opera if he accepted the conducting post promised to him (*Memoirs,* 444–47). The post never materialized.

61. *F-Pan,* AJ[13] 183, "Ouvrages: *Le drapier.*"

62. Monnais, *F. Halévy,* 21; A. Specht, "Nouvelles," *La revue et gazette musicale de Paris,* 24 May 1840; G. Benédit, "Académie Royale de Musique," *La revue et gazette musicale de Paris,* 7 June 1840. Benédit writes that Halévy resigned "voluntarily."

his relationships with key artists and staff. But, as he had come to realize, many of his advantages had transformed into burdens and impediments to his positive public image. In spite of the composer's relief, noted by Monnais, at having relinquished his positions, this likely gave him pause and perhaps some trepidation. His affiliation with the Opéra as a member of the staff and the administration had undoubtedly meant more to him than a source of income and a platform for his own artistic influence: it had to have been a source of great pride as well as personal security, especially because he was well aware that Jews of earlier generations had been barred from professional employment in French institutions.

After releasing his behind-the-scenes control, Halévy of course maintained ties with the theater as a composer, but his influence fluctuated and lessened under subsequent administrations, as is suggested by the reassuring and cajoling manner he adopts in letters to Léon Pillet of the early 1840s, his reference to "les autocrats de l'Opéra" in a letter to his librettist Jules-Henri Vernoy de Saint-Georges in 1847, and the publicized conflicts with Nestor Roqueplan in the 1850s.[63] An account in *Le corsaire* (25 April 1852) depicts Roqueplan directing the conductor, Narcisse Girard, to ignore Halévy's suggestion in a rehearsal of the composer's *Le juif errant*—an insulting gesture that prompted Halévy to snap up his score and exit the theater. Under Roqueplan, Halévy's control over the rehearsals and scheduling of his works diminished markedly.[64] But in 1840, although new challenges lay ahead, Halévy's surrendering of backstage control at the Opéra brought a new kind of power, one that freed him to work with fewer distractions and greater concentration and removed him from career-defeating accusations of conflict of interest. With his renewed focus on composition, the benefits came rather quickly in the rich scores and public acclamation accorded *La reine de Chypre* and *Charles VI*.

---

63. Halévy, *Lettres*, 32–33, 43, 58.

64. See the letter from Nestor Roqueplan to Halévy [end of April 1853], in Halévy, *Lettres*, 108, in which the director reports that he cannot schedule the performances of *Le juif errant* suggested by the composer because of the demanding rehearsals of Louis Niedermeyer's *La fronde*. Several other letters from the 1850s attest to Halévy's frustrations and doubts about Roqueplan's support: in one the director accuses Halévy of having "eyes clouded by black butterflies" (les yeux troublés par des papillons noirs); in another, he appeals to the composer that they work together with understanding and without quarreling; in a third, he reminds Halévy of his profound "respect for our old and mutual friendship" (respect pour notre vielle et mutuelle amitié) (*F-Pn*, MSS, n.a.fr. 14347, fols. 51–52, 53–54, 55–56). For a discussion of the rehearsals of *Le juif errant* and the deteriorating relationship between Roqueplan and Halévy, see Béatrice Prioron-Pinelli, *"Le juif errant," paroles d'E. Scribe et d'H. V. de Saint-Georges, musique de F. Halévy: Un grand opéra français au début du Second Empire* (Weinsberg: Musik-Edition Lucie Galland, 2005), 1:54–60.

Systems Failure in Operatic Paris

THE ACID TEST OF THE THÉÂTRE-LYRIQUE

Katharine Ellis

"Give us another national opera house!" This was the cry that, after repeated stone-walling by theater managers and government commissioners, finally led to the institution of the Opéra-National (1847–48) and then the first Théâtre-Lyrique (1851–70). In the end, neither was inaugurated as "national" or "imperial" in the sense of being publicly funded; but both were predicated on the idea of providing a public service, born as they were of a belief that one should support young operatic composers whose careers in their native France were being stunted by a lack of opportunity for their works—especially innovative ones—to reach the stage. Whereas Paris had a national Opéra and Opéra-Comique, each contractually dedicated to a single type of opera, the *cahier des charges* (contract) for the Théâtre-Lyrique was generically liberal, the emphasis being placed instead on the need for new operas and ballets in various genres and career development for composers. Indeed, the bond between the Théâtre-Lyrique and French operatic renewal was so close that for the rest of the century it went without question that any attempt to found a theater with "Lyrique" in its name was at least in part a venture to foster new compositional talent.[1]

---

1. The theater was called the Opéra-National from 1847 to 1848 and the Théâtre-Lyrique from 1851 to 1870. Thereafter the name was revived several times: Théâtre-Lyrique-Dramatique, 1874–75; Troisième Théâtre-Lyrique Français, 1875; Opéra-National-Lyrique (or Théâtre-National-Lyrique), 1876–77; Théâtre-Lyrique, 1878; Théâtre-Nouveau-Lyrique, 1878; Théâtre-Lyrique, 1888–89; Théâtre-Lyrique, 1893; and Théâtre-Lyrique de la Renaissance, 1899–1900.

AU THÉÂTRE-LYRIQUE.
— Quand je te dis que c'est Morphée !
— Mais, non, ma chère, c'est Orphée, je t'assure.
— Laisse-moi donc tranquille ! je sens bien qu'il
m'endort.

FIGURE 3.1. "At the Théâtre-Lyrique." Caricature by Cham [Amédée de Noé]. *Le charivari*, 18 March 1860.

We might accordingly view the Théâtre-Lyrique as a site of creative instability—an institution with more freedom than any of its predecessors to set a new agenda for French opera. Yet its story tells us something else: born as a venue with a license to concentrate on new French opera in multiple genres, it became an opera house about which Florimond Ronger (alias Hervé) could plausibly quip, "At the Théâtre-Lyrique the dead kill off the living."[2] Classic museum pieces were always intended to be mixed with new works, but in fact they came to predominate. Why? The reasons are complex and interconnecting, but they are best illuminated by reference to Napoléon III's deregulation (*liberté des théâtres*) legislation of 6 January 1864. Beginning the following July, this much-acclaimed law freed Parisian theaters old and new (though not the "imperial" ones) from their contracts with the state and from the generic straitjackets those contracts imposed. Within two years of this legislation taking effect, Paris saw what the state since Napoléon I had tried so assiduously to prevent: direct competition. The Lyrique's manager, Léon Carvalho, was enthusiastically involved. In 1866

2. "Au Théâtre-Lyrique les morts tuent les vivants." Quoted in Nicole Wild, "Théâtre-Lyrique," in *Dictionnaire de la musique en France au XIXe siècle,* ed. Joël-Marie Fauquet (Paris: Fayard, 2003), 1209.

three near-simultaneous productions of the same work appeared at the Opéra, the Théâtre-Italien, and the (now "imperial") Théâtre-Lyrique. Moreover, the work was not a new opera—that was still prevented by the contractual system—but a museum piece by a foreign composer. It was none other than Mozart's *Don Giovanni*.

Can we generalize from an event such as this, the like of which to my knowledge never happened again in nineteenth-century Paris? Yes, I suggest, if we understand it as the last in a series under a system that was already breaking down where opera was concerned. For if we look at the behavior of national opera house managers from 1831, when the Opéra became semi-privatized, we find them straining to reconfigure popular works from the musical museum to fit their own theater's generic definitions. In a shift that amply demonstrates the emergence of canonic imperatives in opera, respect for individual masterworks came to supersede respect for the traditional generic categories of *grand opéra, opéra comique,* and vaudeville by which the Parisian theatrical scene was organized. The reconfiguration of masterworks was closely related to the lazy abuse of the *reprise,* about which critics routinely complained and which Pier-Angelo Fiorentino, for one, hoped would cease after deregulation if the clauses requiring the national theaters to mount new works were properly enforced.[3] And yet in the wake of the 1864 law, we see more of the same. In this article one of my concerns is therefore implicitly counterfactual: I explore what the operatic map of Second Empire Paris might have looked like *without* theatrical *cahiers des charges* and suggest that both before and after 1864 their stipulations for new works were something of a saving grace for opera composers, because in the increasingly conservative environment of the Second Empire they were one of the rare forces that could push unwilling opera managers toward taking risks with unknown works.

Viewing this particular slice of Parisian operatic history from an institutional standpoint reveals multiple fracture lines that might remain imperceptible (or tangential) in histories that embrace individual constituencies—composer and/or librettist, audience or manager. Such fracture lines crop up repeatedly and extend across almost every conceivable problem facing those involved in operatic Paris during a period of transition: tensions between expectation and reality; between French protectionism and international competition; between supply and demand; between love of novelty and the embedding of a stable repertoire; between perceptions of art and of commercial entertainment; and between state control and the free market.[4] The Théâtre-Lyrique occupied a unique position at the intersection of these forces. As an institution it inspired an unusual density of comment because it was new, because its presence was hard-won, and because it had the capacity to alter the dynamic of operatic provision in the capital. It was, in short, an obvious focus for reformist zeal

3. *La France,* 11 January 1864.

4. It should be noted that the problems as outlined here are entirely Parisian. The situation in the French regions was equally fraught, but different. For an overview, see Graham Howard Bould, "The Lyric Theatre in Provincial France (1789–1914)" (Ph.D. diss., University of Hull, 2005).

about how the French should run the flagships of their operatic system. Hence its value as the acid test.

Set up ostensibly to solve a problem of supply, throughout its existence the theater was forced to satisfy very different (and shifting) problems of demand. Despite the efforts of many of its managers, it arguably never achieved its core aim. Yet the exceptional liberality of its *cahier des charges* meant that satisfying a variety of repertorial demands ought, in theory, to have been feasible. Its financial history is not without irony. Unsubsidized until November 1863, a few weeks before deregulation was made law and just eight months before it took effect on 1 July 1864, it was never supported well enough by the government to insulate it fully from market forces. The paltry 100,000 francs it received compared unfavorably with figures higher by a factor of six or more for the Opéra-Comique and the Opéra.

In the standard musicological literature the Théâtre-Lyrique is best known for having mounted Berlioz's *Les Troyens à Carthage* in 1863 under the management of Carvalho and Wagner's *Rienzi* in 1869 under Jules Pasdeloup. For historians of French opera it is celebrated as the first home of Gounod's *Faust* (1859, under Carvalho) and the first theater of the nineteenth century to revive Gluck (the Gluck-Berlioz *Orphée* of 1859, under the same manager). With the exception of *Faust,* all, notably, were recitative operas (and *Faust* would soon be so adapted for the Opéra stage). And all, just as notably, were large-scale, tragic works.

However, with the exception of *Faust,* whose 306 performances between 1859 and 1868 made it the theater's top-ranking success, none of these operas was congruent with the theater's original rationale to act as a theater of apprenticeship for young composers. Nor did they reflect its increasingly dominant reputation as a theater devoted to foreign opera (translated classics by Mozart, Weber, and, increasingly, Verdi).[5] Nor, if the performance statistics are to be trusted, do they form part of what the Théâtre-Lyrique's audiences seem to have wanted most: *opéra comique* and other light opera of various vintages, starting with Grétry's *Richard Cœur-de-Lion* and ending with the works of Adolphe Adam and Victor Massé.[6] As the cartoonist

5. Grétry's *opéra comique* was presented 302 times between 1856 and 1868, making it the second most frequently performed opera. *Richard* racked up performances at a relatively steady rate of around 25 annually; by contrast, Mozart topped the bill for fashionability, with a record 117 performances of *La flûte enchantée* in a single year. Figures are taken from T. J. Walsh, *Second Empire Opera: The Théâtre Lyrique, Paris, 1851–1870* (London: John Calder; New York: Riverrun Press, 1981), 299–322.

6. We can look to performance statistics and repertoire lists to help answer this question, but only if we exercise due caution. Viewed in close-up, such lists are fallible guides to popularity, nor do they necessarily represent a particular manager's aesthetic convictions or his estimations of a work's level of success. And of course, they have to be read in the light of the institutional framework, of which the *cahier* was part, within which managers worked. For instance, when preparation of a new work was delayed, the Théâtre-Lyrique's managers were often constrained to continue presenting repertoire that was past its sell-by date; the same held if singers who were associated with a particular role were temporarily unavailable.

Cham observed (see fig. 3.1), this class of audience and the Gluck-Berlioz Orphée, in particular, did not mix. During its most stable years, then, the essential problem faced by the managers of the Théâtre-Lyrique faced was that it was many things to many people and a slave to many masters.

After the closure of the ill-fated Opéra-National of 1847–48 under Adolphe Adam, Paris's new lyric stage opened in 1851 with a *cahier des charges* that was both complex in its demands and generous in its provision of opportunity. The theater's core repertoire was to be new music, but that music could be *opéra comique* or recitative opera, with prose or verse libretti, and with or without ballets. The manager's focus was channeled toward works by inexperienced composers who needed to cut their teeth on a variety of relatively small-scale projects. By prohibiting any single composer from having more than six acts presented in any one year, the contract ensured a wide distribution of spoils. And, most important of all, it specified that Prix de Rome composers would receive preferential treatment in the two years after the expiry of their award, being offered a two-act work with the libretto to be provided by the manager. Where older repertoire was concerned, clauses permitted two translated works per year, allowed repertoire to be adopted from other French and foreign theaters once it had reached its tenth anniversary, and authorized the presentation of works in the public domain—translated and otherwise—so long as they did not total more than 33 percent of the number of new acts presented by the theater over any two-year period.[7] In addition, the manager had free rights to the revival of works already mounted by the company, thus enabling a nascent Théâtre-Lyrique to begin developing its own repertoire.[8] For composers and managers alike, there was no more flexible deal to be had in operatic Paris.[9]

Even when the terms were tightened in 1854 they remained liberal, requiring an annual minimum of fifteen new acts (a trio of three-act operas along with three works by Paris *débutants*) but retaining the original generic breadth. Nevertheless, the contract also contained warning signs, one of which restricted the new manager, Émile Perrin, to a maximum of six acts per year by any composer who had already seen four of his works staged at the Opéra or the Opéra-Comique. The very fact that such a clause needed to be inserted says much about government administrators' fears that tendencies at the Théâtre-Lyrique might replicate those of the Opéra and the Opéra-

7. I shall henceforth refer to these categories of work as "premieres," "adoptions," and "public-domain works," respectively. Until 1866, when it was extended to fifty years, French copyright extended for a decade after a composer's death.

8. The crucial articles—4, 5, and 6—are given in Wild, *Dictionnaire,* 239.

9. As Albert Soubies and Charles Malherbe explain, after the establishment of the Théâtre-Lyrique, the Opéra-Comique management started to look over its shoulder: the Lyrique's contract was markedly more attractive because of its provision for translations; moreover, while it could dip relatively freely into the Opéra-Comique's own repertoire, the Opéra-Comique could not retaliate. Soubies and Malherbe, *Histoire de l'Opéra-Comique: La seconde salle Favart,* vol. 1, *1840–1860* (Paris: Librairie Marpon and Flammarion, 1892), 214.

Comique, neither of which (the Opéra especially) showed much interest in supporting untried composers.[10] And Carvalho's contract of 1862, which reduced the number of new acts from fifteen to twelve, suggests either weakening resolve, realism, or both on the part of the government's administrative machine.[11] These contracts, all dating from the period before the Théâtre-Lyrique's subsidy was granted, represent a careful balancing act between new repertoire and established works, between the French and the foreign, and between risk and security.

The question of financial security was paramount, for it was not by running at a loss that a private opera house would best serve France's new generation of composers. And audience tastes mattered to the managers of a theater located (at least from 1851 to 1862) on the boulevard du Temple, in a relatively poor part of the city.[12] In this respect, the broad patterns presented by a ranking chart of Théâtre-Lyrique performances from 1851 to 1870 are telling (see table 3.1). Of the five works that garnered two hundred performances or more, only one was a world premiere by a French composer and librettist; and only two of those five works were by living composers. And of all the works that garnered one hundred or more performances (twenty-one works), eight were premieres, six were adopted, and seven were in the public domain.

Different managers nonetheless established different repertorial traditions. Edmond and Jules Seveste (1851–54), Émile Perrin (1854–55), Pierre Pellegrin (1855–56), and Charles Réty (1860–62) took seriously the theater's brief of supporting young composers. All kept strings of new works—often *débutant* one-acters—at different stages of production, ready to be pressed into service at relatively short notice. The Seveste era—from the beginning of the 1851–52 season to July 1854—is indicative: between them, Edmond and Jules put on forty-eight new productions in the various categories stipulated in their contract. Of these, thirty were premieres (fifty-nine acts in total), six were public-domain works (seven acts), and the remainder were adoptions following the tenth-anniversary rule. Réty, whom we can view as occupying an interregnum between Carvalho's two periods of office, filled it with twenty-one premieres (thirty-four acts) and just three public-domain works (eight acts) in thirty-two months.

This practice turned out to be a recipe for bankruptcy. It was Carvalho (1856–60; 1862–68) who altered the dynamic, streamlining the number of productions, lavishing more care on each one, and effectively running the Théâtre-Lyrique on the Italian repertory opera model, in which a production (or an alternating pair) occupied the stage for as long as it remained profitable. Significantly, four of the five productions

10. The measure was probably aimed at Adolphe Adam, a disproportionate number of whose operas—new and borrowed—were given at the Théâtre-Lyrique under the Seveste brothers as well as Perrin and, in his first year, Carvalho. Adam's belated heyday brought near-ubiquity: during January 1853, for instance, his works were performed on four Parisian stages simultaneously.

11. Wild, *Dictionnaire,* 240.

12. The theater would move to a newly built venue on the place du Châtelet in 1862, amid worries that the nature of its repertoire would necessarily change.

TABLE 3.1. Most frequently performed works at the Théâtre-Lyrique, 1851–70

Performances	Work	Details and dates inclusive	Manager
306	**Gounod, *Faust***	o, 5 acts, 1859–68	**Carvalho**
302	Grétry, *Richard Cœur-de-Lion*	oc, 3 acts, 1856–68	Carvalho
243	Verdi, *Rigoletto*	o, 4 acts, 1864–69	Carvalho
201	Weber, *Robin des bois/ Freyschutz*	o, 3 acts, 1855–68	Perrin
200	Mozart, *Les noces de Figaro*	oc, 4 acts, 1858–65	Carvalho
192	**Clapisson, *La fanchonnette***	oc, 3 acts, 1856–68	**Carvalho**
182	Paër, *Le maître de chapelle*	oc, 1 act, 1851–70	E. Seveste
176	**Adam, *Si j'étais roi***	oc, 3 acts, 1852–63	**J. Seveste**
172	Mozart, *La flûte enchantée*	o, 4 acts, 1865–68	Carvalho
170	**Massé, *La reine Topaze***	oc, 3 acts, 1856–66	**Carvalho**
163	Flotow, *Martha*	oc, 4 acts, 1865–69	Carvalho
156	**Maillart, *Les dragons de Villars***	oc, 3 acts, 1856–63	**Carvalho**
144	**David, *La perle du Brésil***	o, 3 acts, 1851–64	**E. Seveste**
138	Gluck, *Orphée*	o, 3 acts, 1859–63	Carvalho
135	Halévy, *Le val d'Andorre*	oc, 3 acts, 1860–70	Réty
133	Adam, *Le sourd, ou l'Auberge pleine*	oc, 3 acts, 1856–64	Artistes en société
132	**Adam, *Le bijou perdu***	oc, 3 acts, 1853–62	**J. Seveste**
126	Rossini, *Le barbier de Séville*	oc, 4 acts, 1851–70	E. Seveste
126	**Gautier, *Flore et Zephyre***	oc, 1 act, 1852–55	**J. Seveste**
124	Halévy, *Jaguarita l'Indienne*	oc, 3 acts, 1855–62	Perrin
100	Weber, *Oberon*	o, 3 acts, 1857–62	Carvalho
38	Wagner, *Rienzi*	o, 5 acts, 1869–70	Pasdeloup
21	**Berlioz, *Les Troyens à Carthage***	o, 5 acts, 1863	**Carvalho**

Boldface = *créations* at the Théâtre-Lyrique; o = opera; oc = *opéra comique*. Raw data taken from T. J. Walsh, *Second Empire Opera: The Théâtre Lyrique, Paris, 1851–1870* (London: John Calder; New York: Riverrun Press, 1981).

that garnered two hundred or more performances were Carvalho's (see table 3.1). The institutional price, however, was a far more erratic rate of turnover. In 1866, his leanest year for new operas, Carvalho mounted just two one-act premieres (by Salomon and Marcelli) and two public-domain works (five acts: *Don Juan* and *The Merry Wives of Windsor*), leaving the bulk of the year's performances to Flotow's *Martha*, which the Théâtre-Lyrique had adopted in December 1865. Such sparse pickings had been preceded, however, by frenetic activity in 1865, which saw seven premieres (sixteen acts), two adoptions (nine acts), and two public-domain works (six acts). In more representative years (1858, 1859, 1863, and 1864), Carvalho balanced four or five premieres (averaging ten and a half acts per year) with one adoption (three or four acts per year) and two or three public-domain works (averaging six acts per year), along with a large number of repertory pieces.

The difference between the practices of the Seveste brothers and Réty on the one hand, and Carvalho on the other, is explained in part by the relative expansiveness of the operas they commissioned: Carvalho's were typically larger and more dramatically weighty enterprises, reflecting a move away from *opéra comique* and toward *grand opéra* (*Faust, Les Troyens, Roméo et Juliette,* and *Mireille* all spanned five acts). But if one takes the act rather than the opera as the unit of measurement (which is how the French government preferred to do its accounting), the increased proportion of operatic time given over to public-domain works in the Carvalho years is plain to see: responsive to public demand for Mozart especially, he was conspicuously adrift from the original 1851 requirement of a 1:2 ratio of public-domain works to premieres. Nevertheless, although Carvalho's first management period became the pivot between a theater run according to supply-side demands and one based more on consumer preferences, his policy did not prevent bankruptcy: it merely staved it off.[13] For all the liberality of its *cahiers,* then, the Théâtre-Lyrique's failure appears almost foreordained. The remainder of this essay provides a sketch of the tensions in people's thinking about the institutions of Parisian opera, as a way of suggesting why.

By the early 1840s it was commonplace to lament that because the Opéra and the Opéra-Comique excluded newcomers (and the Théâtre-Italien was all but closed to all Frenchmen), Paris required another national opera house. In August 1846, when the Opéra-National was granted its license, the Parisian press accordingly typecast it as a theater of apprenticeship. Léon Escudier, editor of *La France musicale* and publisher of a great deal of stage music, was overjoyed. For fifteen years, he wrote, composers,

---

13. In this light, Réty's attempt to move back to the policies of the 1850s appears as doomed idealism, though it is clear that he tried to combine new works with the principle of alternation that Carvalho had spearheaded. Carvalho's practice was noted at the time, and it resulted in his gaining a reputation for *festina lente.* As one critic wrote in 1858, "At the Théâtre-Lyrique the takings for *Les noces de Figaro* are still reaching between 4,000 and 5,000 francs [per night]. It is understandable, then, that M. Carvalho is making slow haste to show us new work. When the *Noces* have reached their 100th performance, perhaps he will decide to celebrate other weddings, with younger, if not necessarily more valiant, couples" (Au Théâtre-Lyrique, les recettes des *Noces de Figaro* se maintiennent entre 4 et 5,000 francs; on comprend que M. Carvalho se hâte lentement pour nous montrer sa pièce nouvelle. Quand les *Noces* seront à leur centième représentation, il se décidera peut-être à en célébrer d'autres avec des mariés plus jeunes, sinon plus vaillants). *La France musicale,* 19 December 1858. Hence the four months' worth of Mozart's *Les noces* in 1865. A full house at the boulevard du Temple theater brought in around 5,500 francs.

musicians, and the general public had been clamoring for precisely this kind of opportunity, only to be shouted down by those with vested interests, for whom such competition would be unwelcome:

> Graduates of the Conservatoire will finish their studies here, and will later be applauded at the royal theaters. Young composers who are rebuffed for no reason by other stages will be able to display their talents in front of a public that will encourage their first attempts. From now on, the monopoly that has stunted artistic progress will be destroyed. From now on, France can count one more musical institution, an institution founded on the principles of devotion and independence.[14]

There were several barbs here, each referring to long-standing debates. Beyond the stifling duopoly of the national theaters for French opera, the problem appeared twofold: first, the restrictions on the generic characteristics of works acceptable at each theater (and the fact that composers were disadvantaged if they were either unwilling to adapt to the needs of either theater or bent on writing works that suited only one of them); and second, the domination in the day-to-day repertoire of men whose works were so popular that they were all but house composers (such as Meyerbeer at the Opéra and Auber at the Opéra-Comique).[15] The first issue was a by-product of the state policy of reducing competition between national theaters by effecting tidy generic separation; the second was exacerbated by the *embourgeoisement* of musical life in Paris, the advent of transient suburban and regional audiences able to access Parisian entertainments by train, and the conservatism that came with the growth of a love of familiar classics.[16]

14. "Les sujets sortis du Conservatoire se formeront à cette école, et viendront plus tard se faire applaudir dans les théâtres royaux. Les jeunes compositeurs, qui sont repoussés sans motifs des autres scènes, pourront révéler leurs heureuses dispositions devant un public qui encouragera leurs premiers essais. Désormais le monopole, qui de tous les temps a été funeste aux progrès des arts, est détruit. La France, dès aujourd'hui, compte une institution musicale de plus, une institution fondée sur les bases de dévouement et d'indépendance." Léon Escudier, "Troisième Théâtre-Lyrique," *La France musicale*, 16 August 1846.

15. He was not alone in thinking thus. As early as 1842, for instance, a sarcastic Émile Dardonville portrayed a new opera house as a nightmare come true for the small number of established composers for whom a restricted market was essential to keeping aspirant composers at bay. See Émile Dardonville, "Méditation!," *Le monde musical*, 17 March 1842. This was the very year that Auber had five of his operas staged at the Opéra-Comique. They provided 141 (40 percent) of the theater's total 348 performances during the year. See Soubies and Malherbe, *Histoire de l'Opéra-Comique, 1840–1860*, 76.

16. The effects of train travel on audience composition have probably been underestimated, though they were occasionally noted in the press as a reason (or excuse) for repetitious programming. See, for instance, Paul Smith [Édouard Monnais], "Revue de l'année 1863," *Revue et gazette musicale de Paris*, 3 January 1864, who reminded readers that the demand for new works in the *ca-*

This last phenomenon was to have a profound impact on the fortunes of the Théâtre-Lyrique, as commentators noted from the outset. Shortly before the first incarnation of the theater opened in November 1847 under Adam's management, a news report in *La France musicale* noted that new works were in rehearsal but that it was the "old repertoire" that could make money for the theater.[17] This was, of course, the unstated (but doubtless understood) calculation underlying the last clause of article 4 in the 1851 *cahier des charges:* that the allowable 33 percent of public-domain works, together with the theater's own repertoire, would neutralize the risks inherent in producing unknown works by unknown composers. Yet as far as the press was concerned, there was another educational rationale for the Théâtre-Lyrique's portfolio of old and new: the institution of a living museum for composers otherwise deprived of the chance to learn from past models. Here, wrote the viscount Adolphe de Pontécoulant, young men would finally be able to learn their Gluck and their Sacchini, thereby compensating for the "extremely superficial" (*extrêmement superficielle*) education they had received at the hands of Conservatoire composition staff.[18] The Théâtre-Lyrique, then, was to provide a neoclassical finishing school along the lines of the Odéon for actors, but—crucially—at no cost to the public purse. From the perspective of an aspiring composer, the idea must have seemed a natural though belated extension of the patronage the state had offered since 1803, when the Prix de Rome in composition was established.

The subventions enjoyed by the national theaters made it relatively easy to invest in the new while maintaining the old. But the system was open to abuse, and as audiences at the main Parisian theaters became less hungry for novelty, older works—especially public-domain translations—took their place at the heart of an emerging repertoire problem. In particular, the *juste-milieu* years of the July Monarchy had brought about a change with which everyone was still living: from 1831, when state opera moved decisively toward the private sector via a change from full underwriting to partial subvention, managers became intensely competitive and market oriented. They avoided the new if they could, milked as much revenue as possible from well-loved works, and knew the value of other people's classics. At the Opéra, a wily Louis Véron took every opportunity to mitigate the more financially demanding terms of his contract: beyond cutting salaries and staff numbers, which he claimed to regret, he reused old backdrops and props when new were required (and, crucially, before any inventory could

---

hier des charges worked to prevent managerial abuse, through stasis, of the new riches brought by a nonresident public buying tickets to a single evening's entertainment. See also A. Lomon, "La force d'inertie," *La France musicale*, 22 September 1861, where the same argument about a transient and easily satisfied population is applied to explain the reluctance of managers to upgrade their facilities.

17. "On répète tous les jours dans la salle Sax des pièces nouvelles, et on s'occupe activement de l'ancien répertoire, qui peut être une source de fortune pour ce théâtre." "Nouvelles," *La France musicale,* 12 September 1847.

18. Le Vicomte de Pontécoulant, "Un infirme de la musique et l'Opéra-National," *La France musicale,* 9 January 1848.

prove it); and, most important, he avoiding putting on new French works.[19] Arguably, his most audacious moment came in 1834, when he requested that a five-act translation of *Don Giovanni,* presented in French as a *grand opéra* with ballets, be regarded for contractual purposes as the equivalent of two French premieres.[20]

Doubtless in this case Véron would have agreed with Castil-Blaze, who rather self-servingly wrote in 1851 (in a review of his own translation of Rossini's *Le bar-bier de Séville* at the Théâtre-Lyrique) that only when their own repertoire was self-sufficient would the French be able to dispense with translations, and that translated works were self-evidently superior because they had been singled out for translation. In addition, as he implied, translated works had benefits: not only were their reputations ready made, but they had been established at someone else's risk. Whatever their aesthetic merits, translations were potential cash cows.[21] Perhaps for the very same reasons, translations at the Théâtre-Lyrique troubled composers, who mobilized their lobbying groups to halt a perceived erosion of their rights.

The Commission des Auteurs Dramatiques argued in 1851 that Edmond Seveste's allocation of two translations per year was one too many, unfairly reducing opportunities for Frenchmen.[22] Castil-Blaze swept its arguments away imperiously: "The Opéra-National is up and running; you requested it, and you will doubtless wish it to live and prosper. Well, it is only with the aid of translations that you will be able to guarantee its existence. Amid the lottery of new operas, the manager needs a few opportunities to play it safe."[23] But Castil-Blaze failed: Seveste's allocation of translations

19. For a graphic discussion of Véron's attempts to save money while appearing to comply with the terms of his contract, see John D. Drysdale, *Louis Véron and the Finances of the Académie Royale de Musique,* Perspektiven der Opernforschung 9 (Berlin: Peter Lang, 2003), 72–73, 127–31. See also Véron's own account in Jacques Bonnaure, ed., *Docteur Véron: L'Opéra de Paris, 1820–1835* (originally published as *Mémoires d'un bourgeois,* 1853–55; Paris: Édition Michel de Maule, 1987), 75 (sets), 92–93 (employee salaries).

20. Correspondence with the Commission de Surveillance of the Opéra and the minister of the interior, March–May 1834. The commission, headed by the Duc de Choiseul, recommended acceding to Véron's request; the minister of the interior refused to do so on the grounds that it would be detrimental to the interests of composers writing for the Opéra. *F-Pan,* AJ[13] 183 (D).

21. "Si vous ne considérez certains opéras traduits comme des modèles qui doivent inspirer l'émulation des jeunes musiciens, regardez-les du moins comme un moyen financier." Castil-Blaze, "Opéra National," *La France musicale,* 5 October 1851.

22. Ibid. Rumor had it that the *Barbier* continued to vex the Commission des Auteurs such that it tried (unsuccessfully if so) to cap the number of performances. The editorial team at *La France musicale* responded trenchantly, advising Seveste to ignore such dictatorial behavior and continue, come what may: "M. Seveste ne peut se sauver qu'avec les traductions, et c'est avec les recettes des traductions qu'il trouvera le moyen de monter les pièces des jeunes auteurs français. Que le ministère avise, et que M. Seveste se mette au-dessus de l'excommunication de MM. les auteurs, ou l'Opéra-National est perdu pour la troisième et dernière fois." "Nouvelles," *La France musicale,* 12 October 1851.

23. "L'Opéra-National est en exercice; vous l'avez demandé, par conséquent vous désirez qu'il vive, qu'il prospère. Eh bien, ce n'est que par le secours de quelques traductions que vous pouvez

was halved. Émile Perrin's management of 1854–55, itself complicated at the outset by his position as manager of the Opéra-Comique, was characterized by similar battles, because the Commission des Auteurs tried to use his monopoly as a reason to effect a complete separation of repertoire (defined not only by genre but as individual works) between the two theaters. Perrin had made it clear that he wished to transfer some of the Opéra-Comique's spare repertoire to the Lyrique, but this was not at all what the commission had in mind. Indeed, clauses 5 and 6 of their proposed *cahier* for the Théâtre-Lyrique would have prohibited *all* adaptations and revivals of works in the public domain.[24]

The Perrin case eloquently suggests how the rivalry of new and old, of classic revival and premiere, and of French versus foreign would become a leitmotif of the theater's existence. The tension reached a peak under Carvalho, when he mounted five Mozart and five Weber operas at a steady rate of one per year and thereby sealed the theater's reputation as a Germanophilic institution.[25] There were disgruntled noises in the press;[26] but as long as the Théâtre-Lyrique remained without subvention, the use of public-domain repertoire would be tolerated as a fact of economic life—proof, if more were needed, of the extent to which a "standard" repertoire, often underpinned by canonic values and likened to a museum, was embedded in French operatic life by the middle of the century.

This view of the Théâtre-Lyrique reached its logical conclusion shortly before deregulation, by which time the theater had indeed gained its modest annual subsidy of 100,000 francs. In 1863 the critic A. de Bory recommended rather starkly that if the theater was to remain "imperial" under deregulation rather than reverting to independent status, it should be prohibited from producing anything except new works

---

assurer son existence. Il faut que, parmi les chances douteuses des opéras nouveaux, le directeur puisse jouer quelquefois à coup sûr." Castil-Blaze, "Opéra-National," *La France musicale,* 5 October 1851.

24. As reported in Léon Escudier, "Le Théâtre-Lyrique," *La France musicale,* 3 September 1854. The situation led to Perrin's resignation, though concessions by the Commission des Auteurs brought him back into the fold. See Walsh, *Second Empire Opera,* 52–53.

25. New productions included *Oberon* and *Euryanthe* (1857); *Preciosa* and *Le nozze* (1858); *Abu-Hassan* and *Die Entführung* (1859); *Così* (1863); *Die Zauberflöte* (1865); and *Don Giovanni* (1866). *Der Freischütz* was already in the repertoire.

26. See especially the comments of a critic who signed himself Aldino Aldini (probably Achille de Lauzières), in 1861, after *Fidelio:* "Faut de l'allemand, pas trop n'en faut. Le Théâtre-Lyrique s'est attaché à nous montrer les pierres gemmes du répertoire germanique" (Aldini, "Théâtre Lyrique: *Fidelio,*" *La France musicale,* 13 May 1860), and his comments on the extent of translated opera in Paris, where the Opéra either acted as a museum or, via new translations, crowded out indigenous composers. In addition, he wrote: "La musique italienne n'a-t-elle pas la salle Ventadour? L'allemande n'a-t-elle pas le Théâtre-Lyrique? libre, celui-ci, de choisir son bien où il se trouve! Encore, s'il l'est de droit, serait-il peut-être convenable qu'il n'en abusât pas." Aldino Aldini, "Les traductions: Un théâtre spécial," *La France musicale,* 17 June 1860. For an attribution to De Lauzières, see Charles Joliet, *Les pseudonymes du jour* (Paris: Achille Faure, 1867), 33–34.

by Conservatoire-trained composers recommended by the government.[27] Translations, he wrote, should be the preserve of the commercial sector: they made money and were of proven artistic value. In fact, a theater devoted to translations, he wrote, would meet "the most heartfelt desires of the true friends of fine music."[28] There is more than a little irony here, with Carvalho suddenly caught between a rock and a hard place. In the wake of *Les Troyens à Carthage*, which had been widely touted as conclusive proof that the Théâtre-Lyrique merited subsidy, discussions around deregulation threatened to disenfranchise the theater from the very repertoire that had made such ventures possible. And 100,000 francs—paltry in relation to the subsidies for the Opéra and the Opéra-Comique—could not possibly bridge the gap.

Notwithstanding the pragmatics of running an opera house (to which I have alluded above), patterns of repertoire on the major lyric stages in Paris showed an increased element of competition. Beginning with the July Monarchy, the proliferation of theaters that presented music had forced aspiring theater managers into ever tighter corners regarding the definition and practical boundaries of the genres they were allowed to present, because in order to secure a license each manager had to demonstrate that what his theater offered would be generically unique within the city. This proliferation had also increased litigiousness between theater managers who perceived others stealing their repertoire, and it had encouraged—indeed, in the face of the imperatives of canonicity and repertorial popularity, it had ensured—an increase in productions of translations, each heavily adapted to fit the generic constraints of the various theaters.[29] The fact that those very imperatives of canonicity, interlaced with an emerging work concept, also demanded fidelity to the work of acknowledged masters gave Paris a uniquely paradoxical operatic scene in which managers wishing to mount highly respected operas had no option but to adapt them, yet in the certain knowledge that they would be vilified for so doing.[30]

The liberality of the Théâtre-Lyrique's *cahier* may be seen in hindsight as evidence of the state's acknowledgment that in respect of opera the back of the licensing system had already been broken, in that licensing according to genre provided no

27. A. de Bory, "Quelques mots à propos de la liberté des théâtres," *La France musicale*, 15 November 1863.

28. Ibid.

29. In respect of the first and second questions, see Mark Everist, *Music Drama at the Paris Odéon, 1824–1828* (Berkeley and Los Angeles: University of California Press, 2002), and especially Everist, "Theatres of Litigation: Stage Music at the Théâtre de la Renaissance, 1838–1840," *Cambridge Opera Journal* 16, no. 2 (2004): 133–61.

30. The problem dated back to the first Mozart adaptations at the Opéra and has reached the modern musicological literature mostly via the berating of Castil-Blaze by a fidelity-conscious Berlioz. It exploded when Véron, Castil-Blaze, and the latter's son presented their *Don Juan* of 1834 at the Opéra and visited the Théâtre-Lyrique for the first time when Adam reorchestrated the theater's second-best-running work, Grétry's *Richard Cœur-de-Lion* (though it should be noted that in 1851 the theater's second production was Castil-Blaze's *Barbier*, by then accepted on its own terms as part of the "repertoire").

guarantee that operatic repertoires would remain distinct. Indeed, hindsight suggests that as early as the mid-1820s, when the Théâtre de l'Odéon's new manager, Claude Bernard, signed a contract to present little more than public-domain *opéra comique* and translations, all bets were effectively off.[31] For the subsequent history of operatic competition between theaters centers not so much on battles over new works but on securing market share in relation to those in the public domain. Litigation over new works was more likely to occur between representatives of spoken and operatic genres, as in 1856, when the Théâtre du Vaudeville reportedly took Carvalho to court over his intention to mount *La traviata* (as *Violetta*) because it represented theft of its property, Dumas's *La dame aux camélias*.[32]

That same year, Grétry's *Richard* had simultaneous runs at the Opéra-Comique, now under Émile Perrin, and at the Théâtre-Lyrique, under Carvalho, both using the late Adolphe Adam's orchestration.[33] Competitive behavior increased in the 1860s: a revival of Pergolesi's *La serva padrona* at the Opéra-Comique in August 1862 (in French as *La servante maîtresse*) was quickly followed in January 1863 by the original at the Théâtre-Italien. Mozart, however, was the main vehicle for competition. When the Théâtre-Italien decided to expand from its traditional Mozart repertoire of *Don Giovanni* and *Le nozze di Figaro* to the otherwise unloved *Così fan tutte* at the end of 1862, it took only until January 1863 for Carvalho to announce his own version—*Peines des amours perdues* (set to the plot of Shakespeare's *Love's Labors Lost*). It was rushed onto the stage by 31 March. Finally, in the wake of deregulation, but at three subsidized theaters, three productions of *Don Giovanni* appeared in the first half of 1866. When the Théâtre-Italien under Prosper Bagier went first, in March, the company knew it was gaining a head start.[34] With a lamentable (but

31. See Everist, *Music Drama*, 46–47. Ironically, as Everist points out, this was precisely the opposite of what Bernard wanted, which was to help Prix de Rome prizewinners stage an *opéra comique* on their return from their time abroad (ibid., 47–48).

32. "Nouvelles," *La France musicale*, 14 December 1856. Carvalho would not produce *Violetta* until 1864, by which time it was indeed a decade old and therefore available to him. However, what is striking about the litigation is that it did not come from the Théâtre-Italien, which mounted the French premiere of *La traviata* on 6 December 1856 and with which it appears Carvalho had decided to compete.

33. However, there is also evidence that nonaggression pacts were in force. Carvalho offered to delay the opening of his season in 1856 (he planned to reprise Antoine-Louis Clapisson's very successful *La fanchonnette*) so that Perrin's revival of Hérold's *Zampa* would not suffer "une concurrence trop dangereuse." "Nouvelles," *La France musicale*, 31 August 1856.

34. As early as January 1866 it was common knowledge that all three theaters were planning productions of *Don Giovanni*; see "Nouvelles," *La revue et gazette musicale de Paris*, 21 January 1866. Moreover, press reports indicate that all three managers had aimed to open during the first fortnight in March. As Marie Escudier noted, "[Bagier] is really making it too easy for his competitors: the Opéra and the Théâtre-Lyrique" ([Bagier] donne vraiment trop beau jeu à ses deux concurrents: L'Opéra et le Théâtre-Lyrique). M. Escudier, "Théâtre Impérial Italien: Reprise de Don Giovanni," *La France musicale*, 4 March 1866.

faithful) production marred still further by Adelina Patti's heavily criticized interpretation of Zerlina, the stage was set for the Opéra to take over almost immediately, as advertised. But Perrin's production—a revision of the 1834 *"grand opéra" Don Juan*—was delayed and did not open until April.[35] Carvalho hung back, waiting until May to put on his *Don Juan* (with Molière's dialogue and multiple entr'actes), coming from behind to win a race in which success hinged on performance and production quality.

> Thus, we have at last reached the end of this celebrated steeplechase, in which three fine companies, three imaginative theaters, raced their Mozart, astride his eternal *Don Juan*. Third out of the starting gate, the Théâtre-Lyrique reached the musical finishing line first, ahead of the Opéra by half a length (the masked trio, in other words) and leaving way behind it the poor old Italiens, which could jump neither the ditches (the scenery) nor the hurdles (the ensembles).[36]

What happened in the spring of 1866 was a regression to a lucrative mean that the licensing system had been set up to prevent, but that would never, in Napoléon I's time, have been envisaged as taking the form of a battle over old works rather than new ones. It also illustrated a change in emphasis that was reflected in concert criticism of the mid-century: as repertories and canons solidified and repeat performances of core works increased, attention shifted from questions of aesthetic merit toward those of performance standards or interpretation. Carvalho appreciated that production and performance quality were of paramount importance when one took over well-known works. Yet such investment was still less risky than investing in the new, as the composer and critic Théodore Ymbert pointed out to readers of *La France musicale* at the end of the *"Don Giovanni* year": "Everyone knows that [new] works of great merit are hard to come by. The wisest course of action is to do without them. It would be better to take the best pieces from the repertoires of the old theaters and to perform them in an altogether superior fashion."[37]

"Les trois *Don Juan*," then, emblematized the cementing of a standard repertoire on Parisian stages. And the fact that the competition took place among three theaters

35. "Nouvelles," *L'art musical*, 1 March 1866.

36. "Enfin, le voilà donc terminé ce fameux steeple-chase où trois bonnes troupes, trois théâtres intelligents ont couru le Mozart en enfourchant son éternel *Don Juan*. Parti le troisième, le Théâtre-Lyrique a musicalement touché le but le premier, distançant l'Opéra d'une demi-longueur (autrement dit, trio des masques) et laissant loin derrière lui les pauvres Italiens, qui n'ont jamais pu franchir le fossé des décors et l'obstacle de l'ensemble." Un Spirite [pseud.], "Théâtre-Lyrique Impérial," *L'art musical*, 17 May 1866.

37. "Tout le monde sait que les pièces d'un grand mérite sont extrêmement rares. Le parti le plus sage est de compter sans elles. Mieux vaudrait prendre aux anciens théâtres les meilleures pièces de leur répertoire, et les exécuter d'un façon tout à fait supérieure." Théodore Ymbert, "Effets de la liberté des théâtres," *La France musicale*, 30 December 1866.

still subject to their imperial *cahiers des charges* brutally exposed the fact that the licensing system would always have been toothless in the face of managers who refused to let principle of generic difference prevent them mounting the public-domain operas of their choosing.[38]

The *liberté des théâtres* of 1864 was supposed to be a watershed in Parisian operatic life. It was loudly demanded in the press with the advent of the Second Republic and again in the late 1850s and early 1860s, seeming to critics and musicians alike to be the only solution to the enduring problem of a lack of opportunity for indigenous opera composers.[39] Deregulation, so the argument went, would encourage a much-needed revivification of operatic life, which had become sterile. In part, those who argued for a free market were frustrated at the barriers to entrepreneurship; in part, they looked (through rose-tinted glasses) to a repeat of the *liberté* of 1791 and the explosion of activity that accompanied the release from monarchical controls; and in part, they despaired that the Théâtre-Lyrique—the only real hope for young composers of large-scale works—was moving inexorably toward a repertory model that favored composers who were either foreign, or dead, or both. It was amid fears of an invasion not only of the Théâtre-Lyrique but also of the Opéra and the Opéra-Comique by older, and translated, repertoire that Napoléon III promulgated his decree.

Yet, beginning on 1 July 1864, a free market came to establish itself around the "imperial" theaters in ways few Parisians had foreseen and even fewer, arguably, had wished for.[40] By contrast with 1791, it was a market that spelled almost immediate failure for any new opera company. Where opera was concerned, in the first instance deregulation conformed to the same expectations of profit and loss established by the subsidized opera houses. On the very day the decree went into effect the Théâtre de la Porte-Saint-Martin mounted its first operas: Rossini's *Barbier* (in the Castil-Blaze

38. It also exposed the extent to which Mozart opera had become a canonic craze in Paris—one that Léon Escudier had lampooned mercilessly as early as a round-up of the year 1858 (the year of Carvalho's runaway success *Les noces de Figaro*) disguised as a set of predictions for 1859: "On bâtira un théâtre qui sera exclusivement consacré à la musique de Mozart. Les chanteurs qui seront âgés de moins de quatre-vingts ans n'y seront point admis. Pour avoir le droit d'assister aux représentations, il faudra faire constater que l'on méprise souverainement toute la musique contemporaine et qu'on a appris par coeur les articles de M. Scudo sur le divin Mozart." L. Escudier, "Année 1859: Ce qui arrivera," *La France musicale,* 26 December 1858.

39. The history is pithily presented in Albert Delpit, "La liberté des théâtres," *Revue des deux mondes,* 1 February 1878.

40. I examine this question in more detail, especially for the French regions (where the premises and debates were very different), in Katharine Ellis, "Funding Grand Opera in Regional France: Ideologies of the Mid-Nineteenth Century," in *Art and Ideology in European Opera,* ed. Clive Brown, David Cooper, and Rachel Cowgill (Woodbridge: Boydell and Brewer, forthcoming).

version) and, two days later, a production of Bellini's *Norma*.[41] New operatic ventures either followed suit with public-domain works—some of them surprisingly old—or suffered. In August and September the Théâtre du Vaudeville mounted Rousseau's *Le devin du village* alongside three short plays, while the Théâtre Saint-Germain, lacking any cross-subsidy from older works and housed in a theater on the wrong side of the river for attracting a decent audience, limped along for three months in 1864 with a repertoire of new one-act pieces.[42] Finally, in the immediate aftermath of deregulation, the Grand Théâtre Parisien lasted just a single season as an operatic venue.[43] None of these ventures succeeded in creating a new audience for opera or in sustaining the new operatic opportunities they seemed to offer to living composers. Only the Fantaisies-Parisiennes (1865–69), which offered an eclectic mix of lyric genres, provided opera with a new venue. Operetta, *opéra bouffe,* and vaudeville, by contrast, found a plethora of new homes, and composition in these genres expanded accordingly.

In the wake of operatic failure within what we might term the "deregulated zone," it took no time at all for the terms of the deregulation debate to change among opera lovers (and those with vested interests) and for deregulation's supporters to eat their words. As news spread of theater closures in Paris and the regions and of composer royalties beginning to fall,[44] feelings of bewilderment and betrayal ran high. The number of Parisian opera critics who had supported deregulation far outnumbered those who had foreseen problems.[45] Some of the passion of the change of heart re-

---

41. In the world of spoken drama a similar thing happened on a grander scale: productions of Molière's *Tartuffe* sprang up in the unlikeliest of places and with the most inappropriate of casts. See F. W. J. Hemmings, *Theatre and State in France, 1760–1905* (Cambridge: Cambridge University Press, 1994), 174. The Théâtre de la Porte-Saint-Martin's *Barbier* and *Norma* were badly received in the press on account of weak performance and production values. See, for example, Léon Escudier, "Le résultat de la liberté des théâtres," *L'art musical,* 7 July 1864, who likened the end result to that of a second-rate regional theater. Édouard Monnais, writing under the name of Paul Smith, noted that such aberrant behavior did not last long: "Dès qu'il eut reconnu que la musique et les opéras ne rempliraient sa caisse, il [the manager] se hâta d'en revenir au genre que le public affectionne." Paul Smith [Édouard Monnais], "Revue de l'année 1864," *La revue et gazette musicale de Paris,* 1 January 1865.

42. The theater reopened for short seasons in 1865 and 1866, playing operettas and *opéras bouffes.*

43. The theater management put on four operas, including Rossini's *Barbier,* Grétry's *Richard,* Duprez's *Jeanne d'Arc* (the composer was the son of the singer Gilbert Duprez), and Borsat's *La leçon d'amour.* In 1874–75 and 1875–85 the theater continued operation, but with no operatic component in its repertoire.

44. See, for instance, the somewhat barbed report by Antoine-Louis Malliot reprinted from the *Nouvelliste de Rouen* in *La France musicale,* 29 January 1865.

45. Because the arguments for deregulation focused so narrowly on the replacement of feudal/monarchical privilege with *la liberté,* it was a difficult concept to argue against in 1860s Paris. However, those who thought consequentially provided prescient warnings. Auguste de Gasperini ("La liberté des théâtres," *La nation,* 13 January 1864, and Gasperini, *La nation,* 14 May 1864) and Édouard Monnais ("De la liberté des théâtres au point de vue musical," *La revue et*

flected the unfounded optimism with which many who called for deregulation had conceptualized it. Within the musical press, the most idealistic vision was of an independent and self-regulating opera industry driven by notions of public interest, with each theater manager respecting certain generic boundaries. *L'art musical,* whose director, Léon Escudier, doubtless hoped deregulation would bring profits for his publishing house, was among those at the forefront, as indeed he had been when at the helm of *La France musicale* before 1860.

However, patriotism came into the argument, too: Escudier's contributor Gustave Chouquet was more anxious for a system in which "false German prophets would no longer suffocate the voices of true Gauls" than for increased profits for the Escudier specialty of Italian opera.[46] Chouquet's brand of idealism led him to envision a market in which competition would generate complementarity rather than rivalry. For him, the kind of competition we have seen operating between managers *within* the licensing system had brought with it a pernicious mixing of genres and works; deregulation would, by contrast, allow a return to niche markets, with each theater having "an easily recognisable physiognomy . . . which distinguishe[d] it from its neighbors."[47] In a later article he set out his hopes more clearly, outlining additions to current operatic provision:

> The abolition of theatrical privileges is not aimed at multiplying theater businesses beyond the needs of the public, still less to advantage commerce that lies beyond the bounds of art. To be fertile and to lead to healthy results, theater deregulation must serve the interests of literature, music, artists, and the people. . . . We shall continue to call for: (1) a *Théâtre lyrique européen,* where we would hear good translations of great works by foreign masters; (2) an *Opéra italien,* where first and foremost opera buffa would be sung—that delicious genre that was the glory of Italian composers and which contemporary Italy is misguided to neglect; [and] (3) a *Théâtre symphonique et orphéonique,* dedicated to instrumental music and choral singing.[48]

---

gazette musicale de Paris, 27 December 1863–7 February 1864) were especially shrewd. Monnais, writing as Paul Smith, was building on arguments he had put forward in the same journal in January and October 1849: he agreed with the principle of deregulation but warned against the idea that it was a panacea.

46. "Les faux prophètes allemands ne pourraient plus étouffer les voix des vrais Galois." Gustave Chouquet, "La liberté des théâtres," *L'art musical,* 24 September 1863. Doubtless Chouquet was thinking of *Tannhäuser;* he may have had the Théâtre-Lyrique's Germanophilia in mind, too.

47. "Une physionomie facile à reconnaître et qui la distingue de ses voisins." Ibid.

48. "L'abolition des priviléges n'a point pour but de multiplier les entreprises théâtrales au delà des besoins du public, encore moins de favoriser des exploitations étrangères à l'art. La liberté des théâtres, pour devenir féconde en heureux résultats, doit servir les intérêts de la littérature, de la musique, des artistes et du peuple. . . . Nous ne cesserons de réclamer: 1° un *Théâtre lyrique européen,* où l'on nous ferait entendre de bonnes traductions des chefs-d'œuvre des maîtres étrangers; 2° un *Opéra*

He demanded cut-price opera and exhorted composers to write socially inclusive music that eschewed complication in favor of simple textures that would appeal to the peasant and laboring classes.[49] Variety, inclusiveness, and public benefit were to be the order of the day—yet all in a context of open competition.

As we have seen, however, at first deregulation brought precisely the opposite response—a feeding frenzy on the classics. On two occasions in July and December 1864, a contributor writing under the *pavillon neutre* "RALPH" in *L'art musical* lamented the fact that theater managers were abusing the new legislation and producing worthless versions of great works.[50] Theaters once devoted to melodrama were now trying to put on Molière and Rossini:

> If the decree freeing theaters from their licenses had to have as its goal, or at least as its result, the opening of all stages—small or large—to the works of masters whom one used not dare touch except respectfully (I would almost say [with] the reverence that masterpieces deserve), then prohibition would have been better. No: this is a misunderstanding of legislator's intention, which was most laudable.[51]

Predicting an industrialization of opera, with substandard replicas attracting ignorant audiences (along the lines, he said, of mass-produced lithography), he drew the debate back to the problem of performance quality, which by December he seemed to regard as insoluble. All in all, deregulation for him had been like most freedoms: "It has put in an uncomfortable position those who ought to have profited from it, especially those who had shouted loudest to secure it."[52]

---

italien, où l'on chanterait surtout des ouvrages bouffes, ce genre délicieux qui a fait la gloire des compositeurs ultramontains et que l'Italie contemporaine a le tort de trop délaisser; 3° un *Théâtre symphonique et orphéonique,* consacré à la musique instrumentale et au chant choral." Gustave Chouquet, "La musique du peuple: Liberté des théâtres—lettre de M. Duruy," *L'art musical,* 12 November 1863.

49. Ibid.

50. A *pavillon neutre,* as defined by Charles Joliet, is a house pseudonym that may be used by any of a journal's contributors. See his *Les pseudonymes,* 67. Within musicology, RALPH is usually identified as Léon Escudier; he is also identified as Gustave Chouquet in the contemporary literature; additionally, Achille de Lauzières is known to have used the name in *La patrie.* However, Joliet identifies RALPH as a *pavillon neutre* for *L'art musical,* which would allow all three men, who were key contributors, to share the name (ibid., 68).

51. "Si le décret qui a donné la liberté aux théâtres devait avoir pour but ou du moins pour résultat d'ouvrir à toutes les scènes, grandes ou petites, les oeuvres des maîtres auxquels on n'osait toucher qu'avec respect, je dirais presque le culte dû aux chefs-d'œuvre, mieux eût valu la prohibition. Non, on s'est mépris sur l'intention du législateur, qui était des plus louables." He was referring to the Théâtre Déjazet and the Porte Saint-Martin respectively. RALPH, "Liberté et licence," *L'art musical,* 28 July 1864.

52. The full text reads: "Cette mesure tant désirée, tant demandée, une fois obtenue, a fait comme la plupart des libertés: elle a mis dans l'embarras ceux qui devaient en profiter, ceux-là surtout qui avaient le plus crié pour l'avoir." RALPH, "Courrier musical," *L'art musical,* 22 December 1864.

The briefest of references to the debates of fifteen years before, when the Théâtre-Lyrique opened, would perhaps have reminded RALPH (and others) that economic realities militated against the success of a neatly segmented market—at least from the point of view of aspiring composers. A look at the theater's history would have done the same, because, as Carvalho's practice illustrated, it was only by careful cross-subsidy within the context of a *cahier des charges* permitting the presentation of several genres at one theater that the Théâtre-Lyrique was able to put on new operas at all. In short, its career as a de facto deregulated theater before 1864 held lessons that went unheeded.

Nevertheless, the move to the classics was a first-wave response to deregulation. A second wave of activity revealed the latent power of operetta and *opéra bouffe*. Here opera composers faced a bitter irony, because the deregulation battle had taken so long to win that by the time victory was declared the rules of the game had changed: opera was no longer in competition just with its *grand* or *comique* self, but with new forms of sung and staged entertainment that were as attractive to audiences as they were cost-effective for theater managers. Those forms came to include the *café concert,* and the seemingly inexorable rise of both traditions cemented a separation between art and entertainment that bedeviled French discourse on stage music for decades.

Among opera's defenders in the mainstream musical press, the signs of a decisive shift toward operetta were detectable as early as 1866.[53] The following year illustrated precisely what was at stake. During the Exposition Universelle, surely the most propitious time for a wave of operatic premieres, Offenbach productions of *opéra bouffe* occupied three deregulated Paris stages—the Bouffes-Parisiens (*Orphée*), the Palais-Royal (*La vie parisienne*), and the Variétés (with the new blockbuster *La Grand-Duchesse de Gérolstein*). Other deregulated stages presented adaptations of Gluck and Mozart as comedies and a parody of Gounod's *Roméo et Juliette.* There was no opera, old or new, on a deregulated stage anywhere in the city. By contrast, the regulated zone now put on three world premieres: Verdi's *Don Carlos* at the Opéra, the twenty-four-year-old Massenet's *La grand'tante* at the Opéra-Comique, and Gounod's *Roméo et Juliette* (eighty-nine performances) at the Théâtre-Lyrique, where Carvalho also presented sixteen performances of a work by the young Victorin Joncières. Setting aside the unpatriotic choice of Verdi over a Frenchman at the country's premier opera house, it is difficult to believe that such works would have seen the light of day had the *liberté des théâtres* extended to the national stages, releasing them from their *cahiers des charges* and thereby relieving them of their subsidies. Whatever the relative weight of older or foreign repertoire to new French works at the Lyrique in terms of numbers of performances, it is emblematic that the original of Gounod's opera was staged under license while the free market embraced its parody. In comparison with

---

53. See, for instance, Théodore de Lajarte's donwnbeat analysis of the year 1866 in "Revue de la musique dramatique," *La France musicale,* 6 January 1867.

the relationship between primary and secondary theaters in the Restoration and July Monarchy years, everything and nothing had changed.

The *café concert* provided a different kind of threat. *Café concert* legislation, which was supposed to have been left unchanged by the terms of the 1864 decree, was not being enforced: costumes and props at such establishments were officially tolerated, to the chagrin of opera composers and to the delight of managers of *cafés concerts,* who knew their market: what their customers (which included a large slice of traditional theatergoers) wanted was lyric theater without the stuffiness of the opera house—a place where song, conversation, smoking, and drinking could all be accommodated together.[54] The success of *cafés concerts,* which spread across France, was such that they became indistinguishable from theaters—apart, that is, from the often free entry, the more risqué acts on stage, and telltale drink shelves behind the seats. In 1867 Paris boasted around 60 *cafés concerts;* by 1872 the number had doubled to over 120. Music lists from the Société des Auteurs, Compositeurs et Éditeurs de Musique of a slightly earlier period show a more pronounced trend: 2,795 *café concert* chansons in 1857; 8,500 in 1866.[55] Even taking scale into account, opera catalogs showed no such expansion. This, for those with an interest in opera, was by far the more dangerous of the twin genies that deregulation had let out of the bottle.

Intensified depression, after 1870, at Second Empire "frivolity" brought around a new cycle of Parisian debate on the deregulation question. The writer and librettist Jules Ruelle had, as chief editor of the *Messager des théâtres et des arts* from 1864, previewed and then praised deregulation in ecstatic terms.[56] Yet, as he wrote in 1875, deregulation had brought nothing but grief.[57] In Paris, both operetta and the *café concert* had, he said, prevailed over serious opera: all independent theaters now presented some form of operetta. They leeched good singers and high-class audiences from the established theaters, forced the established theaters to shut during the summer (otherwise the classic time for *débutant* composers to get their first piece staged), and contributed to the collapsing status of the *opéra comique* tradition. Entertainment, he implied, had got the upper hand over art: it was time to turn the clock back and prevent consumer demand from triumphing over public interest.[58] Three years later his position was somewhat more nuanced, but he still reached the same basic

54. For details on the way in which *café concert* managers tested and retested the regulations, see Hippolyte Hostein, *La liberté des théâtres* (Paris: Librairie des Amateurs, 1867), 162–67; and Albert Delpit, "La liberté des théâtres," *Revue des deux mondes,* 1 February 1878.

55. Figures compiled from the SACEM catalogs in *F-Pn,* Musique: Vmb 5081.

56. The journal was dedicated to representing the interests of those within the music industry: composers, writers, publishers and performers, and was loosely associated with the lobbying groups that represented them.

57. Ruelle admitted that he had been "blinded" by the word "liberté." "La liberté des théâtres," *L'art musical,* 2 September 1875.

58. Ruelle, "La liberté des théâtres," *L'art musical,* 30 September 1875.

conclusion, adding that because opera was a moral and educational force, rather than one of entertainment, it had to be regulated; and just as the state saw the need to regulate education, so it should regulate opera.[59] Albert Delpit, in the *Revue des deux mondes,* concurred, adding that deregulation had skewed the operatic labor market such that the state gave free training to singers who promptly disdained apprenticeship for the national stage in favor of quicker money in operetta or on the *café concert* circuit.[60] "This decree has not produced *a single* serious theater," he moaned. "All it has done is to propagate operetta, which plays everywhere."[61] In the meantime, yet another attempt at a Théâtre-Lyrique (at the Théâtre de la Gaîté) had reopened as a haven for young composers under Albert Vizentini (1876–77) and failed.

The coda to this cautionary tale, then, takes us straight back to the plight of young opera composers. In November 1878 the minister of public instruction and religion, Benjamin-Joseph-Agénor Bardoux, began to assess the feasibility of reinstalling a Théâtre-Lyrique at the Place du Châtelet. As explained to the Conseil Municipal de Paris, his terms of reference could have come out of the 1840s; they were also identical to those used by the Société des Compositeurs in 1876, when they helped lobby for state funding for Vizentini's Théâtre-National-Lyrique. In the wake of what he called a "discernible lowering" (*abaissement sensible*) of artistic standards,[62] Bardoux wrote an open letter to theater managers asking them for their views on the effects of deregulation. But he also had his own solution to part of the problem as he perceived it: a two-year apprenticeship system for young talent stranded between the final stages of state education and the perils of the music profession: "Between the Conservatoire, which is a school, and the Opéra, which is a museum, a single step is not enough; we need at least two, as much for our young singers as for our composers."[63] It was an all too familiar argument dependent for success on high levels of subvention. The measure did not come to fruition, and the Théâtre-Lyrique's history continued with another empty promise of a return to its beginnings.

The problems with the institutions of French opera during this period were multiple and shifting, and many of them were either unforeseen or unintended, or both. Yet all came down to a small number of conflicting desires: tensions between a composer mindset that expected the state to nurture (but not control) artists and to regu-

59. Ruelle, "La liberté des théâtres," *L'art musical,* 26 September 1878.

60. "La liberté des théâtres," *Revue des deux mondes,* 1 February 1878.

61. Ibid.

62. Bardoux, "La restauration du Théâtre-Lyrique," *La revue et gazette musicale de Paris,* 17 November 1878.

63. "Entre le Conservatoire, qui est une école, et l'Opéra, qui est un musée, une seule étape est insuffisante; il en faut au moins deux, aussi bien pour nos jeunes chanteurs que pour nos compositeurs." Quoted in ibid.

late (but not suffocate) the arts, and a public that voted in new ways with its wallet by buying individual items (opera or operetta performances) rather than club membership (an annual loge) and preferring the familiar to the novel. There is no better window onto such Parisian instabilities than the Théâtre-Lyrique's travails. Yet what really matters is the theater's wider significance, within France and more generally as well. I have referred to it as an acid test; but it was also an experiment—in more respects than its architects perhaps intended. For with its history of licenses, subvention, and deregulation intersecting with patterns of canonicity, provision of entertainment, and audience behavior, it was the means by which Parisian opera effectively invented the problem—with which we still live—of public-interest arts funding by a liberal capitalist state.

Jacques Offenbach

THE MUSIC OF THE PAST AND THE IMAGE OF THE PRESENT

Mark Everist

The Théâtre des Bouffes-Parisiens opened in 1855 under less than ideal circumstances for its composer-manager.[1] Jacques Offenbach (see fig. 4.1) was restricted by his license to the performance of music drama in a single act with no more than four singing characters onstage.[2] Furthermore, another theater with an almost identical license, Hervé's Théâtre des Folies-Nouvelles, could have been a direct competitor for the same audiences, composers, and librettists as the Bouffes-Parisiens, despite the fact that such competition was what the licensing system itself had been designed to avoid.[3] And finally, the artistic space between the *opérettes* that Offenbach was permit-

1. For an introduction to the early years of the Théâtre des Bouffes-Parisiens, see Jean-Claude Yon, "La création du Théâtre des Bouffes-Parisiens (1855–1862) ou La difficile naissance de l'opérette," *Revue d'histoire moderne et contemporaine* 39 (1992): 575–600; see also Yon, *Jacques Offenbach* (Paris: Éditions Gallimard, 2000), 128–65. For the repertoire of and other material concerning the Bouffes-Parisiens, see Annie Ledout, "Le théâtre des Bouffes-Parisiens, historique et programmes, 1855–1880" (Ph.D. diss., Université de Paris IV, 2001).

2. The earliest version of Offenbach's license restricted him to three singing characters; *F-Pan*, F²¹ 1136, 4 June 1855. See Yon, *Offenbach*, 137. The loosening of this limitation to four was accomplished in the revision of Offenbach's contract, 22 October 1855. See Nicole Wild, *Dictionnaire des théâtres parisiens au XIXe siècle: Les théâtres et la musique* (Paris: Aux Amateurs des Livres, 1989), 63.

3. For Florimond Ronger (Hervé) and the Théâtre des Folies-Nouvelles, see Eugène Woestyn and Eugène Moreau, *Les Folies-Nouvelles* (Paris: Martinon, [1855]), and Louis-Henry Lecomte, *Les Folies-Nouvelles,* Histoire des théâtres de Paris 4 (Paris: Daragon, 1909).

FIGURE 4.1. Portrait of Jacques Offenbach from the 1860s. *Receuil de pièces* (*F-Pn* Mus. Est. Offenbach J. 002). Bibliothèque nationale de France.

ted to produce and the works of the subsidized theaters—the Académie Impériale de Musique, the Opéra-Comique, and the Théâtre-Italien—had largely been filled five years previously by the Théâtre-Lyrique.[4] However, Offenbach held the lease on two theaters, one on the Champs-Elysées and one—sufficiently far from the boulevard home of the Folies-Nouvelles to reduce direct competition—in the Passage Choiseul; he also enjoyed the support of important state officials connected to the aristocracy and the imperial family, and of a bourgeois audience developed during his time as a salon musician.

Offenbach's artistic and professional aims were clear: he wanted to develop the

4. T. J. Walsh, *Second Empire Opera: The Théâtre Lyrique, Paris, 1851–1870* (London: John Calder; New York: Riverrun Press, 1981).

Bouffes-Parisiens into a theater with a radically different mission and profile from that of the Folies-Nouvelles. He could do this by developing the bourgeois rather than the popular elements of his audience—easy at the Salle Choiseul and the Salle Lacaze—and by setting himself two more complex objectives: to support young composers, especially Prix de Rome laureates returning to the capital, and to position the Bouffes-Parisiens and its emergent genre of *opérette* squarely within the tradition of international comic opera of the past and specifically within that of eighteenth-century *opéra comique*. His first objective tapped into a tradition, dating back at least to the beginning of the licensing system in 1806–7, of aspirant opera managers claiming that their new enterprises would support young composers, an assertion well known to anyone who remembered the attempts to promote music drama at the Odéon in the 1820s or at the Théâtre de la Renaissance in the 1830s.[5] Offenbach's second objective—to return to the music of the past—was an ambitious and idiosyncratic undertaking that had a significant impact on the success of the Théâtre des Bouffes-Parisiens in its first phase. It forms the subject of the present inquiry.[6]

Sources for the Music of the Past

Between 1850 and 1860, Offenbach engaged in a variety of ways with earlier music. As conductor at the Comédie-Française, he was involved in Arsène Houssaye's attempts to revive Molière in ways that might have been familiar to the seventeenth century—by removing two centuries of musical tradition.[7] In his articles published in the journal *L'artiste* in the early part of 1855, and in the announcement of his competition for a new *opéra bouffe* the following year, he exploited the music of the past for his own ends. In addition to attempting to mount productions of largely eighteenth-century comic opera (with variable degrees of success), he used composers from the past to pillory aspects of contemporary musical culture in his *Le carnaval des revues* of 1860.

Offenbach wrote four *causeries musicales* in the journal *L'artiste* in the six months

5. See Mark Everist, *Music Drama at the Paris Odéon, 1824–1828* (Berkeley and Los Angeles: University of California Press, 2002), 210–11; and Everist, "Theatres of Litigation: Stage Music at the Théâtre de la Renaissance, 1838–1840," *Cambridge Opera Journal* 16, no. 2 (2004): 136.

6. Despite its title, Gérard Loubinoux, "Le chercheur d'esprit, ou Offenbach et la mémoire du xviii siècle," in *Retour au xviiie siècle,* ed. Roland Morier and Hervé Hasquin, Études sur le xviiie siècle 22 (Brussels: Éditions de l'Université de Bruxelles, 1994), 63–76, addresses none of the sources or repertoires discussed in this article. It reads those libretti of Offenbach's *opérettes* that depend on eighteenth-century settings—*Le chanson de Fortunio* (1861), *La Foire Saint-Laurent* (1877), *Mesdames de la Halle* (1858, but wrongly assigned by Loubinoux to 1868), and *Madame Favart* (1878)—and attributes the interest in the eighteenth century to Offenbach alone rather than to his librettists.

7. Yon, *Offenbach,* 101, 107, 111. In his bid for the management of the Théâtre-Lyrique in 1854, however, Offenbach made no mention of any interest in the music of the seventeenth or eighteenth century nor (*pace* Wild, *Dictionnaire,* 238–39) in the fate of Prix de Rome laureates. See the letter from Offenbach to Camille Doucet, directeur de l'administration des théâtres, 3 July 1854, *F-Pan,* F[21] 1120/2.

before the Théâtre des Bouffes-Parisiens opened in the Salle Lacaze.[8] One of the tasks they accomplished was to appease those whom Offenbach thought key players in the world of stage music in the mid-1850s. Accordingly, revivals of Halévy's *La juive* and Auber's *La muette de Portici* are praised without reserve, as is the Parisian premiere of Verdi's *Il trovatore;*[9] Émile Perrin's joint direction of the Opéra-Comique and Théâtre-Lyrique comes in for approving comments, and Offenbach throws his weight behind the contemporary vogue for the works of Adolphe Adam.[10] Berlioz is praised for his *L'enfance du Christ,* offered sympathy for being beaten by Louis Clapisson in the competition for the most recent musical nomination to the Institut de France, and praised vicariously through allusions to the shortcomings of the recent revival of *Der Freischütz*—in Castil-Blaze's 1824 version as *Robin des bois*—at the Théâtre-Lyrique.[11] Such attempts to curry favor need to be read alongside the production of such works as the *Décaméron dramatique: Album du Théâtre-Français,* published in October 1854, in which each of the major actresses at the Comédie-Française was presented with a dance for piano composed by Offenbach, a portrait by Hermann Raunheim, and a quatrain by a noted poet of the day, such as Gautier, Dumas, Musset, and others.[12] The articles in *L'artiste* also undertook significant cultural work by praising smaller-scale contemporary *opéras comiques* in terms that stressed their similarities to eighteenth-century classics of the genre. In doing so, they contributed to a view of contemporary *opéra comique* that set it apart from more ambitious contemporary works: the eighteenth century was made to contribute to Offenbach's aesthetic position as he tried to promote his own artistic program.

A year after the publication of the articles in *L'artiste,* and during the first year of the Bouffes-Parisiens' operations, Offenbach advertised a "Concours pour une opérette en un acte" for the composition of an *opéra bouffe,* aimed at composers who had not been performed on any Parisian stage.[13] As part of the announcement for the "Concours," Offenbach published what amounted to a history of *opéra comique* that was slanted so as to throw into relief his own activities at the Bouffes-Parisiens. The announcement constituted not only a partial view of the history of *opéra comique* up to the present, but also a manifesto for the artistic ambitions both of the Bouffes-Parisiens and of its manager and principal composer.

---

8. Jacques Offenbach, *L'artiste,* 14 January 1855, 4 February 1855, 25 February 1855, and 25 March 1855.

9. Halévy: Offenbach, *L'artiste,* 25 March 1855; Auber: Offenbach, *L'artiste,* 14 January 1855; and Verdi: Offenbach, *L'artiste,* 14 January 1855.

10. Perrin: Offenbach, *L'artiste,* 4 February 1855 and 25 March 1855. Adam: Offenbach, *L'artiste,* 14 January 1855.

11. Offenbach, *L'artiste,* 14 January 1855 and 4 February 1855.

12. Yon, *Offenbach,* 131–32.

13. Jacques Offenbach, "Concours pour une opérette en un acte," *La revue et gazette musicale de Paris,* 20 July 1856. The advertisement was also printed in *Le ménestrel,* 27 July 1856, with minimal introduction, and the articles only in *La France musicale,* 20 July 1856. Subsequent reference will be made to the version published in *La revue et gazette musicale de Paris.*

Supported by a series of carefully placed allusions to the music of the past, Offenbach could cast about for works that fell within the limitations of his license, could amplify the repertory of his theater, and could contribute to its cultural capital. He identified four comic operas from the previous century—Rousseau's *Le devin du village,* Pergolesi's *La serva padrona,* Mozart's *Der Schauspieldirektor* and Rossini's *Il signor Bruschino*—that might be of use to the Bouffes-Parisiens.[14] Of these, *Le devin du village* and *La serva padrona* fell foul of the controls placed on the theater's license and were never performed (although the Rousseau may well have got as far as rehearsal); *Der Schauspieldirektor* and *Il signor Bruschino,* however, served as important parts of the repertoire and key aesthetic statements for Offenbach and the Bouffes-Parisiens in the second half of the 1850s.

If putting words into the mouths of dead composers was one of the tricks that Offenbach was using in his manifesto on *opéra comique* that accompanied the advertisement for the "Concours," it was a short step to having composers of the past speak onstage. Offenbach, together with his collaborators Eugène Grangé and Philippe Gille, took his chance in his *Le carnaval des revues* of 1860, a review of the previous year's events.[15] One of the main musical targets was the series of concerts that Wagner had mounted at the Théâtre-Italien—just feet from Offenbach's own Salle Choiseul in the Salle Ventadour—but there were three other targets: the inquiry into pitch that had been reported during 1859, Meyerbeer's continuing success, and—close to Offenbach's heart—the question of the fate of young composers. The sixth tableau of *Le carnaval des revues* begins in the musical corner of the Elysian Fields, a neat classical allusion to *Orphée aux enfers* that would have been missed by no one.[16] Grétry enters humming the aria "Et zig et zog" from *Richard Cœur-de-Lion,* one of the works Offenbach had endorsed four years earlier in his articles in *L'artiste* (see below); from the other side of the stage enters Gluck, singing "J'ai perdu mon Eurydice." The resulting banter concerns the revival of Gluck's *Orphée et Eurydice* at the Théâtre-Lyrique and the contralto who took the title role, Pauline Viardot; the two men then propose a game of dominos. At that point Mozart enters, and Grétry and Gluck greet him by singing "Mon cœur soupire"—the French version of "Voi che sapete." Before they can start their three-way game, Weber arrives, and the other three welcome him

---

14. The inclusion of Rossini's *Il signor Bruschino* (1813) raises the issue of which repertoires Offenbach considered appropriate to his definition of the past. The concept of the "long" eighteenth century does not perhaps allow a finely textured enough view of Offenbach's position, conditioned as it was by his view of the history of *opéra comique* (for which see below). Although Rossini's early *farse* clearly fall into this category—and perhaps Weber's too—the music of the 1820s is much more closely contested, as the discussion of both *opéra comique* and *opera semiseria* in the "Concours" article suggests (Offenbach, "Concours," 230, sec. 1, paras. 5–8).

15. Eugène Grangé and Philippe Gilles, *Le carnaval des revues: Revue de carnaval en 2 actes et 9 tableaux; Les souper de mardi-gras, prologue, Paris, Bouffes-parisiens, le 10 février 1860 . . . Musique de Jacques Offenbach* ([Paris]: Michel Lévy frères, [1860]).

16. Ibid., 14–17.

with a performance of "Chasseur diligent," the French version of the Huntsmen's Chorus from *Der Freischütz*. This quartet of deceased composers—Grétry, Gluck, Mozart, and Weber—serves as the commenting chorus against which the objects of Offenbach's satire are projected.

Apart from the attention given to the *compositeur de l'avenir* in *Le carnaval des revues*—almost too easy a target—Offenbach's most significant victims were Meyerbeer and the quartet of commenting composers themselves. All served as important ways of promoting Offenbach's own aesthetic agenda, especially the support of young composers and the appeal to the musical and dramatic values of the past, exactly those elements that he was trying to develop at his own institution. Offenbach's quartet of composers served here as a fixed point of reference to whom he could have recourse in his constant invocation of earlier values. Their posthumous repudiation of a particular feature of the present functioned as a pointer—as much as Offenbach's explicit statements in the "Concours" article —to the values of eighteenth-century *opéra comique* that by 1860 Offenbach would have claimed were well and truly reestablished in Paris on the boards of his own theater.

The French Tradition

Offenbach's competition to encourage recent laureates of the Prix de Rome was launched in July 1856 and at face value sought to develop his mission to help young composers, which he had set forth in his requests to open a theater the previous year.[17] To have chosen Georges Bizet and Charles Lecocq as winners can be, with hindsight, considered a successful outcome. But when the "Concours" was advertised, Offenbach gave it a context that was no less than the entire history of *opéra comique;* he took advantage of the opportunity to produce a manifesto for the aesthetic project hosted by his own theater and the music drama supported there. He set the competition in the context of a view of contemporary *opéra comique* that valued most the sort of music drama that he himself was allowed and able to play at the Bouffes-Parisiens: works in one act with a limited number of soloists. Conversely, he was suspicious and critical both of the serious elements that had infiltrated *opéra comique* at least since the 1780s and of its more recent growth.

Offenbach's view of the history of *opéra comique* was neatly encapsulated toward the end of his introduction to the "Concours": "One may easily follow the progress of *opéra comique* from its origins to the present. At first, a little brook with limpid water, with new banks it develops little by little as it advances, until it becomes what we see

---

17. There is a tension in all of Offenbach's comments on young composers between Prix de Rome laureates and those novice composers trained outside the Conservatoire, and therefore not eligible to enter the state competition. These included Offenbach himself, not to mention such competitors as Clapisson or Gevaert. Such a tension is clear in the "Concours" text itself. Offenbach, "Concours," 231, sec. 3, paras. 1–3, 7.

today, a wide river, with imposing waves on its vast surface."[18] His metaphor drew an unbroken teleological line from Philidor's *Blaise, le sauvetier* of 1759 to Meyerbeer's *L'étoile du nord* of 1854. Offenbach outlined three phases in the history of the genre. The first ran from Philidor—or from Pergolesi and Duni, because Offenbach was anxious to stress the Italian origins of the genre—to Dalayrac and Grétry. But Offenbach proposed a clear distinction between pre- and post-revolutionary works and pointed to a sudden enlargement of the genre after 1789 that was only accomplished "by denying its own nature" (en se denaturant);[19] he saw this as resulting from the influence of ideas about "political and artistic renovation." While such a view provided a neat point of articulation between his first and second phases, it also gave Offenbach the chance to point to works by Dalayrac and Grétry—"the two most illustrious representatives of *opéra comique*"[20]—and to accuse them of abjuring the genre that had served them so well, with the result that they had embarked on the composition of *Camille, ou Le souterrain* and of *Pierre le grand* and *Guillaume Tell*, respectively. The works of Offenbach's first phase to which he pointed with real approval were Monsigny's *Le déserteur;* Gossec's *La fête du village;* three works by Dalayrac (*Adolphe et Clara, Maison à vendre,* and *Picaros et Diego*); and Grétry's *Le tableau parlant, Zémire et Azor, L'amant jaloux,* and *Richard Cœur-de-Lion.* The last of the four works by Grétry came in for special praise, "applauded every day as if it were written yesterday, although it dates from 1785 [*sic; recte* 1784]," and in Offenbach's discourse on the eighteenth century *Richard Cœur-de-Lion* takes on the role of a signature work for its composer.[21]

Throughout Offenbach's appropriation during the 1850s of the eighteenth century, Grétry remained a key figure. In *Le carnaval des revues,* he was perhaps the central figure among the four composers who comment on the subjects brought before them; but Offenbach had also made extensive use of Grétry five years before in his articles in *L'artiste.* In his review of Albert Grisar's *Le chien du jardinier* at the Opéra-Comique, Offenbach opened up praise for contemporary composers via analogy with his central figure of the eighteenth century.[22] Grisar was identified as "a real comic composer," and in the work under discussion Offenbach took the opportunity to impute to him a love of Grétry: "In this recent score, there is often a reflection of the style of Grétry, much beloved of Grisar."[23] It is impossible to know what Offenbach's evidence for

18. "On peut suivre aisément la marche de l'opéra comique depuis son origine jusqu'à nos jours. D'abord petit ruisseau aux eaux limpides, au frais rivage, il s'étend peu à peu, à mesure qu'il avance, jusqu'à devenir, ce que nous le voyons aujourd'hui, un large fleuve, roulant dans son vaste lit ses ondes imposantes." Ibid., 231, sec. 2, para. 12.

19. Ibid., 231, sec. 1:, para. 2.

20. "Les deux plus illustres représentants de l'opéra comique." Ibid., 231, sec. 1, para. 2.

21. "Que nous applaudissons tous les jours, comme s'il était d'hier, bien qu'il date de 1785." Ibid., p. 231, sec. 1, para. 1.

22. Offenbach, *L'artiste,* 4 February 1855.

23. "Un véritable compositeur bouffe. . . . Dans cette dernière partition, il y a souvent un re-

Grisar's love of Grétry might have been, but that is scarcely the point. Offenbach took the opportunity to praise those contemporary works that he could easily link to his own project of self-identification with the music of the eighteenth century, and eliding Grisar with Grétry accomplished that task very effectively. Grisar was to be included in those works in the third phase of the "Concours" article that were in general terms subject to censure, but Offenbach used analogy with Grétry to protect the work under review that, for him, stood apart from the rest of that phase in the genre's history.[24] In his doubled-edged appreciation of Victor Massé in the "Concours" article, Grétry was used as a point of reference to praise the former's *Les noces de Jeanette*—"a jewel [that] proves the aptitude of the young composer for writing in the old and frank manner of Grétry"—at the expense of Massé's other works.[25] Again, when savaging Clapisson in 1855, he used Grétry as an exemplum of the best of the past (see below). But even Grétry did not escape Offenbach's wrath for having occasionally stepped outside the boundaries that he had set for *opéra comique* of the past. When we read Offenbach's praises by analogy with Grétry, we must remember that his enthusiasm for such works as *Le tableau parlant, Zémire et Azor, L'amant jaloux,* and *Richard Cœur-de-Lion* needs to be read alongside his adverse comments on *Pierre le grand* and *Guillaume Tell,* which he thought betrayed the modishness of post-revolutionary composition.[26]

Offenbach's objections to the overinflated nature of contemporary *opéra comique* were clarified by further comments on the genre that lead straight back to the previous century. A reworking of Charles-Simon Favart's *La chercheuse d'esprit* by Jules Lecomte had just been mounted at the Théâtre du Vaudeville with music by Jean-Baptiste Montaubry that, for Offenbach, "could have been played on the harpsichord of the time of Jean-Jacques [Rousseau], in the salons of Mme de Pompadour, decorated with pastels by Latour and Boucher. If Mme d'Épinay could be resuscitated, she would speak of it in her posthumous memoirs."[27] Perhaps the most colorful of Offenbach's *causeries,* this is a remarkable inclusion in its own right: music at the Vaudeville rarely came in for any comment, favorable or adverse, in his columns, so

---

flet du style de Grétry, que Grisar affectionne, du reste, particulièrement." Offenbach, *L'artiste,* 4 February 1855.

24. In his commentary on Grisar in the "Concours" article, Offenbach praises *Les porcherons* and *Bonsoir, monsieur Pantalon!* in addition to *Le chien du jardinier.* With regard to the other works, he writes that Grisar there "preferred to become the rival of Italian masters" (a préféré devenir le rival des maîtres italiens). Offenbach, "Concours," 231, sec. 2, para. 7.

25. "Un bijou,—prouvent l'aptitude du jeune compositeur à écrire dans la vieille et franche manière de Grétry." Ibid., 231, sec. 2, para. 8.

26. "Pour se faire pardonner ses premiers succès [this is ironic], . . . l'auteur du *Tableau parlant* composa *Pierre le grand* et *Guillaume Tell.*" Ibid., 231, sec. 1, para. 2.

27. "Pourrait se jouer sur les clavecins du temps de Jean Jacques, dans des salons Pompadour, constellés de pastels de Latour et de Boucher. Si madame d'Épinay pouvait ressusciter, elle en parlerait dans ses mémoires posthumes." Offenbach, *L'artiste,* 4 February 1855.

its inclusion here betrayed the importance of the position the author was attempting to develop. It was a marginal event in the Parisian theatrical world of early 1855, but Offenbach's commentary stresses exclusively its eighteenth-century credentials by allusion to the composer of *Le devin du village;* two of the key artists of the ancien régime, Maurice de la Tour and François Boucher; Mme de Pompadour; and Mme d'Épinay. The contemporary nature of Lecomte's and Montaubry's arrangement holds no interest for Offenbach in this literary pastiche of the eighteenth century.

Offenbach called the second phase of his history of *opéra comique* "the reign of the *harmonistes,*" those he said who exhibited "a sovereign contempt for *la petite musique*"—a term that recalled the language (*petites ouvrages, petites pièces*) of his articles in *L'artiste* the previous year.[28] Monarchs in this reign were Nicolo, Berton, Méhul, Catel, Boïeldieu, Lesueur, Cherubini, and, for their early works, Hérold and Halévy. As he attempted to steer a course between trying not to antagonize the musical establishment and promoting his own cause, his argument ran the risk of collapse. Having chastised the generation of his second phase, he then turned to his audience and claimed that these "masters . . . have no less created works of which the French stage can justly be proud."[29] Hérold, however, was held up as a figure of transition, with his *Le pré aux clercs* and *Zampa,* representing—again according to Offenbach—"the transition . . . between *opéra comique* of a light allure and musical drama of lugubrious effect."[30] At this moment, for Offenbach, the original genre of *opéra comique* disappeared in favor of larger works. This was not yet *grand opéra,* but a mixed genre along the lines of Italian opera *semi-seria* and the German-language works that Offenbach thought derived from it: Weber's *Der Freischütz, Oberon,* and *Euryanthe;* Mozart's *Die Zauberflöte;* and Weigl's *Die Schweizerfamilie.*

Offenbach reserved his greatest censure for works of his third phase: those of Auber, Halévy, Thomas, Reber, Gevaert, and Meyerbeer, along with some works of Massé and Grisar. He considered that "the scores of many of our contemporary composers resemble elegant women on the boulevard: they wear too much crinoline. In the daylight, they constitute quite a substantial outfit, and beautifully colored. Close up, *en déshabillé,* at the piano, they are phantoms inflated by wind and sound."[31] This metaphor of the overuse of crinoline echoes one of Offenbach's recurring views

28. "Le règne des *harmonistes* . . . un souverain mépris pour la *petite musique*. Offenbach, "Concours," 230, sec. 1, para. 2. In his approving comments on the current repertoire of one-act *opéras comiques* at the Théâtre-Lyrique and Opéra-Comique, Offenbach alludes to "les petites pièces," "petits opéras comiques," and "ce *repertoiricule* charmant et amusant." See *L'artiste,* 25 March 1855.

29. "Maîtres . . . n'en ont pas moins créé des œuvres dont la scène française doit justement s'enorgueillir." Offenbach, "Concours," 230, sec. 1, para. 4.

30. "Une transition . . . entre l'opéra comique aux allures légères et le drame musicales aux lugubres effets." Ibid., 230, sec. 1, para. 5.

31. "Les partitions de beaucoup de nos compositeurs du jour rassemblent aux élégantes du boulevard, elles portent trop de crinoline. A la lumière, elles forment un ensemble assez substantiel

on contemporary music: that it is overblown beyond the appropriate confines of its genre, especially in the case of *opéra comique,* and it seems clear from his refusal to extend this particular polemic to works at the Académie Impériale de Musique that it is *opéra comique* itself, at both the Théâtre-Lyrique and the Opéra-Comique, that is his target.

As has already been seen, Offenbach did his best not to antagonize those of whom he was critical. In his careful commentary on the works of Thomas, for example, even the pieces on which he was hardest—*Le songe d'une nuit d'été* and *Raymond*—he made sure that their composer knew that he thought them "œuvres magistrales."[32] He even saw redemption for Thomas in *La double échelle* and *Mina.* It is almost possible to smell the fragrance of the salons Offenbach was frequenting in the 1840s and early 1850s in this careful stroking of the culturally rich and powerful as he attempted to position his own works. Massé was praised on several occasions for his *Les noces de Jeanette,* while in his work on *La chanteuse voilée* and *Galathée* he was accused of trying to *faire grand*—an expression that almost defies translation but well expresses the activity that Offenbach found so reprehensible.[33] With Meyerbeer's recent *L'étoile du nord,* Offenbach came to the end of his history and the point at which *opéra comique* had reached its lowest ebb. He set his criticism in the context of the box office's stranglehold over any flexibility that an opera-house manager might wish to exercise. Émile Perrin, the manager of the Opéra-Comique (and until a short time earlier the manager of the Théâtre-Lyrique as well) was praised for mounting productions of Massé's *Les noces de Jeannette* and Grisar's *Le chien du jardinier* but was portrayed in his promotion of Meyerbeer's *L'étoile du nord* as the victim of the preferences of his public, dragged toward productions at the Opéra-Comique of what Offenbach was certain was "absolutely a *grand opéra!*" (un grand opéra tout à fait!).[34] Offenbach also pointed to the libretti of such *opéras comiques* as *La dame blanche, Fra Diavolo, L'éclair, La fille du régiment,* and *Les mousquetaires de la reine* as literary works that existed independently of their music, and also to the transformation of the libretto into something indissolubly linked to its music in works of both the second and third phases of his history of the genre.[35]

In his very last *causerie musicale,* Offenbach pointed with approval to the vogue for what he called *petites pièces* and singled out such works as Ernest Boulanger's *Les sabots de la marquise,* Prosper Pascal's *Le roman de la rose,* Victor Massé's *Miss Fauvette,* and Ferdinand Poise's *Les charmeurs.*[36] Poise, of course, was one of the early composers recruited to Offenbach's own theater, and Massé formed an important link in the

et d'un beau coloris. De près, en déshabillé, au piano, ce sont des fantômes gonflés de vent et de son." *L'artiste,* 14 January 1855.

32. Offenbach, "Concours," 231, sec. 2, para. 5.

33. Ibid., 231, sec. 2, para. 8.

34. Ibid., 231, sec. 2, para. 17.

35. Ibid., 231, sec. 2, para. 15.

36. Offenbach, *L'artiste,* 25 March 1855.

historical chain that Offenbach forged between himself and the eighteenth century in the "Concours" article. Émile Perrin, the director of both institutions licensed to mount productions of *opéra comique,* was credited with the creation of this *réperto-iricule* in the 25 March 1855 *causerie musicale,* but also—in the 14 January article—with the productions of Hérold's *Le pré aux clercs* and Massé's *Galathée* (Meyerbeer's *L'étoile du nord* was mentioned parenthetically). Now, these three works would come in for harsh criticism in the "Concours" article: *Le pré aux clercs,* alongside *Zampa,* as a key work in the transition from the second to third phase in Offenbach's history, and *Galathée* as an example of its composer's attempt to stretch the aesthetic boundaries of *opéra comique* beyond what Offenbach deemed acceptable.[37]

In his attitude toward Perrin's repertory at the Opéra-Comique and the Théâtre-Lyrique, Offenbach's position was hopelessly ambiguous: praising almost without reserve both the repertory that he would shortly be promoting as the future of *opéra comique* and those works that he would then be damning as its worst excesses.[38] These ambiguities remained in his accounts of the works of Adam and Clapisson. Again praising Perrin, Offenbach pointed to productions of Adam's *Le muletier de Tolède, À Clichy,* and the revival of *La reine d'un jour.* In each case, the work was attributed to "l'auteur du *Chalet,*" a conventional form of describing the composer, but Offenbach's use of the convention three times in three lines drove home his implicit point that Adam—a composer at the peak of his career—had been perhaps getting more than his fair share of the stage at the Théâtre-Lyrique. The point was made explicitly when Offenbach suggested that although he was very happy to hear Adam's *charmante musique,* he would also like to hear a work by one of his own young colleagues, a category that would necessarily include Offenbach himself.[39]

Strangely absent from the account of contemporary *opéra comique* in the "Concours" article was the work of Clapisson, who had come in for heavy criticism in the articles in *L'artiste* the previous year, first as the successful rival to Berlioz at the Institut and second as the composer of *Dans les vignes,* which had premiered not long before at the Théâtre-Lyrique.[40] Offenbach's allegiance to Berlioz might well be explained by his hostility to Clapisson. Offenbach's and Clapisson's early careers were mirror images of each other in many respects; both were born outside France (Clapisson's father had been the principal horn in the Teatro San Carlo in Naples), and both came to Paris as string players (Clapisson was a violinist first at the Théâtre-Italien and then at the Académie Royale de Musique). Both then turned to composition, with *opéra comique* as their target, but Clapisson was far more successful during his first

---

37. Offenbach, "Concours," 230, sec. 1, para. 5; and 231, sec. 2, para. 8.

38. Compare, for example, the two *causeries musicales.* Offenbach, *L'artiste,* 14 January 1855 and 25 March 1855.

39. Offenbach, *L'artiste,* 14 January 1855.

40. In the editorial commentary that preceded the copy of Offenbach's advertisement for his "Concours," the exclusion of Clapisson was explicitly recognised with a degree of censure. Offenbach, "Concours," 230.

decade than Offenbach. Offenbach's critique of Clapisson was partial and one-sided. He constantly referred to him as merely a composer of romances and claimed in his commentary on Clapisson's election to the Institut that it "had need of a symphonist, but it was a *romancier* [*un faiseur de romances*] who prevailed."[41] He went further and built a play on words around the title of one of Clapisson's romances, *Le postillon de Madame Ablou*, so that he could claim that both Clapisson and Adam were elected to the Institut because of *Le postillon*, elections that showed that the Académie was "a stickler [*à cheval*] for the principles of art."[42]

In his critique of Clapisson's *Dans les vignes*, Offenbach accused the composer of celebrating his nomination to the Institut by producing a few outdated melodies. He continued by suggesting that in making such an observation, he was not reproaching the composer; but he piled on insult by excusing Clapisson because the melodies were not his own: "he is content to borrow them from the repertory of old French songs, such as 'Le sultan Saladin,' 'Le père Trinquefort,' etc."[43] Offenbach here combined contempt for Clapisson with a subtle promotion of his own cause; accusations of simple borrowing from the past are coupled to a choice of works that is explicitly signaled. To invoke "Le sultan Saladin" is yet again to memorialize Offenbach's key work from the eighteenth century, Grétry's *Richard Cœur-de-Lion*, in which the crusader song "Le sultan Saladin" is quoted at the end of the first act.

Offenbach's primary target in the history of *opéra comique*, Giacomo Meyerbeer, resurfaced four years later when he figured as an object of satire in *Le carnaval des revues*. Offenbach's immediate pretext for the introduction of Meyerbeer into a parody of the events of 1859 was the centenary of the birth of Friedrich von Schiller (born 10 November 1759), for which Meyerbeer had written a *Festmarsch* and a *Festgesang* to a text by Ludwig Pfau; both had been premiered in 1859. The fourth scene of *Le carnaval des revues* began with the entry of the master of ceremonies—who speaks exclusively in a German fit only for the tourist industry and which is consistently misunderstood by Grétry—followed by an individual bearing a banner on which is written "Fête de Schiller." Weber kindly translates and explains how the four composers are to be given a performance of Meyerbeer's *Festmarsch;* Grétry retorts that he has known the march for a decade, declaring that "C'est la Marche du *Prophète*," a convenient swipe at the generic nature of this Meyerbeerian form.[44] The master of ceremonies then collapses into a panegyric to Meyerbeer with which he expects his audience to concur. As he names in chronological order each of Meyerbeer's operas, all of which he describes as "sublime," he waits for the four composers to agree. They readily concur

---

41. "On avait besoin d'un symphoniste, ce fut un faiseur de romances qui l'obtint." Ibid.

42. The full text of this play on words is: "Aussi M. Clapisson a-t-il été nommé au même titre que M. Adam, c'est-à-dire pour cause de *Postillon*, ce qui prouve que l'Académie est à cheval sur ses principes d'art." Ibid.

43. "Il s'est contenté de les emprunter au répertoire des vieux airs français, tels que le *Sultan Saladin*, le *Père Trinquefort*, etc." Ibid.

44. Grangé and Gille, *Le carnaval des revues*, 16.

with this description for *Robert le diable* and *Les huguenots* but are progressively less and less enthusiastic as *Le prophète, L'étoile du nord,* and finally *Le pardon de Ploërmel,* premiered in April 1859, are named. The composers' response to the invitation to express enthusiasm for *Le pardon de Ploërmel* is so muted that it is entirely silent, and the master of ceremonies is obliged to repeat his invitation to comment; the response is the same. He takes his banner with him as he leaves, and the composers sing what is, to judge from the scansion of the text, probably a parody of the opening of the *septuor du duel* "En mon droit j'ai confiance" from act 3 of *Les huguenots:*

En Meyerbeer j'ai confiance;	I have trust in Meyerbeer;
L'Africaine enfin paraitra,	*L'Africaine* will finally appear,
Et le succès lui reviendra! . . .	And success will return to him!
Oui!	Yes!

Offenbach's treatment of this scene echoed the criticism of the turn taken by *opéra comique* in the 1850s so clearly expressed in the 1856 "Concours" article. There Offenbach had identified Meyerbeer's *L'étoile du nord*—then enjoying its first run after its 1854 premiere—as the nadir of the recent tendency to compose *opéra comique* that tended toward the type of work more suitable for the Académie Impériale de Musique. By 1860 and the recent premiere of Meyerbeer's *Le pardon de Ploërmel,* not only was the trend still visible, but the same composer was responsible for perhaps the most high-profile works in that genre. The alignment of Meyerbeer with Schiller in this scene had the effect of placing the composer in the same national frame as Wagner and reminding the audience that—despite his triumphs in French stage music—he was as much a Prussian as Wagner was a Saxon. But that in turn threw the spotlight onto the four composers who served as the commenting chorus in this tableau, none of whom had been born in France.

In the articles in *L'artiste,* in the "Concours" text, and even in his commentary on the music of the past in *Le carnaval des revues,* Offenbach subtly rewrote the history of *opéra comique* in a way that threw his own work into relief. He could do this partly because there was almost no competing view of the historiography of *opéra comique* in the mid-1850s. There was plenty of commentary on the status of the genre and its place in Parisian and provincial musical cultures, but in those texts where one might expect some clear view on the history of *opéra comique,* even if it were no more than the usual "origins and progress" summary, such commentary was missing. The two texts that one might have looked to in order to find some context or competition for Offenbach's comments are remarkably reticent. The two histories by Blondeau (1847) and de la Fage (1844) are either confused in the first case or do not reach the modern period in the second.[45] Fétis's later history of music (1869–76) stops well short of the

---

45. [Pierre] Auguste L[ouis] Blondeau, *Histoire de la musique moderne, depuis le premier siècle de l'ère chrétienne jusqu'à nos jours,* 2 vols. (Paris: Tantenstein et Cordel, 1847); Juste-Adrien Lenoir

beginnings of *opéra comique*.[46] The only history of *opéra comique* from the 1850s was that of Castil-Blaze, which remains unpublished to this day.[47] With Castil-Blaze we find a very different history of *opéra comique*, one that takes its historical credentials very seriously and sees the origins of the genre in the *Jeu de Robin et de Marion* from the end of the thirteenth century.

But Castil-Blaze's text remained unknown, with Offenbach's 1856 "Concours" sketch left commanding the field. The latter's influence was more than obvious in a series of thirty articles published by Louis Meneau in *Le ménestrel* between 19 August 1860 and 14 April 1861. This was a much less ambitious undertaking than Castil-Blaze's, and in its final article it reached a conclusion that owed a great deal to Offenbach's essay, written five years earlier. Here is Meneau's position, ironically encapsulated in a single paragraph:

> Today, the Opéra-Comique has become a branch of the Opéra. One is sometimes astonished to hear, in certain scores which have been the most played in recent years, the orchestra interrupt itself to allow the dialogue to take the place of the music; for, if this dialogue were replaced by recitative, one would have nothing short of a *grand opéra* in which no one would recognize the original genre. It appears that our compatriots compensate with the Opéra-Comique since our premier lyric stage—which ought to be national par excellence, since the whole nation contributes its pennies to its splendor—serves as a pedestal for foreign composers.[48]

Characterizing the Opéra-Comique as a branch (*succursale*) of the Académie Impériale de Musique and claiming that the music of *opéras comiques* had almost eclipsed

---

de La Fage, *Histoire générale de la musique et de la danse,* 2 vols. and atlas (Paris: Comptoir des imprimeurs unis, 1844).

46. François-Joseph Fétis, *Histoire générale de la musique depuis les temps les plus anciens jusqu'à nos jours,* 5 vols. (Paris: Firmin-Didot, 1869–76).

47. Castil-Blaze [François-Henri-Joseph Blaze], *Histoire de l'opéra comique* (MS [1856], F-Po, MS Rés 660). The text was presumably the third in the trilogy of which the first two works were Castil-Blaze, *L'Académie Impériale de Musique: Histoire littéraire, musicale, choréographique, pittoresque, morale, critique, facétieuse, politique et galante de ce théâtre,* 2 vols., Théâtres lyriques de Paris [1] (Paris: The author, 1855); and Castil-Blaze, *L'Opéra-Italien de 1548 à 1856,* Théâtres lyriques de Paris [2] (Paris: The author, 1856).

48. "Aujourd'hui, l'Opéra-Comique est devenu une succursale du grand Opéra. On est parfois étonné, à l'audition de certaines des partitions qui ont été le plus jouées dans ces temps derniers, d'entendre l'orchestre s'interrompre pour laisser le dialogue prendre la place du chant; car si on remplaçait ce dialogue par un récitatif, on aurait bel et bien un grand opéra dans lequel personne ne reconnaîtrait le genre primitif. Il semble que nos compatriotes se dédommagent sur l'opéra-comique de ce que notre première scène lyrique,—qui devrait être nationale par excellence, puisque la nation tout entière contribue de ses deniers à sa splendeur,—serve de piédestal aux compositeurs étrangers." Louis Meneau, "L'opéra-comique, sa naissance, ses progrès, sa trop grande extension," *Le ménestrel,* 14 April 1861.

their spoken dialogue were rhetorical moves that would not have been out of place in Offenbach's "Concours" text. And although Offenbach had stopped short of formally criticizing the presence of foreign composers at the Académie Impériale de Musique (indeed, he had been positive about Verdi's *Les vêpres siciliennes* in 1855), his commentary on "the composer of the future" (le compositeur de l'avenir) in *Le carnaval des revues* has much in common with Meneau's complaint; indeed, it is entirely possible that this edge to Meneau's article was a product of the Paris premiere of *Tannhäuser*, which had taken place a month before the article was published.

With this construction of history in place, Offenbach was able to situate the activities of the Théâtre des Bouffes-Parisiens within it as he sought to justify his announcement of the "Concours." His theater's task was, he said, "to resuscitate the original and true genre" of *opéra comique*.[49] Its success in its first year had been to elide the *opéra comique* of the past with the *farse* of Cimarosa and the early Italian masters. When Offenbach claimed that the repertory of his theater had no other ambition than to *faire court,* he was simply juxtaposing its works with those such as Massé's *Galathée* and *La chanteuse voilée,* in which, as has been seen, Offenbach identified a composer who tried to *faire grand.*[50] Works at the Théâtre des Bouffes-Parisiens were, according to Offenbach, but the first rung on the generic ladder; how, he asked, could composers climb the ladder if that first step did not exist? *Opéras comiques* in three acts, he argued, remained the domain of the proven master, and were an unfair challenge to the *débutant* composer.[51] With this claim Offenbach was able to merge the interests of the young composer with the works, limited by its license, of his own institution.

In his account of the French eighteenth-century tradition of *opéra comique,* Offenbach was not only subtly (re)writing history, but also reconfiguring the present for his own ends by pointing to the betrayal of true *opéra comique* by his colleagues and their immediate predecessors, and by praising works that seemed to embody the characteristics he considered representative of the truth of *opéra comique.* In practical terms, he was forbidden to mount productions of classic *opéra comique,* but that did not stop him from attempting to produce an eighteenth-century French classic: Rousseau's *Le devin du village.*

The fate of Rousseau's *Le devin du village* at the Bouffes-Parisiens demonstrates just how much difficulty Offenbach experienced in his negotiations with the minister of state, and reciprocally, how much difficulty the state encountered in trying to fend off Offenbach's advances. Offenbach had approached François-Louis Crosnier, the manager of the Académie Impériale de Musique, where *Le devin* had originally been performed, and obtained permission to mount it at the Bouffes-Parisiens. At the same time, Offenbach was (quite rightly) doubtful that such permission lay within Crosnier's gift; accordingly, he then wrote to the minister of state to confirm the

49. "De ressusciter le genre primitif et vrai." Offenbach, "Concours," 231, sec. 3, para. 5.
50. "Il n'a d'autre ambition que celle de faire *court.*" Ibid.; emphasis in original.
51. Ibid., 231, sec. 3, para. 6.

permission in March 1856. In his request he noted that rehearsals had already started, that the production had received the institution's greatest care, and that it could not fail to please the public. The work, in one act and with three characters only, appeared to fit the terms of the Bouffes-Parisiens' license perfectly.[52]

The exchange of reports and draft letters prepared within the ministry goes a long way toward showing just how close the system of exclusive licenses was to collapse, as various civil servants attempted to justify refusing Offenbach the permission he needed. An internal report, dated March 1856 and presumably prepared within just a couple of days of the receipt of Offenbach's request, points to a reluctance to authorize "the reduction to the proportions of his theater the great works of the lyric stage."[53] There is a strong sense in this comment that its author took as axiomatic that a work originally destined for the Académie Royale de Musique would be similar to one that could be heard at the Salle Le Peletier in the 1850s: such works as Meyerbeer's *Le prophète* or Verdi's *Les vêpres siciliennes, grands opéras* in five acts on historical themes, with ballets, elaborate sets, a colossal cast, and ostentatious costumes. That *Le devin du village* was in fact a very different sort of work became progressively clearer as the civil servants in the ministry worked on the case, and they finally admitted that it was perhaps a work "that did not have a very great importance."[54] On the other hand, in its use of fourteen numbers and closely integrated recitative, it would have been a significantly more complex undertaking had it been reworked for the Bouffes-Parisiens, and the outcome would have been in marked contrast to other works at the theater. In this initial report a second argument was advanced for refusal: the composer in question was particularly worthy of respect. There can be little doubt that Jean-Jacques Rousseau's reputation was as strong in the mid-1850s as it ever had been, and that he might qualify for perhaps greater protection than other composers active a hundred years before, but this was a strange reason to offer for refusing to allow a production of his best-known work. Attached to this first internal report to the minister was a draft letter which, although it ought to have summarized the two reasons given above, simply introduced a third reason for refusal: that "the work belong[s] to a repertory too different from the one you [are permitted to] exploit."[55]

This first report and its summarizing draft letter clearly met with a mixed reception, for a second version of the letter to Offenbach, dated 12 March 1856 (the date is crossed through) contains very different reasoning. The relevant part reads: "The works of dead masters being placed under the protection of the higher authority, I

---

52. The four groups of documents relating to the negotiations between the ministry and the Bouffes-Parisiens on which this and the following paragraph are based are found in *F-Pan*, F[21] 1136; they are identified numerically in the discussion that follows.

53. "De réduire aux proportions de son théâtre les grands ouvrages de la scène lyrique." *F-Pan*, F[21] 1136/2.

54. See n. 57.

55. "Cet ouvrage appart[ient] à un répertoire trop différent de celui que vous exploitez." *F-Pan*, F[21] 1136/2.

cannot allow the opera in question to be withdrawn from the theater to which it belongs in order to be changed into an *opéra comique* and transferred to a stage of a lower order."[56] Here the reduction of *Le devin du village* to the proportions of a work for the Bouffes-Parisiens was described in different, more specific terms: it was the change into an *opéra comique* that was so objectionable, coupled with the fact that such a change would be accompanied by a move to a stage of a lower order. Plausible reasons, indeed, but they represented subtle changes in emphasis from the earlier report. It was the first of the three reasons given in this document that ought to have been the most important: quite simply that *Le devin du village* "could [not] be withdrawn from the theater *to which it belongs* [auquel il appartient; emphasis added]." One of the tasks of the legislation surrounding the assignment of licenses was to avoid just the sort of appropriation that Offenbach was proposing. However, the opening clause in this paragraph invoking the protection of "l'administration supérieure" for dead composers betrayed the ministry's uneasiness with exercising this particular power. The matter was made even worse in the subsequent and final draft of the letter of refusal, which included the paragraph cited above along with a marginal addition that qualified the works of such dead composers as "meriting respect, even though they are without great importance."[57] Although this finally acknowledged the relatively slender dimensions of *Le devin du village* (so poorly judged in the first ministerial report), the effect of this further clause was to bury the question of theatrical property more deeply into the text and thus minimize its effect.

Offenbach was no stranger to these sorts of refusals. His first work for an established Parisian theater had been *Pépito,* produced at the Théâtre des Variétés two and a half years earlier. This had broken the terms of the Variétés' license and had threatened to impinge on the repertoire of the Opéra-Comique. The minister's action was swift and decisive: *Pépito* came off the stage at the Variétés within a month of the complaint's being made (probably by Perrin, since he had the most to lose from the competition).[58] *Pépito* was revived (within the terms of Offenbach's license) at the Bouffes-Parisiens on 10 March 1856, only five days after his exploratory letter to the minister concerning *Le devin du village* and two days before the first internal report. Offenbach must have been struck by the change in attitude between *Pépito*'s rapid and summary rejection in 1853 and the refusal of permission for a revival of *Le devin du village* in 1856. In 1853 the argument was simple. Furthermore, it had been familiar to theater managers since 1807: they should "be restrained in the future within the limits imposed by their *cahier de charges* as a reciprocal guarantee to each dramatic

56. "Les œuvres des maîtres morts étant placées sous la protection de l'administration supérieure, je ne puis permettre que l'opéra dont il s'agit soit retiré du théâtre auquel il appartient pour être changé en opéra comique et transporté sur une scène d'ordre inférieure." *F-Pan*, F²¹ 1136/3.

57. "Méritant des égards, alors même qu'ils n'ont pas une très grande importance." *F-Pan*, F²¹ 1136/4.

58. Yon, *Offenbach,* 118–19.

enterprise."[59] But in 1856 Offenbach was offered a mixture of excuses, the central one of which was buried in a welter of obfuscation. In the affair of *Le devin du village*, it is difficult to ignore the ministry's equivocal position, which may well have offered encouragement as Offenbach launched a campaign of transgression against his license that was ultimately to prove successful.

Foreign Traditions

Offenbach's attempt to exploit French traditions of the ancien régime had fallen afoul of official interference and the limitations of his license. But only weeks after the debacle with *Le devin du village*, the Bouffes-Parisiens was to have one of the biggest successes of its early years with an eighteenth-century stage work. However, the successful production of Mozart's *Der Schauspieldirektor* as *L'impresario* in May 1856 invoked an entirely different repertoire and set of references from those evolved in Offenbach's engagement with the music of the ancien régime: German opera, and opera by German-speaking composers of the previous century.[60]

In nineteenth-century German-speaking states, the four numbers and overture of *Der Schauspieldirektor* were regarded as a problematic constellation of compositions that did not constitute what was then thought of as opera. Of the various attempts to rework the music, the most successful was that of Louis Schneider and Wilhelm Taubert. This version took the music of *Der Schauspieldirektor*, supplemented it with orchestrations of Mozart's lieder and other vocal works, and provided it with a comic libretto set during preparations for *Die Zauberflöte*. The resulting production, originally entitled *Mozart und Schikaneder* (later revivals of this version returned to the original title), was given for the first time in Berlin in 1845. Offenbach took this version and commissioned Léon Battu and Ludovic Halévy to write a new libretto that kept the action loosely within the domain of opera production, familiar from *Der Schauspieldirektor* and *Mozart und Schikaneder*, but turned it into a simple story of duping a guardian into agreeing to a love match to which he is initially opposed. Musically, *L'impresario* was very close to Schneider and Taubert's 1845 reworking: one number was substantially cut and another resequenced.

The production was successful well beyond what Offenbach might have expected. Its immediate effect was to distance the Bouffes-Parisiens from Hervé's Folies-Nouvelles—all the more desirable in the light of some adverse press in the first couple of months of 1856 that Offenbach was anxious to counter before the launch of

59. "Soient retenus à l'avenir dans les limites que les cahiers des charges imposent, comme une garantie réciproque, à chacune des entreprises dramatiques." F-Pan, F²¹ 1133, 119.

60. The relationship between *Der Schauspieldirektor, Mozart und Schikaneder,* and *L'impresario* is outlined in Mark Everist, "Mozart and *L'impresario*," in *"L'esprit français" und die Musik Europas: Entstehung, Einfluß und Grenzen einer ästhetischen Doktrin*, ed. Rainer Schmusch and Michelle Biget-Mainfroy, Studien und Materialen zur Musikwissenschaft 40 (Hildesheim and New York: Olms, 2007), 420–33, on which the following two paragraphs are based.

his "Concours." The wider impact of *L'impresario* was even more remarkable: commentators borrowed critical discourses from the then commonplace eulogies to *Don Giovanni* and *Le nozze di Figaro* to praise this still-slender work more highly than might have been thought reasonable given the ambitions of the original *Gelegenheitsstück,* in the same way that *Bruschino* (as Rossini's *farsa giocosa* was known in Paris) would be compared favorably with *Il barbiere di Siviglia* and *Guillaume Tell* in 1857. Offenbach's successful appropriation of the past had been a financial and managerial success, and he had struck gold in associating his opera house with arguably one of the most revered composers in Second Empire Paris.

The only point at which Weber and Gluck make any impact on Offenbach's engagement with the music of the past is in the role they play in *Le carnaval des revues.* It could quite reasonably be argued that their presence in this scene is triggered by the fact that their music had been the subject of recent revival at the Théâtre-Lyrique. Weber's presence in the cast might also have been the result of needing a German-speaking character to explain the plays on words in *Le carnaval des revues* that involved Meyerbeer and Wagner. Neither Gluck nor Weber figures in Offenbach's reconfiguration of the comic opera of the past, and it is an open question whether Offenbach knew of the existence of Gluck's *opéras comiques.*

At the beginning of the 1856 manifesto on *opéra comique* presented in the "Concours" article, Offenbach had drawn attention to the important role that Pergolesi had played in the birth of the genre, and he had drawn fiercely nationalistic distinctions between Pergolesi and Grétry and—for a later generation—between Cimarosa and Boieldieu.[61] It is no surprise, then, to read in Albert de la Salle's 1860 account of the first five years of the Bouffes-Parisiens' history that Gevaert had been commissioned to arrange Pergolesi's *La serva padrona* for Offenbach's theater; it was never produced at the Bouffes-Parisiens but was revived at the Opéra-Comique in 1862.[62] In its one-act format and its use of a small number of soloists, *La serva padrona* seemed to be a close fit with the works permitted by Offenbach's license; it was at least as suitable as the two works, *Der Schauspieldirektor* and *Il signor Bruschino,* that did enjoy productions at the Bouffes-Parisiens.

The evidence is elusive, but various factors explain the work's redirection. There already existed a perfectly serviceable adaptation, dating from 1754, of Pergolesi's score as an *opéra comique. La serva padrona* had been translated by Pierre Baurans as *La servante maîtresse* and had enjoyed immense success at the Comédie-Italienne that year. There were therefore questions concerning the rights to the work in its guise as an *opéra comique* that would have posed insuperable problems for the Bouffes-Parisiens if the Opéra-Comique had chosen to challenge the theater: the Comédie-Italienne was viewed as the historical predecessor of the Opéra-Comique, and *La servante maî-*

61. Offenbach, "Concours," 230.
62. Albert de Lasalle, *Histoire des Bouffes-Parisiens* (Paris: Bourdillat, 1860), 44.

tresse as part of its repertoire. But by the time *La servante maître* was revived at the Opéra-Comique in 1862, any claims to it by the Bouffes-Parisiens had been completely forgotten, and the press was pleased to identify the opera as an important landmark in the Opéra-Comique's history and a logical inclusion in its repertory.[63]

As Offenbach cast around for other Italian works, he was drawn to the repertoire of *farse* that Rossini had written for Venice's San Moisè theater between 1810 and 1813. The last of these, *Il signor Bruschino*, formed the basis of the second great foreign success of the Bouffes-Parisiens' early years.[64] Much of the success garnered by *L'impresario* was replicated in *Bruschino*. Unlike with *L'impresario*, however, not only was Offenbach returning to the past (*Il signor Bruschino* had been premiered in 1813), but of course the work's composer was alive, living in Paris, and by the 1850s a national monument. Furthermore, *Bruschino* was the first musical event of any significance publicly associated with the composer since his return to Paris in 1855.

The production was surrounded by a series of discursive moves that associated Rossini with it, that reminded journal readers of the early history of the composer of *Il barbiere di Siviglia* and *Guillaume Tell*, and that praised the Bouffes-Parisiens for having been the first theater to mount a "new" opera of Rossini since 1829 (*pasticci* were excepted).[65] Unlike Offenbach's other appeals to the past, with *Bruschino* (and thanks

63. Lasalle also wrote a "Notice historique sur la *Servante maître*," published with the piano-vocal score of the work that accompanied the 1862 production at the Opéra-Comique; it is dated 16 August of that year (*La servante maître: Opéra comique en deux actes,* paroles françaises de Baurans; musique de Pergolese [*sic*]; partition réduite pour piano et chant par Soumis; seule édition conforme aux représentations de l'Opéra-Comique et précédée d'un notice historique par Albert de Lasalle . . . [Paris: E. Girod, 1862]). Curiously, Lasalle made no reference in this text to the planned performance at the Bouffes-Parisiens, as he had in his book, published two years earlier.

64. The work was premiered under the title *Bruschino* at the Bouffes-Parisiens on 28 December 1857. The piano-vocal score was published as *Bruschino: Opéra bouffe en deux actes,* poème de Mr A de Forges, musique de Rossini, acct de piano par H Salomon . . . (Paris: Léon Escudier, [1857]). Given that we know very little of the chronology of the work on *La servante maître*, it is entirely possible that Offenbach's searches for Italian opera that resulted in *La serva padrona* and *Il signor Bruschino* were coterminous.

65. Claims that Rossini had given the production his blessing were common, and Jules Lovy was typical: "The illustrious composer has not only authorized the performance of his work at the Bouffes-Parisiens, but he has again promised M. Offenbach his assistance and advice, 'considering himself happy,' he added graciously, 'to do something for the one he calls *The Mozart of the Champs-Elysées*'" (L'illustre compositeur a non-seulement autorisé l'exécution de son œuvre aux Bouffes-Parisiens, mais encore il a promis son assistance et ses conseils à M. Offenbach, "s'estimant heureux," a-t-il ajouté gracieusement, "de faire quelque chose pour celui qu'il appelle le *Mozart des Champs-Élysées*"). "Un opéra de Rossini aux Bouffes-Parisiens," *Le ménestrel,* 1 November 1857. In his eulogy to the composer on the occasion of *Bruschino*'s premiere, Henry Boisseaux introduced the composer: "This man, it is Rossini, the composer of *Il barbiere*, the composer of *Guillaume Tell*" (Cet homme, c'est Rossini, l'auteur d'*Il barbiere*, l'auteur de *Guillaume Tell*). Boisseaux, "Premières représentations—Bouffes-Parisiens: *Bruschino*," *La revue et gazette des théâtres,* 31 December

to Rossini's longevity and very early success) he was able genuinely to embody the past on the boards of his own theater. The effect of this cannot be overstated. In comparison with the very real cultural capital that Offenbach earned through his production of *L'impresario,* his musical and theatrical profit from *Bruschino* was immense.

In stark contrast to the Bouffes-Parisiens' production of *L'impresario,* which came as something of a surprise to Parisian theatrical connoisseurs, *Bruschino* was intently tracked in the press. The piano-vocal score was published by the Escudier brothers, who had advertised the forthcoming production incessantly in their house journal, *La France musicale.* Not only were there weekly bulletins on the progress of rehearsals for the six weeks before the premiere on 28 December 1857, but during this period the journal offered the published score of *Bruschino* free to all subscribers beginning on 15 December of that year.[66] The plan was predicated on the work's premiering in early December, but the fact that subscribers to *La France musicale* possessed copies of the work two weeks before its premiere does not seem to have damaged its reception. Enthusiasm for *Bruschino* well before its premiere was not restricted to those who had a vested interest in its success. Jules Lovy, writing in *Le ménestrel,* was typical in pointing to a number of qualities to be expected in the production: the original libretto was not only "une délicieuse bouffonnerie," but had been arranged by Philippe-Auguste-Alfred Pittaud de Forges in a way that had astonished Rossini himself.[67] Finally, Offenbach—as he had in the case of *L'impresario*—had engaged new soloists, one of whom—Charles Duvernoy—had, like his Mozartian predecessors, just won the *premier prix* at the Conservatoire.[68]

The importance of Rossini and the *imprimatur* that he gave to the production cannot be overestimated. A recurring trope in the pre-production commentaries was the juxtaposition of the "high priest of modern music" with "the little temple of the Passage Choiseul" (that is, the Théâtre des Bouffes-Parisiens).[69] This went very well with similar types of hagiography that had accompanied the production of *L'impresario* the previous year.[70] The fact that Rossini—"the high priest of modern

---

1857. Journalists had to look back as far as the *Stabat mater* (known in Paris since 7 January 1842) for comparable Rossini premieres: "Not since the *Stabat* have we seen public curiosity excited in so lively a manner" (Jamais, depuis le *Stabat,* on n'a vu la curiosité publique aussi vivement excitée). "Nouvelles," *La France musicale,* 15 November 1857.

66. The advertising campaign began in *La France musicale,* 15 November 1857.

67. "Le poème primitif est une délicieuse bouffonnerie italienne que M. De Forges a fait entrer dans un cadre nouveau, avec une habilité qui a étonné Rossini lui-même." Jacques Lovy, "Un opéra de Rossini aux Bouffes-Parisiens," *Le ménestrel,* 1 November 1857.

68. Lovy, "Un opéra de Rossini aux Bouffes-Parisiens," *Le ménestrel,* 1 November 1857.

69. "But M. Offenbach is conscious of the obligation and the double responsibility that he incurs in having the name of the high priest of modern music enter his little temple in the Passage Choiseul" (Mais M. Offenbach a le sentiment du devoir et de la double responsabilité qu'il encourt en faisant entrer le nom de grand-prêtre de la musique moderne dans son petit temple du passage Choiseul). "Semaine théâtrale," *Le ménestrel,* 20 December 1857.

70. See Everist, "Mozart and *L'impresario,*" 430–33.

music" could be seen in the neighborhood (he lived no more than a couple of blocks away from the Passage Choiseul on the Chaussée d'Antin) simply enhanced the prestige that the institution could reap from the production.

It is inevitable that *Bruschino* would have been praised to the skies in *La France musicale,* even if the Escudier brothers did manage to resist the temptation to review the work themselves and apparently handed the task over to Achille de Lauzières, who signed himself "A. Aldini."[71] But others were just as quick to praise. Both Jacques-Léopold Heugel in *Le ménestrel* and Henry Boisseaux in the *Revue et gazette des théâtres*—writing for very different audiences—could not have been more positive; they pointed to the quality of the work, its arrangement by de Forges and Offenbach, the performance, and the number of celebrities—musical, political, and social—in the audience.[72] In the same way that *L'impresario* had benefited from analogy with *Don Giovanni* and *Le nozze di Figaro,* *Bruschino* was praised by association with either the pairing of *Il barbiere di Siviglia and La Cenerentola* or that of *Il barbiere* and *Guillaume Tell.*

Boisseaux went further and used the work as an opportunity to renew Paris's praise for the "high priest of modern music." He addresses his review directly to Rossini himself:

> One no longer knows what place you should be assigned in art. To affirm that you are a powerful colorist—what would Weber say? To propose that your orchestration is splendid—what would Beethoven say? To take witness from the *School* that you have infused with science—what would M. Fétis say? To swear in front of all that melody flows in buckets from your work—what would Grétry, Mozart, and Auber say? No, a hundred times no! I shall not judge you. I shall simply repeat, alongside the intelligent critic of *Le Figaro* that you are only a musician, nothing but a musician, but the most perfect of musicians![73]

71. A. Aldini, "Premières représentations I: Bruschino—Rossini (Bouffes-Parisiens)," *La France musicale,* 3 January 1858. The pseudonym is probably based on Comte Antonio Aldini, the minister of state for Italy during the First Empire; his name was in the public consciousness as a result of the publication his memoirs the previous year. *Mémoires du comte Aldini, ministre secrétaire d'État pour le royaume d'Italie, résidant à Paris* (Paris: Allard, 1857).

72. Jacques-Léopold Heugel, "Une partition de Rossini aux Bouffes-Parisiens," *Le ménestrel,* 3 January 1858; Henry Boisseaux, "Premières représentations," *Revue et gazette des théâtres,* 31 December 1857.

73. "On ne sait plus quelle place il faut vous assigner dans l'art. Affirmer que vous êtes un puissant coloriste < . . . > que dirait Weber? < . . . > Soutenir que votre orchestration est splendidement combinée < . . . > que dirait Beethoven? < . . . > Prendre à témoin l'*École* que vous avez la science infusé < . . . > que dirait M. Fétis? . . . Jurer devant tous que la mélodie s'échappe à flots de votre œuvre < . . . > que diraient Grétry, Mozart et Auber? Non, cent fois non! je ne vous jugerai pas. Je répéterai seulement, avec l'intelligent critique du *Figaro* que vous n'êtes qu'un musicien, rien qu'un musicien, mais le plus parfait des musiciens!" Boisseaux, "Premières représentations," *Revue et gazette des théâtres,* 31 December 1857. Boisseaux's choice of this group of composers, with the

The unquestioning praise for Rossini is here hardly the issue; but the consumption of *Bruschino* as a work that could serve as a springboard for such eulogy—by analogy with core repertoire of the Théâtre-Italien and the Académie Impériale de Musique—is testimony to its success.

Offenbach's unsuccessful jousts with the state over *Pépito* at the Variétés and over *Le devin du village* must have made him realize how important state control over his activities could be, no matter how well connected he was personally. His success in negotiating a slight change in his license—increasing the number of soloists in musical works from three to four—when he moved operations to the Salle Choiseul in October 1855 and the ambivalent nature of the refusal to allow him to play *Le devin du village* would also have made him realize that however important such control, it could be manipulated legally or by other means. Lasalle carefully documented no fewer than six changes in Offenbach's treatment of his license between 1855 and the premiere of *Orphée aux enfers* in 1858.[74] The first change—already mentioned—was entirely legal. The remaining breaches of Offenbach's license were illegal, and of these *Bruschino* represented one of the most important stages. The work demonstrates how Offenbach could use the power of a past work—especially when its venerable composer was still alive to authorize it—to generate so much publicity that he could smuggle in generic changes to which he could subsequently point as legitimating the enlargement of the works mounted at his own theater.[75]

The success of *Bruschino*, like that of *L'impresario*, had not come without effort. *Bruschino* was originally made up of an overture and eight numbers separated by *recitativo semplice*, and this entailed not only the reworking of the libretto for the sung numbers but also the replacement of the recitative by spoken dialogue, as

---

exception of Auber, reinforces the view of Rossini as a living composer of the past. By 1858 Auber was in the middle of a career that would last for another fifteen years but had started thirty-five years previously. He is now allied with composers of the past: Grétry, Mozart, Beethoven, and Weber. If Heugel had been thinking of Rossini as a modern composer (rather than as "the high priest of modern music," which is a different concept entirely), he would have chosen Meyerbeer, Halévy, and Verdi as points of reference.

74. Lasalle, *Histoire des Bouffes-Parisiens*, 15–17.

75. Lasalle's careful diagnosis of the six "époques" in the development of the Bouffes-Parisiens' repertoire is distorted by Yon when the latter claims that *Bruschino* "renders official the right to a fifth person or stage and authorizes works of a greater size" (officialise le droit au cinquième personnage et autorise des pièces d'une plus grande dimension; *Offenbach*, 199). This betrays a fundamental misunderstanding of the dynamic of the relationship between the theater and the state. The "époques" identified by Lasalle correspond to progressive transgressions of Offenbach's license that were—as Lasalle observed—"tolerances" (*Histoire des Bouffes-Parisiens*, 16). When Offenbach sought to renew his license in October 1860, the terms of the revision were exactly the same as they had been five years previously (*F-Pan*, F[21] 1136). If Offenbach's license had indeed been subject to change during the late 1850s, the renewal of the license would have had to have taken any such changes into account.

TABLE 4.1. Comparison of Italian and French versions of Rossini, *Il signor Bruschino*

Il signor Bruschino (1813)	Bruschino (1857)
Sinfonia	Ouverture
	Act 1
1. Introduzione "Deh tu m'assisti amore"	1. Introduction et duettino "Hélas! Je désespère" (Corilla, Flavio)
2. Duetto "Io danari vi darò" (Florville, Filiberto)	2. Duetto "C'est moi qui vous rembourserai" (Flavio, Giuseppe)
3. Cavatina "Nel teatro del gran mondo" (Gaudenzio)	3. Air "Tout va bien dans ma citadelle" (Bruschino)
4. Terzetto "Per un figlio già pentito" (Florville, Bruschino, Gaudenzio)	4. Trio "Que d'un père" (Flavio, Bruschino, Bombarda)
	Act 2
5. Recitativo ed aria "Ah voi condur volete—Ah donate il caro sposo" (Sofia)	5. Récitatif et air "O père inexorable—Ah! Pour vous quand l'espoir" (Corilla) [repeat of cabaletta cut]
6. Aria "Ho la testa" (Bruschino, Gaudenzio, Commisario, Sofia, Florville)	6. Quintette [sic] "L'imposture est bien complète" (Bruschino, Bombarda, Giuseppe, Corilla)
7. Duetto "È un bel nodo" (Sofia, Gaudenzio)	7. Rondo "Oui grâce à cette ruse" [= cabaletta only of source duetto] (Corilla)
8. Finale "Ebben, ragion, dovere"	8. Finale "Hélas! Plus d'espérance" (Bruschino, Bombarda, Giuseppe, Corilla, Flavio)

Castil-Blaze had done in his adaptations of Rossini for the Théâtre Royal de l'Odéon in the 1820s—versions that were still in use at the Théâtre-Lyrique in the 1850s (see table 4.1).

The librettist, de Forges, effectively wrote a new narrative around the characters and the music he found in the original; this explains the reassignment of the cavatina "Nel teatro del gran mondo" from Gaudenzio Strappapuppole to Bruschino in the 1857 French version, as well as other changes in the aria "Ho la testa" and in the finale.

It should have been an easy matter to adjust *Il signor Bruschino* to fall in line with the Bouffes-Parisiens' license. In one act and consisting of eight numbers, its physiognomy resembled most works produced at the theater in 1857. Its original cast ran to more than the Parisiens' allotted limit, but the reworking of numbers with more than four characters should have posed no problem. But rather than reworking Rossini to conform exactly to the requirement of his license, Offenbach's strategy was to test its limits, to see how far he could go beyond the terms of his license before the state or his theatrical competitors took action. He did this, however, in ways that would not damage the work if complaints were made—in contrast to the experience with *Pépito* and *Le devin du village,* when they had been either taken off after a curtailed run or withdrawn during rehearsal.

Two examples show how Offenbach accomplished this administrative high-wire act. One of his ambitions was to put himself in a position where he could ultimately mount *opérettes* in two acts—the format of *Orphée aux enfers,* which was to be premiered the following year. *Il signor Bruschino* was in its original form in a single act, and so too were all the works with seven or eight numbers then in the repertory of the Bouffes-Parisiens.[76] Offenbach chose deliberately and unnecessarily to divide the work into two acts, for which there was no musical, dramatic, or practical justification.[77] A work in two acts would have broken the terms of Offenbach's license; yet, had he been challenged, he could simply have abandoned the division, with no change to the content of the work. If unchallenged, he would have had case law on his side as he sought to defend future works in two acts that—like *Orphée aux enfers*—were significantly more ambitious.

Similarly, the *aria Bruschino* originally entitled "Ho la testa" was apparently transformed into a *quintette,* again breaking the terms of Offenbach's license. Here the example is even more subtle than that of the act division: Rossini's original in *Il signor Bruschino* consists of an aria with four additional ancillary parts; although much of the aria consists of duet and trio textures, it employs all five voices in the *stretta,* and removed from its original context, it might well be titled a quintet.[78] But in *Bruschino* this number has only four characters, and the five-part music in Rossini's original is reworked as a quartet (the roles of Florville and the Commissario de polizia are elided), so that the music therefore falls comfortably within the terms of the theater's license.[79] But Offenbach titled it *quintette* in the score (nothing more than an overly technical description of the scoring of Rossini's original) on the page in question and in the *catalogue de morceaux.* He knew that all would recognize that a number with such a title was an infringement of his license, but it would have established a precedent when he mounted future productions with larger ensembles; furthermore, he could defend the number, if required, by showing that it was really a *quatuor* in which no more than four soloists sang at any one time.[80] In the listing of voice types for the number (in both the score and the index), Offenbach adds a tenor to the soprano,

76. Even those works composed just before and after *Bruschino* that aggressively attempted to transgress the theater's license in terms of the number of characters retained a single act: *Les petits prodiges* (19 November 1857) and *Mesdames de la halle* (3 March 1858).

77. As table 4.1 shows, each act consists of four numbers each.

78. Arrigo Gazzaniga, ed., *Il signor Bruschino, ossia Il figlio per azzardo: farsa giocosa per musica in un atto di Giuseppe Foppa, musica di Gioachino Rossini,* Edizione critica delle opere di Gioachino Rossini I/9 (Pesaro: Fondazione Rossini, 1986), 303–17.

79. *Bruschino: Opéra bouffe en deux actes,* 73–76, 79–85.

80. Ibid., 68.

baritone, and pair of basses; although the tenor Flavio/Florville sings in Rossini's original, he is entirely absent from Offenbach's arrangement of the number. In the libretto, however, Offenbach was at the same time more cautious and even more subtle; he called "Ho la testa"/"L'imposture est bien faite" a *morceau d'ensemble,* a terminology that would include a perfectly legal quartet, but also any further ensembles that might include more characters.[81]

Bruschino was the perfect context in which to explore these duplicitous maneuvers. The noise generated by the work allowed enough people to overlook what might be thought minor transgressions. The timing was also fortunate. The source of any objection to breaches of Offenbach's license was likely to be the director of the Opéra-Comique, and Emile Perrin had probably been behind the complaints about *Pépito;* but Perrin had stepped down as director of the Opéra-Comique on 20 November 1857, right in the middle of the public excitement about the impending production of *Bruschino,* and despite the experience Perrin's successor, Nestor Roqueplan, had gained from his work at the Académie Royale de Musique and the Académie Impériale de Musique from 1847 to 1854, he might have been thought not quite as ready to take on the protégé of the emperor's half brother as he might have been later in his tenure of the management of the Opéra-Comique.

In appropriating foreign opera in French translation for the benefit of the Bouffes-Parisiens and in order to circumvent the limitations of his license, Offenbach was inscribing his activities in a tradition common to a wide range of Parisian institutions that supported music drama; the only two exceptions were the Théâtre-Italien—whose license expressly limited its managers to opera in Italian—and the Opéra-Comique. Since 1800 the Académie Impériale de Musique had mounted translations of *Die Zauberflöte, Don Giovanni, Euryanthe, Der Freischütz, Mosè in Egitto, Maometto II, Poliuto, Otello, Lucia di Lammermoor,* and *I Lombardi alla prima crociata.* Although these were occasional productions, other theaters—the Gymnase Dramatique, the Théâtre Royal de l'Odéon, and the Théâtre de la Renaissance—also mounted such productions, and in the case of the Odéon largely depended on them for their survival. The practice would of course continue with the production of *Tannhäuser* at the Académie Impériale de Musique in 1861, and the process of translation would fall out of state control with the repeal of the licensing laws in 1864.

Offenbach saw the appropriation of the stage music of the long eighteenth century as one of several strategies that he could use for the aesthetic positioning of his Théâtre des Bouffes-Parisiens, alongside sycophantic praise for contemporary composers who had little to fear from him, the development of the bourgeois and aristocratic con-

---

81. Lasalle's commentary (*Histoire des Bouffes-Parisiens,* 17) makes it clear that in this case (and perhaps in Yon's as well), Offenbach's strategy of deception had worked well.

tacts that he had built up in the previous decade, and the claims that he could support young composers in a way that no other theater could. In his critical writing in *L'artiste* and in his manifesto accompanying the announcement of the "Concours," he praised the *opéra comique* of the eighteenth century and those contemporaries who emulated it. Even in the context of a parody, such as *Le carnaval des revues,* he could harness the power of eighteenth-century composers to lampoon those, such as the composer of the future, who had little sympathy with *opéra comique.* And finally, although it was difficult to bring to completion plans to produce eighteenth-century music drama at the Bouffes-Parisiens, Offenbach identified perhaps the four key works in the long eighteenth century that seemed to fall within the remit of his theater's license and brought productions of two of them to successful conclusions.

Offenbach always had his sights set higher than his own theater, and even if his first experience at the Opéra-Comique itself was a disaster, he was to abandon the sole management of the Bouffes-Parisiens in 1862 in pursuit of more ambitious goals. By that time the aesthetic identity of the Bouffes-Parisiens was well established, with clear artistic space separating it from the Folies-Nouvelles—as had always been Offenbach's ambition. The consistent and sustained allusion to music drama from the past had successfully done its work.

Carvalho and the Opéra-Comique

L'ART DE SE HÂTER LENTEMENT

Lesley Wright

A long-term director in a state-subsidized theatrical house of nineteenth-century France exercised immense power, even though it was a transitory domination. One of the most influential of these was Léon Carvalho (1825–1897; see fig. 5.1), who presided over the development of French opera for most of the second half of the nineteenth century, first at the Théâtre-Lyrique and later the Opéra-Comique. In 1876 he took over an Opéra-Comique in utter disarray.[1] Only four years later, and even before he

I would like to thank Florence Roth at the Bibliothèque de la SACD for her gracious help and advice and Pauline Girard for her careful reading of this text. And, as always, I am indebted to the personnel of the Bibliothèque nationale de France (at Tolbiac, Musique, and the Opéra).

1. To the Société des Auteurs et Compositeurs dramatiques (for convenience abbreviated as SACD, although the society authorized this only in 1973), Henri Becque reported the state of affairs at the Opéra-Comique in 1876–77: "It seems that when Mr. Carvalho took over the Opéra-Comique, he found only the four walls, and even these four walls needed the much-talked-about renter's repairs, so common in subsidized theaters. No repertory. No work accepted. No troupe, no orchestra, no chorus. The scores were missing, even that of *La Dame blanche*" (Il paraît que M. Carvalho, lorsqu'il a pris l'Opéra-Comique, n'a trouvé que les 4 murs et encore les 4 murs avaient-ils besoin de ces fameuses réparations locatives, si fréquentes dans les théâtres subvention-nés. Plus de répertoire. Aucun ouvrage reçu. Pas de troupe, pas d'orchestre, pas de chœurs. Les partitions, même celle de la *Dame Blanche,* manquaient). Minutes of the meeting of 14 December 1877, Report on the subsidized theaters by Henri Becque, *F-Psc*. The society decided not to assess a penalty even though Carvalho was able to mount only six instead of the requisite ten new acts during his first year (30 September 1876 to 30 September 1877).

99

FIGURE 5.1. Portrait of Leon Carvalho. *L'illustration,* 1 January 1898. Courtesy of Duke University Library.

introduced the three works that quickly became *centenaires*[2]—*Les contes d'Hoffmann* (1881), *Lakmé* (1883), and *Manon* (1884)—commentators were already congratulating this enterprising, if sometimes exasperating, director. They praised him for reviving the house and for finding that elusive balance between honoring the older repertoire of this *éminemment français* genre and giving opportunities to the younger genera-tion of composers. Mindful of the bottom line, though more strongly committed to artistic values, Carvalho also brought back some of the most successful works from the defunct Théâtre-Lyrique, several of which he had first mounted himself. In fact, until he became a scapegoat for the catastrophic fire at the second Salle Favart in 1887, his directorship at the Opéra-Comique was regarded as one of the most successful in nineteenth-century France—profitable, reasonably progressive, and a testament to the enduring appeal of "the charming genre of *opéra comique,* so French, so national."[3]

2. *Centenaires* are works performed more than one hundred times at the same theater.
3. "Le genre charmant, si français, si national de l'opéra-comique." Georges d'Heylli, *Foy-*

In 1898 the librettist Louis Gallet sketched portraits of four of the Opéra's general directors (Perrin, Halanzier, Vaucorbeil, and Ritt), but many of his remarks could easily have described their recently deceased contemporary Carvalho. Gallet pointed out that even the director of the most important theater in the world "has only a very small place in the memory of men once he has disappeared from life or the stage, a lesser place than that of celebrated artists, whose renown, nonetheless, fades so quickly!"[4] Especially in an age before video documentation, a brilliant stage director, too, left behind less to appreciate than did an author or composer. Gallet maintained that nothing remained of a director beyond a name and some scattered anecdotes, though during their lives these figures wielded tremendous power in directing the course of art and the lives of artists, for they were the

judges, the dominators of men, whose impetus is almost irresistible; in front of these men masters [of art] bow down with the healthy fear of godlike omnipotence; . . . their influence, beneficial or harmful, can spread across a large portion of a century, impeding or accelerating the movement of a school, encouraging mediocrities, discouraging superior figures, making the theater a temple or a boutique, according to their particular inclination.[5]

This was the kind of power Carvalho held too. Some grumbled mightily about him as a theater and/or stage director (for he was both), but they did so mostly in the safe havens of private correspondence or retrospective commentary.

This essay examines Carvalho as a central figure of the Opéra-Comique during a particularly brilliant period in its history and focuses on the impact of this director upon composers and others who knew or worked with him and on his image in the press.[6] It will also analyze reactions to Carvalho's first (1876) and second (1891) nominations to the directorship of the Opéra-Comique as well as assessments of his achievements in articles written at the time of his death (1897), when, for example, the author of the column "La vie parisienne" felt justified in stating: "Mr. Carvalho

---

ers et coulisses: Histoire anecdotique des théâtres de Paris; Opéra-Comique (Paris: Tresse et Stock, 1885), 1.

4. "Il ne tient qu'une très petite place dans la mémoire des hommes, une fois disparu de la vie ou de la scène, une place moindre que celle des artistes célèbres, dont le renom, pourtant, s'efface si vite!" Louis Gallet, "Quatre directeurs de l'Opéra," *Revue internationale de musique* 4 (15 April 1898): 208.

5. "Des juges, des dominateurs d'hommes, dont la force impulsive est presque irrésistible, devant lequel les maîtres s'inclinent, avec cette salutaire crainte de la toute-puissance des dieux; . . . leur influence, bienfaisante ou néfaste, put s'étendre sur toute une portion de siècle, ennuyer ou accélérer le mouvement d'une école, encourager des médiocrités, décourager des personnalités supérieures, faire du théâtre un temple ou une boutique, selon leur particulière inclination." Ibid.

6. For a discussion of the role of the opera director in Parisian theaters, see André Michael Spies, *Opera, State and Society in the Third Republic (1875–1914)* (New York: Peter Lang, 1998), especially chapter 2, "The Administration of the Opera," 21–48.

was the director of the Opéra-Comique, and even more than that, he was the Opéra-Comique itself."[7] Despite such assertions, Carvalho himself has not been the center of an extended study. Changing the focus from the institutions he guided or the composers he worked with to the impact of the director himself allows a new understanding of an especially vibrant era for the Opéra-Comique. Documents, anecdotes, and newspaper reports cluster about this magnetic figure and highlight the multiple talents that set him at the forefront of his time: masterful bargaining skills, intelligent management of repertoire, effective personnel management (and people skills), a commitment to artistry as he understood it, and an indefatigable dedication to his work.

Léon Carvaille (called Carvalho) was born in the "colonies" (the island Mauritius, east of Madagascar) in 1825.[8] He came to Paris to study at the Conservatoire, where in 1848 he won an honorable mention in singing. Hired for secondary baritone roles, he showed no more than ordinary talent as singer and actor at the Opéra-Comique, but after he met and married the soprano Marie-Caroline Félix-Miolan (1827–1895), one of the most remarkable French singers of her time,[9] he followed his wife to the Théâtre-Lyrique. There found his true métier: he was an extraordinary director, thanks to his energy, vision, artistry, and staging ability.

Budgeting acumen eluded him at first. During his two terms at the helm, 1856–60 and 1862–68, he steered the Théâtre-Lyrique to prominence among the stages of Paris and persuaded the government to provide a subsidy (starting in 1863). Both his terms ended, however, in financial disarray. Artistic achievements included the premieres of Gounod's *Faust* and *Roméo et Juliette,* Bizet's *Les pêcheurs de perles,* and a heavily cut version of Berlioz's *Les Troyens* (the Carthage acts only). After a stint in Cairo directing the theater of the Khédive, he briefly took over the Théâtre du Vaudeville, where he had the idea of asking Bizet to write incidental music for Alphonse Daudet's play *L'Arlésienne* (1872). When he left this post, he worked as a stage director at the Opéra (1874–75 and beyond) and then succeeded Camille du Locle at the Opéra-Comique in August 1876.

In a newspaper interview published only a few days after the theater burned, Car-

7. "M. Carvalho était et même plus que le directeur de l'Opéra-Comique, il était l'Opéra-Comique lui-même." Santillane [pseud.], "La vie parisienne: Léon Carvalho," *Gil blas,* 30 December 1897.

8. The outlines of Carvalho's biography are well-known and relatively consistent in various sources published during his lifetime. Such material appears, for example, as a footnote to his wife's lengthy biography in Pougin's 1878 supplement to the Fétis dictionary. See François-Joseph Fétis, "Caroline Félix Miolan-Carvalho," in *Biographie universelle des musiciens: Supplément,* ed. A. Pougin (Paris: Firmin-Didot, 1878–80). In an 1885 feuilleton Johannès Weber also mingled the biographies of this couple as he announced the impending farewell performance of Mme Carvalho. "Critique musicale," *Le temps,* 8 June 1885.

9. Mme Carvalho was widely praised for the timbre, range, and suppleness of her voice and for her purity of style. Her husband is supposed to have called her his "subsidy" in the years before 1863 when the Théâtre-Lyrique had no state support. See the discussion of singing and Caroline Carvalho in Hervé Lacombe, *The Keys to French Opera in the Nineteenth Century,* trans. Edward Schneider (Berkeley and Los Angeles: University of California Press, 2001), 41–42.

valho summarized his accomplishments. He reminded the public that ten years earlier the Opéra-Comique had been totally disorganized and lacked a functioning troupe. Worse yet, "the public had forgotten the route to the theater."[10] His task had been to revive the quintessentially French genre, and, despite great difficulties, he felt that in just three years of hard work, helped by a government that increased his subsidy and bought out the end of the developers' forty-year lease on the theater just before the 1879 renovations, he had succeeded. To bring the house and its genre back to life, he had first rebuilt the troupe. He had then turned to the rich repertoire he controlled to woo back the public: "It was by giving perfect renditions of masterpieces that I was able to bring them back to the theater. And it was only in 1879—a year that I attained thanks to the Exposition—that the Opéra-Comique was finally recognized as a good theater!"[11]

In this same interview Carvalho also stressed his service to young French authors. He listed their works, such as Émile Paladilhe's *Suzanne* and Ferdinand Poise's *La surprise de l'amour, L'amour médecin,* and *Joli Gilles.* He underlined the importance of *Les contes d'Hoffmann* (Offenbach), *Jean de Nivelle* and *Lakmé* (Delibes), and *Manon* (Massenet): "All these pieces were interesting artistic events. . . . Everyone remembers these last pieces, and if success has not greeted all the works since *Manon,* undertakings such as *Galante aventure, Egmont, Le roi malgré lui,* etc., have been, nonetheless, works by men of talent worthy of being performed."[12] Even though his most recent productions had not resulted in durable additions to the repertoire, Carvalho defended his job performance: "And if, for three years, I have not had great successes, thanks to my repertoire and my troupe, I have been able to maintain my theater at the highest rank."[13] Neither in this repertoire list nor in a more comprehensive one that his lawyer filed with the court of appeals the next year did Carvalho mention *Carmen,* even though it had become one of the biggest moneymakers at the Opéra-Comique.[14] This silence may confirm his reputed distaste for Bizet's masterpiece. But through his lawyer he did proudly point to his long list of achievements—some forty works premiered, some two dozen masterpieces revived, and the discovery and numerous

10. "Le public avait désappris le chemin du théâtre." Lucien Valette, "L'Opéra-Comique raconté par MM. Ritt, du Locle et Carvalho," *Le voltaire,* 31 May 1887. *F-Po,* Opéra-Comique, Presse 1887 (mai–juin).

11. "C'est à force de lui donner une exécution parfaite des chefs-d'œuvre que j'ai pu le ramener au théâtre. Et c'est en 1879 seulement—année que j'atteignis grâce à l'Exposition—que l'on se décida enfin à reconnaître que l'Opéra-Comique était un bon théâtre!" Ibid.

12. "Toutes ces pièces furent d'intéressantes manifestations d'art. . . . Des dernières pièces tout le monde se souvient, et si le succès ne les a pas toutes saluées depuis *Manon,* elles ont été cependant, entre autres *Galante Aventure, Egmont, le Roi malgré lui,* etc. des œuvres d'hommes de talent dignes d'être représentées." Ibid.

13. "Et si, depuis trois ans, je n'ai pas eu de grands succès, grâce a mon répertoire et à ma troupe j'ai pu maintenir mon théâtre au premier rang." Ibid.

14. Carvalho was fighting charges of negligence brought against him by the state, which used him as a scapegoat for the many fatalities associated with this disaster. In truth, the safety deficiencies had been reported to the government numerous times.

singers cultivated: "There, Sirs, are not his crimes, but his work, his entitlement to the gratitude of the public and the benevolence of the Tribunal."[15]

Even before he was officially named director on 14 August 1876, Carvalho knew the artistic community supported him, and he used this knowledge to his advantage. Backed by a prestigious group, most of whom put up 10,000 francs each in support of his candidacy,[16] he parlayed the memory of his artistically successful directorships at the Théâtre-Lyrique and the dire straits of the Opéra-Comique into a higher sub-sidy from the government (200,000 francs instead of just 140,000). Though he was, in the end, required to purchase the *matériel* for the theater at the assessed value of 317,000 francs, he had also proposed that the state acquire these items, as was the practice at the Opéra. Having failed to persuade the Chambre des députés to do this, he accepted an additional 40,000 francs a year until 1880 for a total subsidy of 240,000 francs per year.[17] To help get the Opéra-Comique on its feet, Léon Gam-betta supposedly diverted this extra sum from the budget for historical monuments. Despite the house's many problems, Carvalho set up from the outset the possibility that he could succeed through canny bargaining with the government.

When Carvalho took over direction of the Opéra-Comique, the public, compos-ers, and artists all applauded the choice. So, too, did some of the musical press, even though many were preoccupied with Bayreuth's first complete *Ring* cycle when the

15. "Voilà, Messieurs, non pas ses crimes, mais ses travaux, ses titres à la reconnaissance du public et à la bienveillance du Tribunal." "Affaire de l'Opéra-Comique. Défense de M. Carvalho. Plaidoirie de Mr. Henri Barboux (1888)." *F-Pn,* 4º Fr. 173 4635, p. 30. The deposition runs to forty-eight pages. The text lists some of the new works Carvalho had presented as part of his duty to the French repertoire: "*Cinq-Mars, les Surprises de l'Amour, l'Amour médecin, Joli Gilles, les Contes d'Hoffmann, Galante Aventure, Jean de Nivelle, Lakmé, Suzanne et Diana, Une Nuit de Cléopâtre, la Taverne de Trabans, Plutus, le Chevalier Jean, Manon, Proserpine, le Roi malgré lui,* etc., etc." He also enumerates about two dozen reprises (including some repertoire moved over from the Théâtre-Lyrique): "*Cendrillon, Joseph, le Déserteur, l'Étoile du Nord, le Pardon de Ploermel, Lalla-Rouk* [*sic*]*, le Pré aux Clercs, le Domino noir, Fra Diavolo, Roméo et Juliette, Philémon et Baucis, la Dame blanche, le Postillon de Longiumeau* [*sic*]*, Richard Cœur de Lion, la Fille du Régiment, le Chalet, les Noces de Jeannette, le Barbier de Séville, les Dragons de Villars, Zampa, le Songe d'une Nuit d'Été, la Flûte enchantée, les Noces de Figaro, la Traviata,* etc., etc." Lists from pp. 30–31.

16. *F-Pan,* AJ[13] 1135, Société du Théâtre National de l'Opéra Comique. See also Jean Gourret, "Léon Carvalho," chap. 9 in *Histoire de l'opéra-comique* (Paris: Éditions Albatros, 1983), 156–57. Of the 200,000 francs that backed Carvalho's nomination, the director himself provided 40,000. The next largest contributor was the wealthy Jules Beer (30,000), a minor composer and nephew of Meyerbeer. Others in this group with direct interest in gaining access to Carvalho's favor and in the success of his enterprise included the publishers Antony Choudens (10,000) and Émile Durand (10,000), and the principal libretto publisher of that time, Calmann-Lévy (10,000). Article 6 reads: "To this society M. Carvalho brings his industry, his intelligence, and his ministrations." His base salary was set at 24,000 francs a year and is confirmed in documents kept by Édouard Noel, general secretary at the theater in the 1880s. See *F-Po,* Opéra-Comique. Arch. 19ᵉ s. [79] 1883–84.

17. Albert Soubies and Charles Malherbe, *Histoire de l'Opéra-Comique: La seconde salle Favart,* vol. 2, *1860–1887* (Paris: Flammarion, 1893), 236–38.

announcement was made. There was a consensus that Carvalho's artistic experience, intelligence, and initiative would provide a guarantee of success at the Parisian bourgeoisie's favorite theater.[18] The editors of *Les annales du théâtre et de la musique* expressed their support as well: "Mr. Carvalho, who is a man of initiative, will not dally for an instant (so we hope at least) with the idea of modifying, however minimally, the genre of Favart; he will not dream of a compromise between this theater and the Opéra; . . . With Mr. Carvalho, the Opéra-Comique will preserve this eminently French genre, typified by *La dame blanche, Le chalet, Le pré aux clercs, Fra diavolo,* and even *Piccolino.*"[19] For the most part they used Daniel Bernard's words to warn Carvalho of the evils of his predecessor's ways: "Mr. Camille du Locle had the best intentions in the world. . . . Alas! he wanted to move too quickly. . . . The best things need to come along at the right *moment psychologically;* we are moving toward serious music for sure, but we are not there yet. We are hastening slowly, and along the way, we do not want to be prevented from smiling a bit."[20] In *L'art musical,* however, Léon Escudier indulged in serious finger-wagging, for he had his doubts about Carvalho, a director of "ideas": "Nothing is more fearsome than an abundance of ideas in a theater whose course has been set out for close to a century."[21] The next day Gustave Lafargue of *Le Figaro* felt it necessary to reassure Escudier that Carvalho was wise enough to insist that the genre observe proper models, such as *La dame blanche* and *Piccolino.* Referring to more recent successes such as *Roméo et Juliette* and *Mignon,* he also remarked pointedly: "Nonetheless, if Messieurs Gounod and Ambroise Thomas come knocking on the door of the Opéra-Comique, Mr. Escudier would certainly permit Mr. Carvalho to open the doors wide to them."[22]

18. For a fine summary of Carvalho's activities and influence up to 1884, see Jean-Christophe Branger, *"Manon" de Jules Massenet ou le crépuscule de l'opéra-comique* (Metz: Éditions Serpenoise, 1999), 24–29.

19. "M. Carvalho, qui est un homme d'initiative, ne s'arrêtera pas un instant, espérons-le du moins, à l'idée de modifier, quelque légèrement que ce fût, le genre de Favart; il ne rêvera pas un compromis entre ce théâtre et l'Opéra. . . . Avec M. Carvalho, l'Opéra-Comique conservera ce genre éminemment français, dont on peut citer comme types *la Dame blanche, le Chalet, le Pré aux clercs, Fra Diavolo,* et même *Piccolino.*" Édouard Noël and Edmond Stoullig, eds., *Les annales du théâtre et de la musique* 2 (Paris, 1877): 212–13. The last opera, by Ernest Guiraud, had its premiere during Perrin's temporary administration on 11 April 1876.

20. "M. Camille du Locle avait les meilleures intentions du monde. . . . Hélas! il a voulu courir trop vite. . . . Les meilleures choses demandent à venir dans leur *moment psychologique;* nous allons vers la musique sérieuse, c'est sûr, mais nous n'y sommes pas encore. Nous nous hâtons lentement, et, pendant la route, nous ne voulons pas qu'il nous soit défendu de rire un brin." Ibid. Quote from music critic Daniel Bernard, writing in *L'union,* a legitimist Catholic paper.

21. "Rien de redoutable comme l'abondance des idées dans un théâtre dont la route est tracée depuis près d'un siècle." Léon Escudier, "Le budget des Beaux-Arts," *L'art musical,* 17 August 1876.

22. "Cependant, si MM. Gounod et Ambroise Thomas viennent frapper à l'Opéra-Comique, M. Escudier permettra bien à M. Carvalho de leur ouvrir, à deux battants, la porte du théâtre." Gustave Lafargue, "Courrier des théâtres," *Le Figaro,* 18 August 1876.

Gustave Lafargue's prediction came to pass, for Carvalho turned immediately to Gounod, a composer he knew could meet deadlines and whose return to the stage after a hiatus of ten years could become a major artistic event. "He realized . . . that it would be important to make a mark with a major new production as soon as possible," and indeed *Cinq-Mars* was in rehearsal by January 1877.[23] Though Carvalho's name alone did not precipitate an immediate escalation in receipts for 1876–77, his ability as an entrepreneur soon turned the fortunes of the house around as soon as 1880. *Les annales* could then exclaim: "Times have certainly changed!"[24] Carvalho had brought the public back to the house. He had struck a balance so that the Opéra-Comique, now fully recovered from the previous directorship, could remain "faithful to the traditions of all its glorious past" and be able "to underline the vitality of our dramatic music, to furnish proven talents new opportunities to present themselves and to extend a hand to unknown composers who were only waiting the right moment to be revealed; to be, in a word, the temple open to all [believers] in the cult of lyric art."[25]

But how did Carvalho accomplish this feat? Certainly he had some good luck. Two of his principal competitors disappeared in 1878 (the Théâtre-Lyrique under Vizentini and the Théâtre-Italien). Not only could he draw their audiences, but he also had access to their stars to raise the quality of his increasingly impressive troupe. He could pick and choose among their proven repertoire to help increase his profit margin. In the case of the Théâtre-Lyrique, the spoils included new works, such as Léo Delibes's *Jean de Nivelle*—the first *centenaire* of Carvalho's directorship—not to mention Jacques Offenbach's *Les contes d'Hoffmann*. His theater raked in high receipts during the 1878 Exposition Universelle by playing audience favorites. And Carvalho also benefited from the suppression of rent paid to private entrepreneurs when the government took possession of the space.

As soon as Carvalho took over the theater, he raced to find appropriate personnel. The uncertainties of the institution's future and the extended closure of the house over the summer of 1876 had led to a general dispersal of the employees. When announcement and gossip columns in music periodicals and daily newspapers speculated on the date the house would open its doors and on the work that would inaugurate the new season, they also commented on Carvalho's feverish activity in his efforts to form a new troupe—auditions every day, artists reengaged, rumors of other artists who might be engaged, contracts with singers who chose to leave other theaters, and so on. In fact, for the next two seasons, Carvalho auditioned and tried out singers constantly and worked tirelessly to improve the caliber of the troupe overall. Not one to waste time,

---

23. Steven Huebner, *The Operas of Charles Gounod* (Oxford: Clarendon Press, 1990), 91–92.

24. "Ces temps sont bien changés!" Noël and Stoullig, *Annales* 6 (1881): 202. Édouard Noël became the administrative assistant at the Opéra-Comique in 1881. See d'Heylli, *Foyers et coulisses,* 74.

25. "Fidèle aux traditions de tout un passé glorieux, pour affirmer la vitalité de notre musique dramatique, fournir aux talents éprouvés de nouvelles occasions de se produire, tendre la main aux compositeurs inconnus qui n'attendent que l'heure de se révéler, être, en un mot, le temple ouvert à tous au culte de l'art lyrique." Noël and Stoullig, *Annales* 6 (1881): 202.

he decided quickly whether a new hire, presented in a repertory work, would be useful or not. He let singers go as necessary. The 1877 season saw an exceptional twenty-seven debuts, but by the end of that year some twenty-one singers had departed.[26]

Lucien Fugère, one of the first true stars Carvalho discovered for his new house, began his career at the Opéra-Comique in September 1877 as Jean in Victor Massé's popular curtain-raiser *Les noces de Jeannette*.[27] He remained a mainstay of the house over the next thirty-plus years. In the context of the director's frantic pace of rebuilding, his forgetfulness (see Fugère's anecdote below) seems distinctly possible. More important, the decisiveness and mutual loyalty to which the singer attests help explain how Carvalho assembled and maintained a first-rate troupe.

The young baritone went to see the Opéra-Comique director on 30 May 1877, announcing that his contract with the Bouffes had finished. Carvalho was stupefied by the news that he had engaged Fugère. "Yes, Mr. Director, I have my contract in my pocket, signed by you. I've come to ask you for a leave of three months to do a season at Néris where I have been engaged by Mr. Danbé for a third year." "Ah! you've been engaged by Danbé," said Carvalho, astonished. And then, smiling, he continued, "It's agreed upon. Off you go, but be here for the season's opening in September." After the singer's debut that autumn, Carvalho exclaimed immediately, "Fugère, I will never be one to let you down."[28]

Fugère's great respect for the director who watched over the first two decades of his career is evident in the posthumous compliments he paid him. Carvalho was in his eyes both a great artist and a great director, "with the triple competence of an extraordinary musician, stage director, and educator. What works, what composers, and what artists he brought to the fore!"[29]

Access to personal loyalty like this gave Carvalho the power to use his soloists to best advantage and to assemble casts with major singers in secondary roles.[30] He could

26. Soubies and Malherbe, *Histoire de l'Opéra-Comique, 1860–1887*, 262–63.

27. *Les noces de Jeannette* had its premiere at the Opéra-Comique on 4 February 1853 and achieved five hundred performances by 18 January 1875. Its thousandth performance occurred on 10 May 1895 during Carvalho's second stint as director. Stéphane Wolff, *Un demi-siècle d'opéra-comique* (Paris: André Bonne, 1953).

28. "Oui, monsieur le Directeur. J'ai mon engagement dans ma poche, signé de vous. Je venais justement vous demander un congé de trois mois pour faire une saison à Néris où je suis engagé par M. Danbé pour la troisième année."—"Ah! vous êtes engagé par Danbé" dit Carvalho étonné. "C'est entendu, dit-il, allez. Mais soyez là pour la rentrée en septembre." "Fugère, ce ne sera jamais moi qui vous quitterai." Raoul Duhamel, *Lucien Fugère* (Paris: Bernard Grasset, 1929), 53–54 (paraphrased, with direct quotations maintained).

29. "Avec la triple compétence d'un musicien, d'un metteur en scène et d'un éducateur extraordinaires. Que d'œuvres, que de compositeurs, que d'artistes il a mis en évidence." Ibid., 187.

30. Alfred Bruneau tells a tale from the early 1890s that lacks the conversation but implies the same modus operandi that Carvalho had used with Fugère in the 1880s. Bruneau and his librettists wanted Blanche Deschamps-Jéhin for the role of Hubertine in *Le rêve* (1892), but they were convinced she would refuse this secondary role as being beneath her, particularly because it had

even reassign roles at the last minute. For example, Carvalho asked Fugère to do him a personal favor in 1884 and switch from singing the coveted lead role of Figaro to that of Bartolo in Rossini's *Il barbiere di Siviglia*. At first the baritone replied: "I, give up Figaro, this role that I love and that I've worked so much on! Truly—but I cannot! Just think. . . . " "My dear Fugère, humor me! Take it on; it's a role that fits you. Do it for me!" At these words, Fugère hesitated a moment, and so Carvalho continued, "It's settled, isn't it?" "Well, so be it, Mr. Director," said Fugère. "I'll play Bartolo and—I promise you to do something with [the role]." "Oh," replied Carvalho, "I'm counting on it; I'm even certain of it." Carvalho had years of casting experience, and most often he was right. Bartolo became, in fact, one of the singer's signature roles. His performance aroused such general admiration that, according to Fugère, Émile Perrin offered him a position at the Comédie-Française.[31]

Carvalho's decisions about casting Offenbach's *Les contes d'Hoffmann* may be seen as authoritarian, but it is likely that he was also intent on assigning his strongest singers to the project, adding their drawing power to that of Offenbach's name. He did impose the tenor Alexandre Talazac upon the composer, who had originally conceived of a baritone in the leading role, thereby forcing the ailing man to do substantial rewriting in the autumn of 1880.[32] Still, as Heather Hadlock has suggested, the choice of this singer, who "belonged to the first generation of tenors that broke with the *opéra comique* tradition of genteel light vocalism," allowed a certain "lyric urgency" to emerge in this role, as it had in Bizet's Don José.[33] Carvalho also chose the coloratura soprano Adèle Isaac as the female lead, and she made a great success of the Doll Song when *Les contes d'Hoffmann* had its premiere in 1881.[34] This was not the case, however, when she played Carmen in the Parisian reprise of Bizet's masterpiece in April 1883. Although some critics maintained that her demure approach to Bizet's gypsy was more appropriate for a proper bourgeois theater than Galli-Marié's

been assigned to another singer before her. Carvalho went to talk to her. The next day he sent news that she had accepted the role graciously. See Alfred Bruneau, *À l'ombre d'un grand cœur* (Paris: Fasquelle, 1931), 30–31.

31. "Moi, laisser Figaro, ce rôle que j'aime et que j'ai tant travaillé! Vraiment... mais je ne peux pas! Songez..."—"Mon cher Fugère, obligez-moi! Prenez Bartholo; c'est un rôle à votre taille. Faites cela pour moi. . . . C'est entendu, n'est-ce pas?" dit Carvalho—"Hé bien, soit, monsieur le Directeur! dit Fugère, je jouerai Bartholo et... je vous promets d'en faire quelque chose."—"Oh, pour cela, dit Carvalho, j'y compte bien; et même, j'en suis certain." Ibid., 71–73.

32. Jean-Claude Yon, *Jacques Offenbach* (Paris: Éditions Gallimard, 2000), 593, 596. Carvalho attended a private concert performance in May 1879 and agreed to stage the work if the Théâtre-Lyrique was not reestablished. Taskin, Carvalho's highest-paid singer, took the four diabolical roles.

33. Heather Hadlock, *Mad Loves: Women and Music in Offenbach's "Les contes d'Hoffmann"* (Princeton, NJ: Princeton University Press, 2000), 9–10.

34. See a substantial sampling of reviews in Arnold Jacobshagen, ed., *Les contes d'Hoffmann: Dossier de presse parisienne (1881)* (Heilbronn: Musik-Edition Lucie Galland, 1995).

seductive play during the premiere, many found fault with Carvalho for casting her.[35] Letters from the Halévy family show that Carvalho's production was also bowing to their wishes as he gingerly mounted a work for which he personally had no real taste.[36] The family wanted him to emphasize musical over dramatic values. Once he and Carvalho had agreed on casting, Bizet's librettist Ludovic Halévy wrote to his cousin Geneviève, Bizet's widow: "Isaac, Bilbaut-Vauchelet, Taskin, and the best tenor possible (I think it will be Stéphane). The reprise will be excellent with this casting, which gives real assurance for [a good] musical performance. . . . We ought to have, under these conditions, an admirable reprise. And the expression is not justifiable. I should say: an admirable first performance. The piece, in truth, was not sung in Paris, and it will be this time."[37]

When Carvalho faced what was left of the Opéra-Comique personnel in August 1876, he also faced a disgruntled group. The orchestra members, who had cost du Locle, the previous director, some 89,000 francs, asked for a hefty raise of 40,000 francs to soothe their unhappiness over several months of unemployment. The chorus asked for a raise as well. The artistic world hoped that Carvalho's proven bargaining skills would effect a compromise and smooth over these exorbitant demands.[38] This faith was well placed, but the director agreed to raise the remuneration of all the *petits employés* by 60,000 francs—a wise investment of his increased subsidy from the government, for he needed their goodwill in order to start his season as soon as possible.[39] During the profitable year of 1879, which included an extended summer

35. For an introduction to criticism of the April 1883 production, see Lesley A. Wright, "Une critique revisitée: L'accueil de *Carmen* à Paris en 1883," in *Musique, esthétique et société au XIXe siècle: Liber amicorum Joël-Marie Fauquet*, ed. Damien Colas, Florence Gétreau, and Malou Haine (Wavre: Mardaga, 2007), 187–97.

36. In 1912 Maurice Lefèvre (critic of *Le clairon* and self-proclaimed leader of a movement in 1882 demanding that *Carmen* be revived in Paris) reported that he heard Carvalho dismiss Lillas Pastia's tavern as a brothel, something that he would never allow on his stage. He also claimed that the librettists, Henri Meilhac and Ludovic Halévy, blamed the first Carmen, Galli-Marié, for the work's failure. See Lefèvre, "Georges Bizet, le musicien," *Musica* 11, no. 117 (June 1912): 102–3.

37. "Isaac, Bilbaut-Vauchelet, Taskin et le ténor le meilleur possible (je crois que ça sera Stéphane). La reprise doit être excellente avec cette distribution qui donne une véritable sécurité comme exécution musicale. . . . Nous devons avoir, dans de telles conditions une admirable reprise. Et l'expression n'est pas juste. Je pourrais dire: une admirable première représentation. La pièce, en effet, n'a pas été chantée à Paris, et elle le sera cette fois." Ludovic Halévy, letter to Geneviève Bizet, [1882], in Françoise Balard, *Geneviève Straus: Biographie et correspondance avec Ludovic Halévy, 1855–1908* (Paris: CNRS Éditions, 2002), 138.

38. Carvalho seems to have deflected the ire of the orchestra members and chorus toward du Locle. They initiated a lawsuit to seek two months' pay in compensation for the four months the theater was closed in 1876. Because their contract had freed them of any obligation to the theater after the first two months it was closed, however, the court did not support their suit. Soubies and Malherbe, *Histoire de l'Opéra-Comique, 1860–1887*, 244–45.

39. See ibid., 238. Personnel changes and reengagements are listed on 238–39.

closure so that the hall could be renovated, he attended yet again to the resulting financial strain upon his personnel; and so the orchestra members (now a much better ensemble than three years earlier) received supplementary pay to tide them over.[40] If Carvalho could cut loose a weak soloist in an instant, he could also be consistently kind to less visible employees, from whom he needed first-rate effort for relatively little pay: "He had exquisite manners. If one of his troupe, be it a simple chorus member, came to see him in his office, he would doff his hat and keep it off to receive him and would listen with the most benevolent attention."[41]

In his first months with the Opéra-Comique Carvalho also showed his ability to exert authority when necessary. On Christmas Eve in 1876, the male choristers went on strike just after the first act of *La dame blanche,* claiming that they needed to provide "religious services." They then left the theater for their church jobs. Even though they continued their strike into the first four days of the new year, ticket revenues were stable. The public wanted to enjoy their holiday entertainments and remained sympathetic to the new director.[42] Carvalho forced the chorus back to work with the threat of a lawsuit and heavy fines. In the end, only the head chorister was punished when he lost his case before the tribunal that March.[43]

Carvalho could also manage his chorus without threats. During rehearsals for the impending premiere of Gounod's *Cinq-Mars,* he noticed that the group lacked the requisite gusto in the finale of the second act. When questioned, one chorus member protested that as ardent republicans they could not develop enthusiasm for the line "Let us save the nobility and France." "Well, then, pretend that you're singing the *Marseillaise,*" retorted Carvalho, giving his chorus a basic lesson in method acting. They followed his advice, and the audience encored this scene at the premiere.[44]

Carvalho could be impatient, explosive, and authoritarian with his employees, even those in prominent positions. Evidence of these traits also showed up in his first season with the Opéra-Comique. For example, when his musical director, Charles Lamoureux, wanted to redo certain passages with the orchestra at the final rehearsal of the William Chaumet's ill-fated *Bathyle* on 3 May 1877, Carvalho nixed the idea. Words were exchanged. Neither would bend.[45] Lamoureux resigned, following through on

40. See ibid., 299.

41. "Il était de manières exquises. L'un des pensionnaires fût-ce même un simple choriste, venait-il le trouver à son cabinet, il le saluait chapeau bas, restait découvert pour le recevoir et l'écoutait avec la plus bienveillante attention." Duhamel, *Fugère,* 187.

42. *F-Po,* Opéra-Comique, Registre 1876–77. For example, on 1 January, the double bill of *Le pré aux clercs* and *Lalla Roukh* brought in 7,163.50 francs, while the 2 January offering of *Les noces de Jeannette* and *Mignon* brought in 7,480.50 francs on a rainy evening.

43. Soubies and Malherbe, *Histoire de l'Opéra-Comique, 1860–1887,* 244.

44. "Eh! bien, [*sic*] figurez-vous que vous chantez la Marseillaise!" Ibid., 251. The premiere of *Cinq-Mars* took place on 5 April 1877.

45. *Bathyle,* to a libretto by Édouard Blau and Louis Gallet, had won the Cressent competition in 1875. It had only nine performances at the Opéra-Comique. Carvalho had clearly been attracted

an action he had threatened and backed down on once before in February after a disagreement with Gounod. After the definitive resignation, Carvalho (in a move that he may well have planned with the composer in anticipation of Lamoureux's departure) turned immediately to Gounod to lead the orchestra for performances of his opera from 5 May to 21 May 1877. The novelty of this arrangement kept gate receipts at a healthy 7,000-plus francs per evening. (They dipped considerably after Gounod left the podium.)[46] Among numerous candidates to succeed Lamoureux, Carvalho selected Jules Danbé, who proved to be an excellent leader for the long term. He stayed in the post from May 1877 until 1898.

Like other directors, Carvalho was also indebted to people, especially the backers who had helped him gain control of the theater in the first place. His largest single investor was the wealthy Jules Beer. Not surprisingly, Carvalho hastened to mount a splendid reprise of Meyerbeer's *L'étoile du nord* in March 1878. Possibly prompted by Carvalho, the music critic Paul Bernard duly noted that

> numerous, meticulous rehearsals all took place under the direction of Mr. Jules Beer, nephew of the illustrious Meyerbeer. Himself a consummate musician, he insisted on fulfilling his pious and artistic duty. No one better than he could have known the intentions of the author nor better replaced the master who was taken away too soon from the admiration of his contemporaries.[47]

Unfortunately the lead soprano, Cécile Ritter, engaged at Beer's request, was overwhelmed by the starring role. After four performances she became "ill," and Carvalho replaced her with a genuine virtuoso, Adèle Isaac. Isaac's success advanced her career markedly while raising box-office receipts on 26 October to the highest level of the profitable year of the Exposition Universelle.[48]

Though Carvalho had considerable personal charm, composers and librettists sometimes found him infuriating. Saint-Saëns claimed he had a veritable mania for leaving his imprint on the works he staged: "He wanted to collaborate on the pieces

---

to the project by the 10,000 francs his theater would receive to subsidize the production. He was probably aware that the work would be unlikely to make money for the theater. Even paired with such warhorses as *Zampa, La dame blanche,* and *Mignon,* receipts stayed low (1,500–2,000 francs per evening); then a heat wave from 8 June to 23 June caused a precipitous drop in all revenues, with even proven repertoire on several of the hottest evenings grossing less than 600 francs. *F-Po,* Opéra-Comique, Registre 1876–77.

46. See Soubies and Malherbe, *Histoire de l'Opéra-Comique, 1860–1887,* 253–54, and *F-Po,* Opéra-Comique, Registre 1876–77.

47. "Les répétitions nombreuses et soignées ont toutes eu lieu sous la direction de M. Jules Beer, neveu de l'illustre Meyerbeer, qui parfait musicien lui-même, a tenu à remplir ce devoir pieux et artistique. Nul mieux que lui n'aurait pu connaître les intentions de l'auteur et remplacer le maître enlevé trop tôt à l'admiration de ses contemporains." Paul Bernard, "Théâtre national de l'Opéra-Comique," *La revue et gazette musicale de Paris,* 31 March 1878.

48. Soubies and Malherbe, *Histoire de l'Opéra-Comique, 1860–1887,* 271.

he presented in his theater. If it was a work consecrated by time and success, he had to leave his mark; even more so if it involved a new work. He announced abruptly that you had to change the era or the country where you had placed the action of your story."[49] Of his own *Le timbre d'argent,* Saint-Saëns complained that Carvalho intended to create a role for his talented wife when he "tormented" the composer and his collaborators to try to make them change the lead character, Fiametta, a mute played by a ballerina, into a lyric role.[50] As is well known, Massenet preempted Carvalho's notorious penchant for tinkering by handing him the score of *Manon* (1884), printed and bound, as they went into rehearsal. Carvalho supposedly replied: "Rest easy, dear friend. We will play your work as if you were already dead."[51] But Massenet was already experienced enough in the theater to do without Carvalho's practiced hand to edit and adjust during the staging. And of course, Offenbach was already deceased when, with the counsel of the composer and critic Victorin Joncières, Carvalho decided to cut the problematic Venetian act of *Les contes d'Hoffmann* shortly before the 10 February 1881 premiere, a decision imposed over the vigorous protests of the librettist, Jules Barbier, and the starring tenor, Talazac. When the director sent his announcement to *Le ménestrel* for publication on 6 February, he justified the massive change as an improvement to the drama: the last two acts made their impact more through spectacle than through music, so he made the "heroic" choice to condense them into one, although he had to waste three sets and a hundred costumes.[52]

Critics agreed that Carvalho staged exquisite *reprises* as part of his campaign to keep subscribers loyal and win back those who had drifted from the fold. Indeed, he acknowledged his fondness for the older repertoire and its emphasis on melody. "I like a good dessert," he asserted in an 1891 newspaper interview. "We are a race who sings. Here we can retain melody, and our musicians, though they respect the poetry more [than before], would be very wrong to let themselves be imprisoned by

49. "Il voulait collaborer aux pièces qu'il représentait sur son théâtre. Fût-ce une œuvre consacrée par le temps et par le succès, il fallait qu'il portât sa marque; à plus forte raison s'il s'agissait d'une œuvre nouvelle. Il vous annonçait brusquement qu'il fallait changer l'époque, le pays où vous aviez situé l'action de votre pièce." Camille Saint-Saëns, "Histoire d'un opéra-comique," in *École buissonnière: Notes et souvenirs* (Paris: Pierre Laffitte, [1913]), 25.

50. In the end, *Le timbre d'argent* (first version 1864–65) was not staged while Carvalho was director of the Théâtre-Lyrique because of his second bankruptcy. After the Franco-Prussian War, the reconstituted Théâtre-Lyrique under Vizentini presented it eighteen times in 1877; for this version Saint-Saëns replaced spoken dialogue with singing. See also David Grayson's essay in this volume.

51. "Soyez tranquille, cher ami, on vous jouera comme si vous étiez un auteur mort." See Félix Galipaux, "Ceux que j'ai connus. Carvalho," clipping from unidentified newspaper, 1888; *F-Pn,* Département des arts du spectacle, Richelieu, coll. Rondel, Ro 2088. Carvalho may have been the one who suggested the subject of *Manon* to Massenet. See Steven Huebner, *French Opera at the fin de siècle: Wagnerism, Nationalism, and Style* (Oxford: Oxford University Press, 1999), 45–46.

52. Yon, *Offenbach,* 621–22.

it."[53] Only a few months after he took the directorship for the first time, he brought back Nicolò Isouard's *Cendrillon* (1810), a tuneful work that had not been staged at the Opéra-Comique since 1848. He interpolated a charming divertissement, with music from *Airs à danser de Lully à Méhul,* a collection that had just been published by the Opéra's librarian, Théodore de Lajarte. Though reviewers found the score a bit pallid and the cast merely adequate, they did praise Carvalho's imaginative insertion: "All our compliments to the artistic sensibility that presided over this charming interlude and all our thanks for the pleasure it gave us."[54] Actually, in addition to giving rein to his visual imagination and adding a novel twist to a work which had played more than a hundred times on that stage, setting the production at the time of Louis XIV allowed Carvalho both to add charm to the entertainment and to recycle costumes left over from the brief run of Delibes's *Le roi l'a dit* (1874).[55]

Once the theater was prosperous, Carvalho systematically set about putting together admirable productions of the most durable repertoire, such as Auber's *Le domino noir* (1848): "This score, unique in its genre must remain in our repertoire. Mr. Carvalho has understood this well, and Friday's *reprise* assures *Le domino noir* a long new lease."[56] No more old sets, no more ripped costumes, and no more cuts. At the time (May 1880) Carvalho was doubtless looking ahead to a celebration of the one thousandth performance of this Opéra-Comique staple, which took place on 3 April 1882. In staging new works, too, especially when he hoped they would join the repertoire of the house, he was often credited as "the lion of the evening, thanks to his intelligent staging and the richness of his costumes and sets."[57]

Carvalho was one of the strongest stage directors of later nineteenth-century Paris.[58] Gaston Jollivet has left a vivid description of the director's artistry, imagina-

53. "J'aime un bon dessert. Nous sommes d'une race qui chante. On peut chez nous garder la mélodie, et nos musiciens, tout en respectant davantage le poème, auraient le plus grand tort de se laisser emprisonner par lui." Maurice Lefèvre, "Le mouvement dramatique et musical II. M. Carvalho," clipping from unidentified newspaper, August 1891; *F-Pn,* Département des arts du spectacle, Richelieu. coll. Rondel, Ro 2088.

54. "Tous nos compliments pour le sentiment artistique qui a présidé à ce charmant intermède, et tous nos remerciements pour le plaisir qu'il nous a procuré." Paul Bernard, "Théâtre national de l'Opéra-Comique: Reprise de *Cendrillon,*" *La revue et gazette musicale de Paris,* 28 January 1877.

55. See Soubies and Malherbe, *Histoire de l'Opéra-Comique, 1860–1887,* 247.

56. "Cette partition, unique dans son genre, doit rester à notre répertoire. M. Carvalho l'a bien compris, et la reprise de vendredi assure au *Domino noir* un nouveau et long bail." H. Lavoix fils, "Théâtre national de l'Opéra-Comique: Reprise du *Domino noir* (21 mai)," *La revue et gazette musicale de Paris,* 23 May 1880.

57. "Quant à M. Carvalho, il a été vraiment le lion de la soirée, grâce à son intelligente mise en scène, à la richesse des costumes et des décors." Paul Bernard, "Théâtre national de l'Opéra-Comique: *Cinq-Mars,*" *La revue et gazette musicale de Paris,* 8 April 1877.

58. Bruneau, *À l'ombre d'un grand cœur,* 29–30, stressed both Carvalho's love of music and the virtuosity of his staging skills as he observed them during the preparation of *Le rêve* for its premiere in 1891.

tion, and versatility in making dialogue come to life.[59] He praised exactly the same attention to detail and close control of interpretation that certain others chafed under, and he compared Carvalho's mastery of the rehearsal to Victorien Sardou's:[60]

> I remember those hours as among the best of my life. What an astonishing man! I can see him still, moving about and saying a few words, always useful to twenty people at once. I can hear him still: "Mademoiselle So and So . . . Wait, you do not know what it is to be tender . . . " and lifting the manuscript from the hands of the stage manager, casting an eye over the text, he demonstrated the amorous, ingenuous, almost baby-like tone he wanted without causing laughter, and it was always profitable for the actress.
>
> An instant later he was haranguing the whole troupe, taking the actors [aside] one by one, reading each role to each person as it should be read, and that without bothering himself about the text, for he serenely made up verses with fourteen syllables (Symbolist before his time) that gave the sense, the color of things; then, after a few seconds of rest, punctuated by a pinch of tobacco, he would leap up on the stage because he had just noticed the extras entering on the courtyard side and, looking them over, he grouped some here in little bunches, and there made other individuals take picturesque poses, at other times yelling to the authors to add a line of verse for this one or a shout for another. In sum, he gave the play life and then increased its charm and truthfulness in expert consultations with costumer and set designer.[61]

59. Jollivet and Albert Millaud were the authors of *Plutus,* which Carvalho staged as a two-act *comédie* while he was director of the Théâtre du Vaudeville; it was premiered there on 14 March 1873. After Charles Lecocq set a libretto based on their play to music, Carvalho staged it again as a three-act *opéra comique* (with libretto by Jollivet and Millaud); it was premiered at the Opéra-Comique on 31 March 1886.

60. Henry Février, for example, documents the hostility between his teacher, André Messager, and Carvalho in the staging of *Le chevalier d'Harmental* (1896); he describes the director as unnecessarily and incessantly interrupting rehearsals as well as intervening everywhere, even in the orchestration. Messager was furious, probably even more so when his opera had only a brief run on the Opéra-Comique stage. See Henry Février, *André Messager: Mon maître, mon ami* (Paris: Amiot-Dumont, 1948), 85–86.

61. "Je me rappelle ces heures-là parmi les meilleures de ma vie. Quel homme étonnant! Je le vois encore, ne tenant pas en place et disant des mots brefs, toujours utiles, à vingt personnes à la fois! Je l'entends encore: 'Mademoiselle Une Telle... Attendez, vous ne savez pas ce que c'est d'être tendre...' Et enlevant le manuscrit aux mains du régisseur, jetant rapidement les yeux sur le texte et donnant sans rire la note amoureuse, ingénue, presque bébé, et c'était une indication toujours profitable à l'actrice... Un instant après c'était toute la troupe qu'il haranguait, prenant ses acteurs un à un, lisant chaque rôle à chacun comme il devait être dit, et cela sans souci de texte, nous faisant avec sérénité des vers de quatorze pieds, symboliste avant l'heure, mais donnant le sens, la couleur des choses, puis, après quelques secondes de repos, ponctuées par une prise de tabac, sautant sur la scène parce qu'il venait de voir la figuration entrer par le côté cour, et passant en revue les figurants, groupant ici des petits paquets, là créant des attitudes pittoresques à des isolés, et entre

In two candid letters to his wife Vincent d'Indy described his experience with Carvalho in October 1881 when the director accepted *Attendez-moi sous l'orme*, a one-act *opéra comique*.[62] The letters show the director's power, decisiveness, musical taste, and modus operandi. We learn that Carvalho began by reading the libretto and assessing its possibilities for the stage before he agreed to hear d'Indy's score. Certainly aware of the young composer's potential, he may well have valued even more the added benefit of a connection with the librettist Jules Prével, also the theater columnist for *Le Figaro*. Although Carvalho had already chosen the female lead before the meeting, d'Indy worried that the music would not please.[63] Composer and librettist arrived at Carvalho's office on 4 October just before 5:00 P.M. Some fourteen people were there, having awaited the "whim of the pasha" for over two hours,[64] but d'Indy and Prével were ushered in immediately. When the lucky pair left, only one individual remained. D'Indy remarked wryly to his wife, "That's where I would have been if I hadn't had the bright idea to get to know some journalists."[65]

Carvalho's charm was widely acknowledged; so too, was his propensity to require sweeping changes, "as it is traditional for every director to require changes."[66] From the outset d'Indy had decided that Carvalho had only theatrical flair and was no musician at all; therefore, the meeting confirmed what the composer had already decided to see. And yet, while listening to the score, the director evidently decided to accept the project, completed the casting process, and used his knowledge of his troupe's vocal abilities and his experience with audience tastes in his theater to home in on what needed to be changed before he would undertake staging. D'Indy had to redo couplets for the character of Pasquin and change the role of Colin because Carvalho thought it too difficult for Barnolt to sing. The director required enough of the old to sweeten the pot so that the new could be swallowed, too: "Well, it's decided. I'll take you . . . try to include some really silly refrains. That's what succeeds. Don't be afraid to compromise your reputation as a serious musician. Enough advanced things will remain in your score so that people will see what school you belong to." Relieved that his favorite scene had passed muster, d'Indy agreed to all the modifica-

---

temps criant aux auteurs d'ajouter à celui-ci une moitié de vers, à cet autre un cri. Bref, communiquant à une pièce la vie avant de lui souffler par surcroît, à la suite de conférences savantes avec le costumier et le décorateur, le charme et la vérité." Gaston Jollivet, untitled newspaper article, 29 April 1898; *F-Pn*, Département des arts du spectacle, Richelieu. coll. Rondel, Rt 1260, Carvalho père et fils.

62. *Attendez-moi sous l'orme* (*opéra comique*, one act, libretto by Jules Prével and Robert de Bonnières after J. F. Régnard) premiered at the Opéra-Comique on 11 February 1882.

63. See letter 80–11 to his wife (Monday, 3 October 1881, 2:30), in Vincent d'Indy, *Ma vie*, ed. Marie d'Indy (Paris: Séguier, 2001), 354.

64. "Le bon plaisir du pacha." Letter 80–12 to his wife (Wednesday morning, 5 October 1881), in ibid., 355–56.

65. "Voilà cependant comme j'aurais été si je n'avais pas eu la veine de connaître des journalistes." Ibid.

66. "Comme il est de tradition que tout directeur doit faire des changements." Ibid.

tions Carvalho imposed: "(besides, I had decided to drink the Opéra-Comique cup to the dregs) and here I am busily trying to come up with brass band ditties ever since yesterday evening."[67] In February 1882 the work began a respectable run of nineteen performances.

Carvalho sometimes refused works he had commissioned even after he had required revisions. This led, not surprisingly, to disputes. For example, on 11 June 1880 Hector Salomon complained to the Société des Auteurs et Compositeurs Dramatiques (SACD) that Carvalho had commissioned his two-act opera *Djémina* (libretto by Pierre Barbier). The composer wanted a three-act libretto but had accepted this one because Carvalho had been so insistent.[68] Upon seeing the score, the director had claimed that the music did not suit the play and refused to put it on. After hearing the work twice, he still refused to change his opinion. Salomon felt Carvalho should not be the only arbiter. He wanted either to be played or to receive the standard indemnity of 1,800 francs. The next week Carvalho appeared before the commission and acknowledged that he had indeed given this libretto to Salomon but that Salomon's music was unsuitable for the genre. Because a second hearing had proven it so, he could not put the work on the performance schedule. The SACD sided with Salomon. On 2 July Carvalho returned once more and told the commission he could not accept their arbitration. Adamant, he left, saying that he would await the composer's lawsuit. On 10 September Salomon returned to the SACD seeking their support for his lawsuit. Because attendance was so poor, they could not conduct serious business. Salomon wrote a letter that was discussed and supported by the commission on 22 October. In a final effort to avoid a lawsuit, however, they suggested a compromise—a *reprise* of Salomon's one-act *opéra comique* entitled *L'aumônier du régiment*. Finally, on 29 October, the minutes record that Carvalho, informed that the commission would support Salomon in his lawsuit, had accepted the compromise "with eagerness." By holding out, he had avoided having to pay damages to Salomon and was able to put on a work that he found acceptable. Still, as Soubies and Malherbe comment, the sixteen performances of *L'aumônier du régiment* in 1881–82 were a poor compensation for the author.[69]

67. "Eh! bien c'est entendu, je vous prends, sous condition de ces trois petites modifications < . . . > cherchez des refrains bien bébètes, c'est ça qui réussit, du reste, m'a-t-il dit, n'ayez pas peur de compromettre votre réputation de musicien sérieux, il restera dans la pièce assez de choses avancées pour qu'on puisse voir à quelle école vous appartenez"; "(du reste je suis décidé à boire la coupe de l'Opéra-Comique jusqu'à la lie) et me voilà depuis hier soir occupé à chercher des flon-flons." Ibid.

68. Soubies and Malherbe, *Histoire de l'Opéra-Comique, 1860–1887*, 331, state that Salomon had awaited the performance of his *Djémina* in vain since 1878.

69. From the minutes of the meetings of 11, 18, and 25 June, 2 July, 10 September, and 22 and 29 October 1880. *F-Psc, L'aumônier du régiment* (with libretto by Henri de Saint-Georges and Adolphe de Leuven) had its premiere at Vizentini's Théâtre-Lyrique, 13 September 1877. With *Le toréador* (Adolphe Adam) and *Les pantins* (Georges Hüe), it formed part of a triple bill at the

Observing that special matinees organized for benefit fund-raising were highly successful and profitable, Carvalho decided to offer Sunday matinee performances on a regular basis. In 1879 he presented five matinees, and in 1880, twenty-four.[70] Once he had solved the initial problem of pulling together an orchestra and chorus for Sunday and holiday afternoons, he was able to augment the repertoire and found "a new source of prosperity and success for the Opéra-Comique." Arousing just as much interest as the evening performances, the matinee performances "responded to the needs of a special public where children are predominant."[71]

Both in the summer of 1876 (between the du Locle and Carvalho directorships) and in 1877 and 1879, the Opéra-Comique had closed during the summer for major repairs and renovations to the facility. It was Carvalho, however, who initiated the two-month summer vacation (1 July to 1 September) as standard practice. The press protested the change,[72] but Carvalho explained to the SACD commission that he lost about 50,000 francs by staying open in the summer.[73] He claimed that reduced-price performances, which he began presenting at the same time the summer closures began, had nothing to do with any bargain struck with the Ministry of Fine Arts. A link between the two seems likely, however, and histories of this theater normally acknowledge one. And so, one Monday evening a month during his ten-month season, Carvalho was instructed to present the best of his repertoire in high-quality productions with ticket prices that ranged from only 50 centimes to 3 francs. With such radically reduced prices, maximum box-office receipts could reach only 2,000 francs, even though daily expenses ran in the neighborhood of 4,500 francs. If the ten "people's performances" required by the government cost 25,000 francs, this was still just half the normal deficit of staying open in the summer. Demand ran strong for these new performances from their beginning: a presentation of Delibes's *Jean de Nivelle* in May 1880.[74] Despite measures put into place to prevent trafficking of these cheaper tickets, journalists noted that the boxes at these performances were filled with clientele who looked interchangeable with the normal audience.

Opéra-Comique on 28 December 1881. Soubies and Malherbe, *Histoire de l'Opéra-Comique, 1860–1887*, 331.

70. Ibid., 303.

71. "Une source nouvelle de prospérité et de succès. Tout aussi suivies et plus peut-être même que les spectacles du soir, elles répondent aux besoins d'un public spécial, où les enfants dominent." Noël and Stoullig, *Annales* 7 (1882): 105.

72. Soubies and Malherbe, *Histoire de l'Opéra-Comique, 1860–1887*, 316, remark with evident disapproval that the strong performers Carvalho had assembled would have permitted the house to stay open in the summer without a dip in revenues.

73. From minutes of the meeting of 4 June 1880. *F-Psc*.

74. See, for example, "Nouvelles des théâtres lyriques," *La revue et gazette musicale de Paris*, 6 June 1880. This little news item announces both the reduced price performances and the summer closure, leaving a connection unspecified. For the text of the official language regulating these reduced-price performances, proposed by Carvalho and ratified by the administration, see Noël and Stoullig, *Annales* 6 (1881): 215 n.

Carvalho had hoped to increase his profit margin through this agreement with the government, so he was particularly challenged by the SACD's response, because they immediately demanded royalties, as if the house had been sold out at normal ticket prices.[75] With tenacity and superb bargaining skills Carvalho gradually imposed his point of view. Even at their first meeting on 4 June 1880, the commission acknowledged that Carvalho might have sought their permission or inserted a protection clause into his treaty had he known the minister would impose these reduced-price performances. The commission decided that if the director obtained the permission of the authors, he could pay royalties for the people's performances on the basis of the average gross in the previous month. Carvalho returned on 18 June 1880, asking that the average used for calculating these royalties be confined to the receipts on Mondays. The commission knew that audiences were generally smallish on this weekday evening and rejected the proposal. They did agree to look at the question again the next year and apply their policy evenly to all theaters. On 23 September 1881 Carvalho asked the commission revisit the question. And finally on 28 October he got the concession he wanted. The commission allowed him to pay royalties on the basis of his actual gross from the people's performances, though he had to change the work if the authors objected to lower royalties.[76]

The government had required people's concerts of the enterprising director, but of his own volition Carvalho began subscription series. On the model of the Comédie-Française and its Tuesday subscription series, he started a Saturday series with a production of *L'étoile du nord* on 5 December 1885.[77] Gaston Calmette of *Le Figaro* reported that the series came about because of a meeting at the home of Émile Durand, where the librettists Henri Meilhac and Philippe Gille, along with the Prince

75. See minutes of the meeting of 28 May 1880. *F-Psc*. Spies (*Opera*, 36) points out that "to some extent, prosperity depended on minimizing operating expenses: physical plant, pay to choruses, soloists, orchestra, administration and substantial royalties due to authors." By 1890 royalties to the SACD were approximately 12 percent of the gross at the Opéra-Comique (ibid., 215). See discussion of the SACD in ibid., 214–19.

76. Carvalho's negotiations over the value of tickets that librettists and composers received free of charge for their own works also show his doggedness. On 6 October 1876 he appeared before the SACD after they decided to use the figure of 150 francs for the standard value. Although he accepted this sum, he countered with a request that he be allowed to play a work in translation every year instead of every other year. The commission denied this request, and so on 1 December 1876 the minutes show that Carvalho had tried to appear at the previous meeting to contest the SACD's assertion that 150 francs was the average cost for free tickets, saying that he had found it to be the maximum. On 22 December he won this small battle, for the commission had promised him his contract would not be more onerous than that imposed on Du Locle. At that time Carvalho also apologized to the commission for losing his temper with Mr. Roger, the general agent of the SACD, when he was in Carvalho's office explaining the society's position. Officially adopted on 29 December, the new ticket formula stood at 102 francs for two-, three-, four-, and five-act works and 58 francs for any one-act works that had not entered the public domain. From the minutes of the meetings, 1876. *F-Psc*.

77. Soubies and Malherbe, *Histoire de l'Opéra-Comique, 1860–1887*, 396.

de Sagan and Carvalho, hatched their plan.[78] Édouard Noël noted that as soon as the Saturday series was announced, the demand was so strong that Carvalho thought it might be necessary to create a second subscription evening.[79] The next year subscription Thursdays were instituted.

Carvalho was powerful, but he was nonetheless answerable to the public, to his backers, to the minister of fine arts, and, as we have seen, to the SACD. He needed all his negotiation skills plus his dynamic personality to bring about compromises that allowed him to modernize his theater in several lucrative ways. To this end, he normalized the presentation of *drames lyriques* and moved away from the obligatory one-act curtain-raisers with which beginners had traditionally been presented at this theater.

The Opéra-Comique had already mounted Gounod's *drame lyrique Roméo et Juliette* in 1873,[80] and thus Carvalho's 1878 request for special dispensation to put on Ambroise Thomas's *Psyché* was not out of line with precedent. Still, moving into the gap left by the closure of Vizentini's Théâtre-Lyrique in January of that year, Carvalho must have intended to claim more and more repertoire that had once belonged to his competitor. Acknowledging unusual circumstances, the SACD decided during the meeting of 3 May 1878 to permit the presentation of *Psyché*. Carvalho explained that the work, which had originally been an *opéra comique,* now had recitatives supplied by the composer.[81] He assured them that in welcoming *Psyché* to his stage after the demise of the Théâtre-Lyrique, he had no intention of modifying the genre, as shown in the list of works he had accepted and was in the process of preparing.[82]

Some found Carvalho's moves ominous, and many were still hoping that the Théâtre-Lyrique would reopen under another entrepreneur. The music critic Paul Bernard thought *Psyché* too grand for the stage. For him it was also "a question of principle regarding the genre we feel is appropriate for the Opéra-Comique, being convinced that [in this house] it is fundamentally an error to perform opera without dialogue too often."[83] Arthur Pougin expressed a similar opinion when he authored a report that same year asking the minister of fine arts to forbid the Opéra-Comique

78. Spies, *Opera*, 233 n. 79.

79. Noël and Stoullig, *Annales* II (1886): 191–92.

80. See a summary of Carvalho's efforts to change his *cahier des charges* in Branger, *Manon*, 24–29; his text focuses on the efforts to dispense with the requirement for spoken dialogue.

81. For a discussion of the various forms of this opera see Mary Jane Speare, "The Transformation of *Psyché*," in "The Transformation of Opéra-Comique: 1850–1880" (Ph.D. diss., Washington University, 1997), 261–300.

82. Minutes of the meeting of 3 May 1878, *F-Psc*. At the same meeting, however, Carvalho also asked for retroactive permission to present Ernest Reyer's *La statue* (1861), another *opéra comique* fitted with recitatives. It, too, was allowed as an exception to the *cahier des charges*.

83. "Une question de principe sur le genre que nous croyons propre à l'Opéra-Comique, étant convaincu qu'au fond c'est une erreur d'y exécuter trop souvent l'opéra sans dialogue." Paul Bernard, "Théâtre national de l'Opéra-Comique: *Psyché*," *La revue et gazette musicale de Paris,* 26 May 1878.

to perform works without spoken dialogue.[84] Carvalho dropped the issue for several years, but in the autumn of 1881 he asked the SACD to study the idea of permitting works without dialogue. He claimed that this change in his *cahier des charges* would serve the interests of certain composers, who were actually refusing to write for his theater because of this restriction.[85] With the decision of 3 March 1882 allowing the change, the SACD acknowledged a natural evolution at the Opéra-Comique after the closure of the Théâtre-Lyrique. Noël and Stoullig's annual summary noted the enlargement of the traditional genre and the great satisfaction of young composers who wanted the opportunity to write *drames lyriques*.[86]

The requirement to present three new one-act curtain-raisers yearly became Carvalho's next target. Support for suppression of this obligation (perhaps managed by Carvalho) surfaced in the press. For example, in 1883 the composer and critic Gaston Serpette expressed sympathy for Carvalho, who had presented a one-act opera by a Hungarian nonentity one mid-June evening that year: "I don't want to speculate on the diplomatic reasons that forced Mr. Carvalho to mount this work and forced on us the boredom of hearing it. The public gave this score, unworthy even of a summer evening, what it deserved."[87] Serpette then launched into an extended discourse on the need to change government regulation of this theater. He blamed the situation on a "ridiculous *cahier des charges:* you impose a certain number of acts on a director, and he has to come up with them, good or bad."[88] Time constraints forced a director to set

84. Arthur Pougin, *Question de la liberté des théâtres: Rapport présenté à Monsieur le Ministre de l'Instruction publique et des Beaux-Arts par la Société des Compositeurs de Musique* (Paris: Société des Compositeurs de Musique, 1878), 29.

85. Minutes of the meeting of 28 October 1881, *F-Psc*. At the same time the SACD took away Carvalho's right to count the Cressent competition opera among the ten new acts that had to be staged each year.

86. Noël and Stoullig, *Annales* 8 (1883): 121. Carvalho would shortly consider staging *Lohengrin,* though he eventually dropped the project; but *Proserpine* (1887), by Saint-Saëns, was sung throughout.

87. "Je ne veux pas rechercher les raisons diplomatiques qui ont fait imposer à M. Carvalho la peine de monter cet ouvrage et à nous l'ennui de l'entendre; le public a fait justice de cette partition indigne même d'une soirée d'été." Gaston Serpette, "Musique," *Le clairon,* 19 June 1883. Serpette's work list, largely a series of operettas, does include a manuscript for a full-length *opéra comique*. In addition, at the beginning of 1880 Carvalho scratched Serpette's one-act *La noce juive* just before the first performance because he found it weak; at that time he implied he would offer Serpette and his librettist, Armand Silvestre, a larger project at a later date. Noël and Stoullig, *Annales* 6 (1881): 234 n. 2. And so it is possible to wonder about the motive behind his championship of the powerful director.

88. "Un cahier des charges ridicule; on impose un certain nombre d'actes et ces actes, il faut qu'il les fournisse, bons ou mauvais." Ibid. Though Serpette names neither the insubstantial work nor its composer, Soubies and Malherbe, *Histoire de l'Opéra-Comique, 1860–1887,* 362–63, reveal it as *Mathias Corvin,* libretto by Paul Milliet and Jules Levallois, with music by Alexandre [Sándor] de Bertha. It received the minimum three performances and was published by Tresse in Paris that year.

aside serious works and produce little ones simply to please the Ministry of Fine Arts: "Mr. Carvalho has given enough proof of his artistic taste; he has raised the musical level of the Opéra-Comique high enough that the bureaucrats of the rue de Valois should let him administer his theater as he wants and not impose these little one-acts."[89]

In May 1884 Carvalho asked the SACD for permission to present a three-act work instead of three one-acts: because his current repertoire was making a great deal of money for the authors, and he still needed to present five new acts before the end of the season. The commission reminded him that his contract ran to 30 September but agreed to examine his request.[90] Carvalho did manage to stage three one-acts that year, though as late as possible before the summer break (23 June 1884). This timing gave fuel to the press who accused him of intending to bury the beginners from the start, but in fact Carvalho had been ill and may not have had the energy to take on as much as usual. Still, he had set up a springboard to his eventual goal with the SACD. The next May he returned to the commission to negotiate a renewal of his contract (which had expired on 28 February) and persuaded them to agree to language that permitted him to bypass presenting new one-acts if he so decided. Each year, however, he still had to mount ten new acts comprising at least three works and meet other requirements as well.[91]

In June 1886 Johannès Weber lamented the metamorphosis of the Opéra-Comique:

> The Opéra-Comique may have kept its name, but in truth it is playing the role of the Théâtre-Lyrique. The transformation has happened, I will not say naturally, but logically. When you set forth on principle, be it erroneous, be it poorly defined, you inevitably wind up leaving the proper path. Mr. Carvalho asked for the authorization to give dramatic works that moved outside the realm of *opéra comique* and belonged more or less to the genre of grand opera. . . . Now the exception has little by little become the rule."[92]

Weber also remarked the seemingly unnoticed disappearance of one-acts and asked whether Carvalho no longer wanted to find young composers who could enrich the

89. "M. Carvalho a donné assez de preuves de son goût artistique, il a élevé le niveau musical de l'Opéra-Comique assez haut, pour que les bureaucrates de la rue de Valois lui laissent administrer son théâtre comme il l'entend, et ne lui imposent plus ces petits actes." Gaston Serpette, "Musique," *Le clairon,* 19 June 1883.

90. Minutes of the meeting of 9 May 1884. *F-Psc.*

91. Minutes of the meeting of 1 May 1885. *F-Psc.*

92. "L'Opéra-Comique garde son nom, mais dans la vérité il remplit le rôle de l'ancien Théâtre-Lyrique. La transformation s'est faite, je ne dirai pas naturellement, mais logiquement. Quand on part d'un principe soit erroné, soit mal défini, on arrive presque inévitablement à quitter la bonne voie. M. Carvalho avait demandé l'autorisation de donner des ouvrages dramatiques sortant du cadre de l'opéra-comique et appartenant plus ou moins au grand opéra. . . . Or l'exception est peu à peu devenue la règle." Johannès Weber, "Critique musicale," *Le temps,* 14 June 1886.

repertoire of his theater. He complained of the presence of *La traviata* at the Opéra-Comique and of the possibility of still more Italian repertoire there, only to conclude that "we should no longer demand the reestablishment of the Théâtre-Lyrique, but of the Opéra-Comique instead."[93] Weber could legitimately accuse Carvalho of expanding the genre, but he had no justification for implying it was a poorly planned move. As an entrepreneur few could match the director in determination or foresight. Unfortunately, his skills did not include second sight, and his brilliant directorship ended temporarily in 1887 with a tragically fatal fire at his theater on 25 May.

After the fire the press began assigning blame, and before the new season began the director and others were facing formal charges. Carvalho, to appease all interests, stepped aside as rumors flew.[94] His choice of a successor, Jules Barbier, became provisional administrator. In December 1887 Carvalho received a sentence of three months in prison and a fine of 200 francs for his role in the disaster—an accumulation of excess scenery that had made the fire more intense, as well as the inflammability of the sets. He and the investment group that supported his enterprise were also held liable for damages running close to 50,000 francs, payable to the families of the many victims. The court of appeals cleared him of all charges in March 1888, but by then Louis Paravey had already taken over as director of the theater.

In March 1891, however, Carvalho was welcomed back with open arms. "A clean sweep has happened. The renter has been evicted by the landlord,"[95] announced the press when the news broke that Carvalho would replace Paravey as director of the Opéra-Comique. A writer using the name Tout-Paris even reported that this appointment represented a sort of "Parisian plebiscite of the most touching kind," for when the papers had announced a few days earlier that Carvalho's business partner Gaudrey had withdrawn (taking with him half of the 600,000 francs necessary to take charge of the theater), offers poured in from smaller investors (industrialists, private citizens, and shopkeepers) willing to stake their 10,000 or 20,000 francs on Carvalho's talents; and so he returned to the ministry with 750,000 francs.[96] Any sense that he had been somehow responsible for the fire at the Opéra-Comique four years earlier had dissipated, and relief that he would guide its fortunes was palpable and widespread. Carvalho could be trusted to work for Art, rather than for his own profit:

93. "Il ne faudra plus demander le rétablissement du Théâtre-Lyrique, mais celui de l'Opéra-Comique." Ibid.

94. The text of Carvalho's letter of temporary resignation to the Minister of Fine Arts is printed in Noël and Stoullig, *Annales* 13 (1888): 130 n. 1.

95. "Le coup de balai est donné. Le locataire chassé par le propriétaire." Amédée Landely [Hettich], "À l'Opéra-Comique," *L'art musical,* 15 March 1891.

96. "Une sorte de plébiscite parisien, et des plus touchants." Tout-Paris [pseud.], "Bloc-notes parisiens," *Le gaulois,* 7 March 1891. ("Tout-Paris" was a pseudonym used by a number of well-known authors.)

[He is] an artist down to the tips of his fingernails, to the ends of his whiskers, to the points of his shirt collars. Despite his age and corpulence, always lighthearted, dashing, alert, witty, eternally youthful. . . . He is an irresistible Parisian. Why? Because he never made a fortune, and he never will. Art consumes him. He will enrich it, he will make the profits rise, he will make the investors glow, he will create great singers and illustrious divas, he will carry men and works on his back—and he will not profit from it.[97]

Carvalho's devotion to art made it possible for journalists to downplay, when they expressed appreciation for his previous deeds and hope for his future accomplishments, the matter of personality:

His somewhat brutal firmness is known. If some suffered from it previously, all will benefit from it today. It is through energy and firmness that the situation . . . of the Opéra-Comique can be turned around. . . . His past bears witness to the present. Without escaping from criticism entirely—who could—he merits our consideration for the tendencies in art that we cannot forget.[98]

Carvalho's plans bore many similarities to his formula in the previous decade. He would be preparing first-rate performances of the traditional repertoire, would never forget that this was a French house devoted to a French genre, and would never close his door to contemporary artists, provided that these artists reconciled themselves with the special genre of the Opéra-Comique. Carvalho equated this genre with clarity, limpid form, and above all, melody—which is "eternal! For there is no music without melody just as there is no painting without drawing."[99] Detractors grumbled more loudly in the 1890s than in the previous decade. Carvalho was now in his late

97. "Artiste jusqu'au bout des ongles, jusqu'à la pointe de ses favoris, jusqu'à la pointe de ses faux-cols légendaires. Malgré l'âge et l'embonpoint, toujours gai, fringant, alerte, spirituel, éternellement jeune. . . . C'est un Parisien irrésistible. Pourquoi? C'est qu'il n'a jamais fait fortune et qu'il ne fera jamais fortune. L'art le dévore. Il enrichira celui-ci, il fera monter les recettes, il fera rayonner les actionnaires, il créera de grands chanteurs, d'illustres cantatrices, il portera aux nues des hommes et des œuvres—et il n'en profitera pas." Le Masque de fer [probably Philippe Gille], "Échos: Instantanés; Carvalho," *Le Figaro,* 9 March 1891.

98. "Sa fermeté un peu brutale est connue. Si quelques-uns eurent à en souffrir autrefois, tous en bénéficieront aujourd'hui. C'est par l'énergie et la fermeté que peut être relevée la situation . . . de l'Opéra-Comique, . . . le passé en lui répond du présent. Sans échapper absolument à la critique,—qui le pourrait—il en mérita les adoucissements par des tendances d'art qu'on ne saurait oublier." Amédée Landely [Hettich], "À l'Opéra-Comique," *L'art musical,* 15 March 1891.

99. "La chose est éternelle! Car il n'y a pas plus de musique sans mélodie que de peinture sans dessin." "M. Carvalho nommé, solution donnée à la question de l'Opéra-Comique," *Le matin,* 7 March 1891. For information on the transition, see ibid. F-Po, Dossier d'artiste: Carvalho. See also Huebner, *French Opera,* 5–6.

sixties to early seventies, and he may well have become less open to progressive tendencies and more prone to authoritarian decisions, though he could still be charming when he wished to be so. A publicity piece associated with the French premiere of Massenet's *Werther* admitted that Carvalho had his detractors, like everybody else. The author then explained that these were generally composers whose works had not been accepted by him or, if they had been accepted and presented, had not succeeded with the public: "But he has still more friends."[100]

The mourning surrounding Carvalho's death at the end of 1897 had something "national" about it, but a few of the disgruntled had their say right then.[101] In *Gil Blas* the composer Émile Pessard, while acknowledging the deceased as a great director and stage director, complained about Carvalho's increasing disorganization and authoritarianism, not to mention his penchant for using his scissors on any new opera.[102] Worse yet, Carvalho capriciously removed works from the performance calendar just when success seemed to be building. Pessard also admitted ruefully that Carvalho managed to get away with this because he was gifted in assuaging the ire of the authors, who entered his office ready to break the windows and left with a smile on their lips.[103]

Several writers were much more charitable, even lyrical in their praise. The librettist and journalist Philippe Gille, mastermind of the profitable Saturday subscription scheme, acknowledged that this valiant and tireless artist was "exposed to many animosities in the unstable and irritable world of artists" but like few others "he also made himself loved, for he had, above all, a feeling for art to which he sacrificed everything."[104] While most other directors passed on "without anyone caring to know their names or wanting to refer to a great work that they had helped bring into the

100. "Mais il a encore plus d'amis." Mirliton [pseud.], "*Werther:* Le directeur M. Carvalho," *Le journal* (January 1893), supplément théâtral illustré. *F-Po*, Dossier d'artiste: Massenet.

101. See Philippe Blay, "Un théâtre français, tout à fait français ou un débat fin-de siècle sur l'Opéra-Comique," *Revue de musicologie* 87, no. 1 (2001): 105–44; and Blay, "Albert Carré et la rénovation de l'Opéra-Comique," *Revue musicale de la Suisse Romande* 57, no. 1 (2004): 42–49.

102. Santillane [pseud.], "La vie Parisienne: Léon Carvalho; Quelques opinions," *Gil blas,* 30 December 1897. Pessard (1843–1917) won the Prix de Rome (1866), taught harmony at the Conservatoire (from 1881), and served as music director of the Maison de la Légion d'Honneur of St. Denis. Like many others, he longed for success in the theater, but he was known more for his songs and instrumental music. Neither of his two works for the Opéra-Comique (*Le char,* 1878; and *Les folies amoureuses,* 1891) had much success.

103. Ibid. In the obituaries we also find unsubstantiated, fantastical stories, like the one about Carvalho, who was known for enjoying exquisite food, sending his wine on a sea voyage because he felt this improved its taste. Marcel Hutin, "Mort de Léon Carvalho," *Le gaulois,* 30 December 1897.

104. "Exposé à se faire bien des inimitiés dans le monde inquiet et irritable des artistes"; "il savait aussi se faire aimer, car il avait, donnant tout, le sentiment de l'art à qui il a tout sacrifié et son repos et sa fortune." Philippe Gille, "Léon Carvalho," *Le Figaro,* 30 December 1897.

world, Carvalho and his memory will remain indissolubly linked to the remarkable musicodramatic period that has just passed."[105]

Victorin Joncières also wrote an eloquent tribute to the director who had presented two of his operas. This artist and innovator had the taste and initiative to discover the talents of so many composers and interpreters. Even into his seventies, Carvalho directed all the pieces he staged, "standing, running, gesticulating, indicating to each person what he had to do during the rehearsals, where he poured out energy without saving himself, from one until five in the afternoon."[106] Joncières described a day that would have foundered many a younger man, for after these long rehearsals Carvalho went to his office to meet with a multitude of visitors. "He received each one with natural urbanity, this innate courtesy of a great lord, which together made him irresistibly charming. In the evening, after dinner, he returned to the theater, where he was the last to leave, between one and two in the morning. This did not prevent him from being up at dawn to take care of the business of the Opéra-Comique." Remembering Madame Carvalho affectionately as well (she had died on 10 July 1895), Joncières wished them both eternal rest and eternal life in the memory of all who knew, loved, and admired them.[107]

Of all those who acknowledged Carvalho's imposing stature in the history of musical art, Louis Gallet was perhaps the most lyrical. In October 1897 he had worked with Carvalho yet again, on *Le spahi* (Lucien Lambert's ill-fated first effort at opera).[108] Now, two months later, he eulogized him. Unlike those who blamed their failures on the director, this highly successful librettist credited him for his contribution. Like Joncières, he especially admired the stage director:

> Carvalho was a painter. . . . He saw groups, faces, gestures as a painter sees them when composing a canvas. Thus, like all creators, he often demolished the next day the toil of the previous day to find something else. . . . In rehearsals he normally

105. "Sans que personne se soucie de savoir leurs noms et puisse citer une grande œuvre dont ils aient aidé l'enfantement, Carvalho et son souvenir resteront indissolublement liés à la belle période musicale dramatique qui vient de s'écouler." Ibid.

106. "Mettant lui-même en scène toutes les pièces qu'il montait, debout, courant, gesticulant, indiquant à chacun ce qu'il avait à faire pendant les répétitions, où il se dépensait sans compter, de une heure à cinq heures de l'après-midi." Victorin Joncières [Félix Ludger Rossignol], "Revue musicale, Léon Carvalho," *La liberté*, 3 January 1898.

107. "Il recevait chacun avec cette urbanité naturelle, cette courtoisie innée de grand seigneur, qui en faisaient un irrésistible charmeur. Le soir, après son dîner, il retournait au théâtre, d'où il ne sortait que le dernier, entre une heure et deux heures du matin. Ce qui ne l'empêchait pas d'être levé dès l'aube, pour s'occuper encore des affaires de l'Opéra-Comique." Ibid.

108. The work had only nine performances. Carvalho tried pairing it with various works to help it along: *Le maître de chapelle* (performances 1, 2, 3, and 7); *Mireille* (performances 4, 7, and 9); *Lalla Roukh* (performances 5 and 6); and *Lakmé* (performance 8). For a discussion of *Le spahi*, see Valeria Wenderoth, "The Making of Exoticism in French Operas of the 1890s" (Ph.D. diss., University of Hawaii, 2004), 238–92.

arrived like an improviser, putting a scene into action without always calculating the rest of what he was deciding on. When, turning the page, he saw that he was going the wrong way, he corrected himself, and finished by so identifying with the work that in the last rehearsals not even the smallest detail escaped him.[109]

With his power, interpersonal skills, extraordinary energy, director's imagination, and business wizardry, not to mention an absolute devotion to art as he understood it, Carvalho must truly have seemed to contemporaries much as Gallet described him: "I think that we can apply to Carvalho and to the colossal work that he achieved the words devised for Dumas the elder: 'He was one of the forces of nature.'"[110] From the perspective of another century, he seems to be one still.

109. "Carvalho était un peintre. . . . Il voyait les groupes, les physionomies, les gestes comme un peintre les voit pour composer un tableau. Aussi, comme tous les créateurs, démolissait-il souvent, le lendemain, la besogne de la veille pour trouver autre chose. . . . Aux répétitions, il arrivait communément en improvisateur, mettant en train une scène sans calculer toujours la suite de ce qu'il réglait. Quand, tournant la page, il s'apercevait qu'il allait à l'encontre du but, il se rectifiait, et finissait par s'identifier à l'œuvre de telle sorte qu'aux dernières répétitions aucun détail, même le plus minime, ne lui avait échappé." *F-Po,* Dossier d'artiste: Carvalho. Quoted in J. L. Croze, "Carvalho," *Le matin,* 30 December 1897.

110. "Je crois bien qu'on peut appliquer à Carvalho et à l'œuvre colossale qu'il a réalisée ce mot trouvé pour Dumas père: 'c'était une des forces de la nature.'"

Finding a Stage for French Opera

David Grayson

When Édouard Noël and Edmond Stoullig, the editors of *Les annales du théâtre et de la musique,* asked their fellow critic Victorin Joncières (see fig. 6.1) to provide a survey of the current state of music in France for their 1880 volume, he eagerly accepted the assignment. He had barely begun, however, when he stopped short, worried that the subjective aesthetic judgments he would inevitably have to render would "offend many sensibilities" and would moreover undermine what he saw as the journal's purpose, which was to provide an "impartial" historical account of Parisian theaters and concerts. He therefore selected a slightly different and "more modest" subject, one upon which he believed his fellow critics would be in agreement: the current condition of French musicians. As we will see, this inquiry quickly homed in on opera, and even more specifically, on the problems that French composers faced in trying to secure performances of their operas.

Joncières the Critic Assesses the Musical Scene (1880)

Joncières made a dire prediction. He foresaw that unless things changed, the French lyric art, which had formerly flourished so robustly, would be ruined. The future for French composers, he believed, was directly dependent on their ability to get their operas produced, and because both the Opéra and Opéra-Comique were neglecting them, their fate was directly tied to that of Paris's third opera company,

FIGURE 6.1. Portrait of Victorin de Joncières, after a photograph by M. Liebert. *L'illustration,* 13 May 1876. Courtesy of Duke University Library.

the Théâtre-Lyrique. Hence the title of his article: "La question du Théâtre-Lyrique."[1]

Joncières's point of departure, which was to consider how living French composers were faring in Paris's opera houses, tacitly accepted the established French view that opera was the most important musical genre and that French composers' reputations were made in the capital's theaters. The notion that writing operas provided composers their principal path to musical celebrity was reflected in the priorities of the Paris Conservatoire and exemplified by the Prix de Rome competition, the culminating exercise for ambitious composition students and designed to test the candidates' po-

1. Victorin Joncières [Félix Ludger Rossignol], "La question du Théâtre-Lyrique," in Édouard Noël and Edmond Stoullig, eds., *Les annales du théâtre et de la musique* (Paris, 1881), 6:i–xviii. Victorin Joncières (or Victorien de Joncières) was the pseudonym of Félix Ludger Rossignol, music critic for *La liberté* from 1871, where he also used the pen name "Jennius" when reporting theater news.

tential as opera composers. According to Joncières, the current French school could boast an unprecedented number of distinguished (opera) composers: "Gounod, Ambroise Thomas, Victor Massé, Massenet, Reyer, Saint-Saëns, Delibes, Guiraud, etc., etc." But equally unprecedented, he noted, was their limited access to Paris's main opera houses. In the eighteen months since Auguste Vaucorbeil had become director of the Opéra, not a single new French opera had been presented there.[2] Joncières contrasted this with earlier times—1836, for example, when the Opéra introduced four new works, comprising nine acts of opera and five of ballet. If the Opéra-Comique was "less stingy" than the Opéra, it still offered only one "important" premiere in 1880: Léo Delibes's *Jean de Nivelle*.[3] In contrast, in earlier times the Opéra-Comique used to introduce a number of new operas annually, amounting to an average of between twenty-five and thirty new acts per year.

Joncières saw French opera composers' counterparts in other countries receiving far better treatment. Apart from Verdi and Wagner, he declared, Italian and German opera composers were inferior to those in France, yet opera companies in these nations had offered their countrymen a considerable number of premieres during the previous year. To illustrate how easy it was for "unknown" composers in foreign lands to secure premieres of their first operas, he cited Arrigo Boito, whose *Mefistofele* had been performed throughout Italy, and Karl Goldmark, who achieved instant celebrity with the premiere of his five-act *Die Königin von Saba* at the Vienna Hofoper.[4] At the Paris Opéra, in contrast, the only new opera productions in 1880 were of Italian works—Verdi's *Aïda* and Rossini's *Le comte Ory*—and neither was a Paris premiere. Meanwhile, important operas by established French composers were waiting in the wings, namely Victor Massé's *Une nuit de Cléopâtre,* Ernest Reyer's *Sigurd,* and Jules Massenet's *Hérodiade,* which seemed at the time to be headed for Italy, having been declined by Vaucorbeil. Other notable French composers, such as Édouard Lalo, César Franck, and Benjamin Godard, had already proven their worth in the concert hall but had yet to be embraced by the opera house.

The Experience of Joncières the Opera Composer

In offering this grim assessment, Joncières was hardly a disinterested observer. Rather, he had an ax to grind: in addition to being a critic, he was also a composer, and, not

2. An editorial footnote indicates that although the statement was literally correct, a new ballet, Charles-Marie Widor's *La korrigane,* was squeezed in at the end of the year, on 1 December 1880, after Joncières had submitted his preface.

3. In addition to the three-act *Jean de Nivelle,* four shorter *opéras comiques* had premieres at the Opéra-Comique in 1880: Hémery's *La fée* (one act) on 14 June, Albert Cahen's *Le bois* (one act) and Théodore de Lajarte's *Monsieur de Floridor* (one act), both on 11 October, and Ferdinand Poise's *L'amour médecin* (three acts) on 20 December. The total for 1880 was thus nine acts of new operas.

4. He neglected to mention that *Mefistofele* was a failure at its 1868 La Scala premiere and was widely performed only after undergoing revisions in 1875 and 1876.

surprisingly, a composer of operas. His first two, the three-act *Sardanapale* (1867) and the four-act *Le dernier jour de Pompéi* (1869), had been staged by the Théâtre-Lyrique and ran for sixteen and thirteen performances respectively, so neither could be considered a real success. A private audition of his third opera, the five-act *Dimitri*, was held at the Opéra on 23 September 1875, and Olivier Halanzier, the director, was reportedly impressed. Nevertheless, he was unwilling to take a chance on a young (thirty-six-year-old) and as yet unproven composer.[5] Claiming that prior commitments prevented the Opéra from staging *Dimitri* within the foreseeable future, he suggested that Joncières instead bring him a short opera, in one or two acts, to serve as a curtain-raiser for a ballet.[6] This was the sort of opportunity typically extended to promising beginners, the short *débutant* opera that could provide its composer exposure but would not have to carry the evening. The implication was that if Joncières could make a success of this "trial," the Opéra would be receptive to a major work. Although this may not have been precisely the outcome for which Joncières had hoped, a commission from the Opéra, even for a short opera, was still a major career break. Meanwhile, his top priority was to place *Dimitri*. This he was able to do rather quickly, when Albert Vizentini selected it for the spring 1876 inauguration of the Théâtre-National-Lyrique (Opéra National Lyrique) at the Théâtre de la Gaîté, his short-lived and ill-fated effort to revive the Théâtre-Lyrique, which had closed a few years earlier.[7]

There was an element of payback in Vizentini's adoption of *Dimitri*, for during the preceding decade Joncières had been a vocal advocate for the reconstitution of the Théâtre-Lyrique as a "third lyric theater" for Paris and had even supported Vizentini's proposal to the minister of public instruction to form such a company.[8] Self-interest surely motivated Joncières's advocacy of the institution that had produced his first two operas, and his reward was the premiere of *Dimitri*, on 5 May 1876. This proved to be mutually beneficial: the opera ran for forty-six performances, with an additional presentation of its ballet at a benefit matinee. At the end of his first, short season Vizentini announced his future plans. In recognition of *Dimitri*'s success, he included another Joncières opera, *Le roi Lear*, among the offerings projected for 1878;[9] but the Théâtre-Lyrique closed on 2 January 1878, and *Le roi Lear* remained an unrealized project.

5. Noël and Stoullig, *Annales* 1 (1876): 54–55; *Annales* 2 (1877): 56–57; and *Annales* 4 (1879): 37–40.

6. Operas such as Auber's *Le philtre* and *Le dieu et la bayadère*, Rossini's *Le comte Ory*, and even Donizetti's *La favorite* commonly served this function. Noël and Stoullig, *Annales* 2 (1877): 32.

7. Vizentini's original plan had been to present an occasional work based on a text that the poet Armand Silvestre had written for the inauguration of the new company and to invite a different composer to set each act. But after abandoning this scheme, he accepted Joncières's *Dimitri*, which had a libretto by Silvestre and Henri de Bornier. The opera's Russian setting was fortuitous, for Vizentini was able to buy at auction the costumes and props that a Russian troupe had been forced to leave behind when it was unable to pay its rent at the Salle Ventadour. Ibid., 287–88.

8. That authorization was granted on 20 November 1875. Ibid., 292–93.

9. Ibid., 308.

Meanwhile, the Opéra prepared to stage Joncières's two-act *La reine Berthe*, which Halanzier had commissioned. It was to have shared the program with *Sylvia*, a new ballet by Léo Délibes, but because Jules Barbier did not finish the libretto in time, the opera was not ready by the date of the ballet's premiere (14 June 1876).[10] *La reine Berthe* finally opened on 27 December 1878, but to bad reviews and audience displeasure. The libretto was judged completely uninteresting and the Wagnerian score, cold, empty, and unoriginal. It didn't help that one of the lead singers was in poor voice. The event was an embarrassment for Joncières, especially because its timing created the impression that even after the success of *Dimitri* at the Théâtre-Lyrique, the influential critic could be entrusted with no more than two acts at the Opéra, where he had failed badly.[11] *La reine Berthe* was withdrawn after only five performances, just two more than the three that had been contractually guaranteed.[12]

The Opéra, the Opéra-Comique, and the Théâtre-Lyrique

Given this personal history, it is hardly surprising that Joncières, writing in 1880, harbored ill will toward the Opéra in particular and lamented the closing of the Théâtre-Lyrique, which he saw, especially under Vizentini, as having admirably fulfilled its mandate to introduce the works of young composers, among whom he counted himself. A more objective assessment of Joncières's compositional career to date might conclude that he had been given major opportunities but had not consistently delivered, with only one success (*Dimitri*) out of four efforts. One wonders how much responsibility he was willing to accept for his failures. Nevertheless, as he surveyed the scene in 1880, he saw only a dubious commitment to new operas on the part of the Opéra and the Opéra-Comique and an unwillingness on the part of the government, at either the state or city level, to subsidize a third lyric theater. Although his harsh critique may have been fueled by personal disappointment, it was supported by the facts. In the eighteen months of its existence, Vizentini's Théâtre-Nationale-Lyrique had produced twelve new works and nineteen revivals, totaling seventy-two acts. In comparison to the state subventions of 800,000 francs to the Opéra and 300,000 francs to the Opéra-Comique, Vizentini received only 200,000 francs (out of which he had had to pay 120,000 francs in rent), and as a condition of the subvention, he was required to open in May—not the best time of year to launch a new season. (The winter season typically began in October.) When the Opéra and Opéra-Comique had shortfalls, the state intervened, but it would not bail out the Théâtre-Nationale-Lyrique. Nor was the city of Paris willing to subsidize it as an Opéra-Municipal. By

10. Ibid., 1–2, 31–32.

11. Noël and Stoullig, *Annales* 4 (1879): 37–40.

12. For its final three performances *La reine Berthe* was preceded and evidently overshadowed by *Yedda,* a highly successful new three-act "Japanese" fairy ballet by Olivier Métra, a popular composer of light music. It went on to have a run of forty-two performances in 1879. *La reine Berthe* swiftly disappeared from the repertoire. Noël and Stoullig, *Annales* 5 (1880): 4–8.

a vote of thirty-five to twenty-five, the city council declined to follow the example of provincial municipalities, which typically supported their own Grands-Théâtres, and rejected the argument that underwriting the company would provide economic benefits by employing city residents and attracting capital.

Surveying the previous twenty years, Joncières observed that the preeminent French composers had been launched not by the Opéra or the Opéra-Comique, but either by the Théâtre-Lyrique ("Gounod, Félicien David, Reyer, Bizet, Maillart, Semet, Poise, Deffès, Delibes, Barthe, etc., etc.") or on the concert stage ("Massenet, Saint-Saëns, Guiraud, Lalo, Widor, Godard, and so many others").[13] With the closing of the Théâtre-National-Lyrique in January 1878, Joncières counseled young composers to abandon all hope of hearing their operas in Paris: "My conclusion is quite simple: no Théâtre-Lyrique, no dramatic music in France. Let us therefore write symphonies, masses, oratorios, or follow the example of Massenet and have our operas produced abroad."[14]

This gloomy scenario may accurately reflect Joncières's personal frustrations, but it did not tell the whole story. First of all, he overlooked a number of opportunities and venues available to young French opera composers. Some of these will be discussed below. But more important, he neglected to mention that, according to the terms of their directors' *cahiers des charges* (the contractual agreement with the minister of fine arts), both the Opéra and the Opéra-Comique were required to present a certain number of new French works as a condition of their annual state subsidies. The real "scandal" was not so much that they were neglecting new works, but rather that their directors seemed not to be fulfilling their contractual obligations—or were using loopholes to circumvent them. As a result, although the institutional system was intended to encourage composers and promote new music, in practice there always seemed to be tension, even conflict, between the aims of the government, the desires of composers, and the needs of the opera directors.

The *Cahiers des Charges:* The Opéra and the Opéra-Comique

In 1875, when the Opéra moved to the Palais Garnier, Halanzier's *cahier des charges* called for an average of one new full-length opera plus either a new ballet or a new

<hr/>

13. On the repertoire of the Théâtre-Lyrique (1851–72) and the regulations governing it, see Nicole Wild, *Dictionnaire des théâtres parisiens au XIXe siècle: Les théâtres et la musique* (Paris: Aux Amateurs de Livres, 1989), 239–41.

14. "Ma conclusion est bien simple: pas de Théâtre-Lyrique, pas de musique dramatique en France. Ecrivons donc des symphonies, des messes, des oratorios, ou suivons l'exemple de Massenet, allons faire représenter nos opéras à l'étranger." Noël and Stoullig, *Annales* 6 (1881): xviii. Alternatively, he might have recommended a great deal of patience. His own four-act *Le chevalier Jean* would premiere at the Opéra-Comique on 11 March 1885, where it had a modest run of twenty-one performances. It found greater success in Germany as *Johann von Lothringen*. His four-act *Lancelot* would premiere at the Opéra on 7 February 1900, but it closed after only eight performances.

one-act opera each year, with an accounting taken every two years.[15] When Vaucorbeil succeeded him, in 1879, the *cahier des charges* was comparable, stipulating an average annual requirement of two new works: an opera in three, four, or five acts and a shorter work, either opera or ballet, in one or two acts. There were loopholes, though, so that, subject to the approval of the minister of fine arts, certain "old" works could be counted as "new." For example, the revival of an opera from the repertoire could be considered a creation if it had not been staged in a number of years and if a new mise-en-scène incurred expenses comparable to those for a premiere. In addition, a foreign opera newly translated into French might count as a creation even if it had been performed abroad.[16] The penalty for failing to present new works was a deduction from the annual subvention equivalent to the expenses that the missing production would have incurred.[17] By 1883 the formula in Vaucorbeil's *cahier des charges* was still comparable, but somewhat more complex, requiring two new works annually, totaling at least six acts, four of which had to be opera.[18] Far more flexibility was granted to Eugène Ritt and Pierre (Pedro) Gailhard, co-directors of the Opéra from 1884 to 1891. They needed only to achieve an average of six new acts of opera or ballet per year over the course of their seven-year appointment and were free to parcel them out as they saw fit.[19]

Thus, although the precise terms of the *cahiers des charges* changed over the years, they essentially boiled down to an average of two new works per year—and that is generally what the Opéra delivered. The directors had to keep an eye on the box office and inevitably worried about the financial risks associated with unproven works. They thus seemed determined to get by with the bare minimum when it came to new music and sometimes met their quotas by the skin of their teeth (or just missed them). For example, in July 1876, when Halanzier found himself in the position of needing to present one new opera before the end of February, he announced the premiere of Massenet's *Le roi de Lahore* for 15 February 1877.[20] This was cutting it close, but even so, he miscalculated, and the premiere came two months late, on 27 April. In July 1878 he came under criticism for having failed to present any creations that year, even though he actually had until 5 January 1879 to stage three new works. He delivered

---

15. Noël and Stoullig, *Annales* 3 (1878): 52.

16. Frédérique Patureau, *Le Palais Garnier dans la société parisienne, 1875–1914* (Liège: Pierre Mardaga, 1991), 65.

17. Noël and Stoullig, *Annales* 5 (1880): 17–18. Under Halanzier the analogous indemnity was 20,000 francs, though less, apparently, for a partial shortfall, as occurred in 1875, when he was fined 2,000 francs for failing to present a new one-act opera. See Noël and Stoullig, *Annales* 1 (1876): 649.

18. Noël and Stoullig, *Annales* 9 (1884): 26. Vaucorbeil complied that year with Saint-Saëns's five-act opera *Henry VIII* and Théodore Dubois's three-act ballet *La farandole*.

19. Steven Huebner, *French Opera at the* fin de siècle: *Wagnerism, Nationalism, and Style* (Oxford: Oxford University Press, 1999), 3.

20. Noël and Stoullig, *Annales* 2 (1877): 34–35.

Gounod's *Polyeucte* on 7 October, Joncières's *La reine Berthe* on 27 December, and Olivier Métra's *Yedda* on 17 January, just twelve days past his deadline.

Joncières's 1880 critique was of course directed not at Halanzier, but at his successor, Vaucorbeil. Upon assuming the directorship in July 1879, the latter announced auspicious plans to produce two new operas by celebrated French composers, Gounod's *Le tribut de Zamora* and Ambroise Thomas's *Françoise de Rimini,* plus three new ballets, by Widor (*La korrigane*), Émile Pessard, and Lalo (*Namouna*). Established composers such as Gounod and Thomas were obviously less of a risk than relative unknowns, and their names even lent luster to Vaucorbeil's inaugural plan. But of the five projected premieres, only the Widor ballet was produced in 1880. Nevertheless, the flexible terms of his *cahier des charges* enabled Vaucorbeil to count the new production of *Aïda,* which opened on 22 March 1880, as a *création,* even if it failed to satisfy the more restricted definition of "new work" (a work by a French composer that has not previously been performed at the Opéra) dictated by the Société des Auteurs et Compositeurs Dramatiques (SACD), to which the Opéra was also contractually bound.[21] In fairness to Vaucorbeil, he programmed *Aïda* only after the Gounod and Thomas premieres had had to be postponed. *Le tribut de Zamora* was originally planned for January 1880, but in a letter to Vaucorbeil of 19 September 1879 Gounod requested an additional six months to revise the score.[22] The premiere was ultimately delayed until 1 April 1881. To replace it, Vaucorbeil first tried to move up the production of *Françoise de Rimini,* but Thomas demurred: the singers he wanted either were unavailable or had yet to be found, and, expecting delays, he did not want his opera to be introduced late in the season. Originally scheduled for November 1880, *Françoise de Rimini* did not open until 14 April 1882. Vaucorbeil next approached Massenet, whose *Hérodiade* was nearly completed, but the composer's choice for the title role, the baritone Jean Lassalle, was unavailable.[23] It was only after reaching this third impasse that Vaucorbeil traveled to Italy to secure Verdi's permission to produce *Aïda,* though this left a host of French composers feeling slighted. Saint-Saëns stepped forward. In an open letter published in the journal *XIXe siècle,* he announced that his *Étienne Marcel,* having been performed in Lyon in February 1879, would take only three months to prepare, but his offer fell on deaf ears.[24]

The greater flexibility accorded Vaucorbeil's successors, Ritt and Gailhard, to spread out new works did not insulate them from criticism, and they came under sharp attack for offering only one new work, Thomas's three-act ballet *La tempête,*

---

21. Patureau, *Le Palais Garnier,* 158–60. The Opéra production was not even the Paris premiere of *Aïda* in French translation. It had previously been produced by the Théâtre-Lyrique, Salle Ventadour, on 1 August 1878.

22. Some accounts claim that it was Vaucorbeil who insisted on revisions.

23. Lassalle had made an impression in the Opéra premiere of Massenet's *Le roi de Lahore* in 1877.

24. Noël and Stoullig, *Annales* 5 (1880): 45–53.

during 1889, the year of the Exposition Universelle.[25] However, they made up for it, at least contractually, with three *créations* in 1890 and another three in 1891.[26]

The Opéra-Comique was required to present even more new music than the Opéra. In 1876, when Léon Carvalho assumed the directorship, he was bound by the same terms as his predecessors: to present new operas totaling ten acts per year. (In contrast to the Opéra, the Opéra-Comique did not offer ballets during this period.) Given the trying circumstances of his first year, this quota was not enforced. Nevertheless, the Commission des Beaux-Arts took pains to remind him that the main purpose of the state subsidy was to promote new works by young composers and that these must not be sacrificed in favor of the old repertoire.[27] If thereafter Carvalho fulfilled this obligation, he seems at times to have done so only grudgingly. In 1884, for example, he was obliged, both by the terms of his *cahier des charges* and by an agreement with the SACD, to program three one-act *opéras comiques*, which he did by putting all three on the same bill with a two-act opera that had entered the repertoire a year before. He still came under criticism for scheduling them so late in the season (on 23 June), at a time of year when audiences had rather less interest in novelties (and when the press was presumably less attentive).[28]

The requirement to present new operas was not always regarded as a burden. Louis Paravey, who succeeded Carvalho at the Opéra-Comique in 1888 (following the brief interim directorship of Jules Barbier), understood that prestige and publicity could attach to a successful premiere and recognized that potential in Lalo's *Le roi d'Ys,* which had been completed thirteen years earlier, in 1875, but remained unperformed. Carvalho may have been correct in considering the company's theater, the Salle Favart, too small to accommodate the work, but Paravey was not bound by this constraint: the Salle Favart had burned down in 1887, and the Opéra-Comique had found a temporary home in the theater formerly occupied by the Théâtre-Lyrique in the Place du Châtelet.[29] *Le roi d'Ys* opened on 7 May 1888 and was an immediate and

25. Annegret Fauser, *Musical Encounters in the 1889 Paris World Fair* (Rochester, NY: University of Rochester Press, 2005), 92–95.

26. Saint-Saëns's *Ascanio,* Paul Véronge de la Nux's *Zaïre,* and Léon Gastinel's ballet *Le rêve* (totaling nine acts) in 1890; and Massenet's *Le mage,* Wagner's *Lohengrin,* and Louis Bougault-Ducoudray's *Thamara* (totaling eleven acts) in 1891. Strictly speaking, the two-act operas by Véronge de la Nux and Bougault-Ducoudray, both Prix de Rome laureates, do not figure in the annual average of six acts stipulated in the *cahier des charges.*

27. Noël and Stoullig, *Annales* 3 (1878): 140.

28. Noël and Stoullig, *Annales* 10 (1885): 68–72. The three one-act operas performed on 23 June 1884 together with Théodore de Lajarte's *Le portrait* (which had been created on 18 June 1883) were Adolphe Deslandres's *Le baiser,* Georges Pfeiffer's *L'enclume,* and Rodolphe Lavello's *Partie carée.* On Carvalho's tenure at the Opéra-Comique, see also Lesley Wright's contribution to this volume.

29. Noël and Stoullig, *Annales* 14 (1889): 83–88. In 1899 the hall was renamed Théâtre Sarah-Bernhardt.

lasting success. Paravey also made a splash the following year with the spectacular premiere of Massenet's *Esclarmonde* on 15 May 1889. Acclaimed as the highlight of the year, it coincided with the start of the Exposition Universelle and the opening of the Eiffel Tower.[30] Similarly, two years later, in 1891, when Carvalho reclaimed the directorship, he too wanted to inaugurate his new administration with a striking novelty and to that end offered the premiere of Alfred Bruneau's *Le rêve* on 18 June, just three months after taking the reins.[31]

The Prix de Rome and Other Competitions

The stipulation in the *cahiers des charges* requiring new works was not the only instrument by which the government imposed new music on its subsidized theaters. Another provision of Vaucorbeil's *cahier* stipulated that every other year the Opéra's required short work (a one- or two-act opera or ballet) be commissioned from a former Prix de Rome winner.[32] From the government's perspective this policy made good sense as a simple matter of supply and demand. The annual Prix de Rome competition, administered by the Académie des Beaux-Arts, was calculated to select that year's most promising opera composer. (Its final round required the contestants to compose a lyric scene, an unstaged mini-opera referred to as a cantata.) It therefore seemed apropos that a commensurate performance outlet be provided to the winners once they had completed the required residency at the Villa Medici in Rome, proven their worth through the compositions (called *envois*) that they were required to submit annually as evidence of their progress, and then gone on to fulfill their initial promise.[33] Because the competition was held annually but the Opéra commission was awarded only biennially, perhaps a calculation was made that only half of the winners would ultimately be deserving of this honor.

It appears that the policy was first put into practice in 1881, the very year in which Joncières's appeal on behalf of young French opera composers was published. That year the music section of the Académie des Beaux-Arts selected a slate of six candidates for this opportunity: Émile Paladilhe (awarded the Prix de Rome in 1860), Théodore Dubois (1861), Charles Ferdinand Lenepveu (1865), Émile Pessard (1866), and Henri Maréchal and Charles Édouard Lefèbvre (1870).[34] From this slate the minister chose

30. Fauser, *Musical Encounters,* 62–78.

31. Noël and Stoullig, *Annales* 17 (1892): 119. Carvalho assumed the directorship on 6 March 1891.

32. The fine for failing to stage the commissioned work was 5,000 francs per act. See Patureau, *Le Palais Garnier,* 65.

33. On the relationship between the Prix de Rome and opera composition see David Grayson, "Debussy on Stage," in *The Cambridge Companion to Debussy,* ed. Simon Trezise (Cambridge: Cambridge University Press, 2003), 61–62.

34. In the 1870 competition, Maréchal and Lefèbvre received, respectively, the first and second Premier Grand Prix. Of other potential choices from the preceding two decades, Jules Massenet (Prix de Rome 1863) and Gaston Salvayre (1872) had already had performances at the Opéra. Gaston

two of the oldest, Dubois and Pessard, who had been prizewinners approximately two decades earlier. The works commissioned from them were to have been staged in 1882 and 1883,[35] but the projected schedule proved to be unduly optimistic: Dubois's three-act ballet *La farandole* was created on 14 December 1883, and Pessard's two-act opera, *Tabarin*, on 12 January 1885. The potentially onerous nature of these government-imposed commissions became apparent in 1891 when the transfer of the directorship from Ritt and Gailhard to Eugène Bertrand was negotiated. Although Ritt and Gail-hard insisted on retaining control until the very last day of their appointment, they agreed to allow their successor to proceed with whatever arrangements he needed to facilitate the inauguration of his administration with the Paris premiere of Reyer's *Salammbô*. Their only condition was that he also bear the financial responsibility for the production of Louis Albert Bourgault-Ducoudray's *Thamara*, the imposed two-act opera that had been commissioned from the 1862 winner of the Prix de Rome, whose premiere was to take place on 28 December 1891.[36]

Earlier, responsibility to perform new works by Prix de Rome winners had fallen to the Opéra-Comique (by a decree of 26 June 1832) and the Théâtre-Lyrique (decree of 9 May 1851), though the applicable *cahiers des charges* stipulated only that, in selecting or commissioning new operas, preference be given to Prix de Rome winners.[37] When Léon Carvalho became director of the Théâtre-Lyrique in 1862, his *cahier des charges* became more binding in this regard, even though it reduced from fifteen to twelve the number of acts of new opera that he was required to produce annually.[38] As a condi-

---

Serpette (1871), after being rebuffed by the Opéra-Comique, had turned to operetta, while Victor Sieg (1864), a church organist, focused on religious compositions, salon pieces for piano, music for beginners, and pedagogical works. Antoine Tadou (1869) had written incidental music for François Coppée's *Le luthier de Crémone*, staged by the Comédie-Française in 1876, but he earned his living as a violinist in orchestras and in the Quatuor Tadou, which he founded. As a composer he was known chiefly for his chamber and orchestral music. No Premier Grand Prix had been awarded in 1867 or 1877, and other winners, especially the more recent ones, had presumably not yet demonstrated that they could be entrusted with a commission from the Opéra. On the details of the process through which the minister of fine arts was involved in the selection of Prix de Rome winners for performance at the Opéra, see Patureau, *Le Palais Garnier*, 212–22.

35. Noël and Stoullig, *Annales* 7 (1882): 6.

36. Noël and Stoullig, *Annales* 17 (1892): 15–16.

37. Wild, *Dictionnaire*, 239, 330. The actual language of the decrees describes the Prix de Rome laureates as winners of the first prize in musical composition at the Conservatoire. At the Opéra-Comique the article read: "Les premiers prix de composition musicale au Conservatoire auront un tour de faveur, à l'expiration de leur temps de pensionnat, pour la représentation d'un ouvrage de leur composition sur le théâtre royal de l'Opéra-Comique." Ibid., 330. At the Théâtre-Lyrique, the analogous article limited the period of preferential treatment to the two years following their return from Rome and specified that the director provide the composer with a two-act libretto: "Les premiers prix de composition musicale au Conservatoire auront un tour de faveur dans les deux années qui suivront l'expiration de leur pensionnat, pour la représentation d'un ouvrage en deux actes dont le directeur devra fournir le poème." Ibid., 239.

38. Ibid., 240.

tion of his annual subvention of 100,000 francs, a clause was added stipulating that he present each year a three-act opera by a Prix de Rome laureate who had not yet had an opera performed in Paris. The first beneficiary of this regulation was Georges Bizet, recipient of the Prix de Rome in 1857. However, his *Les pêcheurs de perles,* introduced on 30 September 1863, was in fact already in the pipeline, having been commissioned by Carvalho in April 1862, months before he assumed the directorship and before the terms of his *cahier* had been finalized. Carvalho next turned to Edmond Chérouvrier, winner of the Second Grand Prix in 1858; his three-act *opéra comique Le roi des mines,* was produced on 22 September 1865 and closed after five performances.

In order to provide a mechanism for fulfilling this requirement (and to guarantee a libretto of quality), in July 1863 Camille Doucet, the newly appointed director general of state theaters, established a competition, initially conceived as an annual event, for a three-act opera based on a given libretto and composed by a qualifying Prix de Rome laureate. The contestants themselves elected three of the five judges (Carvalho and an administrative appointee completed the jury), and the winning entry was to be staged by the Théâtre-Lyrique.[39] The five competitors, who set *La fiancée d'Abydos,* Jules Adenis's adaptation of Byron's *The Bride of Abydos,* were Adrien (Grat-Norbert) Barthe (awarded the Prix de Rome in 1854), Jean Conte (1855), Samuel David (1858), Emile Paladilhe (1860), and Théodore Dubois (1861). Their efforts were auditioned in two sessions held in the Petite Salle of the Conservatoire in late October and early November 1864, and the jury's unanimous choice was by the oldest contestant, Adrien Barthe.[40] His opera had its premiere on 30 December 1865. Despite good notices, it was not a success. It closed after nineteen performances and marked the end of Carvalho's accommodation of Prix de Rome laureates. He tended to have more box-office success with translations of foreign operas than with new French works, with the conspicuous exception of Gounod's *Roméo et Juliette.*[41] It is hardly surprising, then, that when Carvalho selected a new work such as Jean Adolphe Hippolyte Devin-Duvivier's three-act *opéra comique Déborah* for performance on 14 January 1867, it was because the composer paid for the production. *Déborah* closed after three performances.[42] Joncières's *Sardanapale,* which opened a month later, on 8 February, had the benefit of the celebrated Swedish soprano Christine Nilsson as the female lead, but its sixteen performances hardly constituted a success.

The conductor Jules Pasdeloup, who succeeded Carvalho as director of the

39. T. J. Walsh, *Second Empire Opera: The Théâtre Lyrique, Paris, 1851–1870* (London: John Calder; New York: Riverrun Press, 1981), 162–63.

40. *La revue et gazette musicale de Paris,* 30 October 1864; Paul Smith [Édouard Monnais], *La revue et gazette musicale de Paris,* 6 November 1864; and *Le ménestrel,* 6 November 1864.

41. Prominent examples are Verdi's *Rigoletto* and *Violetta* (*La traviata*), Mozart's *La flûte enchantée* (*Die Zauberflöte*) and *Don Juan* (*Don Giovanni*), Weber's *Robin des bois* (*Der Freischütz*), and Flotow's *Martha.* See Albert Soubies, *Histoire du Théâtre-Lyrique* (Paris: Librairie Fischbacher, 1899), 47.

42. Walsh, *Second Empire Opera,* 218–19.

Théâtre-Lyrique in August 1868, may have been a dedicated promoter of contemporary French concert music, but he did relatively little for new French opera. Rather, his signal achievement was the Paris premiere of Wagner's *Rienzi* (6 April 1869), which enjoyed a run of thirty-eight performances. During the course of his relatively short directorship, which ended on 31 January 1870, he introduced only three new French operas, none of them a success. The first, *En prison* (5 March 1869), a one-act *opéra comique,* was by Ernest Guiraud, winner of the Prix de Rome in 1859. Rather than being a boost to his career, the production actually took place against Guiraud's wishes. The score had for some years been "imprisoned" by the Théâtre-Lyrique, accepted but shelved, and Guiraud worried that, having made a good impression at the Opéra-Comique in 1864 with his one-act *opéra comique Sylvie,* this "sin of his youth" would damage his reputation.[43] Evidently Pasdeloup was more concerned about his *cahier des charges.* The second new opera was Ernest Boulanger's three-act *opéra comique Don Quichotte* (10 May 1869), based on a libretto by Jules Barbier and Michel Carré that had been declined by Offenbach.[44] Boulanger, remembered today primarily as the father of Nadia and Lili, had won the Prix de Rome back in 1835, as a result of which his *Le diable à l'école,* in one act, had been performed at the Opéra-Comique in 1842. The third new work created during Pasdeloup's reign, Joncières's *Le dernier jour de Pompéi* (21 September 1869), also turned out to be the last new opera produced by the Théâtre-Lyrique. The living composers who benefited most from the Pasdeloup regime were not Frenchmen, but Wagner and Verdi, whose *Le bal masqué* was heard sixty-five times.[45]

If a composer hadn't won the Prix de Rome, an alternative path to the stage—this time, to the Opéra-Comique—was through a privately endowed competition, the Concours Cressent. This triennial competition was created through the bequest of a wealthy amateur, Anatole Cressent, who had died from an equestrian accident: Cressent's 100,000 francs were augmented by 20,000 francs from his family. The competition guidelines established a preliminary contest for a one- or two-act libretto, and the following year the competing musical settings of the winning libretto were to be judged. The Opéra-Comique agreed to stage the prizewinning opera, for which it would receive 10,000 francs. *Bathyle,* Édouard Blau's libretto for a one-act *opéra comique,* was selected in 1874 for the first competition, and in December 1875 Ambroise Thomas, president of the competition, announced the winning composer: William Chaument.[46] The opera was created at the Opéra-Comique on 4 May 1877 and received nine performances. Samuel Rousseau's *Dianora* (one act), winner of

43. H. Moreno [Henri Heugel], *Le ménestrel,* 14 March 1869.

44. Soubies, *Histoire du Théâtre-Lyrique,* 53.

45. The Théâtre des Italiens gave the Paris premiere of Verdi's *Un ballo in maschera* in 1861, but Pasdeloup's production was the first in French. The translation was by Édouard Duprez, who had also done the translations of *Rigoletto* and *La traviata* that were performed at the Théâtre-Lyrique.

46. Noël and Stoullig, *Annales* I (1876): 658–59.

the second competition, was presented on 22 December 1879 and was even less successful, receiving only five performances. The third winning opera was by Georges Hüe, recipient of the 1879 Prix de Rome. His *Les pantins* (two acts) was staged on 22 December 1881 and was fairly quickly dropped—that is, until the librettist, Édouard Montagne, invoked a provision of the award that guaranteed ten performances.[47] The fourth winner, Edmond Missa, had received only honorable mention in the 1881 Prix de Rome competition, but his two-act *opéra comique Juge et patrie,* created at the Opéra-Comique on 17 November 1886, was greeted in the pages of *Les annales du théâtre et de la musique* with the prediction that the Cressent competition had finally found an opera that would remain in the company's repertoire. This pronouncement proved to be misguided: *Juge et partie* was withdrawn after twelve performances, only a couple more than the obligatory ten.[48] Ten performances were again the fate of the next winner, Gaston de Maupeou's *L'amour vengé,* which Louis Paravey, the director of the Opéra-Comique, presented on 31 December 1890, but with great reluctance and only after persistent ministerial pressure.[49] Ten performances were also accorded Lefèvre-Derodé's *Le follet,* created on 1 May 1900.[50] This string of unsuccessful operas, together with the increasing prestige symphonic music was enjoying—owing in part to its emphasis in the curriculum of the Schola Cantorum—must have contributed to the decision to change the nature of the competition. Starting in 1904 the Prix Cressent was awarded to symphonic compositions instead of operas.[51]

Other competitive opportunities that likewise were not restricted to Prix de Rome laureates were the separate competitions for new operas announced by Paris's three state-supported opera houses on 1 August 1867 in connection with the Exposition Universelle.[52] The terms of the three competitions were somewhat different, but the opera houses were uniformly slow to stage the winning works. The Opéra competition was held in two stages. An initial competition was for a libretto in three acts,

47. Noël and Stoullig, *Annales* 8 (1883): 109–10.

48. Noël and Stoullig, *Annales* 12 (1887): 131; and Albert Soubies, *Soixante-neuf ans de l'Opéra-Comique en deux pages: De la première de "La dame blanche" à la millième de "Mignon," 1825–1894* (Paris: Librairie Fischbacher, 1894), table. These two sources disagree as to the number of performances: Soubies lists twelve, while the *Annales* counts thirteen—ten in 1886 and three in 1887. Missa's *Juge et patrie* was more successful than the one-act opera with which it shared the bill: *Le signal,* by Paul Puget, the 1873 Prix de Rome laureate, was dropped after three performances.

49. Noël and Stoullig, *Annales* 16 (1891): 120.

50. Noël and Stoullig, *Annales* 26 (1901): 93–94. Charles Lefèvre used the names Lefèvre (de Reims) and Lefèvre-Derodé to avoid confusion with the composer Charles Édouard Lefèbvre, joint winner of the 1870 Prix de Rome.

51. Jane Fulcher, *French Cultural Politics & Music: From the Dreyfus Affair to the First World War* (New York: Oxford University Press, 1999), 30–31, 105.

52. See Camille Doucet, *Le ménestrel,* 11 August 1867, for the announcement of the terms of the three competitions. Additional terms and details are in "Concours d'opéras," *Le ménestrel,* 15 September 1867.

and from among sixty-eight submissions, the jury selected *La coupe du roi de Thulé,* by Louis Gallet and Édouard Blau.[53] Composers were then given fifteen months to set it. Forty-two scores were anonymously submitted, and in November 1869 Eugène Diaz de la Peña was declared the winner.[54] A rumor circulated that Victor Massé, who was not only Diaz's teacher but also a member of the jury, had actually written most of the score. Coming in a close second was the entry by Jules Massenet, followed in ranked order by Ernest Guiraud, Adrien Barthe, the Prince de Polignac, and, in either sixth or seventh place, Georges Bizet. It took more than three years for the Opéra to stage Diaz's work, which, during rehearsal, underwent revision by Massé and the baritone Jean-Baptiste Faure, among others.[55] It opened on 10 January 1873 and was not a success, although it enjoyed a run of twenty performances.[56]

For the Opéra-Comique competition a libretto was commissioned from Jules-Henri Vernoy de Saint-Georges, one of the most celebrated and productive librettists of his time and co-director of the Opéra-Comique in 1828–30. It was to have been made available on 30 August, but Saint-George's late delivery of the three-act libretto, *Le Florentin,* necessitated an extension of the composers' deadline. The winning setting was by Charles Lenepveu (awarded Prix de Rome in 1865). Massenet had entered this as well as the Opéra competition and was said to have been ranked third among the sixty-three anonymous submissions.[57] When the result was announced, in November 1869, a premiere in early 1870 was optimistically anticipated.[58] The opera was not staged until 25 February 1874, however, and was a failure, withdrawn after only eight performances.[59] Ironically, a competing setting by Émile Pichoz reached the stage far sooner when a single performance was given at the Théâtre de la Monnaie in Brussels on 29 April 1870.[60]

For the Théâtre-Lyrique competition, forty-three scores were anonymously submitted, and the composers were free to choose their own libretti. This complicated the adjudication process because a double jury was needed to evaluate the text and music. The prize went to Jules Philippot for his one-act *opéra comique Le magnifique,* with a libretto by Jules Barbier.[61] Second and third place went respectively to Émile-

53. "Le concours d'Opéra," *Le ménestrel,* 19 April 1868.

54. "Concours de Grand Opéra," *Le ménestrel,* 28 November 1869.

55. Winton Dean, *Bizet,* 3rd ed., revised reprint (London: J. M. Dent & Sons, 1978), 78–79.

56. Albert Soubies, *Soixante-sept ans de l'Opéra en une page: Du "Siège de Corinthe" à "La Walkyrie" (1826–1893)* (Paris: Librairie Fischbacher, 1893), table.

57. Demar Irvine, *Massenet: A Chronicle of His Life and Times* (Portland, OR: Amadeus Press, 1994), 53.

58. Extensive cuts were envisioned from the start: Lenepveu's score contained three and a half hours of music, and with the spoken dialogue and intermissions it would have made for a six-hour entertainment. Gustave Bertrand, "Semaine théâtrale," *Le ménestrel,* 7 November 1869.

59. Soubies, *Soixante-neuf ans de l'Opéra-Comique,* table.

60. Jules Salès, *Théâtre Royal de la Monnaie, 1856–1970* (Nivelles: Éditions Havaux, [1971]), 59.

61. Eugène Gautier, "Le concours du Théâtre-Lyrique," *Le ménestrel,* 4 July 1869.

Adolphe Canoby's *La coupe et les lèvres,* in five acts, and Édouard Lalo's *Fiesque,* in three. Philippot's opera took even longer to reach the stage than the winners of the Opéra and Opéra-Comique competitions, for the Théâtre-Lyrique closed before it could be produced. Nevertheless, the commitment to stage it was honored by the company's successor, Albert Vizentini's Opéra National Lyrique. *Le magnifique* opened on 24 May 1876, less than three weeks after the inauguration of the opening season, but nearly nine years after the announcement of the competition and nearly seven after the opera had been declared the winner. It proved to be no more successful than the winners of the companion competitions and ran for only four performances. Thus, although these various competitions—the Théâtre-Lyrique competition of 1863, the three opera competitions of 1867, and the Concours Cressent—provided young composers with opportunities to have their operas produced, the competition process failed to produce operas of lasting, or even immediate, value.

Private Performances, "Ephemeral" Companies, and Other Alternatives: French Opera Abroad, in the Provinces, and in the Capital (but in Translation)

Those who failed to win a competition, whether the Prix de Rome, the Prix Cressent, or some other, had to turn elsewhere. Of course, money could buy access of sorts, as when a wealthy physician rented the Opéra-Comique's Salle Favart on 4 May 1876 for a single Thursday matinee performance of the opera *Les héroïques,* a three-part *drame lyrique,* with a libretto by his daughter Antonine Perry-Biagioli and music by his twenty-two-year-old son Henry Perry-Biagioli.[62] One supposes that the same financing supported the concert performance of excerpts from this opera, which Édouard Colonne conducted at the Concerts du Châtelet on 6 February, three months earlier, presumably to generate publicity, draw press notices, and entice an audience to the opera. Even more exclusive was a private concert performance of *Partisan,* a three-act *opéra romantique* by M. le comte d'Osmond, an amateur composer, presented on 1 May 1875 by the Concerts du Conservatoire at the Salle de la rue Bergère.[63] More ambitious but less well connected, the composer and librettist Pauline Thys (Thys-Sébault) rented the Théâtre de l'Athénée-Comique on 23 April 1876 for a single Sunday matinee audition of her three-act opera *Le Mariage de Tabarin.* Hoping to interest an opera company in her work but recognizing the impracticality of asking the cast to learn three acts of prose for a single performance, she offered it as a *roman lyrique,* a narrated novel interspersed with twenty-one musical numbers.[64]

The salon, rather than the theater, was the usual venue for such events—privately funded performances of works that would otherwise be denied a hearing, or audi-

62. Noël and Stoullig, *Annales* 2 (1877): 202–4.
63. Noël and Stoullig, *Annales* 1 (1876): 511.
64. Noël and Stoullig, *Annales* 2 (1877): 690–91.

tions before an audience but primarily intended to secure a commitment from an opera director. Indeed, salon performances had contributed significantly to the dissemination of Wagner's music in Paris.[65] Jacques Offenbach famously invited three hundred guests to a salon performance of portions of *Les contes d'Hoffmann* on 18 May 1879. Singers from the Opéra and the Opéra-Comique were accompanied by a piano, and the chorus consisted of the composer's "charming" daughters and their friends.[66] Chabrier's *Gwendoline* had already been created at the Théâtre de la Monnaie in Brussels but had not yet been heard in Paris when Winnaretta Singer, the future Princesse de Polignac but then the Comtesse de Scey-Montbéliard, hosted a concert performance of it in her home on 22 May 1888 with singers from the Opéra accompanied by a chamber orchestra.[67] The salon was also a place where composers informally shared their operas in progress. On 18 October 1893, for example, Ernest Chausson invited a small group of friends and colleagues to his home to hear Vincent d'Indy play and sing the third act of *Fervaal* and Claude Debussy, a scene from *Pelléas et Mélisande* (act 4, scene 4).[68]

Even if the two main Paris opera houses rejected a new opera, it might still find a stage through one of the "ephemeral" Parisian opera companies that cropped up periodically, taking over a theater for a limited season. These companies could hardly expect to compete with the Opéra or Opéra-Comique in terms of star power or production values. Unless they could feature a superstar, such as Adelina Patti, for example, their survival depended on popular "standard" operas that were guaranteed to draw an audience or alternatively, operas of quality that the two state-subsidized houses had neglected or rejected. In particular, premieres of new operas might draw concentrated (and hopefully favorable) attention from the press and, with luck, would attract an audience as well. Thus, as discussed above, Albert Vizentini inaugurated his Théâtre-National-Lyrique in May 1876 with the auspicious premiere of Joncières's *Dimitri*, but he had a much bigger success later that year with the creation of Victor Massé's *Paul et Virginie*. Launched on 15 November 1876, it ran for 121 performances and saved the company from imminent ruin. Before it was accepted by Vizentini, *Paul et Virginie* had been considered in turn by the Théâtre de la Gaîté and the Opéra-Comique. Posterity has not been kind to it, but the critic Édouard Noël attributed its success to a combination of factors. Based on Bernardin de Saint-Pierre's well-known

65. For example, the "Petit Bayreuth" (founded by two zealous amateurs, a judge and a painter), Judith Gautier's marionette theater (dubbed the "Bayreuth de poche" by Wagner himself), and the weekly Wagner soirées organized by the conductor Charles Lamoureux, the publisher Wilhelm Enoch, and the critic Victor Wilder, a French translator of Wagner's librettos. See Martine Kahane and Nicole Wild, *Wagner et la France* (Paris: Éditions Herscher, 1983), 55–56.

66. Noël and Stoullig, *Annales* 5 (1880): 567–69.

67. Sylvia Kahan, *Music's Modern Muse: A Life of Winnaretta Singer, Princesse de Polignac* (Rochester, NY: University of Rochester Press, 2003), 371.

68. Jean-Pierre Barricelli and Leo Weinstein, *Ernest Chausson: The Composer's Life and Works* (Norman: University of Oklahoma Press, 1955), 35–36.

roman of 1788, it had a familiar title and a libretto by Michel Carré and Jules Barbier that made the most of the subject. Massé was also a known commodity, and the music displayed his usual charm while also exhibiting the more modern dramatic style associated with Gounod. It was thus satisfying to both the experts and the general public. Finally, the performance itself was superb, with first-rate direction, splendid sets, magisterial conducting by Vizentini, and triumphant singing by Cécile Ritter, Nadine Engally, and especially Victor Capoul.[69]

In 1877 Vizentini offered nine new operas totaling twenty-one acts, but none approached the success of *Paul et Virginie*.[70] Saint-Saëns's *Timbre d'argent* was another opera that Vizentini adopted after others had rejected it. During the previous decade it had been promised in turn by at least five different opera companies, not only the Opéra and the Opéra-Comique (under Camille du Locle), but the Théâtre de la Renaissance under Léon Carvalho, the former Théâtre-Lyrique under Jules Pasdeloup, and the Salle Ventadour (Troisième Théâtre-Lyrique Française) under Prosper Bagier.[71] *Timbre d'argent* received mixed reviews and ran a disappointing eighteen performances; yet of the nine creations that year, it was surpassed only by the twenty-five performances of Gaston Salvayre's *Le bravo*. The others enjoyed no more than thirteen performances—or as few as one. The enduring popularity of *Paul et Virginie* was not enough to save the company, which folded on 2 January 1878, after twenty months of operation.

Even the most unlikely organizations were sometimes willing to gamble on a premiere. For example, the sporadic summer seasons of the Opéra Populaire at the Théâtre du Château-d'Eau justified its name with a generally predictable "popular" repertoire, dominated by *Le trouvère, La traviata, Le barbier de Séville, Lucie de Lammermoor, Martha,* and the like. Still, it occasionally slipped in a new opera, such as Alfred Bruneau's *Kérim* (in three acts), which it introduced on 9 June 1887. Bruneau had won the Second Grand Prix de Rome in 1881, and *Kérim* was the first of his operas to reach the stage.

A new opera was always a risk, especially for an unsubsidized ephemeral company, but the odds were considerably better if it had already proved successful elsewhere. For French works, this would typically have been either in Brussels or in one of the provincial theaters. By offering the Paris premieres of such operas, the smaller companies could hope to scoop the Opéra and Opéra-Comique. Of course, the strategy might just as easily backfire. Such was the case with *Pétrarque,* a five-act opera by the

---

69. Noël and Stoullig, *Annales* 2 (1877): 318–33.

70. Vizentini's nine creations of 1877 were Camille Saint-Saëns's *Timbre d'argent* (23 February); Gaston Salvayre's *Le bravo* (18 April); Willent-Bordogni's *Rafaello le chanteur,* Charles de Courcelles's *La promise d'un autre,* and Jean-BaptisteWeckerlin's *Après Fontenoy* (28 May); Antony Choudens's *Graziella* and Hector Salomon's *L'aumônier du régiment* (13 September); Eugène Gautier's *La clé d'or* (14 September); and Henri Kowalski's *Gilles de Bretagne* (24 December).

71. Noël and Stoullig, *Annales* 3 (1878): 209.

hapless Hippolyte Duprat, a former naval surgeon. The Théâtre-Lyrique accepted *Pétrarque* around 1870, but the only copy of the score was destroyed in a fire during the Commune (1871), and the composer had to recreate it from memory. By this point the Théâtre-Lyrique had folded, and Duprat was unable to interest another company in his opera. Giving up on Paris, he turned to the provinces, and *Pétrarque* was performed successively in Marseille, Toulon, Avignon, and Lyon. When Husson, the director of the Grand Théâtre de Marseille, moved to Paris and, together with Louis Martinet, formed the Opéra Populaire at the Théâtre de la Gaîté, he recalled the success that *Pétrarque* had enjoyed in Marseille and staged the Paris premiere on 11 February 1880. It certainly made an impression, beginning at eight and ending at two in the morning! Pruning and condensation could not save it, and it closed after thirteen performances.[72] A similar fate befell Saint-Saëns's *Étienne Marcel*, created in Lyon on 19 February 1979 but unsuccessful five years later in Paris. It opened the fall season of Garnier's Opéra Populaire at the Théâtre du Château-d'Eau on 20 October 1884 but closed after only ten performances.[73]

On other occasions, however, the strategy worked. Santerre's five-month season of Théâtre-Lyrique at the Chateau-d'Eau opened on 13 October 1888 with the Paris premiere of Benjamin Godard's *Jocelyn*, which had been created in Brussels eight months earlier, on 25 February. It ran for thirty-two performances. Saint-Saëns's *Samson et Dalila* followed a similar but far more circuitous path. Created in German translation in Weimar on 2 December 1877, it received a concert performance in Brussels in 1878 and was staged in Hamburg in 1882. In France, though, there had been only partial performances: act 2 at Pauline Viardot's little theater in Bougival in August 1874 (with sets and costumes, but with Saint-Saëns at the piano in place of the orchestra) and act 1 in concert by the Concerts Colonne on 26 March 1875. Years later, Henry Verdhurt selected it to open the new Théâtre des Arts in Rouen, of which he was director.[74] For the premiere, on 3 March 1890, numerous Parisians were on hand to witness its success. Eighty-seven subscribers arrived via special trains and stayed in commandeered hotel rooms.[75] Eight months later, on 31 October, when Verdhurt wanted a gala event to inaugurate his Théâtre-Lyrique at the Éden-Théâtre, he offered the Paris premiere of *Samson et Dalila*, recreating the success it had enjoyed in Rouen.

72. Noël and Stoullig, *Annales* 6 (1881): 282–89. The table on p. 298 indicates twelve performances beginning on 13 January.

73. Noël and Stoullig, *Annales* 10 (1885): 307. See also Brian Rees, *Camille Saint-Saëns: A Life* (London: Chatto and Windus, Random House, 1999), 254–55.

74. Christian Goubault, "La decentralisation de l'art lyrique à Rouen (1830–1900)," in *Regards sur l'opéra: Du "Ballet comique de la reine" à l'Opéra de Pékin*, ed. Elisabeth Bernard (Paris: Presses Universitaires de France, 1976), 69–70; Pauline Viardot, "La jeunesse de Saint-Saëns," *Musica* (June 1907): 84, quoted in Myriam Chimènes, *Mécènes et musiciens: Du salon au concert à Paris sous la IIIe République* (Paris: Fayard, 2004), 302.

75. Rees, *Saint-Saëns: A Life*, 286.

After five weeks (and fifteen performances of *Samson*), the company folded from lack of funds, bringing an end to yet another attempt to sustain a Théâtre-Lyrique.[76] Verdhurt's loss, however, was Saint-Saëns's gain. This first Paris production aroused sufficient interest that *Samson* entered the repertoire of the Opéra two years later, on 23 November 1892.

Strange as it may seem, some French operas were introduced to Paris in Italian translation. Although the Théâtre-Italien officially closed in June 1878, sporadic short seasons of Italian opera continued to crop up, offered by various companies in various theaters and under various directors. One of these, at the Théâtre des Nations under the celebrated baritone Victor Maurel and the Corti brothers from La Scala (and later under Maurel alone), operated for thirteen months, from 27 November 1883 through December 1884.[77] In 1881 Maurel had sung the title role in the La Scala premiere of Verdi's revised version of *Simon Boccanegra*, and, wishing to repeat the role in Paris, he selected this opera to inaugurate his Théâtre-Italien.[78] The repertoire also included Flotow's *Martha* and familiar operas by Rossini, Bellini, Donizetti, and Verdi.[79] But when ticket sales failed to cover the company's expenses, Maurel formulated and publicized a plan to alternate Italian operas with new French operas (sung in Italian, of course), evidently hoping to broaden his audience base and garner the support of the municipal government. In response, many French composers came forward, clearly preferring to hear their operas in Italian rather than not at all. Maurel announced his acceptance of five operas: Gaston Salvayre's *Richard III*, Victorin Joncières's *Le chevalier Jean*, Mme la baronne Legoux's *Joël*, Eugène Diaz's *Benvenuto Cellini*, and Théodore Dubois's *Aben-Hamet*.[80] Salvayre's opera had already been translated into Italian, as *Riccardo III*, for its premiere in St. Petersburg on 21 December 1883. Rather

76. Noël and Stoullig, *Annales* 16 (1891): 513–16, 521–22.

77. As a singer Maurel had made an auspicious debut at the Opéra in 1868, shortly after graduating from the Paris Conservatoire, but he became dissatisfied with the roles he was assigned and felt eclipsed by the baritone Jean-Baptiste Faure. He therefore left Paris the following year and for the next decade performed in major opera houses abroad. He returned to the Opéra in 1879 and continued to sing there until 1894.

78. Noël and Stoullig, *Annales* 9 (1884): 217–19.

79. Rossini's *Il barbiere di siviglia*, Bellini's *I puritani* and *La sonnambula*, Donizetti's *Lucrezia Borgia* and *Lucia di Lammermoor*, and Verdi's *Ernani, Rigoletto, Un ballo in maschera, La traviata*, and *Il trovatore*.

80. Noël and Stoullig, *Annales* 10 (1885): 117–18. Mme la baronne Legoux, born Eugénie-Lucie Chausson and married to Baron Jules Legoux, published musical compositions under the pseudonym Gilbert Des Roches. Her opera *Joël*, with a libretto by Louis Gallet, was being studied at the Opéra-Comique when the theater (Salle Favart) burned down on 25 May 1887, so the anticipated performances did not take place. It was premiered instead in Nice on 11 April 1889. That same year the vocal score of *Joël* was published in Paris by V. Durdilly with both French and Italian texts. The second language may be the legacy of the opera's provisional acceptance five years earlier by the Théâtre-Italien, but it was fitting, in any case, given that V. Durdilly represented Ricordi in Paris. The composer's death, on 14 January 1891, was reported in the international press.

than these, however, it was *Erodiade*, an Italian translation of Massenet's *Hérodiade*, that became the first French opera to have its Paris premiere at the Théâtre-Italien. As Joncières noted in his gloomy assessment of the plight of French opera composers, Vaucorbeil, the new director of the Paris Opéra, had rejected *Hérodiade*, forcing Massenet to court foreign opera houses. *Hérodiade,* in its original three-act version, thus had its highly successful French-language premiere at the Théâtre de la Monnaie in Brussels on 19 December 1881, followed three months later, on 23 February 1882, by its Italian-language premiere at La Scala. It was next given in Nantes, on 29 March 1883, and on 5 April Massenet conducted two excerpts from it—the ballet of the Phoenicians and Hérode's arioso "Vision fugitive," sung by the baritone Jean Lassalle—at a gala concert held at the Paris Opéra and sponsored by the Parisian press to benefit flood victims in Alsace-Lorraine.[81] Aside from this charity gala, the Paris Opéra remained indifferent to *Hérodiade,* and the work was not staged there until 1921. Maurel saw his opening and was thus able to offer, on 1 February 1884, the Paris premiere of *Hérodiade,* in its revised, four-act version, albeit in Italian. The cast included not only Maurel, but also the de Reszke brothers, Jean and Édouard. During the run, their sister, Joséphine de Reszke, also joined the cast. The production was a great success, leading one critic to comment, "If the need for an Italian theater appears not to have been proved to many people, the evening of 1 February should at the very least help to justify its existence."[82] Maurel created a second French opera, Dubois's *Aben-Hamet,* at the end of the year, on 16 December 1884. Despite its success, this proved to be Maurel's last production. Financial difficulties caused this incarnation of the Théâtre-Italien to fold soon thereafter, bringing an end to Maurel's short-lived plan to promote new French operas—in Italian.

Reference has already been made to French operas that were introduced abroad: *Samson et Dalila* in Weimar, *Riccardo III* in St. Petersburg, and *Gwendoline, Jocelyn,* and *Hérodiade* in Brussels. Also created at the Théâtre de la Monnaie were Reyer's *Sigurd* (1884) and *Salammbô* (1890), Litolff's *Les templiers* (1886), Paul and Lucien Hillemacher's *Saint-Mégrin* (1886), D'Indy's *Fervaal* (1897) and *L'étranger* (1903), and Chausson's *Le roi Arthus* (1903), among others. The Théâtre de la Monnaie, a world-class company with a predilection for French opera, was a manageable train ride from Paris and offered perhaps the most desirable foreign stage to operas snubbed by the French capital. Other rejected operas were embraced by the provincial theaters.[83] Their composers surely still held out hope for a performance in Paris, preferably at the Opéra or the Opéra-Comique, although, as we have seen, they sometimes had to settle, at least initially, for one of the city's ephemeral opera companies.

81. Noël and Stoullig, *Annales* 9 (1884): 11.

82. "Si la necessité d'un théâtre italien ne paraît pas démontrée à beaucoup de gens, la soirée du 1er février doit tout au moins contribuer à justifier son existence." Noël and Stoullig, *Annales* 10 (1885): 120.

83. On one of the most important of these provincial theaters, at Rouen, see Goubault, "Decentralisation," 47–85.

Theoretically, at least, another option was afforded French opera composers by the Société des Grandes Auditions Musicales. This organization was founded in 1890, with the Comtesse Greffulhe as its president, to promote French works that were known abroad but unknown in France. Its manifesto, published in *Le Figaro* on 10 April 1890, explicitly acknowledged the difficulties that French opera composers faced and echoed Joncières's dire prophecy of a decade earlier—that, unable to get their works performed in Paris, French opera composers were forced to export them. The manifesto even named the prominent composers in this predicament: Reyer, Gounod, Salvayre, Saint-Saëns, Chabrier, Litolff, Godard, Lenepveu, the Hillemacher brothers, Dubois, Massenet, and "the Master of old," Berlioz.[84] Indeed, the work that apparently inspired this agenda was Berlioz's *Béatrice et Bénédict,* which had had its premiere in Baden-Baden in 1862 and was subsequently performed in Weimar (1863), Carlsruhe (1888), and Vienna (March 1890), but to date had not yet been seen in Paris. It was thus the first work to be presented by the Société, in June 1890, followed in 1892 by the first French performance of Berlioz's *Les Troyens à Carthage.* These performances benefited not the composer, but his posthumous reputation. Other dead French composers were similarly promoted. In 1893 the Société presented two eighteenth-century French operas,[85] and in 1894 a festival honoring the recently deceased Gounod was held.[86] Thus, although the Société purported to be sympathetic to the plight of living French composers, in practice they were not the immediate—or even primary—beneficiaries of the organization's efforts. Despite a direct appeal to Parisians' "feelings of artistic patriotism" and an articulated ambition "to be a center for French composers, to secure for our country the first performance of their works, too often held abroad," it was more generally and even primarily dedicated to giving "complete performances" of works that had not yet been heard in France, "by composers old and new"—and not exclusively French ones.[87] Over the years the Société thus presented choral works of Bach, Handel, Beethoven, and Elgar, concert music by Russian composers, and the Paris premieres of operas by Wagner, Strauss, and contemporary Italian composers.[88] Living French composers had to wait until

84. The manifesto was reproduced in H. Moreno [Henri Heugel], "Semaine théâtrale: La Société des Grandes Auditions musicales de France," *Le ménestrel,* 13 April 1890, and is quoted extensively in Chimènes, *Mécènes et musiciens,* 569–73.

85. Gretry's *Les deux avares* and Monsigny's *Le déserteur.* See Chimènes, *Mécènes et musiciens,* 574–83.

86. This program included operatic excerpts and fulfilled the Société's aim to promote new music by featuring the premiere of "Repentir," a scene in the form of a prayer for mezzo-soprano and orchestra, billed as the composer's last work.

87. Anne de Cossé Brissac, *La comtesse Greffulhe* (Paris: Perrin, 1991), 87.

88. The choral works were Handel's *Israel in Egypt* in 1891, portions of Bach's Christmas Oratorio in 1892, Beethoven's *Missa Solemnis* in 1903, and Elgar's *Dream of Gerontius* in 1906. As for Russians, the 1892 program featured music by Glinka, Rimsky-Korsakov, Tchaikovsky, Anton Rubinstein, Borodin, and Glazunov. Wagner's *Tristan et Isolde* was premiered in 1899, *Le crépuscule des dieux (Götterdämmerung)* in 1902, excerpts from *Parsifal* in 1903, and Strauss's *Salome* in 1907.

1894, when they were served by a single concert conducted by Colonne and featuring orchestral works by Debussy, Fauré, Magnard, d'Indy, Bordes, Chausson, and Dukas.[89] Notwithstanding, their operatic aspirations were still being ignored. In 1905 the Comtesse Greffulhe considered presenting Chaussons's *Le roi Arthus* (expenses could have been reduced by borrowing the sets and costumes from Brussels), but the plan was abandoned. Thus, although the plight of living French opera composers was lamented in the Société's manifesto of 1890, in the end the organization did absolutely nothing to help them.

Opera in Concert and Concerts at the Opéra

When no theater was available to the French opera composer, the concert hall could fill the breach. Multiple interests were served through concert performances of operatic excerpts. In the case of operas that had not yet been staged, successful concert performances of vocal or instrumental selections might draw the attention of an opera director and a potential audience. Even if a new opera was already scheduled for theatrical performance, concert previews could pique audience interest. For this purpose, even a different work by the same composer would do. For example, knowing that the Théâtre-Lyrique was to stage the premiere of Gaston Salvayre's opera *Le bravo* in the spring of 1877, Édouard Colonne conducted his *symphonie biblique, La résurrection,* at the Concerts du Châtelet four months in advance, on 3 December 1876.[90] Both institutions stood to benefit from the attendant publicity. Concert performances of excerpts from Wagner's operas—by the Concerts Pasdeloup, Concerts du Conservatoire, Concerts Colonne, and Concerts Lamoureux—certainly played a large role in their acceptance by French audiences and ultimately led to staged productions.[91] Unlike Wagner, however, French composers did not have to overcome a deep-seated, politically charged audience hostility.[92] Among the French operas repeatedly excerpted in concert programs prior to their Paris stagings were Reyer's

---

The Société's 1905 season of Italian opera focused on recent verismo operas, seven of which received Paris premieres: Pietro Mascagni's *L'amico Fritz;* Umberto Giordano's *Andrea Chénier, Fedora,* and *Siberia;* Ruggero Leoncavallo's *Zazà;* Francesco Cilea's *Adriana Lecouvreur;* and Lorenzo Filiasi's *Manuel Menendez.* Rossini's *Il barbiere di Siviglia* was the eighth opera.

89. François Lesure, *Claude Debussy: Biographie critique* (Paris: Klincksieck, 1994), 154. The concert was given at the Palmarium du Jardin d'acclimatation on 29 May 1894.

90. Noël and Stoullig, *Annales* 2 (1877): 795–96.

91. See Kahane and Wild, *Wagner et la France,* 158–65, for a listing of such concert performances between 1841 and 1914.

92. This hostility was displayed, for example, when Pasdeloup included the Prelude to Wagner's *Lohengrin* at a concert on 7 November 1880 and portions of the audience heckled while others cheered. In response, Pasdeloup announced that he would repeat the Prelude, but only at the end of the concert so that those who wished to avoid the encore could escape. About two hundred to three hundred audience members did leave, noisily and ostentatiously. Noël and Stoullig, *Annales* 8 (1883): 703–4.

Sigurd, Lalo's *Le roi d'Ys*, Chabrier's *Gwendoline*, Saint-Saën's *Samson et Dalila*, and Massenet's *Hérodiade*.

On the other hand, a competitive aspect might intrude when concert series sought to capitalize on the popularity of current or recent opera productions. Less than a month after the successful premiere of Godard's *Jocelyn* at the Théâtre-Lyrique (13 October 1888), Colonne inaugurated the fifteenth season of his Concerts du Châtelet on 4 November with excerpts from the same opera. They were so warmly received that he repeated them the following week. The critic Édouard Noël considered these concert performances superior to what he had heard in the opera house,[93] which may have been the point. Colonne had been involved in negotiations to stage the opera at the Odéon, but the Théâtre-Lyrique thwarted his plans. He exacted revenge from the podium. A decade earlier, Colonne had also piggybacked on the resounding success of the Lyon premiere of Saint-Saëns's *Étienne Marcel,* which took place in February 1879. He presented excerpts from the opera on 16 and 23 November of the same year and attracted a full house, reportedly turning away a thousand people. The participation of the celebrated baritone Jean-Baptiste Faure obviously helped.[94] Five years later, on 26 October 1884, Colonne inaugurated his eleventh season with the opera's ballet, just six days after its Paris premiere by Garnier's Opéra Populaire. Noël again praised Colonne's performance at the expense of the production by the ephemeral opera company.[95]

Turnabout is fair play, and on 17 November 1895 the Opéra inaugurated its own series of Sunday matinee concerts, in direct competition with the established concert series. The stated aim of the Concerts de l'Opéra was "to give young composers the opportunity to have their works heard, without any cost to them. Half of [each] concert program, at least, will be devoted to [these young composers]; during the other segment of the concert, we will present selected historic and modern compositions, the knowledge of which will serve as training for the *jeunes*."[96] The series was not a financial success (nor was it intended to be), and it lasted for only two seasons.[97] The first ended in April 1896, and the second ran from January to April 1897: ten programs in all, adding up (with repetitions) to twenty-two concerts. Excerpts from new or recent operas figured in most programs. The very first (17 and 24 November 1895) included act 2, scene 3, from D'Indy's *Fervaal*, conducted by the composer. *Fervaal* had already been announced by the Théâtre de la Monnaie, though it would not be

93. Noël and Stoullig, *Annales* 14 (1889): 397–98.

94. Noël and Stoullig, *Annales* 5 (1880): 559.

95. Noël and Stoullig, *Annales* 10 (1885): 345–46.

96. Quoted in Elinor Olin, "Concerts de l'Opéra, 1895–97: New Music at the Monument Garnier," *Nineteenth-Century Music* 16 (1993): 255.

97. Perhaps it was to forestall the accusation that he was squandering state money that the co-director Eugène Bertrand decided to announce: "Our concerts are not an enterprise in which a financial interest enters into play. We are quite resolved to endure the losses, which may well result." Ibid., 259.

staged there until 12 March 1897, and the eventual Paris premiere would be at the Opéra-Comique (19 May 1898), not at the Opéra. The third program (29 December 1895 and 5 January 1896) included a portion of *Le duc de Ferrare* by Georges Marty, chorus master at the Opéra and, with Paul Vidal, organizer of the concerts. Marty's opera was to have been presented by the Opéra-Comique, but Carvalho considered its subject immoral.[98] It was finally staged on 30 May 1899 by the Milliaud brothers' Théâtre-Lyrique de la Renaissance. The eighth program (3 and 10 January 1897) offered excerpts from Henri Maréchal's *Ping-Sin*, which would be created at the Opéra-Comique on 3 January 1918. And the final program (7 and 14 March 1897) included the second tableau from act 1 of Théodore Dubois's *Circé*, an opera that Carvalho had commissioned for the Opéra-Comique but then rejected. It appears never to have been staged. The point is that none of these four *opéras inédits* was destined for a stage premiere at the Opéra. The Concerts de l'Opéra thus allowed the institution to claim credit for promoting new operas (and assuage critics of its subvention) while avoiding the much larger cost and risk associated with their actual staging. The tactic worked. President Félix Faure attended the fifth program and afterward congratulated the directors, Bertrand and Gailhard, for promoting French music by performing new works by seventeen French composers.[99] Philanthropists are rarely selfless, and it is hard to regard the enterprise without some degree of cynicism, especially because the "historic" portion of the programs—operatic excerpts (in many cases, just short dances) by Lully, Destouches, Rameau, Gluck, Spontini, Piccini, Sacchini, and others—seemed correspondingly calculated to answer those critics who lamented the Opéra's neglect of the great classical masters.[100]

The Case of Debussy's *Pelléas et Mélisande*

Claude Debussy's protracted struggle to secure the premiere of *Pelléas et Mélisande*, which eventually took place on 30 April 1902 at the Opéra-Comique, provides a useful summary of the frustrations encountered by young French opera composers and of the range of venues available to them.[101] At one point Debussy had a vague understanding that Count Robert de Montesquiou would arrange a salon performance at his "Pavillon des Muses," but this opportunity never materialized, and Debussy probably did not pursue it in earnest. Above all, he was intent on introducing his opera only in a complete staged (and preferably public) production. He thus rejected a request from London for what his friend Pierre Louÿs referred to as a "symphonic suite" drawn

98. Noël and Stoullig, *Annales* 21 (1896): 26.

99. Noël and Stoullig, *Annales* 22 (1897): 10–11. The president also attended the eighth program (during the second season) and again thanked the Opéra directors for the contribution their concert series made to French art. Noël and Stoullig, *Annales* 23 (1898): 4.

100. Patureau, *Le Palais Garnier*, 263.

101. On Debussy's efforts to secure the premiere of *Pelléas*, see David Grayson, *The Genesis of Debussy's "Pelléas et Mélisande"* (Ann Arbor, MI: UMI Research Press, 1986), 39–54.

from the opera.[102] Most likely this was a request that he extract music from the opera to provide incidental music for a staging of the Maurice Maeterlinck play that had furnished his libretto. As he explained to his publisher, Georges Hartmann, having conceived the work as an opera, he refused to do something that would have seemed like a denegation of it.[103] He also vetoed Eugène Ysaÿe's proposal to conduct vocal excerpts at a concert in Brussels. Having failed to persuade the Théâtre de la Monnaie to accept the opera, Ysaÿe argued the case for concert excerpts passionately.[104] A composer's early works, he insisted, should be heard in "the atmosphere in which they are born," and a partial performance is surely better than none at all. Above all, he feared that by the time *Pelléas* was staged, Debussy's style would have changed. Moreover, a good concert performance might arouse the interest of a theater director, as happened with Wagner. He also felt that *Pelléas* would gain prestige in the public's eye by virtue of its promotion by his concert series, which had a reputation for being daring and progressive. Perhaps anticipating that his arguments would fall on deaf ears, he pledged to continue doing everything in his power to find an opera house willing to stage the opera. He was in touch with Ghent and Bruges and thought they would be ideal. Neither possibility materialized.

What was unusual in the case of *Pelléas* was Debussy's flirtation with the avant-garde theater, whence his libretto came. Shortly after the opera's completion in August 1895, Paul Larochelle offered to produce it at the Théâtre-Libre. Among other motivations, this was a way for him to get the name of the librettist, the celebrated and fashionable Maeterlinck, on his marquee. In announcing his plans for the 1895–96 season Larochelle expressed his ambition to spare no expense to make the Théâtre-Libre a lyric as well as a dramatic theater, to which end he was prepared to hire an orchestra of seventy and a chorus of fifty.[105] In September 1895 he announced plans to stage three other lyric works—Xavier Leroux's *L'épave*, Chausson's *Le roi Arthus*, and Camille Erlanger's dramatic legend *Saint Julien l'hôpitalier*;[106] and in October he even told the press, falsely, that *Pelléas* was in rehearsal.[107] Lugné-Poe, director of the rival Théâtre de l'Œuvre, the company that in 1893 had given the stage premiere of Maeterlinck's *Pelléas*, was alarmed by these announcements. He still bore a grudge

102. Letter to Debussy of 27 November 1895, in Claude Debussy, *Correspondance (1872–1918)*, ed. François Lesure and Denis Herlin, annotated by François Lesure, Denis Herlin, and Georges Liébert (Paris: Gallimard, 2005), 290.

103. Letter of 9 August 1898, in Debussy, *Correspondance*, 414–15.

104. Ysaÿe, letter to Debussy, 17 October 1896, in François Lesure, "La longue attente de *Pelléas* (1895–1898)," *Cahiers Debussy* 15 (1991): 9–10.

105. "Echos divers et communication," *Mercure de France* 15 (August 1895): 256.

106. "Nouvelles diverses," *Le ménestrel*, 29 September 1895. A similar announcement, appearing in *Oueste-Artiste* on 19 October, identified the Leroux opera as *William Ratcliff*, presumably a different work. The notice is cited in Debussy, *Correspondance*, 273.

107. *Le Figaro*, 11 October 1895; quoted in Claude Debussy, *Esquisses de "Pelléas et Mélisande" (1893–1895)*, ed. François Lesure (Genève: Minkoff, 1977), 8.

against Larochelle for having "stolen" Villiers de l'Isle-Adam's *Axël,* and he had no intention of "losing" *Pelléas* to him as well. Maeterlinck interceded on Lugné-Poe's behalf and wrote to Debussy on 17 October 1895 to convey both the director's and his own distress over Larochelle's announced production.[108] Debussy decided to terminate negotiations with Larochelle and instead discuss with Lugné-Poe the possibility of the Théâtre de l'Œuvre staging his opera. Lugné-Poe's company was no more accustomed to producing operas than was the Théâtre-Libre, but it had earlier staged plays with substantial incidental music. For example, the previous year it had presented Henri Bataille and Robert d'Humières's *La Belle au bois dormant,* with incidental music by Georges Hüe; and their forthcoming production of Ibsen's *Peer Gynt* was to require an orchestra of around sixty to play Grieg's incidental music. Debussy confided to the soprano Julia Robert, whom he may have been considering for the role of Mélisande, that discussions with the Théâtre de l'Œuvre seemed to be quite serious.[109] Nevertheless, this prospect too came to naught, perhaps because of the expenses involved.

Unable to reach an agreement with the avant-garde theater, rejected by the Monnaie (and perhaps by other Belgian opera houses as well), indifferent to the salon, unwilling to extract excerpts for the concert stage or as incidental music, and ignored by the Parisian opera companies, Debussy had to content himself with the modest gratification that neglected composers habitually derive from playing their music to informal gatherings of friends. When *Pelléas* was finally accepted by the Opéra-Comique, it had less to do with the terms of a *cahier des charges* or his having won the Prix de Rome in 1884 than it did with the progressive leadership of the company's new director, Albert Carré, who took over in January 1898. What Debussy had working for him were important professional and personal contacts. In Hartmann he had a publisher who was generous, energetic, and influential. It was apparently Hartmann's idea to approach Carré through André Messager, who had recently been appointed music director and conductor of the Opéra-Comique. Debussy and Messager had been friends since 1893, and Messager had performed Debussy's music as both pianist and conductor. Debussy played portions of *Pelléas* for Messager, who liked what he heard and arranged an audition for him with Carré. This too had a favorable outcome. In May 1898 Carré accepted *Pelléas* "in principle," although Debussy still had to wait until 3 May 1901 to receive the director's written commitment that *Pelléas* would be performed in 1902.

For *Pelléas,* the path to the stage was a long and arduous one, and during this journey Debussy, like so many other ambitious and frustrated French composers, must surely have identified with Joncières's plaint. After the success of *Pelléas,* however, everything changed for him, and if he ended his career as a one-opera composer, it was not for lack of opportunities. In 1908 he signed a contract with Giulio Gatti-Casazza

108. Debussy, *Correspondance,* 284–85.
109. Ibid., 291.

granting the Metropolitan Opera first performing rights to his Poe double bill, *Le diable dans le beffroi* and *La chute de la maison Usher,* and an option on his next opera, *La légende* (later, *L'histoire*) *de Tristan.* Unlike the many composers seeking a stage for their operas, Debussy was finally in the enviable position of having a major opera house awaiting the delivery of his operas—and willing to pay for the privilege. Obviously, his talent warranted it, even if he was unable, for a variety of reasons, to deliver.

Every aspiring opera composer needs a break to get a start, and given the enormous expenses associated with operatic production, it is hardly surprising that opera companies tend to be risk averse. To be sure, both Joncières and the young Debussy faced challenges in placing their operas, but one could argue that the system worked for both of them, and that their relative successes were commensurate with their talents. The frustrations that Joncières voiced in 1880, while broadly relevant, responded to a very particular historical moment and moreover reflected his personal history; but it is also important to recognize that he was surveying the scene from a particular perspective—that of the composer. My own account has privileged the composer's outlook as well, but I have also tried to acknowledge the crucial interests and perspectives of some of the other involved institutions and parties: government agencies and officials, opera companies and concert organizations (along with their performers, administrators, and staffs), music schools, publishers, patrons, and finally, audiences. It was within this complex social nexus that French opera flourished.

PART II

Cultural Transfer

Auber's *Gustave III*

HISTORY AS OPERA

Sarah Hibberd

In the introduction to his illustrated *L'histoire de France* (1833), Henri Martin insisted that history was a faceted mirror in which the viewpoints of people of the past and of the present day would be reflected, and which every reader could break and reconstitute according to his own convictions.[1] In the same year the context of political chaos that followed the July Revolution was foregrounded in Auber's *Gustave III, ou Le bal masqué* (see fig. 7.1), an opera which arguably presented history in a similarly kaleidoscopic fashion.[2] In this specifically styled *opéra historique* the past was brought

These ideas were first explored in a paper presented at the symposium on music in France (1830–1940), Melbourne University, 14–17 July 2004, in a session devoted to *Gustave III;* the other speakers were Anna McCready and Mark Pottinger. I am grateful to participants in the session, and to Dan Grimley and Ingrid Sykes, for stimulating discussion about the opera. A longer version of this essay appears in my *French Grand Opera and the Historical Imagination* (Cambridge: Cambridge University Press, 2009).

1. Henri Martin, "Avertissement," in *L'histoire de France depuis les temps les plus reculés jusqu'en juillet 1830: Par les principaux historiens et d'après les plans de MM. Guizot, Augustin Thierry et de Barante* (Paris: L. Mame, 1833–36), 1:1–12, 7; cited in Beth Segal Wright, *Painting and History during the French Restoration: Abandoned by the Past* (Cambridge: Cambridge University Press, 1997), 169.

2. Anselm Gerhard offers the kaleidoscope—"the craze of the 1820s"—as a metaphor for "the confusing multiplicity of [*grand opéra*'s] motives and conventions." *The Urbanization of Opera: Music Theater in Paris in the Nineteenth Century,* trans. Mary Whittall (Chicago: University of Chicago Press, 1998), 15. I am using the term here to suggest the fluidity and diversity of the political context in which we might understand the genre.

FIGURE 7.1. Charles Antoine Cambon's stage design for act 5 of Auber's *Gustave III* (1833), "Salle de bal." Bibliothèque nationale de France.

alive in a way that resonated with audiences, whatever their political persuasions. Critics identified a myriad of veiled allusions to diverse aspects of recent French history in their reviews—from the ancien régime, through the revolutionary period and Empire, to the Bourbon Restoration and the July Monarchy.

The opera sets the story of the Swedish king's assassination in March 1792 at a masked ball: his closest friend, Ankastrom, who has come to suspect the king of seducing his wife, is encouraged to shoot Gustave by a group of aristocratic conspirators who are resentful of his removal of their hereditary privileges. At the end of the opera the other characters discover what the audience already knows: nothing has happened between Gustave and Amélie beyond their reluctant admission of mutual love, and ironically, when Ankastrom shoots him Gustave has just handed Amélie a letter in which he confirms her husband as governor of Finland, thus ensuring the end of their liaison.[3]

3. It premiered on 27 February 1833. The librettist was Eugène Scribe; the composer, Daniel Auber; the choreographer, Taglioni; the scene designers, Feuchère, Diéterle, Alfred, Ciceri, Philastre,

The opera's lively contemporary reception and obvious political resonances with late eighteenth- and early nineteenth-century Paris have given rise to a number of modern studies. Herbert Schneider, Charles Pitt, Maribeth Clark, and Anna Mc-Cready have each explored parallels with the political situation in Paris.[4] In particular, Clark has posited a conflation of the eighteenth and nineteenth centuries, Stockholm and Paris, bourgeoisie and aristocracy effected in the music, dance, and costumes of the ball scene that precedes the assassination. McCready has also observed the easy fusion of the eighteenth and nineteenth centuries in the opera, interpreting the plot as a metaphor for the demise of the Bourbons (and of the ancien régime) and the ball scene as standing for the escapist self-indulgence of the period, with hedonistic pleasure being iconized in place of monarchy.[5] Mark Pottinger has addressed the purely historical dimension of the work, filtering the narrative strategies of the libret-

---

and Cambon; and the costume designers, Lami and Lormier. Published materials relating to the premiere include the libretto, *Gustave III, or Le bal masqué* (Paris: Jonas, 1833); the full score, *Gustave ou Le bal masqué* (Paris: Troupenas, [1833]; reprint, New York: Garland, 1980), and the mise-en-scène (reprinted in H. Robert Cohen, *The Original Staging Manuals for Ten Parisian Operatic Premières, 1824–1843/Dix livrets de mise en scène lyrique datant des créations parisiennes, 1824–1843* [Stuyvesant, NY: Pendragon Press, 1998], 13–55). Manuscript materials include an orchestral score, *F-Po*, A. 505a (I–VII), and *matériel* boxes, *F-Po*, Mat. 19 309 (1–194). For a full listing of librettos and scores (including arrangements) relating to the opera, see Herbert Schneider, *Chronologisch-thematisches Verzeichnis sämtlicher Werke von Daniel François Esprit Auber (AWV)* (Hildesheim: Olms, 1994), 1:697–760.

4. Herbert Schneider, program notes for a performance at Compiègne in 1991 (*F-Po*, dossier d'œuvre), and "Scribe and Auber: Constructing Grand Opera," in *The Cambridge Companion to Grand Opera*, ed. David Charlton (Cambridge: Cambridge University Press, 2004), 168–88; Charles Pitt, liner notes for Daniel Auber, *Gustave III, ou Le bal masqué*, French Lyrique Orchestra, cond. Michel Swierczewski, with Laurence Dale, ARN 368220 (Paris: Arion, 1993); Maribeth Clark, "Finding the Merit in the Masked Ball from *Gustave, ou Le bal masqué*," in "Understanding French Grand Opera through Dance" (Ph.D. diss., University of Pennsylvania, 1998), 118–79, and in revised form in "The Role of *Gustave, ou Le bal masqué* in Restraining the Bourgeois Body of the July Monarchy," *Musical Quarterly* 88, no. 2 (2005): 204–31; and Anna McCready, "Assassination and the Historical Ball: Auber's *Gustave III* and the Duc de Berry," in "Gilding the Lily: Music and Monarchy in Paris (1814–1833)" (Ph.D. diss., King's College, University of London, 2003), 157–207 (a shorter version of the chapter was delivered as a paper at the symposium on music in France [1830–1940], Melbourne University, 14–17 July 2004). Other scholars have stepped back from the political relevance of the opera to compare Auber's setting of the story with those of other composers, notably Verdi's *Un ballo in maschera* (1859). Scribe's adaptation of his literary sources is discussed in relation to subsequent operas on the same story in Federico d'Amico, "*Il ballo in maschera* prima di Verdi," *Verdi: Bollettino dell'Istituto di studi verdiani* 1, no. 3 (1960): 1251–1328; and in Gerhard, *Urbanization*, 409–56.

5. I read and commented on an early version of McCready's dissertation chapter in the mid-1990s. Her specific focus on the Bourbon metaphor and her critical dismissal of Auber's music encouraged me to look more closely at the opera's perceived political significance and to examine the broader musicodramatic aesthetic of Auber, Scribe, and their collaborators.

tist Eugène Scribe and the historian Jules Michelet through the rhetorical modes of Hayden White.[6]

Contemporary critics, however, offered more diverse political interpretations than these modern studies acknowledge. Futhermore, they were generally agreed that the political resonances were ultimately forgotten in the unprecedented magnificence of the ball scene at the heart of the opera. Reviews are characterized by unease about this apparent disjunction between the political and the spectacular, a feeling in which they are joined by modern commentators. This essay will explore these two dimensions of the opera and suggest that they might be understood as being closely entwined, in a manipulation of the temporal that goes beyond simply drawing parallels between the eighteenth and nineteenth centuries. After situating the libretto in the context of the historical sources referenced by Scribe and the critics, I will examine the diverse political interpretations of events offered by critics and suggest that in the ball scene the creators of the opera are proposing an alternative mode of history writing to that of predetermined linear narrative: history as synchronic moment. A kaleidoscope of conflicting personal actions gestures both backward and forward in time, and a new level of self-awareness is introduced into the process of writing history. Drawing comparisons with Jules Michelet's retrospective ideas about the revolutions of 1789 and 1830 and the task of the historian, I conclude that what amounts to the dissolving of politics into spectacle in the ball scene is not merely a sign of selling out to popular appeal, or of Scribe and Auber's lack of dramatic vision, as has been suggested by contemporary and modern commentators. It can instead be viewed as a defining characteristic of an aesthetic that offers a more complex understanding of the relationship between past and present—and a cathartic response to the events of the 1790s.

Libretto as Historical Document

Parisians were already familiar with the person and the story of Gustaf III when Scribe wrote his libretto in the late 1820s: a confirmed Francophile, Gustaf had spent time with the French royal family in Paris and Versailles before taking up the crown of Sweden; his involvement in the French Revolution, on behalf of the counterrevolutionaries, was well documented, and his literary and political writings had been published in France.[7] William Coxe's writings on his travels in the Baltic at the end

6. Pottinger also shows how the tonal and thematic associations in the opera help to articulate the narratives of the plot. "The Staging of History in France: Characterizations of Historical Figures in French Grand Opera during the Reign of Louis-Philippe (D. F. E. Auber, Louis Niedermeyer, F. Halévy, Giacomo Meyerbeer)" (Ph.D. diss., City University of New York, 2005), especially chapter 3 (a shorter version of this material was delivered as a paper at the symposium on music in France [1830–1940], Melbourne University, 14–17 July 2004). I am grateful to Mark Pottinger for sharing his thoughts on the opera, and excerpts from his dissertation, while I was preparing this essay.

7. J. B. Dechaux, ed., *Collection des écrits politiques, littéraires et dramatiques de Gustave III, roi de Suède, suivie de sa correspondance* (Stockholm: C. Delén, 1803–5). See also Inger Mattsson,

of the eighteenth century and John Brown's 1818 history *The Northern Courts,* both of which included lengthy sections on Gustaf, had been translated into French soon after their initial publication and were referenced by Scribe and by some of the critics reviewing the opera.[8]

On one level the libretto was received as another work of historical scholarship and judged on the truth of its portrayal of events. Scribe's eagerness to prove his scholarly credentials is evidenced by copious footnotes referencing his sources and expanding on points of interest through act 1, by his highlighting of real episodes that found their way into the libretto, and even the printing of an excerpt from Brown.[9] Some critics queried the accuracy of Scribe's interpretation, and the critic in the legitimist *La gazette de France* even suggested that the assassination might just as easily have been prompted by popular hostility (filtered through ideas from the French Revolution) rather than aristocratic disaffection.[10] But Jules Janin, writing in *Le journal des débats,* enthusiastically completed Scribe's version of history, detailing at colorful length what happened after the assassination—notably the beating, execution, and quartering of Ankastrom and the display of his head on a spike for five weeks—before then declaring his unease with the way in which such terrible and violent history was routinely turned into opera.[11] Such fascination with gruesome detail seemed

---

ed., *Gustavian Opera: An Interdisciplinary Reader in Swedish Opera, Dance and Theatre, 1771–1809* (Stockholm: Royal Swedish Academy of Music, 1991). A number of plays about Swedish history were staged during the Restoration, including Brault's *Christine de Suède (drame historique;* Théâtre-Français, June 1829), and Soulié's *Christine à Fontainebleau (drame;* Odéon, October 1829). During the Empire a play entitled *Gustave,* intended for performance at the Théâtre-Français, had been suspended owing to its similarities with current events in Sweden; see David Chaillou, *Napoléon et l'Opéra: La politique sur la scène, 1810–1815* (Paris: Fayard, 2004), 196–97.

8. William Coxe, *Travels in Poland, Russia, Sweden and Denmark: Interspersed with Historical Relations and Political Inquiries* (London: Cadell and Davies, 1784), trans. P. H. Mallet as *Voyage en Pologne, Russie, Danemarck, etc.* (Geneva: Barde, Manget et Cie, 1786). Coxe's discussion of Gustaf is in vol. 3, chap. 4 (the book pre-dates the assassination, discussion of which is not included). See also John Brown, *The Northern Courts, containing Original Memoirs of the Sovereigns of Sweden and Denmark since 1766,* 2 vols. (Edinburgh: Constable; London: Fenner; 1818), trans. Jean Cohen as *Les cours du Nord, ou Mémoires originaux sur les souverains de la Suède et du Danemarck depuis 1766,* 3 vols. (Paris: A. Bertrand, 1820). Brown engages with other historians, including Coxe, whom he cites. He discusses the assassination and its aftermath (including Ankastrom's confession, torture, and death) at length in vol. 3. Cohen adds footnotes glossing Brown's interpretation of events.

9. The libretto published in 1833 by Jonas—and its reprint in the series *La France dramatique au dix-neuvième siècle, choix de pièces modernes* (Paris: Tresse, 1845)—includes footnotes in act 1 referencing Brown (in Cohen's translation), and an "account of the death of Gustaf III excerpted from the work on Sweden by Mr. Coxe" (relation de la mort de Gustave III extraite de l'ouvrage de M. Coxe sur la Suède) at the end (83–87), which (presumably misattributed by the publishers, as suggested in Schneider, "Scribe and Auber," 181), is actually drawn from Brown, *Les cours du Nord,* 3:107–16.

10. *La gazette de France,* 1 March 1833.

11. J. J. [Jules Janin], *Journal des débats,* 1 March 1833.

to confirm the truth of the past by virtue of its immediacy—which for many must have resonated with personal and collective memories. Other critics took the libretto as a cue to inform their readers about aspects of Gustaf's rule or to muse on the phenomenon of revolution or on the function of royalty in Europe, treating the libretto as just another historical source.[12] The critic for *La quotidienne* quipped that even without their scholarly trimmings Scribe's rhymed historical verses seemed more authentic than the 1830 Charter.[13]

Brown's *The Northern Courts*, the principal source (in its French translation) for Scribe's libretto, sets the tone of the opera: Gustaf had staged a coup d'état in 1772, taking power from the government, ending Catherine the Great's attempt to damage Sweden, and establishing absolute rule. Although Brown depicts Gustaf rather unsympathetically as cold, calculating, and hypocritical, he nevertheless makes explicit the strong relationship between the king and his people in the face of a corrupt and greedy aristocracy, and both he and Coxe term the coup a "revolution"—after which, according to Brown, Gustaf required the fallen nobles (at bayonet point and within cannon range) to join him in singing psalms to praise God.[14]

Scribe underscores this fundamental alliance between king, people, and *patrie*, establishing Gustave in the first act as a cultured and popular citizen-king. The opening chorus—consisting of diplomats, court officials, bourgeois and peasant deputies, a painter, a sculptor, and a ballet master—tells Gustave, "Your happy people watch over you,"[15] and when he receives a petition from the deputies he vows, "It is up to me to listen to your worries and dry your tears."[16] It is only a group of aristocratic conspirators—notably Dehorn and Warting—who complain about his popular image, about how they, "the great men of the empire," are "confused, without regard, with all his subjects: bourgeois, soldiers, ballet masters!"[17]

The seeds of fate are planted when one of the ministers asks Gustave to sign a document banishing the sorceress Arvedson from Stockholm (she is rumored to harbor conspirators). The king decides first to visit her and witness her powers. The sorceress predicts the king's murder by the next man to shake his hand, and from this point the pull of fate is felt not only in the unfolding of the plot, but also in the music. Auber's characteristic injection of dancelike numbers throughout the score—and a number of specific foreshadowings of the rhythms of the dances from the ball scene that provides the cover for the assassination—led the critic in *Le moniteur universel* to complain that Auber was preoccupied with the ball (and by implication the pro-

12. P., *Le moniteur universel*, 28 February 1833; *Le constitutionnel*, 3 March 1833.

13. *La quotidienne*, 4 March 1833. The Charter of 1830 (a revision of that of 1814) had launched the July Monarchy, setting out the rights of king and people.

14. Brown, *Northern Courts*, 1:316.

15. "Ton peuple heureux veille sur toi." Scribe, *Gustave III*, act I, scene 1.

16. "C'est à moi d'écouter vos chagrins et de tarir vos larmes." Ibid.

17. "Les grands de l'empire . . . confondus sans égards avec tous ses sujets: des bourgeois, des soldats, des maîtres de ballet!" Ibid.

cesses of fate) from the very first scenes: "This thought follows him everywhere, to the point that the four first acts are nothing more than an introduction to the fifth."[18] Anticipations of the galop, the culminating frenzy of the dancing, in the quintet that closes act 4, and in Gustave's solo at the beginning of the final act—this time as "real" music, with harps, triangle, and woodwind, making itself heard as the ball gets under way in the adjoining opera house—tighten the spatial as well as the temporal teleological effect.[19]

Historical Truth

In spite of this increasingly powerful pull of fate in the plot and the score, the linearity and inexorability of the narrative are disrupted at another level by the intrusion of the present into the retelling of the past. Specifically, the obvious similarities between Louis-Philippe and Gustave open up the example of alternative endings and call into question the reliability of any narrative of events.

Most obviously, the atmosphere of legitimist, Bonapartist, and republican plotting that was plaguing the Orléanist regime seemed to mirror that depicted in the opera, but with the important difference that in France such plots had been unsuccessful. The duchesse de Berry, who had been involved the previous year in insurrections in the Midi and the Vendée in order to put her son (the last true Bourbon heir, conceived just before the assassination of her husband) on the throne, had finally been captured in January 1833.[20] The critic for *La gazette de France* suggested that the French were particularly squeamish about conspiracy at that time.[21] In fact, there had been an assassination attempt on Louis-Philippe just four months earlier, on the Pont Royal on 19 November 1832, and more attempts were to follow in the next two years.[22] Journalists had been quick to turn it into political capital: an article for *La nouvelliste,* reprinted in the official paper *Le moniteur universel,* suggested that "the attack . . . revealed this love of order, this weariness of division, this generosity, these feelings of care for the king in all classes of Parisians. . . . Never . . . have anti-republican feel-

---

18. "Cette pensée le poursuit partout, en telle sorte que les quatre premières actes ne sont, pour ainsi dire, qu'une introduction au cinquième." P., *Le moniteur universel,* 2 March 1833. Schneider suggests that the presence of the ball scene earlier in the score serves as "a preparation for the apotheosis and perversion in the murder at the end of the opera." Schneider, "Scribe and Auber," 183.

19. These anticipations of the motif are found in Auber, *Gustave,* 535, 581, 588.

20. Philip Mansel, *Paris between Empires, 1814–1852* (London: John Murray, 2001), 301. For a detailed contemporary account of the duchesse de Berry's adventures, see comtesse de Boigne, *Les mémoires de la comtesse de Boigne,* vol. 2, *De 1820 à 1848* (Paris: Mercure de France, 1999), 350–468.

21. *La gazette de France,* 1 March 1833.

22. According to the comtesse de Boigne, the assassin was a republican sympathizer named Bergeron who initially escaped but was finally arrested, tried, and acquitted. *Mémoires,* 433. The comtesse de Boigne's account of the assassination attempt is cited in McCready, "Assassination," 168.

ings burst through all classes of the people with such force."[23] It was reported that even the two chambers of peers and deputies went straight to the Tuileries once they heard the news: "Respect could not contain the lively demonstration of their feelings, expressed by unanimous cries of *vive le Roi!*"[24] The king's apparently cool and confident reaction to the attempt—the critic writing in *La nouvelliste* noted the "admirable sang-froid" of the *roi populaire*—anticipated Gustave's bravado in act 1 when threats against him are reported. Following the premiere of *Gustave*, *Le charivari* reported that the interior minister M. d'Argout (Antoine Maurice Apollinaire, comte d'Argout) had voiced his fears to the Opéra director, Louis Véron, that the onstage pistol shot would not only remind audiences of the shot on the Pont Royal, but would also encourage further allusions to Louis-Philippe's government to be discovered in the libretto, such as the fact that the singer who was playing the role of Ankastrom looked rather like M. Athalin (Louis, baron Athalin), a general at the Tuileries palace, for example, or that Louis-Philippe was given to shaking hands with his (potentially murderous) subjects.[25] Other critics associated Gustave's assassination with that of the duc de Berry, the Bourbon heir to the throne, on the steps of the Opéra in 1820, which indeed echoed the murder of the Swedish king in many details: "This dénouement recalls the tragic end of a prince who was also assassinated at the Opéra, and whose last words had been to ask for mercy for his assassin; the duc d'Orléans, who was at this performance, could remember it."[26]

The unpredictable nature of events and the conflicting ways in which they were reported prompted a certain amount of musing in reviews of *Gustave* about how one might recognize the truth of events—past or present—and whether such narratives could ever be reliable.[27] The critic in *La gazette de France* observed that four months after the assassination attempt on Louis-Philippe that had been so widely reported in the press, it remained unclear as to whether there had been an assassin at all: "We

23. "L'attentat . . . a révélé dans toutes les classes de la population de Paris cet amour de l'ordre, cette lassitude des partis, cette générosité, ces sentimens d'attention pour le Roi. . . . Jamais . . . les sentimens anti-républicains n'ont éclaté dans toutes les classes du peuple avec autant de force." P., *Le moniteur universel*, 21 November 1833.

24. "Le respect n'a pu contenir la vive manifestation de leurs sentimens, qui se sont exprimés par des cris unanimes de *vive le Roi!*" Reprinted in *Le moniteur universel*, 20 November 1833.

25. *Le charivari*, 1 March 1833.

26. "Ce dénouement a rappelé la fin tragique d'un prince assassiné aussi à l'Opéra, et dont les dernières paroles ont été pour demander la grâce de son assassin; M. le Duc d'Orléans, qui assistait à cette représentation, a pu se rappeler." *La quotidienne*, 4 March 1833. The assassination of the duc de Berry is recounted in detail in comtesse de Boigne, *Mémoires*, 28–46; and parallels with Gustave's murder are examined in McCready, "Assassination," 160–67.

27. This was a theme of much historiographical writing as well. For example, in response to a new edition of a life of Napoleon, a critic noted that until now he had been villainized (e.g., by Walter Scott) or put on a pedestal; so how was one to find true, impartial history, and how would one recognize it? "Histoire de Napoléon par M. Saint-Maurice (2e édition)," *Le corsaire*, 26 September 1831.

are sure of only one thing: no one was assassinated."[28] It followed that if one could not establish the truth of current events, how could one ascertain historical truth? Thus, the manner in which the opera fused events of the past and present encouraged reflection not only on the linearity of history's stories, but also on the nature of truth and the degree to which history can be fixed at all.

The Chaos of History

Gustave was more profoundly an *opéra historique* than Scribe and Auber had perhaps anticipated: the final act not only represented a specific episode from Swedish history, but also evoked a dazzling array of moments from France's past, from the revolutionary decade to the July Monarchy, subsuming historical narratives into a kaleidoscope of political opinion and memory. Thus the apparently straightforward narrative of the opera—the playing out of Gustave's fate—was displaced by a new mode of history writing, filtered through the experience of *living* history.

Critical reception of the ball scene gloried in this kaleidoscopic approach and willfully collapsed geographical, temporal, and sociopolitical distinctions. First, the Swedish setting was subsumed into ancien régime France, an easy shift given that Gustaf had modeled his court on the example of eighteenth-century Versailles. Critics claimed that the stairway at the beginning of the act 5, scene 3, for example, was copied from French examples (variously Fontainebleau, the Palais-Royal, and Versailles),[29] and that Gustave's costume resembled the garb of a French abbé.[30] Janin, after claiming to have been transported from Stockholm to Paris, even suggested that the eighteenth-century French element might have been made still more explicit. For example, Auber should have worked the revolutionary song "Ça ira" into his score because, Janin alleged, it was in vogue on the eve of the assassination, brought to Sweden from France by the conspirators.[31]

Second, as has been documented, aspects of France's past and present were skillfully

28. "On n'est sûr que d'une chose, c'est qu'il n'y a pas eu d'assassiné." *La gazette de France,* 1 March 1833.

29. *La quotidienne,* 4 March 1833; J. J. [Jules Janin], *Journal des débats,* 1 March 1833; and L-V [Ludovic Vitet], *Le temps,* 4 March 1833, respectively. During the Restoration and the July revolution the Palais-Royal had acquired dual dynastic and revolutionary significance, further contributing to the confusion of political symbols; see Mansel, *Paris between Empires,* 234.

30. J. J. [Jules Janin], *Journal des débats,* 1 March 1833. The gallows under which Gustave and Amélie met in act 3 had been identified by several critics, including Janin (*Journal des débats,* 4 March 1833), as Montfaucon, the execution site on the northeast edge of Paris that had been used until the beginning of the seventeenth century (demolished in 1761)—a symbol of pre-guillotine days in France.

31. McCready argues that Auber does indeed embed "Ça ira" in the score. "Assassination," 186–90.

brought together in the music.[32] Dances such as the minuet and the quadrille (and the high degree of masquerade) gestured back to the previous century and to the traditional series of balls held during the ancien régime. But with the spectacular galop, a dance invented during the 1820s and at its height in the early 1830s, contemporary Paris was evoked, and more recent balls were recalled—notably one held earlier in the 1833 season at which members of the audience had taken the stage, causing a near riot.[33] By implication, class distinctions were also blurred—eighteenth-century aristocratic and nineteenth-century bourgeois entertainments merged not only for the participants, but also in the makeup of the audience in this new "bourgeois" era at the Opéra.[34]

Third, parallels with a variety of past French rulers supplemented the implied references to Louis-Philippe. For Vitet in *Le temps,* the extravagances of the scene could have come from the court of Louis XIV.[35] The Opéra's director, Louis Véron, claimed that the actors were overawed by the re-creation of the court of Louis XV and were thus unable to express their emotions with true ardor.[36] The critic for *Le constitutionnel* compared Gustave and Amélie to Louis XVI and Marie-Antoinette, while suggesting that the ball scene more generally recalled the age of Louis XIII. *Le moniteur universel*—seeking perhaps to distance the story from that of the Bourbons—pointed obliquely to similarities with Robespierre and Napoleon: Gustaf had destroyed the power of the nobility by abolishing the senate and, tormented by an ambition to make his country great again, had employed a combination of powerful royal and revolutionary symbols in his propaganda.[37] In *Le corsaire,* comparisons were extended

---

32. The ideas summarized in this paragraph are drawn from Clark, "Finding the Merit," 118–79.

33. Clark describes how "the barrier between performers and audience dissolved" when dancers performing the ballet-pantomime *Carnaval de Venise* were pushed aside by costumed members of the audience who sought to alleviate their boredom by adding a galop; Clark, "Role of *Gustave*," 208.

34. Odile Krakovitch makes the point that this era "was truly that of 'popular theatre,' of mixed classes, of spectacle integrated into everyday life." Krakovitch, *Hugo censuré: La liberté au théâtre au XIXe siècle* (Paris: Calman-Lévy, 1985), 45. The scene also evoked other theatrical works that combined historical assassinations and balls, such as Casimir Delavigne's *Marino Faliero* (based on Schiller) and *Lucrèce Borgia;* Hugo's *Hernani* and *Marion de Lorme;* and Planard and Hérold's *opéra comique Le pré aux Clercs,* based on Mérimée's *La chronique du règne de Charles IX.* Janin lists these works in *Journal des débats,* 11 March 1833.

35. L-V [Ludovic Vitet], *Le temps,* 4 March 1833.

36. Louis Véron, *Mémoires d'un bourgeois de Paris* (Paris: Librairie nouvelle, 1857), 3:178. However, Véron went on to observe that "the elegance, the coquetry of this epoque . . . were more suited to the tone of comedy . . . the slightest violent gesture could excite by provoking the explosion of a white cloud [of powder]" (les élégances, les coquetteries de cette époque . . . se prêtent mieux au ton de la comédie . . . le moindre geste violent peut exciter le rire en provoquant l'explosion d'un nuage blanc); Véron, *Mémoires* (1857), 3:178–79.

37. Brown's description of Gustaf's failed attempt to conquer St. Petersburg and the parallels he draws with Napoleon's Russian campaign are cited in the Lyon edition of the libretto, 11. Moreover, the crowd of nobles that surrounds Ankastrom and his wife in act 3, as Gustave makes his escape, has echoes of the counterrevolutionary White Terror of 1794 (which resurfaced in 1815), during

beyond France to include Peter the Great (Russia), Frederick II (Austria), Joseph II (Prussia), and Charles XII (Sweden).[38] Parallels between the "popular" monarchs Gustave and Louis-Philippe were apparently so evident—as suggested above—that the critic of *Le charivari* instead focused on the few *dis*similarities between the two rulers.[39]

Even the close relationship between king and people, established in act 1 and confirmed at the end of the opera, conjured up a range of parallels beyond that to Louis-Philippe. Louis XVI had also—nominally—become a constitutional *roi des Français* in 1791. More than that, sympathy for Louis following his execution clouded the question of his guilt. Michelet was later to claim that by killing the defenseless monarch, the Jacobins had unleashed sympathy that purified the monarchy in the public imagination, allowing regicide to be understood as patricide.[40] Perhaps more overwhelmingly, at a time when monarchy as an institution was under threat, this portrait of a king who had seized power but was sensitive to the needs of the people and in conflict with the nobility, and who was a patron of the arts, recalled the figure of Napoleon, who had come to power on the back of the revolution, and whose seal as consul read "in the name of the French people."[41] Ludovic Vitet devoted an entire article in *Le temps* to describing the life of the Swedish monarch in which parallels with the emperor were suggested.[42] Following the humiliation of a Restoration secured by foreign powers in 1814–15, there had been a growing nostalgia in some quarters for the patriotic glories of Napoleon's early reign—encouraged by the 1820s best seller *Le mémorial de Sainte-Hélène*, in which the emperor is presented as an idealistic liberal.[43] This nostalgia was even encouraged by Louis-Philippe, who perhaps hoped to capitalize on the rekindling of proud memories of France's recently glorious

---

which reactionary royalist forces targeted real and suspected Jacobins and gangs of aristocratic youths wandered the streets and beat known Jacobins.

38. *Le corsaire,* 1 March 1833.

39. *Le charivari,* 1 March 1833. For example, it was pointed out that Louis-Philippe would never find himself caught in snow without an umbrella, as Gustave is in the third act, and that he survived an assassination attempt.

40. Jules Michelet, *Histoire de la révolution française,* vol. 1 (1847; Paris: Pléiade, 1952), cited in Susan Dunn, "Michelet and Lamartine: Regicide, Passion, and Compassion," *History and Theory* 28, no. 3 (1989): 275.

41. "Au nom du peuple français." Lynn Hunt, *Politics, Culture, and Class in the French Revolution,* new ed. (Berkeley: University of California Press, 2004), 229. The Napoleon cult was flourishing in the early years of the July Monarchy; the year 1830–31 was the theaters' "single most Napoleonic year." Maurice Samuels, *The Spectacular Past: Popular History and the Novel in Nineteenth-Century France* (Ithaca, NY: Cornell University Press, 2004), 120.

42. L-V [Ludovic Vitet], *Le temps,* 1 March 4 March 1833.

43. Emmanuel [comte de] Las Cases, *Le mémorial de Sainte-Hélène* (Paris: Gallimard, 1963). This enthusiasm was also manifest in Bérenger's nationalistic poems and in the large number of plays about Napoleon after the lifting of censorship in 1830. For more on nostalgia for Napoleon, see Mansel, *Paris between Empires,* 239–41.

military past in order to move forward and cement the relationship between king, people, and *patrie*.[44]

The manner in which critics conjured up competing interpretations and metaphors suggests that this scene presented a reading of history that overwhelmed the single event of Gustave's murder and evoked a kaleidoscope of more resonant and relevant moments from French history of which the audience had collective and individual, imagined and remembered, memories. This picture of the past effectively subverts historical determinism and reliable, linear narrative in a manner that mirrors the style of historical storytelling favored by Henri Martin in the same year. A convincing case might be made for the ball scene as a metaphor for the fall of the Bourbons (with either the 1789 or the 1830 Revolution or the 1820 assassination) or for the defeat of Napoleon in 1814–15. In this sense, the scene gestured nostalgically to the ancien régime, to the moment of the outbreak of revolution, and to Napoleon's glory days, all moments of recent history when France was, in different ways, the envy of Europe.[45] Alternatively, the ball could be seen more directly as a comment on Louis-Philippe's changing fortunes by allusion to historical example. Something of each of these possibilities seems to have been appreciated by the critics, according to their political preferences, in what amounted to a smorgasbord of interpretation in the press.

The Suspended Present

Having spelled out their preferred political allusions, however, reviewers then assessed the overall impact of the ball scene. They were agreed that the spectacle ultimately overwhelmed the political references altogether, making one forget the drama. Few tried to reconcile the political with the spectacular. The lengthy (twenty-minute) scene—which comprised an allemande, a *pas des folies,* a march-minuet combination, two marches, and a galop—was arguably experienced as a suspended moment, a divertissement that existed outside the dramatic flow of the plot and outside time and that had its own momentum. Moreover, it drew the audience into the frenzied

44. Three "cults" of Napoleon have been identified: the official cult, promoted by himself and his heirs, which portrayed him as a charismatic leader and war hero; the popular cult, developed during the Restoration and fused with republicanism, which depicted a revolutionary emperor whose power was sanctioned by the people; and the political cult, which emphasized him as a usurper, dictator, and foreigner who nevertheless restored the greatness of France. Robert Gildea, *The Past in French History* (New Haven, CT: Yale University Press, 1996), 89–95. For those who resisted the glorification of Napoleon, the words uttered by the conspirators in the opening chorus—"Tyran, qui prends le nom de roi"—might still have carried echoes of the self-appointed emperor.

45. This apparent separation of content and form seems to mesh with Catherine Join-Diéterle's understanding that monarchical operas of the July Monarchy no longer focused on specific political concepts, but rather offered a framework for royal magnificence, confirming a generalized nostalgia for the past; see Join-Diéterle, "La monarchie, source d'inspiration de l'opéra, à l'époque romantique," *Revue d'histoire du theatre* 35, no. 4 (1983): 430–41.

experience as potential participants. The critic for *Le constitutionnel* suggested that if the orchestra had not been in the way, the audience would have been tempted to join in.[46] The evocation of the visual and musical atmosphere of a real ball (contemporary or historical) increased the ease with which barriers between fantasy and reality, past and present, were broken down.

The critic for *Le moniteur universel* described the spectacle:

> What richness can equal the vast decoration of the ball room, a thousand candles shed a magical clarity on a crowd of masques in magnificent, bizarre, original, and infinitely varied costumes, illuminating groups who pass without colliding who mark out, draw back, move together, spin, losing themselves in the midst of the most ravishing, intoxicating, graceful, unexpected dancing, in a deafening galop that will drive Paris wild.[47]

The hypnotic effect of both the visual and the musical dimensions of the scene created the illusion of suspended time. The spectacle incorporated embedded pantomime scenes and mesmerizing, endlessly varying—though carefully synchronized—dancing.

For Vitet in *Le temps,* the *ronde* at the end of the galop "distilled movement" and was comparable to a work by Michelangelo or Callot—it was like a "gigantic painting, a prodigious fresco, in which the painter and designer had been unable to sketch in the details," a spectacle that should be judged purely by its impact.[48] For the reviewer in *Le corsaire* it was more like *A Thousand and One Nights* in its blend of exotic costumes from the mystical East as well as more familiar commedia characters and the strikingly bizarre.[49] The more peculiar of these were listed in the *Journal des débats* and included a barrel, a guitar, and a bunch of asparagus.[50] The mesmeric quality of the music derived in part from the simple additive structures of binary, rounded binary, and rondo forms, typical of dance numbers, and from its strong rhythms.[51]

46. *Le constitutionnel,* 3 March 1833.

47. "Quelle richesse peut égaler cette vaste décoration de la salle de bal, ces mille bougies répendant une clarté magique sur une foule de masques aux costumes magnifiques, bizarres, originaux, variés à l'infini, sur ces groupes qui se croisent sans se heurter jamais, qui se dessinent, s'éloignent, se rapprochent, tourbillonnent, se perdent au milieu de tout ce que la danse a de plus ravissant, de plus enivrant, de plus gracieux, de plus imprévu, dans une galope étourdissante qui fera la folie de Paris." P., *Le moniteur universel,* 2 March 1833.

48. "Un tableau gigantesque, une fresque prodigieuse où le peintre et le dessinateur n'ont pu pointiller des détails," L-V [Ludovic Vitet], *Le temps,* 4 March 1833.

49. *Le corsaire,* 1 March 1833.

50. J. J. [Jules Janin], *Journal des débats,* 1 March 1833. Some costumes—though not all those referenced in the press—are listed in the mise-en-scène, 50–53.

51. Clark, "Finding the Merit," examines the structure of each dance and points to the associations they encapsulated, notably the ancien régime implications of the minuet; she concludes that the combined effect of these numbers was to collapse the past into the present.

The galop was particularly infectious: it began at full tilt following the promenading of dancers during the marches, and its additive increases within an irregular structure of repeated themes and returns contributed to a sense of community as the dancers seemed to move spontaneously as one person.[52]

This idea of a suspended present evokes the idea of carnival, which has been understood as offering an "*instant* par excellence" that arguably celebrates "nothing but itself."[53] This is a notion that has been specifically identified with revolutionary times in contemporary and early nineteenth-century descriptions of revolutionary festivals, and more recently in Lynn Hunt's politically charged concept of the "mythic present"—the "sacred moment of the new consensus" after revolution.[54] This "moment" was temporally ambiguous and in flux.

The historian Jules Michelet forged a more explicit connection between the timelessness of revolution, dance, and history in his writings between 1831 and 1848 in an attempt to inspire a sense of communality and excitement about—and hope for—the future among his readers. Since at least 1831 he had been interested in the relationship between social cohesion and freedom, seeing them come together in the 1830 revolution: "After the victory we sought the hero, and we found an entire people. . . . [It was] the work of human freedom."[55] Writing from the vantage point of France's next uprising in 1848—when a number of historians (including Alphonse de Lamartine, Edgar Quinet, and Louis Blanc) were reassessing the significance of 1789 in the light of recent events—Michelet sought to rekindle memories of the early, idealistic stages of the 1789 and 1830 Revolutions to spur reconciliation and action among his contemporaries.[56] In his *L'histoire de la révolution française* (begun in 1847), he did this by underscoring the relationship between freedom and social unity through the metaphor of dance. Specifically, he evoked the image of a farandole to recall the "movement of the Federations" across France—a process during which regional diversity was for Michelet translated

52. Indeed, its contagion spread across Paris: at the Théâtre des Variétés a *galoppade populaire* was performed at the end of the evening's program of four plays, and according to a review of a performance the previous evening, the whole place began to dance. *Le corsaire,* 30 March 1833.

53. Jean Starobinski, *L'invention de la liberté, 1700–89* (Geneva: Skira, 1987), 85–86, elaborates on the idea of carnival. A number of critics made explicit comparisons between the scene and a Venetian carnival, including Vitet, *Le temps,* 4 March 1833, and P., *Le moniteur universel,* 2 March 1833.

54. Mona Ozouf, *La fête révolutionnaire, 1789–99* (Paris: Gallimard, 1976), and *L'homme régénéré: Essais sur la révolution française* (Paris: Gallimard, 1989); Hunt, *Politics, Culture, and Class,* 27. Here, different factions and regimes chose to celebrate different symbolic events of the period— the storming of the Bastille, the regicide, the establishing of the Republic—thus contributing to an amorphous, ambiguous, constantly shifting phenomenon.

55. "Après la victoire on a cherché le héros, et l'on a trouvé tout un peuple. . . . [C'était] l'œuvre de la liberté humaine." Jules Michelet, *Introduction à l'histoire universelle* (Paris: Hachette, 1831), 463–64.

56. Ceri Crossley, *French Historians and Romanticism: Thierry, Guizot, the Saint-Simonians, Quinet, Michelet* (London: Routledge, 1993), 235.

into *patrie* with the creation of *départements:* "the enormous farandole which was formed, little by little, from the whole of France."[57] He presented the Fête de la Fédération in July 1790 as a culminating, suspended moment of national openness and transparency and spontaneous social reconciliation after the Revolution: "Time has perished, space has perished."[58] For Michelet, this precarious balance and euphoria had been recaptured in the "lightning flash" of 1830, when "a thousand confusions are resolved, find their true connections and, in coming together, are illuminated."[59] But, as in 1790, although on one hand this movement had gathered the people into a transcendent, celebratory unity, a collective self-awareness, on the other hand such unity also contained the seeds of disillusion and further conflict. For Michelet, the spontaneity captured by the 1830 Revolution had not only echoed the events of 1790, offering a new sense of national destiny, but also illuminated the historian's vocation: to reanimate an engagement with social reality.[60] Although social unity and the freedom from time or place signified by revolution (and dance) had proved unsustainable in the face of historical progress, Michelet believed that the historian had the power to retrieve such a state and inspire a different outcome.[61]

Although the process of writing might have been for Michelet the means of "overcoming time and otherness, of appropriating the world," the ball scene in *Gustave* arguably encapsulated more immediately the contradictions of revolution and, by extension, the complex processes of history.[62] In 1833 history was—explicitly or implicitly—revolutionary history. Indeed, the ball scene might be viewed as a prism through which memories of 1789 and 1830 were refracted for 1833 audiences: action was suspended in a moment that stood outside time, before violent action propelled us into historical and dramatic chaos, returning us to the narrative of Swedish (and by implication, French) history.

57. "La farandole immense qui s'est formée peu à peu de la France tout entière." Michelet, "De la religion nouvelle: fédération générale (14 juillet 90)," in *L'histoire de la révolution française,* vol. 1 (1847; Paris: Pléiade, 1952), 423. Crossley discusses this passage from *Histoire de la révolution française* in *French Historians and Romanticism,* 238–41.

58. "Le temps a péri, l'espace a péri.'" Michelet, "De la religion nouvelle: Fédérations (juillet 89–juillet 90)," in *Histoire de la révolution française,* 406. For more on this interpretation, see Lionel Gossman, "The Go-Between: Jules Michelet, 1798–1894," *MLN* 89, no. 4 (1974): 532.

59. "'Mille choses embrouillées s'y résolvent, y retrouvent leurs vrais rapports et . . . s'illuminent." Michelet, "Préface de 1869," in *Histoire de France,* in *Œuvres complètes* (Paris: Flammarion, 1893), 1:iv.

60. This idea is developed in Crossley, *French Historians and Romanticism,* 199, 241–44.

61. Explaining the contradictions of history also fascinated Edgar Quinet, who—looking back at the 1789 revolution from 1865—observed "such astounding contradictions, such heroic beginnings, such magnanimous promises and such misjudgments, how can they all be reconciled?" Cited and translated in Linda Orr, *Headless History: Nineteenth-Century French Historiography of the Revolution* (Ithaca, NY: Cornell University Press, 1990), 67. Indeed, Orr goes on to suggest that for Quinet, the very chaos of history was its essence: the contradictions of the Revolution and of modern society were caused by "an eternal misunderstanding." Ibid.

62. Gossman, "The Go-Between," 530.

The state of contemplation is at once escapist and nostalgic. The scene enabled the majority of critics to forget the political drama. The critic for *Le moniteur universel* noted there were specific complaints that the weighty ideas of the conspirators had disappeared through the opera, swallowed up by quadrilles and waltzes, and that the conspiracy itself had been transformed via musical forms into a type of "burlesque mystification."[63] *Le constitutionnel* agreed that everyone was instead mesmerized by the dancers.[64] But Janin's assessment of Auber's music was tinged with nostalgia: he characterized the score as "music of memory rather than imagination, of regret rather than hope," pointing to a more complex, engaged experience.[65] Indeed, he fully approved of the way in which politics had been subsumed by spectacle to the point that the whole act seemed to exist independently of Scribe and Auber: "It creates itself."[66] His conception was arguably one of history transfigured as art, with a cathartic, even redemptive quality. When he suggests it is an opera about memory and regret, we might understand him to imply this bigger picture of French history, in a fusion of political awareness and aesthetic beauty.

Assassination

After the dancing, the mood suddenly changes: a D pedal under tremolo strings takes us from D major into G minor and focuses our attention on the conspirators. Gustave's page, Oscar, reassures Ankastrom—unaware that he is addressing the king's assassin—that Gustave has arrived. When the king unmasks, the descent into the tragic fateful conclusion accelerates, and the narrative is punctuated by further melodramatic, visual gestures, by mocking echoes of the galop theme, and by an increasingly insistent repeated (tonic) E in the bass line. During the ensuing duet Amélie warns Gustave, accompanied by a variation on the rhythm of the galop, that Ankastrom might appear. But Gustave lingers and eventually hands Amélie the letter in which—as she declaims on a resonant E—he names her husband governor of Finland, thus putting an end to their liaison before it has truly begun. When a group of conspirators starts to sing, the words of Amélie and Gustave become indecipherable, and the shot is finally fired amidst the visual and aural commotion.

A pattern of building confusion and pace is diverted by an almost unnoticed yet

---

63. *Le constitutionnel,* 3 March 1833.

64. *Le moniteur universel,* 2 March 1833.

65. "Musique de souvenir plutôt que d'imagination, musique de regrets plutôt que d'espérance." J. J. [Jules Janin], *Journal des débats,* 1 March 1833.

66. "Ce cinquième acte là se fait tout seul; il existe par lui-même." J. J. [Jules Janin], *Journal des débats,* 4 March 1833. In his previous article he had—rather less enthusiastically—complained about how the violence and horror of history had been translated into beautiful and dramatic scenes in operas. But he had also admired the fact that the eighteenth century had "died well" in *Gustave*—as captured in the galop.

significant and symbolic act: the shot fired by Ankastrom, which becomes visible and audible in the reaction of a shocked and repentant people.[67] Once Oscar has confirmed what has happened—in a monotone declamation echoing the rhythm of the fateful galop—the personal tragedy of the protagonists is expanded into collective shock: individual motivation and anguish are ultimately subsumed by the voice of the people in a spectacular visual and (implied) aural confusion (see the stage directions below).

The full score published by Troupenas in 1833 gives a shorter version of the final scenes than that found in the published libretto.[68] The cuts, made presumably during rehearsals, draw the focus away from individual characters—notably Ankastrom and Amélie—and give priority to an essentialized king and to the chorus, promoting the collective over the individual experience.[69] Such phrases as "Adieu Suède" are omitted while "Gloire et patrie" is retained, serving to reclaim patriotism for the (implied) French nation while avoiding the specificities of revolutionary, republican, or royalist sentiments and denying the assassin a voice. Many critics saw these final scenes as anticlimactic at best; but the concluding tableau, with its stage directions detailing each character's reaction to the events, encourages the audience to experience the shock of the onstage characters, in whose ears the dance music still metaphorically rings:[70]

The grenadiers who carry Gustave on their crossed rifles begin slowly to walk towards the granite stairway, preceded by servants who hold torches: this is the principal group. To the right, Ankastrom and the conspirators, at whom the soldiers aim the points of their bayonets; Gustave only just lifts himself, and with his hand seems to say: Stop! To the left, Amélie, Oscar, the gentlemen of the court who have removed their masks and who are pale, in their costumes and with terror on their faces. At the back, the other people from the ball grouped variously and trying to glimpse the features of the king. Everywhere there is disorder, confusion:

67. A similar effect is created at the end of Scribe and Auber's earlier collaboration, *La muette de Portici* (1828). See Sarah Hibberd, "*La muette* and Her Context," in *The Cambridge Companion to Grand Opera*, ed. David Charlton (Cambridge: Cambridge University Press, 2004), 149–67.

68. Schneider tells us that Auber had to complete the last three acts after rehearsals had begun. "*Gustave III, ou Le bal masqué,*" in *The New Grove Dictionary of Opera*, ed. Stanley Sadie, (London: Macmillan, 1992), 2:584. It seems likely that cuts were made during this process, with most of the extra words not having been set at all. Later editions of the libretto retain the original, lengthier text.

69. In *grand opéra*, the individual is still an essential: as Michelet practiced in his own history writing, "Social will [is] refracted through the individual lives which built sociality." Crossley, *French Historians and Romanticism*, 192. This idea is also central to Pottinger, "Staging of History."

70. Its continuation, although signaled in the stage directions, does not appear in the published score. This example of an impressionistic description of the chaos rather than an accurate description of what happened is typical of the mises-en-scènes of the period.

and in the other rooms where the news has not yet reached, the distant sound of joyful instruments, while the orchestra at the front sounds a lugubrious and funereal rumbling.[71]

Writing in 1831, a moment of profound crisis in French spiritual life, Michelet asserted that the modern self, in order to rediscover its wholeness, required the support of history as a guarantor of meaning.[72] With *Gustave III,* Auber, Scribe, and their collaborators provided a message from the past that spoke to everyone, whatever their political views, but that also helped to expiate the events of the Revolution and especially the Terror by tapping into personal and collective memories, disrupting the predetermined and linear approach to history writing, and suggesting the pull of the moment. In the ball scene, with its sense of self-propulsion, drawing in participants and audience alike, containing past and present, the political was arguably transfigured as spectacle. It crystallized the struggle between a need to distance oneself from the past—to forget it or to make it other—and a desire to identify with and embrace a variety of pasts and their connections with the present in order to move forward. It also encapsulated the contradiction between overloaded remembrance of the past through allusions and carnivalesque delirium of forgetting everything but the present moment. The conclusion of the opera suggests that, foreshadowing Michelet's *L'histoire de la révolution française,* the ball scene offered "the chance to pass through multiplicity and succession to oneness and eternity."[73]

But more than that, opera has a nonreferential aspect, a purely aesthetic dimension.[74] Right from its premiere, the ball scene offered so many parallels with events in various past and present geographical, social, and political spaces, blurring fact with

71. "Les grenadiers qui portent Gustave sur leurs fusils croisés se mettent lentement en marche et se dirigent vers l'escalier de granit, précédés de domestiques qui tiennent des torches: c'est là le groupe principal. À droite, Ankastrom et les conjurés, sur lesquels des soldats ont dirigé la pointe de leurs baïonnettes; Gustave se soulève à peine, et de la main semble leur dire: Arrêtez!—À gauche, Amélie, Oscar, les seigneurs de la cour qui ont ôté leurs masques et qui sont pâles, en habit de fête et la terreur sur le visage.—Au fond, les autres personnes du bal différemment groupées et cherchant à apercevoir les traits du roi. Partout le désordre, la confusion: et dans les autres salles où la nouvelle n'est pas encore parvenue, le son lointain des instruments joyeux, tandis que sur le devant l'orchestre fait entendre un roulement lugubre et funèbre." Scribe, *Gustave III,* act 5, scene 5.

72. Michelet, *Introduction à l'histoire universelle.* This view of history was developed in his *Précis de l'histoire de France* (Paris: Hachette, 1833), and through *Histoire de France,* 17 vols. (Paris: Hachette and Chamerot, 1833–67). See also Crossley, *French Historians and Romanticism,* 197–200.

73. Crossley, *French Historians and Romanticism,* 243.

74. James Treadwell elaborates on this idea in the context of modern stagings in "Reading and Staging Again," *Cambridge Opera Journal* 10, no. 2 (1998): 205–20. This article was a response to David Levin, "Reading a Staging/Staging a Reading," *Cambridge Opera Journal* 9, no. 1 (1997): 47–71. Treadwell makes the point that meanings which gather around an interpretation are not

fiction and experience with imagination, that it ultimately confused all boundaries, buckling under the burden of suggestion and prompting its transfiguration as "pure" spectacle in the present. It is precisely this explosion of specific, self-consciously detailed references into wonderment that clinches the historical experience, undercutting the idea of determinism and order. This approach can be viewed as a defining characteristic of Scribe and Auber's aesthetic, one rooted in the ways of thinking about the Revolution and its aftermath at the beginning of the July Monarchy exemplified by Michelet. Aestheticizing can here be understood as a political act: with *Gustave III* opera made history triumphantly in its own image.

---

necessarily related to directorial intention or to a critical conception of what the work is about in the abstract.

Analyzing Mise-en-Scène

HALÉVY'S *LA JUIVE* AT THE SALLE LE PELETIER

Arnold Jacobshagen

Opera is a multimedia art, and thus the character of an individual work cannot be reduced simply to the fixed form of the notated score or the libretto. This has led recent musicological scholarship to focus increasingly on a broader range of sources for the study of operas of earlier periods, including materials relating to their performances. How these sources contribute to our understanding of opera can be seen, for example, in the Rossini complete edition. Thus, Elizabeth Bartlet's edition of Rossini's last opera, *Guillaume Tell*, contains—in addition to the four-volume score and a critical commentary—an edition of the various versions of the libretto, a separate volume on the iconography of the staging in Paris in 1829, and, finally, an edition of the (ostensibly) original Parisian staging manual. This broadening of editorial principles to include collections of somewhat heterogeneous texts and images in the context of a composer's *opera omnia* exposes issues all too often ignored in editions of operas and other works, where the score is usually seen a priori as the sole carrier of textual substance.

Even the notion of historically informed performances of nineteenth-century opera—which is extending its reach to the works of Wagner and Verdi—continues to focus primarily on the interpretation of the score. Yet from the nineteenth century on, if not before, the staging of an opera was always an integral aspect of a work, whose character and individuality were realized only by way of decisions made in the performative arena (costumes, scenery, staging, etc.) in conformance to a unifying artistic concept. It has long been accepted that Richard Wagner's idea of the *Gesamtkunstwerk* allocates a key role to staging; more recently, scholars have shown the degree to

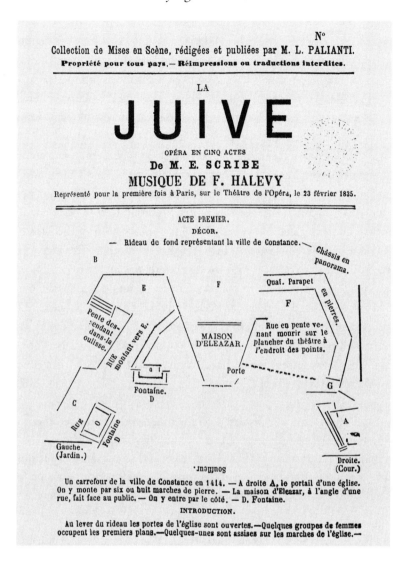

LA

JUIVE

OPÉRA EN CINQ ACTES

De M. E. SCRIBE

MUSIQUE DE F. HALEVY

Représenté pour la première fois à Paris, sur le Théâtre de l'Opéra, le 23 février 1835.

ACTE PREMIER.

DÉCOR.

— Rideau de fond représentant la ville de Constance. —

Châssis en panorama.

B

E F Quai. Parapet

en pierres.

Pente descendant dans la coulisse.

RUE montant vers E.

MAISON D'ELEAZAR.

F

Rue en pente venant mourir sur le plancher du théâtre à l'endroit des points.

Porte

G

Fontaine. D

C

Rue

Fontaine D

A

Gauche. (Jardin.)

Souffleur.

Droite. (Cour.)

Un carrefour de la ville de Constance en 1414. — A droite **A**, le portail d'une église. On y monte par six ou huit marches de pierre. — La maison d'Eléazar, à l'angle d'une rue, fait face au public. — On y entre par le côté. — D. Fontaine.

INTRODUCTION.

Au lever du rideau les portes de l'église sont ouvertes. — Quelques groupes de femmes occupent les premiers plans. — Quelques-unes sont assises sur les marches de l'église. —

FIGURE 8.1. Title page of Louis Palianti's mise-en-scène for *La juive*. The three-dimensional scenery does not correspond to the original production of 1835 and is reminiscent of later staging practices. Bibliothèque Historique de la Ville de Paris. Photograph by the author.

which Giuseppe Verdi from the 1860s onward sought to influence every detail of a production of his work. This intense desire on the part of both Wagner and Verdi for complete control over all musical and scenic aspects of their operas shares a historical precedent: both composers were profoundly influenced by their decades-long engagement with Parisian *grand opéra* as the first form of music drama to develop a modern concept of musical staging while at the same time enjoying ideal conditions in terms of financial support, personnel, and stage technology. The practice in Paris of producing so-called *livrets de mise en scène* provides us with a remarkable set of sources on staging whose relevance for the historical reconstruction and the musicodramaturgical analysis of the works with which they are concerned is no longer in dispute.

The Parisian staging manuals have long been regarded as indispensable sources for the reconstruction of nineteenth-century French opera. H. Robert Cohen, in the late 1970s, was the first scholar to awaken musicological interest in these sources. Since then Cohen has published many important articles, facsimile editions, and, together with Marie-Odile Gigou, a catalog of the collection of *livrets de mise en scène* at the Bibliothèque de l'Association de la régie théâtrale in Paris.[1] As early as 1978 Cohen described these manuals as "a permanent documentation of the staging in order to allow exact reproduction in the case of a reprise,"[2] and in 1991 he concluded that opera direction was characterized by the continuous conservation of the original staging from the Paris premieres: "Staging in Paris and the French provinces throughout the nineteenth century and well into the twentieth was an art of preservation rather than creation. *Régisseurs* strove to conserve, to the extent possible, the original *mise en scène* of an opera's premiere as transcribed in the production book. Staging, in a word, was *not* intended to be altered."[3] Recent scholars on Paris opera, such as Rebecca Susan Wilberg, Karin Pendle, Stephen Wilkins, and Cormac Newark, have fully endorsed Cohen's assumptions and have emphasized the importance of the staging manuals. According to Wilberg,

> the value of these manuals was based on the nineteenth-century aesthetic of considering the entire work in all its facets—music, libretto, and staging—as part of an integral whole. It was assumed that the general scenic design, positioning of characters and sets, and blocking of the original performance would be followed exactly in all subsequent productions, both at the Opéra and elsewhere.[4]

1. H. Robert Cohen, "On the Reconstruction of the Visual Elements of French Grand Opéra," in *International Musicological Society: Report of the Twelfth Congress, Berkeley 1977*, ed. Daniel Heartz and Bonnie Wade (Kassel: Bärenreiter, 1981), 463–80; Cohen, "La conservation de la tradition scénique sur la scène lyrique en France au XIXe siècle," *Revue de musicologie* 64 (1978): 253–68; Cohen, "On Preparing Critical Studies of the Original 'mise en scène' of Nineteenth-Century Operas," in *Opera & Libretto*, vol. 2, ed. Gianfranco Folena, Maria Teresa Muraro, and Giovanni Morelli (Florence: Leo Olschki, 1993), 215–24; Cohen, *The Original Staging Manuals for Twelve Parisian Operatic Premières/Douze livrets de mise en scène lyrique datant des créations parisiennes* (Stuyvesant, NY: Pendragon Press, 1991); and Cohen, *Cent ans de mise lyrique en France (environ 1830–1930): Catalogue descriptif des livrets de mise en scène, des libretti annotés et des partitions annotées dans la Bibl. de l'Association de la régie théâtrale (Paris)* (New York: Pendragon Press, 1986).

2. "Enregistrements permanents de la mise en scène en vue de la reconstitution exacte lors de la reprise de l'œuvre." Cohen, "La conservation," 253.

3. Cohen, *Original Staging Manuals* (1991), xxiii.

4. Rebecca Susan Wilberg, "The 'Mise en Scène' at the Paris Opéra, Salle Le Peletier (1821–1873) and the Staging of the First French 'Grand Opéra': Meyerbeer's *Robert le Diable*" (Ph.D. diss., Brigham Young University, 1990), 9.

More recently, Newark went so far as to state that "in the nineteenth century, libretto and music (i.e. those parts of opera musicology has traditionally sought to pin down in critical editions) were both more likely to change in the later stages of production and re-production than set and costumes."[5]

In an earlier article I expressed some reservations about the supposed perpetuity of the original staging.[6] Based on the observation that the *livret* for Daniel François Esprit Auber's *Fra Diavolo* (1830) reproduced in facsimile in Cohen's anthology could not possibly be a document from the 1830s, I have compared this source with others and tried to demonstrate that the staging of this work underwent continual changes during its more than eight hundred performances at the Opéra-Comique. In the present article I will reconsider the function of stage-direction books, focusing on *grand opéra* and the staging of Fromental Halévy's *La juive* (1835).[7]

The production book by Louis Palianti for *La juive* is included in Cohen's first facsimile edition of staging manuals and presented as "the original mise en scène" of 1835 (see fig. 8.1).[8] Karin Pendle and Stephen Wilkins, who have analyzed parts of the document, assert that it was published in the year of the first performance.[9] Cormac Newark, in his 1999 Oxford dissertation on the staging of *grand opéra*, as well as in a recent article on the mise-en-scène of *La juive*, tried to situate the document even more precisely and claimed that it was published "some time after the final dress rehearsal, owing to the absence of what were originally planned as the first two scenes of Act III, cut before the official first night."[10]

Nevertheless, the document has to be dated quite differently: in fact, as will be shown in the following, Palianti's *livret* was published more than thirty years after the premiere of *La juive*. The first clear evidence is given in the second line of the title page: the modern copyright statement ("Rights for all countries—reprinting or translation not permitted" [Propriété pour tous pays.—Réimpressions ou traductions

---

5. Cormac Newark, "Staging Grand Opéra: History and the Imagination in Nineteenth-Century Paris" (Ph.D. diss., Oxford University, 1999), 25.

6. Arnold Jacobshagen, "Staging at the Opéra-Comique in Nineteenth-Century Paris: Auber's *Fra Diavolo* and the *livrets de mise en scène*," *Cambridge Opera Journal* 13, no. 3 (2001): 239–60.

7. On *La juive*, see Diana R. Hallman, *Opera, Liberalism, and Antisemitism in Nineteenth-Century France: The Politics of Halévy's "La Juive"* (Cambridge: Cambridge University Press, 2002); Fromental Halévy, *La juive*, vol. 100 of *L'avant-scène opéra* (1987); Karl Leich-Galland, ed., *Fromental Halévy: "La juive"; Dossier de presse parisienne (1835)* (Saarbrücken: L. Galland, 1987).

8. L[ouis] Palianti, comp., *Collection de mises en scène, "La juive": Opéra en cinq actes de M. E. Scribe, musique de F. Halévy; Représenté pour la première fois à Paris, sur le Théâtre de l'Opéra, le 23 février 1835* ([Paris]: The author, [c. 1868]). Also reprinted in Cohen, *Original Staging Manuals* (1991), 137–50.

9. Karin Pendle and Stephen Wilkins, "Paradise Found: The Salle le Peletier and French Grand Opera," in *Opera in Context: Essays on Historical Staging from the Late Renaissance to the Time of Puccini*, ed. Mark A. Radice (Portland, OR: Amadeus, 1998), 190 n. 60.

10. Cormac Newark, "Ceremony, Celebration, and Spectacle in *La juive*," in *Reading Critics Reading*, ed. Roger Parker and Mary Ann Smart (Oxford: Oxford University Press, 2001), 181–82; Newark, "Staging Grand Opéra," 167.

TITRES DE QUELQUES MISES EN SCÈNES

RÉDIGÉES

PAR M. L. PALIANTI.

Envoyer par la poste, à M. L. PALIANTI, un mandat de *cinq, six, neuf, douze* ou *quinze francs*, et courrier par courrier, la Mise en Scène demandée est expédiée. — MM. les correspondans se chargent également, sur demande, de faire parvenir, franc de port, ces Mises en Scène.—Il ne reste plus que *deux* exemplaires complets des cinq premiers volumes, contenant 85 ouvrages ou 240 actes. Le prix des cinq volumes complets est de 250 fr.

GRANDS OPÉRAS ET TRADUCTIONS.

La Muette de Portici (manuscrit)....	5 actes.
Les Huguenots.............id.........	5 id.
Guido et Ginevra.........id.........	5 id.
Les Martyrs..............id.........	5 id.
Robert-le-Diable.........id.........	5 id.
Guillaume Tell...........id.........	4 id.
Le Siège de Corinthe................	4 id.
Le Juif errant......................	5 id.
Gustave III...... (manuscrit).......	5 id.
Le Siège de Corinthe ..id...........	3 id.
La Favorite.........................	3 id.
Dom Sébastien.......................	5 id.
L'Âme en Peine......................	2 id.
Le Prophète.........................	5 id.
La Reine de Chypre..................	5 id.
Le Juif Errant......................	5 id.
L'Enfant Prodigue (manuscrit).......	5 id.
Charles VI...........id.............	5 id.
L'Eau Merveilleuse..................	2 id.
Le Naufrage de la Méduse............	3 id.
La Chaste Suzanne...................	4 id.
Norma...............................	3 id.
Une Aventure de Scaramouche.........	3 id.
Robert d'Evereux....................	3 id.
Niza de Grenade.....................	3 id.
Linda de Chamouni...................	3 id.
Don Pasquale........................	3 id.
Maria Padilla.......................	3 id.

OPÉRAS COMIQUES.

Lestocq............(manuscrit)..	3 actes.
Fra-Diavolo.............id.........	3 id.
Zampa...................id.........	3 id.
La Fiancée..............id.........	3 id.
Marguerite..............id.........	3 id.
La Figurante............id.........	3 id.
Le Cheval de Bronze.....id.........	3 id.
Les Deux Nuits..........id.........	3 id.
L'Ambassadrice..........id.........	3 id.
La Double Échelle.......id.........	3 id.
Le Perruquier de la Régence id.....	3 id.
L'An mil................id.........	3 id.
Le Brasseur de Preston..............	3 id.
La Dame d'Honneur...................	3 id.
La Mantille.........................	1 id.
Régine..............................	2 id.
Le Planteur.........................	2 id.
Polichinelle........................	1 id.
Les Treize..........................	3 id.
La Reine d'un Jour..................	3 id.
La Symphonie........................	1 id.
Les Travestissemens.................	1 id.
La Fille du Régiment................	2 id.
Carline.............................	3 id.
La Perruche.........................	1 id.
L'Élève de Presbourg	1 id.
Zanetta.............................	3 id.
Le Cent Suisse......................	1 id.
Le Guittarrero......................	3 id.
Les Deux Voleurs....................	1 id.
Frère et Mari.......................	1 id.
La Main de Fer......................	3 id.
Mlle de Mérange.....................	1 id.
Le Code Noir........................	3 id.
Les Dix.............................	1 id.
Le Roi d'Yvetot.....................	3 id.
La Part du Diable...................	3 id.
Le Puits d'Amour....................	3 id.
Lambert Symnel......................	3 id.
Mina................................	3 id.
Cagliostro..........................	3 id.
La Sirène...........................	3 id.

L'Esclave de Camoens................	1 actes.
Les Deux Gentilshommes..............	1 id.
Les Mousquetaires de la Reine.......	3 id.
Le Trompette de M. le Prince........	1 id.
Le Caquet du Couvent................	1 id.
Gibby la Cornemuse..................	3 id.
Ne Touchez pas à la Reine...........	3 id.
Le Bouquet de l'Infante.............	3 id.
Gastibelza..........................	3 id.
Haydée..............................	3 id.
Gille Ravisseur.....................	1 id.
Il Signor Pascarello................	3 id.
Le Caïd.............................	2 id.
Les Monténégrins....................	3 id.
La Fée aux Roses....................	3 id.
Le Val d'Andore.....................	3 id.
Le Moulin des Tilleuls..............	1 id.
Giralda.............................	2 id.
Les Porcherons......................	3 id.
Le Songe d'une Nuit d'Été...........	3 id.
La Chanteuse Voilée.................	1 id.
La Dame de Pique....................	3 id.
Bonsoir, M. Pantalon................	1 id.
Raymond ou le Secret de la Reine....	3 id.
Mosquita la Sorcière	3 id.
Le Carillonneur de Bruges	3 id.
Galathée............................	1 id.
La Croix de Marie...................	3 id.
Madelon.............................	3 id.
Le Père Gaillard....................	2 id.
Le Paysan...........................	1 id.
Marco Spada.........................	3 id.
Les Noces de Jeannette..............	1 id.
La Tonelli..........................	2 id.
Le Sourd............................	3 id.
Le Nabab............................	3 id.
Colette.............................	3 id.
Les Papillotes de M. Benoist	1 id.
L'Étoile du Nord....................	3 id.
Les Trovatelles.....................	1 id.
Les Sabots de la Marquise...........	1 id.
Le Chien du Jardinier...............	1 id.

DRAMES ET COMÉDIES.

Ruy-Blas............................	5 actes.
Claude Stoeq........................	5 id.
Le Naufrage de la Méduse............	5 id.
Le Verre d'Eau......................	5 id.
Les deux Serruriers.................	5 id.
Les Pontons.........................	5 id.
Une Chaîne..........................	5 id.
Mademoiselle de Belle-Isle..........	5 id.
La Main droite et la Main gauche....	5 id.
La Folie de la Cité.................	5 id.
Les Mousquetaires...................	5 id.
Clarisse Harlow.....................	3 id.
Les Ennemis de la maison	3 id.

VAUDEVILLES, ETC.

Lekain à Draguignan.................	1 actes.
Maurice.............................	2 id.
Ninon, Manon et Maintenon...........	3 id.
La Canaille.........................	3 id.
Phœbus..............................	3 id.
Amandine............................	1 id.
Les Premières armes de Richelieu....	2 id.
Louisette...........................	2 id.
Le Chevalier du Guet................	2 id.
La Grâce de Dieu....................	5 id.
Les Mémoires du Diable..............	5 id.
L'homme blasé.......................	2 id.
L'Amour dans tous les quartiers.....	3 id.

FIGURE 8.2. An advertisement for Louis Palianti's *Collection de mises en scène*. Besides printed editions, the theater agent offered manuscript copies for some major works dating from the 1820s and 1830s. *La juive* was not in his collection until the 1860s, neither printed nor in manuscript. Bibliothèque-musée de l'Opéra. Bibliothèque nationale de France.

TABLE 8.1. Performances of *La juive* in Paris at the
Salle Le Peletier

Year	Number of performances	Year	Number of performances
1835	46	1855	20
1836	12	1856	8
1837	14	1857	6
1838	9	1858	8
1839	13	1859	9
1840	11	1860	8
1841	13	1861	3
1842	12	1862	18
1843	9	1863	12
1844	8	1864	9
1845	9	1865	–
1846	9	1866	15
1847	8	1867	4
1848	8	1868	13
1849	7	1869	5
1850	–	1870	–
1851	9	1871	5
1852	3	1872	14
1853	–	1873	15
1854	–		

interdites]) is not to be found in any issue of the *Collection de mises en scène* published before 1868.[11] A further proof for the late publication of the *livret* can be found in Palianti's various catalogs, printed on the back pages of many issues of his series: at least until the 1860s, these advertising blurbs simply don't mention any mise-en-scène for *La juive* (see fig. 8.2). In fact, the *livret* of *La juive* was one of the last mise-en-scènes that Palianti ever published—presumably around 1868, when he apparently used the new copyright statement for the first time, but certainly before 1870, when the *livret* entered the Bibliothèque Nationale, five years before Palianti's death. It would therefore correspond to the production mounted between 1866 and 1873, when *La juive* was staged for the last time at the Salle Le Peletier (see table 8.1).

11. Among the issues of Palianti's *Collection de mises en scène,* only four titles bear this mention: David's *Mademoiselle Sylvia,* first performed in 1868, *dépôt legal* at the Bibliothèque Nationale in 1868; Auber's *Le premier jour de bonheur,* first performed in 1868, *dépôt légal* in 1868; Halévy's *La juive,* first performed in 1835, *dépôt légal* in 1870; Méhul's *Joseph,* first performed in 1807, *dépôt légal* unknown.

A more accurate transcription of the original staging of *La juive* than the one by Palianti is the mise-en-scène published by the Bureau de Commission Théâtrale of the former stage director Louis Vieillard Duverger, presumably not long after the premiere in 1835 (see fig. 8.3).[12] Astonishingly, no scholar on *La juive* has taken this staging manual into account.[13] There are some peculiarities also in the title of this document, such as the music's being attributed to Auber instead of Halévy, who was still—at least in the eyes of theater agents and stage directors in the provinces—a relatively unknown composer in 1835, just before his first major success with *La juive*. The surviving publications by Duverger all follow the same layout: they consist of only two pages printed on both sides, in quarto, divided into two columns, and separated into individual chapters: *mouvemens de scène, decorations, costumes,* and *accessoires.* The price for one mise-en-scène was fairly high (6 francs), which might be the reason many more manuscript copies than original prints have survived. Duverger's stage manuals were always accompanied by separate pictures of scenery (see fig. 8.4) and costumes.

The question of the dating of production documentation would be of less significance if the assumption about productions being preserved as exactly as possible for as long as possible were true. If we compare Duverger's indications carefully with the other sources of the opera's premiere, there can be little doubt that they correspond to the *La juive* of 1835, whereas Palianti's indications, as we will see, do not. To start with the front page of the Palianti booklet, the most astonishing difference concerns the scenery, which corresponds neither to the indications given in the libretto, nor to the illustrations from act 1 that we know (see fig. 8.5).[14] Eugène Scribe's libretto unmistakably indicates: "On the right, the entrance of a church. On the left, the jewelry shop."[15].

The illustration furnished by Duverger demonstrates exactly this disposition (see fig. 8.4). In Palianti's mise-en-scène, on the other hand, the house of Eléazar is located right in the center of the stage. What is more, the decoration described in Palianti not only consists of a painted canvas on a substage chariot running the width of the stage, but is a three-dimensional structure with considerable depth, occupying several sections of the stage. (This has serious consequences for the cortège at the end of act 1, when the stage is filled with horses and hundreds of people.) The scenery depicted by Palianti offers a multilevel playing area, making extensive use of the so-

---

12. L[ouis]-V[ieillard] Duverger, *Mise en scène et décorations de "La juive": Grand opéra en cinq actes, paroles de M. Scribe, musique de M. Auber [sic]; Représenté à l'Académie Royale de Musique, le 23 Février 1835* ([Paris]: Bureau de Commission Théâtrale, [c. 1835]). On Duverger, see Jacobshagen, "Staging at the Opéra-Comique," 245.

13. A copy of Duverger's publication, however, is to be found at *F-Pn,* 4° Yf. 614 (40*bis*).

14. The most prominent illustration is a coloured lithograph by Cicéri. See Catherine Join-Diéterle, *Les décors de scène de l'Opéra de Paris à l'époque Romantique* (Paris: Picard, 1988), 37.

15. "À droite du spectateur, le portail d'une église. À gauche, à l'angle d'une rue, la boutique d'un orfèvre joaillier." Eugène Scribe, *Théâtre complet,* 2nd ed. (Paris: A. André, 1835), 14:387.

L.-V. Duverger,

Bureau de Commission Théâtrale, rue Rameau, n° 6.

MISE EN SCÈNE ET DÉCORATIONS
DE
LA JUIVE,

Grand opéra en cinq Actes, Paroles de M. Scribe, Musique de M. Auber,

REPRÉSENTÉ A L'ACADÉMIE ROYALE DE MUSIQUE, LE 23 FÉVRIER 1835.

Le prix des 5 Planches lithogr. et coloriées, représentant les décorations, est de 28 fr.; 15 Costumes, Personnages et divers ornemens coloriés : 6 fr.; Mise en Scène 6 fr.; total 40 fr.

MOUVEMENS DE SCÈNE.

ACTE PREMIER.
Scène Ire.

Au lever du rideau, les fidèles sont agenouillés près et devant le grand portique de l'église, à droite du public, 1er plan; hommes, femmes et enfants entendent l'office; on voit, çà et là, se promener dans les rues quelques personnes.

Après le 1er chœur, les fidèles se lèvent et emplissent le théâtre. Éléazar, donnant le bras à Rachel, sa fille, rentre chez lui (à gauche du public), se dirigeant d'abord sur l'avant-scène gauche du public, et passant à travers la foule.

Albert, sergent des gardes, a vu dans le fond un homme rôder du côté de la maison du Juif; il l'aborde et reconnaît en lui le prince Léopold, déguisé en homme du peuple. La scène est alors :

Scène II.

Peuple tout au fond.

1.	2.
LÉOPOLD.	ALBERT.
(Souffleur.)	

Lorsqu'on a entendu dans l'église, à droite du public, le *Te Deum laudamus*, tous deux s'éloignent vers le côté gauche du fond.

Les chœurs, le peuple rentrent en scène par toutes les coulisses. Les fidèles qui étaient dans l'église sortent et traversent de droite à gauche; on voit des dames de haute condition vêtues de leurs longues robes de soie, coiffées de hauts bonnets pointus à la cauchoise avec voile; quelques petits pages portent le bas de leurs robes. Hommes, femmes et enfants de toutes conditions regagnent leurs logis.

Ce mouvement achevé, Ruggiero, magistrat, enveloppé de son long manteau en velours noir et couvert de son chaperon noir, suivi de deux officiers et de l'officier crieur, arrive du fond et vient lire au peuple la proclamation touchant les fêtes que l'empereur donne.

Le principal crieur monte sur les marches de la fontaine, à gauche du public, 1er plan, au son de la trompette; et même roulement de tambours au lointain. La proclamation lue, le peuple se livre à la joie (chœur), quand on entend très distinctement le bruit en mesure des ouvriers ciseleurs chez le Juif Éléazar. Surprise de Ruggiero et du peuple.

Scène III.

Mouvement. Deux gardes qui étaient au fond, suivis du peuple, se sont fait ouvrir la porte du Juif, qu'ils tirent de chez lui. Rachel le suit tout éplorée; on les menace. La position de la scène est alors :

Peuple.	Deux gardes.	Habitans.
Femmes.	Le crieur.	Femmes.
1.	2.	3.
ÉLÉAZAR.	RACHEL.	RUGGIERO.

Après le motif du chœur et de continuelles menaces envers le Juif et Rachel, on voit d'autres personnes sortir du temple; on leur fait place et on aperçoit le cardinal Brogni, revêtu de son chapeau rouge et manteau écarlate herminé, suivi d'un ou deux pages, de deux ou trois autres cardinaux, de deux évêques avec robe, camaille violet et rochet; ils descendent les marches du portail de l'église. Après ces entrées la position de scène est :

Peuple.		Habitans.		Femmes.
Deux gardes.				Évêques.
				Cardinaux.
1.		2.	3.	4.
RACHEL.		ÉLÉAZAR.	BROGNI.	RUGGIERO.

À ces mots: *Sois libre, Éléazar!* le cardinal s'est rapproché

de lui, ensuite Rachel est venue derrière Éléazar, près du cardinal, pendant son air: *Si la rigueur et la vengeance*, etc.

À la fin de son air, le cardinal sort par la gauche du public, suivi des évêques et des cardinaux, de Ruggiero et de la foule qui les suit et se disperse à droite et à gauche.

Scène IV.

Tandis que le Juif reconduit sa fille en sa maison, on voit sortir un ouvrier portant un portefeuille et se retirant avec Éléazar par le 3e plan, à droite du public.

La scène reste vide une seconde.

Scène V.

On voit au fond le prince Léopold, toujours déguisé; près de lui un domestique portant une mandoline, que Léopold prend pour chanter sa romance. Après la romance, le domestique reprend l'instrument et s'esquive. Rachel sort de chez elle.

Scène VI.

1.	2.
RACHEL.	LÉOPOLD.

À la fin de leur duo et de leur scène, Léopold, la remettant sur le seuil de sa porte, à gauche du public, lui dit adieu et sort par la gauche, 3e plan. Aussitôt Rachel a saisi le bras de sa servante et est sortie par la droite du public, 3e plan, ou par la gauche.

On entend le tintement des cloches; les chœurs d'hommes entrent gaiment en scène, joyeux preuve d'une joie délirante. Chaque homme porte sa petite cruche pour puiser le vin coulant de la fontaine, à gauche du public, 1er plan. Les uns ont des bouteilles de terre cuite, d'autres des vases, des gobelets de métal.

Chœur brillant, animé, devant être chanté par de bonnes voix et des acteurs et choristes intelligents. Durant ce chœur, ils se précipitent les uns et les autres vers la fontaine et reviennent rapidement en ligne pour répéter : *Du vin, du vin, du vin.*

Vers la moitié de ce chœur, un buveur a laissé sa cruche au pied d'un habitant qui est à la fontaine; en y revenant, il voit qu'on s'en est emparé; il se fâche et menace; une querelle violente est sur le point de s'engager lorsque le motif du chœur revient. Cette pantomime doit être exécutée avec intelligence. Les dames du chœur, qui s'étaient tenues dans le fond, reviennent vers la fin du chœur, et, dans les théâtres où il y a un ballet, les femmes vont inviter leurs maris à danser avec elles.

Divers pas de danse et d'ensemble (1).

On aperçoit ensuite dans le lointain, vers le fond, à gauche du public, des habitants accourant, élevant leurs toques, leurs chaperons, s'écriant : *Noël, le cortège s'avance.* Grande joie parmi le chœur, annonçant la marche du cortège impérial. En ce moment, Éléazar et Rachel reparaissent dans la foule, descendent en scène par la droite du public, et se placent sur les marches de l'église, à droite du public, comme prêts à y entrer. Sur ces entrefaites, Ruggiero et deux gardes sont rentrés en scène et, saisis d'horreur en voyant le Juif et sa fille aux portes du temple, courent sur eux; on sépare Éléazar de sa fille, on menace de le jeter au lac; Rachel éplorée, tâche d'intéresser cette foule, lorsque Léopold avance, se fait connaître aux gardes, dont une seconde était arrivée du fond, et ordonne qu'on les rende libres, à ces mots: *Lâchez fuyez, tous.* Après l'action de ce morceau d'ensemble, le son des trompettes se fait entendre. Les chœurs courent au fond, au-devant du cortège dont

(1) La danse pourra facilement se passer dans les théâtres où il n'y a point de ballot.

FIGURE 8.3. Title page of Louis Vieillard Duverger's mise-en-scène for *La juive*, on which the music of this brand-new opera is erroneously attributed to Auber instead of Halévy—a clear hint that the document was conceived for immediate practical use rather than for permanent conservation. *F-Pn*, 4° Yf. 614 (40 *bis*). Bibliothèque nationale de France.

FIGURE 8.4. Scenery of act 1 of *La juive* as depicted by Duverger's mise-en-scène and corresponding to the indications given in the libretto. Bibliothèque nationale de France.

called *praticables,* platforms on which actors could stand and move, such as ramps, staircases, and so on. And Palianti demands a rounded panorama drop instead of a flat one at the back of the stage, a device not to be found in any of Palianti's *livrets scéniques* published before the late 1860s and hence another clear indication that this cannot be considered the "original mise-en-scène."

With regard to the setting of act 1 and the procession at the end of it, Duverger's description of scenery indicates the "prospect of a grand square with adjacent streets. The city of Constance is in the back, with its gothic monuments and churches; left to the public, second *plan,* the house of Eléazar. *Nota.*—Give the complete width and depths of the stage."[16] The procession starts at the back of the stage, from the left side as seen by the public, and slowly advances on the other side to the front of the stage, where it moves again to the left. At the same time as the cortège starts, the chorus moves to both wings of the theater, thus taking the position that has been

16. "Vue d'une grande place et rue adjacentes. La ville de Constance forme le lointain: on voit ses monuments gothiques, ses églises; un peu à la gauche du public, 2e plan, le logis d'Éléazar. NOTA.—Donner toute la largeur et toute la profondeur possibles au théâtre pour que le cortège, au final, se déploie somptueusement. Le défilé commence par le fond, à gauche du public, et fait la tour." Duverger, *Mise en scène,* 3.

FIGURE 8.5. *La juive,* finale of act 1; colored lithograph by Pierre Luc Charles Cicéri. Bibliothèque-Musée de l'Opéra. Bibliothèque nationale de France.

---

standard for choruses since the time of Lully:[17] "The chorus members rush backward to the cortège, of which only the front is seen; all the chorus members assemble along the wings."[18]

According to Palianti's indication, however, the scene is quite different: "The procession starts from the back left F, moves on toward the audience, turns left, and continues down the street E."[19] Because half of the stage's depth is occupied by a three-dimensional stage picture, there is not as much space for the cortège as in the original mise-en-scène. Why was the depth of the stage reduced in the later production? There is one obvious reason for this very important change: the implausibility of the perspective that the earlier version offered. It seems that after some time, spectators got used to the splendor of costumes and coats of armor, and they started to perceive shortcomings in other respects. One of the greatest problems with the original staging was the fact that the masses of armed people destroyed the illusion

17. See Lois Rosow, "Performing a Choral Dialogue by Lully," *Early Music* 15 (1987): 325–35.

18. "Les chœurs courent au fond, au-devant du cortège dont la tête se voit; et là commence le défilé du cortège; tous les chœurs se rangent aux ailes." Duverger, *Mise en scène,* 1–2.

19. "Le cortège part du fond gauche F, descend face au public, fait par le flanc gauche et continue sa marche par la rue E." Palianti, *Collection de mises en scène,* 5.

of the painted scenery to the rear of the stage. If most critics were enthusiastic about the staging in the beginning, they became more and more skeptical after a while. Very telling in this respect are Henri Trianon's remarks about the painting in theatrical scenery from 1836, one year after the premiere: "Isn't it absurd to see, in *La juive,* men on horseback at the same height as the second floor of these awkwardly sketched carton houses on the scenery, where everything seems to be calculated to spoil the impression and the spectacle of the cortège?"[20]

A harsh sentence, indeed, on a production that is reported to have been one of the most splendid ever seen at the Paris opera! Notwithstanding this, there was only one possible solution for this problem, and it is exactly the solution described in Palianti's manual: the masses were arranged in front of buildings of proportionate dimensions, which therefore had to be closer to the spectators. Let us have a look at the detailed description of the cortège in the two *livrets.* According to Duverger, the procession consisted of thirteen groups of people preceding the entrance of Cardinal Brogni and, finally, Emperor Sigismond:

1. The trumpeters.
2. The standard-bearer.
3. The crossbowmen.
4. The diverse guilds, with a standard-bearer each.
5. Soldiers.
6. Heralds-at-arms.
7. The cardinal's trumpeters, his standards with two crosses.
8. The members of the council.
9. Three bishops and their crucifers.
10. Their domestics.
11. Four cardinals.
12. Five pages bearing the signs on cushions.
13. Twelve guards of the council.

Then the cardinal Brogni, on horseback, under a baldachin carried by four officers and followed by his gentlemen; finally the emperor, on horseback, followed by his armed officers.[21]

---

20. "N'est-il pas absurde de voir dans *La juive,* les hommes à cheval de niveau avec le deuxième étage de ces maisons de carton, si maladroitement jetées sur la scène, où tout semble déjà avoir été calculé pour gêner le déploiement et les évolutions du cortège qui va passer." Henri Trianon, "De la peinture en décoration théâtrale," *Revue du théâtre* 7 (1836): 5, quoted in Join-Diéterle, *Les décors de scène,* 188.

21. "1. Les sonneurs de trompe. 2. Les porte-bannières. 3. Les arbaletiers. 4. Les Corporations diverses, chacune une bannière. 5. Hommes d'armes. 6. Hérauts. 7. Sonneurs du cardinal, ses bannières aux deux croix. 8. Les membres du concile. 9. Trois évêques, leurs porte-croix. 10. Leurs domestiques. 11. Quatre cardinaux. 12. Cinq pages portant les insignes sur des coussins. 13. Douze gardes du concile. Ensuite le cardinal Brogni, à cheval sous un dais porté par quatre officiers et suivi

This is, incidentally, almost exactly the same as the procession demanded by Scribe in the libretto.[22] The complete list in Palianti, in contrast, is much longer. It comprises a total of twenty separate groups, and there are at least five horses and altogether more than 300 people on stage (about 240 in the cortège and at least 60 chorus members, who are already onstage when the procession starts):

1. The Emperor's trumpeters, preceded by three lavishly armed and equipped guards on horseback.—2. A standard-bearer.—3. Twenty crossbowmen.—4. A standard-bearer.—5. Two cardinals followed by two clerks.—6. Two more cardinals followed by two clerks.—7. A standard-bearer accompanied by bishops and various guildsmen.—8. A standard-bearer accompanied by two more bishops and several abbots.—9. Three sheriffs.

During the cortège, the chorus occupies the scene until no. 7. Here the cortège marches slower and more silently, in order to let the soloists sing: *O mon Dieu que j'implore.—O mon Dieu que j'implore—Que toujours elle ignore etc., etc.*

Almost without interruption, the cortège goes on at the beginning of the ensemble: *Non jamais dans ces lieux, spectacle plus pompeux.*—10. A hundred and twenty soldiers richly armed, covered with gold mail and wearing short coats.—11. Six trumpeters. (The instruments are adorned with richly encrusted standards.)—Another stop without completely interrupting the march.—12. Six trumpeters.—13. Six standard-bearers.—14. Twenty crossbowmen. 15. Three cardinals followed by their pages and their clerks.—16. Under a magnificent baldachin carried by four heralds (a fifth carries the horse's bridle): LE CARDINAL BROGNY on horseback, followed by his pages and his gentlemen and preceded by heralds bearing the pontifical vestments on rich velvet cushions.—17. Ten soldiers.—18. Three heralds-at-arms on horseback.—19. Twenty pages of the emperor.—20. EMPEROR SIGISMOND, in the most stunning armor. He sits on a superb horse with all the luxury imaginable.[23]

---

de ses gentilshommes; puis enfin l'empereur, à cheval, suivi de ses officiers armés de pied-en-cap." Duverger, *Mise en scène*, 2.

22. "Le cortège défile dans l'ordre suivant: Les sonneurs de trompe de l'empereur, les porte-bannières et les arbalétiers de la ville de Constance, les maîtres des différens métiers et confréries, les échevins, les archers de l'empereur, puis les hommes d'armes, les hérauts, les sonneurs du cardinal, ses hallebardiers, ses bannières et celles du Saint-Siège; les membres du concile, leurs pages et leurs clers; le cardinal à cheval, avec ses pages et ses gentilshommes; les hallebardiers, les hérauts d'armes de l'empereur, portant les bannières de l'empire; puis enfin l'empereur Sigismond, à cheval, précédé de ses pages, entouré de ses gentilshommes, et de ses écuyers, et suivi des princes de l'empire." Scribe, *Théâtre complet*, 408.

23. "1° Les sonneurs de trompe de l'empereur, précédées de trois gardes à cheval richement armés et équipés.—2° Un porte bannière.—3° Vingt arbalétiers.—4° Un porte bannière.—5° Deux cardinaux suivis de deux clercs.—6° Deux autres cardinaux suivis de deux clercs.—7° Un porte bannière accompagné d'évêques et des maîtres de différents métiers.—8° Un porte bannière accompagné de deux autres évêques et de quelques supérieurs de confréries.—9° Trois échevins. . . . Le chœur occupe le temps du cortège jusqu'au no. 7. Là, le cortège marche plus silencieusement et

As we know from the press reports, the cortège had already been amplified in former times. When *La juive* was mounted in 1847, after a renovation of the Salle Le Peletier, the journal *L'illustration* published two caricatures by Cham entitled "The procession of La Juive will be enlarged" (La procession de la Juive sera augmentée). Whereas the first one depicts "L'empereur Sigismond d'autrefois" on horseback and in full armor, the second one shows "L'empereur Sigismond d'aujourd'hui" sitting on a hobbyhorse, followed by cut-out figures of his officers on wheels pulled by the horse.[24]

As we have already seen, in the first production there was more space onstage than in the later one described by Palianti. So how can we explain in what ways the procession in the late 1860s was much more lavish than the earlier one? According to Duverger's description, the curtain fell at the exact moment when the greatest number of people was onstage: there is no hint that anybody might leave the stage before the emperor is seen. In the later production, however, a "ramp descending to the backstage" (pente descendant dans la coulisse) at the left, not seen by the spectators, allowed the head of the procession to disappear, so that a greater number of people could successively crowd the scene. It would also allow the same extras— and maybe even the same horses—to reappear, either in new costumes or in those already seen.

The different arrangement of the procession also marks an aesthetic shift between the 1830s and the 1860s. In the original staging, the overall image is that of a crowd advancing slowly from the back to the front of the stage. This corresponds to the then dominant aesthetics of tableau—showing one basically static picture that alters only by degrees of intensification. The second staging has a clearly articulated musical dramaturgy. It moves the procession from the right to the left and consists of a series of different pictures, set into motion by the altering rhythm of the music.[25] The first nine

---

plus doucement pour laisser chanter aux artistes les solos: *O mon Dieu que j'implore.—O mon Dieu que j'implore—Que toujours elle ignore etc., etc.* . . . Le cortège, qui ne s'interrompt presque pas, recommence à l'ensemble: *Non jamais dans ces lieux, spectacle plus pompeux.*—10° Cent vingt soldats richement armés et couverts de cottes et de juste au corps en maille d'or.—11° Six trompettes. (Les instruments sont ornés de tabliers richement armoiriés.—Nouvelle halte sans cependant arrêter tout à fait la marche.—12° Six trompettes.—13° Six porte bannières.—14° Vingt gardes arbaletiers. 15° Trois cardinaux suivis de leurs pages et de leurs clercs.—16° Sous un magnifique dais porté par quatre hérauts (un cinquième tient la bride du cheval): LE CARDINAL BROGHY à cheval, suivi de ses pages et de ses gentilshommes et précédé des hérauts portant sur de riches coussins de velours les vêtements pontificaux.—17° Dix soldats.—18° Trois hérauts d'armes à cheval.—19° Vingt pages de l'Empereur.—20° L'EMPEREUR SIGISMOND, sous une armure des plus éblouissantes.—Il monte un superbe cheval harnaché et cuirassé avec tout le luxe imaginable." Palianti, *Collection de mises en scène,* 5.

24. H. Robert Cohen, *Les gravures musicales dans "L'illustration," 1843–1899* (Québec: Presses de l'Université Laval, 1983), 1:139.

25. Palianti, *Collection de mises en scène,* 5.

groups from the list make their appearance during the chorus "De ces nobles guerriers," in a 6/8 Allegro brillante.[26] When the soloists then sing alone, the procession has to slow down, and probably the horses have to stand still.[27] An especially detailed narrative occurs when the emperor passes the church, at the very end of act 1:

> When it passes in front of the church, whose doors opened a few seconds before, from the interior begins the "Te Deum." Choirboys (eight at least) on the steps of the altar wave illuminated censors in front of the emperor. The emperor stops and bows before the house of God. The bells sound at full volume. The organ is heard. Shouts of joy and the "Noels" of the people mingle with this noise.
>
> The emperor turns to his procession, surrounded by his entourage, his squires, and the noblemen of the empire in glittering apparel and armor.
>
> At the moment the emperor appears, Léopold hides his face with his cloak, seeks to hid himself from the gaze of all, and loses himself in the crowd. Rachel follows him with an uneasy eye and shows her surprise.
>
> Eléazar, who has looked upon the cortège with disdain, drags his daughter away.
>
> The curtain falls quickly on this tableau and before the last great characters of the cortège have disappeared. There remain a few soldiers of various ranks to pass by.
>
> From the appearance of the emperor, the people shout with joy and wave their headdresses. [?][28]

Also in act 2, besides important divergences in scenery, the characters onstage and their acting do not correspond. Duverger reports that eight or nine people were at the table, some standing, others sitting. The women were placed on the right

26. Fromental Halévy, *La juive,* vol. 36 of *Early Romantic Opera,* ed. Philip Gossett and Charles Rosen (New York: Garland, 1980), 176.

27. "Le cortège marche plus silencieusement et plus doucement pour laisser chanter aux artistes les solos: *O mon Dieu que j'implore.—O mon Dieu que j'implore.—Que toujours elle ignore, etc., etc.*" Palianti, *Collection de mises en scène,* 5.

28. "Lorsqu'il passe devant l'église, dont les portes se sont ouvertes quelques instants avant, on attaque dans l'intérieur le TE DEUM.—Des enfants de chœur (huit au moins) sur les marches du temple, agitent alors devant l'Empereur les encensoirs allumés.—L'Empereur s'arrête et s'incline devant la maison du Seigneur.—Les cloches sonnent à toute volée.—Les orgues se font entendre.—A ce bruit se mêlent les cris de joie et les NOEL du peuple. . . . L'Empereur se remet en marche suivi et entouré de ses gentilshommes, de ses écuyers et des grands de l'Empire sous des habits et sons des armures éblouissants. . . . Au moment ou paraît l'Empereur, Léopold se cache la figure avec son manteau, cherche à se soustraire à tous les regards et se perd dans la foule.—Rachel le suit d'un œil inquiet et témoigne sa surprise. . . . Eléazar qui a regardé le cortège avec dédain, entraîne sa fille. . . . Le rideau baisse vivement sur ce tableau et avant que les derniers grands personnages du cortège aient disparu.—Il reste encore à défiler des soldats de diverses armes. . . . Dès la présence de l'Empereur, le peuple laisse éclater sa joie et agite ses coiffures." Ibid.

and the men on the left.[29] According to Palianti, however, there were eight persons in addition to the principals, all of them seated at the table, but the sexes were not separated.[30] More astonishing, there were only two men and six women, compared to seven men and five women in the premiere;[31] this had important consequences for the chorus that these reduced forces would have to sing. Palianti further indicates three domestics standing at a distance behind the table in order to assist Éléazar during the service: According to the libretto, and also according to Duverger, Eléazar is doing everything on his own. If the servants' presence onstage already contradicts the original intentions, it would certainly do so even more if they also were to sing during the ceremony to reinforce the choir. But according to the libretto, the only servants to appear in act 2 are those accompanying the princess Eudoxie, who unexpectedly enters the Jew's house in order to purchase a rare jewel from Éléazar as a present for Léopold. Specific to Palianti is the very detailed description of lighting cues, especially at this very moment. As Karin Pendle and Stephen Wilkins have already pointed out, "Changes in lighting from the *rampe* or footlights—the row of gaslights that lined the apron below floor level—underscore important dramatic turning points."[32] Palianti indicates lighting changes not only for the sake of realism, but also for psychological effects. For instance, Leopold's terrified recognition of his wife when she enters is emphasized by the indication "daylight at the footlights" (jour à la rampe), referring to a sudden brightening. Lighting effects of this kind for psychological purposes were of course completely unknown in the 1830s.[33] The same goes for the very detailed descriptions of mimetic expression, with which Palianti's manual abounds—this was not common practice in *livrets* published as early as the 1830s.

The different staging of the masses in these two productions becomes even more apparent if we consider the second cortège in *La juive*, in act 5, preceding the execution of Rachel. Once again, Palianti's list is very much longer than Duverger's. What is more, Duverger suggests economizing on costumes by demanding exactly the same extras that appeared in act 1: "With the exception of the emperor and the baldachin of the cardinal, one would do well to make the whole of the act 1 cortège reappear for the dénouement."[34]

This suggestion, of course, mainly applies to the directors of provincial theaters.

29. Duverger, *Mise en scène*, 2.

30. Palianti, *Collection de mises en scène*, 6.

31. See Hallman, *Opera, Liberalism, and Antisemitism*, 177.

32. Pendle and Wilkins, "Paradise Found," 197.

33. Gas lighting was first used at the Opéra in 1822 for special effects in Isouard's *Aladin ou la lampe merveilleuse,* and it was generally introduced onto the stage of Salle Le Peletier in 1833, shortly before the première of *La juive.*

34. "Excepté l'empereur et le dais du cardinal, on fera bien de faire reparaître tout le cortège du 1er acte pour le dénouement." Duverger, *Mise en scène,* 4.

If Louis Véron had spend more than 60,000 francs for a total of 524 costumes,[35] Palianti would have needed many more: about 300 were already in use in act 1, about the same number in act 3, and even more in act 5 (not to speak of those required in acts 2 and 4).

Among the examples showing the differences between Duverger and Palianti with regard to perspective, the most interesting one concerns the final scene of the opera.[36] In 1835 there was only a painted imitation of a furnace, mounted on a wooden structure, with a mattress onto which Cornélie Falcon, the actress playing the female protagonist, was presumably flung at least forty-six times in the course of the opera's first season alone. Duverger describes this incident: "The cauldron of boiling water is in the middle of the stage, toward the fourth *plan*. . . . This cauldron is presented alone; two men in this *carré* receive the actress or the one of exactly the same size who will replace her; but it is preferable that the actress undertake this action for greater truth and interest."[37]

Palianti's description of the corresponding events reads somewhat differently. In his mise-en-scène an enormous bronze vat can be seen, placed on top of a real brick furnace; the fire under the vat is already lit, and a raging inferno has been blazing in the furnace since the beginning of the act. In the ultimate event, however, two boys in hangmen's costume, each twelve or thirteen years old, appear on the platform and simply throw a puppet into the steaming tank: "For the purposes of illusion and perspective, it is two children of twelve or thirteen who, on a platform, appear dressed as executioners. It is also a fake Rachel, or a dummy that is thrown into the cauldron."[38]

It is beyond the scope of the present article to compare all the other very remarkable differences between the two sources: suffice it to state that there can be no

35. John Drysdale, *Louis Véron and the Finances of the Académie Royale de Musique,* Perspektiven der Opernforschung 9 (Frankfurt am Main: Peter Lang, 2003), 188. According to his *cahier des charges,* Véron was not allowed to use old costumes. Even if we take into account the costumes needed in acts 2, 3, and 4 (with the emperor's banquet and the ballet in act 3 being particularly lavish), there might have been at least some costumes not yet seen before the dénouement even in the premiere, in addition to those needed for the *penitents* and the executioners.

36. As in act 1, Duverger insisted on using the entire stage: "Donner au théâtre toute la largeur possible." This indication is perfectly matched by the scenery of act 5. The tent, ready to receive the members of the Concile, is restricted to the stage's *premier plan;* the stage is otherwise empty except for the furnace on the *quatrième plan.* Duverger, *Mise en scène,* 4.

37. "La cuve d'eau bouillante est au milieu du théâtre, vers le 4° plan. . . . Cette cuve est seulement figurée; deux matelats dans ce carré reçoivent l'actrice ou celle de même taille exactement qui la remplacerait; mais il est préférable que l'actrice se prête elle-même à cette action pour plus de vérité et d'intérêt." Ibid.

38. "Pour l'illusion et la perspective, ce sont deux enfants de douze à treize ans qui, sur la plate-forme, paraissent habillés comme les exécuteurs. C'est aussi une fausse Rachel ou un mannequin que l'on précipite dans la cuve." Palianti, *Collection de mises en scène,* 14.

doubt about the importance of the changes that the staging of *La juive* underwent in nineteenth-century Paris. Instead of a conclusion, I would like to raise some general issues on which discussion might be necessary. One is the problem of the authorship of these documents.[39] Furthermore, it is important to distinguish between documentation aimed at internal use in the theater and documentation prepared for external use in the French provinces or elsewhere. Whereas the former was normally the duty of the humble *sous régisseurs* (such as Palianti at the Opéra-Comique),[40] the latter was the domain of theater agents (such as Duverger), who normally didn't have full insight into all the details of a production. If we compare the manuals published by Duverger, it seems that they report what a cautious and professionally trained spectator could analyze by himself by carefully watching the spectacle, but they do not stem directly from the production process itself. With the notable exception of Solomé, stage directors themselves have rarely transcribed what they intended in the form of a *livret,* and there is little evidence that around 1830 they would care about what their colleagues would do in the future. Most Parisian productions completely disappeared after a short time, and only in very rare cases could the stage directors expect right from the premiere that their indications could be of any interest even in the near future. The dissemination of information about production, in general, was completely within the responsibility of theater agencies such as Duverger's Bureau de Commission Théâtrale. The physical form of these publications—as newspaper insertions, folded sheets, or pamphlets—and the fact that they were evidently not available in bookstores, but only through specialized theatrical agencies, show clearly that they were intended primarily for practical and immediate use, not for extended conservation of an immutable production. The orientation toward the present is also evidenced by the fact that sample copies were not regularly deposited in the Bibliothèque Nationale.

It is true that stage manuals published by theater agents were often later copied in manuscript. But it doesn't seem that these copies were generally prepared with an eye toward any subsequent production. Most examples of such manuscript copies at the library of Bibliothèque de l'Association de la régie théâtrale (ART) do not show any evidence of ever being used for practical purposes. Many of these copies in fact belonged to the collections of individual theater professionals (such as Eugène Lespinasse, Louis Picot, Alexandre Lapissida, Émile Bertin, Charles Belin, or Charles Ferrand Michaud). In any case, stage directors, *régisseurs,* and other professionals such as prompters, *chefs de chant,* and *chefs de chœurs* would normally work with different

39. On this issue, see Arne Langer, *Der Regisseur und die Aufzeichnungspraxis in der Opernregie im 19. Jahrhundert,* Perspektiven der Opernforschung 4 (Frankfurt am Main: Peter Lang, 1997).

40. This was the post Palianti held at the Opéra-Comique at the time of his publication on *La juive.*

types of material, namely, annotated libretti interpolated with pages showing the stage directions and, in later periods, annotated piano-vocal scores.

Without doubt there was a strong sense of conservation with respect to staging in the nineteenth century. But the question is, what was actually conserved? The libretto, or the staging manual? In analyzing mise-en-scène, we should therefore try to establish whether there are really direct intertextual relations among different staging manuals that can be identified with specific productions, or whether they only refer directly to the libretto, to the description of scenery, or other sources. Although the tradition of printed stage directions continued well into the twentieth century, mainly for operettas and works of lighter genres, we should not overlook that for many of the most successful French operas, including *Carmen, Les contes d'Hoffmann, Lakmé, Les dragons de Villars, Mireille,* and others, there is no trace of any printed *livret de mise en scène* at all.[41]

Most Parisian productions completely disappeared after a short time, and only in rare cases could the directors expect right from the premiere that their indications would be of any interest in the future. Even when a work entered the repertoire, it is generally agreed, operatic productions changed over time: important cuts were made regularly, and, less often, new music was added. Given this common practice, why should libretto and music be more likely to change than stage direction, the most transitory aspect of an operatic production? Staging, at least, was subject to permanent technical improvement, aesthetic changes, and different social and political contexts.

A difficult aspect of the manuals concerns whether they document "a composerly desire to gain control over the visual aspect of opera," as some scholars have argued.[42] We know from Giacomo Meyerbeer's letters and diaries that the composer met with Duverger during the time of *Robert le diable* and *Les huguenots,*[43] and even more

41. A careful reading of the ART catalog reveals that as the century went on, lesser-known works were even more likely to be accompanied by a printed mise-en-scène. At a time when all the country's major cities had a railway connection to the capital, many theater professionals would have seen *Carmen* in Paris or elsewhere and wouldn't have needed a transcription of its overall scenic effect. It is true that neither *Carmen* nor *Les contes d'Hoffmann* was an outright triumph when it appeared for the first time, but even then, both certainly drew more public attention than passing fads such as Clapisson's *Code noir,* Balfe's *Le puits d'amour,* or Massa's *Royal-cravate,* all *opéras comiques* that all disappeared forever after their first season despite the fact that carefully prepared *livrets de mise en scène* had been published. *Code noir* was given thirty-two times in 1842, *Le puits d'amour* twenty-eight times in 1843, and *Royal-cravate* only eight times in 1861. See Albert Soubies, *Soixante-neuf ans à l'Opéra-Comique en deux pages, de la première de "La Dame blanche" à la millième de "Mignon," 1825–1994* (Paris: Librairie Fischbacher, 1894).

42. See Cormac Newark, "Staging Grand Opéra," 24–25. See also Roger Parker, "Reading the *livrets,* or the Chimera of 'Authentic' Staging," in *Leonora's Last Act: Essays in Verdian Discourse* (Princeton, NJ: Princeton University Press, 1997), 126–48.

43. See Giacomo Meyerbeer, *Briefwechsel und Tagebücher,* vol. 2, ed. Heinz Becker (Berlin: De Gruyter, 1970), 174–75, 275.

regularly with Palianti several months after the premiere of *Le prophète*.[44] With re-gard to this last work, Meyerbeer himself delivered to the theater agent the technical information about the roller skates required for the skating interlude and the electric arc lamp invented to create the effect of a sunrise, both in act 3 of that opera, and on more than one occasion the composer urged Palianti to accelerate the preparation of the staging manual. In October 1849, almost half a year after the premiere, Meyerbeer corrected Palianti's indications and wrote comments on them; the two men met two days later for a final discussion. Palianti's *livret* for *Le prophète* is certainly the most detailed printed description of a *grand opéra* production published since Solomé's for *La muette de Portici*. It seems obvious that Palianti had no direct insight into the stag-ing material used at the Opéra; but as an experienced professional, he could analyze most of what happened on the stage by himself.

For many of the earlier *grands opéras*, however, documentation is much more limited. Palianti, at least, never printed a mise-en-scène for *Les huguenots, Guillaume Tell,* or *Robert le diable,* to mention only the three most often performed works at the Opéra throughout the whole nineteenth century. Besides the fact that he was too young and lived outside Paris when these works appeared, a provisional explanation could be that these operas, after years in the repertoire (and subsequent to enormous changes and cuts), were so well-known that nobody really needed the little amount of extra information that a staging manual could offer, in addition to the directions given in the printed libretto or the brief description published by Duverger. But why, then, did Palianti publish one for *La juive* as late as the 1860s? Maybe he felt that in addition to the new scenery, some of the changes made over time were so noteworthy that it might be helpful to write them down, such as, for example, the introduction of a rounded panorama drop, the advanced lighting effects, or the welcome substitu-tion for the suffering prima donna of a water- and heat-resistant dummy. In any case, the fact that a new mise-en-scène was printed clearly shows that the original one was not considered at all sacrosanct. On the contrary, it was simply inadequate for present purposes. Therefore, the idea of an "authentic" and immutable staging has to be seen in relative terms: as a retrospective projection of modern concepts, but certainly not as a part of nineteenth-century operatic reality.

44. Giacomo Meyerbeer, *Briefwechsel und Tagebücher,* vol. 4, ed. Heinz Becker and Gudrun Becker (Berlin: De Gruyter, 1985), 490; Meyerbeer, *Briefwechsel und Tagebücher,* vol. 5, ed. Sabine Henze-Döhring Becker (Berlin: De Gruyter, 1998), 41, 59, 91, 93, 103.

Lucia Goes to Paris

A TALE OF THREE THEATERS

Rebecca Harris-Warrick

Donizetti's opera *Lucia di Lammermoor* had an unusual career path in Paris. It not only made the rounds of three different opera houses over a period of nine years—the Théâtre-Italien (1837), the Théâtre de la Renaissance (1839), and the Opéra (1846)—but did so with its original story line and music relatively intact, despite being translated into French starting with its second incarnation. The opera was a huge success with the Parisian public every time it was mounted and during its tour of Paris generated an enormous paper trail of librettos, scores, arrangements, correspondence, theatrical documents, and journalistic reports. This complex, well-documented history makes for a rich point of entry into many of the questions, both institutional and aesthetic, that agitated the Parisian operatic world between 1835 and 1846. At the Théâtre-Italien *Lucia* not only figured in the eternal debates about the relative merits of Italian versus French opera and the status in Paris of this particular theater, but also became a focal point for the narrower question of whether it was better to import operas composed in Italy or to commission Italian composers to write new works for Parisian audiences. The translated *Lucie*'s resounding success at the Théâtre de la Renaissance suddenly made this theater a threat to the subsidized opera houses, but the opera itself also reopened vexing questions about the validity of translations and about Italian versus French attitudes toward the construction of librettos. The performing materials for *Lucie* in its move to the Opéra show that these questions remained live ones there as well, as did the question of whether or not this opera should have a ballet. At the Opéra a debate emerged as to whether the opera should be performed there at all,

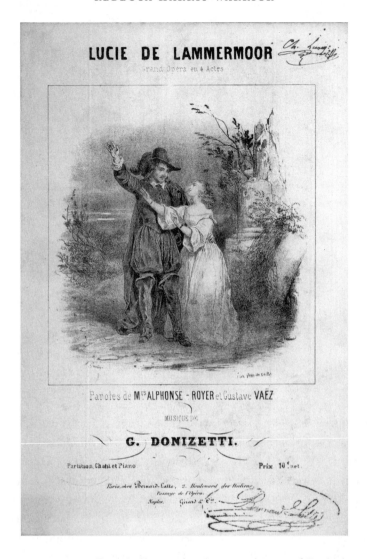

FIGURE 9.1. Frontispiece to the piano-vocal score of *Lucie de Lammermoor* (Paris: Barnard Latte, n.d.) showing Lucie and Edgard at the end of act 1. Courtesy of Cornell University Library, The Sidney Cox Library of Music and Dance.

since it had already been done in two Parisian theaters. And, of course, critical reception of this opera in its various venues offers a means for examining the shifting French views on Donizetti and his music—which evolved from seeing *Lucia* as derivative and conventional to accepting it as a work whose musical merits were beyond question. It nonetheless comes as a surprise, given our own mad-scene-centric view of this opera, that as far as Parisian critics were concerned, it might more accurately have been entitled *Edgard de Ravenswood*.

When the opera first arrived in Paris, two years after its premiere in Naples, Lucy

Ashton and Edgar Ravenswood were by no means new to Parisian audiences: most reviewers of the opera took it for granted that their readers knew Walter Scott's novel *The Bride of Lammermoor*—first translated into French as *La fiancée de Lammermoor* in 1819—not to mention its various theatrical spinoffs (see table 9.1). In fact, after *Lucia di Lammermoor* premiered in Naples in September 1835, an event that was reported in several Parisian papers,[1] the *Le ménestrel* (8 November 1835) grounded Donizetti's new opera for its readers by explaining that the plot was drawn from Scott's novel and that this was also the same story as the play that had made the reputations of the actors Frédérick Lemaître and Marie Dorval a few years earlier.[2] In Paris, Donizetti's opera became such a guaranteed box-office success that various performers chose to use parts of it in benefit performances, only some of which are listed in table 9.1. And this outline does not even touch on the various concerts around Paris in which individual arias or ensembles were sung or piano fantasies on the opera's themes were played by visiting virtuosos such as Thalberg and Liszt—or the myriad balls where people danced to *Lucia* quadrilles. Moreover, Parisian music lovers could purchase the piano-vocal score in either the French or Italian version or in any number of different instrumental arrangements, not to mention acquire printed orchestral parts, various iterations of the libretto, and a staging manual.

The very active Parisian press generated enormous numbers of articles about the opera every time it was performed, many of them very lengthy; these form the primary basis of this study. Whereas I cannot claim to have read every word written about *Lucia* in the French press, I have aimed to collect as many as possible of the articles written between 1835 and 1846—primarily those about performances of the opera, but also some written about the Parisian operatic scene in general. To date I have been able to gain access to some twenty-five different periodicals representing both the specialized musical press and general newspapers, although not always to the dates covering every performance at each theater. The appendix provides excerpts from these articles, transcribed in the original French; they are numbered for reference in the main text, where they are paraphrased or translated. My proximate goal has been to summarize the main threads in the critical reception of this opera over the first nine years of its performance in Paris. The larger project is someday to make all the primary data I have collected available to scholars in the hope that it will prove useful for future studies of Parisian operatic life during the 1830s and 1840s.

---

1. See, *inter alia*, *Le ménestrel*, 13 September and 8 November 1835; *Le temps*, 7 September 1835; and *La revue musicale*, 8 November 1835.

2. This play, which maintained the plot and the characters of the novel more faithfully than did Cammarano's libretto for Donizetti, although it ended with a spectacular scene in which Edgard and Lucy were drowned by a rising tide, was an enormous success: it had twenty-nine performances between its premiere on 22 March and the end of April alone, and the text of the play was published by Bouquin-Delasouche in mid-April. (This information comes from the March and April listings of performances in *Le Figaro*, which reviewed the production on 26 and 27 March 1828.)

TABLE 9.1. Lucy Ashton in Paris: a partial survey

1819

Walter Scott's novel, *The Bride of Lammermoor* was translated into French for the first time as *La fiancée de Lammermoor,* the same year it was published in English. There were many subsequent editions, in separate volumes and as part of collected works editions of Walter Scott, the first of which was published in Paris between 1822 and 1830 (*La fiancée de Lammermoor* was in vol. 16).

1827

A. Dartois and François Antoine Eugène de Planard, *Le Caleb de Walter Scott, pièce en un acte, mêlée de couplets,* music by Adolphe Adam, Théâtre des Nouveautés.

1828

22 March: Victor Ducange, *La fiancée de Lammermoor,* three-act *mélodrame,* Théâtre de la Porte Saint-Martin.

Edgard . . . . Frédérick Lemaître
Lucie . . . . Marie Dorval

1829

12 December: Michele Carafa, *Le nozze di Lammermoor,* two-act opera semi-seria, Théâtre-Italien. Three performances only, never revived.

1835

26 September: Premiere of Donizetti's *Lucia di Lammermoor,* Naples, Teatro San Carlo. The premiere was noted in the French press.

Edgardo . . . . Gilbert Duprez
Lucia . . . . Fanny Tacchinardi-Persiani
Enrico . . . . Domenico Cosselli

1837

12 December: Paris premiere of *Lucia di Lammermoor,* Théâtre-Italien.

Edgardo . . . . Giovanni Battista Rubini
Lucia . . . . Fanny Tacchinardi-Persiani
Enrico . . . . Antonio Tamburini

1838

19 April: Last scene of *Lucia di Lammermoor* performed at the Opéra, in Italian, as part of a benefit for Laure Cinti-Damoreau. Repeated at the Opéra on 5 May, as part of a benefit for the ballerinas Fanny and Thérèse Elssler, and at the Odéon on 30 August, as a benefit for the "incendiés du Vaudeville" (performers from the burned-out Théâtre du Vaudeville).

Edgardo . . . . Gilbert Duprez
Chorus of the Théâtre-Italien

1839

6 August: Premiere of *Lucie de Lammermoor,* French libretto by Alphonse Royer and Gustave Vaëz, Théâtre de la Renaissance.

TABLE 9.1. (*continued*)

Edgard . . . . Achille Ricciardi
Lucie . . . . Anna Thillon
Asthon . . . . Auguste Hurteaux

1841

24 April: Acts 3 and 4 of *Lucie* (in French) at the Opéra, as part of a benefit for Gilbert Duprez.

Edgard . . . . Gilbert Duprez
Lucie . . . . Julie Dorus-Gras
Asthon . . . . Jean-Etienne Auguste Massol

1846

20 February: Premiere of *Lucie de Lammermoor* (in French) at the Opéra.

Edgard . . . . Gilbert Duprez
Lucie . . . . Maria Nau
Asthon . . . . Paul Barrhoilhet

The Théâtre-Italien

By December 1837, when *Lucia di Lammermoor* opened at the Théâtre-Italien, four of Donizetti's operas had already been performed there, most successfully *Anna Bolena,* which had been mounted every season from 1831 onward. Donizetti himself had visited Paris from January to March 1835 to oversee the premier of his *Marin Faliero.*[3] Bellini's untimely death in September 1835 had dealt a severe blow to the Théâtre-Italien, and by the fall of 1837 many critics were complaining that the theater's repertoire was getting stale, that the same works were being continually recycled (see excerpt 1 in the appendix). But writers were divided as to whether the Théâtre-Italien should refresh its repertoire by commissioning operas, as it had in 1835 with *Marin Faliero* and Bellini's *I puritani,* or whether it should import operas that had already proven successful in Italy. *Le constitutionnel* reported that whereas it saw Italian operas composed in Paris as an homage to the Parisian public for which Parisians should be grateful, audiences tended to prefer operas that had already acquired a reputation (excerpt 2). As if to prove the point, the *Le courrier français* opened its review of *Lucia* with the remark, "At last we are returning to Italian music from Italy, and

---

3. William Ashbrook, *Donizetti and His Operas* (Cambridge: Cambridge University Press, 1982), 87–93. The other two operas that had been performed in Paris were *L'ajo nell'imbarazzo* (1832) and *Gianni di Calais* (1833); for a list of the Théâtre-Italien's repertoire year by year, see Albert Soubies, *Le Théâtre-Italien de 1801 à 1913* (Paris: Librairie Fischbacher, 1913), especially the unpaginated chart at the end of the book.

giving up on works fabricated in Paris or London. . . . The funeral procession is stopping; the massacre of the innocents is interrupted" (excerpt 3). *La quotidienne* attributed the failure of Carafa's opera on the same story, *Le nozze di Lammermoor,* to the fact that it had been composed in Paris, and suggested that had the opera come from Naples or Venice it would have succeeded (excerpt 4). Louis Viardot, writing in *Le siècle* (14 December 1837), requested that two other Donizetti operas that seemed to be getting good press in Italy, *Parisina* and *L'elisir d'amore,* be brought to Paris soon.[4]

But pleasure in some quarters that an already successful opera was now being offered to the Parisian public did not necessarily translate into favorable reviews. Press reaction to *Lucia* in 1837 acknowledged that the opera was filling the Théâtre-Italien night after night, and lavished praise upon all three of the main performers—including Fanny Tacchinardi-Persiani, who was new to Paris that fall—but critics were generally cautious about the qualities of the opera. Known anti-Italian papers such as *Le courrier des théâtres* were typically scathing, and excerpt 5 contains a particularly snide passage from *Le corsaire* claiming that this opera was Donizetti's 55,919th score and that the music was inert and without soul. On the other end of the spectrum, a few reviewers, such as Gérard de Nerval, found enough merit in the work to predict that it would become a staple of the Théâtre-Italien's repertoire (excerpt 6). But most of the reviewers were lukewarm about the opera, insofar as it was separable from the performance. *La gazette de France* said that the quality of the singers masked the mediocrity of the music, even while allowing that this opera provided a good vehicle for them (see the second paragraph of excerpt 8). The usual complaints about Donizetti as an imitator of Rossini or even of Bellini were trotted out, as were remarks about his music as facile and shallow. *Le national,* in one of the milder passages of this nature, commented that this opera, like Donizetti's other works, is full of borrowings from himself, Rossini, and other composers, and that every now and then, just when he seems on the verge of doing something interesting, he falls back into his usual monotonous and predictable style (excerpt 7). *La gazette de France* opined that the music is appropriate to the dramatic situations but gives the listener the impression of having heard it elsewhere (excerpt 8). One of the most amusing comments comes from *L'artiste,* reviewing the opening of the season at the Théâtre-Italien in the fall of 1839, which was that the act 2 finale "will always be considered the beautiful simulacrum of a masterpiece" (excerpt 9).

As was generally the case in the Parisian press, reviewers devoted a great deal of attention to the libretto. Critics took it for granted that their readers were familiar with Scott's novel, and many writers took Cammarano to task for disfiguring his literary model. *Le constitutionnel*'s remarks may serve as an example:

4. Louis Viardot was to become co-director of the Théâtre-Italien following the sudden death of Severini in January 1838. He married the soprano Pauline Garcia in 1840.

You should not expect to find Walter Scott in signor Cammarano. What would happen to librettos and writers of librettos if they were obliged to be geniuses, great poets, or to respectfully reproduce the creations of illustrious poets and men of genius? The job would be too difficult; no one could manage. Signor Cammarano thus did not even try; . . . he made the poetic characters who fill Scott's novel with their loves, their passions, and their misfortunes unrecognizable . . . and those he did not disfigure, he simply left out. . . . Don't ask Signor Cammarano about the old and faithful Caleb Balderston; the signor erased him with a stroke of the pen. Yes, my poor Caleb, we have to do without you. . . . (Excerpt 10)

Le charivari pointed out that in addition to Caleb, Lucy's mother had been left out as well, "this haughty and proud parvenue, who talks of 'misalliance' and 'the little folk' with such aplomb," her politically ambitious father, and her adolescent brother, replacing them all with "a tall young man modeled on the 'ferocious brothers' of melodrama" (excerpt 11). *Le temps* went so far as to accuse Cammarano of simply trading on the reputation of Walter Scott by applying the names of his characters to a plot that could have come straight from the boulevard theaters (excerpt 12).

Partly because the libretto took so many liberties with its literary model, but also out of long-standing habit, reviewers felt obliged to provide a relatively detailed synopsis of the plot, often tying it to the major musical numbers, as in the following from the *Le courrier français:*

The opera opens with a short introduction, whose first notes are struck quietly on the cymbals, supported by a muffled thump from the bass drum. The curtain rises: after a brilliant chorus, the unnatural brother, Enrico, appears and complains that his sister persists in loving Edgardo di Ravenswood, the enemy of the Ashton family. He learns that Edgardo has reappeared in the environs, that he has saved Lucia from danger, and that Lucia meets him every day. While the brother deplores his sister's conduct in a peaceful andante, the chorus announces that a pale, silent man has been seen in the ruined vestibule of the tower; it is Edgardo. The peaceful andante gives way to an allegro agitato, and the brother leaves the stage, boiling with rage, swearing vengeance. This number is well constructed, well done, little endowed with invention, or rather, suspiciously reminiscent. . . . The following number is a cavatina sung by Lucia and worked out with exquisite care. A harp introduction precedes the young girl's entrance, and the flute accompanies her as she regrets not having the tireless wings of the wind to follow her lover. Edgardo is not far away; he comes to sing a tender duet with her. This duet seemed to us the best piece in the work. The stretta is charming, notwithstanding the eternal pizzicato that underlies the melody.

In the second act there is a big duet between Enrico and Lucia, divided into three movements. The parts we appreciated the most were the beautiful violin phrases, which trace a design with rare elegance, but on the whole, the duet is long and cold. The brother deceives his sister, telling her that Edgardo has married another woman. Poor Lucia resigns herself to marrying Lord Arturo Bucklaw. The wedding chorus is very pretty; unfortunately, the groom does not resemble the chorus: he sings very badly and in that regard he has competition from a certain Raimondo, tutor and confidant to Lucia, who can't open his mouth without going out of tune. He is recognizable for that reason, by his white gloves, and by his black pants. The wedding takes place. Lucia signs the fatal document, and no sooner has she signed than Edgardo appears on the doorstep of the Gothic manor. Enrico and Edgardo reach for their swords; the tutor exhorts them to respect divine majesty, and both of them understand the worthiness of the observation, even if it is sung out of tune. Edgardo returns to Lucia the ring she had given him and cries in despair: "Maledetto sia l'istante / Che di te mi rese amante" [Cursed be the moment / That made me your lover.]

On the word "maledetto" the singer finds the means to produce an effect that the composer had only weakly set up. We have so many beautiful finales, but the one in *Lucia di Lammermoor* is merely adequate. It begins well and finishes not badly, but nothing exceptional happens. . . .

The third act consists of a duet between Enrico and Edgardo, a chorus, an aria sung by Lucia, and a final scene sung by Edgardo. Lucia has gone mad; in her madness she has killed her husband, Arturo. There is nothing left for her to do but die, and Edgardo cannot fail to follow her. He does not get pulled into the quicksand on the shore, as does Walter Scott's hero; he purely and simply stabs himself, as any operatic hero is wont to do. (Excerpt 13)

Criticisms of Cammarano's libretto for *Lucia,* of which there were many, opened the door for the more general and very familiar complaint that Italian librettists knew nothing about dramatic construction. This was an ongoing issue in Paris, and Italian operas performed in French theaters had to be revised in accordance with French dramaturgical conventions.[5] In the case of *Lucia,* one of the perceived weaknesses concerned the final scene. *La gazette de France,* for instance, wondered what became of Enrico at end of the opera, given that he doesn't reappear after the mad scene: "I don't even know if Lord Henry wasn't perhaps killed by Edgard de Ravenswood in a duel. At least he doesn't return, which means that all the characters are dead at the end of the opera except Raimond" (excerpt 14). Étienne-Jean Delécluze, writing in the *Journal des débats,* took a more favorable view of the concision of the libretto but pointed out that "the author [of the libretto] gave no details regarding the background of the action or of the characters of the *dramatis personae,* which means that there are hardly fifty measures of recitative in the opera."[6]

5. See M. Elizabeth C. Bartlet, "From Rossini to Verdi," in *The Cambridge Companion to Grand Opera,* ed. David Charlton (Cambridge: Cambridge University Press, 2003), especially 266–73.

6. "Comme je l'ai déjà dit, l'auteur n'a donné aucuns détails sur les antécedens de l'action ni du caractère des personnages, en sorte que c'est à peine s'il y a cinquante mesures de récitatif dans

The numbers critics singled out as either having the best music or attracting the most applause from the audience were, more often than not, ones involving Edgardo—especially the act 1 love duet with Lucia, the act 2 finale (when Edgardo suddenly appears at Lucia's wedding), and Edgardo's death scene (see excerpts 5, 6, and 9).[7] The mad scene was criticized as trite: *Le charivari* and *Le siècle* were only two of the papers to claim that these days all Italian operatic heroines seemed to go mad (excerpts 15 and 16), and *Le Temps* pointed out that Lucia shared the conventional visual markers of the "inevitable" stage madness: a white dress, a pale face, floating hair, and jerky movements (excerpt 17). *Le national* (15 December 1837) thought that the music of the mad scene was inappropriate to Lucia's ravings. Only *La gazette de France* appeared to recognize that the mad scene was a "frightening" challenge for a singer (excerpt 18). Persiani was generally praised for her performance of it, notwithstanding the scene's perceived banality, and Delécluze, the reviewer for the *Journal des débats* (14 December 1837), even singled out the mad scene as among the three best pieces in the work, his other favorites being the act 1 duet and the act 2 finale. His, however, was decidedly a minority opinion; most reviewers passed over the mad scene in only a few words. All that *La revue et gazette musicale de Paris* (11 December 1837) had to say, for instance, was that in act 3 there was a "cavatina by the dying Lucia." In fact, on the basis of the reviews from Paris in the 1830s and 1840s no one could possibly have predicted the centrality the mad scene was to acquire in the opera's subsequent reception history.[8]

Reviewers were more inclined to highlight Lucia's entrance aria in act 1. This was *not* the now familiar "Regnava nel silenzio," but the very florid "Perché non ho del

---

l'opéra." *Journal des débats,* 14 December 1837. In Delécluze's view, the lack of what he called "esprit" in this libretto actually made it easier to set to music.

7. Contemporary opinion in Italy was apparently quite similar: see the reviews of *Lucia*'s Neapolitan premiere in Annalisa Bini and Jeremy Commons, eds., *Le prime rappresentazioni delle opere di Donizetti nella stampa coeva* (Milan: Skira, 1997), 513–32.

8. Regarding staged madness in Paris, see the section "Women in White" from Sarah Hibberd, "'Dormez donc, mes chers amours': Hérold's *La somnambule* (1827) and Dream Phenomena on the Parisian Lyric Stage," *Cambridge Opera Journal* 16, no. 2 (2004): 112–14. Much has been written about Lucia's madness; see especially Mary Ann Smart, "The Silencing of Lucia," *Cambridge Opera Journal* 4, no. 2 (1992): 119–41, and Romana Margherita Pugliese, "The Origins of *Lucia di Lammermoor*'s Cadenza," *Cambridge Opera Journal* 16, no. 1 (2004): 23–42. The mad scene is central to current visual representations of Lucia, as even a quick perusal of the covers of recordings shows. In the special issue of *L'avant-scène opéra* devoted to *Lucia* (see n. 12), over twenty of the photographs (by far the majority) showing various sopranos in the role depict the mad heroine, starting with the cover photo of Joan Sutherland in a bloodstained nightgown. (Nineteenth-century engravings, by contrast, generally feature either the love duet or the act 2 finale.) Several of the articles in this issue also focus on questions surrounding madness, and some recent productions of the opera have set it in an insane asylum. Pugliese historicizes this interest by arguing that the addition to the mad scene of the famous cadenza with flute, which she dates to Nelly Melba's performances at the Paris Opéra in 1889, "enabled the opera to reinvent itself, adapting to a changed set of expectations regarding the representation of madness." Pugliese, "Origins," 35.

vento," which Donizetti had composed for *Rosmonda d'Inghilterra* but which Persiani had chosen even before coming to Paris to interpolate into *Lucia*.[9] Given the fact that this substitution remained in the text of the opera when it was translated into French, Donizetti presumably acquiesced in the change or perhaps even approved it. Attentive Parisians did have the means of knowing that a substitution had taken place, because the first score of the opera published in Paris (by Latte, in Italian) contained both the original aria and, in an appendix, its replacement. The substitution, however, generated no comment in the press.[10] A passage from *La quotidienne* summing up the musical qualities of Donizetti's score is shorter—and more favorable—than most such discussions from 1837, but it does provide a sense of the relative degree of attention generally given by the critics to the various musical numbers, and particularly their appreciation of the act 2 finale (excerpt 19). The cautious and even sometimes hostile attitudes of the critics did not prevent *Lucia* from being a box-office success, although performances were cut short by the fire that destroyed the theater and killed one of its directors, Carlo Severini, on 13 January 1838. After the company moved into the Salle Ventadour at the end of January, *Lucia* was among the first works to be revived.

Théâtre de la Renaissance

Two years later, when *Lucia* became *Lucie* for performance at the Théâtre de la Renaissance (see fig. 9.1), the criticisms aimed at the Italian libretto seemed to have an impact on the team of Alphonse Royer and Gustave Vaëz, who did not just translate the libretto, but adjusted it in various ways. This time Donizetti *was* in Paris, where he had come to prepare *Les martyrs* for performance at the Opéra, so he participated in the reworking of the opera.[11] The changes Donizetti and his French librettists made to *Lucia* were small by comparison with the substantial revisions involved in transforming *Poliuto* into *Les martyrs,* or, earlier, works such as Rossini's *Maometto II* into *Le siège de Corinth*. In fact, the relatively minor degree of alteration *Lucia* experienced as it passed through the three Parisian opera houses—almost all the new

9. Ashbrook, *Donizetti*, p. 627, n. 109, says this happened in Italian productions "at least by May 1837." Hilary Poriss, "A Madwoman's Choice: Aria Substitution in *Lucia di Lammermoor,*" *Cambridge Opera Journal* 13, no. 1 (2001): 2, nn. 7 and 8, cites a Venetian libretto from 1836–37 that contains this substitution; she also lists other substitute arias later inserted into the same spot.

10. The Italian libretto, published in Paris by Lange Lévy in 1837 (copy consulted: *F-Pn*, Th^B 1640), includes only the text "Perché non ho del vento." On its title page it says that the engraved score can be found "chez Bernard-Latte" (pl. no. B. L. 1421; copies consulted: *F-Pn*, L. 3885, and *F-Po* [treble clef], 4087). This score, published in Paris but in Italian, gives the names of the singers from the Naples premiere, not from the Théâtre-Italien.

11. Donizetti resided in Paris between 21 October 1838 and 14 December 1840, except for a brief trip to Bergamo during the summer of 1840. During that time he oversaw productions of *Roberto Devereux* and *L'elisir d'amore* at the Théâtre-Italien, reworked *Les martyrs* for the Opéra and *Lucie* for the Théâtre de le Renaissance, and composed *La fille du régiment* for the Opéra-Comique and *La favorite* for the Opéra.

music Donizetti composed for *Lucie* was recitative—is something that sets it apart from other translations of Italian operas that had careers in France.

Royer and Vaëz's revisions to the libretto—for instance, eliminating Alisa entirely, removing the duet in which Raimondo convinces Lucia to marry Arturo, and transforming the Wolf's Crag scene at the start of act 3 by moving it to later in the act, changing its setting, and eliminating the storm—have often been attributed to the limited resources of the Théâtre de la Renaissance.[12] That, however, is not the explanation the two authors gave in their introduction to the published French libretto, which they framed as an open letter to Donizetti. On the contrary, they stated:

> Everyone knows that it is not the richness of the spectacle that makes for success at the Théâtre-Italien;[13] we have simplified still further the performance of the piece by avoiding set changes in the middle of the acts, which French dramatic convention does not easily accept. The new scenes that you composed with us, in order to make this imitation of the libretto meet the demands of our theater, are for your opera a true naturalization. (Excerpt 20)

By "our theater" the authors appear to mean French theatrical conventions, not the Théâtre de la Renaissance, which is nowhere mentioned in this introduction; in fact, it appears that Donizetti and the two French librettists had prepared the translation for performances in the French provinces and that the arrangement for a Parisian premiere only came later.[14] One of the spots Royer and Vaëz adjusted in order

---

12. In *Donizetti and His Operas*, 381, Ashbrook introduces his summary of the changes with the remark, "The score is considerably changed, principally to accommodate the limited resources, financial as well as artistic, of the company at the Renaissance." A more detailed, number-by-number comparison in chart form of the Italian and French versions may be found in *Lucia di Lammermoor*, vol. 55 of *L'avant-scène opéra* (1983): 26–27. The elimination of the duet between Lucia and Raimondo may not have been Royer and Vaëz's doing, for it appears not to have been performed at the Théâtre-Italien either, even though it was included in the libretto published for the Parisian performances; not a single one of fifteen reviews from December 1837 checked to date—most of which give a detailed account of the musical numbers—mentions such a duet. On the contrary, the synopses describe act 2 as proceeding from the duet between Enrico and Lucia directly to the wedding scene (see, for example, excerpt 13).

13. Complaints about the sets, costumes, and acting abilities of many singers at the Théâtre-Italien were legion during this period.

14. "Le public de nos provinces, privé de chanteurs italiens, attendait avec impatience qu'une traduction française pût lui transmettre quelques-unes de vos belles inspirations. Nous avons choisi la *Lucia di Lammermoor* comme l'œuvre la plus poétique et la plus passionnée qu'ait enfantée votre génie musical, et nous avons essayé de lui adapter une forme et des paroles qui permissent aux théâtres de nos grandes villes de la populariser en France." This letter is dated 12 January 1839 and alludes to the new music Donizetti had composed for this revision. It was included in the first French libretto, published in 1839 by Bernard Latte (copy consulted: *F-Po*, Liv. 19 [583]), whose title page calls the work a "grand opéra en trois actes (d'après le libretto italien), paroles de MM. Alphonse Royer et Gustave Vaez"; it does not mention the Théâtre de la Renaissance and lists

to "naturalize" the opera was its ending. In their revised version, Asthon (as Enrico was called—and spelled—in French) *does* come back in the last scene, sword in hand, ready to fight the duel he and Edgard had set up at the start of the act. But he arrives between the two verses of the cabaletta, after Edgard has stabbed himself, just in time to be forgiven by Edgard and to express his remorse.[15] The rearrangements in acts 1 and 3 that eliminate the scene changes can also be read as an effort to make the narrative more coherent. One of the time-honored principles of serious French drama, and one scrupulously observed on the French operatic stage in the seventeenth and eighteenth centuries, was the *liaison des scènes,* the principle that within an act the stage could never be empty—at least one character had to remain from one scene to the next. As a corollary, there could be no change of setting within an act.[16] Royer and Vaëz rearranged act 3 in accordance with these principles. Cammarano's design had Enrico leave his sister's wedding celebrations not only in the middle of the party, but in the middle of a violent storm, to ride off to Edgardo's ruined tower in order to issue a challenge, then ride back in time to observe his sister go mad; the French libretto kept the whole act inside the Asthon castle ("une galerie de communication entre les appartements du château d'Asthon. Au fond les jardins illuminés"). At the start of the act the offstage guests are heard celebrating (scene 1) while Asthon and Gilbert enter the stage (scene 2); then Edgard arrives to call on Asthon, rather than the other way round (scene 3). After their confrontation the party resumes, this time with the guests visible (scene 4), only to be interrupted by Raimond's announcement that Lucie has murdered her husband (scene 5); the rest proceeds the same way in the two versions. Perhaps these changes were made to help theaters save money on sets, but long-standing dramatic principles also appear to have been in play.

---

the roles without attributing them to specific singers. The manuscript libretto submitted by Anténor Joly for approval by the censors states that it was "received" at the Théâtre de la Renaissance on 6 April 1839 and sent to the Ministry of the Interior one month later (*F-Pan*, F[18] 1261).

15. This ending can be heard on the French version recorded live at Martina Franca—*Lucie de Lammermoor,* Orchestra Internazionale d'Italia, cond. Maruizio Benini, with Patrizia Ciofi and Alexandru Badea, CDS 204/1–2 (Genova: Dynamic, 1998)—although the other and in most respects superior recording (*Lucie de Lammermoor,* Orchestre et Chœur de l'Opéra National de Lyon, cond. Evelino Pidò, with Natalie Dessay and Roberto Alagna, 7243 5 45528 2 3 [Virgin Classics, 2002]) does not bring back Asthon at the end and omits the extra bars of recitative Donizetti wrote to accommodate him.

16. These principles derive from adherence to the Aristotelian unities of action and time. Whereas spoken tragedy did not admit changes of place (a unity not enunciated by Aristotle but adopted nonetheless by d'Aubignac and other seventeenth-century theorists) until well into the eighteenth century and then only between acts, French opera from its initiation permitted changes of place between acts—and even within, provided they were brought about by the action of a character, such as a magic spell. Regarding the construction of acts and scenes in French tragedy, see Jacques Scherer, *La dramaturgie classique en France* (Paris: Librairie Nizet, n.d.), especially part 2, chap. 5 ("Les liaisons des scènes"), and Jean-Pierre Perchellet, *L'héritage classique: La tragédie entre 1680 et 1814* (Paris: Honoré Champion, 2004), part 1, chap. 4, especially 124 and 136.

Another change that seems to have been made in the interest of providing greater dramatic coherence was enlarging the role of Gilbert (Normanno). In *Lucia* Normanno opens the opera by leading the male chorus in its search for Edgardo and in revealing to Enrico that Lucia and Edgardo are in love. He disappears for the rest of the act, then resurfaces briefly at the start of act 2 and again as one of the spectators to the mad scene, following which Raimondo accuses him of being the cause of the tragedy, in a very brief *scena* (thirty bars) that is often cut. Gilbert, however, not only appears in every act, he is the catalyst for much of what happens. He is a kind of double agent, accepting money both from Asthon to keep him informed, and from the lovers to watch over their rendezvous. Gilbert's asides during Asthon's double aria in Royer and Vaëz's reworking of act 1, scene 3, reveal his duplicity and venality:[17]

Asthon, Gilbert, les chasseurs rentrant

CHOEUR DE CHASSEURS
Le soleil hors de la plaine   [= "Come vinti da stanchezza"]
Nous fait chercher un abri [. . .]

Dans une sombre avenue
Parut à notre vue
L'ennemi par vous d'ici chassé, [. . .]

ASTHON
Qui donc?

LE CHOEUR
        Edgard.

ASTHON
                Encore?
Oh! rage qui dévore!
C'en est fait, il doit périr.

GILBERT
Oui, c'est le parti le plus sage
(*à part*) Et qui me plaît davantage;
Enfin, bien, très bien. [Libretto: "Ce coup-là va m'enrichir."]

ASTHON
A moi, viens, ouvre tes ailes,   [= cabaletta: "La pietade in suo favore"]
Je t'évoque, ange du mal [. . .]
[text swears vengeance against Edgard]

---

17. The text presented here follows the 1839 libretto for its layout and rubrics but incorporates textual variants found in the piano-vocal score deriving from this production (Paris: Bernard Latte, [1839]). No critical edition has yet been prepared of either *Lucia* or *Lucie*.

GILBERT, *à part* [during the repeat of the cabaletta]
A prix égal, à ne rien feindre,
Je le sauve de bon cœur.

[CHORUS OF HUNTERS: The sun shining in the plain forced us to seek
shelter . . . On a dark road we caught sight of the enemy you have driven from here.
ASTHON: Who? CHORUS: Edgard. ASTHON: Again? Oh, devouring rage!
That's it, he has to die. GILBERT: Yes, that's the right decision. (Aside) And one
that pleases me more; very good. (The libretto continues, "This business is going to
make me rich.") ASTHON: Come, open your wings, I invoke you, angel of evil . . .
GILBERT (aside): To be honest, for the same price I'd be happy to save him.]

In act 1, scene 5, Asthon, who learns from Arthur that Edgard is about to be sent
on a mission to France, countermands his order to Gilbert to assassinate Edgard.
Gilbert remains alone onstage in a scene that forms the liaison between Asthon's
departure and Lucie's first appearance:

GILBERT, *seul*
Il part, c'est me voler; pour tuer notre amant
J'aurais eu de mon maître une assez ronde somme . . .
Diable soit du scrupule! avec un pareil homme
Pas moyen de gagner sa vie honnêtement.
⠀⠀⠀⠀Mais dans l'allée obscurcie,
Là-bas, voici venir la charmante Lucie.
Doucement, sir Gilbert, chaque rôle à son tour;
Prenons l'air attendri d'un confident d'amour.

[GILBERT, *alone*
He's leaving—and stealing from me. For killing our little lover
I would have had a nice round sum from my master.
The devil take scruples! With such a man
it's not possible to earn an honest living.
⠀⠀⠀⠀But in the dark pathway
I see the charming Lucie coming.
Be careful, Sir Gilbert, every role in turn.
Let me adopt the tender mien of a lover's confidant.]

Neither the conversation between Asthon and Arthur, who fears that Lucie may love
Edgar, nor Gilbert's monologue has an equivalent in the Italian libretto.

At the start of act 2 we learn that Gilbert has been engaged in much more than
intercepting letters: he has been to France with Edgard, planting doubts in his mind
about Lucie's fidelity. Furthermore, he has stolen Lucie's ring from Edgard's finger
while he slept and had an expert copy made. This he produces later in the act to show
Lucie that Edgard has betrayed her. When Edgard makes his dramatic entrance just

after Lucie has signed the marriage contract, it is Gilbert who ushers him in. Gilbert even sings the music in the sextet that had been assigned to Alisa in the Italian version of the opera. And at the very end of the opera, Gilbert arrives with Asthon for the duel, carrying the swords.

These changes not only give Gilbert much more presence in the opera than Normanno ever had, they also change the tone of several scenes. Given the French concern for the qualities of librettos, it seemed likely that reviewers in 1839 would comment on Gilbert's greatly enlarged role. But they did not; critics tended to observe only in a general way that the libretto had been improved (see the positive but imprecise comments in excerpts 21–23). Admittedly, the alterations to Gilbert's role mostly affect the recitative, and reviewers who were being guided by their ear would probably not have noticed the modifications these changes entailed in vocal scoring within the well-known set pieces. But to me Gilbert remained a puzzle, because his blatant venality seemed even to border on the comic tradition of the grasping servant looking out only for himself. Whereas such a character could seem palatable on the stage of the Théâtre de la Renaissance, which had a very mixed repertoire, it was hard to imagine him passing unchanged onto the stage of the Académie Royale de Musique. In fact, Gilbert put me in mind of Don Gaspar, the buffo chamberlain in *L'ange de Nisida*, the next opera Donizetti intended for the Théâtre de la Renaissance and which also had a libretto by Royer and Vaëz. When the Théâtre de la Renaissance folded and Donizetti salvaged *L'ange de Nisida* by transforming it into *La favorite* for the Opéra, Don Gaspar's role had to be radically toned down,[18] and I thus expected to find that a similar process might have operated in 1846 when *Lucie* was taken up into the repertoire of the Opéra. The evidence, however, is ambiguous. The 1846 libretto is virtually the same as the one printed in 1839 for the Théâtre de la Renaissance, but the case of *La favorite* shows that the text of a libretto might retain for decades passages that had been cut within days of the premiere. The performing parts for *Lucie* that were prepared for the Opéra tell a more complex story. All of Gilbert's music was copied into the original layer, but the smarmiest bits, such as the monologue quoted above from the end of act 1, were crossed out, and in other places his words were modified to make him less objectionable and to raise the tone. Given that the *Lucie* sources have not yet received serious study, it is not possible to date these changes securely. But at the very least these modifications show that at the Opéra there was uneasiness about the character of Gilbert.[19]

For most of the libretto, Royer and Vaëz's job was to craft a French text that

---

18. Regarding the role of Don Gaspar in the two operas, see Rebecca Harris-Warrick, "Historical Introduction," in Gaetano Donizetti, Alphonse Royer, Gustave Vaëz, and Eugène Scribe, *La favorite: Opéra en quatre actes,* ed. Rebecca Harris-Warrick, critical ed. (Milan: Ricordi, 1997), 1: xvii–xx.

19. These annotations appear in the archival manuscript score (*F-Po,* A549a.I-III) and the surviving performing parts (*F-Po,* Mat. 19 [328]). The only solo vocal role still among the set is for Gilbert.

would fit the rhythms of Donizetti's already composed music. This meant, by and large, that the translation could not be literal, and there are many instances of interesting textual choices, even on a micro level, that not only meet the rhythmic exigencies, but also accord with the librettists' larger enterprise of "naturalizing" the opera. For example, in the French text of the famous sextet, unlike in the Italian, Edgard does not read remorse in Lucie's face, but focuses instead on the ring he has on his finger as a token of her pledge to him ("De son vœu j'ai là le gage, / Mais l'effroi sur son visage / Du parjure est le présage" [I have the proof of her vow here [on my finger], but the fear in her face is a sign of betrayal]). Moreover, as the musical demands of the ensemble fragment his line into small phrases, the accompanying words demand gestures of pointing to his finger: "J'ai son gage, . . . j'ai là son gage, . . . oui, là! là!"[20] This insistence on gesture not only sets up the visually dramatic moment during the *tempo di mezzo* in which Edgard tears off the ring and throws it at Lucie's feet before violently pulling the one he had given her off her finger, but also follows through on the plot thread set up by Gilbert's having used a counterfeit ring to convince Lucie of Edgard's infidelity. It thus appeals to French taste in two ways: by increasing plot coherence and by heightening the *coup de théâtre*.[21]

Another textual choice raises an issue about how the opera was intended to be performed. At the start of act 3, where the chorus is celebrating the wedding of Lucie and Arthur—in the Italian version this is the "D'immenso giubilo" chorus—Royer and Vaëz added four more lines of text that have no equivalent in the Italian: "Le ciel pâlit déjà / Dansons encore, / Pour nous l'aurore / Trop tôt viendra" (The sky is starting to brighten, let's keep dancing; dawn will come all too soon). The music Donizetti had already composed for the Naples premiere is very clearly dance music, as the stage directions also tell us ("Dalle sale contigue si ascolta la musica di liete danze" [From the adjoining rooms joyful dance music is heard]), but this newly added French text seems explicitly designed to invite a ballet, and it certainly would have been easy enough to insert more dance music into this spot. The Théâtre de la Renaissance production did not provide a ballet, although a writer for the *Gazette de France* (29 August 1839) suggested it should do so, partly because the theater seemed to have the means—after all, some other performances on its stage did include dance. But whatever the circumstances at the Renaissance, it looks as if Royer and Vaëz were at least trying to set up a spot where a ballet could logically be inserted, should a theater decide to have one. If a single sentence from the *Coureur des spectacles* (17 February 1846) is to be believed, the Opéra itself considered working a ballet into *Lucie* when it was performed there in 1846. But in the event, a different solution prevailed: no ballet was added inside the work, but instead a ballet was performed after the curtain

20. Gaetano Donizetti, *Théâtre de la Renaissance / Lucie de Lamermoor* [sic], piano-vocal score (Paris: Bernard Latte, [1839]), 86.
21. Cammarano's scene has less visual intensity: Edgardo gives his ring back to Lucia, then asks her for the ring she wears, which he throws down and tramples.

came down on the opera. At first this was a potpourri of favorite *pas* from a variety of works, but soon the decision was made to put on a short ballet-pantomime, such as *Paquita,* or a single act from a longer ballet, such as *La péri*.[22] Théophile Gautier's take on this choice was that Léon Pillet, the director of the Opéra, must have decided that because people were accustomed to seeing *Lucie* without a ballet, it would have seemed odd to add one (excerpt 31).

One issue that did exercise quite a few critics was whether translations of operas were a good idea at all. This, of course, was a major debate that had been going on in Paris for decades, and in this particular set of reviews the question of translation was not just an aesthetic issue—it was inextricably bound up with the institutional politics of the various theaters. Excerpts 24 and 25 present two contrary opinions. The first, from *La gazette de France,* offers a strongly negative view that seems to be based on principle: "Whatever gave Donizetti the bizarre idea of having one of his best works translated? . . . Lucia can only lose by leaving her native country. Every copy is inferior to the original." However, this opinion is underpinned by the writer's desire to protect the repertoire of the Théâtre-Italien in its pure form. The other passage, from *L'écho français,* argues that the French should be given access to *more* foreign opera, German as well as Italian, and that the unsubsidized Théâtre de la Renaissance, which had just succeeded beyond everyone's expectations in mounting a translated opera, now had a mission to broaden the available repertoire. Gautier also saw the Théâtre de la Renaissance as both a new opera house and a new theater for serious spoken drama (excerpt 26), whereas Berlioz wished that it might become an opera house where the composer was finally in charge (excerpt 27).

Mark Everist has recounted the sad story of how the official theaters attacked the Théâtre de la Renaissance because, with its combination of plays, *opéras comiques,* and now serious opera, it was impinging on the repertoire of all four government-subsidized theaters.[23] However, for a brief moment in 1839 the theater basked in almost universal acclaim and allowed audiences to dream that opera in Paris might achieve a more varied configuration. The reviewers seem to have been flabbergasted that the Théâtre de la Renaissance could have succeeded in putting on *Lucie de Lammermoor* as well as it did; *La France musicale* was not alone in having expected a failure (excerpt 28). In sharp distinction to the cautious or even negative tone the reviewers had taken when *Lucia* had premiered in 1837, this time most of them accepted its merits—or, at least its popularity—as a given. (By way of example, excerpt 29 shows that *Le corsaire* still harbored doubts about the opera, whereas *La France musicale* called the score "brilliant and dramatic.") Because the opera was already well-known, only a few critics included the traditional plot synopsis in their write-ups.

22. The ballets that accompanied *Lucie* are all listed in the register of performances in the manuscript "Journal de l'Opéra" (*F-Po*).

23. Mark Everist, "Theatres of Litigation: Stage Music at the Théâtre de la Renaissance, 1838–1840," *Cambridge Opera Journal* 16, no. 2 (2004): 133–61.

The success of the opera appeared all the more astonishing because the singers were young and virtually untried: the English soprano Anna Thillon was only nineteen, and the young Italian tenor, Achille Ricciardi, had only recently arrived in Paris. By most reports, both did very creditable or even praiseworthy jobs (depending on the writer), despite the fact that Ricciardi apparently mangled the French. Only the baritone, Auguste Hurteaux, was generally seen as a disappointment. The two leads could not compete vocally with the stars at the Théâtre-Italien, but they apparently did hold their own—and when in the fall of 1839 *Le ménestrel* compared *Lucia* at the Théâtre-Italien with the new *Lucie* (excerpt 30), it offered the startling opinion that "judging by the general impression of the drama, both as a musical whole and as a spectacle, the advantage rests entirely with the Théâtre de la Renaissance."

Académie Royale de Musique

After the Théâtre de la Renaissance closed early in 1840, *Lucie de Lammermoor* began touring the provinces, and the Parisian publishers were spurred by its success into putting out still more arrangements, fantasies, and quadrilles based on its favorite tunes. But for the next several years, the only place to hear *Lucia* whole in Paris was, once again, at the Théâtre-Italien, where the opera remained consistently in the repertoire.[24] However, in January 1846 Léon Pillet, the director of the Opéra, wrote to the minister of the interior to request permission to perform the French version of *Lucie* at the Opéra. This was an unusual proposal, and Pillet justified it on the grounds of needing to vary the repertoire of short operas that could be performed before a ballet. He went on to explain that the work would essentially be a revival, in that it had not only had a run several years previously in Paris, but that parts of it had been performed at the Opéra in benefit concerts (see the years 1838 and 1841 in table 9.1). He added that because the singers had also been performing *Lucie* in the provinces, they already knew their roles. In fact, he went on, "it is astonishing that I have been neglecting for so long such an obvious way of varying my repertoire." The president of the theatrical commission, however, was not pleased. He objected to the idea of translations on the stage of the Opéra, wondered why the Opéra would want to enter into direct competition with the Théâtre-Italien, and asked why a foreign composer should be preferred to a French one for a slot at the Opéra. He nonetheless recommended approval on the condition that *Lucie* not count among the number of works the Opéra was required to put on, and the performances went ahead on this basis.[25]

24. According to Soubies, *Le Théâtre-Italien, Lucia* was performed annually until 1855 (excepting 1852), with four performances during December 1837, seventeen in 1838, ten in 1839, six in 1840, six in 1841, twelve in 1842, eleven in 1843, four in 1844, seven in 1845, three in 1846, and nine in 1847.

25. All four of the relevant documents may be found in *F-Pan*, AJ[13] 183. The libretto for the Opéra production, which was published by Bernard Latte in 1846 (copy consulted: *F-Po*, Liv. 19

The debate at the official level found reflection in the press. *Le corsaire* claimed that it had been advising the Académie Royale de Musique for a long time to take over works from the Théâtre-Italien and was happy to see that someone was finally listening (excerpt 32). On the other hand, the critic in the *Journal des débats* (who in this instance was not Berlioz) remarked that he was not going to take the extreme position that only French operas should be performed at the Opéra, but in his opinion works already performed in other theaters in Paris did not belong there (excerpt 33). The *Coureur des spectacles* probably represented the view of a large portion of the audience in saying that people were eager to go see an opera that had already been a success and which they knew in advance they would like (excerpt 34). And the public did flock to see *Lucie* once it opened on 20 February; in its first four weeks alone the opera was performed a dozen times, notwithstanding the fact that the baritone, Paul Barrhoilhet, was sick and had to be replaced by lesser singers. *Le corsaire* predicted a new era of prosperity for the Opéra (excerpt 35), and in April *Le ménestrel* reported that Pillet was planning to put on more translations of Italian operas and was at that moment in Italy recruiting singers. To many observers, supporters and detractors alike, it appeared that the Opéra was in the process of becoming a second Théâtre-Italien (excerpt 36).

Even though reactions to their performances constituted a large part of virtually all reviews, so far this account has deliberately neglected the singers, primarily because interpreting the critics' comments is so problematic. However, it is not possible to discuss the critical reception of *Lucie de Lammermoor* in 1846 without mentioning Gilbert Duprez, whose performance as Edgard dominated the press reports. Duprez had created the role at San Carlo in 1835, during his years in Italy, but by time the Théâtre-Italien put *Lucia* on in Paris he had returned to France, been engaged at the Opéra, and made a brilliant debut in *Guillaume Tell*. And even though Duprez sang

---

[293], is virtually identical to the one from the Théâtre de la Renaissance. However, until all the sources for the two versions are sorted out (librettos both printed and in manuscript, printed piano-vocal score, printed orchestral parts, several editions of *morceaux détachés,* manuscript full score, manuscript performing parts, and a few pages in Donizetti's hand—not counting the sources, printed and manuscript, associated with the Théâtre-Italien), it will not be possible to make firm claims about how the two versions may have related to each other or how the work's contents changed over time. The numerous layers in the Opéra's manuscript sources do show, nonetheless, that the French version got at least partially re-Italianized at some point: for example, a French translation of "Regnava nel silenzio" (with two different versions of the text) was added to the manuscript score (see n. 19) as a substitution for Lucie's entrance aria, "Que n'avons nous des ailes"; the original layer says that this substitution was "pour Mme De Lagrange," who briefly sang the role of Lucie at the Opéra in December of 1848 (*La revue et gazette musicale de Paris,* 24 December 1848). Whether that substitution was a one-off or a permanent change remains to be determined. (Anna de Lagrange was French but, with her very flexible and agile voice, specialized in Italian coloratura roles and spent most of her career outside of France. Regarding her career and vocal qualities, see the review in *La revue et gazette musicale de Paris,* 27 March 1853, of her debut at the Théâtre-Italien as Rosina in the *Barber of Seville.*)

bits of *Lucia* in Paris at various benefit performances (see table 9.1), Rubini was the tenor who set the standard for the role as far as Parisian audiences were concerned. So when it was announced that Duprez would try to recreate his early Neapolitan triumph on the stage of the Opéra, the Parisian musical world was electrified. By 1846, however, if the press accounts are to be believed, Duprez's voice was showing serious signs of wear. *Le constitutionnel* (5 March 1846), among others, attributed his decline to his having had to perform roles composed for Nourrit, and critics were not optimistic about his ability to take on a role they saw as challenging, even if it had been written for him. But by virtually all accounts, Duprez triumphed, and excerpts 37–40 show a tiny sampling of the encomiums his performance in the role generated. Even taking into account the critics' inability to resist the meta-narrative of death and resurrection, the ecstatic tone is striking. Poor Maria Nau could not compete; even when reviewers had one or two favorable sentences about her, they buried them in the midst of brilliant fanfares about Duprez (excerpts 38–41).

It is hard to detach the Duprez story from contemporary assessments of the roles themselves, but it is nonetheless clear that in Paris from 1837 to 1846, the title character in this opera was seen as secondary to her leading man. Of the three sopranos who initiated the runs of performances at the various theaters in Paris, only Persiani received anything approaching equal time in the press, and even then the critics did not seem to find the scenes in which Lucia appeared as dramatically compelling as Edgardo's. Even in 1846 the mad scene continued to be mentioned in passing, if at all—the only thing *La gazette de France* had to say about it in a lengthy review was that Nau sang it with brio and in tune (excerpt 41). On the other hand, *La France musicale* considered Edgard's death scene "le sublime de l'art" (excerpt 39). For by this time it is also clear that *Lucia di Lammermoor* was well on its way to becoming canonic; *Le constitutionnel* even remarked that "everyone knows Donizetti's score by heart" (excerpt 40). Only the most curmudgeonly of critics dared to say anything negative about the music, and several called it Donizetti's masterpiece. But critical reception was yet again intertwined with the personal. *Lucie de Lammermoor* opened at the Paris Opéra within three weeks of Donizetti's forced removal to the sanatorium in Ivry, where he was to be kept for the next sixteen months, only to finally leave so he could return to Bergamo to die. In February 1846 word of his deteriorating mental state spread quickly and even colored some of the responses to *Lucie*. Gustave Héquet compared Donizetti to a harmonious lyre that had been broken before its time (excerpt 42). And Théophile Gautier expressed his wish for another resurrection in addition to Duprez's, while recognizing that a new dawn would not arrive (excerpt 43). The madness that moved him to eloquence, and which he attributed to the struggles of artistic creation, was not Lucia's, but Donizetti's.

APPENDIX
Excerpts from Press Reports on Performances in Three Parisian Theaters

Théâtre-Italien (1837)

EXCERPT I. THÉOPHILE GAUTIER, «LA PRESSE», 21 DECEMBER 1837

Enfin, voici un opéra nouveau. Il était temps! Si résignés et si patients que soient les habitués des Bouffes, ils commençaient à être bien fatigués de l'audition des mêmes chefs-d'œuvre, chantés par les mêmes acteurs; . . . les acteurs eux-mêmes s'endormaient en scène, excédés de dire toujours les mêmes phrases. *Lucia di Lammermoor* va réveiller un peu toute cette somnolence.

EXCERPT 2. «LE CONSTITUTIONNEL», 15 DECEMBER 1837

Marino Faliero n'est-t-il pas né en Italie. Donizetti l'a écrit en France, tout exprès pour les menus plaisirs des dilettanti parisiens, c'est un hommage rendu à notre public et dont nous reconnaissons volontiers toute la courtoisie; mais en général nos dilettanti tiennent peu à ces cadeaux de primeur; ils aiment tout autant qu'on leur donne des ouvrages éprouvés en Italie et dont la réputation est toute faite. Cela les arrange mieux et met leur admiration plus à l'aise. *Lucia di Lammermoor* ne pouvait avoir l'inconvénient de les faire hésiter et de laisser leur jugement en balance. Les échos péninsulaires avaient d'avance apporté le bruit de son succès transalpin jusqu'à notre boulevard Italien. Nous n'avions plus qu'à nous laisser faire et à être du même avis que l'Italie, c'est ce qui vient d'arriver.

EXCERPT 3. «LE COURRIER FRANÇAIS», 14 DECEMBER 1837

Enfin l'on en revient à la musique italienne d'Italie, et l'on renonce au régime de celle qui se fabriquait à Paris ou à Londres. Ce n'est pas notre faute, si l'on n'a pas reconnu plus tôt l'abus de ce régime débilitant, somnifère et anti-digestif, qui menait tout droit à l'atonie, de l'atonie à l'étisie, et de l'étisie à la mort. Mais, depuis le succès des *Puritains,* on n'était préoccupé que d'une idée, on ne connaissait qu'une nécessité; on voulait avant tout trouver en chaque opéra une tunique pour Rubini, un manteau pour Lablache, une cuirasse pour Tamburini, et un long voile, blanc ou noir, pour Mlle Grisi. . . .

Ne réveillons pas les morts! Que la terre soit légère aux *Ernani,* aux *Marino,* aux *Briganti,* aux *Malek-Adhel* et aux *Ildegonda*! La funèbre procession s'arrête; le massacre des innocents est interrompu. Voici qu'on a demandé à l'Italie l'un des nouveaux opéras qu'elle attendait avec le plus de plaisir et croyait doués de la force vitale la plus énergique: l'Italie, qui n'est pas trop riche, hélas! a désigné *Lucia di Lammermoor,* composée, il y a deux ou trois ans, pour Duprez et Mme Tacchinardi-Persiani par le maëstro Donizetti. Depuis que Rossini se tait, depuis que Bellini a succombé, Donizetti, le fécond, le facile et l'ingénieux Donizetti porte en ses mains le sceptre musical.

EXCERPT 4. «LA QUOTIDIENNE», 18 DECEMBER 1837

Lucia di Lammermoor a été écrite à Naples, il y a deux ou trois ans, pour Duprez, et cette Mme Persiani, que nous venons d'y applaudir. Il y a sept ans que M. Caraffa composa *Le Nozze di Lammermoor* sur un libretto du poète Barochi. Sa musique était fort remarquable, mais elle n'obtint que peu de succès, parce que nous avons le ridicule de ne pas croire à la musique italienne faite à Paris; si M. Caraffa, nous eût envoyé sa partition de Naples ou de Florence, nous l'aurions trouvée ravissante; c'est, du reste, un préjugé dont plusieurs maëstri de talent ont subi les tristes conséquences, le seul Bellini en a triomphé dans les *Puritani,* mais Marliani, Mercadante, Gabussi et Costa en ont été les victimes.

EXCERPT 5. «LE CORSAIRE», 17 DECEMBER 1837

Lucia de Lammermoor qui a été donnée ces jours-ci au Théâtre-Italien, est un des trois chefs-d'œuvre que la munificence de MM. Robert et Séverini offrent tous les ans aux stalles et aux loges de leur théâtre, par reconnaissance et par ordre de Monsieur le ministre des beaux-arts. Ce chef-d'œuvre n'a donné aucun démenti à ses frères aînés. Comme eux il a mérité les encouragements de la presse. Le public a baillé à l'unanimité. . . . Ce poème tragique se vendait deux sous à la porte, sous ce titre *argument,* entre deux marchandes d'oranges.

Cet argument est imité de Walter-Scott. Il est fort connu. Il a des bottes en buffleterie de garde nationale, bottes *des Puritains,* des gants de boxeur, et une épée en métal de casserole, à la chute des reins; voilà pour la couleur locale.

Quant à la musique, c'est autre chose. Il est prodigieux qu'elle ne soit pas plus médiocre.

Dans le foyer, plusieurs personnes en lunettes, affirmaient que *Lucia di Lammermoor* était la 55,919ᵉ partition de M. Donizetti, musicien à part qui parcourt tous les ans sept à huit lieues de poèmes d'opéras. On conçoit qu'un pareil *Maëstro,* chemin de fer de la double-croche, se fatigue quelquefois, lui et son public.

On a cependant remarqué au premier acte, un assez joli duo, et au second acte, un final qui ne doit son effet qu'à la voix de Rubini. Le reste a passé sans qu'on s'en aperçut. C'est du Rossini à l'eau tiède. . . . C'est avec peine que nous avons vu de grands artistes tels que MM. Rubini et Tamburini s'épuiser à animer une musique inerte qui manque à la fois d'âme, de souffle et de vie.

EXCERPT 6. GÉRARD DE NERVAL, «LA PRESSE», 28 DECEMBER 1837

Le succès de l'opéra de Donizetti se consolide de plus en plus: cette partition restera au répertoire assurément, et nous y reviendrons volontiers encore après plusieurs auditions. On reconnaît là-dedans l'habilité et toute la facilité de l'auteur d'*Anna Bolena,* l'œuvre qui approche le plus des beaux ouvrages de Rossini. L'instrumentation, riche et claire, relève fort heureusement ce que les motifs ont parfois de pâle et de commun. Les chœurs nous ont paru en général bien traités, et parmi les morceaux que nous avons le plus remarqués, il faut citer en première ligne le finale du deuxième acte, dont l'*andante* admirable est suivi d'un vigoureux *allegro,* parfait d'expression et de situation. Dans le duo qui termine le premier acte, on ne peut trop admirer la simple et touchante mélodie à trois temps qui en forme la *cabalette,* et l'*addio* original et expressif jeté à la fin.

Dans le troisième acte, tout est goûté et applaudi avec raison; cependant nous pensons que la plus grande part dans les éloges doit être attribuée aux exécutants. Du reste *l'andante* de l'air final de Rubini et le *majeur* du chœur funèbre qui suit sont admirables de facture et d'effet scénique. C'est sans contredit une des meilleures inspirations de Donizetti.

EXCERPT 7. «LE NATIONAL», 15 DECEMBER 1837

C'est sur ce canevas que Donizetti a brodé une musique assez gracieuse, qui, sans faire époque dans le monde musical, sera cependant agréable aux amateurs et aux habitués du Théâtre-Italien, et variera le répertoire si monotone des bouffes. . . . La plus grande partie de ses œuvres, tant *Lucia* que *Marino Faliero, Anna Bolena,* est faite de remplissages, d'imitations, de réminiscences de lui-même, de Rossini et d'autres; une autre partie, la *coda* des duos, des airs et des chœurs, est celle dont le copiste de tout compositeur italien peut faire la besogne. Quelquefois on croit le voir prendre l'essor, on s'apprête à l'écouter attentivement, mais il retombe bientôt et reprend sa marche accoutumée et avec elle la monotonie de ses travaux de fabrique.

EXCERPT 8. «LA GAZETTE DE FRANCE», 18 DECEMBER 1837

La musique du maestro Donizetti est, comme toutes les œuvres de ce compositeur, quelque chose d'élégant, de gracieux, de facile, sans élévation ni profondeur. Sauf deux ou trois morceaux qui portent un caractère d'originalité, tout le reste n'offre que des motifs très habilement arrangés, fort bien appropriés aux situations, mais qu'on croit avoir entendus ailleurs et qui manquent par conséquent du mérite de la nouveauté.

. . . M. Donizetti a beaucoup d'obligations à Rubini, Tamburini, et Mme Persiani. La musique, quelle qu'elle soit, ne paraît jamais médiocre quand elle a de pareils interprètes. Le Théâtre-Italien, s'il ne compte pas dans *Lucia* un ouvrage du premier ordre, a acquis du moins un moyen de plus de mettre en évidence d'une manière très heureuse trois de ses premiers talents, et surtout Mme Persiani, dont on ne connaissait pas encore tout le mérite.

EXCERPT 9. «L'ARTISTE», 2E SÉRIE, T. 4 (1839)

D'ailleurs, à côté de quelques desseins employés en partie avant lui, et de l'allegro du duo du troisième acte, dont le moule est dans *Ricciardo e Zoraïde,* le reste de la partition est aussi original qu'il est permis à Donizetti d'en faire. Les duos et les airs sont d'un beau caractère, et le finale du deuxième acte, avec son magnifique *andante* et sa péroraison énergique, pourra toujours être considéré comme le beau semblant d'un chef d'œuvre.

EXCERPT 10. «LE CONSTITUTIONNEL», 15 DECEMBER 1837

Il signor Salvador Cammarano est l'auteur des paroles. Il ne faut pas s'attendre à retrouver Walter Scott dans il signor Salvador Cammarano. Que deviendraient les livrets et les faiseurs de livrets, s'ils étaient obligés d'être eux-mêmes de grands génies, de grands poètes, ou de reproduire respectueusement les créations des poètes illustres et des hommes de génie? Le métier serait par trop difficile; on n'y pourrait plus tenir. Il signor Salvador Cammarano n'y a donc pas mis de façons; il a rendu méconnaissables, par la toute puissance du livret, les poétiques personnages qui occupent de leurs amours, de leurs passions et de leurs infortunes le célèbre roman de Walter Scott: Edgar de Ravenswood, Arthur Bucklaw, Henri Ashton, Raimon Bidebent, et enfin la pâle et mélancolique Lucie de Lammermoor. Les personnages qu'il n'a point défigurés, il les a complètement fait disparaître, et ceux-là ne sont certainement pas les plus malheureux et les plus à plaindre. Ne demandez donc point au signor S. Cammarano le vieux et fidèle Caleb Balderston; il signor l'a supprimé d'un trait de plume. Oui, mon pauvre Caleb, il faut nous passer de toi: ainsi le veulent le livret et M. Cammarano.

EXCERPT 11. «LE CHARIVARI», 15 DECEMBER 1837

L'auteur du libretto s'est approprié une partie de la terrible légende si dramatiquement mise en scène par l'illustre romancier écossais; mais il n'en a conservé que les incidents tristes et lugubres. Il a rejeté toutes les scènes de passion tendre, de comique naturel, de joyeuses illusions, toutes les demi-teintes en un mot qui, dans le beau tableau de Walter-Scott, adoucissent la sombre couleur du fond.

Ainsi, il a fait disparaître ce bon Caleb, une des plus heureuses entre les heureuses créations de l'auteur de *Waverly*, et qui restera comme un type de finesse naïve et de bonhomie comique à l'égal de l'immortel Sancho-Pança.

Le signor Poeta a laissé également de côté la mère du Lucy, cette fière et orgueilleuse parvenue qui parle de *mésalliance* et de *petites gens* avec autant d'aplomb qu'une de nos baronnes de pacotille de la cour citoyenne.

Il n'est pas non plus question de lord Ashton, l'ambitieux conseiller, espèce de girouette peinte en bronze qui, malgré ses airs de rigide gravité, tourne sans cesse au vent de la faveur, et change avec tant de facilité ses amitiés et ses opinions politiques; véritable doctrinaire du 16e siècle.

Enfin, le jeune frère de l'héroïne, l'enfant espiègle dont la figure rosée fait un si agréable contraste au milieu des autres figures assombries par la haine, l'ambition et le désespoir, a disparu pour faire place à un grand jeune homme taillé sur le modèle des *frères féroces* du mélodrame.

Lucia di Lammermoor est donc un opéra-séria, dans la plus funéraire acception du mot.

EXCERPT 12. «LE TEMPS», 23 DECEMBER 1837

Cet excès de modestie qui a porté *il signor poeta* italien à mettre son poème sous le patronage tout puissant de la grande renommée du baronnet écossais, pourrait même, à la rigueur, passer pour un excès de prudence, et ce calcul de titre, cet emprunt de personnages, n'être qu'une rouerie habile pour faire passer, sous le manteau d'un nom justement et universellement révéré, les stériles inventions d'un génie *poétique* aux abois.

Voyez, en effet, jusqu'à quel point le *poème* en question ressemble plutôt à la *Bride of Lammermoor*, par exemple, qu'à mille autres de ces compositions romanesques qui dorment aujourd'hui, plus ou moins illustres, plus ou moins poudreuses, dans le répertoire des théâtres du boulevard, ou dans les cabinets de lecture les plus en vogue du quartier du Temple et du Marais!

EXCERPT 13. «LE COURRIER FRANÇAIS», 14 DECEMBER 1837

Donc l'opéra commence par une petite introduction de quelques mesures, dont les premières notes sont frappées à demi-voix par les cymbales, appuyées d'une note sourde de grosse caisse. La toile se lève: après un chœur brillant, le frère dénaturé, Enrico, se présente et se plaint de sa sœur qui s'obstine à aimer Edgardo di Ravenswood, l'ennemi de la race des Ashton. Il apprend qu'Edgardo a reparu dans les environs; qu'il a sauvé Lucia d'un péril, et que Lucia le revoit tous les jours. Tandis que le frère déplore la conduite de sa sœur dans un paisible andante, le chœur lui annonce qu'un homme pâle et silencieux s'est montré dans le vestibule ruiné de la tour; un fauconnier l'a reconnu; c'est Edgardo. Alors le paisible andante fait place à l'allegro agitato, et le frère quitte la scène, bouillant de fureur, altéré de vengeance. Tout ce morceau est bien coupé, bien fait, peu saillant d'invention, ou plutôt fort suspect de réminiscences. Le chœur des chasseurs, qui racontent l'apparition d'Edgardo, déclame sur un ton léger, peu en harmonie avec la situation; mais l'école italienne n'y regarde pas de si près. Le morceau suivant est une cavatine chantée par Lucia et travaillée avec un soin exquis. Une ritournelle de harpe précède l'entrée de la jeune fille; la flûte l'accompagne lorsqu'elle regrette de ne pas avoir l'aile infatigable des vents pour suivre toujours et partout celui qu'elle aime. Edgardo n'est pas loin; il vient chanter avec Lucia un duo plein de tendresse et de fraîcheur: ce duo nous paraît le morceau capital de l'œuvre; la stretta en est charmante, malgré l'éternel pizzicato sur lequel se détache la mélodie.

Au second acte, il y a d'abord un autre grand duo d'Enrico et de Lucia, divisé en trois mouvements; ce que nous en avons goûté le plus, ce sont les belles phrases de violon qui s'y dessinent avec une rare élégance; mais, en somme, le duo est long et froid. Le frère trompe la sœur, en lui disant qu'Edgardo a épousé une autre femme. La pauvre Lucia se résigne à épouser lord Arturo Bucklaw. Le chœur nuptial est très joli; par malheur, le prétendu ne ressemble pas au chœur; il chante fort mal, et, à cet égard, il a pour digne concurrent un certain Raimondo, précepteur et confident de Lucia, lequel n'ouvre pas la bouche sans détonner: on le distingue à cet avantage, à ses gants blancs et à sa culotte noire. Le mariage se conclut; Lucia signe l'acte fatal, et à peine a-t-elle signé qu'Edgardo franchit le seuil du gothique manoir. Enrico et Edgardo mettent flamberge au vent; le précepteur les engage à respecter la majesté divine, et chacun d'eux comprend la justesse de l'observation, quoique faite d'une voix fausse. Edgardo rend à Lucia l'anneau qu'il avait reçu d'elle et s'écrie avec désespoir: "Maledetto sia l'istante / Che di te mi rese amante."

Sur ce mot, *maledetto*, le chanteur trouve moyen de produire un effet que le compositeur n'avait que faiblement préparé. Nous avons tant de beaux finales! Celui de *Lucia de Lammermoor* n'est que suffisant: il débute bien et ne finit pas mal: toutefois rien n'y sort des proportions communes. Le rideau baissé, on rappelle Rubini, et Rubini reparaît avec Tamburini et Mme Persiani. On ne dira pas que les triomphateurs du Théâtre-Italien soient égoïstes: ils tiennent pour maxime qu'en fait de triomphe, quand il y en a pour un il y en a pour deux, pour trois, pour quatre: ils ne se décident à le consommer seuls que quand ils ne peuvent pas faire autrement.

Le troisième acte se compose d'un duo d'Enrico et d'Edgardo, d'un chœur, d'un air chanté par Lucia, et d'une scène finale chantée par Edgardo. Lucia est devenue folle; dans sa folie elle a tué son époux, Arturo: il ne lui reste plus qu'à mourir, et Edgardo ne saurait manquer de la suivre de près. Il ne s'abîme pas dans les sables mouvants du rivage, comme le héros de Walter Scott; il se poignarde purement et simplement, comme tout héros d'opéra est susceptible de le faire.

EXCERPT 14. «LA GAZETTE DE FRANCE», 18 DECEMBER 1837

Je ne sais pas même si lord Henri n'a pas été tué en duel par Edgard de Ravenswood; du moins il ne reparaît plus, en sorte que tous les personnages sont morts à la fin de la pièce, excepté Raimond.

EXCERPT 15. «LE CHARIVARI», 15 DECEMBER 1837

Au troisième acte, la pauvre jeune fille devient folle comme l'héroïne d'*Anna Bolena,* du *Bravo,* de *Marino Faliero,* des *Puritani,* etc., etc.; car depuis long-temps la folie est le dénoûment obligé de tous les libretti italiens. C'est comme le mariage sur nos théâtres.

EXCERPT 16. «LE SIÈCLE», 14 DECEMBER 1837

La scène de la folie est un peu longue, un peu froide, comme celle d'*Anna Bolena,* comme celle des *Puritani,* comme toutes les scènes de cette espèce; mais elle se termine par un chant, *Spargi qualche pianto,* le plus orné, le plus brillant qui se puisse imaginer.

EXCERPT 17. «LE TEMPS», 23 DECEMBER 1837

Au troisième acte, après une scène de provocation entre Ashton et Ravenswood, arrive l'inévitable scène de folie. Le théâtre, qui a abusé de tout, a surtout fait des scènes de folie un usage tout à fait exorbitant; soyez surs que sur notre théâtre moderne, toute femme à qui survient une contrariété imprévue ou un chagrin violent, tournera à la folie avec une déplorable facilité. Les symptômes de cette cruelle épidémie dramatique sont effrayants de simplicité.—Une robe blanche, un visage pâle, un peigne qui tombe et qui laisse flotter au hasard une maigre chevelure sur les épaules,—voilà pour les signes extérieurs.—Un grand air accompagné de gestes heurtés et d'effets quelque peu outrés; des prosopopées plus ou moins poétiques consistant à ressusciter les êtres chéris plus ou moins morts dans les scènes précédentes,—voilà pour la littérature de ces coups de théâtre qui, à force d'avoir été répétés sur tous les tons et dans toutes les circonstances de la vie passionnée et conventionnelle du théâtre, ne produisent plus aujourd'hui qu'un effet médiocre, même sur les imaginations les plus jeunes et les moins blasées.

Voilà le résultat dramatique de la scène de folie de la Lucia. Quant à son mérite musical, et surtout quant à la manière dont l'air en question a été chanté par madame Persiani, c'est une autre affaire! Une pareille voix eût fait passer, bien plus! eût fait applaudir bien d'autres banalités cent fois plus démonétisées encore qu'une scène de folie!

EXCERPT 18. «LA GAZETTE DE FRANCE», 18 DECEMBER 1837

La scène de folie qui suit a fourni à Mme Persiani l'occasion de déployer, sinon un talent profond comme actrice, du moins (ce qui est la première condition à l'Opéra-Italien) une rare perfection et une très belle expression dans le chant. Dans cette longue scène, elle a attaqué des difficultés, effrayantes pour toute autre qu'elle et elle en a triomphé avec le plus grand bonheur.

Heureusement que Donizetti est arrivé pour dissimuler toutes les pauvretés de ce ridicule libretto, en y prodiguant la richesse de ses mélodies. *Lucia di Lammermoor* est une digne rivale donnée à *Anna Bolena,* qui est elle-même une belle tragédie lyrique. Son introduction est peu importante, comme l'ouverture qui lui sert après de ritournelle; mais la cavatine de Tamburini est fort belle, et surtout admirablement chantée. L'entrée de Lucia est annoncée par un délicieux solo de harpe, qui prépare à merveille, par un récitatif simple, la ravissante cavatine *Perchè non ho del vento l'infaticabil volo.* Mme Persiani y a trouvé des trésors di fioritures et d'agréments, elle y a déployé toutes les richesses de sa méthode et toute la légèreté de sa voix. Rubini n'a pas de cavatine à chanter, mais le premier morceau de son rôle est un beau duo: *Sulla tomba che rinserra,* dans lequel Mme Persiani a bien fait sa partie; au second acte, le duo: *Il pallor funesto orrendo,* chanté par Tamburini et Mme Persiani a été fort goûté; ils en ont surtout attaqué la strette: *Soffrira nel pianto . . . languia nel dolore,* avec une grande énergie; mais le morceau capital de l'acte, et même de l'ouvrage, c'est le beau final dans lequel l'apparition d'Edgardo de Ravenswood fait un si grand effet. Rubini s'était montré souvent pathétique et touchant, mais il ne s'était jamais montré aussi tragique, que dans ces cruels reproches: "Calpertando l'esangue mia spoglia / All'altare più lieta ne andrà." Ce morceau, comme effet de musique dramatique, peut soutenir la comparaison avec les plus belles scènes de ce genre. Il y a au troisième acte un très beau duo entre Tamburini et Rubini; c'est une énergique scène de défi, que les deux acteurs ont aussi bien jouée que chantée, surtout dans le moment où leur fureur est à son comble: *O sole più rapido a sorger t'appresta.* . . . La scène de folie de Lucia est touchante, elle rappelle quelques mélodies de celle d'*Anna Bolena,* dont l'auteur s'est peut-être trop souvent inspiré. La pièce se termine par un grand air que Rubini chante avec une mélancolie et une douleur profondes.

Edgard de Ravenswood ne meurt pas comme dans le roman au milieu des sables mouvants de Wolfhope [*sic*]; il eût été difficile de faire disparaître Rubini de manière à ce qu'il ne restât plus de lui au baisser du rideau, que la plume noire de son chapeau; on a mieux aimé le faire mourir d'un coup de son poignard, et même lui faire chanter une reprise de l'air après sa mort: nous pensons que Rubini fera bien de ne se tuer qu'après la cabalette, ce sera aussi musical et plus vraisemblable.

Théâtre de la Renaissance (1839)

On sait que ce n'est pas la richesse du spectacle qui fait les succès au Théâtre-Italien de Paris; nous avons d'ailleurs simplifié encore la représentation de la pièce en évitant au milieu des actes les changements de décors que la forme dramatique française n'accepte pas volontiers; les scènes nouvelles que vous avez composées avec nous, pour approprier cette imitation du libretto aux exigences de notre théâtre, sont pour votre opéra une véritable naturalisation.

EXCERPT 21. HECTOR BERLIOZ, «JOURNAL DES DÉBATS», 9 AUGUST 1839

MM. Alphonse Royer et Gustave Vaëz ont fait leur traduction avec talent et conscience; le libretto italien n'a subi que de légères modifications qui toutes lui ont été avantageuses, et pour lesquelles M. Donizetti a écrit quelques nouvelles pages. Il n'arrive pas souvent aux compositeurs étrangers de voir leur musique adaptée à des traductions aussi élégantes, aussi fidèles et aussi peu gênantes pour les chanteurs.

EXCERPT 22. «LE CORSAIRE», 8 AUGUST 1839

Nous devons ajouter que les auteurs du *libretto* se sont associés au triomphe du chanteur et du musicien, par leur versification pleine d'images poétiques et de suavité. Grâces leur en soient rendues! Il est si rare d'entendre chanter au théâtre quelque chose qui ait le sens commun!

EXCERPT 23. «LE TEMPS», 11 AUGUST 1839

La traduction de MM. Royer et Vaëz est la meilleure peut-être qu'on ait faite de l'italien pour un de nos théâtres. Le drame a été, du reste, corrigé avec talent par les traducteurs; aussi le dialogue est-il presque entièrement nouveau, et Donizetti a-t-il refait tous les récitatifs.

EXCERPT 24. «LA GAZETTE DE FRANCE», 8 AUGUST 1839

Quelle fantaisie a donc pris à M. Donizetti de faire traduire un de ses meilleurs ouvrages? N'a-t-il pas redouté les chances du parallèle? Sa *Lucia* ne pouvait que perdre en quittant le pays natal. Toute copie est inférieure à l'original. Quelle entreprise que de lutter contre Rubini, Mme Persiani et Tamburini! Ne devait-il pas craindre que le public ne répondit, comme cet empereur romain à qui on proposait d'entendre un homme très habile à contrefaire le chant du rossignol: Excusez-moi, j'ai entendu le rossignol lui-même.

Les traductions d'opéras étrangers ont quelquefois été heureuses, mais jamais elles n'ont pu soutenir le parallèle avec les œuvres originales. Malgré le mérite des artistes de notre grand opéra français, *Don Juan* n'est pas à comparer à *Don Giovanni,* et les essais de ce genre qu'on a faits sur le *Barbier* et autres opéras de Rossini ont beaucoup laissé à désirer. Ces translations sont bonnes pour qui n'a pas l'oreille habituée à la douceur de la mélodie italienne. Beaucoup de gens se contentent de lire Virgile et Milton dans l'abbé Delille. Grand bien leur fasse.

EXCERPT 25. «L'ÉCHO FRANÇAIS», 13 AUGUST 1839

Il existe une foule de chefs-d'œuvre lyriques dont, chaque hiver, la moitié à peine nous est offerte par les Italiens. L'école allemande nous est à peu près inconnue: *Oberon,* de Weber; *Fidelio,* de Beethoven; la *Flûte enchantée,* de Mozard [*sic*], et tant d'autres opéras aux effets puissants, à l'ensemble magnifique, attendaient jusqu'à ce jour une scène qui pût, en les recevant, en les nationalisant parmi nous, remplir une lacune immense. . . . La Renaissance serait comme ces temples de Rome où tous les dieux étrangers trouvaient un autel et une statue. Grâce à elle, *notre éducation musicale se compléterait.* . . . Car, à notre époque de haute civilisation, il ne nous est pas permis d'ignorer ce qui se produit à Naples, à Florence, à Vienne, à Berlin; et Paris, si bienveillant pour les talents qui viennent à lui, doit une égale hospitalité à tout ce qui se produit hors de son sein.

EXCERPT 26. THÉOPHILE GAUTIER, «LA PRESSE», 14 AUGUST 1839

Le théâtre de la Renaissance vient de *renaître* réellement et de mériter son titre. Depuis *Ruy Blas,* il n'avait pas vu de succès pareil; il vient enfin d'entrer franchement dans la voie qui lui convient. Il faut que ce théâtre soit alternativement un second Opéra et un second Théâtre-Français. Pas de vaudevilles avec flonflons.

EXCERPT 27. HECTOR BERLIOZ, «JOURNAL DES DÉBATS», 9 AUGUST 1839

Il ne s'agissait que de savoir si nous pouvions espérer enfin un théâtre lyrique proprement dit; destiné à la musique et rien qu'à la musique; aussi éloigné de sacrifier à la danse et à la peinture comme l'Opéra, que peu disposé à se laisser ronger par le dialogue, comme l'Opéra-Comique; un théâtre enfin où le compositeur fût réellement *maître* dans la véritable acception du mot.

EXCERPT 28. «LA FRANCE MUSICALE», 11 AUGUST 1839

On se partageait déjà par anticipations les dépouilles du théâtre de la Renaissance, et voilà que tout-à-coup un éclatant succès est venu le relever dans l'opinion publique, et lui ouvrir une nouvelle carrière. . . . Il est parfaitement inutile d'analyser la brillante et dramatique partition de Donizetti. Une popularité européenne lui est acquise; voilà de la musique expressive et mélodieuse!

EXCERPT 29. «LE CORSAIRE», 8 AUGUST 1839

Tout a été dit depuis longtemps sur la *Lucia* de Donizetti. C'est une œuvre jugée, et quelle que soit l'opinion toute relative que l'on puisse en avoir, en la mettant en parallèle avec les magnifiques productions de Rossini, la *Lucia* n'en restera pas moins comme l'une des créations les plus complètes du fécond, et peut être trop fécond Maëstro. C'est donc bien moins le mérite intrinsèque d'un poème et d'une musique déjà connus que nous avons à constater aujourd'hui, que le résultat de l'excursion hardie tentée par la Renaissance sur le domaine du théâtre Italien, audace qui a été couronnée hier par le plus éclatant succès. . . . L'épreuve est décisive; la Renaissance vient de prendre rang parmi les théâtres lyriques, et de prouver ce que l'on pouvait avec le seul secours d'une volonté ferme, du zèle et de la persévérance.

EXCERPT 30. «LE MÉNESTREL», 6 OCTOBER 1839 (REVIEW OF THE SEASON OPENER AT THE THÉÂTRE-ITALIEN, «LUCIA DI LAMMERMOOR»)

Il ne faut pas oublier que le beau résultat des auditions de *Lucia* doit être en grande partie attribué aux chanteurs de prédilection [Persiani, Rubini, Tamburini] que nous venons de nommer. Car, sous le rapport de l'impression générale du drame, tant comme ensemble musical que comme spectacle, l'avantage reste tout entier au théâtre de la Renaissance; aussi considère-t-on les soirées des Bouffes comme d'élégants concerts où des chanteurs admirables viennent se faire entendre successivement. Les adhérences dramatiques n'arrivent là qu'en sous-ordre.

Opéra (1846)

EXCERPT 31. THÉOPHILE GAUTIER, «LA PRESSE», 23 FEBRUARY 1846

La représentation s'est terminée par un divertissement de danse composé de plusieurs pas, où figuraient Mlle Adeline Plunkett, Robert, M. Hilariot, et Petipa, le tout terminé par une polka générale. On avait pensé que la danse s'encadrerait mal dans l'opéra de *Lucie de Lamermoor* à cause de sa couleur élégiaque et de l'habitude où l'on est de la voir privée de cet ornement.

EXCERPT 32. «LE CORSAIRE-SATAN», 23 FEBRUARY 1846

Depuis long-temps, nous conseillons à l'Académie royale de s'emparer des chefs-d'œuvre dont le Théâtre-Italien sèvre ses abonnés, soit incurie, soit caprice. Puisque M. Vatel a le bon esprit de laisser pourrir dans ses cartons *Don Juan, Othello, Lucie,* pour se préparer à grands frais l'immense déception du *Proscrit;* c'est à M. le directeur de l'Opéra à réhabiliter la gloire de Mozart, de Rossini, de Donizetti. La soirée de vendredi, soirée solennelle et fructueuse pour notre première scène, est le plus éclatant témoignage de la justesse de nos prévisions.

EXCERPT 33. «JOURNAL DES DÉBATS», 3 MARCH 1846

Il y aurait bien quelque chose à dire contre l'accueil fait par l'Académie royale à cette partition de *Lucie de Lammermoor.* Sans doute nous ne poussons pas le patriotisme musical jusqu'à n'admettre sur notre première scène lyrique que des œuvres exclusivement françaises; la prétention serait singulière à l'égard d'un théâtre dont le répertoire n'a pendant si longtemps vécu que des emprunts faits à l'Italie et à l'Allemagne; nous voudrions seulement que l'Opéra eût au moins la primeur de ces importations, et qu'il se refusât désormais à accepter des traductions d'ouvrages étrangers déjà jouées sur un autre théâtre de Paris; mais nous n'insisterons pas sur cette observation

EXCERPT 34. «LE COUREUR DES SPECTACLES», 21 FEBRUARY 1846

L'affluence qui était, hier, à l'Opéra, donnait déjà gain de cause à l'idée de transporter *Lucie de Lammermoor* sur ce théâtre. Le public y ayant vu une addition favorable à l'agrément, comme à la variété du répertoire, avait voulu contribuer au succès de son exécution. Par la musique qui court, il y en a si peu qu'il soit prudent d'arrêter sur la route, qu'on est heureux d'en rencontrer qui soit tout éprouvée, et qu'on soit sûr d'applaudir sans se compromettre. Celle de l'ouvrage dont il s'agit a fait plus que son tour de France, elle est connue à l'Étranger; elle a pris son rang, et le gardera. La question était donc, hier, de savoir comment le public parisien y jugerait deux chanteurs pour qui cette partition n'est pas nouvelle.

EXCERPT 35. «LE CORSAIRE-SATAN», 23 FEBRUARY 1846

La fiancée de Lammermoor a triomphé à l'Opéra comme elle avait déjà triomphé sur tous les théâtres et dans toutes les langues. Cette fois la province avait pris l'initiative, et la belle traduction de MM. Alphonse Royer et Gustave Vaëz avait arrêté plusieurs entreprises sur la pente du précipice. *Lucie* tiendra désormais brillamment sa place dans le répertoire de l'Opéra, à côté de sa plus jeune sœur *la Favorite;* et recommencera une ère nouvelle de prospérité et d'éclat.

EXCERPT 36. «LE MÉNESTREL», 26 APRIL 1846

L'apparition de Mme Rossi-Caccia a été tout un événement pour le public de l'Académie Royale de Musique. . . . Nul doute à nos yeux que Mme Rossi-Caccia ne soit une précieuse acquisition pour M. Léon Pillet, qui aura de plus la ressource de s'en servir pour les rôles à roulades, surtout ceux de la *Lucie,* d'*Othello* et de *Norma* dont la traduction arrivera inévitablement rue Lepelletier.

17 MAY 1846

Restent maintenant les deux transfuges italiens, Bettini et Anconi. A l'heure qu'il est, remarquons en passant que tous nos chanteurs français brillent sur les scènes de Naples, Milan, Venise, etc., tandis que l'Académie Royale de Musique ne sera bientôt qu'un second Théâtre-Italien. On a tant de foix crié et répété: "Allez chercher des chanteurs en Italie!" que notre personnel menace de tourner au macaroni.

EXCERPT 37. THÉOPHILE GAUTIER, «LA PRESSE», 23 FEBRUARY 1846

Lucie de Lammermoor a été pour Duprez une résurrection; au troisième acte, la salle enthousiasmée l'a redemandé à grands cris, pendant plus de dix minutes, et, à la fin de la pièce, on lui a fait une ovation véritable. Jamais public ne fut plus agréablement surpris. . . .

Pendant cette représentation d'un succès si inattendu, une idée nous traversait la tête. Nous nous disions: Il faut croire que toute la faute n'était pas à Duprez, puisque, à la première musique italienne qu'il chante, la voix lui revient; le vacarme algébrique des opéras modernes n'est pas fait pour des poitrines humaines. . . . C'étaient ces opéras qui n'avaient pas de voix et non Duprez.—Toutes les fois qu'on lui a donné une mélodie, il a chanté. *Guillaume Tell* ne l'a jamais vu médiocre.

La scène de la malédiction, la scène du désespoir, qui est à elle seule tout le quatrième acte, ont été rendues par Duprez avec un feu, une âme et un pathétique au delà de tout éloge. Il est impossible de trouver des accents à la fois plus déchirants et plus harmonieux.

38. «LE MÉNESTREL», 1 MARCH 1846

L'apparition de Duprez dans la *Lucie* fera époque dans nos annales dramatiques, chacun est resté foudroyé sous le coup des notes vibrantes de la *Malédiction* et da la grande scène finale, alors qu'on soupçonnait l'illustre chanteur complètement dépourvu de moyens. Du-

prez renaît de ses cendres et il a de ces moments d'inspiration qui dépassent toute idée. . . .
Mlle Nau de son côté y a déployé de grandes qualités vocales.

EXCERPT 39. «LA FRANCE MUSICALE», 22 FEBRUARY 1846

[After two paragraphs about Duprez:] Après la quatrième acte, la salle était complètement transportée; nous ne pouvons dire l'expression profonde de sensibilité et de douleur avec laquelle Duprez interprète cette dernière page de la partition de Donizetti; c'est le sublime de l'art, au double point de vue de l'action dramatique et de la science vocale. Cet acte seul suffira pour amener tout Paris à l'Académie Royale de Musique. À la fin de la pièce, on a fait à Duprez une nouvelle ovation; le public en masse a redemandé l'artiste, la toile s'est levée, et il a paru pour la seconde fois au milieu des acclamations les plus enthousiastes.

Dans le rôle de Lucie, Mlle Nau a été délicieuse au premier acte; elle a merveilleusement dit son air et son duo avec Duprez. On l'a énergiquement applaudie; malheureusement elle ne s'est pas soutenue dans la scène de folie du troisième acte, ce qui n'empêche pas que le rôle de Lucie ne lui fasse honneur.

EXCERPT 40. «LE CONSTITUTIONNEL», 5 MARCH 1846

[After several paragraphs about Duprez's vocal difficulties:] Tout le monde sait par cœur la partition de Donizetti. Nous n'ajouterons donc que peu de mots sur l'exécution. Duprez a mis une telle passion, une telle vérité dans le largo du finale, et dans toute la scène de la malédiction, qu'un véritable frisson a couru dans la salle. Mais c'est surtout dans l'air des Tombeaux que le chanteur s'est surpassé. L'art des nuances et des contrastes ne va pas plus loin. Dans les quelques phrases détachées où Edgard dialogue avec les chœurs, Duprez ne chanta pas, il pleure, il sanglote; on oublie réellement l'artiste pour ne plus voir que l'amant désolé qui s'enfonce un poignard dans la poitrine pour rejoindre sa Lucie. Inutile de dire que Duprez est rappelé tous les soirs après le second acte et à la fin de la pièce.

Mlle Nau dit la cavatine du premier acte avec une facilité, une perfection de vocalise, dont la critique la plus exigeante doit se montrer satisfaite. Le premier jour, soit émotion, soit fatigue, la jeune et intelligente cantatrice a fléchi dans la scène de la folie. Mais, aux représentations suivantes, elle a pris brillamment sa revanche. Mlle Nau déploie surtout dans l'andante de cet air difficile, beaucoup de sensibilité, beaucoup d'âme, et supplée par la grâce, le naturel et le goût, à ce qui peut lui manquer de force et d'énergie.

EXCERPT 41. «LA GAZETTE DE FRANCE», 6 MARCH 1846

[After several paragraphs praising Duprez:] Mlle Nau a partagé avec Duprez les honneurs de la représentation. Elle a chanté la grande scène de la folie avec autant d'éclat que de justesse d'intonation. On l'a redemandée à la fin de l'acte, et ces témoignages de la faveur publique étaient de fort bon aloi, ce qui n'arrive pas toujours. À peine le rideau tombait sur la dernière note de l'opéra, que les mêmes acclamations ont rappelé Duprez, qui est venu à son tour recueillir des battements de mains enthousiastes. C'est pour ces deux artistes un très-grand succès.

EXCERPT 42. GUSTAVE HÉQUET, «LE NATIONAL», 5 MARCH 1846

Lucie de Lammermoor est le chef-d'œuvre de M. Donizetti. Jamais ce maître n'a été si heureusement inspiré; jamais il n'a eu tout à la fois plus de passion et plus de grâce. Nulle part il n'a fait une telle dépense d'idées. Hélas! faut-il donc s'en rapporter aux bruits qui courent, et cette lyre si harmonieuse, brisée avant le temps, serait-elle pour toujours devenue muette? Ah! ne nous hâtons pas de le croire! Ce serait pour l'art une perte trop cruelle et un trop douloureux mécompte!

EXCERPT 43. THÉOPHILE GAUTIER, «LA PRESSE», 23 FEBRUARY 1846

À propos de *Lucie,* puissions-nous bientôt aussi annoncer une autre résurrection. L'âme harmonieuse [i.e., Donizetti] qui trouva ces beaux chants sommeille, obscurcie et fatiguée, traversée de rêves étranges, qui vont se dissiper sans doute; la fraîche rosée d'une nouvelle aurore la réveillera de son assoupissement, et la mélodie reviendra babiller sur ces lèvres d'où ne sortent plus que des mots sans suite. Voilà le secret de ces facilités prodigieuses: une fatigue immense et pour résultat la folie!

Cette musique sans tradition

WAGNER'S *TANNHÄUSER* AND ITS FRENCH CRITICS

Annegret Fauser

Strangely enough, Paris has become the only city, for which I hold a
certain interest of curious sympathy . . . and even today, I prefer it to all other
places in the world . . . I could bring myself, as a cultural-historical study,
to go to a new opera by Meyerbeer or Gounod in a Parisian theater, for whose
circumstances, abilities, and audience it is calculated; in Berlin, Vienna
and Munich I would find this impossible.

RICHARD WAGNER, LETTER
TO KING LUDWIG II OF BAVARIA, 18 JULY 1867

"If God would only bestow such a flop upon me!" According to Richard Wagner,
these words were uttered by Charles Gounod soon after the scandalous fiasco of
the Parisian premiere of *Tannhäuser* in March 1861 (see fig. 10.1).[1] In February, a

I am grateful to M. Elizabeth C. Bartlet, Mark Evan Bonds, and Tim Carter for their helpful
and insightful comments on earlier versions of this essay, and to my research assistant, Alicia C.
Levin, for her indefatigable help in locating and providing copies of contemporary reviews in
French newspapers and periodicals. The epigraph is from *König Ludwig II. und Richard Wagner:
Briefwechsel,* ed. Otto Strobel (Karlsruhe: G. Braun, 1936), letter no. 337, 2:185–86, 189: Sonderbarer
Weise ist dieses Paris zu der einzigen Stadt geworden, für welche ich eine gewisses Interesse neu-
gieriger Teilnahme hege . . . und noch heute ziehe ich es allen Orten der Welt vor. . . . Ich könnte
mich überwinden, eine neue Meyerbeer'sche oder Gounod'sche Oper in einem der Pariser Theater,
für dessen Verhältnisse, Leistungen und Publikum sie berechnet ist, als culturhistorische Studie
noch mit durchzumachen; in Berlin, Wien und München wäre mir diess durchaus unmöglich. I
am grateful to Peter Jost for locating this letter and sharing a copy with me.

1. "Mir wurde von [Gounod] berichtet, daß er in der Gesellschaft überall mit Enthusiasmus für

« Monsieur, c'est un lit à musique : rien que du *Tann-häuser*, on dort parfaitement là-dedans.

FIGURE 10.1. "Exposition des Beaux-Arts appliqués à l'industrie." Caricature by Cham [Amédée de Noé]. The caption reads: "Sir, this is a musical bed: nothing but *Tannhäuser;* one sleeps perfectly in it." *L'illustration,* 21 November 1863. Courtesy of Duke University Library.

month before that fateful event at the Opéra, the chronicler of the Belgian periodical *Le guide musical* wished for a dispute similar to the scandal surrounding the 1830 premiere of Victor Hugo's play *Hernani,* if only to shake the Parisians out of their current complacency and indifference toward the arts. "At least," he wrote, "it would be life."[2] And the event was lively indeed. Few incidents in music history created such waves—politically, culturally, aesthetically, and biographically—as the three performances of Wagner's *Tannhäuser* at the Académie Impériale de la Musique in Paris on 13, 18, and 24 March 1861. Within a couple of days, Wagner's unsuccessful revi-

---

mich eingetreten sei; er solle ausgerufen haben: 'Que Dieu me donne une pareille chûte!'" Richard Wagner, *Mein Leben: 1813–1868,* ed. Martin Gregor-Dellin (Munich: List Verlag, 1994), 653–54.

2. "Tout ce bruit autour du *Tannhäuser* [sic] ne doit point déplaire aux personnes qui s'affligent de l'indifférence qui règne à Paris en matière d'art et de littérature. Plût au ciel, qu'à l'occasion du nouvel opéra de Wagner, on vit se renouveler les luttes des Gluckistes et des Piccinistes, ou les querelles plus récentes des classiques et des romantiques! Au moins ce serait de la vie. Est-ce vivre que nous faisons?" "France," *Le guide musical,* 14 February 1861. The anonymous correspondent for *L'indépendance belge* (17 March 1861) used the same analogy: "C'est le champ de bataille des classiques et des romantiques transporté du Théâtre-Français à l'Opéra." In *Le Figaro*'s "Petite chronique des théâtres" (28 March 1861), we read: "Depuis les orages soulevés par *Hernani* . . . jamais, dans une salle de spectacle parisienne, pareil charivari ne s'était produit."

sions of his opera for Paris became the subject of legend, and they have remained so ever since.

The plot of this tale is all too familiar to music lovers past and present: In the standard telling of the story, Wagner, the greatest German composer since Beethoven, came to Paris to have his *Tannhäuser* performed on the stage of the Opéra, then the most important music theater in Europe. Unfortunately, the administration of the house asked for revisions, in particular the addition of a ballet in act 2, in order to accommodate the taste of its spoiled audience. Aristocrats habitually attended the opera after dinner in time to see their favorite ballerinas perform onstage before the subsequent, more private entertainment in bed. Wagner, however, steadfastly refused to compromise his artistic integrity on the altar of convention. Nevertheless, as a concession to Parisian taste, he used the presence of a well-trained corps de ballet to revise the Venusberg scene in act 1, significantly enlarging the scope of the bacchanal. Alas: Parisian prejudice prevailed when the members of the Jockey Club were prevented by Wagner's artistic vision in act 2 from ogling their favorite ballerinas. They took their revenge, whistling and shouting throughout the remainder of the opera, drowning out Wagner's music with their racket. This scandalous behavior only escalated during the next two performances. A cruel cabal in the French press further encouraged the opera's rejection by Parisian audiences, and so, after the third evening of the battle, Wagner capitulated in the face of overwhelming hostility. In an open letter to Alphonse Royer, the director of the Opéra, he wrote:

> The opposition which has manifested itself against *Tannhäuser* proves to me how right your observations were, at the beginning of this undertaking, about the absence of a ballet and of other conventions of the stage to which the regular subscribers of the Opéra are accustomed. I regret that the nature of my work has prevented me from conforming to these requirements. Now that the vigor of the opposition against it does not even allow those in the audience who want to hear it to give it the attention necessary for its appreciation, I have no other honorable recourse than to withdraw it.[3]

A few weeks after the withdrawal of his *Tannhäuser* from the stage of the Opéra, Wagner left Paris in disgust, never to return to the French capital again. Soon, with

3. "L'opposition qui s'est manifestée contre le *Tannhäuser* me prouve combien vous aviez raison quand, au début de cette affaire, vous me faisiez des observations sur l'absence du ballet et des autres conventions scéniques auxquelles les abonnés de l'Opéra sont habitués. Je regrette que la nature de mon ouvrage m'ait empêché de le conformer à ces exigences. Maintenant que la vivacité de l'opposition qui lui est faite ne permet même pas à ceux des spectateurs qui voudraient l'entendre d'y donner l'attention nécessaire pour l'apprécier, je n'ai d'autre ressource honorable que de le retirer." "Nouvelles diverses," *Le ménestrel*, 31 March 1861.

the help of King Ludwig II of Bavaria, he established himself first in Munich and then in Bayreuth. In the end, history would prove Wagner right and show the Parisians for what they were: superficial pleasure seekers mired in operatic conventionality who were unable to recognize true art.

My rendering of this tale may seem like a caricature, but for over a century it remained the dominant version circulating in German and Anglo-Saxon literature after it was cemented in Wagner's own words, first in his report about the premiere for the *Deutsche Allgemeine Zeitung* in April 1861 and later in his autobiography.[4] The Wagnerian master narrative was only slightly revised in France through the documents presented by Georges Servières in his 1895 monograph on the Parisian *Tannhäuser*.[5] This changed, however, when in the 1980s musicologists began to develop two new areas of interest: on the one hand, led by the Berlioz renaissance, scholars began to focus on French nineteenth-century music as an area of research and performance, whether for the music of Gounod, Massenet, or Méhul; and on the other, sketch studies grew into one of the main scholarly projects of the period, expanding traditional work on Beethoven to the examination of sketches by Schumann, Wagner, and Rossini. Thus the iconic Parisian opera scandal of the nineteenth century received fresh attention. In the early 1980s Carolyn Abbate went into the Parisian archives and explored many of the materials relating to the Parisian *Tannhäuser*. She presented them in two carefully documented source studies that showed for the first time in detail the literary and musical changes Wagner made for the Paris premiere.[6] In the mid-1980s Gerald Turbow and Jane Fulcher revised the political aspects of the narrative and revealed that the Jockey Club's attack in fact served as a pretext for political protest against the patron of the performance, the French emperor Napoléon III.[7] Yet even in opening up new alleys of inquiry as regards sources and political reinterpretation,

4. For bibliographical references, see Carolyn Abbate, "The 'Parisian' *Tannhäuser*" (Ph.D. diss., Princeton University, 1985), 315.

5. Georges Servières, *Tannhœuser à l'Opéra en 1861* (Paris: Librairie Fischbacher, 1895). Although Servières attempts a more nuanced and complete rendering of the events, drawing on a rich fund of primary documents, his story—especially when examining the Parisian press—remains close to the Wagnerian master narrative.

6. Carolyn Abbate, "The Parisian 'Vénus' and the 'Paris' *Tannhäuser*," *Journal of the American Musicological Society* 36 (1983): 73–123; Abbate., "The 'Parisian' *Tannhäuser*." Ulrich Drüner's interpretation of the Parisian *Tannhäuser* offers an alternative reading of the Parisian "Vénus" in his "La version parisienne du *Tannhäuser* de Richard Wagner ou l'introduction du psychologique dans le grand opéra," in *Le théâtre lyrique en France au XIXe siècle,* ed. Paul Prévost (Metz: Éditions Serpenoise, 1995), 163–80.

7. Gerald D. Turbow, "Art and Politics: Wagnerism in France," in *Wagnerism in European Culture and Politics,* ed. David C. Large and William Weber (Ithaca, NY: Cornell University Press, 1984), 134–66; Jane F. Fulcher, *The Nation's Image: French Grand Opera as Politics and Politicized Art* (Cambridge: Cambridge University Press, 1987), 189–98.

much of the recent scholarly work in effect maintained and even strengthened the century-old Wagnerian master narrative, explaining the reasons for the Parisian rejection of Wagner in political rather than the aesthetic terms of the 1850s, celebrating Wagner the progressive—if not in his own political attitude, then at least in his impact on republican and socialist writers such as Jules Champfleury or avant-garde artists such as Charles Baudelaire—while condemning Wagner's adversaries and ridiculing his critics with choice quotations and summary dismissal.

In contrast, Manuela Schwartz, in her 1999 study on French reception of Wagner, pointed out that the scandal served to politicize the composer himself, turning him from a cosmopolitan with ambivalent political alliances into a German nationalist.[8] In addition, Katharine Ellis's careful reading of French music criticism illuminates the complexities of the aesthetic debate that has surrounded Wagner's music since the 1850s.[9]

Thus, changing the traditional perspective and challenging the Wagnerian master narrative—by taking Wagner's critics seriously instead of disregarding them as incompetent, spiteful, or reactionary—may well reveal that theirs was not simply an unreflecting hostility toward Wagner and his new musical language, but, rather, a mirror of their deep concerns about the future of opera, the primary genre of French cultural life, its institutional context, and its musical and poetic language.[10] Many of the critics went to great lengths to explain to their readers why Wagner's *Tannhäuser* represented a wrong turn in opera. A careful and close reading of Parisian criticism surrounding Wagner's second Parisian sojourn shows in fact that the notorious nature of Wagner's own theories and music served as a prism that turned a spotlight onto a deep-seated polemical undercurrent about the nature of French opera, especially because Wagner was not French. Therefore any perceived danger to the genre could be discussed in time-tested terms of national difference rather than internal artistic conflict.

8. Manuela Schwartz, *Wagner-Rezeption und französische Oper des Fin de siècle*, Berliner Musik Studien 18 (Sinzig: Studio Verlag Schewe, 1999), 2–7. Schwartz also points out that the French press was by no means as monolithic in its rejection of Wagner's opera as has been assumed. She cites the case of Ursula Eckart-Bäcker who, in her study of nineteenth-century French music criticism, focused only on the negative reviews (Schwartz, *Wagner-Rezeption,* 5). See Ursula Eckart-Bäcker, *Frankreichs Musik zwischen Romantik und Moderne* (Regensburg: Bosse, 1965), 77–100.

9. Katharine Ellis, "Wagnerism and Anti-Wagnerism in the Paris Periodical Press," in *Von Wagner zum Wagnérisme: Musik, Literatur, Kunst, Politik,* ed. Annegret Fauser and Manuela Schwartz, Transfer: Deutsch-Französische Kulturbibliothek 12 (Leipzig: Leipziger Universitätsverlag, 1999), 51–83.

10. James Ross raises this point in his discussion of the reception of Debussy's *Pelléas et Mélisande.* See Ross, "Crisis and Transformation: French Opera, Politics and the Press, 1897–1903" (D.Phil. diss., Oxford University, 1998), 187.

Wagner in Paris

The story of Wagner's Parisian *Tannhäuser* began long before the ill-fated premiere in March 1861. It goes back to the young Richard Wagner's first visit to Paris, between 1839 and 1842, when he tried to establish himself as an opera composer in the musical capital of the nineteenth century. Cherubini, Meyerbeer, Spontini, and Rossini had shown that foreign composers could impose themselves on the French musical stage. In 1840 Wagner came close to placing his *Liebesverbot* with the Théâtre de la Renaissance, but he lost out to Donizetti's *L'ange de Nisida*.[11] That same year, inspired by a short story by Heinrich Heine, Wagner sketched the outline for a one-act opera on the topic of the Flying Dutchman that was intended as a one-act curtain-raiser for a ballet at the Opéra such as *Giselle*.[12] Although the Opéra's administration was interested in the subject, it had other artists in mind to create the work, and 9 November 1842 saw the premiere of Pierre-Louis Dietsch's fantastic opera in two acts, *Le vaisseau fantôme, ou Le maudit des mers*.[13]

When Wagner returned to Paris twenty years later, in September 1859, he was no longer an unknown hopeful from Germany, but a controversial *chef d'école*. In particular, after the publication around 1850 of the so-called Züricher Kunstschriften— *Art and Revolution* (1849), *The Artwork of the Future* (1850), and *Opera and Drama* (1851)—he had become one of the most discussed composers alive. In 1852 François-Joseph Fétis dedicated a series of articles to Wagner's theoretical "system," whose terms would shape the discussion in France for several decades.[14] But although the debate about Wagner's ideas was lively, his music remained virtually unknown in Paris. Thus one of his first acts of self-promotion in Paris was to remedy this lack of musical awareness with three concerts of his own music, which he conducted in January and February 1860. Except for the *Tristan* Prelude, Wagner played it safe: he selected those extracts from his operas that were the closest to the style of French *grand opéra* (see table 10.1). His medley from *Tannhäuser* opened with the march from act 2, the arrival of the guests at the Wartburg, which was modeled on similar marches composed by Meyerbeer and Halévy. After the first concert he added to his program another piece attractive to French tastes that was to become known as the *Romance de l'étoile* ("O du mein holder Abendstern"). The poetic images, the elegiac tone, the regular

---

11. Mark Everist, *Giacomo Meyerbeer and Music Drama in Nineteenth-Century France* (Aldershot: Ashgate, 2005), 309–41.

12. Martine Kahane and Nicole Wild, eds., *Wagner et la France* (Paris: Editions Herscher, 1983), 21.

13. Dietsch, of course, was one of the players in the Paris *Tannhäuser,* twenty years later, for he became the musical director of the Opéra. Not only Dietsch, but also various other players of the 1840s reappeared in the *Tannhäuser* scandal, whether composers such as Berlioz and Rossini or Édouard Monnais, who—under the pen name of Paul Smith—wrote a harsh review in *La revue et gazette musicale de Paris.*

14. On Fétis's Wagner reception and its fallout, see Ellis, "Wagnerism and Anti-Wagnerism."

TABLE 10.1. Program for the concerts organized and conducted by Richard Wagner
at the Théâtre-Italien, 25 January 1860, 1 February 1860, and 8 February 1860

Der fliegende Holländer:
      Ouverture
Tannhäuser:
      March and Chorus
      Introduction to act 3 and Pilgrims' Chorus
      Romance de l'étoile (Jules Lefort) [1 and 8 February only]
      Ouverture
Tristan und Isolde:
      Prelude
Lohengrin:
      Introduction and Bridal Chorus
      Wedding Celebration

---

phrase structure, and the harp accompaniment of this *romance* were all musical signi-
fiers familiar to his Parisian audience from countless operas of the past decades.[15]

But even though the concert featured the more traditional elements of his music,
its reception took place in the context of what was perceived as Wagner's "system" for
the "music of the future." Thus, Léon Escudier's review of the concerts carried the title "La musique de l'avenir à Paris," and Paul Scudo declared that Wagner's sobriquet
"musicien de l'avenir" had now become an "indelible epithet."[16] Through his negative
concert review for the *Journal des débats,* the French "musician of the future," Hector
Berlioz, became embroiled in the fight, attacking Wagner's system on the grounds
of its lack of tradition and beauty.[17] Parisian audiences quickly became divided into

15. On the musical structure and subject matter of operatic *romance,* see David Charlton, "The
romance and Its Cognates: Narrative, Irony and *vraisemblance* in Early Opéra Comique," in *Die
Opéra Comique und ihr Einfluß auf das europäische Musiktheater im 19. Jahrhundert,* ed. Herbert
Schneider and Nicole Wild, Musikwissenschaftliche Publikationen der Hochschule für Musik und
Darstellende Kunst Frankfurt/Main 3 (Hildesheim: Georg Olms Verlag, 1997), 43–92. That local
taste was one of Wagner's main selection criteria when he put together his concert programs becomes obvious in his *Lettre sur la musique,* which he published later that year together with prose
translations of his four operatic texts: *The Flying Dutchman, Tannhäuser, Lohengrin,* and *Tristan
and Isolde.* See Richard Wagner, *Quatre poèmes d'opéras: Le vaisseau fantôme—Tannhæuser—
Lohengrin—Tristan, précédés d'une "Lettre sur la musique,"* new ed. with a preface by Gustave Samazeuilh (Paris: Mercure de France, 1941).

16. Léon Escudier, "La musique de l'avenir à Paris," *La France musicale,* 29 January 1860. "Le
titre de *musicien de l'avenir* lui reste acquis comme une qualification indélébile": Paul Scudo, "Revue musicale," *La revue des deux mondes,* 1 March 1860.

17. David Cairns, *Berlioz,* vol. 2, *Servitude and Greatness, 1832–1869* (London: Penguin, 1999),
654–60.

Wagnerians and anti-Wagnerians, with polemic reviews and pamphlets published by Wagner himself as much as by his supporters—especially Champfleury—and detractors.[18] Reported the young Georges Bizet to his publisher, Choudens: "Berlioz finds the music of Wagner abominable, Reyer finds it splendid—it is clear that one of them has it completely wrong."[19]

Such was the notorious pervasiveness of the *Zukunftsmusik* epithet that it quickly found entrance into the rich culture of Parisian parodies in the form of a short number composed by Jacques Offenbach for his *Le carnaval des revues,* which premiered on 10 February 1860, just two days after Wagner's last concert.[20] The piece in question is a melodrama, *Le musicien de l'avenir,* in which Wagner meets Grétry, Weber, Mozart, and Gluck in Elysium. After explaining his revolutionary theories to his august predecessors, the musician of the future offers a glimpse of what such music might sound like with a *Symphony of the Future.*[21] Offenbach based his proto-Stravinskyan score of that "symphony" on the "Quadrille des lanciers," one of the best-known dances of the nineteenth century. Offenbach's satire was so successful that it was included in a gala performance at the Théâtre-Italien in April that year at the request of the emperor and was still played at the time of the *Tannhäuser* premiere.[22] Other comic attempts at the sounds of the future followed suit, with works such as H. Thiéry's revue *Il pleut, il pleut, bergère,* with a "great symphony" by the composer Tanne-tout-le-monde in "scie majeur."[23] Both the composer's name, which translates roughly as "getting on everybody's nerves," and the key of the symphony (here spelled *scie,* i.e., a saw, rather than *si*—a comment on the ugliness of the sound) played with perceptions of the music of the future as dissonant and enervating. Caricaturists also had their fun. One of Cham's caricatures in *Le charivari* shows, for example, a mother crying over the fact that her child was to hear naught but such music in the future (see fig. 10.2).[24] Indeed, before Wagner's operas ever reached the Parisian stage, his *musique de l'avenir* was performed as an ongoing saga onstage as well as off.

18. Ellis, "Wagnerism and Anti-Wagnerism," 59–62.

19. "Berlioz trouve la musique de Wagner abominable, Reyer la trouve splendide—il est bien évident que l'un des deux se trompe complètement." Hervé Lacombe, *Georges Bizet* (Paris: Fayard, 2000), 269.

20. Jean-Claude Yon, *Jacques Offenbach* (Paris: Éditions Gallimard, 2000), 228. The *Carnaval des revues* was the first piece of Offenbach's to be staged after he became a French citizen.

21. Siegfried Kracauer, *Jacques Offenbach und das Paris seiner Zeit* (Frankfurt am Main: Suhrkamp, 1994), 199.

22. Kracauer, *Jacques Offenbach,* 200. Servières (*Tannhœuser,* 111) offers 27 April 1860 as the date of the gala performance.

23. Servières, *Tannhœuser,* 111.

24. Cham was the pseudonym of the caricaturist Amédée de Noé (1818–79). He published his caricatures in *Le charivari, L'illustration,* and *Le journal amusant,* among other periodicals. See John Grand-Carteret, *Les mœurs et la caricature en France* (Paris: À la Librairie Illustrée, 1888), 628.

— Chère amie, tu pleures sur le berceau
de ton enfant ?
— Hi ! hi ! je crois bien !... hi ! hi ! je suis
allée hier au soir entendre M. Wagner. Si
vous croyez que c'est pas triste de savoir
la musique que l'avenir réserve aux oreilles
de ce pauvre petit.

FIGURE 10.2. A mother weeping at the cradle of her infant at the prospect of the music of the future. Caricature by Cham [Amédée de Noé]. *Le charivari*, 4 March 1860. Reproduced in John Grand-Carteret, *Richard Wagner en caricatures* (Paris: Librairie Larousse, [1892]), 223. Courtesy of Duke University Library.

By the spring of 1860 Wagner had thus established himself as the latest celebrity in the musical world of Paris, if not quite in the way he desired. As Gerald Turbow has pointed out, Wagner was "the darling of the progressives."[25] But he also moved in more conservative circles, which included the wife of the Austrian ambassador, Pauline von Metternich, who became his principal patron in Paris during these months. During a reception at the imperial court, she suggested to Napoléon III that he support her protégé's thus far fruitless attempts to have an opera performed in Paris. The emperor reacted quickly and on 12 March ordered the performance of *Tannhäuser* at the Opéra.[26] This imperial decree secured Wagner a lavish production on the first national stage, but it also linked him inextricably with the authoritarian and widely despised figure of the emperor, an association that laid the foundation for the *Tannhäuser* scandal a full year before the premiere. Nor did it help that Wagner's opera was the

25. Turbow, "Art and Politics," 147.
26. Schwartz, *Wagner-Rezeption*, 4.

FIGURE 10.3. M. Despléchin, stage design for *Tannhäuser,* act 1, scene 2. Engraving by Auguste-Paul-Charles Anastasi and Jules Worms. *L'illustration,* 16 March 1861. Courtesy of Duke University Library.

publicly cited reason for the Opéra's refusal to put on Berlioz's still unperformed *Les Troyens* and for the delay of the premiere of Gounod's *La reine de Saba.*

Nevertheless, imperial patronage secured for Wagner all that the Opéra could muster in resources and support. Stars such as Fortunata Tedesco, Marie Sass, and Antonio Morelli were cast for the roles of Venus, Elisabeth, and Wolfram, and on Wagner's request, the Opéra hired the German tenor Albert Niemann to sing the title role. The stage design by Édouard Despléchin was sumptuous and the costumes lavish (see fig. 10.3). Lucien Petipa was to serve as the ballet's choreographer and Eugène Cormon as stage director. The production was overseen by Alphonse Royer, who had a good deal of experience with the adaptation of foreign works for the French opera stage, including Verdi's *I Lombardi* in 1847. It was as close to a dream team as Paris had to offer at that time, and everybody expected a major success if only because of the splendid quality of the production.[27]

The adaptation of foreign-language works for the stage of the Opéra was not unusual. Only four years prior to *Tannhäuser,* in 1857, the Opéra had produced the

27. Servières (*Tannhœuser,* 26) mentions that Wagner would have preferred Jean-Baptiste Faure for the role of Wolfram, but Faure had gone to Britain to spend the season at Covent Garden.

French version of *Il trovatore*. But whether the composer was Verdi or Weber, Mozart or Donizetti, when a foreign work was performed on France's premier opera stage, it was translated not only in terms of language, but also in terms of theatrical convention.[28] This process of cultural transfer was part and parcel of these productions, to the point that in 1834 the Opéra could advertise Mozart's *Don Juan* as a version in which "Mozart's text has undergone no changes," even though the work was extended to five acts with significant transformations, including the reworking of the title role for the tenor Adolphe Nourrit; the insertion into act 1 of a ballet based on medleys of Mozart's themes; and Donna Anna's falling in love with Don Giovanni, her subsequent suicide, and a danced epilogue portraying Anna's funeral.[29] Such extensive reworking to suit the conventions of the Paris Opéra may seem extreme from today's perspective, but it needs to be understood in the frame of a cultural practice that conceived of opera as a theatrical event tailored toward a specific audience at a specific moment in time; this was not the Wagnerian concept of music drama as an autonomous work of art, a fixed text to be performed according to the author's intentions.[30] Although works of dead composers were arranged by French producers, librettists, and composers to fit their latest home in Paris, living composers such as Verdi often used the opportunity to revise their works for the new context, seeking and often following the advice of the Opéra's creative team. In 1847 Verdi completely reworked his *I Lombardi alla prima crociata* as *Jérusalem,* a four-act opera with ballets included.

Wagner's concept of music drama as a work created solely by the musician-poet proved a serious obstacle to the process of adapting *Tannhäuser* for the Parisian stage. But his reluctance to conform to institutional convention was less pronounced than legend would have it. As Carolyn Abbate has shown, Wagner was delighted to use the opportunity to make changes to the Venusberg scene, and he was far more amenable to the question of the act 2 ballet than later events might imply. Early on Royer had suggested that the finale of act 2—after the arrival of the guests at the Wartburg and before the song contest—would be an ideal place for the traditional act 2 ballet. Al-

28. On the adaptation of Weber's *Freischütz* for the Odéon, see Annegret Fauser, "Phantasmagorie im deutschen Wald? Zur *Freischütz*-Rezeption in London und Paris 1824," in *Deutsche Meister—Böse Geister? Nationale Selbstfindung in der Musik*, ed. Hermann Danuser and Herfried Münkler (Schliengen: Edition Argus, 2001), 245–73. For Berlioz's 1841 adaptation of *Freischütz*, see Frank Heidlberger, *Carl Maria von Weber und Hector Berlioz*, Würzburger Musikhistorische Beiträge 14 (Tutzing: Hans Schneider, 1994).

29. Katharine Ellis, "Rewriting *Don Giovanni,* or 'The Thieving Magpies,'" *Journal of the Royal Musical Association* 119 (1994): 214.

30. Hervé Lacombe discusses the more fluid work concept as collaborative performance, which prevailed in nineteenth-century France, in his *The Keys to French Opera*, trans. Edward Schneider (Berkeley and Los Angeles: University of California Press, 2001). See also Mark Everist, "Lindoro in Lyon: Rossini's *Le barbier de Séville*," *Acta Musicologica* 63 (1992): 50–85; and Everist, *Music Drama at the Paris Odéon, 1824–1828* (Berkeley and Los Angeles: University of California Press, 2002), 218–26.

though Wagner refused categorically to include a ballet within the opera, he agreed to the intercalation of a newly composed ballet divertissement by Théodore Labarre, *Graziosa*, after act 2.[31] Wagner could have avoided a great deal of controversy had he not made his disdain for the local custom known in an article about the ballet question published in the *Journal des débats* in July 1860, and had he not demanded that the first few performances of *Tannhäuser* be given without the intercalation of *Graziosa*.[32]

From a Parisian standpoint, Wagner made one tactical mistake after another during the lead-up to the premiere, gambling away any general goodwill toward the controversial musician of the future. He demanded to conduct the first three performances of his opera in lieu of Louis Dietsch, the house conductor, whom he found wanting. Rehearsal time was excessive by any contemporary standards. He was rude to the musicians and singers and was perceived as arrogant by the Parisian press because he refused to pay the traditional visits to important journalists.[33] He snubbed the professional claqueurs, depriving them of their income, then hastily brought some of them in at the last minute. His negative views of French composers such as Auber, Halévy, and Berlioz were widely circulated and found offensive. The court case about the rights to the work's translation into French a week before the premiere only added to the general uproar. The press followed the events closely, reporting that opera, "this week, was not in the house at the rue le Pelletier [*sic*], but at the Palais de Justice."[34] As one journalist observed, "One speaks so much about *Tannhäuser* that its first performance is expected with the liveliest curiosity."[35] Into all of this commotion were mixed "the three magic words"—*musique de l'avenir*—which, according to Charles de Lorbac, served only to divide the French press and public into two camps even before the premiere.[36]

Wagner's Critics: Rereading the Parisian Reception of *Tannhäuser*

This volatile mix exploded at the tumultuous premiere on 13 March, when *Tannhäuser* was greeted by laughter, shouts, noise, and loud abuse. The subsequent two perfor-

31. Servières, *Tannhœuser,* 94, 107.

32. Abbate, "The 'Parisian'" Tannhäuser," 270.

33. He also refused to offer complementary tickets to the press for his 1860 concerts, as Paul Scudo pointed out: "M. Wagner n'a pas daigné, comme c'est l'usage, nous convier à la fête de son esprit." "Revue musicale," *La revue des deux mondes,* 1 February 1860.

34. "L'Opéra, cette semaine, n'était pas dans la salle de la rue le Pelletier [*sic*], mais bien au Palais de justice." "Actualités," *La France musicale,* 10 March 1861.

35. "En somme, on parle tant du *Tannhäuser,* que la première représentation est attendue avec la plus vive curiosité." *Journal de débats,* 13 March 1861.

36. "Grâce à trois mots magiques, et dont M. Wagner décline pourtant la responsabilité, *Musique de l'avenir,* l'auteur du *Tannhaüser* [*sic*] a eu le rare bonheur de partager la critique française en deux camps, avant la représentation de son œuvre, et d'appeler sur sa personne la curiosité, l'intérêt même d'un public qui le connaît à peine de nom." Charles de Lorbac, "Richard Wagner," *Le Figaro,* 21 February 1861.

mances were even more turbulent. Journalists from newspapers and music periodical alike reflected both on the riotous events of the evenings and on their meaning for French opera. Although Wagner's ideas elicited intense debate in the French press in the decade before this performance, these discussions came into sharp focus over *Tannhäuser*, possibly the most important Parisian premiere at the Opéra between Verdi's *Les vêpres siciliennes* in 1855 and his *Don Carlos* in 1867.[37] Given that the soubriquet of the "music of the future" dominated the entire discourse leading up to the *Tannhäuser* premiere, from Offenbach's *Symphony of the Future* and Cham's caricatures to Wagner's own *Lettre sur la musique,* it is no surprise that it became a central issue in the reviews. By asking whether Wagner's *Tannhäuser* was indeed the music of the future, critics could examine a notorious case to analyze how invention and convention related to new styles in music and, more specifically, opera.[38] Through the lens of this controversy, reviewers revisited questions of opera's aesthetic foundation, musical form and style, institutional framework, and modes of reception. Because of the prominence of the scandal and the preceding and consequent exposure of music criticism in the national press, the debate about *Tannhäuser* became itself a performance, self-consciously styled as a key debate similar to the famous eighteenth-century *querelles.* Not only did Wagner's *Tannhäuser* and its reception provide the press with newsworthy tidbits to report, it also served to validate music criticism as a vital arbiter of national culture.

Wittiness became one of the hallmarks of the press reception, contrasting French *esprit* with the Germanic dullness ascribed to Wagner's writings and music. Once more, Wagner and his opera were the subject of caricatures in *Le charivari,* where we find, for example, Venus sobbing about her depressing fate as the only person in Paris who loves Tannhäuser (see fig. 10.4). But wit was also displayed in the feuilletons of the daily press. Whether it was Pier Angelo Fiorentino comparing the song competition in act 2 to the end-of-year competition at the Conservatoire "where one hears the same piano piece twenty-seven times in a row," Léon Gatayes predicting a duel between Wagnerians and anti-Wagnerians where opponents "will cross their scores

37. The fact that I am citing two works written by Verdi rather than Gounod, Thomas, or Auber points toward the crisis of French opera in the middle of the nineteenth century. When *L'Africaine* was premiered in 1865 it was as a posthumous work, presented a year after Meyerbeer's death and four years after Scribe's; Gounod's *La reine de Saba* (1862), the work premiered at the Opéra immediately after *Tannhäuser* and *Graziosa,* did not come even close to Gounod's success with *Faust* (1859) at the Théâtre-Lyrique. Indeed, many of the key premieres of French music-theater during those years took place at the Théâtre-Lyrique and the Opéra-Comique. See Lacombe, *Keys to French Opera;* Anselm Gerhard, *The Urbanization of Opera: Music Theater in Paris in the Nineteenth Century,* trans. Mary Whittall (Chicago: University of Chicago Press, 1998), especially 345–87. For Wagner criticism prior to the *Tannhäuser* premiere, see Ellis, "Wagnerism and Anti-Wagnerism." See also Katharine Ellis, *Music Criticism in Nineteenth-Century France: "La revue et gazette musicale de Paris," 1834–1880* (Cambridge: Cambridge University Press, 1995), 206–18.

38. On convention in French opera, see Gerhard, *Urbanization of Opera,* 8–12; Lacombe, *Keys to French Opera,* 252–301.

— Maman Vénus, qu'est-ce que tu as
donc à être triste comme ça depuis quelques jours?
— Si tu crois que ça m'amuse d'aimer
le *Tannhäuser* à moi toute seule! Personne
pour vous aider, merci!

(17 mars 1861.)

FIGURE 10.4. Venus weeping because of *Tann-häuser*. Caricature by Cham [Amédée de Noé]. *Le charivari*, 17 March 1861. Reproduced in John Grand-Carteret, *Richard Wagner en caricatures* (Paris: Librarie Larousse, [1892]), 227. Courtesy of Duke University Library.

and ram them through their bodies," or Arthur Pougin characterizing Wagner's apparently nebulous writing style as "reflecting the sunshine of his country," reviewers sharpened their pens and used the occasion to perform deliberately their role as *French* writers and critics.[39] To be sure, if national culture was defined above all by *esprit,* which the critic Gaston de Saint-Valry in his review explicitly linked to Voltaire, then the critics' strategy of peppering their reviews with sarcasms and witticisms could be read as a performative act in a contest not over French opera versus Wagner's, but over critics' skill with the pen.[40]

Even in the battle between Wagnerians and anti-Wagnerians, the successful use

39. "Ces concours du Conservatoire où l'on entend vingt-sept fois de suite le même morceau de piano": Pier Angelo Fiorentino, "Théâtres," *Le constitutionnel,* 18 March 1861. "On croisera les partitions et on se les passera au travers du corps": Léon Gatayes, *L'univers musical,* 14 March 1861. "Le style rappelle le soleil de son pays": Arthur Pougin, "M. Richard Wagner," *La jeune France,* 3 March 1861.

40. Gaston de Saint-Valry, "Revue dramatique," *Le pays,* 19 March 1861.

of wit became a yardstick for critics' powers of persuasion. The assiduous Wagnerian Auguste de Gasperini saw Parisian wit as the signal flaw that precluded any serious discussion of music and aesthetics in the French press: "To be amusing, witty, this is the first condition required of today's critic; and whichever the journal in which he reigns—whether *Le moniteur* or *Le constitutionnel, La presse* or *L'opinion*—he must, under threat of immediate devaluation, primarily search for merriment and the mocking word, with the rest coming as an extra."[41] Léon Leroy, for his part, sarcastically characterized one fellow writer's feuilleton as empty pyrotechnics before revealing Benoît Jouvin's famous malapropism in his review in *Le Figaro,* where he had confused the auditory with the olfactory nerves.[42]

Journalists also evoked Parisian wit as one reason behind the inevitability of Wagner's failure, for the German composer had committed the cardinal sin of boring his French audience with his theories, his plot, his poetry, and his music while alienating his French hosts with his boorish behavior. By blatantly and openly disregarding the tastes of his audience and the conventions of French *grand opéra,* according to his critics, Wagner had made himself a target of both the audience's disapproval and the journalists' attack; therefore, the reviews turned to lessons on the institution of French *grand opéra* and its audience. Much was at stake, because if Wagner was successful in his critique of convention, then the central position of Paris as a musical capital was in jeopardy. Thus Paris as a cultural center played a big role in these reviews. Albert Wolff reminded his readers that "Paris is not only the capital of France, but the center of the artistic world."[43] Instead of adopting an appropriate humility in the face of such an august performance context, Wagner showed hubris:

> No, Wagner is not one of those foreign composers who—like Rossini, Meyerbeer, Donizetti, and Verdi, paying homage to our tastes, our enlightenment, our impartiality—has come loyally and without flattery to present to us his views about

41. "Être plaisant, spirituel, telle est la première condition exigée du critique de nos jours; et quel que soit le journal où il règne, au *Moniteur,* ou au *Constitutionnel,* à la *Presse* ou à l'*Opinion,* il doit sous peine de démonétisation immédiate, chercher d'abord la gaîté et le mot pour rire, le reste venant de surcroît." Auguste de Gasperini, "Courrier musical," *Le journal de Francfort,* 4 April 1861.

42. "Le compte-rendu pyrotechnique de M. de Saint Victor est sans doute fort brillant, comme de coutume, mais ne contient pas un mot de critique raisonnée, au point de vue de la musique—si ce n'est que le feuilletoniste déclare préférer le chœur de pèlerins de *Jérusalem* à celui de *Tannhauser*. . . . Nous demandions tout à l'heure ce que M. de Saint-Victor entendait par 'une voix bien modulée' nous demanderons maintenant ce que signifie cette autre phrase de M. Jouvin, toujours à propos du *Tannhauser:* 'La musique brutale et banale est celle qui ébranle seulement le nerf OLFACTIF.' Auditif, M. Jouvin, auditif, s'il vous plaît!—à moins que par un autre phénomène de votre organisation, vous ne perceviez les sons musicaux par le nez." Léon Leroy, "La cabale et les critiques," *La causerie,* 31 March 1861.

43. "Paris n'est pas seulement la capitale de la France, c'est le centre du monde artiste." Albert Wolff, "Le courrier de Paris," *Le Figaro,* 24 March 1861.

the future of art and to submit to our judgment original compositions written under the inspiration of a new ideal. . . . But no, for the year that he has spent among us, the author of *Tannhäuser* plays with intolerable grandiloquence the role of the misunderstood man, of the messiah of a new art, of the pathbreaking genius. He pours contempt on works that form the object of our admiration; he writes books in which the name of Rossini is omitted with an affectation that would be impertinent if it were not so entirely puerile.[44]

At least on the surface of the negative reviews, Wagner's offense was therefore not the simple fact that he was trying to be innovative as a composer or that he was a foreigner, but that he so openly disdained that what his audience and critics enjoyed seeing and hearing in their theaters. "Richard Wagner's greatest mistake," Édouard Monnais observed, "was to ignore what might please or displease the French public."[45] Such pride deserved punishment in many eyes. Some were up front about their intent, especially Oscar Comettant, who spelled out Wagner's crime and punishment *expressis verbis:*

Of course, if Mr. Wagner had not shown, in his numerous writings published in Germany and in France, his disdain for the works of the great masters past and present, and if he had not sustained with such incredible pride his system of opera composition as the *nec plus ultra* of the beautiful, and if he had not made his operas out to be the only ones worthy to be listened to by serious minds, the Parisian public—naturally benevolent and polite—would have been content to remain silent before the misshapen, dull, and wrongheaded work of the unfortunate composer. But to a pretension without limits and which nothing justifies, an exemplary lesson needs to be taught.[46]

44. "Non, Wagner n'est pas un de ces compositeurs étrangers qui, comme Rossini, Meyerbeer, Donizetti, Verdi, rendant hommage à nos goûts, à nos lumières, à notre impartialité, est venu loyalement et sans flatterie nous exposer ses vues sur l'avenir de l'art, et soumettre à notre jugement des compositions originales, écrites sous l'inspiration d'un nouvel idéal. . . . Main non, l'auteur du *Tannhauser* [*sic*], depuis un an qu'il est parmi nous, joue avec une jactance intolérable le rôle d'homme incompris, de messie d'art nouveau, de génie initiateur; il déverse le mépris sur les œuvres qui font l'objet de notre admiration; il écrit des livres où le nom de Rossini est omis avec une affectation impertinente, si elle n'était avant tout puéril." "Feuilleton," *L'ami de la religion,* 21 March 1861.

45. "Le plus grand tort de Richard Wagner, c'est, à nos yeux, d'ignorer ce qui peut plaire ou déplaire à un public français." Paul Smith [Édouard Monnais], "Théâtre impérial de l'Opéra: *Tannhœuser,*" *La revue et gazette musicale de Paris,* 17 March 1861.

46. "Certes, si M. Wagner n'avait pas manifesté, dans de nombreux écrits publiés en Allemagne et en France, son mépris pour les œuvres des grands maîtres passés et présents, et s'il n'avait pas soutenu avec un incroyable orgueil son système de composition lyrique comme le *nec plus ultra* du beau, et posé ses opéras comme les seuls dignes d'être écoutés par les esprits sérieux, le public parisien, naturellement bienveillant et courtois, se fût contenté de rester silencieux devant l'ouvrage informe, terne et faux du compositeur malheureux. Mais à une prétention sans limites et que rien

The Parisian journalists responded in this strong and concerted fashion not only because Wagner had offended French taste, but because his competing aesthetics called into question everything they prized. The aesthetic position of Wagner's opponents was strongly influenced by the eclectic philosopher Victor Cousin, whose 1853 tract *Du vrai, du beau et du bien,* was cited by Scudo in his 1860 review of the Wagner concerts.[47] If Comettant worried about Wagner's claim to the *"nec plus ultra* of the beautiful," then a key concept of French aesthetics was indeed under attack. This probably seemed to justify the critics' concerted action, often described as a cabal.[48]

Whether the French reviewers simply picked up on current debates or had agreed upon certain critical tactics for their feuilletons, a significant number of reviews share common topics, discursive strategies, and even formulations—not only those written by the ringleaders of anti-Wagnerian invective such as Alexis Azevedo, Oscar Comettant, Pier Angelo Fiorentino, Benoît Jouvin, and Paul Scudo, and but also those of the more equanimous albeit equally negative critics such as Paul Bernard, Franck-Marie (Franco Maria Pedorlini), Stéphen de la Madeleine, Joseph d'Ortigue, and Arthur Pougin (table 10.2). Wagner himself had provided the starting point for a significant number of these topics and strategies: he published his *Lettre sur la musique* in late 1860, three months before the premiere, enough time for it to be circulated among and discussed by Parisian critics. Not only did this text synthesize Wagner's most provocative ideas about opera and drama; it also contained, thanks to the translator, Paul Challemel-Lacour, some mistranslations that made matters worse by insulting Italian music.[49] Three issues in particular served to provoke the *Tannhäuser* reviewers: Wagner's discussion of melody and the introduction of his metaphor of the *mélodie de la forêt* for his *unendliche Melodie;* his open disdain for current opera, its conventions, and its traditions (including his disavowal of his earlier compositions as pandering to public taste); and his discussion of the symphony as dramatic music.[50] These three themes, which intersected with Fétis's criticism (by then a commonplace) that Wagner lacked form, melody, and rhythm, became key issues in the press reception, in which Wagner's own writing was used against him.

Among the critics who referred to and often cited Wagner's *Lettre sur la musique*

---

ne justifie, il fallait une leçon exemplaire." Oscar Comettant, "Académie Impériale de Musique: *Tannhauser,*" *L'art musical,* 21 March 1861.

47. Ellis, "Wagnerism and Anti-Wagnerism," 59. Gasperini ("Courrier musical," *Le journal de Francfort,* 4 April 1861) sarcastically refers to Cousin's omnipresence in French criticism when he concludes that "M. Cousin's eclecticism ran all through it" (l'éclectisme de M. Cousin a passé par là).

48. Servières (*Tannhœuser,* 60–63) identified Scudo as the ringleader.

49. See Peter Jost, "Zu den französischen Übersetzungen von Wagners Schriften zu Lebzeiten," in *"Schlagen Sie die Kraft der Reflexion nicht zu gering an": Beiträge zu Richard Wagners Denken, Werk und Wirken,* ed. Klaus Döge, Christa Jost, and Peter Jost (Mainz: Schott, 2002), 32–47, especially 38.

50. Wagner, *Quatre poèmes d'opéras,* 13–110.

TABLE 10.2. Selected reviews of *Tannhäuser* from Parisian periodicals

Critic	Journal	Comment
Charles Baudelaire	*Revue européenne* (1 April 1860)	Favorable review praising Wagner as the founder of a new art
Paul Bernard	*Le ménestrel* (24 March 1861)	Negative review of poem and music
Gustave Chadeuil	*Le siècle* (26 March 1861)	Negative review of poem and music
Pier Angelo Fiorentino	*Le constitutionnel* (18 March 1861)	Criticizes unsuccessful music and plot; labels Wagner a "symphonist"
M. Franck-Marie [Pedorlini]	*La patrie* (24 March 1861)	Mixed review; critical of poem and musical structure, but celebrates Wagner as a "great musician" following in steps of Bach and Beethoven
Adolphe Giacomelli	*La presse théâtrale et musicale* (17–21 March 1861)	Claims critics mounted a cabal and did not understand Wagner's music
J.-L. Heugel	*Le ménestrel* (17 March 1861)	Criticizes music as formulaic and without beauty
Benoît Jouvin	*Le Figaro* (18 March 1861)	Criticizes music as unnatural and unintelligible, music insulting to its audience
Léon Leroy	*La causerie* (31 March 1861)	Mostly positive review; attacks the "cabal"
Paul de Saint-Victor	*La presse* (18 March 1861)	Criticizes Wagner's music as mainly monotonous; calls to rally under the "classical flag of the Latin genius"
Paul Scudo	*La revue des deux mondes* (1 April 1861)	Author is leader of anti-Wagner cabal and follower of Victor Cousin; review attacks Wagner's music, poem, system, and behavior

were both his more passionate critics such as Azevedo, Comettant, Scudo, and Wilhelm, and those—such as de la Madeleine, d'Ortigue, and Pougin—whose responses seem more balanced in their rejection.[51] Wagner was taken to task first and foremost over the "melody of the forest," which was then applied to reading the score. Thus Scudo's attack on the Venusberg scene used Wagner's own terminology, including the contrast between the *unendliche Melodie* (to which he aspired) and the (wrongly translated) "Italian melody," for it seems that Challemel-Lacour translated *welche Melodie* as "Italian melody," probably confusing *welch* and *welsch,* an old German term for Italian:[52] "This first scene of *Tannhäuser,* which was written in Paris and reveals the maestro's latest manner, cannot be compared to anything that exists in music. It is chaos, it is nothingness, but scientific chaos and nothingness; it is the great *melody of the forest* that has nothing in common with the Italian melody."[53] The "scientific" quality of Wagner's music was not a new charge, and metaphors were often industrial, in a manner already familiar from Berlioz criticism: this became a way of disputing any natural beauty of Wagner's "new manner," mocking his own reference to nature in the *Lettre sur la musique.* Paul Scudo described the *Tannhäuser* overture as a "vast music machine," while J.-L. Heugel likened Wagner's tendency toward extended use of formulaic accompaniment patterns to the transatlantic telegraph cable.[54] Jouvin, in his review for *Le Figaro,* compared Wagner's vocal lines to a bobbin that never empties itself of its endless thread, and he concluded that it was "music against nature."[55] And any music that was not based on the "charm and the sentiment of the melody"—so wrote Heugel, playing on the familiar trope—would lead to a path *"without future for music."*[56]

51. Paul Scudo, "Revue musicale," *La revue des deux mondes,* 1 April 1861; Joseph d'Ortigue, "Théâtre de l'Opéra," *Journal des débats,* 23 March 1861; Arthur Pougin, "M. Richard Wagner," *La jeune France,* 3 March 1861; Wilhelm [Édouard Monnais], "Revue musicale," *Revue contemporaine,* 31 March 1861; Stéphen de la Madeleine, "Revue des Théâtres Lyriques," *L'univers musical,* 31 March 1861; Alexis Azevedo, "Musique," *L'opinion nationale,* 19 March 1861; and Oscar Comettant, "Académie Impériale de Musique: *Tannhauser,*" *L'art musical,* 21 March 1861.

52. Jost, "Zu den französischen Übersetzungen," 38.

53. "Cette première scène du *Tannhäuser,* qui a été écrite à Paris et qui révèle la dernière manière du maître, ne peut se comparer à rien qui existe en musique. C'est le chaos, c'est le néant, mais le chaos et le néant scientifiques; c'est cette grande *mélodie de la forêt* qui n'a rien de commun avec la mélodie italienne." Scudo, "Revue musicale," *La revue des deux mondes,* 1 April 1861.

54. "Une vaste machine de musique": Scudo, quoted in Ellis, "Wagnerism and Anti-Wagnerism," 60. "Une formule d'accompagnement . . . se prolonge indéfiniment, à l'instar du câble transatlantique": J.-L. Heugel, "Académie Impériale de la Musique: *Tannhauser,*" *Le ménestrel,* 17 March 1861.

55. "La phrase de M. Wagner . . . est un fil sans fin . . . Figurez-vous une bobine qu'on déviderait toute une soirée, une *bobine inépuisable*"; "la musique de l'avenir, cette musique contre nature." Benoît Jouvin, "Théâtre: *Le Tannhauser,*" *Le Figaro,* 21 March 1861.

56. "Le charme et le sentiment de la mélodie"; "sans avenir pour la musique." J.-L. Heugel, "Académie Impériale de la Musique: *Tannhauser,*" *Le ménestrel,* 17 March 1861.

If nature served as the foundation to true beauty—an idealist claim shared by both Wagner and his detractors—the classical qualities of proportion, clarity, and variety were conjured in these reviews as the pillars of genuine art against which Wagner's *Tannhäuser* was to be judged, for nature alone was not enough for the French critics: "Who among us would accept this so-called *melody of nature* which nobody could repeat? Nature has only noises, and art alone gives them sense. The melodic idea is for noise and notes what the plan of a palace is for marble and stones, what a painting's design is for its colors."[57] The critics homed in on form as a marker of successful operatic music. Their critical approach thus became threefold: they denounced most of Wagner's music as formless and monotonous, they contrasted it with form as an essential element of music, and they used traditional form—when it could be identified in *Tannhäuser*—as surefire proof of form's irrepressibly musical quality.

The charges of monotony and formlessness were closely linked. Monotony was seen as the direct result of any deviation from good operatic practice; thus, for Sylvain Saint-Étienne, it was the consequence of Wagner's Germanic poetic procedures, while most other critics blamed the abandoning of distinct forms, the disproportionate length of pieces such as Tannhäuser's Rome narration, and the recitative-like style of the vocal lines for the impression of the "great ocean of monotony."[58] Fiorentino saw the Rome narration as a twenty-page travelogue, monotonous and declamatory, "aggravated by all the incidents, all the encounters and all the emotions of a trip to Rome, there and back."[59] Another scene that allowed Wagner's reviewers to criticize such "monotony" was the song contest in act 2, which, according to Bernard, was an "eminently musical subject" that Wagner treated without inspiration.[60] Saint-Valry compared it to an endless disputation between philosophers at the Sorbonne. What is the point, Saint-Valry asked his reader, of having Tannhäuser interrupt Wolfram in the song contest if it is only to interject more of the same? One would have hoped rather that Tannhäuser would "sing some honest-to-goodness Italian melody, bursting with tenderness and voluptuousness."[61]

Saint-Valry's demand for contrast harks back to the notion of *varietas,* an aesthetic

57. "Qui de nous accepterait cette prétendue *mélodie de la nature,* que personne ne pourrait redire? La nature n'a que des bruits, et l'art seul leur donne un sens. L'idée mélodique est aux bruits et aux notes ce que le plan d'un palais est au marbre et aux pierres, ce que le dessin d'un tableau est aux couleurs." Wilhelm [Édouard Monnais], "Revue musicale," *Revue contemporaine,* 31 March 1861.

58. "Océan de la monotonie." Benoît Jouvin, "Théâtres," *Le Figaro,* 21 March 1861.

59. "Vingt pages d'une narration monotone et déclamatoire, aggravé de tous les incidens, toutes les rencontres, et toutes les émotions d'un voyage à Rome, aller et retour." Pier Angelo Fiorentino, "Théâtres," *Le constitutionnel,* 18 March 1861.

60. "Sujet éminemment musical." Paul Bernard, "*Tannhauser,*" *Le ménestrel,* 24 March 1861.

61. "[On croit que Tannhæuser] va chanter quelque franche mélodie italienne, frémissante de tendresse et de volupté. C'était bien la peine d'interrompre Wolfram pour continuer exactement dans le même style; la mélopée, le plein-chant l'emportent, l'amour sensuel est célébré d'une façon aussi accablante que l'autre." Gaston de Saint Valry, "Revue dramatique," *Le pays,* 19 March 1861.

key concept in French music, which had found its way into the aesthetics of *grand opéra*.[62] Critics linked variety to character development on the one hand, and to musical form and structure on the other. D'Ortigue deplored the absence of "a form, a frame, a melody, a rhythm, a syntax that are distinguishable, perceptible."[63] Without form—so Scudo reminded his readers—there was no beauty, which was, after all, "the first aim of art."[64] Similarly, Franck-Marie argued that because of the lack of clear-cut form, Wagner's music was naught but a "long psalmody," in which "nothing remains graven on memory."[65] For Franck-Marie, Wagner's resistance to form was the result of his enmity toward operatic convention; he maintained that all opera was, by definition, naught but convention:

> The form that Wagner gives to his airs only serves to increase the tedium that results from the absence of any dramatic element in his subject. Enemy of all convention, the master does not want that singers set themselves apart to perform a cavatina, an aria, a duet. The action stops during that time, he thinks, and it is not at all natural that a person should step aside in that manner from those who surround her in order to repeat a long *a parte*. . . . Opera is founded solely on conventions of all kinds; why not admit, among so many others, one more when it can offer so much variety and interest to singing?[66]

Oscar Comettant similarly reflected on the needs of the musical stage, defining its essence as riveting drama based on variety and contrast and invoking Aristotelian rules of dramatic structure:

62. Herbert Schneider, "Scribe and Auber: Constructing Grand Opera," in *The Cambridge Companion to Grand Opera,* ed. David Charlton (Cambridge: Cambridge University Press, 2003), 168–88. Schneider cites both a letter by Scribe and a passage from Auber's memoirs that emphasize the importance of "variety" for an opera (168, 170). See also Lacombe, *Keys to French Opera,* 87–143, on the construction of mid-century French opera.

63. "Une forme, un cadre, une mélodie, un rythme, une syntaxe saisissables, perceptibles." Joseph d'Ortigue, "Théâtre de l'Opéra," *Journal des débats,* 23 March 1861.

64. "La beauté, premier but de tous les arts"; "la forme, sans laquelle l'esprit humain ne peut rien comprendre." Paul Scudo, "Revue musicale," *La revue des deux mondes,* 1 April 1861.

65. "Wagner ne déterminant jamais ses mélodies d'une manière précise, par des formes bien arrêtés, sa partie chantée n'est plus qu'une longue psalmodie se déroulant à satiété. Rien ne se grave dans l'esprit, car rien ne se détache sur ce fond d'harmonie uniforme par trop de continuité." Franck-Marie [Perdolini], "Revue musicale," *La patrie,* 24 March 1861.

66. "La coupe que Wagner donne à ses airs ne fait qu'accroître l'ennui qui résulte de l'absence tout élément dramatique dans le sujet. Ennemi de toute convention, le maître ne veut pas que les chanteurs s'isolent pour exécuter une cavatine, un air, un duo. L'action s'arrête pendant ce temps, pense-t-il, et il n'est point naturel qu'un personnage s'écarte ainsi de ceux qui l'entourent pour répéter un long *à parte*. . . . L'opéra n'est fondé que sur les conventions de toutes sortes; pourquoi dès lors, au milieu de tant d'autres, n'en pas admettre une de plus lorsqu'elle peut donner tant de variété et d'intérêt au chant?" Franck-Marie [Perdolini], "Revue musicale," *La patrie,* 24 March 1861.

What one wants from theater is a gripping drama, clearly set up, well developed, with a strong dénouement, and which permits a musician to give full scope not to his own sentimental dreams that affect none but himself, but to the well-characterized emotions of the heart. And because variety is one of the key elements of musical theater, one needs, next to the grand manifestations of passion, graceful pieces of various characters that charm the ear and hold the attention.[67]

In the journalists' view, Wagner's music itself served as the ultimate proof of their aesthetic position. Even his harshest critics heaped lavish praise (albeit sometimes grudgingly) on those segments of *Tannhäuser* that conformed to the conventions of French *grand opéra*. These reviewers did not use their praise as a means to soften the blow they were dealing Wagner, but rather to strengthen it. For Heugel, the traditional pieces served as a "condemnation of the culprit by the culprit himself," and Saint-Valry asked whether they were "not the most significant condemnation of his unhappy inventions."[68] The march in act 2 was compared to similar compositions by Auber, Meyerbeer, and Halévy, to whom Wagner was sometimes judged a close second and at other times an equal. For the septet at the end of act 1, scene 4, comparisons were drawn to the music of Bellini, Donizetti, and Verdi, with Wagner's music emerging not unfavorably. Thus Heugel considered the "andante of the septet a fragment that Bellini and Donizetti would have signed with both hands, entrusting the voices with [the melodic lines] that Wagner gave to the violins."[69] And Bernard characterized the same extract ("à l'italienne") as an ensemble "in which the voices were married with a rare success. The musician of the future arrives, in this respect, at effects that Verdi, the *sound-colorist*, could rightfully envy."[70] By thus homing in on the traditional aspect of the score—whether in terms of form or musical texture—these

67. "Ce qu'on veut au théâtre, c'est un drame saisissant, clairement exposé, bien conduit, dénoué avec force, et qui permette au musicien de donner un libre essor, non à ses rêveries sentimentales et dont personne autre que lui n'est affecté, mais aux émotions bien caractérisées du cœur. Et comme la variété est un des éléments par excellence de la musique théâtrale, il faut, à côté des grandes manifestations de la passion, des morceaux gracieux de différents caractères qui charment l'oreille et tiennent l'attention en éveil." Oscar Comettant, "Académie Impériale de la Musique: *Tannhauser*," *L'art musical,* 21 March 1861.

68. "La condamnation du coupable par le coupable lui-même": J.-L. Heugel, "Académie Impériale de la Musique: *Tannhauser*," *Le ménestrel,* 17 March 1861. "Les quelques morceaux réussis de *Tannhæuser* qui semblent procéder de l'éducation première du compositeur ne sont-ils pas la condamnation la plus caractéristique de ses malheureuses inventions?": Gaston de Saint-Valry, "Revue dramatique," *Le pays,* 19 March 1861.

69. "L'andante du septuor, un fragment que Bellini et Donizetti auraient signé des deux mains, en confiant aux voix ce que M. Wagner fait chanter aux violons." J.-L. Heugel, "Académie Impériale de la Musique: *Tannhauser*," *Le ménestrel,* 17 March 1861.

70. "Les voix se marient, alors avec un rare bonheur. Le musicien de l'avenir arrive, sous ce rapport, à des effets que Verdi, le *sonoriste coloré*, pourrait à bon droit lui envier." Paul Bernard, "*Tannhauser*," *Le ménestrel,* 24 March 1861.

critics responded to Wagner's own declaration in the *Lettre sur la musique,* where he claimed that he no longer made concessions to the frivolous tastes of the audience.[71] Jouvin explicitly referred to this attitude in his review, in which his praise of the act 2 march was framed with a scathing assessment of Wagner's condescension: "The musician has such contempt for anything that resembles a melody even from afar, for the periodic and rhythmic phrase, that he considers the march in question as a sin of his youth, as a cowardly concession to the routine taste of an irreverent public."[72]

French opera, for Wagner, was indeed "an institution whose particular purpose is almost exclusively to offer a distraction and an amusement to a population that is as bored as it is pleasure-seeking."[73] By attacking the institution of French opera and its audience, Wagner raised hackles. How much so becomes clear in the almost ubiquitous reference in the reviews to French audiences as arbiters of taste. Descriptions of the audience as "impartial" (Monnais), "competent" (Fiorentino), "benevolent, welcoming, and courteous" (Comettant), and "intelligent and generous" (Wolff) are liberally strewn across the negative reviews, defending audiences' taste against Wagner's charge by highlighting their "generous" and "enthusiastic" applause for the right kind of music.[74]

But these operatic numbers in *Tannhäuser* could also be used to broaden the critical discussion to questions about genre by setting French definitions of opera against Wagner's evocation of the symphony in his *Lettre sur la musique.* For Wagner's adversaries, opera and symphony were mutually exclusive genres, and to introduce symphonic procedures into opera went against its dramatic essence. Franck-Marie called the traditional numbers "sublime pages, written with all the inspiration and skill of the genius." He continued by identifying them as "pieces which by their nature detach themselves from the action and only enter the general framework of the drama in the guise of symphonic hors-d'œuvre."[75] Comettant used a long segment of his review to contrast the theater's need for "gripping drama"—created by musical numbers of great variety—with the opposing aesthetic aim of symphonic unity:

71. "Ces concessions que mon premier modèle, mon vénéré maître, Weber, se croyait encore obligé de faire au public d'opéra, vous ne les rencontrez plus, je puis, je pense, m'en flatter, dans mon *Tannhœuser.*" Wagner, *Quatre poèmes d'opéras,* 106.

72. "Le musicien a un mépris tel pour tout ce qui ressemble de près ou de loin à de la mélodie, pour la phrase périodique et rythmée, qu'il considère la marche en question comme un péché de jeunesse, comme une concession sans courage faite à l'esprit routinier du public profane." Benoît Jouvin, "Théâtres," *Le Figaro,* 21 March 1861.

73. "Je voyais dans l'opéra une institution dont la destination spéciale est presque exclusivement d'offrir une distraction et un amusement à une population aussi ennuyée qu'avide de plaisir." Wagner, *Quatre poèmes d'opéras,* 34.

74. See, for example, Scudo, "Revue musicale," *La revue des deux mondes,"* 1 April 1861.

75. "Des pages sublimes écrites avec toute l'inspiration et la science du génie. Qu'on remarque que nous citons justement des morceaux qui, par leur nature, se détachent de l'action et ne rentrent dans le cadre général du drame qu'en guise de hors-d'œuvre symphoniques." Franck-Marie [Perdolini], "Revue musicale," *La patrie,* 24 March 1861.

Now, the invention of Mr. Wagner consists of turning opera into an instrumental symphony with the obbligato accompaniment of singers. . . . How can a musician of the worth of Mr. Wagner (because, after all, Mr. Wagner is a man of infinite talent) hold to such terms? Has Mr. Wagner forgotten that the great interest—so to speak, the only interest—of the symphony resides in the developments of a given theme that serves, so to speak, as the thesis for the comments of the composer[?] Can one imagine a symphony without unity of thought, and without this ingenious treatment of the parts that establishes itself as a piquant and often witty conversation between the various instruments on the given subject of the conversation, on the theme[?] Of course not, and nobody doubts it. However, these ingenious developments of a main theme are simply impossible once the music is required to follow dramatic and scenic action. In fact, as the action proceeds little by little, the characters necessarily express different feelings, and the music that expresses them is obliged to change character; consequently, no more unity of sentiment, and no more possible developments of a gestational musical idea.[76]

Not only Wagner's music but also the characters of his dramas were judged in this generic binary between symphony and opera. By using legends instead of the more traditional historic plots of French *grand opéra*—another controversial change Wager advocated in the *Lettre sur la musique*—Wagner was seen as eliminating human interest from his dramas. Instead he replaced them with "abstractions" (according to Azevedo, Comettant, and Wilhelm) without flesh and blood. When de la Madeleine compared *Tannhäuser* to the librettos of *La juive* (Scribe), *La reine de Chypre* (Saint-Georges), and *Les huguenots* (Scribe and Deschamps), Wagner's poem seemed "primitive" and "naive."[77] De la Madeleine and other critics thus contrasted Wagner's sup-

76. "Or l'invention de M. Wagner consiste à faire de l'opéra une symphonie instrumentale, avec accompagnement obligé de chanteurs. . . . Comment un musicien de la valeur de M. Wagner (car, après tout, M. Wagner est un homme d'infiniment de talent) peut-il tenir un langage pareil? M. Wagner a-t-il oublié que le grand intérêt, pour ainsi dire l'unique intérêt de la symphonie, réside dans les développements d'un thème donné qui sert, pour ainsi dire, de thèse aux commentaires du compositeur. Peut-on imaginer une symphonie sans unité de pensée, et sans ce travail ingénieux des parties qui s'établit comme une conversation piquante et souvent spirituelle entre les divers instruments, sur le sujet donné de la conversation, sur le thème? Non, certes, et cela n'est douteux pour personne. Eh bien, ces développements ingénieux d'un motif principal sont tout simplement impossibles dès que la musique doit suivre d'action dramatique et scénique. En effet, au fur et à mesure que l'action s'avance, les personnages expriment nécessairement des sentiments différents et la musique qui les exprime est obligée de changer de caractère; par conséquent, plus d'unité de sentiment et plus de développements possibles d'une idée musicale mère." Oscar Comettant, "Académie Impériale de la Musique," *L'art musical*, 21 March 1861.

77. "Examinons donc tout d'abord son libretto; jugeons-le en lui-même, puis comparons-le à tous ces pauvres poëmes dont on a fait la pauvre musique de *la Juive*, de *la Reine de Chypre*, des *Huguenots* et de *la Muette*. . . . On voit que M. Wagner n'aime pas les imbroglios trop compliqués; ce deuxième acte est d'une simplicité primitive. Le troisième est encore plus naïf." Stéphen de la Madeleine, "Revue des Théâtres Lyriques," *L'univers musical*, 21 March 1861.

posed naiveté with the professionalism of the librettists of French *grand opéra*. Gustave Chadeuil similarly looked to successful models of the past when judging Wagner's proposed changes to the genre, mocking his attempts to replace "prosaic" historical persons with "poetic" legendary figures: "Mr. Wagner does not want to represent just any ordinary lover, whether Arnold in *Guillaume Tell* or Raoul in *Les huguenots*. He wants to represent love."[78] By creating "allegorical characters" that inhabit "an imaginary world," wrote Franck-Marie, Wagner did not relate "the rigorous conditions of human truth; and opera must be human before anything else, because it is drama, that is, life, true reality, and not a dream."[79] Contrasting Wagner's libretto and genre theory with classic Aristotelian theories of drama, the critics pulled the rug out from under Wagner's own reference to Greek tragedy in his *Lettre sur la musique* as validation for his dramatic theories. Classic French tragedy—whether theatrical or operatic—was held up as a mirror to the arrogant German upstart who sought to supplant appropriate historic subjects with legends of a "German simplicity that falls into puerility."[80]

By casting the debate over *Tannhäuser* in nationalist terms that had been familiar for over a century, the journalists could defend the honor of French art without engaging in the question of musical progress in France itself. For conservative critics, Wagner's work—dangerous as it was—also proved a boon. As the often long theoretical elaborations of the nature of French opera show, Wagner's opera served as a substitute for French works, where attacks on musical and dramatic change might be more problematic. If the traditional mold of the number opera, with its clear-cut melodic phrases and ensembles, were reworked by a French composer, then such complete rejection could be more problematic. But by identifying these characteristics as either German or idiosyncratically Wagnerian, French (and Italian) music could be defined by its past masterworks and timeless rules of clarity, elegance, and form. Furthermore, *Tannhäuser* provided a weapon for future criticism, for now any deviation from the French tradition could either be celebrated as a French (and therefore elegant) form of progress or criticized as foreign infiltration. The latter was the focus of the hostile reviews of Charles Gounod's *La reine de Saba* (1862).[81] But when Reyer's new opera *La statue* was given at the Théâtre-Lyrique on 11 April, a few weeks after the *Tannhäuser* debacle, de la Madeleine recontextualized Reyer's style in a modern, French school that developed melody without falling into the excesses of Wagner:

78. "M. Wagner ne veut pas représenter un amoureux quelconque, soit l'Arnold de *Guillaume Tell*, soit le Raoul des *Huguenots*. Il veut représenter l'amour." Gustave Chadeuil, "Revue musicale," *Le siècle*, 26 March 1861.

79. "Tous ces personnages allégoriques, ces fictions plus ou moins brillantes puisées dans un monde imaginaire, ne sauraient convenir aux conditions rigoureuses d'une vérité humaine, et l'opéra doit être humain avant tout, parce qu'il est le drame, c'est-à-dire la vie, la réalité vraie et non le rêve." Franck-Marie [Perdolini], "Revue musicale," *La patrie*, 24 March 1861.

80. "Une simplicité allemande qui tombe dans la puérilité." Benoît Jouvin, "Théâtres," *Le Figaro*, 21 March 1861.

81. Steven Huebner, *The Operas of Charles Gounod* (Oxford: Clarendon Press, 1990), 64–65.

Today we have the researchers about whom I spoke last Thursday—the likes of Félicien David, Gounod, Berlioz, Reyer, and even Mr. Wagner himself—who present their melodic thought in a more complicated guise, more closely linked on the one hand to the harmony, which defines its tessitura, and, on the other, to the words of which it is the most complete and most passionate expression. It is these qualities, whose excess has been blamed so strongly on Mr. Wagner, which today make the fortunes of *La statue* at the Théâtre-Lyrique.[82]

These brief glimpses into the passionate debate over the Parisian *Tannhäuser* show that much was at stake for the institution of the Paris Opéra and its guardians. By all accounts, Wagner was the first musician in the history of the Opéra who refused so blatantly to bend to the dictates of the genre as determined by the French. Not only did he resist actively the translation of *Tannhäuser* into the generic framework of *grand opéra*, but his theoretical writings had also challenged the genre and its music famously as "effect without cause." For Wagner's critics, the missing ballet—the pretext for the Jockey Club's protest—was inconsequential and rarely mentioned. What was essential, however, was to demonstrate that Wagner's music of the future had no such future in Paris, not only because he failed to consider his audience, but also because his music lacked beauty. Although the political circumstances and Wagner's own refusal to compromise certainly contributed to the rejection of *Tannhäuser,* its core challenge to the Opéra rested in the work itself. Critics whose aesthetic position held up the tradition of French and Italian opera had no choice but to condemn this kind of music of the future lest they jeopardize the true future of a genre which was the nation's image.

For the critics, both in the theater and in the press, this end justified the means. Two intertwined themes dominated the post-mortem debate: was the French public right to react so violently to Wagner's opera, and was Wagner victim of a cabal? The first was more disturbing for the critics than the second. Rumors of a cabal were dismissed as musings of disgruntled Germans.[83] Moreover, three of his fiercer detractors—Bernard, Heugel, and Jouvin—accused Wagner and his acolytes of turn-

---

82. "Nous avons aujourd'hui ces chercheurs dont je parlais jeudi dernier, les Félicien David, les Gounod, les Berlioz, les Reyer, et M. Wagner lui-même, qui présentent leur pensée mélodique sous un aspect plus compliqué, plus étroitement lié, d'une part à l'harmonie qui lui sert de tessiture, et, de l'autre, à la parole, dont elle est l'expression plus complète et plus passionnée. Ce sont ces qualités, dont l'excès a été si vertement blâmé chez M. Wagner, qui font aujourd'hui la fortune de *la Statue* au Théâtre-Lyrique." Stéphen de la Madeleine, "Six nouveaux morceaux de chant par M. Edmond Michotte," *L'univers musical,* 2 May 1861.

83. See, for example, Albert Wolff, "Courrier de Paris," *Le Figaro,* 24 March 1861: "Dans les salons et dans les cafés, on n'a cessé depuis huit jours de discuter la musique de l'avenir. Les Allemands étaient généralement d'avis que la cabale française avait fait tomber l'œuvre de leur compatriote. Je

ing the *Tannhäuser* debacle into a martyr's trial. What seemed more problematic to Parisian critics was the continued and increasing misbehavior of the audience in the opera house during the three performances of *Tannhäuser*. Although some defended the mischief-makers as truly French—because they could not stand to be bored and insulted by Wagner—many others, including d'Ortigue, Pougin, and Francis Sept-Fontaines, saw this as inappropriate for French dignity. In particular, Pougin—who was otherwise highly critical of Wagner's ideas and score—was horrified by such improper behavior from a people at the zenith of cultural sophistication:

> And so! In our France, in this hospitable land to which all the foreign geniuses come in order to ask for the supreme consecration of their renown, it is here that a conscientious artist, full of faith, convinced—rightly or wrongly—of the worth of his doctrines, an artist who for close to twenty years has impassioned an entire people, comes to invite us to pronounce ourselves openly, with frankness, on the merit of his works, and in order to welcome him, we the royal people, we the elegant people, we the enlightened people, we the polite people, we the witty people, can only offer insult, disdain, sarcasm, and irony. Truth be told, I would have believed my compatriots to be more just, more benevolent, and more sensible.[84]

For Pougin, the Parisians had missed an opportunity not only to show themselves as cultivated, but also to judge the work in a calm and sophisticated manner for what it was worth. Instead, because of the unmeasured reaction of the audience and critics, Wagner's star remained high in the firmament of the operatic sky, and the threat he posed was, in fact, far from neutralized. The critics' own betrayal of the ideals of *justesse* and moderation in their reviews jeopardized their otherwise legitimate criticism of a perceived incompatible dramatic system, proposed by an artist who openly showed his disdain for native French culture. Because of their extremeness, the reactions of Scudo, Heugel, Azevedo, d'Ortigue, Fiorentino, and others were dismissed as reactionary and incompetent by their contemporaries Baudelaire, Champfleury, Gasperini, and Léon Leroy, whose ideology of musical progress meshed seamlessly with the Wagnerian master narrative. Instead of protecting the institutionalized opera they fought so hard to defend against the threat of Wagner, the critics discredited

---

considère comme un devoir de protester contre ces accusations injustes. La question de nationalité n'a rien à voir dans le *Tannhäuser,* qui n'est qu'une question de plus ou moins de trombones."

84. "Eh quoi! en notre pays de France, en cette terre hospitalière à laquelle tous les génies étrangers viennent demander la consécration suprême de leur renommée, voici qu'un artiste consciencieux, plein de foi, convaincu—à tort ou à raison—de la valeur de ses doctrines; un artiste qui pendant près de vingt ans a passionné tout un peuple, vient nous inviter à nous prononcer ouvertement, franchement sur le mérite de ses œuvres, et nous ne trouvons pour l'accueillir, nous le peuple roi, nous le peuple élégant, nous le peuple éclairé, nous le peuple poli, nous le peuple spirituel, que l'injure, le dédain, le sarcasme et l'ironie! En vérité, je croyais mes compatriotes plus justes, plus bienveillants et plus sensés." Arthur Pougin, "Chronologie musicale," *La jeune France,* 31 March 1861.

their own aesthetic position and opened the door to precisely the "music without tradition" (in Saint-Valry's words) that they feared.

The 1861 *Tannhäuser* scandal had disastrous consequences for the institution of French *grand opéra*. Once the Wagnerian ideology of musical progress began to dominate aesthetic and musicological discourses not only in the nineteenth century but also in the twentieth, the tables were turned. Instead of judging music drama by the tenets of French classicist aesthetics, music critics and musicologists dismissed the operas of Auber, Meyerbeer, and Halévy—so beloved by Wagner's critics—as overly determined by the very convention and the very institution that Wagner attacked in his *Lettre sur la musique*. Wagner's Parisian critics were far more astute than posterity ever gave them credit for: their attack on *Tannhäuser* was indeed a cabal, because only a concerted, last-ditch effort could help preserve an operatic tradition that had become obsolete by the late 1850s. The price for their rather spectacular failure was high: ridiculed themselves, they were left behind in the dust of history, for it was Wagner's music—not that of Auber, Rossini, Meyerbeer, and Halévy—that dominated the artistic future they helped to shape in this March of 1861.

La sylphide and Les sylphides

Marian Smith

This is a tale of two *Sylphides,* that is, two ballets about sylphides.[1] The first was created in 1832; the second, nearly eighty years later. Both were set some time in the hazy
romantic past, and both involved white-clad sylphs dancing ethereally. Both featured
a ballerina whose portrayal of a sylph caused a great sensation: Marie Taglioni in the
nineteenth century and Anna Pavlova in the twentieth. And—perhaps because the
second ballet was deliberately created to look like the first—the two "are often mis-
taken for one another."[2]

Despite their similarities in appearance, however, these two works came out of
entirely unlike circumstances, and they differ from one another in crucial ways. In
this essay I will emphasize the distinctions between the two apparently similar ballets,
proposing a reading that goes roughly as follows: the first ballet is a typical "story
ballet," the type that was the mainstay of the Opéra, the most powerful institution
for ballet in Europe at the time. The second was a new sort of experimental work
brought to Paris by an upstart troupe of young Russians eager to break away from the
old established repertoire of their home company, the Imperial Ballet, which by then
had seized the mantle of the Paris Opéra to become Europe's ballet juggernaut; this
new work was plotless, relatively short, and, despite its nostalgically romantic appear-

---

1. A sylph is a being or spirit who inhabits the air. A sylphide is a young or little sylph. In this
essay I use the terms *sylph* and *sylphide* interchangeably.
2. " . . . que l'on confond souvent." André David, *Le combat,* 19 December 1957.

ance, quite radical in form and style. Thus was the sylph plucked from one culture and transferred to another, a symbol of ballet's romantic age in Paris helping to usher in ballet's modern age in the same city.

My goal in this chapter is simple: to shed light on the disparate natures of these two works by describing them and recounting their genesis stories, and thereby to remind readers not only of the modernity of *Les sylphides,* but also of the standard practices for ballet at the Opéra in the 1830s. That practice is worth remembering specifically in the light of these two sylph ballets, because the second one, by borrowing only the ethereal, otherworldly aspect of the first and then becoming terribly famous, has created a misleading impression of *La sylphide.* A further complicating factor is that *Les sylphides* looked so old-fashioned in comparison to the other antiestablishment ballets its choreographer, Michel Fokine, was creating around the same time ("a pale anemone blooming delicately amid the colorful violence of *Scheherezade, Cléopâtre,* and *Prince Igor*")[3] that it passed—from the very beginning—for a reasonable facsimile of a ballet from the 1830s, even though it was not.

La sylphide, *1832*

Let us begin with the genesis and first production of *La sylphide.* The ballet made its premiere, along with several other works (including *Fernand Cortez, La tentation, Le serment, Nathalie,* and a revival of *Moïse*), in 1832. This was in keeping with the Opéra director's contractual obligation to stage, each year, one *grand opéra,* one *grand ballet,* two *pétits operas,* and two *pétits ballets.*[4] The ballet's libretto—written by the tenor Adolphe Nourrit, who bore in mind the young Marie Taglioni (see fig. 11.1) as the otherworldly character of the title role—was based upon the conflict between the everyday world and the alluring, mysterious magical realm of the supernatural. Inspired by Charles Nodier's novel *Trilby,* Nourrit fashioned a plot about a Scottish farmer, James, who falls in love with a sylphide and shocks his fellow villagers by leaving his mortal fiancée, Effie, and pursuing his new beloved. At the end, owing to an

---

3. Grace Robert, *The Borzoi Book of Ballets* (New York: A. A. Knopf, 1946), 217.

4. Louis Véron's contract also stipulated that he could be exempted from some of these requirements if he showed the "proper pomp and spectacle" in one or more of the new works. Louis Véron, *Mémoires d'un bourgeois de Paris* (Paris: G. de Gonet, 1853–55), 3:173–78. Véron was unable to fulfill these requirements, and fewer works were required of later directors, though the Opéra was still required to produce both operas and ballets. The contract of Edmond Duponchel, for example, stipulated that he produce two ballets and two operas per year: (1) a *grand opéra* in three, four, or five acts, of about three hours' duration, not replaceable by works of any other nature or duration; (2) a second opera in two acts, or two operas of one act, in which latter instance one of the operas could be replaced by a translated foreign work; and (3) two ballets of at least two acts each; one of which could be replaced by two one-act ballets, or by a one-act opera and a one-act ballet, or by a two-act opera. The requirements made of Léon Pillet, Henri Duponchel, and Nestor Roqueplan in a contract of 1847 are identical to these (*F-Pan,* AJ[13] 180).

MARIAN SMITH

FIGURE 11.1. Eugène Lami's costume design for Marie
Taglioni in *La sylphide*, 1832. Bibliothèque-Musée de
l'Opéra. Bibliothèque nationale de France.

evil spell cast at a witches' sabbath, James inadvertently brings about the death of his
beloved sylphide (see appendix).

The role of the sylph fit Marie Taglioni's style of ethereal dancing perfectly, and
it carried on the sort of otherworldly identity she had assumed in *Robert le diable* in
1831 as the ghostly Abbess Hélène (as well as offering "white" scenes reminiscent of
that opera's famous moonlit cloister scene).[5] In this ballet her remarkable technique
and apparent weightlessness became the toast of Paris.

The subject matter of *La sylphide* and Taglioni's stunning performance in the bal-

5. *La sylphide* was one of the first nineteenth-century ballets to include "white" scenes (inspiring
the term *ballet blanc,* coined in the late nineteenth century and popularized in the twentieth). A

258

let struck many in the audience as quite innovative. As one critic saw it, the story of *La sylphide* followed the new literary fashion, even as the staging signaled a return to the era of the marvelous that had prevailed earlier in the century when classically themed ballets were the order of the day at the Opéra: "Transported from *The Odyssey* to *Waverly,* the Opéra has taken its flight from Taygete [in Greece] to Ben Lomond [in Scotland], and discarded the tunic and chlamyde for the plaid and the tartan." Taglioni's new style of dancing was crucial to the ballet's success, he continued, and the layout of the ballet was deliberately arranged to emphasize the contrast "between the *noble* and serious dancing style of Mlle [Lise] Noblet [Effie] and the more original, more idealized talent of Mlle Taglioni [the Sylphide]; this ballet, one could truly say, places her on a pedestal. Everything is calculated to bring out her grace and lightness, qualities which never fail to inspire enthusiastic applause."[6] Jules Janin, the critic for the *Journal des débats,* who openly detested the old-style *danse noble,* described the natural grace of Taglioni's dancing:

> Imagine our joy one evening when, unsuspecting and by pure chance, like finding a pearl by the roadside, we were presented not with the *danse noble,* but with a simple, easy, naturally graceful Taglioni, with a figure of unheard-of elegance, arms of serpentine suppleness and legs to match. . . . When we first saw her so much at ease and dancing so happily—she danced like a bird singing—we could not understand it. "Where is the *danse noble?* asked the old men. The *danse noble* is as foreign to Taglioni's style as natural dancing is to that of her rivals. She uses her hands when she dances! See how she bends her body, how she walks. . . . She has given us a new art, she has initiated us into a new pleasure, for she has completely reformed the ballet of her time.[7]

This ballet's fashionably romantic subject matter and the fresh new dancing style of its star—not to mention the foregrounding of its innovative qualities in some latter-day dance writing in which *La sylphide* is depicted as a revolutionary work—need not deter us from recalling what made it typical of the Opéra's ballet output of the period. First, it depended upon three modes of bodily expression: classical dance,

---

"white scene" is usually danced by females in white on a dimly lit stage. See Marian Smith, "The Disappearing Danseur," *Cambridge Opera Journal* 19, no. 1 (2007): 33–57.

6. "Transporté de l'*Odysée* à *Waverly,* l'Opéra a pris son vol du taygête au Ben-lhomond, et dépouillé la tunique et la chlamyde pour le plaid et le tartan. . . . Tout son charme est dans l'exécution scénique, heureusement arrangée pour faire contraster la danse noble et sérieuse de mademoiselle Noblet [Effie] avec le talent plus original, plus idéalisé de mademoiselle Taglioni; c'est, à vrai dire, un piédestal élevé à cette idole des *dilettanti* de la danse. Tout est calculé le manière à faire briller cette grâce, cette légèreté, auxquelles n'ont jamais manqué les applaudissemens d'enthousiasme." *L'artiste,* 1832.

7. *Journal des débats,* 24 August 1832. Translated by Ivor Guest in *The Romantic Ballet in Paris,* rev. 2nd ed. (London: Dance Books, 1980), 115–16.

national dance (balleticized folk dance nowadays referred to as "character dance"), and pantomime, though Taglioni's new brand of "idealized" dancing did expand its range of classical dance, as Janin so delightedly pointed out.[8] These three expressive modes were used to tell a fairly elaborate story involving six characters (Effie, James, the Sylphide, Gurn, Madge, and Anne Reuben) and a good many Scottish villagers, witches, and sylphides as well. The high number of corps de ballet parts called for (seventy-eight) is typical of ballets of the July Monarchy and quite in keeping with the Opéra's institutional commitment to spectacle. So were *La sylphide*'s special effects, which included sylphs flying on wires, and its use of what Carl Dahlhaus has identified as the "pantomimic intelligibility" typical in works at Opéra of this period, that is, the "striking, 'speechlike' arrangements of the agents—among whom Véron also includes the chorus" as a primary expressive means. In this approach, dramatic events "must be comprehensible as visible action without regard for the text."[9] Props handled by the characters figured into this form of expression too, and in *La sylphide* they were typically meaningful as well as plentiful. They included the plaid draped by the Sylphide about her waist when she wishes to suggest her eagerness to replace Effie as James's bride,[10] the objects arranged around the witches' cauldron (bellows, a pan, the skimmer, two spheres, skulls, a transparent vase containing writhing reptiles, and a bag filled with dried herbs), the poisonous substances thrown into it (toads, a snake, lizards, an old howling cat, wolf's teeth, hemlock, cat ears, and goat feet), the large book of cabalistic signs the witch Madge opens in front of it (on a makeshift pulpit formed by hideous animal pets), and the nestful of little birds that the Sylphide hankers after. This visual approach also entailed the transfer from one character to another of meaningful objects, including the bridal bouquet placed in Effie's hands, the veil placed on her head, and the scarf that was bewitched by Madge and then fatally draped by James around the Sylphide's shoulders.[11]

Making a story intelligible pantomimically could also entail the stark differentiation of groups of characters from one another, and *La sylphide* does so in spades. Here we have three groups—witches, Scottish villagers, and sylphides—each with its own predominant style of dancing, distinctive costumes, and particular home place (respectively, the mouth of a cave, a Scottish farmhouse, and a woods). Each group engages in its own typical behaviors (the witches ride on broomsticks, jump

8. Self-standing dramatic ballets such as *La sylphide* were officially called "ballet-pantomimes," as opposed to the danced divertissements often called "ballets" and performed within operas and ballet-pantomimes.

9. Carl Dahlhaus, *Nineteenth-Century Music*, trans. J. Bradford Robinson (Berkeley: University of California Press), 126.

10. This action, missing from today's productions but stipulated in Alexander Bennett's 1835 *répétiteur*, in Bennett's view makes more sense than having the Sylphide wrap the plaid around her shoulders, as she sometimes does today, because it shows that she wishes to resemble her mortal rival.

11. These details are given in the libretto.

grotesquely, and hold a satanic Sabbath, and one tells fortunes; the villagers do Scottish dances and hold a wedding celebration; the sylphs fly and dance ethereally in the woods). And it is obvious when one of these life forms trespasses into another's territory.

The music for *La sylphide,* also in keeping with the Opéra's practice (as I have described elsewhere at length),[12] was commissioned to conform to the ballet's particular dramatic requirements—its various moods, its stage action, its setting. The composer selected for the task was Jean-Madeleine Schneitzhoeffer (1785–1852), a versatile musician who served as a timpanist and as *chef du chant* at the Opéra, and who had already supplied six ballet scores for the house.[13] And, like several of the other composers of ballets for the Opéra during this period (including Alexandre Montfort, Casimir Gide, François Benoist, and Édouardo Deldevez), Schneitzhoeffer had been trained at the Conservatoire (and had taught there as well), and he enjoyed close connections to the established musical institutions of Paris (having played timpani, for example, for the Royal Chapel). Similarly typical was his interest in composing opera, though his only such work, *Sardanapale,* remained unfinished.

Schneitzhoeffer's score for *La sylphide* conforms well to the description of ballet music published in a music dictionary of 1826 describing the genre's two main components, dramatic music and dance music:

> [Each] situation, each passion which comes momentarily to predominate, requires a new rhythm, new motifs, changes of tone and of phrasing. The skillful composer, despite the difficulties of these requirements, knows how to make a pleasing ensemble out of this mixture. . . . As for the dance airs, one conceives that they must be characteristic and analogous to the place where the action transpires; thus the dance airs of the Indians, the Scots, the Hungarians must have the character of the music of their countries.[14]

In the dramatic scenes, Schneitzhoeffer does indeed follow the action from moment to moment. For example, for an exchange between the Sylphide and James in act 1,

12. See Marian Smith, *Ballet and Opera in the Age of "Giselle"* (Princeton, NJ: Princeton University Press, 2000).

13. *Proserpine* (1818); *Le séducteur au village* (1818); *Zémire et Azor* (1824); *Mars et Vénus* (1826); *Le sicilien,* with Fernando Sor (1827); and *L'orgie,* with Michel Carafa (1831) He was also the composer of *La tempête* (1834).

14. "Chaque situation, chaque passions qui vient momentanément à prédominer, demande un nouveau rythme, de nouveaux motifs, des changements de ton et des périodes. L'habile compositeur, malgré ces exigences, sait former de ce mélange un ensemble agréable. . . . Quant aux airs de danse, on conçoit facilement qu'ils doivent être caractéristiques et analogues au lieu où se passé l'action; ainsi les airs de danse des Indiens, des Écossais, des Hongrois, doivent avoir le caractère de la musique de leur pays." Pierre Lichtenthal, *Dizionario e bibliografia della musica* (Milan, 1826), translated and augmented by Dominique Mondo as *Dictionnaire de musique* (Paris: Troupenas, 1839), 1:115–16.

scene 4, he composes a poignant 12/8 largo of eleven bars' duration as the Sylphide worries that James "loves Effie too much." She falls into a desperate despair (thirty bars of agitato) and tells James that she will die. After he evinces his love for her (adagio, 4/4), the Sylphide dances with joy (6/8). Schneitzhoeffer also provided ambient sounds when called for, such as the burst of wind act 1, scene 4, and the Sylphide's beating wings in the opening scene.

Dance music is plentiful too in this score, and, typically, some but not all of it is "characteristic and analogous to the place where the action transpires"—for instance, a dance number in the first act, including a section quoting the Scots melody "The White Cockade."[15]

Another typical feature of Schneitzhoeffer's score was its use of borrowed music, though the composer used less of it than some critics would have liked.[16] One snippet is from the F Major Fugue by J. S. Bach from Book II of *Das wohltemperierte Clavier,* used at the beginning of act 2; each subject entry of the fugue coincides with the entrance of a group of witches, who have come to celebrate their late-night sabbath. (Fugues were occasionally associated with malign characters in ballet; Adolphe Adam, for instance, wrote a fugue for the scene in *Giselle* in which the Wilis attack Albrecht.) When referring to the witch Madge, Schneitzhoeffer gave bits of Paganini's "Le Streghe" (The Witches) to a solo violin. Schneitzhoeffer also used a few measures of "Che farò senza Euridice," from Gluck's *Orfeo ed Euridice,* at the moment James realizes his beloved Sylphide has died. The practice of using a short segment of a well-known texted melody, known as an *air parlant,* had played an important role in the Opéra's ballet scores for decades and helped the composer fulfill his task of helping the audiences follow the action.

Thus, *La sylphide* may be read as a ballet typical of those created at the Opéra in the age in question: it told a story, and in order to do so, it made use of an elaborate set with many props, special effects, a stageful of characters categorizable into groups that could be readily distinguished from one another visually, and a tailor-made score.

The Genesis of *Les sylphides*

Let us now turn our attention to *Les sylphides,* a set of relatively short dances that took shape incrementally over the course of three years in the hands of Michel Fokine (1880–1942), a premier danseur in the Imperial Ballet and a choreographer bent on reform. This ballet began in 1907 in Russia as a series of tableaux, most of them programmatic, under the name *Chopiniana* (for it was choreographed to Glazunov's suite of the same name consisting of orchestrated piano works of Chopin) and wound up as an abstract piece, inspired in part by the 1832 *La sylphide,* and danced in Diaghi-

---

15. Alexander Bennett, "The Ballet Called *La Sylphide,*" unpublished manuscript, 91.
16. On borrowed music in ballets, see Smith, *Ballet and Opera,* chapter 4.

lev's first Saison Russe in Paris in 1909 at the Théâtre du Châtelet under the name *Les sylphides.*

In the ballet itself, and in Fokine's peppery comments in his memoirs about its genesis, we may see a refraction of the passionate struggle taking place in the Maryinsky ballet company between two factions: Fokine and his followers (known variously as the "Fokintsy" and "the innovators"), and the "Imperialitsy," led by Nikolai Legat and the prima ballerina Matilde Kschessinska, celebrated for her stunning technique (and likely the subject of a satirical portrait in the character of the mechanical-doll ballerina of Fokine's *Petroushka,* 1911). The Fokintsy, who counted among their number Bronislava Nijinska and Vaslav Nijinsky, believed that ballet had come to emphasize empty virtuosity without dramatic expressiveness.[17] Fokine laid out the polarization as he saw it in a famous letter to the *Times* of London in 1914, drawing a distinction between "the new ballet" and "the older ballet" and declaring five principles of reform:

1. Movement must be appropriate to the "period and character of the nation represented" instead of based on ready-made and established dance steps.
2. Dance and gesture must serve the dramatic action, instead of used as "mere divertissement or entertainment."
3. Performers should be expressive from head to foot, "replacing gestures of the hands by mimetic of the whole body" and employing conventional gesture "only where it is required by the style of the ballet."
4. The group, or corps de ballet, should express the appropriate sentiment of the ballet instead of, as in the old ballet, being "ranged in groups only for the purpose of ornament."
5. Dancing is equal in stature to music and scenic decoration in ballet. It does not serve as a slave to either. Nor, "in contradistinction to the older ballet," does the new ballet "demand 'ballet music' of the composer as an accompaniment to dancing; it accepts music of every kind, provided only that it is good and expressive. It does not demand of the scenic artist that he should array the ballerinas in short skirts and pink slippers. It does not impose any specific 'ballet' conditions on the composer or the decorative artist, but gives complete liberty to their creative powers."[18]

Fokine also wrote at some length in his memoirs about his frustration with the establishment at the Maryinsky, arguing (not for the first time in the history of the theater) that expressiveness and portrayal of emotion and character should take precedence over vacuous virtuosity. He wrote of truth and naturalness, embracing the idea

17. See Suzanne Carbonneau, "Michel Fokine," in *International Encyclopedia of Dance,* ed. Selma Jeanne Cohen (New York: Oxford University Press, 1998), 3:14–28.
18. Fokine, letter to the *Times,* 6 July 1914; reprinted in Roger Copeland and Marshall Cohen, *What Is Dance? Readings in Theory and Criticism* (New York: Oxford University Press, 1983), 260.

of barefoot dancing, finding it less artificial than "toe dancing" (more often called "pointe dancing" today).[19] In this regard he was no doubt influenced by Isadora Duncan, whose performances in Russia, the first of which took place in 1904, sent shock waves through the ballet establishment there. In addition, Duncan sometimes performed to the music of Chopin played on the piano, a practice not lost on the eager young Fokine.[20]

In any case, lest there be any doubt about *Chopiniana* as a reform ballet—for it has nothing of the pointedly modern look of some of Fokine's other early works—Fokine himself averred that in *Chopiniana* he expressed his notions about reform even more plainly than in his prose writings: "From the outset I myself pictured the ballet as most varied in content and form, expressive of life. I recognized the dramatic, the abstract, the character, and the classic dance; and I believe that, in this ballet, I expressed my sentiments more clearly than in any other, more clearly even than in my own program of reforms."[21]

THE FIRST VERSION, FEBRUARY 1907

Indeed, the first *Chopiniana* (created for a charity event at the Maryinsky) did cover a broad span, consisting of five separate tableaux danced to piano pieces of Chopin. Fokine's own description of its five scenes is worth quoting at some length, for it gives a clear sense both of the ballet's variety of content and form (so "expressive of life," as the choreographer saw it), and of the importance he placed on the lack of spectacular feats in the pas de deux (no. 4), a genre then expected to feature virtuosic display.[22]

1. Polonaise in A Major, op. 40, no. 1 (a Polish ball in a luxurious palace): "In gorgeous costumes, a large ensemble performed Polish ballroom dances. (Whenever I endeavor to prove the connection existing between a national dance and the life which created it, I always think of the Polonaise as the best example. It was created in the period of the fullest bloom of the Polish nation; it reflects and exemplifies its majesty, luxury, pride, and at the same time its chivalrous homage to the fair sex.)"

2. Nocturne in F Major, op. 15, no. 1 (Chopin in Majorca): "The curtain opens disclosing Chopin sitting at the piano in a monastery on the island of Majorca, where, during the night, the ill composer suffers nightmarish hallucinations. He sees dead monks rising from their graves and slowly approaching him to the ac-

19. Fokine, *Memoirs of a Ballet Master,* ed. Anatole Chujoy, trans. Vitale Fokine (Boston: Little, Brown, 1961).

20. Fokine chose Glazunov's existing suite of orchestrated Chopin pieces, as well as its title, *Chopiniana,* for his new work, asking the composer to orchestrate one more number, the Waltz in C sharp Minor, op. 64 no. 2 (a work that Duncan had used in her performance as well). See Noël Goodwin, "Sight and Sound: Fokine and Chopin," *Dance and Dancers* (November 1991): 15–17.

21. Fokine, *Memoirs,* 105.

22. Ibid., 100–105.

companiment of a monotonously beating rain. Frightened, he rushes away from the piano, trying to seek safety from the horrible visions. He finds salvation in his Muse. Again he sits at the piano and finds calm in the sounds of the Nocturne.

"Chopin was portrayed by an excellent pantomimist, Alexis Bulgakov, who was made up to resemble the composer. The Muse was portrayed by a beautiful dancer, Anna Ourakova, who specialized in Good Fairy roles. The male dancers played the roles of the monks. The female dancers, in light, transparent gauze costumes, interpreted the music of the Nocturne."

3. Mazurka in C sharp Minor, op. 50, no. 3 (a wedding in a Polish village): "An unfortunate young girl is being married to an elderly man whom she does not love. In the course of the general dancing, her beloved finds his way to her. As a result of his passionate pleas, she throws the wedding ring at the unwanted suitor and flees with her beloved. The part of the bride was danced by Julie Sedova."

4. Waltz in C sharp Minor, op. 64, no. 2 (a plotless pas de deux): "The Waltz was danced by Anna Pavlova and Michael Oboukhov. Pavlova appeared in a Taglioni costume from the sketch by Léon Bakst. It was a simple reproduction of the etchings of the 1840 period. Oboukhov was attired in a very romantic black velvet costume from the ballet 'Fairy Doll,' also from a sketch by Bakst.

"The choreography differed from all other *pas de deux* in its total absence of spectacular feats. There was not a single *entrechat,* turn in the air, or pirouette. There was a slow turn of the ballerina, holding her partner's hand, but this could not be classified as a pirouette because the movement was not confined to the turn but was used for a change of position and grouping.

"When composing, I placed no restrictions on myself; I simply could not conceive of any spectacular stunts to the accompaniment of the poetic, lyrical Waltz of Chopin. I was totally unconcerned whether this romantic duet would bring applause or satisfy the audience or the ballerina, for I did not think of methods for guaranteeing success."

5. Tarantella in A flat Major, op. 43 (a public festival, with the Bay of Naples and Vesuvius in the background): "This was performed by Vera Fokina assisted by a large ensemble. I tried to project the authentic character of the national dances which Vera and I had observed on our trip to Italy, when we studied them in detail on the island of Capri."

Fokine was also intent on proving a few points in regard to toe dancing: he had not renounced it, he did understand it, and moreover, its proper use eschewed needless display:

Before I created *Chopiniana* it had already been pointed out to me that . . . I had renounced toe dance and had devoted myself exclusively to barefoot dancing. I wished to demonstrate, therefore, that I loved not only the dramatic, but the dance in its pure form; that I recognized the toe dance, and the ballet skirts—but only in their proper place, and not in the place they then occupied in the ballet.

It was in the waltz pas de deux in particular that he meant to establish that even though toe dancing was not natural or realistic, it could still be deployed in a tasteful and expressive manner:

> Toe work I recognized as one of the means of the dance, a more poetic form, removed from the realistic life of some dancing. However, when a dancer jumps and performs feats on her toes, unrelated to and unconnected with the subject of the moment, for the sole purpose of demonstrating that she is the possessor of "steel" toes, I fail to see any poetry in such an exhibition. . . . With the production of the "Chopiniana" Waltz I wanted to show how I understood the unique beauty of the classic dance.[23]

So keen on creating noncharacteristic choreography was Fokine that he had commissioned Glazunov to orchestrate another Chopin piece for the purpose, to be added to the four numbers the composer had already orchestrated. Not coincidentally, he chose the waltz in C sharp Minor, op. 64, no. 2, to which Isadora Duncan had famously danced. ("I needed *that* waltz," wrote Fokine, "because most of the other waltzes suggested character dancing.")[24]

THE SECOND VERSION: "DANCES SUR LA MUSIQUE DE CHOPIN," MARCH 1908

Fokine's next version of the ballet (performed at a charity evening at the Maryinsky under the title "Danses sur la musique de Chopin") was, he said, "in substance an elaborate evolution of the same waltz and a repetition of the earlier experiment on a much greater scale." He erased the ballet's characteristic qualities, putting all of the ballerinas throughout the whole piece in long, diaphanous white tutus instead of character costumes; he rechoreographed the Nocturne as an abstract ensemble dance instead of a depiction of Chopin in Majorca; he jettisoned the tarantella scene altogether; and he stripped the polonaise of its characteristic dancing and moved the music to the beginning to serve as an overture. The effect of the new overture, according to Nijinska, was breathtaking, for it drew attention to the ballet's dreaminess:

> The overture: the pompous "Polonaise" attunes the Theatre. In the audience there is an air of festivity in the anticipation of a brilliant performance. But there is a long pause . . . and then, to the soft sounds of Chopin's dreamy "Nocturne," the mood in the Theatre changes . . . as the curtain is slowly raised an eerie enchantment descends over the Theatre and envelops the spectators and the dancers onstage.[25]

23. Ibid., 105.
24. Ibid, 99; emphasis added.
25. Bronislava Nijinska, *Early Memoirs,* trans. and ed. Irina Nijinska and Jean Rawlinson (Durham, NC: Duke University Press, 1992), 251.

In this new version of *Chopiniana,* Fokine left intact only the choreography of the plotless waltz pas de deux, which had been conceived as an abstract number to begin with, and now added four new Chopin pieces (orchestrated by one Maurice Keller): the Waltz in G flat (op. 70, no. 1), the Mazurka in D (op. 32, no. 2), the Mazurka in C (op. 67, no. 3), and the Prelude in A (op. 28, no. 7). The choreography for each of these was a plotless solo dance. As Fokine put it proudly, "This ballet contains no plot whatsoever. It was the first abstract ballet."[26] It featured Nijinsky in the only male role and twenty-three female dancers in white costumes ("twenty-three Taglionis," as Fokine described them).[27]

By narrowing the focus of the ballet, he explained, he could show up his critics—again—by proving his mettle as a choreographer of classical and *pointe* dancing; he could "repudiate the accusation that I was rejecting the toe dance, that either I did not understand it or I did not love it, and that I was destroying the old ballet. I did understand the toe dance, but I understood it differently from my contemporaries."[28] Another incentive for altering the ballet thus, said Fokine, was his wish to present two ballets widely separated in style in the course of one evening; therefore, this "reverie Romantique" appeared with *Egyptian Nights* (later called *Cleopatra*), a strikingly modern piece calling for profile positions, flat palms, angular lines, and a snake dance for Pavlova (featuring a live snake, which, after curling up around Pavlova's arm and remaining motionless during the premiere, was returned to the zoo and replaced with a better-behaved prop snake made of oilcloth).[29]

But Fokine was particularly compelled by this approach because of his desire to restore ballet to its former greatness—to the heights of the Taglioni era, a time he compared very favorably to his own decadent, empty era:

> I had come to the conclusion that, in the pursuit of acrobatic feats, ballet and the toe dance had lost the very important purpose for which they were created.
>
> When I looked at the etchings and lithographs of ballerinas of the romantic period—Taglioni, Grisi, Cerrito, and others—I clearly saw that their dancing and goals were entirely different from those of the present. For theirs was not the demonstration of physical strength but of pure poetry.
>
> It is easy to understand the colossal difference between the romantic and the modern periods of the ballet if we compare their pictorial representations. Following the poetic romantic ballet, there was a period of decline. In my "reverie Romantique," as I called my new "Chopiniana," I tried to return to the ballet the conditions of its period of highest development.[30]

26. Fokine, *Memoirs,* 102–5.
27. Ibid., 129.
28. Ibid., 128.
29. Ibid., 127–28.
30. Ibid., 128–29.

THE THIRD VERSION: «LES SYLPHIDES», JUNE 1909

The ballet remained largely unchanged in its third and now best-known incarnation, which became a part of the Imperial Ballet repertoire and made its Western debut in Paris at the Théâtre du Châtelet in Paris during the first Saison Russe in June 1909. The company's director, Serge Diaghilev, had altered the ballet a little, discarding the Polonaise overture and replacing it with the mysterious, hushed Prelude op. 28 no. 7, which set the mood for a peaceful, dreamy atmosphere entirely different from the mood evoked by the jauntier Polonaise in St. Petersburg. Diaghilev also commissioned new orchestrations for all but the C sharp Minor Waltz—for which he kept the Glazunov version—including two from Stravinsky (see fig. 11.2).[31] And he changed the title to *Les sylphides,* surely to draw his Parisian audience's attention to the ballet's similarities to *La sylphide.*[32]

The number-by-number description of *Les sylphides,* in which I have paraphrased and quoted the words of George Balanchine and Francis Mason, offers a good sense of what the ballet looked and sounded like at its Parisian premiere:[33]

> Overture (Prelude op. 28 no. 7). The mood of the music is quiet and contemplative. The curtain rises (before the overture ends) on a secluded wood near an ancient ruin; sylphs are grouped about the scene in a still tableau. The light is soft and bluish white. (One observer in 1909 reported that "when the curtain went up . . . the whole house gasped with admiration and surprise . . . the dancers were like blue pearls.")[34]
>
> Nocturne op. 32 no. 2. Some of the *danseuses* begin to dance; they are joined by the principal dancers, who stand in a cluster at the back.
>
> Waltz op. 70 no. 1. One *danseuse* dances a solo to "music suggestive of beautiful and controlled happiness."
>
> Mazurka op. 33 no. 3. The music is "not as soft; it is bolder, more open and

31. He may have done so because he had no access to the Keller arrangements, or because, as Richard Buckle has put it, he "could not leave a score alone." Buckle, *Diaghilev* (New York: Atheneum, 1979), 148. As Goodwin points out, the arrangements commissioned by Diaghilev were never published, so subsequent productions have necessitated the creation of new arrangements: "This subtly alters the look of the ballet according to treatment of the music, from the richly swooping Glazunov-Keller arrangements in the Soviet *Chopiniana* to the sharp instrumental clarity of Britten's reduced version in 1940 for Ballet Theatre and, somewhere in between, the partly brighter colouring of the Roy Douglas arrangement long used by the Royal Ballet companies and many others." Goodwin, "Sight and Sound," 17.

32. The title *Chopinina* is retained in some Russian productions of this ballet, as is the Polonaise overture.

33. George Balanchine and Francis Mason, *Balanchine's Complete Stories of the Great Ballets,* rev. and enlarged ed. (Garden City, NY: Doubleday, 1977), 653–58.

34. Valerien Svetlov, *Le ballet contemporain,* trans. Michel Calvocaressi (Paris: M. de Brunoff, 1912), 98–99; translated and quoted in Buckle, *Diaghilev,* 148. Svetlov was reporting on the dress rehearsal, for which the house was full.

FIGURE 11.2. Program of the premiere of *Les sylphides*. F-Po, Carton 2238.

PROGRAMME

————

Soirée du Samedi 19 Juin 1909

————

BORIS GODOUNOW
Opéra de Modeste Moussorgsky
2e Acte–3e Acte: 2e Tableau
Boris
M. Chaliapine

| *Le Tsarevitch Fédor* | *La Nourrrice* | *Xenia* |
| Mme Pétrenko | Mme Karénine | Mme Pavlova |

Chouisky   *Pimène*
M. Davidow   M. Zaporojetz

————

LES SYLPHIDES
Rêverie Romantique en un acte
Musique de Chopin
Groupes et danses de M. Fokine
Décor peint par M. Yarémitsch d'après la maquette de M. A. Benois
Costumes de M. A. Benois

Nocturne, op. 32   Instrumenté par M. *I Stravinsky*
    Mlles Anna Pavlova, Karsavina, Baldina, Alexandra Fédorova, Smirnova.
    M. Koslow.
    Mmes Barasch, Constantinova, Dobrolubova, Anna Fédorova, Fokina,
    Goloubéva, Léonova, Léontiéva, Loukachévitch, Nijinska, Olkhina, Sadonova,
    Scholar, Soboleva, Sprichinska, Tchernicheva, A. Vassilièva, Vlassova.

Valse, op. 70   Instrumentée par M. *A. Tanéïew*
    Mme Karsavina.

Mazurka, op. 33   Instrumentée par M. *N. Sokolow*
    Mlle Anna Pavlova.

Prélude, op. 28   Instrumenté par M. *A. Tanéïew*
    Mlle Baldina.

Valse, op. 64   Instrumenté par M. *A. Glazounow*
    Mlle Pavlova et M. Koslow.

Grande Valse Brillante, op. 18   Instrumenté par M. *I Stravinsky*

---

free," and so is the choreography, in which "the ballerina bounds diagonally across the stage" in great forward leaps.

Mazurka op. 67 no. 3. The *danseuses* form a decorative tableau around the stage, and then the danseur performs a solo.

Prelude op. 28 no. 7 (also used for the overture). The "sylphs form picturesque groups, the girls kneeling about central figures." A ballerina enters softly, pauses, and seems to listen to a distant call. She moves among the groups "adroitly and sweetly, but completely removed from them in her rapt attention to what she might hear."

Waltz op. 64 no. 2. Now the danseur carries the ballerina across the stage; she appears to be lighter than air. After she is released, the pas de deux begins. As the momentum of the music increases, the ballerina responds with "unhesitating swiftness and flight to the inspiration from the music and the night."

Waltz op. 18 no. 1. After a moment of silence and an empty stage, the dancers return to this buoyant waltz; they fill the stage with movement "like the swift fluttering of butterfly wings." The principal dancers appear and dance short solos. At the end, all are standing still in the same tableau with which the ballet begins.[35]

This choreographic manifesto, delivered sweetly to the strains of Chopin, broke convention after convention. It ensured that no solo ended in the same fashion as any other; it avoided specific hand gestures; it erased obvious distinctions between corps and solo dancers, integrating them choreographically and even calling for them to wear the same costumes. It removed all formal positions from the flowing port de bras, eliminated applause breaks, and made defiant use of *pointe* dancing, eschewing obvious displays of virtuosity even though the poses and flowing steps required great control and strength.[36] Moreover, aside from being the first abstract ballet of the twentieth century (according to Fokine), it was, as Balanchine and Mason asserted decades later, the first "ballet as a whole (with precedents from Ivanov and Gorsky) in which movement itself projected from important music was a prime factor rather than a propulsive accompaniment."[37]

Yet Fokine's concerns as a reformer were not communicated to the French audience in Martial Teneo's program-book essay.[38] Instead, the essay, like Diaghilev's new title,

---

35. Of Nijinsky's performance in *Les sylphides,* Cyril Beaumont said the dancer "was a very great artist, and every role that he created was quite different from the other ones. You see some dancers who have very considerable talents technically, perhaps even mimetically, but on the other hand you can see it's just the same dancer wearing a different costume. But with Nijinsky that wasn't the case at all. In *Schéhérazade* he was rather gross and seemed to broaden his body, and when you saw him in *Carnaval* as Harlequin, he was very slim and mercurial and something quite different. Again when you saw him in *Les Sylphides,* there he was a wonderful romantic person. He seemed to epitomize the romantic movement." John Drummond, *Speaking of Diaghilev* (London: Faber and Faber, 1997), 126.

36. See Buckle, *Diaghilev,* 149. See also Sondra Lomax, "Fokine's Manifesto and *Les sylphides,*" in *New Directions in Dance,* ed. D. T. Taplin (Toronto: Pergamon Press, 1979), 113–20, in which the author shows specifically how the ballet enacts Fokine's five principles of anti–Imperial Ballet reform.

37. George Balanchine and Francis Mason, *Balanchine's Complete Stories of the Great Ballets,* rev. and enlarged ed. (Garden City, NY: Doubleday, 1977), 656.

38. Teneo, *bibliothécaire* of the Opéra from 1912 till 1922, was a composer, librettist, and music critic. Nor did the ballet look particularly radical to the audience, though some critics remarked on its plotlessness and use of preexisting music. See, for example, the review by one Nozière, *Le théâtre: Revue bimensuelle illustrée* (1909): 12–15. Buckle points out that a critic in *L'intransigeant* (undated

emphasized *Les sylphides*' connectedness to France. It explained to the audience that Fokine's choreography was meant to represent Chopin's music in bodily form: "[He] has succeeded in his enterprise: presented on a romantic set, his reverie is charming and makes visible the hazy sense of amorousness that Chopin instilled in his works."[39] Teneo further stated that *Les sylphides* constituted a continuation of the great traditions of French ballet of the past, oddly positing a connection between Auguste Vestris and Nijinsky and invoking the long tenure of Marius Petipa in Russia (never mind that Fokine wished to erase some of the hallmark features of Petipa's choreography):

> [This work] evokes, through the talent of the dancers, the character of our late eighteenth-century *école de danse,* so admirably carried on for fifty-five years in Russia by the illustrious ballet master [Marius Petipa]. . . . Seeing Nijinsky, incomparable in his flexibility and lightness, brings to mind Vestris, "the god of the dance," as he was called by his father, so proud of the jumps and entrechats made stylish by his son.[40]

So what we find in *Les sylphides* is a work by a reform-minded choreographer that began as a demonstration of the breadth of ballet's possibilities, in its next phase focused on the poetic qualities of romantic ballet as Fokine perceived them, and in its final tweaking by Diaghilev and under a name reminiscent of *La sylphide* was presented to Parisians—with the help of Teneo's essay—in a fashion pointedly aimed at awakening pride in their ballet history and invoking family ties that connected the Ballets Russes to Paris.

Having taken a look at the two ballets separately, let us conclude by noticing how little of her original surroundings the sylph brought back with her back to Paris in 1909. In the first ballet she was the instigator of a conflict that helped reveal both an

---

press clipping) noted that the visiting company had had the "Russian impudence" to orchestrate Chopin. See Buckle, *Diaghilev,* 151.

39. "A réussi dans son entreprise: présentée dans un décor romantique, sa *rêverie* est charmante et rend sensible la vapeur amoureuse que Chopin répandit dans ses œuvres." Program book, 19 June 1909, *F-Po,* Carton 2238.

40. "[Cette œuvre] évoque, par le talent des danseurs, le caractère de notre école de danse a la fin du 18e siècle si admirablement continué en Russie, cinquante-cinq ans durant, par l'illustre maître de ballet Petitpas. . . . À voir M. Nijinsky dont la souplesse et la légèreté sont incomparables, on se prend à songer à Vestris fils, le '*diou* [*sic*] de la danse' comme l'appellait son père si orgueilleux des sauts et des entrechats mis à la mode par son descendant." Program book, 19 June 1909, *F-Po,* Carton 2238. Nijinska, however, wrote: "The advance publicity for the Saison Russe had hailed Nijinsky as a new Vestris, but once the public saw Nijinsky 'lifted to heaven, weightless, above a group of sylphs,' all comparison with Auguste Vestris vanished." *Early Memoirs,* 275, quotation uncited. Auguste Vestris (1760–1842) was a virtuoso *danseur* whose technique was considered almost miraculous.

unreal world and a real one. Such otherworldly or exotic figures—usually in the form of unattainable females, longed for by mortal, unexotic men of the sort the Opéra's male clientele could identify with—never kept the stage to themselves for an entire ballet. Their role was to interact and attract, to play against beings of another sort. Fokine's sylphs, on the other hand, occupied a world without witches or Scottish villagers or any other sorts of opposing groups. It was simply a group of sylphs in long white dresses and a sole male, forming beautiful pictures in a moonlit setting, whose story, if there was one, was known only to themselves. In other words, *La sylphide* had all the components of a typical story ballet of the 1830s: characters with well-defined personalities, an identifiable geographical setting, and obvious conflicts. *Les sylphides* had none of these things, but instead explored the pure and mysterious world of the "white" scene and, in its modern way, self-consciously occupied a world of ballet itself. Moreover, the music for the first sylph was conceived after the story had been written and was custom-made to help impart her story to the audience. Fokine's sylphs, on the other hand, as dancers in one of the first of the "new ballets" as defined by Fokine, were animated by music that had come into existence on its own, not for the sake of ballet. Because narrative itself was missing from *Les sylphides,* so was the sort of music that had in the 1830s been intended to explain it.

Thus ends the tale of the two sylph ballets. For the average theatergoer, of course, the benefits of untangling the differences between them may seem of little account. Just as no grave consequences ensue when the audience mistakes the operettas of Gilbert and Sullivan for the Donizetti operas that inspired them, so may we enjoy these two sylph ballets without grasping how or why Michel Fokine fashioned his ballet in the image of the earlier work. Yet in looking behind the deliberately wrought likenesses of *Les sylphides* to *La sylphide,* we find the features of two disparate theatrical cultures, both justly celebrated into the present day. Following the sylph as she took wing and flew from one century to the next allows us to enter more fully into her beautiful, complicated, and mysterious worlds.

APPENDIX
Plot Summary of *La sylphide* from *Le courrier des théâtres,* 13 March 1832

Note: In keeping with custom, the story of this ballet was summarized in newspaper reviews of the ballet's premiere.

Acte Ier. C'est dans une ferme de l'Écosse. James et Gurn, deux jeunes montagnards, sont endormis. Une Sylphide est aux genoux de James, caressant son sommeil et le couvrant de baisers. James se réveille. Il ne voit rien. Cependant ces apparitions mystérieuses se sont souvent renouvelées dans ses rêves. Il demande à Gurn s'il n'a vu personne. Gurn n'a rien aperçu. Alors entre dans la ferme Effie, la fiancée de James, appuyée sur le bras de sa mère, Anne Beuden [*sic*]. Gurn court au-devant d'elle, mais Effie ne songe qu'à James; elle le voit préoccupé. Je pensais à toi, lui répond James. Ils se mettent à genoux et reçoivent la bénédiction de leur mère. Gurn s'éloigne au désespoir. Les compagnes d'Effie viennent lui offrir les présens de noces et rient du chagrin de Gurn. James toujours occupée de la Sylphide la cherche partout des yeux; il aperçoit derrière les groupes de jeunes filles une figure hideuse, c'est la vieille sorcière Madge. Elle examine la main d'Effie et lui prédit qu'elle n'est point aimée de James autant qu'elle l'aime. La mère Anne emmène ensuite sa fille pour le preparer à la cérémonie des fiançailles. James resté seul pense encore à son apparition mystérieuse. À ce moment un coup de vent ouvre la fenêtre; la Sylphide paraît blottie dans un coin. Elle apprend à James l'amour qu'elle a pour lui; elle n'a plus qu'à mourir s'il la repousse. Le fiancé d'Effie détourne les yeux; puis la voyant à ses pieds enveloppée dans le manteau de son amante, l'esprit l'abandonne, il la relève, la presse sur son Cœur et lui donne un baiser. Gurn qui l'épiait a été chercher Effie pour lui prouver l'infidélité de James. À l'instant où ils entrent, James fait cacher la Sylphide dans un fauteuil et la recouvre de son plaid. Gurn a tout vu; il va le relever, mais la Sylphide a disparu; le montagnard demeure confondu. On célèbre les fiançailles de James et d'Effie, les danses commencent, James oublie d'inviter son amante; puis viens l'heure de la cérémonie. James alors ôte de son doigt l'anneau qu'il va échanger avec sa cousine. La Sylphide, sortie de l'âtre, lui arrache l'anneau. La raison de James se trouble, il craint de perdre sa Sylphide, et s'échappe avec elle derrière la foule pressée autour d'Effie. Surprise générale lorsqu'on vient à l'appeler; désespoir d'Effie, qui voit s'accomplir a prédiction de la sorcière.

Acte II: Le théâtre représente un forêt. À gauche est l'entrée d'une caverne. La vieille sorcière Madge célèbre un sabbat avec toutes ses compagnes, et chacune se retire en emportant un talisman; Madge s'est réservé une écharpe. Alors, paraît au-dessus des rochers la Sylphide guidant les pas de James. Elle s'arrête au milieu de la forêt, dont les brouillards dissipés laissent voir la profondeur. En vain James veut l'entourer de caresses, elle lui échappe toujours. Puis du sein du feuillage sortent une foule de sylphides au ailes bleues et roses. James est enivrée de ce délicieux spectacle; mais insensiblement les Sylphides s'éloignent, et, une à une, se perdent dans les églantiers. James alors songe à ses fautes passées; il voudrait trouver un moyen de retenir pour jamais auprès de lui la Sylphide qui l'a rendu infidèle. Madge sort de la caverne et lui donne son écharpe, à l'aide de laquelle les ailes de la Sylphide tomberont d'elles-mêmes. En revenant sur ses pas James aperçoit la Sylphide jouant avec un nid d'oiseau. Elle court à lui pour lui ravir l'écharpe. James profite d'un instant pour l'envelopper dans le tissu magique, qu'il ne desserre que lorsque les ailes sont tombées. La Sylphide pâlit, les forces l'abandonnent, elle meurt. Madge vient jouir de son triomphe. Les Sylphes et les Sylphides descendent et enlèvent leur malheureuse compagne, ce qui forme un tableau ravissant. James accablé jette un dernier regard sur la Sylphide, voit à travers les arbres de la foret la noce qui défile au son des cloches, pour célébrer le mariage de Gurn et d'Effie, et enfin, épuisé par tant de coups, tombe sans connaissance.

Act 1: A farm in Scotland. James and Gurn, two young highlanders, are sleeping. A Sylphide is at James's knee, gazing admiringly at him and covering him with kisses. James wakes up. Now he sees nothing, but this mysterious apparition has been haunting his dreams. He asks Gurn if he saw anyone. Gurn saw nothing. Then Effie the farm girl, James's fiancée, enters on the arm of his mother, Anne Reuben. Gurn hastens to her side, but Effie can think only of James; she sees that he is preoccupied. "I was only thinking of you," says James. They kneel and receive the blessing of their [sic] mother. Gurn, in despair, draws away.

Effie's friends arrive, offering wedding gifts and scoffing at Gurn's sorrow. James is preoccupied by thoughts of the Sylphide and looks around for her everywhere. Behind the groups of girls he finds a hideous figure: it is old Madge, the witch. Madge tells Effie's fortune, examining her hand and telling her that James does not love her as much as Effie would wish. Mother Anna then leads Effie away to prepare for the betrothal ceremony. James is now alone again, still thinking of his mysterious dream.

At this point a strong gust of wind opens the window, and the Sylphide appears, huddled in a corner. She tells James of her love for him; she will die if he rejects her love. Effie's fiancé turns his eyes away; then he sees her at his feet wrapped up in the cloak of his beloved; his wits abandon him; he lifts her up, presses her to his heart, and gives her a kiss. Gurn, who has been spying, goes to find Effie so he can show her this proof of James's infidelity.

Just as they arrive, James hides the Sylphide in an armchair and covers her up with a plaid. Gurn saw everything, but when he pulls the plaid away, the Sylphide has disappeared. The highlander is confounded. Everyone celebrates the engagement of James and of Effie; the dances begin. James forgets to invite his fiancée to dance.

Then comes the hour for the ceremony. James removes his ring, which he is going to exchange with his cousin [Effie]. The Sylphide, emerging from the hearth, snatches it away from him. James's mind is disturbed; he fears losing his Sylphide and escapes with her behind the throng that surrounds Effie. General surprise when they realize he is gone. Despair of Effie, who sees that the witch's prediction has come true.

Act 2: A forest. On the left is the mouth of a cave. The old witch Madge and her companions celebrate a sabbath; each one departs, carrying a talisman. Madge reserves a scarf for herself. Then, above the rocks, the Sylphide appears, guiding James's steps. She stops in the middle of the forest, the depth of which is just becoming apparent as the fog dissipates. In vain James seeks to embrace the Sylphide, but she keeps eluding him. Then, from the foliage there appears a bevy of sylphides with pink and blue wings. James is intoxicated by this delicious spectacle.

But, imperceptibly, the sylphides move away and, one by one, disappear amongst the wild roses. James then contemplates his past faults. He would like to find a way to keep the Sylphide forever by his side, this Sylphide who rendered him a faithless lover.

Now Madge emerges from the mouth of the cave and gives him the scarf, which will cause the wings of the Sylphide to fall off. James then retraces his footsteps and finds the Sylphide playing with a bird's nest. She runs up to him, hoping to have the scarf for herself. James benefits from this moment, wrapping her up in the magic fabric, which he loosens only when the wings fall. The Sylphide fades; her life force grows dim; she dies. Madge arrives so she can exult in her triumph. The sylphs and sylphides descend from above, hovering in the air, and carry away their luckless companion. This forms a charming tableau. Overwhelmed, James takes one last look at the Sylphide and sees, through the trees, a nuptial party filing by as wedding bells ring: they are celebrating the marriage of Gurn and Effie. Finally, exhausted by so many blows, he falls unconscious.

Questions of Genre

MASSENET'S *LES ÉRINNYES* AT THE THÉÂTRE-NATIONAL-LYRIQUE

Peter Lamothe

In September 1875 Albert Vizentini applied to the Ministry of Public Instruction for authorization to open a new opera house in Paris. He had taken over the directorship of the Théâtre de la Gaîté from a defeated Jacques Offenbach two months earlier with the intention of performing larger-scale works than the vaudevilles, *opérettes*, and spoken dramas that at the time made up its repertoire. The stagnation of the Paris Opéra repertoire and the recent failure of the Théâtre-Lyrique (Salle du Châtelet) suggested an opportune time for his venture, and financial problems at the Gaîté necessitated its reorganization in order to regain profitability.[1]

The opening of an independent opera house in Paris to serve as an alternative to the Opéra or the Opéra-Comique was not unusual. The Gymnase-Dramatique had served such a role (1820–24), as had the Théâtre de l'Odéon (1824–28), the Théâtre des Nouveautés (1827–31), the Théâtre de la Renaissance (1838–41), the Opéra-National (1847–48 and 1851), and the Théâtre-Lyrique (1852–72, situated in the Châtelet since 1862).[2] Later the Eden Théâtre (1883–94) would follow in this trend. To the infrequent

1. Jane Fulcher has demonstrated that under the Second Empire, the Paris Opéra served to "incarnate the nation's patrimony, the treasures of its cultural past"; see Fulcher, *The Nation's Image: French Grand Opera as Politics and Politicized Art* (Cambridge: Cambridge University Press, 1987), 166. With such a goal, the Opéra often had entire years without a premiere, including 1872, 1874, and 1875.

2. A summary of the various attempts at establishing secondary lyric theaters may be found in Nicole Wild, "Musique et théâtres parisiens face au pouvoir (1807–1864) avec inventaire et histo-

(but not unprecedented) combination of a double troupe performing both opera and *opéra comique,* Vizentini added a Thursday concert series of excerpts from symphonies, operas, and oratorios.[3] The combination of genres at the Théâtre-National-Lyrique seems to have been calculated to ensure the fledgling institution's fiscal stability with a diversity of programming, in order to help it to compete with the entrenched state-run theaters. Seen in light of the more rigid approach to repertoire at the Opéra and Opéra-Comique (instigated by tradition as well as by legislation and their *cahiers des charges*), the broader aims of the Théâtre-National-Lyrique allowed it to serve as a sort of laboratory for the exploration of institutional identity and for the meaning of genre. The theater's freedom to examine these issues was most strongly exemplified in the 1876 production of Leconte de Lisle's play *Les Érinnyes,* with a newly expanded score by Jules Massenet, for this substantial musical contribution contained not a single line of aria or recitative. Leconte de Lisle's *tragédie antique* had first been performed on 6 January 1873 at the Théâtre de l'Odéon, where it had played to moderate success, reaching twenty-five performances that season (see fig. 12.1). The reasons such a nonoperatic work was given as the second major premiere on the new stage of the Théâtre-National-Lyrique illustrate both the pressures of opening a new opera theater in nineteenth-century Paris and the evolution of the genre of the *drame lyrique* in France.

The theater owed its existence to the tireless efforts of Albert Vizentini, Offenbach's former conductor at the Gaîté and a friend of Massenet since childhood.[4] Having been made director of the Gaîté in June, Vizentini applied for authorization to

---

rique des salles," 3 vols. (Ph.D. diss., Université de Paris IV, 1987). The Théâtre Lyrique is discussed in T. J. Walsh, *Second Empire Opera: The Théâtre Lyrique, Paris, 1851–1870* (London: John Calder; New York: Riverrun Press, 1981). For further information on the Théâtre-Lyrique, see Katharine Ellis's contribution to this volume. The production of opera at the Théâtre de l'Odéon is discussed in Mark Everist, *Music Drama at the Paris Odéon, 1824–1828* (Berkeley and Los Angeles: University of California Press, 2002); Everist discusses a similar crossover by a spoken theater into the lyric repertoire in "Theatres of Litigation: Stage Music at the Théâtre de la Renaissance, 1838–1840," *Cambridge Opera Journal* 16 (2004): 133–61. The dates of these theaters and the details of their repertoires can be found in Nicole Wild, *Dictionnaire des théâtres parisiens au XIXe siècle: Les théâtres et la musique* (Paris: Aux Amateurs de livres, 1989).

3. The Théâtre-National-Lyrique, alternatively known as the Opéra-National-Lyrique and the Théâtre-Lyrique-National, is also the subject of David Grayson's contribution to this volume. The Odéon (1824–28) and the Théâtre de la Renaissance (1838–40) had each held double troupes for opera and spoken drama, and the earlier Théâtre-Lyrique (1848–1870) had a double troupe for opera and *opéra comique.*

4. Massenet recalled Vizentini as a dear friend from childhood in *My Recollections,* trans. H. Villiers Barnett (Freeport, NY: Books for Libraries Press, 1970), 120 (translation of *Mes Souvenirs* [Paris: L. Lafitte, 1912]). For information on Albert Vizentini, see François-Joseph Fétis, *Biographie universelle des musiciens et bibliographie générale de la musique: Supplément et complément [à la 2. éd.],* ed. Arthur Pougin (Paris: Firmin-Didot, 1878–80), 1134–35. Because Vizentini was a longtime affiliate of Offenbach, he appears frequently in Jean-Claude Yon's very thorough biography *Jacques Offenbach* (Paris: Éditions Gallimard, 2000).

FIGURE 12.1. Marie Laurent as Klytemnestra in the 1873 production of *Les Érinnyes* at the Théâtre de l'Odéon. *Le monde
illustré*, 1 February 1873. Courtesy of Library of Congress.

form a new opera house in September 1875. The minister of public instruction named
him director of the Théâtre-Lyrique (Salle de la Gaîté) for a four-year period beginning 20 November 1875, though he continued to operate the hall with the repertoire
and personnel of the Gaîté until spring of 1876 in order to buy time to organize
the new opera house. Over the next seventeen months, the theater would produce
twenty-five premieres and twenty-eight revivals of operas and *opéras comiques,* including the premieres of Saint-Saëns's *Le timbre d'argent,* Victor Massé's *Paul et Virginie,*
Jules Philippot's *Le magnifique,* Eugène Gautier's *La clé d'or,* Gaston Salvayre's *Bravo,*
and Jean-Baptiste Wekerlin's *Après Fontenoy.*

The work Vizentini selected for the grand opening of the theater on 5 May 1876
was Victorin Joncières's newly composed *grand opéra, Dimitri,* the plot of which is

best known to us today through Mussorgsky's *Boris Godunov*. The new work hit its mark, enjoying a stunning critical and financial success that gave hope to Vizentini's ambitious venture. But the theater needed more than one work to maintain its income. Thus *Dimitri* alternated with Molière's *Le bourgeois gentilhomme* and *Monsieur de Pourceaugnac*, spoken dramas performed with Lully's divertissements. These were already in the repertoire of the Gaîté before the opening of the Théâtre-National-Lyrique.[5] Unfortunately, the financial success of *Dimitri* was not repeated by the Molière plays, and Vizentini rushed to bring a second major work to the public.

That work was *Les Érinnyes*, a work that thwarted the genre expectations created by Joncières's five-act opera. Massenet's score was originally written as incidental music (*musique de scène*) for a *drame antique* in two parts by Charles-Marie Leconte de Lisle (1818–1894), founder of the Parnassian movement in poetry and mentor to such prominent writers as Stéphane Mallarmé, Comte de Villiers de L'Isle-Adam, and Catulle Mendès.[6] The drama was an adaptation of the first two tragedies of Aeschylus's trilogy *The Oresteia* and represented Leconte de Lisle's first foray onto the stage. Premiered at the Théâtre de l'Odéon on 6 January 1873, the music garnered much critical acclaim and quickly made it to the concert hall, in spite of the critics' reservations about the play. Massenet's 1876 version expanded the original score, nearly tripling it by adding choruses and a three-part ballet divertissement, as well as *mélodrames*. Thus, a major spoken drama without recitatives or arias was given at a theater that had been recently renamed the *Opéra*-National-*Lyrique*. The only points of resemblance in this score to opera or *opéra comique* were the choruses, ballet, and melodrama that complemented its orchestral interludes. (See table 12.1 for a list of the number and nature of movements in the 1876 score.)

Given the tapering off of spoken dramas from the Gaîté's repertoire after *Dimitri*, we might wonder why such a *musique de scène* as *Les Érinnyes* was premiered at all. A part of the answer can be found in the column "Nouvelles des théâtres lyriques" in the 30 April 1876 edition of *La revue et gazette musicale de Paris*: "As we have said, *Les Érinnyes* will be performed the day after *Dimitri*, but for a short time, because this work (which is not an opera) will not become part of the repertoire of the Théâtre-Lyrique, and M. Vizentini is only playing it to honor an engagement already

---

5. "Le 23 janvier le théâtre de la Gaîté donnait la première représentation du *Bourgeois gentil-homme* de Molière, accompagné des divertissements et de la musique de Lulli, c'est-à-dire tel qu'il avait été joué devant Louis XIV, et que le 2 avril il offrait à son public *Monsieur de Pourceaugnac*, accompagné aussi des divertissements et de la musique de Lulli." Édouard Noël and Edmond Stoullig, eds., *Les annales du théâtre et de la musique* 2 (Paris, 1877): 340. For context on these performances of Lully's incidental works, see Katharine Ellis, *Interpreting the Musical Past: Early Music in Nineteenth-Century France* (Oxford: Oxford University Press, 2005), 137–40.

6. Regarding Leconte de Lisle, see Robert T. Denommé, *Leconte de Lisle* (New York: Twayne, 1973), and Irving Putter, *Leconte de Lisle and His Contemporaries* (Berkeley: University of California Press, 1951). Regarding the Parnassians, see Renée de Thiès, *Des poètes parnassiens: Entretiens* (Paris: J. Grassin, 1995).

TABLE 12.1. The movements in the 1876 score of Massenet, *Les Érinnyes*

N° 1. Prélude

Acte I: Klytaimnestra
   N° 2. Mélodrame [entry of Érinnyes]
   N° 3. Chœur
   N° 4. A. Chœur du retour
      B. Divertissement
         I. Danse grecque
         II. La Troyenne regrettant la patrie perdue
         III. Final
      C. Reprise du chœur [entry of Agamemnôn]
   N° 5. A. Mélodrame
      B. Mélodrame
      C. Mélodrame [with chorus of Vieillards]
Acte II: Orestès
   N° 6. Entr'acte
   N° 7. Scène religieuse et chœur
   N° 8. Invocation d'Elektra: Mélodrame
   N° 8 bis. Mélodrame
   N° 9. Mélodrame et chœur
   N° 10. Les apparitions: Mélodrame

This table is based on a comparison of the 1873 orchestral score, *F-Pn* MS 4274, with the piano-vocal score (Paris: G. Hartmann, 1876). Movements in bold were significantly revised or added for the 1876 version.

undertaken by the Théâtre de la Gaîté for three performances only."[7] Yet Vizentini had directed the Gaîté's productions since October, and he could certainly have found room for three performances before the opening of the opera house. While we may never know his precise motives, delaying the premiere of *Les Érinnyes* until the opening of the Théâtre-National-Lyrique was advantageous for several reasons. One was the opportunity to use the subvention of 300,000 francs accorded by the Ministère des Beaux-Arts to the Théâtre-National-Lyrique to offset any losses from the creation of the new staging. Any losses from staging such a large work would likely have strained the Gaîté's smaller budget too far, for that theater already had considerable

---

7. "*Les Érinnyes* feront, comme nous l'avons dit, les lendemains de *Dimitri,* mais pendant peu de temps, car cet ouvrage, qui n'est point un opéra, ne fait pas partie du répertoire du Théâtre-Lyrique, et M. Vizentini ne le joue que pour faire honneur à un engagement pris jadis, pour trois représentations seulement, par le théâtre de la Gaîté." "Nouvelles des théâtres lyriques," *La revue et gazette musicale de Paris,* 30 April 1876.

debts—which were inherited by the Théâtre-National-Lyrique. A second advantage lay in the work's sensational nature. Although the play was known for appealing primarily to those initiated into the poetic values of the Parnassians (the group from which the "art for art's sake" movement in France developed), the graphic depiction of violence might have added a voyeuristic element to its appeal as well.[8] By the end of the drama, Agamemnôn and Klytaimnestra have died on the stage (contrary to the long-standing tradition in European drama of deaths occurring offstage). After killing his mother, Orestès rages during a ten-minute monologue while her body, its eyes open and its wounds bloody, remains exposed onstage. He then meets his doom at the hands of the Furies themselves. It so overwhelmed the audiences that the weekly *L'éclipse* published its 19 January 1873 edition with a cover illustration cleverly depicting the carnage. At the center of the illustration stands a Grecian vase, surrounded by the characters' names written in the Greek alphabet. The vase teeters precariously as the figures painted upon it, having come to life, eviscerate each other mercilessly. Vibrant red, yellow, and blue ink overprinted on the black-and-white page intensifies the violence of the image.

And although the reputation of the playwright might not appeal to the broadest audience, the composer's growing status and the score's reputation would. The music was by this time critically acclaimed and well-known through both the Concerts Populaires and concerts at the Théâtre du Châtelet.[9] The expansion of Massenet's popular score into a major event broadened its already significant appeal, and any alterations of an existing work would be far less expensive than a commission for a complete original opera. Finally, the performance of *Les Érinnyes* required actors from the spoken theater, and because Vizentini's new company consisted solely of opera singers, he was compelled to borrow the two lead performers from the Porte-Saint-Martin and the remainder of the cast from the Odéon.[10] In doing so, he gave his already taxed troupe the luxury of additional time to learn new roles for the upcoming works (Jules Philippot's one-act *opéra comique Le magnifique;* Adolphe Adam's three-act *opéra comique Le sourd ou L'auberge pleine;* and Carl Maria von Weber's *Obéron,* adapted as a three-act *opéra fantastique*) under less pressure. And the pressure was

8. Regarding the Parnassians and the development of the "art for art's sake" credo, see Robert T. Denommé, *The French Parnassian Poets* (Carbondale: Southern Illinois University Press, 1972).

9. A concert version had appeared, without Massenet's prior knowledge, in the program of the Concerts Pasdeloup on 17 February 1873. See François Oswald, "Bruits de coulisses," *Le gaulois,* 18 February 1873; and Demar Irvine, *Jules Massenet: A Chronicle of His Life and Times* (Portland, OR: Amadeus Press, 1994), 68.

10. "*Les Érinnyes* will be played three times, after which Mme Marie Laurent and M. Taillade will return to the Porte-Saint-Martin to create *L'espion du roi* there" (*Les Érinnyes* se jouent trois fois, après quoi Mme Marie Laurent et M. Taillade retournent à la Porte-Saint-Martin pour y créer *l'Espion du roi*). Noël and Stoullig, *Annales* 3 (1878): 298. The two artists cited had created the roles of Klytaimnestra and Orestès, respectively, at the Odéon in 1873.

Depuis la pièce des *Erinnyes* les restaurants de l'Odéon ne donnent plus que des racines grecques.

FIGURE 12.2. *Depuis la pièce les Érinnyes . . . : dessin humoristique. L'éclipse,* January 1873. Département des Arts du spectacle. Bibliothèque nationale de France.

considerable for the fledgling institution, given Vizentini's promise to the minister of public instruction in his letter of 6 November 1875: "My program is summed up in these words: produce, produce, and always produce."[11] Indeed, Émile Blavet noted in his review of *Dimitri* that the troupe simultaneously rehearsed *Dimitri* on the stage, *Le magnifique* in the foyer, and *Obéron* in Vizentini's office![12]

Although *Les Érinnyes* lacked arias and recitatives, it did combine an extensive orchestral prelude and entr'acte with a substantial ballet (justified as part of Agamemnôn's court entertainment), a significant role for a chorus, and *mélodrame*. Table 12.1

11. "Mon programme se résume en ces mots: produire, produire et toujours produire." Albert Vizentini, letter to Henri Wallon (the minister of public instruction), 6 November 1875. See Wild, *Dictionnaire,* 342.

12. "Une fois sa troupe à peu près formée, Vizentini, . . . faire répéter en même temps *Dimitri* sur la scène, le *Magnifique* au foyer et *Obéron* dans son cabinet." Un Monsieur de l'orchestre [Arnold Mortier], "La soirée théâtrale: *Dimitri,*" *Le Figaro,* 6 May 1876.

shows just how substantial were the additions Massenet made for this "second pre-miere" of the work, most notably in the addition of the ballet and chorus, but also in the expansion of melodrama. Although the manner in which *Les Érinnyes* straddled genre boundaries provided practical advantages for Vizentini, it led to some confusion in its critical reception, starting with the genre labels applied to the work. The irony of a premiere at this newest Parisian opera house that was completely devoid of solo singing and ensembles was not lost on critics, who discussed the genre of the work at length. Many called it by Leconte de Lisle and Massenet's term, a *drame antique*, which gave no indication as to the increased importance of the music for a play whose initial score was already substantial.[13] Conversely, Édouard Noël and Edmond Stoul-lig, in their summary list of the works premiered on that stage in 1876, called the work a two-act opera. Albert de Lasalle referred to it as a "hybrid work," while Oscar Comettant and G. Stradina used the descriptor *tragédie lyrique*.[14] And several critics called it a *drame lyrique,* the term most often used to describe it in the *Courriers des théâtres* columns.[15]

The genre of *drame lyrique* had its origins as a more serious sibling of the *opéra comique* of the late eighteenth and early nineteenth centuries, in which drama with a moralizing tone about modern life and ordinary people might be encapsulated in an entertaining setting (Méhul's *Mélidore et Phrosine,* for example). But by the 1880s *drame lyrique* would have strong associations with Wagnerism in France. Indeed, Arthur Pougin noted polemically in an article about the genre in his *Dictionnaire historique et pittoresque du théâtre* (1885) that

> *drame lyrique* is the term frequently given to a serious opera, in which the dra-matic, moving, and impassioned sentiments are carried to their highest power. Twenty or twenty-five years ago, one still considered *Les huguenots, Guillaume Tell, La juive,* [and] *Le prophète* as beautiful *drames lyriques;* since then, a new musical school, the excessive school of the Wagnerians, has changed all this; the masterpieces which we cited are considered no more than simple operas by the new iconoclasts, and it is not necessary to say with what contempt this word is used by

13. See Auguste Vitu, "Premières représentations," *Le Figaro,* 17 May 1876. Adolphe Jullien, "Opéra-National-Lyrique: Les Érinnyes," *La revue et gazette musicale de Paris,* 21 May 1876, calls the work a *drame antique* in the rubric of the review yet describes the work as a *drame lyrique* in the text. Noël and Stoullig initially refer to the work as a *drame antique* (*Annales* 2 [1877]: 296), but change their genre designation for the summary list on p. 341.

14. Albert de Lasalle, "Chronique musicale," *Le monde illustré,* 20 May 1876. G. Stradina, *L'art musical,* 18 May 1876, calls it a *tragédie* in the rubric of the review, yet a *tragédie lyrique* in the text. See also Oscar Comettant, "Revue musicale," *Le siècle,* 22 May 1876.

15. See Un Monsieur de l'orchestre [Arnold Mortier], "La soirée théâtrale," *Le Figaro,* 15 May 1876; Adolphe Jullien, "Opéra-National-Lyrique: Les Érinnyes," *La revue et gazette musicale de Paris,* 21 May 1876; Adrien Laroque, "Revue des théâtres," *Le petit journal,* 13 May 1876; Charles Darcours, "Courrier des théâtres," *Le Figaro,* 13 May 1876; "Les théâtres," *Le siècle,* 14 May 1876; and Victor Wilder, "*Dimitri,*" *Le ménestrel,* 14 May 1876.

them; the apparently much more noble label of *drame lyrique* is reserved exclusively for the works of Richard Wagner, for which it had been impossible to go without a special designation.[16]

Yet neither of these understandings of the genre applies here, raising the question: in what sense was *Les Érinnyes* a *drame lyrique*?

Although the majority of the nineteenth-century French music and theater dictionaries define the *drame lyrique* in terms of its original or Wagnerian varieties, the Larousse *Grand dictionnaire universel du XIXe siècle* (1870) defines the genre as "an opera, a work entirely set to music, or dramatic work mixed with singing," which fits *Les Érinnyes* remarkably well.[17] Indeed, this catchall definition would seem to fit nearly anything in which drama and music are mixed, including all forms of opera and the vast majority of incidental music. But the vague broadness of this definition seems to have been connected to trends in music criticism, as the critical response to *Les Érinnyes* demonstrates. And in light of the vagueness of this usage, reviewers contextualized it for their readers. In his "Courrier des théâtres" column in *Le Figaro*, Charles Darcours prepared his readers for the shape of the work by comparing it to a *drame lyrique*, "or better, a *melo*-drama in the true and olden conception of the word, a scenic genre rarely used by us, but well-known in Germany, where Mendelssohn has particularly popularized it."[18] Similarly, Albert de Lasalle noted the German affinity for such techniques in his review of *Les Érinnyes* in *Le monde illustré*, stating that it was

> one of the hybrid works that please the Germans so much, in general, and some French in particular. There were no sung pieces properly speaking among these

---

16. "Drame lyrique est la qualification qu'on donne souvent à un opéra sérieux, dans lequel le sentiment dramatique, pathétique, passionné, est poussé à sa plus grande puissance. Il y a vingt ou vingt-cinq ans, on considérait encore *Les huguenots, Guillaume Tell, La juive, Le prophète,* comme de beaux drames lyriques; depuis lors, une nouvelle école musicale, l'école des wagnériens à outrance, a changé tout cela; les chefs-d'œuvre que nous venons de citer ne sont plus considérés par les nouveaux iconoclastes que comme de simples opéras, et il n'est pas besoin de dire avec quel mépris ce mot est employé par eux; la qualification, beaucoup plus noble, paraît-il, de drame lyrique est exclusivement réservée aux œuvres de Richard Wagner, pour lesquelles il eût été impossible de se passer d'une désignation spéciale." Pougin, "Drame lyrique," in *Dictionnaire historique et pittoresque du théâtre* (Paris: Firmin-Didot, 1885), 309.

17. "Opéra, pièce toute en musique, ou pièce dramatique mêlée de chant." "Drame lyrique," in *Grand dictionnaire universel du XIXe siècle,* ed. Pierre Larousse, vol. 6 (Paris: Administration du Grand dictionnaire universel, 1870), 1188.

18. "*Les Érinnyes* ont été transformées en drame lyrique, ou mieux, en *mélo*-drame dans la véritable et ancienne acception du mot, genre scénique peu usité chez nous, mais très connu en Allemagne, où Mendelssohn l'a particulièrement popularisé." Darcours, "Courrier des théâtres," *Le Figaro,* 13 May 1876. Mendelssohn's music for *A Midsummer Night's Dream* had been heard in Paris since 1844, when it was premiered on the stage of the Odéon.

melodramas, and the roles are left to spoken actors, but there were an introduction, entr'actes, choruses, ballet airs and other *intermèdes*. There exist, in this form, considerable works: *Egmont* and *The Ruins of Athens,* by Beethoven; *A Midsummer Night's Dream,* by Mendelssohn; *Struensée,* by Meyerbeer; and (it has been too much forgotten) *The Siege of Missolonghi* [*sic*], by Hérold.[19]

In the same way, while discussing the score of *Les Érinnyes* for *Le Figaro,* Bénédict cited Beethoven's *The Ruins of Athens,* Weber's music for Schiller's play *Jeanne d'Arc,* and Meyerbeer's music for the play *Struensée,* authored by his brother Michael Beer.[20] And Adolphe Jullien situated Massenet's score as a *drame lyrique* amidst Mozart's music for *Thamos, King of Egypt,* Beethoven's *Egmont,* Meyerbeer's *Struensée,* Schumann's *Manfred,* and Gounod's 1873 score for Jules Barbier's play *Jeanne d'Arc.*[21] In reminding their readers of such expansive incidental scores, critics were able to shift their readers' horizon of expectations from opera and *opéra comique* to line up with the type of *drame lyrique* that *Les Érinnyes* represented. And in doing so they created a niche for the incidental form of the *drame lyrique* that was based on both domestic and foreign scores well-known to the Parisian public, thus providing a strong sense of historical precedent for works appearing from 1876 onward.

These discussions of genre were especially relevant in light of the general malaise that affected French opera in the 1870s. The deaths of Berlioz, Meyerbeer, Bizet, Halévy, and Scribe had thinned the ranks of successful composers and librettists in Paris. Thomas and Gounod were aging, and their successors had not come into view.

19. "Une de ces œuvres hybrides qui plaisent tant aux Allemands, en général, et en particulier à quelques Français. Point de morceaux de chant proprement dits dans ces mélodrames où les rôles sont laissés aux acteurs déclamants, mais une introduction, des entr'actes, des chœurs, des airs de ballet et autres intermèdes. Il existe, sous cette forme, des œuvres considerables: *Egmont* et *les Ruines d'Athènes,* de Beethoven; *le Songe d'une nuit d'été,* de Mendelsshon [*sic*]; *Struensée,* de Meyerbeer; et (on l'a trop oublié) *le Siège de Missolonghi* [*sic*], d'Hérold." Albert de Lasalle, "Chronique musicale," *Le monde illustré,* 20 May 1876.

20. Bénédict [B. Jouvin], "La partition 'des Érinnyes,'" *Le Figaro,* 17 May 1876.

21. "On the other hand, one could study this genre of musical composition, which is conventionally called the *drame lyrique,* and review the masterpieces already written in this genre by the greatest masters from *Le roi Thamos* and *Egmont* to *Struensée* and *Manfred.* One could also examine the essential elements of this genre and its more or less absolute value as artistic creation, its wide currency with the public; but I dealt with all these questions when *La gazette musicale* asked me to review one of the first attempts at the *drame lyrique,* Gounod's *Jeanne d'Arc*" (On pouvait, d'autre part, étudier ce genre particulier de composition musicale, auquel on est convenu de donner le nom de *drame lyrique,* passer en revue les chefs-d'œuvre déjà écrits dans ce genre par les plus grands maîtres, depuis *Le roi Thamos* et *Egmont* jusqu'à *Struensée* et *Manfred,* sans oublier d'examiner les conditions essentielles de ce genre et son plus ou moins de valeur absolue comme création d'art, son crédit plus ou moins grand auprès du public;—mais j'ai traité moi-même toutes ces questions lorsque la *Gazette musicale* me chargea de juger un des derniers essais de drame lyrique, la *Jeanne d'Arc* de M. Gounod). Adolphe Jullien, "Opéra-National-Lyrique: *Les Érinnyes,*" *La revue et gazette musicale de Paris,* 21 May 1876.

Ernest Reyer had never attained their status, and the generation of Massenet, Saint-Saëns, and Delibes had yet to rise to prominence. As Wagner's influence grew, so did fears of musical influence of contemporary German composers and of German cultural incursion, particularly after the Franco-Prussian War. The lack of an outstanding composer to serve as a figurehead for the future of French opera was combined with the ossification of the genre of *grand opéra* and the corresponding sluggishness of repertoire at the Paris Opéra.[22] The critical rethinking of the *drame lyrique* fit into this scenario as a potential alternative for the future of the French stage, paralleling the developments in *opéra comique* and in the operas seen at the earlier Théâtre-Lyrique under the direction of Carvalho.[23]

Seen in this context, the lineage constructed by the critics for the *drame lyrique* is significant both for what it includes and for what it excludes. All the scores in question combine instrumental preludes and interludes with sections of *mélodrame,* choral singing, and/or aria-like solo or duet passages. Although German composers figured in the list of precedents, they were considered "safe" in comparison to Wagner: all were long dead and had been part of the classical canon in France for decades.[24] Moreover, the presence of the New German School composers Mendelssohn and Schumann could be viewed by some as an alternative (non-Wagnerian) German tradition with which to interact in order to revitalize the tradition of French stage music.[25] In addition to the German composers, the lineage cited above also included scores by the prominent and successful Parisian opera composers Meyerbeer and Gounod, each of whom had contributed to the repertoire of the Opéra.

Alternatively, the genre could be read as one in which French composers of

22. Although the Paris Opéra continued to produce new works such as Verdi's *Don Carlos* (1867) and Thomas's *Hamlet* (1868), its administration often failed to produce a new work each year, taking full advantage of the fact that the count was made every two years. During the nineteen months of the Théâtre-National-Lyrique, no fewer than twenty-five premieres of operas and *opéras comiques* took place in Vizentini's theater, compared to only two at the Opéra: Mermet's *Jeanne d'Arc* (1876) and Massenet's *Le roi de Lahore* (1877). It would seem that the low rate of production at the Paris Opéra prevented many younger and lesser-known composers' works from reaching the public.

23. From 1850 the Opéra-Comique saw a new trend toward works that were more serious in tone, including Thomas's *Mignon* (1866) and Bizet's *Carmen* (1875). In a similar vein, the Théâtre-Lyrique saw the premieres of such progressive works as Gounod's *Faust* (1859) and *Roméo et Juliette* (1867) and Bizet's *Les pêcheurs de perles* (1863).

24. The most recently deceased, Schumann, had been dead for twenty years.

25. Regarding the influence of various German and Austrian composers, including Mendelssohn, on the members of the Société Nationale, see Michael Strasser, "The Société Nationale and Its Adversaries: The Musical Politics of *l'invasion germanique* in the 1870s," *Nineteenth-Century Music* 24 (2001): 225–51, especially 238. Strasser also draws attention to the positive reviews given to French performances of music by these German and Austrian composers by the critic Oscar Commetant, an outspoken detractor of Wagner's music (249). For more on Mendelssohn reception in France, see Jean de Solliers, "Zur Mendelssohn-Rezeption in Frankreich," *Beiträge zur Musikwissenschaft* 15 (1973): 209–12.

the 1870s had eclipsed their German peers. Besides *Les Érinnyes,* the 1870s saw the premieres of such works as Bizet's score for *L'Arlésienne* (Théâtre du Vaudeville, 1 October 1872), Gounod's two scores *Les deux reines de France* (public premiere at the Salle Ventadour, 27 November 1872) and *Jeanne d'Arc* (Théâtre de la Gaîté, 8 November 1873), Massenet's music for *La vie de bohème* (Odéon, 19 November 1875) and *Notre Dame de Paris* (Théâtre des Nations, 4 June 1879), Henri Maréchal's music for *L'ami Fritz* (Comédie-Française, 4 December 1876), and Léo Delibes's music for *Ruy Blas* (Comédie-Française, 4 April 1879). These scores became seminal works for a growing body of large-scale incidental scores which reached a critical mass in the mid-1880s.[26]

Perhaps most unusual is the critics' reluctance to connect these *drames lyriques* with the *chœurs* of the Comédie-Française. Between 1852 and 1864 five very substantial scores were produced on that stage that underpinned the substructure of the genre of *Les Érinnyes.* Charles Gounod composed the score for François Ponsard's adapted five-act tragedy *Ulysse* (premiered on 18 June 1852 under Offenbach's music directorship), and Edmond Membrée wrote the music for Jules Lacroix's adaptation of Sophocles' *Œdipe roi* (18 September 1858). Jules Cohen contributed three scores: those for Racine's *Athalie* (8 April 1859) and *Esther* (5 July 1864), and one for the *Psyché* of Corneille, Molière, Quinault, and La Fontaine (14 August 1862). The rubric of "choruses" is rather misleading, for it was not meant to describe their contents to the contemporary audience, but was instead calculated to emphasize their continuity with ancient Greek traditions. Substantial instrumental passages and the consistent support of the chorus by the orchestra, coupled with the frequent use of *mélodrame,* made these works closely related to the incidental form of the *drame lyrique.* Their exclusion from the lineage may well have been meant specifically to distance such works as *Les Érinnyes* from the tradition of incidental music: any music performed at the Comédie Française, the central venue for the preservation of seventeenth-century

26. The latter four of these works are closer to the model of Hérold's *Le dernier jour de Missolonghi,* because they feature a relatively small number of sung excerpts interspersed with spoken dialogue, rather than the more thoroughgoing use of music seen in the scores that feature *mélodrame.* The incidental works premiered in the 1880s that featured extensive *mélodrame* included Charles-Marie Widor's *Conte d'avril* (Odéon, 22 September 1885) and *Les jacobites* (Odéon, 21 November 1885), Ernest Chausson's *La tempête* (Petit Théâtre des Marionnettes, 5 November 1888) and *Les oiseaux* (Petit Théâtre des Marionnettes, 16 April 1889), and Gabriel Fauré's *Caligula* (Odéon, 8 November 1888) and *Shylock* (Odéon, 17 December 1889). Incidental works of the same decade which featured a mix of song and spoken drama included Delibes's *Garin* (Comédie-Française, 8 July 1880), *A quoi revent les jeunes filles* (Comédie-Française, 29 November 1880), and *Barberine* (Comédie-Française, 27 February 1882); Henri Maréchal's *Smilis* (Comédie-Française, 23 January 1884); Alfred Bruneau's *Elza* (Palais du Trocadéro, 3 June 1884); Louis Bourgault-Ducoudray's *Fils de Jahel* (Odéon, 14 October 1886); and Emmanuel Chabrier's *La femme de Tabarin* (Théâtre Libre, 11 November 1887). Also significant are the revivals of Mendelssohn's *Le songe d'un nuit d'été* (Odéon, 14 April 1886) and Bizet's *L'Arlésienne* (Odéon, 5 May 1885), works that featured extensive *mélodrame* and orchestral passages.

French classical tragedy, would implicitly be incidental (that is, not intrinsic) to the spoken dialogue of the drama. In overlooking these *chœurs* in their construction of the lineage of the *drame lyrique,* the critics could strengthen associations between the *drame lyrique* and operatic forms and thus establish the fitness of the *drame lyrique* to join grand opéra and *opéra comique* as a genre suitable for a new lyric theatre.

Although the use of the term *drame lyrique* to describe major scores for spoken plays never became the standard definition of the term, the inclusion of what we would call incidental works under the rubric of *drame lyrique* was not a short-lived phenomenon of the 1870s. Through the end of the century, this subgenre of incidental music remained embroiled in the dialogues surrounding opera and Wagnerism. In 1891 Charles-Marie Widor revised and expanded his 1885 incidental score for *Conte d'avril,* an adaptation of Shakespeare's *Twelfth Night.* Some six years after Pougin's polemical definition of the term *drame lyrique,* and fifteen years after the premiere of Massenet's expanded score for *Les Érinnyes,* Widor's score received the same genre designation from the journalists as Massenet's, and once again readers were provided with a constellation of comparable incidental scores. Adolphe Aderer compared the work to Bizet's *L'Arlésienne* (premiered in 1872 and revived in 1885), Massenet's *Les Érinnyes* (premiered in 1873 and revised in 1876), Francis Thomé's *Roméo et Juliette* (1890), Mendelssohn's *A Midsummer Night's Dream,* and Beethoven's *Egmont.*[27] Similarly, the incidental score that Gabriel Fauré wrote for the adaptation of Jean Lorrain and André-Ferdinand Hérold's *Prométhée* (1900) received an analogous genre label, nuanced as a *tragédie lyrique.* With this rubric, Fauré reflected both the relevant theatrical subgenre (tragedy as opposed to drama) and hinted at the substantial number of sung roles mixed into this work, which was originally meant to be *musique de scène,* by its reference to the eighteenth-century operatic genre and to Lully's *tragédies lyriques* on libretti similarly drawn from Greek mythology.[28]

27. "M. Porel is going to return this work to the stage, and he has commissioned Charles Widor to do for *Conte d'avril* that which Bizet has done for *L'Arlésienne,* Massenet for *Les Érinnyes,* Francis Thomé for *Roméo et Juliette,* etc., etc., and which Mendelssohn did for *A Midsummer Night's Dream* and Beethoven for *Egmont.* So *Conte d'avril* will expand the repertoire of *drames lyriques*" (M. Porel va remettre cet ouvrage à la scène et il a chargé M. Ch. Widor de faire pour *Conte d'avril* ce que Bizet a fait pour l'*Arlésienne,* Massenet pour les *Érinnyes,* Francis Thomé pour *Roméo et Juliette,* etc., etc., et ce qu'avaient fait Mendelssohn pour le *Songe d'une nuit d'été* et Beethoven pour *Egmont. Conte d'avril* vient ainsi augmenter le répertoire des drames lyriques). [Adolphe Aderer], "Spectacles et concerts," *Le temps,* 9 March 1891.

28. Fauré's work was received as an incidental work, rather than as an opera, by Paul Dukas in his review of 31 October 1900 for *La revue hebdomadaire,* cited in Pierre Menneret, "La musique de scène en France de Napoléon III à Poincaré, 1852–1914" (Ph.D. diss, Paris Conservatoire, 1973), 115. With regard to Lully, it is interesting to note that the operagoing public in Paris in 1900 knew his music only through performances of his incidental music at the Comédie-Française and the Gaîté, both under Offenbach's baton. Lully's operas were known only through published scores at that time, though Rameau's *tragédie en musique Dardanus* had been performed at the salon of the Princesse de Polignac in 1895, providing Parisian audiences with a point of sonic reference for

Elinor Olin has established at length how the genre label of *drame lyrique* was utilized by nationalistic French critics who sought to defend their musical traditions against Wagnerian influence.[29] Hervé Lacombe has further followed the implications of the term through nineteenth-century French theatrical and musical dictionaries.[30] Tracing the above-referenced incidental *drames lyriques* demonstrates the degree to which the usage of this rubric for incidental works remained in current usage throughout the crisis of Wagnerism in France, serving both as a means of distinguishing these unusual *musiques de scène* from shorter scores in the same genre, and as a means to reclaim the French identity of this genre label from the Wagnerians. Such fluency and change in the definition of genre by critics and musicians had been almost unthinkable before 1864. The Napoleonic Code, which regulated theaters, had granted permission to perform certain genres to specific theaters, in seeking to reduce the competition (and the consequent economic impact) of purely entrepreneurial theaters with the state-sponsored theaters such as the Opéra, the Opéra-Comique and the Comédie-Française. The implications of the Napoleonic Code of 1807, which delegated unique rights for specific genres to each of the principal theaters in Paris, gave the genres a fixity of meaning in practice (if not in the letter of the law) that had hindered reinterpretations of their meaning.[31]

Vizentini's Théâtre-National-Lyrique barely outlasted its production of Massenet's hybrid score. Its life span was unusually short even for Paris's ephemeral secondary opera stages. By 2 January 1878 the doors had closed on the enterprise after a number of significant productions that included the premieres of Saint-Saëns's *Le timbre d'argent* and Victor Massé's *Paul et Virginie*. During its brief existence, Vizentini's theater produced 377 performances of revived works and a substantial 161 performances of new works. In part because of the debts left over from the Théâtre de la Gaîté, Vizentini never was able to break even, regardless of nearly 477,000 francs in subventions spread out over the seventeen months of productions at the Théâtre-National-Lyrique and receipts totaling 1.4 million francs.[32] On 29 December 1877 Vizentini submitted his resignation, effective 1 January 1878.

French baroque opera. For a detailed study of the role of the salon of the Princesse de Polignac in Parisian musical life, see Sylvia Kahan, *Music's Modern Muse: A Life of Winnaretta Singer, Princesse de Polignac* (Rochester, NY: University of Rochester Press, 2003).

29. See Elinor Nichols Olin, "*Le ton et la parole:* Melodrama in France, 1871–1913" (Ph.D. diss., Northwestern University, 1991).

30. See Hervé Lacombe, "Definitions des genres lyriques dans les dictionnaires français du XIXème siècle," in *Le théâtre lyrique en France au XIXeme siècle*, ed. Paul Prevost (Metz: Serpenoise, 1995), 297–334.

31. For a reprinting of this and other legislation concerning French theater from 1790 to 1872, see Alfred Bouchard, *La langue théâtrale* (Paris: Arnaud et Labat, 1878), 337–76.

32. The subvention figures for the Théâtre-National-Lyrique are drawn from Noël and Stoullig, *Annales* 3 (1878): 255–56; the figures for the total receipts at the theater are drawn from Noël and Stoullig, *Annales* 4 (1879): 215.

Although Vizentini's musicotheatrical laboratory failed not long after Massenet's hybrid work found a home there, the legacy of experimentation in fusing music and theater continued—though in some surprising places. In light of the string of failures at entrepreneurial opera houses in nineteenth-century Paris, the need for more adventurous programming on the operatic stages was taken up by the Opéra-Comique, beginning under Léon Carvalho (1876–87 and 1891–97) and expanding under Albert Carré (1898–1913), where such works as Massenet's *Werther* (1893) and *Manon* (1894), Bruneau's *Le rêve* (1891), *L'attaque du moulin* (1893), and *L'ouragan* (1901), Gustave Charpentier's *Louise* (1900), and Debussy's *Pelléas et Mélisande* (1902) were premiered. Similarly, under the director Paul Porel (1884–92) the state-run Théâtre de l'Odéon took up the incidental form of the *drame lyrique* as its signature. Porel worked closely with Édouard Colonne and his orchestra (as well as the rival orchestra directed by Charles Lamoureux) to provide accompaniment for some two hundred performances of major incidental works per year. These included Mendelssohn's score for Racine's *Athalie* (1884), the wildly successful revival of *L'Arlésienne* (1885), Charles-Marie Widor's music for *Les jacobites* and *Conte d'avril* (both 1885), Mendelssohn's *A Midsummer Night's Dream* (1886), Benjamin Godard's music for the Shakespearean adaptation *Beaucoup de bruit pour rien* (1887), the revival of Lully's score for *Psyché* (1887), Fauré's music for *Caligula* (1888) and *Shylock ou le marchand de Venise* (1889), a version of Beaumarchais's *Le mariage de Figaro* featuring entr'actes derived from Mozart (1889), Beethoven's score for *Le comte d'Egmont* (1890), and Francis Thomé's music for *Roméo et Juliette* (1890). That the Opéra-Comique and the Théâtre de l'Odéon were increasingly successful in combining drama and music in fresh and innovative ways that won both critical acclaim and popular acceptance suggests that Vizentini had been ill-advised to mix so many disparate genres in a single theater. Yet despite its failures, the Théâtre-National-Lyrique contributed significantly to the rethinking of what French opera could and should be during a period in which French music struggled to develop a clearer identity.

PART III

The Midi and Spain, *or* Autour de Carmen

Carmen

COULEUR LOCALE OR THE REAL THING?

Kerry Murphy

As an institution the Paris Opéra-Comique was from its early beginnings a site for the exploration of *couleur locale*.[1] However, as has been widely discussed, with Bizet's *Carmen* the representation of *couleur locale* became suddenly more complex. This article explores the concepts of authenticity and exoticism that have been and continue to be raised about the representation of Spanishness in *Carmen*. Was *Carmen* "a fantasy about Gypsies," "an intuitive but not a lived work," as Raoul Laparra claims?[2] Or did it represent "the real Spain" for the audience of its day?[3] And if it did, just what was the "real" Spain to a Parisian of the 1870s? To what extent, to paraphrase Benedict Anderson, was Spanish style merely "the style by which . . . [it was] imagined"?[4]

Part I of this chapter provides an overview of the cultural material that was likely

I would like to acknowledge the generous assistance of a University of Melbourne research grant. I would also like to thank Lesley Wright and Richard Langham Smith for their valuable comments on an earlier draft of this article, and Nathalie Castinel for her help in locating material in Melbourne.

1. See Hervé Lacombe, "The Writing of Exoticism in the Libretti of the Opéra-Comique, 1825–1862," *Cambridge Opera Journal* 11, no. 2 (1999): 135–58.

2. "Une fantaisie bohème"; "une œuvre d'intuition mais non une œuvre vécue?" Raoul Laparra, *Bizet et l'Espagne* (Paris: Delagrave, 1935), 43, 42.

3. "Une espagne pour de vrai." Charles Vimenal, *L'art* 2 (1875): 33.

4. Benedict Anderson, *Imagined Communities: Reflections on the Origin and Spread of Nationalism* (London and New York: Verso, 1991), 6.

FIGURE 13.1. Gustave Doré, *Andalucian Dancers;* wood engraving; in Charles Davillier, *Spain,* illustr. Gustave Doré, trans. J. Thomson (New York: Scribner, Welford and Armstrong, 1876). Courtesy of University of Melbourne Baillieu Library.

to have informed knowledge of Spain in nineteenth-century France and discusses the presence of actual Spanish musicians and artists in Paris. Part II uses this background to evaluate critics' expectations of Spanishness in *Carmen* and to ask to what extent *Carmen* confounded or reinforced these expectations.

I. French Views of Spain

The strong presence of Spain in nineteenth-century French cultural life has been much written about, and some interesting new material from Spanish scholars has appeared in the past few years.[5] French interchange with Spain in the nineteenth century began with Napoléon's invasion and occupation of 1808–13. During the first half of the century large numbers of Spaniards immigrated to France for a variety of political reasons.[6] During the 1820s and 1830s Spain became an obsession with romantic writers such as Victor Hugo and Alfred de Musset, and their vivid evocations of an exotic, oriental Spain, land of passion and eroticism, inspired other romantic artists and musicians and provided stereotypes of Spanishness that quickly became ubiquitous. It was southern Spain, and in particular Andalusia, with its Moorish heritage, that featured most strongly, a bias that affronted some Spanish writers of the time who felt, for instance, that, the French undervalued the new European city of Madrid.[7]

The figure of the Gypsy came to symbolize Spanish orientalism. By the 1830s the collective French imagination did not make much of a distinction between Gypsies and Spaniards.[8] Mérimée's 1845 novella *Carmen* firmly reinforced this symbolization and also the notion of the eroticism of the female Gypsy, with her overt sexuality and promiscuity.[9] Mérimée borrowed much of his material on Gypsies from the Englishman George Borrow's 1840 accounts of his travels in Spain.[10] Interestingly, Mérimée chose not to follow Borrow's claim that despite their overt sensuality, female Gypsies were extremely chaste and faithful in their relationships; but Mérimée's view clearly had appeal and remained popular for many years in France.

By the late 1830s the vogue for Spain in the dramatic arts was everywhere. L. F. Hoffmann's book *Romantique Espagne* gives an appendix listing a staggering number of works based on Spanish themes during the first half of the century.[11] If we just look at the theaters for 1837, for instance, we find:

---

5. See Celsa Alonso, "La réception de la chanson espagnole dans la musique française du XIXe siècle," 123–60; Montserrat Bergada, "Les pianistes espagnols au Conservatoire de Paris au XIXe siècle," 195–234; and Encina Cortizo, "La zarzuela espagnole du XIXe siècle: Relations et divergences avec le théâtre français du XIXe siècle (1832–1866)," 62–122; all in *Échanges musicaux franco-espagnols, XVIIe–XIXe siècles: Actes des rencontres de Villecroze,* ed. François Lesure (Paris: Klincksieck, 2000).

6. See Montserrat Bergada, "Musiciens espagnols à Paris entre 1820 et 1868: État de la question et perspectives d'études," in *La musique entre France et Espagne: Interactions stylistiques (1870–1939),* ed. Louis Jambou (Paris: Presses de l'Université de Paris-Sorbonne, 2003), 19–20.

7. Gil Reicher [Gilberte Guillaumie-Reicher], *Gautier et l'Espagne* (Paris: Hachette, [1935?]), 484.

8. Léon-François Hoffmann, *Romantique Espagne: L'image de l'Espagne en France entre 1800 et 1850* (Paris: Presses Universitaires de France, 1961), 122.

9. Merimée's novella *Carmen* originally appeared in *La revue des deux mondes,* October 1845; it was republished in 1847 as one of four novellas in a book also titled *Carmen.*

10. See the excellent article by George T. Northup, "The Influence of George Borrow upon Prosper Mérimée," *Modern Philology* 13, no. 3 (1915): 143–56.

11. Hoffmann, Appendice III, in *Romantique Espagne.*

Hippolyte Auger, *Le corrégidor de Séville, mélodrame,* Théâtre de la Gaîté

Charles Briffault, *François Ier à Madrid,* verse with epilogue

Cogniard frères, *Micaela, drame-vaudeville,* Folies-Dramatiques

Louise Collet, *L'abencérage,* opera in two acts, Théâtre de M. le comte de Castellane

Charles Desnoyers and A.-L. Boulé, *Rita l'espagnole,* drama, Théâtre de la Porte Saint-Martin

Théophile Deyeux, *Le muet de Barcelone,* drama, Théâtre des Folies-Dramatiques

Fabrice Labrousse and Saint Ernest, *Don Pèdre le mendiant,* drama, Théâtre de l'Ambigu-Comique

Hippolyte Monpou (music) Alexandre Dumas (words), *Piquillo, opéra comique,* Opéra-Comique

J. B. Rosier, *Maria Padilla, chronique espagnole,* Théâtre du Vaudeville[12]

The influence of Spanish literature on French literature during the nineteenth century was also significant. The Spanish-Moorish novel was a popular model for French writers of fiction: authors such as Casimir Delavigne, Leconte de l'Isle, and Alphonse Daudet were all indebted to Spanish writers. Spanish novels and plays were also widely available in translation.[13]

DANCE

From an early period, Spanish dances had been inserted into ballets and *grand opéra,* for instance the performance in 1836 by the sisters Fanny and Theresa Elssler of a cachucha in the ballet-pantomime *Le diable boiteux* (choreography by Jean Corali, music by Casimir Gide); Fanny Elssler's performance of a cachucha inserted into the reprise of *Les huguenots* in 1837; and a performance by the Noblet sisters (Lise and Félicité, whose stage name was Alexis Dupont) of a cachucha in a reprise of *La muette de Portici,* also in 1837.[14]

From the 1830s Paris also had many visits from Spanish dancers, who made guest appearances at, for instance, the Opéra balls, and later entire dance companies came. Hervé Lacombe has traced the impact and reception of the visiting Spanish dance companies during the mid-century (1847–57). He points out that the popular vaudeville *Les folies d'Espagne,* written especially to incorporate visiting Spanish dancers, was performed fifty-two times at the Théâtre de la Gymnase during this time.[15]

12. This list has been drawn up from Hoffmann, Appendice III, in *Romantique Espagne,* and some titles given in Patrick Berthier, preface to Théophile Gautier, *Voyage en Espagne suivi de España,* ed. Patrick Berthier (Paris: Éditions Gallimard, 1984), 8–9.

13. See Paul Patrick Rogers, "Spanish Influence on the Literature of France," *Hispania* 9 (1926): 205–35. This article includes an extensive list of French works that demonstrate Spanish influence.

14. See Berthier, preface to Gautier, *Voyage en Espagne,* 9.

15. Hervé Lacombe, "L'Espagne à Paris au milieu du XIXe siècle (1847–1857): L'influence

In 1840 a Spanish newspaper reported that the bolero and cachucha, accompanied by castanets, were danced everywhere in Parisian popular music venues.[16] It was elsewhere noted that one danced the fandango and the bolero in salons, something that would have been unthinkable in Madrid at the time.[17] A Frenchman, Émile Guimet, wrote from Spain in a letter to his mother, "In the theater they perform grand ballets as at the Opéra, in the balls they dance the polka and no fandango, or bolero."[18]

Spanish dance was also integral to French *opéras comiques* of the mid-century and earlier. In his survey of French *opéras comiques* based on Spanish themes (1840–70), Hervé Lacombe discusses the way in which the genre was typically constructed from stereotypes and highlights the features that became the markers of Spanishness.[19] In particular, he notes the use of dance, the use of instruments onstage (castanets, guitar, and *tambour de basque*) and the appearance of Gypsies, smugglers, toreadors, and/or bandits, and the like. However, the evocation of Spain was strictly coloristic; Lacombe mentions that the only real toreador he came across in this period was actually a retired one in Adam's *opéra comique* of the same name, and that there was no blood, no playing with death associated with him, nor any bulls.[20] There is, however, at least one other *opéra comique* with a toreador as a central character: *Les nuits d'Espagne* (1857), by M. Semet, with words by Michel Carré. The story revolves around a Dr. Morelo who wants to marry his daughter Carmen to a toreador from Cádiz—a bizarre sort of toreador, no macho specimen this, but rather a late eighteenth-century Parisian dandy. Carmen, for her part, prefers a young English officer she danced with at Gibraltar. The second act is set around a bullfight in Cádiz. The bullfight takes place, and as might be expected, our dandy toreador does not fare well and is wounded—and wounded in a place, not named, that makes it impossible for him to sit down. Rather than stay standing, he takes himself to bed, and of course Carmen makes off with her English officer.[21] This *opéra comique* does, then, include a

---

d'artistes espagnols sur l'imaginaire parisien et la construction d'une 'hispanicité,'" *Revue de musicologie* 88, no. 2 (2002): 399.

16. Popular entertainment at the Variétiés, Palais Royal, Salle Jullien, etc. Article in *Semanario pintoresco Español,* quoted in Alonso, "Réception," 131.

17. As stated in Victor Giraud, *La vie tragique de Lamennais* (Paris: Presses Universitaires de France, 1933); quoted in Alonso, "Réception," 131.

18. "Dans les théâtres on donne de grands ballets comme à l'Opéra, dans les bals on danse la polka et aucun fandango, aucun boléro." Émile Guimet, *L'Espagne, lettres familières, avec des postscriptum en vers, par Henri de Riberolles* (Paris: L. Cajani, 1864), 49. At the end of each of his letters Guimet inserted a small verse written by his traveling companion, Henri de Riberolles.

19. Hervé Lacombe, "L'Espagne à l'Opéra-Comique avant *Carmen:* Du *Guitarrero* de Halévy (1841) à *Don César de Bazan* de Massenet (1872)," in *Échanges musicaux franco-espagnols, XVIIe–XIXe siècles: Actes des rencontres de Villecroze,* ed. François Lesure (Paris: Klincksieck, 2000), 168.

20. Ibid., 166.

21. "Théâtre-Lyrique: *Les nuits d'Espagne,* opéra comique en deux actes, paroles de M. Michel Carré, musique de M. Semet (première représentation le 26 mai 1857)," *La revue et gazette musicale de Paris,* 31 May 1857.

bullfight—but one that, in accordance with Lacombe's argument, is associated with comedy rather than tragedy.

An interesting sideline to the *opéras comiques* with Spanish themes is that from mid-century, the Spanish zarzuela was transformed into a genre referred to by Spanish critics as *ópera cómica española*.[22] Spanish composers visiting Paris came back enamored of the French *opéra comique,* and for a few decades most works of the indigenous genre were nothing but translations, arrangements, and imitations of mid-century French *opéra comique,* albeit with new music (often more Italianate than French) and usually added national nuances.[23]

During the troubled Spanish civil wars throughout the century, many Spaniards took refuge in Paris, and some studied at the Conservatoire.[24] In the Second Empire, with Louis Napoléon's Spanish wife, the empress Eugénie, the Spanish presence in Paris intensified even more. The guitarist Ferdinand Sor and the Garcia family played a significant role in diffusing national song.[25] Innumerable collections of Spanish songs (boleros, tiranas, and Andalusian songs) were available, either in the form of arrangements of popular airs by artists such as Sor and Narciso Paz or songs by well-known Spanish composers.

The Spanish musicologist Celsa Alonso emphasizes the importance of the lyric Spanish song in conditioning the French imaginative vision of a picturesque Spain.[26] Manuel Garcia's song *El contrabandista,* for instance, inspired a phenomenal number of French artworks, both in literature and in music.[27] This song was extremely popular in Spain too.

Spanish composers and performers resident in Paris also picked up on the French passion for Spanish dances and helped make them better known. Some volumes of songs were published with the price not in French francs, but in Spanish currency (*duros*), indicating that they were perhaps destined for export back to Spain.[28] In the 1840s Spanish singers, aware of the vogue for Spanish music in Paris, visited and performed chiefly at the salons, where they sang songs of José Melchor Gomis and

22. Cortizo, "La zarzuela espagnole," 104.

23. Ibid., 121.

24. See Bergada, "Musiciens espagnols"; and Bergada, "Les pianistes espagnols." See also Bergada, "Espagne," in *Dictionnaire de la musique en France au XIXe siècle,* ed. Joël-Marie Fauquet (Paris: Fayard, 2003), 434–38.

25. Alonso, "Réception," 138.

26. "La chanson lyrique espagnole . . . conditionnant la vision imaginative que l'intellectualité française se forgea de . . . [l'Espagne] comme nation romantique, pittoresque et tendant au cliché littéraire." Ibid., 131.

27. Ibid., 132.

28. Ibid., 139. In fact, the bolero model that came to France has been shown to have been influenced by the French even earlier, with the visit of the Lefevre dance company to Spain during the French Napoleonic occupation. See Antonio Álvarez Cañibano, "The Company of the Lefevre Family in Seville," in "The Origins of the Bolero School," ed. Javier Suárez-Pajares and Xoán M. Carreira, special issue, *Studies in Dance History* 4, no. 1 (1993): 21–37.

Sebastián Iradier, amongst others. Iradier, the former singing teacher of Empress Eugénie, renewed contact with her in Paris and had an official title bestowed on him as her teacher. From this moment on his songs began to be published in several languages, and they became extremely popular.

This crossover of cultures makes any discussion of authenticity quite complicated. The Spanish were clearly writing for and playing to a market eager to buy a certain type of Spanish music, one that perpetuated romantic stereotypes of a picturesque nature. French composers too were contributing to this market, and their product can in some ways be seen as a commercially driven one, an aspect that did not pass unnoticed at the time either.[29] Yet Spaniards were also writing for fellow Spaniards living in Paris (and perhaps back in Spain as well), and many of their collections were not newly written works but arrangements of well-known Spanish songs—some of which had apparently been practically forgotten in Spain itself. This all becomes rather confusing, but a few things are clear. First, there was an enormous amount of Spanish song of one sort or another around in Paris at the time. And second, the bulk of the songs (and other salon pieces as well) were composed in what can be called a picturesque genre, a genre generated by homesickness or commercial demand (or both).[30] Acquaintance with this music was something that French composers and critics could not have avoided.

VISUAL ARTS

French knowledge of Spain's visual arts started early in the century when Napoléon's generals brought back what can only be called plundered loot, much of which had later to be returned. In 1838, at the height of the Spanish craze in the boulevard theaters during the July Monarchy, Louis Philippe (himself a great lover of Spain) opened to the public his Musée Espagnol at the Louvre.[31] This was the biggest collection of Spanish painting outside Spain, and it had an immense impact on French artists during this time, inspiring many to make trips to Spain.[32] The French interest in Spanish art intensified during the Second Empire and is seen in particular in the works of painters such as Henri Regnault, who spent the late 1860s in Spain, and Édouard Manet, for whom a visit to the Prado in 1869 and, most important, the works of Velásquez were a revelation.[33]

---

29. Alonso, "Réception," 150, suggests that music editors at the time encouraged the writing of *andalouseries des soirées françaises* for commercial reasons.

30. Bergada, "Musiciens espagnols," 29, raises this point.

31. See excellent coverage of this *musée* in Ilse Hempel Lipschutz, *Spanish Painting and the French Romantics* (Cambridge, MA: Harvard University Press, 1972).

32. See Jean François Revel, "Théophile Gautier et le goût pour l'Espagne en France au XIXe siècle," introd. to Théophile Gautier, *Voyage en Espagne* (Paris: Julliard, 1964), 9–24, for an excellent summary of the development of the taste for Spanish art in France in the nineteenth century and the importance of Louis Philippe's collection.

33. Édouard Manet, *Voyage en Espagne*, ed. Juliet Wilson-Bareau (Caen: L'Échoppe, 1988).

Photographs of Spain would also have been available. The French photographer Jean Laurent, for instance, who had settled in Spain in 1843, opened a branch of his photography shop in Paris in 1868, from which he sold prints of Spain and Portugal.

As with the *opéra comique,* the exchange was not one-sided. After 1850 several groups of Spanish artists established themselves in Paris, many to study at the École des Beaux-Arts. They specialized in painting in what was called the *genre andalou,* with folkloric scenes of dances and fêtes.[34] As one might imagine, this art became very popular. It was in a way a visual reflection of the *couleur locale* of the *opéra comique:* visual vignettes of colorful Spanish life. At the same time, the Hispanophile Gustave Doré was providing haunting Spanish genre scenes drawn from life to accompany articles written between 1862 and 1873 by Baron Charles Davillier for the popular travel journal *Le tour du monde.* In 1874 they were collected together and published as a book, *L'Espagne.*[35] I shall return to Davillier below, but first a few words about another famous French travel writer on Spain (one of many, it should be said): Théophile Gautier.

Gautier's *Voyage en Espagne* was popular throughout the nineteenth century and went through ten editions between 1843 and 1875. Throughout the century his book and poems helped reinforce a romantic, picturesque view of Spain.[36] A close reading of his book shows, as Patrick Berthier has noted, that for Gautier the heart of Spain was "L'Andalousie," which he saw as "Arabian Andalusia."[37] During his travels, Gautier was annoyed by aspects of Spanish life that departed from what he *wanted Spain to be.* For instance, he was irritated when he saw Spanish women imitating French fashions.[38] He famously complained that Spanish dancing existed only in Paris, although fortunately he finally found some in Seville, as part of some locally observed national celebrations. He still deplored the loss of knowledge of national dance among the upper and middle classes.

After the outbreak of the Franco-Prussian war there was a lull in the intensity of

34. There was a reaction against this later in the century when the Spanish artists Ignacio Zuloaga, Isidro Nonell y Monturiol, and Dario Regoyos visited Paris and proposed a demystification of the "Cliché espagnoliste"; see Alonso, "Réception," 143.

35. Charles Davillier, *L'Espagne* [with 309 woodcuts by Gustave Doré], (Paris: Hachette, 1874).

36. Although accused at the time it appeared of presenting an exaggeratedly romantic view of Spain, the Spanish artist Ignacio Zuloago claimed toward the end of the century that Gautier didn't exaggerate—"he was just lucky to have had the chance to pass through our country during the most picturesque moment of its history" (a eu la chance de traverser notre pays au moment le plus pittoresque de son histoire); quoted in Reicher, *Gautier et l'Espagne,* 488.

37. Berthier, preface to Gautier, *Voyage en Espagne,* 17.

38. To meet this desire for French fashion, there was a huge migration of French jewelers, perfumers, hairdressers, and dress designers to Spain at the beginning of the 1860s. See Émile Témime, "Les Français en Espagne au milieu du XIXe siècle: Une migration privilégiée," in *Exil politique et migration économique: Espagnols et Français aux XIXe–XXe siècles,* ed. CNRS, Groupement de Recherche (0030) (Paris: Éditions du CNRS, 1991), 55–69.

the Spanish cultural presence in France, but it resurfaced with great gusto with the Exposition Universelle of 1878. Nevertheless, writings on Spain continued to appear with great regularity during the 1870s. Among these were Davillier's accounts of his travels in Spain. In his narrative, Davillier presents a more realistic and prosaic view of Spain than anyone before him had done. He recounts what he sees on his travels in ethnographic fashion, intermingled with historical information and quotations from Spanish and French literature on Spain. An extraordinarily well-informed narrator who appears careful not to present stereotypes, he explains that he took Doré with him because he felt the painter "could make us acquainted not with the Spain of the *opéra comique* and keepsakes, but the real Spain."[39] Davillier stresses the vast differences between the various areas of Spain and the various groups of Gypsies; for instance, he does not talk just about Andalusian Gypsies, nor does he privilege Andalusia. He resists the romantic merging of Gypsy and Spaniard typical earlier in the century: "The Gypsy type is usually characterized and differentiated so much from that of the Spaniard that nothing is easier than to pick them out at first glance."[40] Davillier's account of the tobacco factory in Seville is very evocative, particularly his description of the excitement at the end of the day when the unfortunate women, cooped up inside with the smell of tobacco all day, emerged from their workplace, "impatient to regain the pure air outside, and to regain a moment of liberty."[41] It reminds one of the scene in act 1 of *Carmen,* as do many other sections, making it seem very probable that Meilhac and Halévy and perhaps also Bizet were familiar with Davillier's writings and Doré's illustrations,[42] given that these illustrated articles had been appearing regularly over the ten years immediately prior to *Carmen.* And like other French travelers, Davillier is fascinated by Spanish dance. He provides extensive historical information on the various dance types, including even liturgical dances in Toledo and Seville.

The complicated and turbulent political events of Spain were constantly before the eyes of any interested nineteenth-century Parisian reader. Most of the daily press either contained regular articles from foreign correspondents, often entitled "Lettres d'Espagne," or provided weekly bulletins on the political troubles. The *Revue des deux mondes* provided articles by writers such as Gautier,[43] Georges Sand, Charles

---

39. "Non pas celle des opéras-comiques et des keepsakes, mais l'Espagne vraie." Davillier, *Le Voyage en Espagne* (Paris: Stock, 1980), 8.

40. "Le type de gitanos est d'ordinaire caractérisé et diffère tellement de celui des Espagnols que rien n'est plus facile que de les distinguer à première vue." Ibid., 162.

41. "Impatientes de respirer l'air du dehors et de retrouver un moment de liberté." Davillier, *L'Espagne,* 333.

42. Some of these illustrations owe a considerable amount to Goya. Yet they can also be quite sentimental and almost kitschy, as many of the representations of young children show. Jean-Louis Martinoty is also of the opinion that many scenes in *Carmen* were directly inspired by Doré's illustrations, see "De la réalité au réalisme," in *Carmen,* vol. 26 of *L'avant-scène opéra* (1980): 100.

43. Gautier even brings the civil war into his vaudeville *Voyage en Espagne* (12) when the character Bénito comments: "Heavens, Guzman, when I see my beautiful country, Spain, being con-

Didier, and later, during the 1860s and 1870s, the journalist Charles de Mazade, who regularly finished his "Chronique" with a section on Spain in which he showed great sympathy for the Spanish people, subjected as they were to the ravages of the wars. Many French writers on Spain spoke of a country with a great past, and a recoverable great past. Indeed, two accounts of the Spanish exhibit at the Exposition Universelle of 1867 stated that despite the country's political troubles, Spain put on an impressive show. Léon Droux claimed that with a degree of peace Spain would return to its former glory, for "the past of a nation feeds into its future."[44] Similarly, Charles Lucas, who expressed astonishment at the quality of items sent by Spain in the category of "public works," concluded that "Spain, so celebrated for her architectural past, has the right to expect even more in the future."[45] Not all approved of the Spanish exhibit, however. The critic for *Le monde illustré*, for instance, found it distressingly prosaic because it lacked the picturesque stereotypes he associated with Spain, and he lamented most the absence of "the costumes of their toreadors, of their manolas, and of their lovers covered by their sombreros!"[46]

SPANISH MUSIC

Those who wrote on Spain's music were not so sanguine about the resurrection of a glorious past. For most French music critics, the value of contemporary Spanish music lay in its popular song, and in its dance in particular.[47] Hervé Lacombe is absolutely correct in his emphasis on the centrality of dance to French discourse about

---

stantly torn apart by civil wars, when I see twenty different parties seizing a part of government for themselves, I say to myself: 'There is nothing we can do when a country is being pulled in so many different directions in this way'" (Tiens, Guzman, quand je vois mon beau pays d'Espagne incessamment déchiré par des guerres civiles; quand je vois vingt partis tirer chacun à soi un morceau du gouvernement, je me dis: "il n'y a rien à faire pour nous quand un pays est tiraillé ainsi").

44. "Le passé d'un peuple répond de son avenir." Léon Droux, *L'Espagne à l'Exposition universelle de 1867* (Paris: Dentu, 1867), 9.

45. "L'Espagne, si célèbre par son passé architectural, a droit à attendre plus encore de l'avenir." Charles Lucas, *L'Espagne à l'Exposition universelle de 1867, aperçu des nombreux et intéressants envois de la Direction générale des travaux publics de Madrid* (Paris: Chez l'auteur, 1867), 20.

46. "Les costumes de leurs toréadors, de leurs manolas et de leurs amoureux couverts de leurs sombreros." *Le monde illustré*, 28 September 1867.

47. Some, such as Henri Blanchard, were a little condescending about this; it was not, after all, art music: "À l'exception de quelques airs de danse et de chansons populaires, l'Espagne n'a pas de musique nationale." Henri Blanchard, "[Revista musicale] de *La nacion* [Observations d'Emilio Arrieta sur la musique nationale espagnole; José Ciebra, *Maravilla*]; Audition d'un grand opéra [d'André Simiot]; *Les trois sultanes*, aux Variétés [Morceaux d'ensemble et chœurs par Nargeot, airs par Creste; Delphine Ugalde]," *La revue et gazette musicale de Paris*, 31 July 1853. Others, however, privileged it for its spontaneity and verve.

Spanish music.[48] Henri Blanchard, for instance, reviewing a Spanish *drame lyrique,* *Maravilla,* by José Ciebra, remarked that the music seemed to be designed more "for choreography than the human voice."[49] Blanchard, who often wrote harshly of Spanish music in *La revue et gazette musicale de Paris,* constantly claimed that there was no national opera in Spain, only imitation Italian opera. Even the Spanish devotee Émile Mathieu de Monter wrote, in one of a series of articles called "La musique dans les beaux arts," that "music in this country is more a popular taste than a widely cultivated art and science."[50] Adrien de La Fage, in a long series of scholarly articles on music in Spain published in the *La revue et gazette musicale de Paris* of 1861, did argue for a heritage of great church music but made no claims for a national opera school.[51] In an article of 16 June 1861 La Fage lamented (probably in reference to the *opéra comique* imitations) that contemporary Spanish music appeared to be imitating rather than inventing, and he quoted his friend the Spanish composer and scholar Soriano Fuertes as saying: "Previously, we were the model for all people; today we are the parody of such a model. In the sixteenth century Spain was alive for the whole world; now, she doesn't even exist for herself."[52]

This quotation is very interesting. I have already discussed how certain images such as dancers, castanets, guitars, bandits, smugglers, bullfights, and so on came to represent Spain in the popular French imagination. But did these images ever become a parody of Spanishness? Certainly, a number of French writers of the time were aware of the clichéd nature of the reproduction and repetition of these stereotypes.

Despite contributing to the French romanticization of Spain through his travel book *Voyage en Espagne,* Gautier also mocked the artificiality of the popular picturesque portrayal of Spain in the vaudeville he wrote of the same name, which was premiered on 21 September 1843. A character in the vaudeville, Reniflard, exclaims:

48. Lacombe, "L'Espagne à Paris," 406.

49. "Pour la chorégraphie que pour la voix humaine." Henri Blanchard, "Théâtre Impérial Italien: *Maravilla,* drame lyrique en espagnol et en trois actes, libretto et partition de M. José Ciebra (première représentation le samedi 4 juin 1853)," *La revue et gazette musicale de Paris,* 12 June 1853.

50. "La musique est dans ce pays plutôt un goût populaire qu'un art et une science largement cultivées." Émile Mathieu de Monter, "La musique dans les beaux-arts; Les monuments et les traditions poétiques; Visites d'un dilettante aux musées de l'Europe; Deuxième partie Espagne et Portugal X; L'Espagne (suite)," *La revue et gazette musicale de Paris,* 8 November 1874.

51. Lacombe, "L'Espagne à Paris," 178, cites the Escudier brothers' statement in their *Dictionnaire de musique théorique et historique* (Paris: E. Dentu, 1872) that learned music in Spain was at a standstill and that musical potential now lay with popular repertoire.

52. "Alors nous étions le modèle de tous les peuples, [XVIe siècle] aujourd'hui nous en sommes la parodie! Au XVIe siècle, l'Espagne était vivante pour le monde entier; maintenant elle n'existe pas même pour elle!" Adrien de La Fage, "De la musique en Espagne (8e et dernier article)," *La revue et gazette musicale de Paris,* 16 June 1861.

For two years now, I have been doing nothing but devour my base: Victor Hugo, Alfred de Musset, Prosper Mérimée, Lord Byron, I read and reread you; you went to my head—you inspired me with the love of local color—Oh! Local color—All I dreamt of was gothic villages—of orange trees with their golden apples, pomegranate trees with their coral fruit, of bandits, smugglers, Gypsies, and especially Andalusian women with their sunburned breasts, pale like a beautiful Autumn evening [direct quote from Musset's *L'Andalouse*]—You know the rest—I came to Spain to study local color and to make a pleasure trip—Oh!

AIR

I am thirsty for local color
I am hungry for the blue sky of Spain
All I dream of is oriental women
Golden sun and fiery looks.

He finishes, however, by saying:

Good God! The wind from the mountain
I know, will drive me crazy.
In short, the Spain I dream of
is the Spain of Monsieur Monpou's songs.[53]

It is interesting that Gautier objectifies and indeed ironizes about *couleur locale* here. He is thirsty for it, and he wants to find it, to study it. But what is it exactly? He seems to suggest that it is partly an artificial French literary creation that does not really conform to reality. A similar sort of irony is expressed by Émile Guimet and his friend Henri de Riberolles in their letters from Spain in 1865. In Valladolid the weather was bad, "the sky was grey, the wind blew from the North, it was terribly cold—What a Siberia this Iberia is!" And Riberolles's verse on Madrid starts: "We are at Madrid. Alas! Where are our dreams? Hugo, Musset, Gautier, whose pupils we were, what mocking muse dictated your songs!" It is snowing (in April), and instead of the expected scent of

---

53. "Depuis deux ans, je m'occupais sans relâche à dévorer mon fonds < . . . > Victor Hugo, Alfred de Musset, Prosper Mérimée, lord Byron, je vous ai lus et relus; vous m'avez monté la tête < . . . > vous m'avez inspiré l'amour de la couleur locale < . . . > Oh! la couleur locale < . . . > Je ne rêvais que villes gothiques < . . . > Je ne rêvais qu'orangers aux pommes d'or, que grenadiers aux fruits de corail, que bandits, contrebandits, gitanos, et surtout qu'Andalouses au sein bruni, pâles comme un beau soir d'automne < . . . > Vous savez le reste < . . . > Je suis venu en Espagne étudier la couleur locale, et faire un voyage d'agrément. Oh! L'Espagne!; Air "J'ai soif de la couleur locale / J'ai faim de l'Espagne au ciel bleu / Je ne rêve que d'Orientale / Soleil d'or et regard de feu!"; "Vrai Dieu! Le vent de la montagne / Je le sens, va me rendre fou / Bref, je ne rêve que d'Espagne / sur les airs de monsieur Monpou." Théophile Gautier and Paul Siraudin, *Un voyage en Espagne: Vaudeville en 3 actes* (Paris: Tresse, 1843), 2–3.

orange blossom and jasmine, all they smell is onion and garlic.[54] Once again, the same list of literary names is evoked, although now Gautier is himself part of the tradition.

In 1857 the critic Léon Lespès despairingly asked composers of *opéras comiques,* "Why don't you go to China or India, Lapland or Patagonia, leave off that country where *the eye of a young girl gleams under the mantilla.*"[55] The stereotypes of the popular Spanish theater were beginning to annoy some people; Davillier referred scornfully to those "so-called Andalusian songs where *Grenade* rhymes with *serenade, Inésille* with *résille* and *toréador* with *matador.*"[56] The critic Ralph for the journal *L'art musical* was one of many to complain about despised rhyming patterns of "alcades" and "cavalcade," "mantille and Castille," and so on.[57]

In 1867 Émile Mathieu de Monter wrote a curious article on Spain as part of an extensive series on the Exposition Universelle in *La revue et gazette musicale de Paris.* The flowery rhetorical style carries a slightly patronizing edge. "Who was it that claimed that the picturesque Spain was dead?" he asks. "Who did you want to convince that the *opéra comique* has inherited the mantillas, the cigarettes, the castanets, and the corsets?" "[Who claims that] local color has gone out of fashion on the other side of the mountains?" Yet he answers his rhetorical questions himself: "Yes, absolutely, the joyous Andalusia, the superb Aragon, the pious Galicia, the noble Castille have faithfully conserved their traditions."[58] However, seven years later, in the series "La musique dans les beaux-arts," Monter seems gloomier about the preservation of national customs in Spain. He now regretfully acknowledges that despite the fact that the soul of the nation was in "le chant populaire,"[59] and that it was hard to find

54. "Le ciel est gris, le vent souffle du nord, il fait un froid terrible. . . . Quelle Sibérie, que cette Ibérie": Guimet, *L'Espagne,* 9. "Nous sommes à Madrid. Hélas! où sont nos rêves? Hugo, Musset, Gautier, dont nous sommes élèves, Quelle muse railleuse a dictée vos chansons?": ibid., 13. Fortunately their trip improves later on.

55. "Allons en Chine, aux Indes, en Océanie, en Laponie, en Patagonie, mais n'allons plus dans ce pays où *l'oeil d'une jeune fille brille sous la mantille.*" Léon Lespès, "Théâtre Impérial de l'Opéra Comique: Don Pèdre," *La France musicale,* 4 October 1857; quoted in Lacombe, "L'Espagne à l'Opéra-Comique," 168.

56. "Prétendues chansons andalouses, où, sous prétexte de couleur locale, *Grenade* rime avec *sérénade, Inésille* avec *résille, toréador* avec *matador.*" Davillier, *Voyage,* 56.

57. Ralph, "Les espagnols à Paris," *L'art musical,* 29 June 1865.

58. "Qui donc a prétendu que l'Espagne pittoresque était morte? . . . A qui a-t-on voulu faire croire que l'opéra-comique avait hérité des mantilles et des cigarettes, des castagnettes et des basquines?"; "la couleur locale [est] passée de mode de l'autre côté des monts?"; "oui certes. La joyeuse Andalousie, l'Aragon superbe, la pieuse Galice, la noble Castille, ont fidèlement conservé leur traditions." Émile Mathieu de Monter, "Exposition universelle de 1867: Espagne," *La revue et gazette musicale de Paris,* 26 May 1867.

59. "Le chant populaire . . . L'âme de la nation y est déposée." Émile Mathieu de Monter, "La musique dans les beaux-arts; Les monuments et les traditions poétiques; Visites d'un dilettante aux musées de l'Europe; Deuxième partie Espagne et Portugal X; L'Espagne (suite)," *La revue et gazette musicale de Paris,* 1 November 1874.

anything "more essentially Spanish than castanets, it was only with "le peuple" that such music could be found, for "the society people repudiated [traditional areas] a long time ago as being in 'bad taste'" and sang in their salons not the songs of Iradier, but the tunes of French operetta.[60] Monter now claims that "nothing resembles Spain less than the Spain of the *opéra comique* . . . that accessory shop of rejects is part of the Spanish morgue."[61] He nevertheless expends much time evoking with great enthusiasm what Spain was like in the past and expresses nostalgia for the "extinct races!," "abandoned customs," and "faded figures!"[62]

Although it is true that in the nineteenth century the French had their own images of Spain that surfaced in the popular imagination in certain stereotyped ways, many were aware that these stereotypes did not really bear much resemblance to contemporary Spain. The French were also, as already mentioned, exposed to Spanish music by resident Spanish musicians. Yet one has to wonder to what extent the Spanish musicians resident in Paris were incorporating knowledge of the French stereotypes of the Spanish into their performance and playing up to the expectations of their French audience.

The French were also exposed to Spanish music by visiting Spanish troupes. Many critics referred to the division at these events between the Spaniards and the French in the audience, between those who understood what was going on and those who did not.[63] The critic D. A. D Saint-Yves, commenting on a concert of what he called "Spanish operettas," wrote that although the Spaniards in the audience expressed "demonstrations of joy," he could not respond in the same way since "the language of *Le Cid* is all Hebrew to us."[64] The use of "nous" rather than "moi" suggests Saint-Yves believed there were other French in the audience who felt the same. What audience were the visitors playing to? Although some critics responded ambivalently to vocal works sung in Spanish, there was widespread admiration always for Spanish dance: dance was, after all, a universal language. However, the crossover between the two cultures throughout the century meant that the whole notion of what represented the "real Spain" was unclear for the French and indeed for the Spanish themselves.

60. "La 'société' . . . a depuis longtemps répudié [ses coutumes] pour cause de 'mauvais genre.'" Émile Mathieu de Monter, ""La musique dans les beaux-arts; Les monuments et les traditions poétiques; Visites d'un dilettante aux musées de l'Europe; Deuxième partie Espagne et Portugal X; L'Espagne (suite)," *La revue et gazette musicale de Paris*, 25 October 1874.

61. "Rien ne ressemble moins que l'Espagne à l'Espagne d'opéra-comique . . . ce magasin d'accessoires au rebut fait partie de la morgue espagnole." Ibid.

62. "Races éteintes! coutumes délaissées! figures évanouies!" Ibid.

63. See Ralph, "Les Espagnols à Paris," *L'art musical*, 29 June 1865.

64. "Manifestations joyeuses"; "la langue du Cid est pour nous de l'hébreu." D. A. D. Saint-Yves, "Vaudeville: *Les petites comédies de l'amour,* comédie en un acte, mêlée de chant, par MM. Dutertre et A. Lemonnier, musique de M. de Groot; *Le Nid,* comédie en un acte, part M. Gust. Bondon," *La revue et gazette musicale de Paris*, 18 June 1865.

II. *Carmen*, Spain, and the Critics

It seems reasonable to assume that critics came to *Carmen* with their knowledge of Spain broadly informed by what has been outlined here: French romantic literature, French *opéra comique,* and romance stereotypes, but also knowledge of Spanish music, art, and dance as performed and published by Spaniards in France. In the period immediately before *Carmen,* the romantic stereotypes of Andalusian oriental Spain were being tempered by more realistic portrayals of the whole country, which involved an understanding of its distressing political life. Critics were also familiar with Prosper Mérimée's novella.

Because the reviews of *Carmen* were extremely mixed, it must be borne in mind that exceptions can sometimes be found to the general trends that I have outlined, and that the reviews are not always consistent with one another.[65]

WHAT IMPRESSION OF SPAIN DO THE REVIEWS GIVE?

A few things stand out. First of all, nearly all the critics are eager to show their detailed knowledge of Mérimée's novella *Carmen,* and most admire it greatly.[66] A few critics thought that it worked well as an *opéra comique* libretto and admired the skillful adaptation by Henri Meilhac and Ludovic Halévy, who were renowned librettists.[67] A few felt that its power had been weakened,[68] though the majority believed that what could be countenanced in a literary genre—in particular, one in which the passionate story is framed by the distancing objectification of a narrator—becomes too realistic when turned into the flesh and blood of living and breathing characters on the

65. This is pointed out also by Lesley Wright in her excellent introduction to her edition of *Georges Bizet, "Carmen": Dossier de presse parisienne* (Heilbronn: Lucie Galland, 2001), i–x. This press dossier has been used extensively in the preparation of this article, as has the extra list of reviews of *Carmen* given in Wright, *"Carmen": Dossier,* 165–69. As is now increasingly being pointed out, the reviews were overall more positive than negative with a few often-quoted exceptions. See, on this point, Wright, introduction to ibid.; and Robert L. A. Clark, "South of North: *Carmen* and French Nationalisms," in *East of West: Cross-Cultural Performance and the Staging of Difference,* ed. Claire Sponsler and Xiaomei Chen (New York: Palgrave, 2000), 205.

66. Only one critic, Simon Boubée, seriously questions Merimée's representation of the female Gypsy as promiscuous, claiming that the oddest thing about the female Gypsy is that her physical appearance doesn't relate to her character, for despite her burning gaze (*expression brûlante*) and lascivious looks, she is chaste and faithful. Boubée continues, however, in quite a disturbing way, by explaining the fidelity not in terms of her morality, but in relation to her lack of any moral sense, because she has no heart, no faith, no religion, and doesn't know how to love. Boubée, *Gazette de France,* 6 March 1875, in Wright, *"Carmen": Dossier,* 36.

67. M. Savigny, "Les théâtres," *L'illustration,* 13 March 1875, in Wright, *"Carmen": Dossier,* 108; Émile Abraham, "Théâtres: Opéra-Comique," *Le petit journal,* 6 March 1875.

68. The strongest argument for this is put by Simon Boubée, "Revue musicale," *Gazette de France,* 8 March 1875, in Wright, *"Carmen": Dossier,* 37.

stage.[69] The critics did not necessarily object to the violence of Mérimée's story; rather, they did not think it a good fit for the genteel stage of the Opéra-Comique.[70] This is not just a matter of the difference between a literary and a theatrical genre, because some critics also suggested that the story would be fine, even "old hat" (*fade*), at one of the boulevard theaters such as the Ambigu-Comique.[71] Blaze de Bury, in the *Revue des deux mondes,* described what he called the "melodrama" of the card scene in *Carmen* as belonging to the Théâtre de la Porte Saint-Martin.

The critics were uniformly keen to show their familiarity with the Spanish language. L. F. Hoffmann comments that it was very chic to use Spanish words in France in the first half of the nineteenth century, even when perfectly good French equivalents existed.[72] The reviews of *Carmen* are so bristling with Spanish words that at times they verge on the comical. Their use was clearly intended to display the critics' knowledge, but it also suggests that some Spanish words were well-known and formed part of an educated Frenchman's vocabulary, so to that extent they may not have been necessarily markers of exoticism.

The critics by and large expected the representation of Spain in *Carmen* to relate to the popular stereotypes they knew so well.[73] There was much discussion of *couleur locale*—Spanish color, Spanish rhythms, Spanish themes, Spanish style—but the word Spain is used almost as a generic term, referring to commonly recognized tropes. As Simon Boubée commented, we have "a Spain that is more Spanish than reality."[74]

However, the critics' reactions to the issue of *couleur locale* were quite complex. They all acknowledged the expected appearance of the stereotypes, the Gypsies, the smugglers, the bullfight, the castanets, and so on. Some welcomed them as familiar friends or as inevitable but unavoidable accoutrements.[75] As Paul Bernard commented of the third act entr'acte, "It is the absolute reign of castanets and *tambour de basque,*

69. On this point see in particular Paul Bernard, "Théâtre National de l'Opéra-Comique," *La revue et gazette musicale de Paris,* 7 March 1875, in Wright, *"Carmen": Dossier,* 25.

70. See, for instance, Victorin Joncières, "Théâtres," *La liberté,* 5 March 1875, in Wright, *"Carmen": Dossier,* 41; Léon Escudier, "Théâtre de Opéra-Comique," *L'art musical,* 6 March 1875, in Wright, *"Carmen": Dossier,* 105; Daniel Bernard, "Théâtres: Opéra-Comique," *L'union,* 8 March 1875, in Wright, *"Carmen": Dossier,* 73; and Paul Bernard, "Théâtre National de l'Opéra-Comique," *La revue et gazette musicale de Paris,* 7 March 1875, in Wright, *"Carmen": Dossier,* 25.

71. François Oswald, "Musique," *Le gaulois,* 6 March 1875, in Wright, *"Carmen": Dossier,* 17.

72. "Le grand chic était d'employer des mots espagnols même lorsqu'ils avaient d'excellents équivalents en français." Hoffmann, *Romantique Espagne,* 54.

73. There is sometimes a direct link made between the music of the opera and the visual arts; for instance, Blaze de Bury refers to the Picador chorus as enabling one to "relive in song the Spain of Zamacoïs and de Fortuni" (revivre en chansons l'Espagne de Zamacoïs et de Fortuni). Blaze de Bury, "Revue musicale," *Revue des deux mondes,* 15 March 1875.

74. "Une Espagne plus *espagnole* que nature." Simon Boubée, "Revue musicale," *Gazette de France,* 8 March 1875, in Wright, *"Carmen": Dossier,* 40.

75. François Oswald [Oswald François], "Musique," *Le gaulois,* in Wright, *"Carmen": Dossier,* 14.

but could it have been otherwise?"[76] When Victor Fournel of *Le correspondant* gave a list of all the stereotypes used, he included a few, such as the chorus of Andalusian girls smoking cigarettes and the final knife thrust, that he felt went a little beyond the expected; he remarked that Bizet had used "all he could find that was the most titillating amongst the banality [of the stereotypes]" in order "to enliven the bourgeois taste without shocking it."[77]

There was a feeling that these signs of Spanishness were now almost a part of everyday life. Achille de Lauzières commented that local color was easy to do. There are "thousands of Spanish songs that are on everyone's lips and played on all the guitars!"[78] Johannès Weber's review in *Le temps* went so far as to say that the opening dance in the second act didn't really give any sense of local color, because today you would find boleros, polkas, and waltzes in all *opéra comique,* so they didn't really give a sense of where the action takes place.[79]

Some critics were bored by the all too familiar stereotypes, which to them revealed an inability on the part of the *Carmen* team to represent onstage the harsher reality found in Mérimée. As Simon Boubée commented, "M. Bizet used a lot of Spanish color, as it is commonly known: a bolero air, some castanets, a *tambour de basque,* and the trick is done"; but where is that "harsh flavor, that violent scent of ferocity that comes to your lips when you read Mérimée's masterpiece?"[80] Bizet's colleague Ernest Reyer stated with some unease that although he understood that Bizet had to use the familiar stereotypes of local color,[81] it might have been preferable to have tried something a little newer. Why, for instance, after making Carmen sing like a Spaniard, didn't he think of also making her sing a Gypsy air?[82]

There were, on the other hand, a few who felt that the *Carmen* team had broken

76. "C'est le règne absolu des castagnettes et du tambour de basque, mais pouvait-il en être autrement?" Paul Bernard, "Théâtre National de l'Opéra-Comique," *La revue et gazette musicale de Paris,* in Wright, *"Carmen": Dossier,* 27.

77. "Ce qu'il y a de plus piquant dans la banalité"; "réveiller le goût bourgeois sans le dérouter." Victor Fournel, "Les œuvres et les hommes, *Le correspondant,* 10 March 1875, in Wright, *"Carmen": Dossier,* 99.

78. "Des mille mélodies espagnoles qui sont sur toutes les lèvres et sur toutes les guitares." M. de Thémines [Achille de Lauzières], "Revue musicale," *La patrie,* 8 March 1875, in Wright, *"Carmen": Dossier,* 58.

79. J[ohannès] Weber, "Critique musicale," *Le temps,* 9 March 1875, in Wright, *"Carmen": Dossier,* 87.

80. "M. Bizet a fait beaucoup de couleur espagnole comme on l'entend vulgairement: un air de boléro, des castagnettes, un tambour de basque et le tour est joué"; "saveur âcre, ce violent arôme de férocité qui vous vient aux lèvres à la lecture du chef d'œuvre de Mérimée?" Simon Boubée, "Revue musicale," *Gazette de France,* in Wright, *"Carmen": Dossier,* 39.

81. "N'a guère pu se dispenser de chercher la couleur espagnole." E[rnest] Reyer, "Revue musicale," *Journal des débats,* 14 March 1875, in Wright, *"Carmen": Dossier,* 117.

82. "Pourquoi, après avoir fait chanter Carmen comme une Espagnole, n'a-t-il pas pensé . . . de lui faire chanter aussi un air de ce pays de Bohême?" Ibid., 118.

the boundaries of conventional expectation and instead of "the anodyne Spain of M. de Saint Georges" had given us a "harsh and wild Andalusia . . . where love deals in sunlight [and] where jealousy deals in thrusts of a knife."[83] Or, as Pierre Véron commented in reference to the costumes, *Carmen* provided "a picturesque reality that scarcely resembles the stupid bourgeois images of Spain that the Opéra-Comique used to display."[84] Armand Gouzien, in *L'événement,* was of the opinion that the *Carmen* team had indeed conserved the wildness and strangeness of the original model and stated that the tableau of the Gypsies in the second-act posada scene "presented a startling truth to which the musician also added his luminous colors."[85] The use of the term "truth," which is not a word one expects to encounter in reference to the representation of conventional *couleur locale* in *opéra comique,* points to a different understanding of the work. Such terminology in *Carmen* reviews is used almost invariably in reference to the mise-en-scène and décors, both aspects of the production that were uniformly praised. However, at times, as above, the music was seen as reinforcing the realism of the setting. Another example can be found in Adolphe Jullien's discussion of the second act: he noted its color and animation, which he attributed to "extremely realistic staging and costumes, and also to the music, to this *romanesca* that begins muted and slowly and finishes in a whirlwind, to the sound of outbursts of laughter, castanets, and *tambour de basque.*"[86] A few critics found themselves in the position of admiring the realism even though they did not necessarily like it. The critic for *La petite presse,* for instance, commented: "The costumes have been designed by Detaille. They are not very pretty but apparently they are very exact."[87] Detaille was a very well-known artist at the time who principally drew realistic drawings of

83. "L'Espagne anodine de M. de Saint-Georges"; "Andalousie âpre et fauve . . . où l'amour donne des coups de soleil, où la jalousie donne des coups de couteau." Paul de Saint-Victor, "Revue dramatique et littéraire," *Le moniteur universel,* 8 March 1875, in Wright, *"Carmen": Dossier,* 45. I must stress that I am here chiefly looking at cases where the expectations of the representation of Spain have been broken. There were, as is well-known, critics who felt that the character of Carmen broke violently with *opéra comique* conventions, but this had more to do with her sexuality than with her portrayal as a Spaniard. Oscar Comettant does mention the character of Carmen in relation to Spain, but just to say that he thought this type of character would only exist in Spain in the popular cafés of Seville: "Andalouses . . . comme il ne s'en trouve . . . que dans les tapis francs de Séville." Comettant, "Revue musicale, *Le siècle,* 8 March 1875, in Wright, *"Carmen": Dossier,* 67.

84. "Une pittoresque réalité qui ne ressemble guère aux Espagnes bourgeoises et bébêtes que l'Opéra-Comique d'autrefois exhibait." Pierre Véron, "Théâtres: Opéra-Comique; Carmen," *Le charivari,* 6 March 1875, in Wright, *"Carmen": Dossier,* 9.

85. "Saisissante vérité et le musicien y a ajouté ses plus lumineuses couleurs." Armand Gouzien, "Critique musicale," *L'événement,* 6 March 1875, in Wright, *"Carmen": Dossier,* 12.

86. "Mise en scène et aux costumes d'une grande exactitude, et aussi à la musique, à cette *romanesca* qui commence en sourdine et lentement, pour finir en tourbillonnant, au bruit des éclats de rire, des castagnettes, des tambours de basques." Adolphe Jullien, "Revue musicale," *Le français,* 15 March 1875, in Wright, *"Carmen": Dossier,* 122.

87. "Les costumes de dragons ont été dessinés par Detaille. Ce n'est pas très joli, mais il paraît que c'est très exact." "Théâtre des Beaux-Arts," *La petite presse,* 6 March 1875.

battle scenes and military figures. The fact that the Opéra-Comique directors had gone to the trouble of employing him as well as another well-known artist, Clairin, who designed Carmen's costumes, impressed the critics considerably. Charles Vimenal commented in his review for the exclusive journal *L'art* that Bizet was very lucky to find a theater director who was concerned with "real paintings and exact costumes, not designed by more or less talented designers from the industry but by painters with true talent—at last, an authentic Spain that seemed astonished at its appearance on the stage of *Le domino noir*."[88] To give one final example, Blaze de Bury remarked in his review on the current interest in ethnology, where "one looks for truth, one *presents things as they are*."[89] For him as for many other critics, it was the opening of the second act of *Carmen* that most impressed with its veracity: "Go and see the second act of *Carmen*, you will think you are in Spain, the décors, the costumes, the tone, the gestures, the facial expression, all is there."[90] He continued that the originality of the mise-en-scène was also due to Bizet and showed him to be as much an archaeologist as musician: "The Gypsy race is performing their arabesques against an old oriental background of monotonous and heavy sounds that emerge from behind the scenes with, in the distance, a suggestion of military music; you cannot help but think of the colorful civilization of modern Spain emerging from its Jewish, Arabian, and Egyptian origins."[91] With the strong and obviously approving terms "vrai," "vérité," "exact," "exactitude," and "justesse," the critics perceived in the staging an attempt to portray a picture of Spain that went beyond the conventional *opéra comique* mise-en-scène. Whereas such ethnographic work, to use Bury's term, had for many years been common at the Opéra, it was a surprise to encounter it at the Opéra-Comique.

I mentioned earlier the similarity between some of the scenes in *Carmen* and the verbal descriptions in Davillier and Doré's *L'Espagne*. One could speculate that many of the critics were familiar with this source (more probably as the serialized articles in *Le tour du monde* than the 1874 book) and saw it as a travel narrative, and thus as a reflection of the real Spain, which, if also reflected in *Carmen*, would have given

88. "Véritables tableaux et des costumes exacts, dessinés non par des industriels plus ou moins habiles mais par des peintres d'un vrai talent, enfin une Espagne pour de vrai, et qui semblait tout étonnée de son apparation sur la scène du *Domino noir*?" Charles Vimenal, *L'art* 1, no. 2 (1875): 33. See also "Musique," *La revue de France*, 13 March 1875: "Mise en scène et costumes d'une grande exactitude"; and Albert de Lasalle, "Chronique musicale," *Le monde illustré*, 20 March 1875: "La pièce est très pittoresque, grâce surtout à la justesse de ses décors et de ses costumes espagnols"; in Wright, *"Carmen": Dossier*, 138:

89. "On cherche le vrai, on fait *Nature*." Blaze de Bury, "Revue musicale," *Revue des deux mondes*, 15 March 1875, in Wright, *"Carmen": Dossier*, 130.

90. "Allez voir ce second acte de *Carmen*, c'est à se croire en Espagne: décors, costumes, le ton, le geste, l'air du visage, tout y est." Ibid.

91. "Sur un fond vieil orient de sons monotones et sourds tendu derrière la coulisse, la gent bohème brode ses arabesques et se dessine le chant militaire dans le lointain; vous diriez la civilisation picaresque de l'Espagne moderne émergeant de ses origines judaïques, arabes, égyptiennes." Ibid.

FIGURE 13.2. Gustave Doré, *Gipsy Dancing the Vito Sevillano;* wood engraving; in Charles Davillier, *Spain*, illustr. Gustave Doré, trans. J. Thomson (New York: Scribner, Welford and Armstrong, 1876), 312. Courtesy of University of Melbourne Baillieu Library.

it too an aura of authenticity or *vérité*. Figure 13.2 (above) and figure 13.3 show the similarities that I am talking about:

In an article on the influence of Spain on Manet, the art historian Juliet Wilson-Bareau comments that in Manet's early portraits, Spanish guitarists were portrayed in some sort of national dress, but because they subsequently became so much part of civilized, cultured life, Manet later did away with the costume. Wilson-Bareau

FIGURE 13.3. Lithograph of the stage design for act 2 of Bizet's *Carmen*. Courtesy of Éditions Choudens

suggests that this change is because, during the late Second Empire, reflections of Spain were absorbed and adopted into the French milieu and Parisian social life to such an extent that they were no longer exotic.[92] It would be interesting to know to what extent this change also reflected a change in artists' behavior. Monserrat Bergada describes how the guitarist Pagans, for instance, used to often dress up in regional Spanish costumes, or even as a toreador, when he played in the salons (to the delight of his hostesses).[93] At what point did he stop doing this?

Such deadening of exoticism certainly resonates with some of the observations of the music critics on the mundanity of the Spanish *couleur locale*. Moreover, their familiarity with actual Spanish dances and songs is reflected in the way in which *Carmen*'s overtly Spanish numbers, such as the Habanera and the Séguedille, are generally not portrayed by the critics as being exotic, even though, as is well known, some thought the acting that accompanied the dancing offensive. It is interesting that in a few years the Habanera and Séguedille would become the most frequently

92. Juliet Wilson-Bareau, "Manet and Spain," in *Manet/Velazquez: The French Taste for Spanish Painting,* ed. Gary Tinterow and Genevieve Lacambre (New York: Metropolitan Museum of Modern Art; New Haven, CT: Yale University Press, 2003), 249–50.

93. Bergada, "Musiciens espagnols," 24.

arranged and most popular numbers from *Carmen* in Spain,[94] which again raises the complex issue of cultural exchange.

On the whole, critics' expectations of the representation of Spain were largely fulfilled. The opera referred to accumulated French notions of Spanishness shared by critics and creators alike. It also referred to shared experiences of the actual Spanish presence in Paris. However, it went further and in the staging and costumes (reinforced in places by the music) introduced a Spain that critics saw as going beyond the conventional stereotypes and being closer to the "real" Spain. What they meant by the real Spain is an interesting question. I have suggested that what they saw as the real Spain was perhaps related to the ethnographic work of Davillier, although in certain cases (Blaze de Bury, for instance) it would have related to their own visits to Spain. But maybe, on another level the opera seemed closer to reality because its dramatic, adventurous presentation went beyond the *opéra comique* stereotypes.

Despite its birth in France, *Carmen* has, curiously, elicited almost proprietary responses in a number of Spaniards. On the first performance of *Carmen* in Spain, for instance, the critic of the paper *El imparcial* stated, "At last, *Carmen* was presented in her homeland."[95] More recently, Teresa Berganza has famously claimed that in her interpretation of Carmen, she wanted to present to the public the "image of the authentic Spain" and escape the representation of a "journalistic Spain" and "the stupid and simplistic travel-agency image of castanets and tambourines."[96] A recent colloquium on *Carmen* held in Seville had speakers arguing passionately about the representation of Andalusia in the opera. The theater director Salvador Tavora, in particular, reacted strongly against Bizet's representation of the cigarette girls: "I believe that it is important to buy back the myth of the misrepresentation given by the aggressive and inaccurate image of the cigarette girls of Seville . . . it is important for the history of our so manipulated and so misunderstood country, Andalusia."[97] It is extraordinary that the artwork *Carmen* can arouse such a reaction. The image of Spain portrayed in Mozart's *Don Giovanni*, for instance, would never be criticized in

---

94. See Michael Christoforidis, "Georges Bizet's *Carmen* and Spanish Nationalism," in *Romanticism and Nationalism in Music,* ed. Anastasia Siopsi (Corfu, forthcoming).

95. *El imparcial,* 3 November 1887. Quoted in Christoforidis, "Georges Bizet's *Carmen.*"

96. "Je cherchais à offrir au public l'image d'une Espagne authentique"; "une Espagne de feuilleton": quoted in Dominique Maingueneau, *Carmen: Les racines d'un mythe* (Paris: Du Sorbier, 1985), 140. "Une image simpliste et stupide: castagnettes et tambourins pour agence de voyage": Teresa Berganza, "Ma Carmen," in *Carmen,* vol. 26 of *L'avant-scène opéra* (1980): 117.

97. "Je crois qu'il est important de racheter le mythe de la déformation donnée par une image agressive mais inexacte des cigarières de Séville . . . c'est important pour l'histoire de notre terre, si manipulée et si mal comprise: l'Andalousie." Salvador Tavora, "Carmen, regards Croisés," in *Actes du colloque Carmen miradas cruzadas* (Seville: Institut Culturel Français de Seville, 2002), 78.

the same way for its relationship to the "real" Spain. One could say that Bizet should be free to portray the cigarette girls of Seville in *Carmen* in whatever way he likes; he was writing an opera, after all, not a social history of Spain. As a critic commented at the time of *Carmen*'s premiere in Madrid in 1887, the "true aficionado will savor the beauties of *Carmen* without making an exhaustive study of her baptismal record." Yet this baptismal record continues to be interrogated, and in a 1997 poll in the European Union, Carmen topped the lists in the popular imagination as the symbol of Spain.[98] However, study of the representation of Spain in *Carmen* reveals that authenticity clearly has value as social myth, quite apart from its accuracy. And these myths will continue, as Lilyane Drillon concluded in her paper at the colloquium in Seville:

> If a country, a town, is capable of being the breeding ground of myths that are so important and universally known . . . it is because that country or that town is, fortunately, alive, and much more alive that those that are unremarkable. They are the cradles of dreams that have a life and a culture strong enough to survive the interpretations that can be made of them and continue to be the cradle of future creations.[99]

98. José F. Colmeiro, "Exorcising Exoticism: *Carmen* and the Construction of Oriental Spain," *Comparative Literature* 54, no. 2 (Spring 2002): 127.

99. "Si un pays, une ville est capable d'être la pépinière de mythes aussi importants et universellement connus . . . c'est parce que ce pays ou cette ville est, heureusement, vivant, et beaucoup plus vivant que tous ceux qui ne se font pas remarqués. Ce sont des . . . berceaux de rêves qui ont une culture et une vie assez fortes pour survivre aux interprétations qui peuvent être faites [*sic*] d'eux et continuer à être le berceau de créations futures." Lilyane Drillon, "Carmen, regards Croisés," in *Actes du colloque Carmen miradas cruzadas* (Seville: Institut Culturel Français de Seville, 2002), 17.

Spanish Local Color in Bizet's *Carmen*

UNEXPLORED BORROWINGS AND TRANSFORMATIONS

Ralph P. Locke

Bizet's greatest opera had a rough start in life. True, it was written and composed to meet many of the dramatic and musical expectations of *opéra comique*. It offered charming and colorful secondary characters that helped "place" the work in its chosen locale (such as the Spanish innkeeper Lillas Pastia and Carmen's various Gypsy sidekicks, female and male), simple strophic forms in many musical numbers, and extensive spoken dialogue between the musical numbers.[1] Despite all of this, the work

I am grateful for many insightful suggestions from Philip Gossett and Roger Parker and from early readers of this paper—notably Steven Huebner, David Rosen, Lesley A. Wright, and Hervé Lacombe. I also benefited from the suggestions of three specialists in the music of Spain: Michael Christoforidis, Suzanne Rhodes Draayer (who kindly provided a photocopy of the sheet-music cover featuring Zélia Trebelli), and—for generously sharing his trove of Garciana, including photocopies of the autograph vocal and instrumental parts for "Cuerpo bueno" that survive in Madrid—James Radomski. The Bibliothèque nationale de France kindly provided microfilms of their two manuscripts of "Cuerpo bueno" (formerly in the library of the Paris Conservatoire). Certain points in the present paper were first aired briefly in one section of a wider-ranging essay, "Nineteenth-Century Music: Quantity, Quality, Qualities," *Nineteenth-Century Music Review* 1 (2004): 3–41, at 30–37. In that essay I erroneously referred in passing to Bizet's piano-vocal score as having been published by Heugel; the publisher was, of course, Choudens.

1. Many Gypsies today prefer to be known as Roma. I preserve "Gypsy" (*gitano*, etc.), as is customary, for literary and operatic characters based on widely held notions about them, whether these notions are accurate or not. In Spain, in any case, *gitano* (of which Gypsy is the rough English equivalent) remains more acceptable to the *gitanos* themselves than words such as *Zigeuner* are in

was treated slightingly in 1875—or even rejected outright—by many in the audience and most of the critics.[2]

But, like its title character, *Carmen* is a survivor. Within a few years it resurfaced, outfitted with competent if sometimes leaden recitatives by the composer Ernest Guiraud (Bizet having died in the meantime). In that form it went on to triumph on the world's stages.[3] In time, the original spoken-dialogue version became a central item of the repertoire at the very locale where it had first failed to please, Paris's Théâtre de l'Opéra-Comique. Today *Carmen* remains one of the most frequently performed, recorded, and filmed operas. It is also possibly the one opera—indeed the one "classical" work—that is most often alluded to or freely adapted in popular culture, from various Olympic figure-skating routines to *Carmen: A Hip Hopera* (2001), based on the work's libretto (and a tiny bit of its music) and featuring the pop diva Beyoncé Knowles and the screen actor Mekhi Phifer.[4]

Carmen's ongoing success clearly derives in large part from the very features that made it exceptional—and initially problematic—within the *opéra comique* repertoire of the 1870s. These include a plot of quite serious intent; an ending that is more or less tragic for the main characters and fatal for the opera's (anti-?)heroine; musical numbers that play with formal layouts deriving from diverse traditions within and outside the lyric theaters of Paris; a musical style that makes imaginative use of orchestral color and unconventional harmonic and tonal procedures; and, not least, the feature that is the topic of this chapter: music that plainly sets out to evoke, in one way or another, Andalusian Spain, its primary native population, and the distinctive Gypsy (or Rom) minority living in its midst.[5]

Germany and Eastern Europe. See further Ralph P. Locke, *Musical Exoticism: Images and Reflections* (Cambridge: Cambridge University Press, 2009).

2. Lesley Wright, *Georges Bizet, "Carmen": Dossier de presse parisienne (1875)* (Weinsberg: Lucie Galland, 2001).

3. The opera received its premiere in March 1875, Bizet died in June of that year (on the evening of the thirty-third performance), and Guiraud's recitatives were first heard in October (in Vienna), after which they gradually helped the work conquer the world. The history of the work has been often and well told, as, for example, in Winton Dean, *Bizet*, 3rd ed., rev. reprint (London: J. M. Dent and Sons, 1975), 129–31; and Hervé Lacombe, *Georges Bizet: Naissance d'une identité créatrice* (Paris: Fayard, 2000), 630–747, 7–10 (on the work's fate after Bizet's death). The so-called critical edition by Fritz Oeser, 2 vols. (Kassel: Alkor-Verlag, 1964; also in a one-volume piano-vocal score, rev. 1969), is misleading on many important points. Oeser's sometimes spectacularly ignorant solutions have unfortunately—and despite warnings from scholars—been incorporated into certain productions and recordings. Editions that are more reliable include a piano-vocal score by Robert Didion (Mainz: Schott, 2000) and score and parts by Richard Langham Smith (London: Edition Peters).

4. *Carmen: A Hip Hopera*, DVD, directed by Robert Townsend (New Line Home Video, 2001).

5. Reasons of space preclude my giving attention to all the numbers in the opera that are obviously, or at least arguably, Spanish- or, more specifically, Spanish Gypsy–sounding. Besides the entr'acte to act 4 and three numbers touched upon more briefly here (the Habanera, the Séguedille,

Evidence of Spanishness

"On the Spanish element [in *Carmen*] much unnecessary ink has been spilt."[6] With these brusque words, in 1948, Winton Dean attempted to pulverize and wash away the many prejudiced attacks (and ill-informed encomia) that Bizet's masterpiece has suffered in the critical and scholarly literature. Dean's aim was to help us to appreciate the evidence for Spanish style in the work and to consider various plausible ways of interpreting that evidence.

In the intervening sixty years, more has been said on the subject and more ink spilled, sometimes confusing the matter further. Yet the two primary pieces of evidence—one song each by Manuel García (1775–1832) and Sebastián Iradier (1809–1865)—have rarely been looked at closely for what their words or music, or both, might reveal about which version of them Bizet knew and how he reshaped aspects of the two songs to his own purposes.[7] The present study clears the ground one more time and takes that first closer look at the García and Iradier songs, with special emphasis on the García (whose source history is more tangled than that of the Iradier) and the resulting entr'acte.

Dean wrote that "the chief significance of the alien elements [in Bizet's score] lies in the complete transformation they undergo in their passage through Bizet's creative imagination: they emerge as much his own as the rest of the score."[8] I endorse that sentence almost wholeheartedly. My one hesitation: I wish to avoid any suggestion that Bizet has somehow flattened out the distinctive folk and regional—non-French, nonoperatic—stylistic features that he found in Spanish musical sources. As commentators have long agreed—from Julien Tiersot and Edgar Istel to Susan McClary, Lesley Wright, James Parakilas, Steven Huebner, and Hervé Lacombe—certain numbers in this opera tell as foreign—indeed, as exotic. And thus they also tell *us* something about the characters and situations we are seeing and how we, the audience, are to respond to what we are seeing and hearing acted out onstage in movement, gesture, word, and song.

---

and the "Chanson bohème"). one might explore in detail the "fate" theme (with three augmented seconds in its "scale"), Carmen's taunting "Tra la la" song to Zuñiga, Escamillo's Toreador Song (especially its opening section in bolero rhythm), Don José's "Halte-là," Carmen's dance-song with castanets for Don José, and the music that opens the final act (outside the bullfighting arena). The question of how Spanish Gypsies are represented in numbers that do not sound foreign is addressed (with regard to the chorus that opens act 3 and Carmen's Card Aria) in Locke, *Musical Exoticism*, 160–74; the Card Aria discussion first appeared in Ralph P. Locke, "A Broader View of Musical Exoticism," *Journal of Musicology* 24 (2007): 506–11.

6. Dean, *Bizet*, 228.

7. A third song seems a likely source for the major-mode section of Carmen's "Tra la la" song in act 1. See Edgar Istel, *Bizet und "Carmen": Der Künstler und sein Werk* (Stuttgart: J. Engelhorns Nachf., 1927), 126–27.

8. Dean, *Bizet*, 232.

From 1804 Aria to Song

Bizet based the entr'acte to act 4 on the Andalusian-style serenade "Cuerpo bueno, alma divina" from Manuel García's light opera of 1804, *El criado fingido* (The Man in Servant's Disguise).[9] In figure 14.2 I lay out the basic facts about the song's most authoritative or influential surviving versions.[10]

García's song is musically startling for its day, notably in the way that it undermines certain tenets of common-practice harmony (e.g., by avoiding the raised seventh degree).[11] It is also verbally fresh (see figure 14.3). Most striking to a non-Spanish-speaker, only the last vowel or couple of vowels of the lines rhyme (e.g., *divina/dormida*; this is permitted in Spanish and is called *rima asonante* or sometimes half-rhyme), and certain lines do not rhyme at all (*fallezco/acaba*). One can understand why Bizet was attracted to García's song, a vivid transcribed fragment or close imitation (the distinction hardly matters) of folk culture and one that had been made accessible to the cosmopolitan, musically literate world through the artistry of Spain's leading operatic composer-performer.

The idea that Bizet's entr'acte originated in the García song was proposed by Julien Tiersot in 1925 and became even more plausible when, in 1959, Mina Curtiss revealed that Bizet had owned a copy of *Échos d'Espagne* (1872), a volume of heavily edited and arranged Spanish songs that included this very song by García (see fig. 14.1).[12]

A close comparison of Bizet's entr'acte with the version of "Cuerpo bueno" that he knew (reprinted here as ex. 14.1) would seem an obvious next step. But the possibility of doing so in reliable fashion has been somewhat clouded by the confusing fact that until now two other versions of García's song have been more readily available than the *Échos d'Espagne* version. As a result, several recent comparisons have—misleadingly—been drawn with these versions, rather than with the one that Bizet knew from *Échos d'Espagne*. These two other versions are the one in the 1804 opera and the one that was published first in 1831 and, again and again thereafter (with slight adjustments), in song anthologies and a music encyclopedia.

---

9. The original title was "Cuerpo bueno, alma jitana" (Precious body, Gypsy soul).

10. I will not generally repeat citations here that are present in full in figure 14.2 or, for the Iradier song, in figure 14.6.

11. Another García song, *Rosal* (published in Paris in the *Caprichos líricos españoles* [1830], though the songs had mostly been composed years earlier) ends, in aforementioned classic Hispanic fashion, "on the dominant chord"—as such a procedure would be heard in non-Hispanic contexts. Celsa Alonso would instead describe such a passage as relying on the *cadencia andaluza*. Alonso notes that the song "El Riqui-Riqui" is an early example of a composed *guaracha*. "Las canciones de Manuel García," booklet notes to Ernesto Palacio, tenor, and Juan José Chuquisengo, piano, *Manuel García: Yo que soy contrabandista y otras canciones* (Almaviva CD DS 0114), 23, 25.

12. See Julien Tiersot, "Bizet and Spanish Music," trans. Theodore Baker, *Musical Quarterly* 13 (1927): 581; and Mina Curtiss, *Bizet and His World* (New York: Alfred A. Knopf, 1958), 401, 472.

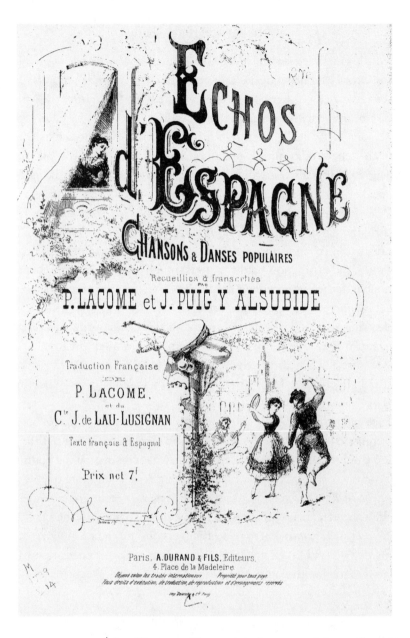

FIGURE 14.1. *Échos d'Espagne: Chansons & danses populaires,* coll. and transc. P. Lacome and J. Puig y Alsubide (Paris: Durand et Fils, n.d.). Courtesy Sibley Music Library, Eastman School of Music.

FIGURE 14.2. Short history of Manuel García, "Cuerpo bueno, alma divina."

- Manuscript: *F-Pn*, MS 13337. The entire 1804 opera is now in the Madrid Biblioteca municipal, MS 194-3 (libretto) and MS 223-1 (vocal and orchestral parts). An incomplete orchestral score of García's opera is in *F-Pn*, MS 13807. See James Radomski, *Manuel García, 1775–1832: Chronicle of the Life of a Bel Canto Tenor at the Dawn of Romanticism* (Oxford: Oxford University Press, 2000), 308.

- First published in *Regalo lírico [A Gift of Song]: Colección de boleras, seguidillas, tiranas y demás canciones españolas por los mejores autores de esta nación* (Paris: Paccini, 1831), no. 5. Apparently based on *F-Pn*, MS 13337. No. 6 in this volume is García's "El contrabandista," soon to achieve great popularity.

- *Échos d'Espagne: Chansons et danses populaires,* coll. and transcr. P. Lacome and J. de Lau-Lusignan [and J(osé) Puig y Alsubide] (Paris: Durand, [1872]), 78–82; pl. no.: D. S. et Cie. 1341. Later issues, with pl. no. [1341], are catalogued in various libraries with the date "1900–25?" "Cuerpo bueno" is, as Lacome points out in his preface, the only song in the volume attributable to a composer. A footnote thanks García's daughter and son, who, like their late sister, María Malibran, had attained enormous prominence in the French and international vocal world:

  > Ce POLO est tiré d'un opéra de Manuel Garcia.* Les Éditeurs ont reçu de Madame Pauline Viardot-Garcia et de Monsieur Manuel Garcia (fils) la gracieuse autorisation de le publier dans ce recueil.
  >   *EL POETA CALCULISTA [recte: *El criado fingido*]

  The song lyrics in this volume were translated by Paul Lacome, now better known as the composer of the Spanish-style vocal duet "Estudiantina," upon which Émile Waldteufel based his waltz of that title. The piano part was "transcribed" (i.e., reworked) by Puig y Alsubide. (Some writers confuse Lacome with Bizet's friend and student Paul Lacombe; however, the two Pauls were born a year apart.)

- Eduardo Ocón, *Cantos españoles: Colección de aires nacionales y populares* (Malaga and Leipzig, 1874 [see Josep i Martí y Perez et al., "Spain, II: Traditional and Popular Music," in *The New Grove Dictionary of Music and Musicians,* ed. Stanley Sadie, 2nd ed. (London: Macmillan, 2001), 24:152; and Celsa Alonso, ed., *Cien años de canción lírica española,* vol. 1, Música hispana, Serie C, Antologías 8 (Madrid: Instituto Complutense de Ciencias Musicales, 2001), viii, n. 7] or 1888 [OCLC holdings]; 2nd ed. 1906 [*New Grove*], 3rd ed. 1903 [OCLC]); 100 pp., with words in Spanish and German; reprinted, with words in Spanish only and without the introductory matter (Madrid: Unión Musical Española, 1952, 59–61).

- An adaptation of either the 1831 or the Ocón version appeared in Isidoro Hernández, *El cancionero popular: 12 cantos populares para piano con letra, 1a serie* (Lodre, 1875, 7–9; reprinted, Madrid: Unión Musical Española, 1963).

- The Ocón version was reprinted, with slight changes, in Rafael Mitjana, "La musique en Espagne," in *Encyclopédie de la musique et dictionnaire du Conservatoire,* ed. Albert Lavignac and Lionel de la Laurencie, part 1, vol. 4 (Paris: C. Delagrave, 1920), 2296–98. García's "El contrabandista" appears in Mitjana's article as well.

- Celsa Alonso, ed., *Canciones y caprichos líricos,* Música hispana, Serie C, Antologías

FIGURE 14.2. (*continued*)

1 (Madrid: Instituto Complutense de Ciencias Musicales, 1994), 3–5. Based on the *F-Pn* manuscript and the 1831 Paccini print. Alonso also prints García's "El contrabandista." Alonso includes "Cuerpo bueno" again in her *Antología (siglo XIX): La canción andaluza,* Música hispana, Serie C, Antologías 3 (Madrid: Instituto Complutense de Ciencias Musicales, 1996).

- Carol Mikkelsen, ed., *Spanish Theater Songs: Baroque and Classical Eras* (Van Nuys, CA: Alfred, 1998), 49–53. Based on the Ocón version.

- James Radomski, *Manuel García: 1775–1832: Chronicle of the Life of a Bel Canto Tenor at the Dawn of Romanticism* (Oxford: Oxford University Press, 2000), 54–56, 325–41. Based primarily on Madrid Biblioteca Municipal MS 223-1, and so includes the extensive vocal introduction that sets up the "performed" song ("Paseando cierto día en tiempo de vacaciones . . . / Los que hice en tal caso") and the subsequent cabaletta. Radomski also prints García's "El contrabandista."

- CD recording: *Manuel García: Yo que soy contrabandista y otras canciones,* with Ernesto Palacio, tenor, and Juan José Chuquisengo, piano; DS 0114 (Almaviva, 1995). The performers use the edition in the two Alonso volumes, based on *F-Pn,* MS 13337 and Paccini 1831, except that Palacio raises the fourth scale degree in the cadenza (perhaps applying *ficta* rules?). To my knowledge no recording has been made of the version that, as demonstrated in the present chapter, was almost surely the one that Bizet knew (published in *Échos d'Espagne,* 1872) and upon which he based the entr'acte to act 4 of *Carmen.*

The earliest source of the song is the version in *El criado fingido.*[13] Although the opera was performed to acclaim in Madrid in 1804 (with García singing the title role and thus this aria), it was never published. Almost two hundred years later, in 2000, James Radomski transcribed from several manuscript sources the whole aria of which "Cuerpo bueno" is a part and published it in his pathbreaking book on García as performer and composer. As a result, one can easily see now that "Cuerpo bueno" was not an independent song in this opera; rather, it served as the central cantabile movement of a multimovement aria.

The song also turns out to have a fascinating and specific dramatic function that nobody had guessed. The aria as a whole begins with the tenor hero, Vicente—who is disguised as his brother's *criado* (manservant)—conversing with another character (his own sister, Jacinta, who, somewhat implausibly, does not recognize him).[14] The "servant" tells Jacinta that one day, when he was on school vacation, he fell in love with a nameless beauty (who was leaning out from her balcony) and sang her a

13. *Fingido* is the Spanish equivalent of the Italian *finto* (false, feigning, pretending), as in Mozart's *La finta giardiniera.*

14. Vicente was one of García's middle names. This suggests a further layer of identity play in *El criado fingido.*

Note: Transcription and translation based on Radomski, *Manuel García;* F-Pn, MS 13337; and Madrid Biblioteca municipal MSS 194-3 and 223-1. The text of the polo appears in boldface, with some of the lines that precede and follow it in the opera aria shown in regular type.

Vicente (disguised as the servant of his actual brother, and conversing with his sister):
(Andante, G minor)

Paseando cierto día	One day, walking around
En tiempo de vacaciones	During [school] vacation,
Asomada a sus balcones,	I saw, leaning out from her balcony,
Yo vi la mayor beldad. . . .	The greatest beauty. . . .

(Allegro [*recitado*], modulating)

. . . Aquella noche misma	. . . That very night,
Tomando una guitarra	Taking a guitar,
Cuando todos tranquilos reposaban,	When everyone was quietly resting,
Yo junto a sus balcones	I [placed myself] next to her balcony
Con aire de Andaluz y su gracejo,	[And,] with an Andalusian manner and grace,
Del silencio tan sólo acompañado,	Accompanied only by silence,
Mi voz dirijo al objeto amado.	Aimed my voice at the beloved object.

(Allegretto [*polo*], E minor [resting mainly and ending on the dominant])

Cuerpo bueno, alma divina [*Madrid MS:* jitana]	**Precious body, divine [*originally: Gypsy*] soul**
¡Qué de fatigas me cuestas!	**What hardship you make me bear!**
Despierta si estás dormida,	**Awake, if you are sleeping**
Y alivia por Dios mis penas.	**And ease, for God's sake, my suffering.**
Mira, que si no fallezco.	**Look, if I don't die [faint?],**
La pena negra me acaba.	**Dark sorrow will finish me off.**
Tan sólo con verte ahora,	**Only if I can see you now,**
Mis pesares se aliviarán.	**Can my cares be lifted!**
Ay, ay, qué fatigas,	**Ay, ay, what hardship,**
Ay, ay, qué ya espiro.	**Ay, ay, I'm dying.**

(Allegro [cabaletta], G major)

. . . Un papel me tira, y marcha . . .	. . . A piece of paper she throws me, and leaves. . .
A mi padre le doy cuenta,	I tell my father.
El me riñe, yo no cedo	He scolds me, but I don't give in.
Y mis libros echo al fuego,	And I throw my books into the fire,
Y huyo asi de su rigor.	And thus I run away from his harshness.

EXAMPLE 14.1. Manuel García, "Cuerpo bueno, alma divina." Facsimile of the version published in *Échos d'Espagne*, marked here to coordinate with fig. 14.4. The facsimile continues with an anonymous "Malagueña" on the next pages of *Échos d'Espagne*.

EXAMPLE 14.1. (*continued*)

79

(*continued*)

EXAMPLE 14.1. (*continued*)

EXAMPLE 14.1. (*continued*)

81

(*continued*)

EXAMPLE 14.1. *(continued)*

MALAGUENA

Transcrite et traduite
par **P. LACOME.**

Le morceau suivant a été transcrit avec une absolue fidélité, sous la dictée de trois men-
diants aveugles. Cette *Malagueña* peut être considérée comme un type très remarquable de ce genre bizarre et étrange, appartenant plus à l'Afrique qu'à l'Europe, aux
Maures qu'aux Espagnols, mais qui, dans son apparente monotonie arrive à des effets
de charme inexprimables.

(continued)

EXAMPLE 14.1. (*continued*)

Ce chant est une sorte de psalmodie qui se plaque sur un accompagnement très rhytmé, sans relation de mesure apparente, en obéissant surtout au rhytme prosodique.

Hélas!cesse un tel langage!
Ni tam _ po _ co da_me, da_me,

EXAMPLE 14.1. (*continued*)

85.

serenade—"Cuerpo bueno." The "servant" then promptly sings it by way of explanation. The aria concludes with an up-tempo cabaletta in which the "servant" jauntily
tells Jacinta that his "father" disapproved of the attachment, so the young man moved
out of the family home and gave up being a student (and presumably took up his
present "occupation"). (I enclose "servant," "father," and "occupation" in quotation
marks because the story Vicente is telling is a lie.) Figure 14.3 gives a condensed version of the text of the whole aria; the words of the "Cuerpo bueno" movement are
presented in boldface in their entirety.

Whereas the 1804 aria long lay unknown (including, as I shall demonstrate, to
Bizet), a version of its cantabile section, largely similar to the original but differing
in details that are crucial for present purposes, became available in print as an independent number shortly before García's death, in an anthology of Spanish songs by
various composers published by Paccini in 1831 and entitled *Regalo lírico* (A Gift of
Song). This 1831 version is plainly based on a source copied out by the composer at
some point as a separate item—perhaps the autograph manuscript (largely identical to
the 1831 Paccini print) that survives in the Bibliothèque nationale as MS 13337, or some
other manuscript that is now lost. To add to the confusion, two subsequent versions
of the song, both clearly indebted to the 1831 Paccini print, appeared in collections
published in 1874 by Eduardo Ocón and 1875 by Isidoro Hernández.[15] Those were the
very two years in which Bizet was composing and revising his opera. The possibility thus exists that Bizet managed to see and use the Ocón or Hernández version of
"Cuerpo bueno"—or proofs thereof, or materials soon to be used in them—though
the tight time frame (and the fact that the two collections were published in Spain,
not France) makes this unlikely. In contrast, the 1831 Paccini print itself (or the closely
related MS 13337, which at the time was presumably in the possession of García's
daughter Pauline Viardot) could, at least in theory, have been a source for Bizet.

In order to pin down with greater assurance which version(s) of "Cuerpo bueno"
Bizet knew and used, I tried to find significant or even tiny variants in the vocal part,
but its music turns out to have been transmitted unchanged in the various manuscript
and published versions.[16] By contrast, there are notable differences in both the rhythm
and the harmony of the accompaniment and in the prelude and postlude (see table 14.1),
some quite significant:

15. I erroneously stated in Locke, "Nineteenth-Century Music," 32, that Tiersot knew not
only the *Échos d'Espagne* version but also, through Mitjana's article in the Lavignac *Encyclopédie*,
"some relatively early (pre-Lacome/Puig and pre-Ocón) version"; Rafael Mitjana, "La musique en
Espagne," in *Encyclopédie de la musique et dictionnaire du Conservatoire*, ed. Albert Lavignac and
Lionel de La Laurencie (Paris: C. Delagrave, 1913–31), part 1, vol. 4 (1920): 2296–98. As table 14.1
demonstrates, Mitjana's version turns out to be based heavily on Ocón's and thus has no independent documentary interest.

16. Some intriguing disparities in the Spanish words leave, of course, no revealing trace in
Bizet's purely instrumental entr'acte.

- The 1831 edition and all succeeding versions except *Échos* use as a prelude García's orchestral introduction to the opera aria's cantabile section but strip it of hemiola. The prelude in the *Échos* version—though for the most part newly composed, presumably by the arranger—does incorporate hemiola. Conversely, García's prelude uses a conjunct augmented second in the right hand, a strikingly Andalusian feature that the newly written prelude in the *Échos* version, for whatever reasons, avoids.
- The 1831 edition and all succeeding versions except *Échos* have only eighth notes on the second and third beats in the song's accompaniment, whereas the *Échos* version uses sixteenths on the second beat, following what García had done in the (then unpublished) opera-aria version.
- The 1831 edition and all succeeding versions except *Échos* employ similar tonal procedures, most notably a bass line that leaps about, in functional manner.
- The 1831 edition and all succeeding versions except *Échos* end with two brisk measures of chords in the tonic, whereas in both the opera aria and the *Échos* version the song ends with a sixteen-measure coda that brings the harmony back from i to end, as the song began, on V. (I shall return to the question of whether the $\hat{5}$ in the bass is actually a dominant or an Andalusian-style tonic.)

The conclusion is inescapable: the editors of *Échos d'Espagne* based their version of the García song on the opera-aria version that is today preserved in a manuscript in the Bibliothèque nationale, Département de la Musique, MS 13807 (or else on some nearly identical manuscript that has since disappeared).[17] MS 13807 is the sole surviving autograph orchestral score of the entire aria (and of several other numbers from *El criado fingido*); in the mid-nineteenth century, it, like MS 13337, was presumably in the care of García's daughter Pauline Viardot, a noted collector of manuscripts and devoted protector of her father's memory.[18]

The most striking evidence for linking the version in *Échos d'Espagne* to MS 13807, besides the features noted above, is that the prelude of *Échos d'Espagne* version, as well as its more or less identical postlude—though presumably composed by the song's arranger, José Puig y Alsubide—turns out to have been based on several measures from García's original postlude in the opera aria, a postlude that, as noted above, had been replaced by two measures of tonic confirmation in the version in MS

17. It is conceivable, though implausible, that the editors may have based their version on the orchestral and vocal parts that one may assume were in the possession of one of the Madrid theaters throughout the nineteenth century and can now be consulted at the Madrid Biblioteca municipal, MS 194-3 (libretto) and MS 223-1 (vocal and orchestral parts). These parts were much less easily available to the Parisian publisher Paccini than were the manuscripts in Paris. In any case, they do not diverge significantly (in ways relevant to the questions under discussion) from *F-Pn,* MS 13807.

18. On Viardot's collecting, see Mark Everist, "Enshrining Mozart: *Don Giovanni* and the Viardot Circle," *Nineteenth-Century Music* 25 (2001–2): 165–89.

TABLE 14.1. Comparison of the most significant versions of García's "Cuerpo bueno"

Source	Tempo	Prelude	Key	Accompanimental rhythm	Bass and upper voices	Coda
Madrid MS	Andante	García's (w/ hemiola)	e/B	[♪ ♫♫]	5̂ pedal (sometimes ♭6̂) w/sliding 6ths	Yes (ends on 5̂)
Paris MS 13807	All[egret]to	García's (w. hemiola)	e/B	[♪ ♫♫]	5̂ pedal (sometimes ♭6̂) w/sliding 6ths	Yes (ends on ^5̂) but partly crossed out
Paris MS 13337	None indicated	García's (w/o hemiola)	e/B	[♪ ♩]	functional	No (ends on i)
Paccini 1831	None indicated	García's (w/o hemiola)	e/B	[♪ ♩]	functional	No (ends on i)
Échos 1872	Andantino, ♪ = 126	New (by Puig?), based on contrary-motion material in García's coda	c/G	[♪ ♫♫]	5̂ pedal w/ sliding 6ths	Yes (ends on 5̂)
Ocón 1874	Larghetto, ♪ = 126, 6/8 meter	García's (w/o hemiola)	d/A	[♪ ♩]	partly functional, partly 5̂ with sliding first-inversion chords	No (ends on i)
Bizet 1875	Allegro vivo, ♩. = 80	New, w. contrary motion	d/A	[♩ ♫♫] in the introductory measures, then [♪ ♩] over "gallop" in the harp part	5̂ pedal w. sliding thirds	N.a.; ends on 5̂

Hernández 1875	Based on Ocón, but with vocal line now becoming the right-hand piano part (*para piano y letra*), and with new variants in harmony (including unresolved 7th chords)		
Mitjana 1920	Andantino	d/A	Nearly identical to Ocón (note their common error in the words, mm. 65-67), but with different editorial choices (the 3/8 meter is restored; some bass notes displaced by an octave)
Alonso 1994	Combines Paris MS 13337 (variants in bass notes, as indicated in Alonso's critical report) with Paccini 1831 and 1996		
Mikkelsen 1998	Based on Ocón		
Radomski 2000	Based on Madrid manuscript parts and the (largely identical) orchestral score, Paris MS 13807		

Close examination of musical features of the three manuscript versions and the 1831 print makes clear that the last is the source from which almost all later publications of "Cuerpo bueno," including one that appeared in the Lavignac *Encyclopédie*, are directly or indirectly derived. (The Paccini 1831 edition and all succeeding versions except *Échos* have the authentic prelude [ultimately from the manuscripts], but they have no hemiola in the prelude [whereas *Échos* and the aria manuscripts do], they have no sixteenths in the accompaniment of the song proper [whereas *Échos* and the aria manuscripts do], they have harmonies that are more similar to each other [including a changing bass line, whereas *Échos*'s harmonies are almost exactly those of the aria manuscripts—sixths moving above an unchanging dominant pedal], and they have no coda bringing the harmony from i back to V [whereas *Échos* and the aria manuscripts do].) All, that is, except the version that Bizet knew, in *Échos d'Espagne*, which preserves notable features from García's original opera version (pedal bass on B, with harmony in sliding sixths over it in strumming rhythm; and a chunk of García's coda, ending on the dominant). The *Échos d'Espagne* version, however, was not entirely faithful to the opera version either. The editors "transcribed" (i.e., arranged) it, the most notable change being the substitution of a new prelude derived from contrary-motion motion material in García's coda.

---

*The holograph vocal and instrumental parts (Biblioteca Nacional, Madrid).

†Holograph full score of large sections of the opera (*F-Pn*).

‡Holograph piano-vocal score of "Cuerpo bueno" (*F-Pn*).

13337, in the published anthology of 1831, and in all other versions based on that 1831 print, such as the aforementioned ones published in Spain in 1874 (Ocón) and 1875 (Hernández).

Furthermore, a number of the unique variants in the *Échos d'Espagne* version recur in Bizet's act 4 entr'acte, enough to make amply clear that the younger composer knew García's song in that version and not any other:

- Bizet's eight-measure prelude, though musically unrelated to either García's own prelude (in the opera aria) or the mostly new prelude by Puig in the *Échos* version, resembles the one in that version in avoiding the augmented second. (Bizet seems to have preferred to save that powerful symbol of southern Spain for the main melody **b,** to be discussed below.)
- Though the body of the entr'acte does not use an accompanimental rhythm of second-beat sixteenths, such as is found in the opera-aria version and in the *Échos* version, Bizet's new prelude does use that rhythm (with its implication of rapid guitar strumming), and in frank manner.
- Bizet's harmony throughout the body of the entr'acte is built almost entirely on a dominant pedal, just as it was in the opera aria and in the *Échos* version of the song (and no other versions).
- The upper voices of the accompaniment merely slide up and down in thirds, as if played by a hand moving along a guitar fretboard (against a repeated open-string low note, the aforementioned dominant)—and very much like the sliding sixths in the opera-aria and *Échos d'Espagne* versions.

It can therefore now stand as proven by internal musical evidence that Bizet used Puig's version—as published in *Échos d'Espagne,* which we already know that he owned—rather than any other as the basis for his entr'acte.

From Song to Bizet's 1875 Entr'acte

I have started with a number of fine details and disparities in order to identify the version of the song that Bizet knew. Once that is accepted, we are free to tackle the long-neglected task of comparing more closely that particular version to Bizet's entr'acte.

I have also thus far scanted some basic similarities between García's song and Bizet's free adaptation because they are common to all the versions of the song and thus would not have helped us identify the particular version that he used. In the remainder of this section I will focus on various features of García's song as it appeared in *Échos d'Espagne,* whether or not they are peculiar to that version.

The cantabile that our half-comic, half-romantic hero in the 1804 version says he sang to his balcony beauty is, as authorities on Spanish music agree, a decent imitation of a *polo,* a traditional Andalusian song in quick triple meter with melismatic passages on the cry "Ay!"[19] Indeed, the character in the opera himself, in the section leading up to the song itself, announces to his sister that he struck (what he took to be) a suitably Andalusian pose as he lifted his guitar and sang:

Con aire de Andaluz y su gracejo,
Del silencio tan sólo acompañado,
Mi voz dirijo al objeto amado.

[And,] with an Andalusian manner and grace,
Accompanied only by silence [and my guitar],
Aimed my voice at the beloved object.

One can immediately see from this how far García's opera is from folk culture: the main character is not so much inventing his story, and his serenade, from whole cloth as piecing them together from ethnic/regional stereotypes that were already widespread both within and outside Spain in 1804.[20]

The vocal melody of this song—identical or nearly so, as I said, in all versions—likewise has something of an "Andalusian manner and grace," for it is composed in what is sometimes called, even by Spanish musicologists, the Andalusian mode (or Andalusian scale), a tonal practice that has recently been renamed "dual tonicity" by Peter Manuel.[21] That is to say, the tune generally uses the pitches of the minor mode, but it tends to hover around the dominant, thereby tonicizing it at least as strongly as the nominal tonic, and may even end on that (tonicized) dominant.[22]

The result is a frequent occurrence of what is sometimes called a Phrygian relationship between the main note (the tonicized dominant) and the note above it (the flatted sixth degree—not, as in true Phrygian, the flatted second degree). In example 14.1 (García's song), the section that I have marked *l* ends with an emphatic juxtaposition

19. E.g., Radomski, *Manuel García*, 53; and Faustino Nuñez, "Polo," in *Diccionario de la música española e hispanoamericana*, ed. Emilio Casares Rodicio, José López-Calo, Ismael Fernández de la Cuesta, and María Luz González Peña ([Madrid?]: Sociedad General de Autores y Editores, 1999–2002), 8:873–74.

20. Grace was not, of course, the only characteristic that Andalusia could connote. In 1829, when the aging Manuel García gave his final performances in Paris, the music critic François-Joseph Fétis pondered whether he sang more like a "Castilian nobleman" or an "Andalusian muleteer." Quoted in Radomski, *Manuel García*, 252.

21. Peter Manuel, "From Scarlatti to 'Guantanamera': Dual Tonicity in Spanish and Latin American Musics," *Journal of the American Musicological Society* 88 (2002): 311–36. Cf. Peter Van der Merwe, *Roots of the Classical: The Popular Origins of Western Music* (Oxford: Oxford University Press, 2004), 46, 63–64, 102–3, 144–54, and 159–64.

22. More precisely, the song accepts some variability about whether the sixth and seventh scale degrees are flatted or not; in this regard, it resembles many other works that were composed—even in other centuries—in the minor mode, e.g., by J. S. Bach.

of the lowered sixth degree (A flat) and the dominant (G). In the last phrase of the song, though, García's vocal line finally comes to rest on the tonic. (See section *p*, before the coda, in ex. 14.1.)

But the *Échos d'Espagne* version of the song offers a largely different coda that does bring the music back to a very Andalusian-sounding conclusion on the dominant. In addition, this coda, which also serves as a prelude in the *Échos* version, features contrary motion between the two hands, one bar of which even amounts to literal voice exchange (see the first measures, marked *k*, in ex. 14.1).

I would suggest that this is where Bizet got the idea of beginning his adaptation of García's song with a few measures of music that, though largely independent of anything else in that song (besides possibly borrowing García's second-beat sixteenths), feature treble and bass chords moving in contrary motion to each other. But already in the first measures of the Bizet we begin to encounter details attributable to some combination of compositional genius and protomodernist experiment: the contrary motion here results in far harsher harmony than was typical for 1875 (much less 1804), harshness only slightly weakened for most of us by a lifetime of familiarity with these memorable measures. I draw attention particularly to the pandiatonic cluster of notes in the second beat of measure 2 in example 14.2.

Viewed as a formal whole, García's *polo* is a loose concatenation of different ideas that bear at most a family relationship to each other. The diagram presented in figure 14.4 shows that the six different ideas are stated either just once or else two or more times in succession; each idea thus treated then moves on to the next, but, except for the one in the prelude, none of them ever returns. The individual units also vary a good deal in phrase length, as the diagram shows, some stretching out an inherent eight-bar phrase by adding an extra measure or two of accompanimental vamp or by holding on to the final note in a vocal phrase for two or even four measures. The result is a sense of spontaneity and, perhaps, relaxation.

In contrast, Bizet creates an obsessive eight-bar structure for his piece that persists almost throughout. In the diagram of the Bizet aria (see fig.14.5), I try to keep things visually simple by not noting phrase lengths except in the few instances where a passage is *not* eight measures long. Only one of those exceptions is a flexibly structured developmental episode (**g**, fourteen measures long). The others are relatively rigid: an episode of eight-plus-eight measures, one of four measures, and a concluding one of nine measures, which is simply an eight-measure episode stretched by an extra measure toward the end as the piece collapses to silence.

Even more interestingly, Bizet actually offers three different melodies in turn—I call them **b, c,** and **f** in the diagram—over an identical eight-measure accompanimental pattern, labeled **x.** The first two, **b** and **c,** return several times, a bit rondolike, whereas **f** is stated just once. I do not find any mention in the Bizet literature of the astonishing fact that all three of these tunes, whenever they appear, are supported by the identical accompaniment. And yet surely, from the 1875 premiere onward, conductors, harpists, and players in the string section cannot fail to have noticed. If one

EXAMPLE 14.2. Georges Bizet, *Carmen,* entr'acte to act 4, from his own piano reduction in the Choudens piano-vocal score, marked here to coordinate with figure 14.5.

(*continued*)

EXAMPLE 14.2. (*continued*)

EXAMPLE 14.2. (*continued*)

301

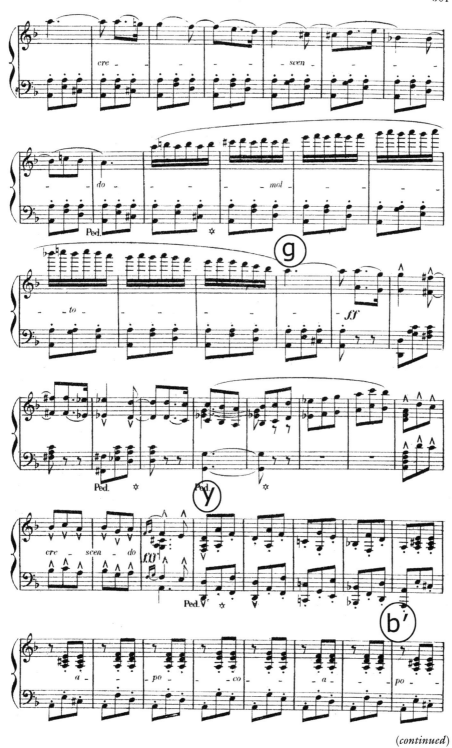

(*continued*)

EXAMPLE 14.2. (*continued*)

302

Enchaînez le N.º 25.

FIGURE 14.4. Structural diagram of Manuel García, "Cuerpo bueno, alma divina," as printed in *Échos d'Espagne* (1872).

k	prelude on $\hat{5}$ bass (including two measures of contrary motion)—7 + 4 mm. Presumably composed by the arranger, freely using material from the postlude of García's *polo* as found today only in the full aria (as transcribed in Radomski, *Manuel García*, 325–41, mm. 178–83)
l	"Cuerpo bueno" / "Tu dors[,] la belle amoureuse": 8 + 4 mm.
m	"Mira, que si non fallezco" / "Entends ma voix": 8 + 4 mm.
n	"Ay! ay! que faitigas" / "Hélas! parais!": 2 + 4 mm. (then just the 4)
o	coloratura with angled cresc./decresc. marks: 4 mm. (then 5)
cadenza	"Ah! yo espiro!" / "Ah!": 1 (long, free; equivalent to 4 mm.) + 4 mm.
p	cadential phrase to i
k'	postlude = prelude: 7 + 4 + 5 mm. (i.e., back to $\hat{5}$ bass)

```
k l l l l m  m  n  n  o  o  cadenza   p  p          k'
i-------------------------------------i---------------i
↑                         ↑              ↑
but sitting on 5̂:         functional     ending on 5̂ again
"dual tonicity"           tonality (PAC)
```

takes into consideration all the repetitions of **b** and **c,** the one statement of **f,** and the statements of the accompaniment without any melody atop (for example, the leftmost **x** in the bottom portion of figure 14.5 and the two in the coda), one tallies no fewer than thirteen statements (104 measures) of accompanimental pattern **x,** amounting to almost two-thirds of the entr'acte (if one discounts the eight-bar intro, which uses entirely different music).

Prejudicially Simplistic or Imaginatively Respectful of Spanish Folk Tradition?

How shall we interpret this stern self-constraint? Susan McClary has proposed that Bizet, in this and other numbers in *Carmen,* engages "static bass lines" and other "simplistic [processes]" that reflect the "timelessness" and "lack of interest in progress" that were, at the time, thought by Europeans to be typical of the Orient, including Spain and, especially, Spanish Gypsies.[23]

23. Susan McClary, *Georges Bizet: Carmen* (Cambridge: Cambridge University Press, 1992), 52. McClary's statement that "at the end, [Bizet] gives the main tune a decisively tonal harmonization to secure it" (*Georges Bizet: Carmen,* 106) is untrue; the music retains its modal quality to the last note. Nor is the "the concluding major [dominant] triad" understandable as "a picardy alteration of the phrygian tonic" (ibid.), because that A chord has been in the major mode throughout the

FIGURE 14.5. Structural diagram of Georges Bizet, *Carmen*, entr'acte to act 4.

Note: All passages are eight measures long unless otherwise indicated. Passages from the 1872 version of García's "Cuerpo bueno" are identified by italic letters.

a   pandiatonic (m. 2, beat 2: e–f–g cluster) but with variable $\hat{7}$ over $\flat\hat{5}$–$\flat\hat{4}$–$\flat\hat{3}$–$\flat\hat{4}$ whole-step tetrachord bass; hemiola makes the 8 mm. sound like 4 mm. of 3/2; based, arguably, on the prelude (presumably by the 1872 arranger) to García's "Cuerpo"

x $\hat{5}$-bass line and arpeggiated accompaniment: based on *l* in García's "Cuerpo"

b   octave-spanning descending melody

c   rising wind melody in sixteenth notes: based on *o* and ***cadenza*** in García's "Cuerpo"

d   episode mostly in III: 16 mm.

e   extension using trills and triplet runs (and modulating back to i)

f   yet a third descant (in addition to **b** and **c**) over the **x** bass line, using ♪♪♪♪ rhythm

g   development of **b**: 14 mm. (including, at the end, 4 mm. of mainly unison playing)

y   descending-tetrachord bass line and accompaniment ($\hat{8}$–$\flat\hat{7}$–$\flat\hat{6}$–$\flat\hat{5}$), without melody; analogous to the whole-step bass in the prelude (**a**): 4 mm.

b'   **b** but faltering toward the end, with fermata; melody hints at an augmented second

e'   accompaniment silent during triplet runs

x'   coda, dominant confirmation (quiet): 9 mm.

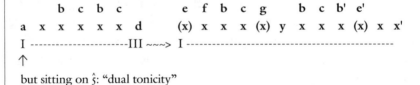

but sitting on $\hat{5}$: "dual tonicity"

An alternative explanation here seems more plausible and perhaps less censorious: Bizet imagined he was creating a kind of strophic-variation form (with a few contrasting episodes—including the fourteen-measure developmental one, **g**) that captured a practice central to much Spanish traditional music: setting up a repeating phrase of strummed and/or arpeggiated chords in the guitar (or guitars) and then adding vocal melodies (often with extended melismas) on top. (Of course, variation over a bass line or chordal pattern had also long been a distinctive feature of much composed music in Spain, as exemplified by the *diferencias* of Narváez or, later, Cabanilles, or the *roma-*

---

entr'acte. McClary's argument, a recurring one in her book, is echoed somewhat uncritically in Manuel, "From Scarlatti to 'Guantanamera,'" 316 n. (with specific reference to her on 55).

EXAMPLE 14.3. "Rondeña o Malagueña (Rasgueada)," as printed in Edoardo Ocón, *Cantos españoles* (1874 and later editions).

nesca, the *passamezzo antico,* or the chords associated with the *folia* melody.) In 1874, as Bizet was completing *Carmen,* the aforementioned anthology of Spanish folk songs edited by Eduardo Ocón appeared in Málaga and Leipzig, probably just a bit too late to be of any use to Bizet. It included (in addition to "Cuerpo bueno") a number of skeletal versions of heavily improvised musical events in various traditional Spanish genres, and some of the results display dissonance levels more intense than those in the songs that we know Bizet had encountered in *Échos d'Espagne.* (See ex. 14.3, whose "strummed" [*rasgueada*] chords sometimes involve intense harmonic clashes over a dominant open-fifth pedal—in other words, a $\hat{5}$ $\hat{9}$ pedal against a flat submediant chord—and then, after several repetitions, are topped with a vocal melody.)

But Bizet had only to look at the facing page in his copy of *Échos d'Espagne*—that is, the beginning of a different "Malagueña" (see the last three pages in example 14.1) —to find at least a simple example of a varied melody, in this case instrumental, over a repeated or, as in the case here, slightly altered chordal pattern (see passages marked **1** and—the varied restatement—**2**).

Writers, even Spanish ones, are perfectly content to state that the opening number of act 2—the "Chanson bohème" for Carmen, Frasquita, Mercédès, and the dancing Gypsy women—is in many ways an effective, imaginative re-creation of a flamenco performance, with the tempo building from *andantino* to *animato* to *plus vite* to a final *presto.* I would propose that in the entr'acte to act 4, Bizet has likewise captured—

but in a compressed, laconic, and emblematic rather than an expansively theatricalized manner—aspects of improvisational performance in Spanish traditional music. In this case, though, he allows the music to fade away to a whispered, mysterious final A major chord, the dominant in D minor. (This final chord links smoothly to the bright D *major* music of the opening of act 4 proper, outside the bullfight arena.)[24]

Tiersot did note that elsewhere in the entr'acte Bizet absorbs various "subordinate figurations gleaned from the [Spanish] songs [available to him]," but he gives few specifics.[25] And he made almost the opposite point when he praised Bizet's main melody—**b**—as "vastly superior" to the melodies in García's song because of its "singularly greater amplitude."[26] Edgar Istel specifically named the melody in García's song that I have labeled **m** as Bizet's source for the (indeed, singularly ample) melody **b**. This intriguing possibility was not generally picked up from Istel—either for confirmation or for refutation—by later writers. Both *l* and **m** end with the same augmented-second-invoking cadence, so there is no denying a similarity. Istel's proposal suggests, though not in so many words, that Bizet had peeled off the melody **m** from the **y** accompaniment and placed it instead over the **x** accompaniment: a remarkable, almost combinatorial approach to the collection of stylistic gestures available to him within García's "Cuerpo bueno." Istel's reason for preferring **m** to *l* as Bizet's model for **b** presumably derives from the fact that **m** begins at the upper $\hat{5}$ and descends. But then—as if to avoid going too low for the singer's tessitura—it jumps up an octave for the crucial cadence involving $\flat\hat{6}$–$\flat\hat{7}$–$\hat{5}$. This leap interrupts the effect of a single descending octave span, the very "ample" span that posterity, including Tiersot, has found so captivating in Bizet's melody **b**. Furthermore, it deserves to be noted that Bizet, if he turned the page in the "Malagueña," would have found a melody that, like his **b,** describes an entire octave descent from the upper fifth degree to the lower, and one that even ends with the same augmented-second melodic cadence that he surely found attractive in the García song and would use at the end of melody **b**.[27] (See the passage marked **3** in ex. 14.1, seventh page.)

The differences between the "Malagueña" melody (passage **3**) and Bizet's melody **b** are striking and revealing. The "Malagueña" melody—played by a mandolin over the guitar's descending broken thirds—uses the escape-note figure formulaically, at the end of every single measure. Bizet instead builds variety into his melody: first a straight scalar descent, then a reversal and ascent, and finally that special melodic cadence with the lowered sixth and raised seventh.[28] Similarly, it is interesting to

---

24. Lesley A. Wright, "A Musical Commentary," in *Carmen: Bizet,* ed. Nicholas John, English National Opera Guide 13 (London: John Calder, 1982), 34.

25. Tiersot, "Bizet and Spanish Music," 581.

26. More accurately, he was contrasting it in this regard to the vocal lines in both "Cuerpo bueno" and García's "El contrabandista." Ibid., 580.

27. Istel, *Bizet und "Carmen,"* 124–25.

28. Perhaps one hears a reflection of the *principle* of formulaic repetition in the slashing figure that recurs three times in a row in melody **f.**

compare this to Bizet's melody **f**: it too is a variant of a scalar descent from the upper fifth scale degree to the lower fifth, and it, too, repeats a single figure with emphatic literalness; but because that figure is two measures long, there are only three repetitions, not, as in the "Malagueña," an irritating eight.

Another artful touch: although each time **b** appears, it comprises two statements of the whole four-measure phrase just described, those two statements are not identical. Bizet always saves the distinctive escape-note vocal cadence for the end of the second statement (i.e., the eighth measure). The last time melody **b** appears in the entr'acte, Bizet puts a fermata over the escape note itself, D, as if finally allowing himself to linger on an aspect of (if we may use the language of the day) Spanish "national music" that he found "curious," "characteristic," or "touching."

Other Borrowings from "Cuerpo bueno"

Before leaving the act 4 entr'acte, I would like to point out three other of its crucial features that clearly derive from the García song. We have already seen that the music sits most of the time on the dominant, exactly as did the version of the García song that Bizet knew (and only that version). Interestingly, though, Bizet reworks the accompaniment, borrowing the chordal pitches and voicing from that version but spreading them across the bar by use of a triplet rhythm that, as Tiersot notes, is found in many other songs in the *Échos d'Espagne* anthology. I suspect, though, that this triplet rhythm was more familiar to him from a song that, although not in that anthology, was at the time García's biggest single hit: "El contrabandista" (see ex. 14.4).[29]

Besides the contrary motion in the introduction (**a**) and the tune and harmony of the first tune (**b**), two other specific passages are clearly indebted to García's "Cuerpo bueno." In "Cuerpo bueno," section ***m*** is a melodic phrase under which a descending tetrachord bass creates a dramatic departure from the previous sixty-one measures of uninterrupted sounding of the dominant in the bass. The equivalent passage in Bizet's entr'acte—letter **y** in figure 14.5—cranks the contrast up a notch by harmonizing García's descending tetrachord bass with parallel triads and by offering no melody over them to distract from their brazen voice leading. And Bizet, efficient

---

29. García's two famous opera-singing daughters, Maria Malibran and Pauline Viardot, each reportedly interpolated it at times into the lesson scene of Rossini's *Barber of Seville;* Berlioz loved the song and taught it to the poet Alfred de Vigny; and Liszt composed (in 1836), published (with a dedication to George Sand), and performed on various prominent occasions an amazing and all too rarely performed *Rondeau fantastique* upon this very song. Liszt's piece was greatly praised by Berlioz in the *Journal des débats,* 12 March 1837. Cf. Radomski, *Manuel García,* 68. The Liszt is now available on a CD containing also five other Spanish-style pieces by Liszt: Franz Liszt, *Rapsodie espagnole and Other Pieces on Spanish Themes,* Leslie Howard, piano, CDA67145 (London: Hyperion, 1997). The song deals with a smuggler of contraband goods, someone much like the opera's Dancaïre and Remendado.

EXAMPLE 14.4. Manuel García, "El contrabandista," mm. 106–24, showing triplet accompaniment not present in García's "Cuerpo bueno" but incorporated by Bizet into *Carmen*, entr'acte to act 4 (see ex. 14.2).

as ever, states the four-measure phrase only once, then slams back into his relentless eight-measure statements of the chordal phrase **x**.

The other element Bizet lifts from "Cuerpo bueno" is the quasi-melismatic passage—letter **c** in figure 14.5—stated initially by the piccolo and clarinet and later by the flute. Two recent writers have related it to the prelude of García's song, but both were using versions of the song that Bizet did not know.[30] In any case, there are, as Raoul Laparra noted back in 1935, two closer analogues within the vocal line of the song itself: some four-bar melismatic passages and a lengthy cadenza (**o** and *p,* respectively, in fig. 14.4).[31]

Once one correctly identifies which passage in the song is the likely source for Bizet's wind passage (**c**), one can proceed to note the artful ways in which Bizet reworks it. Both passages are built more or less entirely of two figures: rapid, almost warbling adjacent-note alternations (in *o*) and four-note turns (in *p*). But Bizet, rather than rigidly separating these two- and four-note figures as García does, combines them as the passage draws to a close (see ex. 14.5, m. 5), demonstrating a subtlety of compositional technique that we might not have appreciated without the García song for comparison.

Pitch content, too, is treated with greater suppleness. Whereas García's quick vocalises in the cadenza are almost entirely built on the top notes of what we might call the descending melodic minor mode (except for a sharped leading tone in two turns around the upper tonic),[32] Bizet increases variety by beginning his wind phrase (**c**) in the ascending minor and switching to the descending minor at the highest notes of the phrase. Indeed, I would suggest that such conventional nomenclature tends to flatten out the felt tension between the raised and lowered versions of the relevant

30. Radomski, *Manuel García,* 53; Carol Mikkelsen, ed., *Spanish Theater Songs: Baroque and Classical Eras* (Van Nuys, CA: Alfred, 1998), 49. Radomski's and Mikkelsen's claim of influence here—though factually erroneous because Bizet did not know García's introduction—may have been prompted by a good insight into the similarity in structural function: Bizet's wind solo, like García's introduction, serves as a kind of frame for the main tune, except that it follows the tune instead of preceding it. Istel, like Mikkelsen, relies on Ocón's transcription, in D minor (with the distinctive tempo marking of Larghetto). This leads Istel to adduce the identity of key (D minor) as proof that Bizet knew and used the García song; but the version that Bizet used is in C minor. Or did Ocón adopt the key from Bizet? Though intriguing and by no means implausible, this seems unlikely, because Ocón adopts the metronome mark from *Èchos d'Espagne:* ♪ = 126. However, in more significant respects—e.g., the prelude, the accompanimental figuration, and the harmonies—his version is closer to that published by Paccini in 1831.

31. Laparra focused on similarities—the rise and eventual fall, and, as he calculates it, the dependence on eight-measure phrases even in the cadenza—but did not note Bizet's departures from the model. Raoul Laparra, *Bizet et l'Espagne* (Paris: Librairie Delagrave, 1935), 60–62. I consider the four-bar passages to be closer analogues because, unlike García's prelude, they do not baldly state the interval of an augmented second; Bizet, as noted earlier, was careful in this song to avoid engaging too often what may have struck him as too abrupt or stereotypical a gesture. Cf. Jean-Pierre Bartoli, "L'orientalisme dans la musique française du XIXe siècle, la *ponctuation,* la seconde augmentée, et l'apparition de la modalité dans les procédures exotiques," *Revue belge de musicologie* 51 (1997): 137–70.

32. In my article "Nineteenth-Century Music," the equivalent parenthetical phrase about the ornamentally raised leading tone (p. 33) erroneously appears after instead of before the name Bizet, thus seeming to refer to the latter's entr'acte rather than the García song.

EXAMPLE 14.5. Bizet, *Carmen,* entr'acte to act 4: wind melody marked to show the artful combination of two-note alternation and turn from García's sections *o* and *p.*

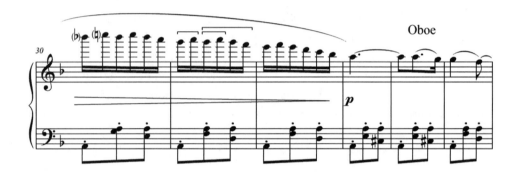

notes (the sixth and seventh degrees), especially because the C natural in m. 30 effectively turns a dominant seventh chord into a highly unusual dominant *minor* seventh. We may also note that Bizet was careful to omit the major third of this a[7] chord from the orchestral part in that measure, allowing the solo wind instruments to decide the mode of the chord. This careful stratification of texture further enhances the spotlit, soloistic nature of the wind instruments' role, perhaps even inviting some rhythmic flexibility in performance at that moment. (If any conductor has ever permitted the wind players such freedom, little sign of it can be heard on available recordings.)

Complex "Others" or Primitive "Us"?

All these additional features of the entr'acte, along with those discussed earlier, help us see that Bizet was applying a good deal of artistic complexity to his vision of Spanish traditional music. Such a conclusion may seem unsurprising: a master composer, thirty-six years old and at the top of his game, could hardly let himself pen a page of music that was not interesting in several mutually enriching ways. But the richness, and rich Spanishness, of these few powerful pages of music may have implications for how we think about the opera's locale and its inhabitants.

Describing this entr'acte as one of several numbers in the opera that make use of "static bass lines" in combination with "extensive melodic chromaticism" and/or "modal references," Susan McClary relates these devices to "orientalist" attitudes:

> The structures of [these numbers in *Carmen* and other] Orientalist pieces are usually simplistic, since complex formal processes are counted among the unique accomplishments of the West. The static bass lines of much of this music betray a Western belief in the timelessness, the lack of interest in progress among "Orientals." But what the "Orient" offers in exchange for progress and intellectual complexity is the sensuality the West tends to deny itself. Orientalist scores exploit color in place of the "purely musical ideas" that were the pride of nineteenth-century Absolute music. They foreground timbres alien to the standard orchestra or use the orchestra to mimic exotic instruments, such as the guitar or sinuous, nasal winds, as in the *entr'acte* to Act IV.[33]

Much of this matches what I hear and sense in various parts of the opera. But what I find in this particular entr'acte, as shown in figure 14.5 and the previous paragraphs, is not simplicity, much less timelessness. Quite the contrary, I find complexity and grim, forward-moving urgency of a different nature than that which one hears in a Beethoven sonata-form movement (though maybe also a little of the latter, in **g,** which I have described as "development"). If we can agree with McClary that the use of a "simplistic" musical process implies that the culture to which the composer attaches it is somehow primitive or naively simple—or, at best, wallowing in sensual self-indulgence—then perhaps the complexity, intensity, headlong drive, and suppleness that we find in Bizet's entr'acte, after having looked at it closely and contrasted it with the Spanish music materials that it incorporated and transformed, may be fairly described as implying that that culture exhibits intelligence, determination, even emotional depth. Bizet, far from exoticizing the Gypsies and the Spanish soldiers into inconsequentiality or beastliness, may have tapped in this entr'acte a vein of profound empathy for them and their joys and struggles, yearnings and delusions; he may even have seen aspects of himself and his fellow French citizens in these "Others."

My point fits well, I think, with one made by James Parakilas: that the score of *Carmen* "uses all the usual Spanish stereotypes and gives them all a serious twist."[34] This entr'acte and certain other Spanish-tinged numbers in the work grab hold of some of the standard devices—including the relaxed lyricism heard in García's "Cuerpo bueno"—of dancelike salon song and other kinds of Spanish and Spanish-style entertainment music, and tighten, elaborate, even refract or distort them in ways

---

33. McClary, *Georges Bizet: Carmen*, 52.

34. James Parakilas, "How Spain Got a Soul," in *The Exotic in Western Music,* ed. Jonathan Bellman (Boston: Northeastern University Press, 1998), 137–93 (164).

that signal that Spain and its inhabitants are no longer to be taken as decorations that exist for the distraction of lazy, smug audiences.

In this sense, much of what Manuel de Falla said about the Spanish portraits by Debussy, and particularly *Soirée dans Grenade* (from the *Estampes* for piano, 1904), can be applied as well to several of Bizet's numbers, and especially the entr'acte to act 4:

> The evocative nature of *Soirée dans Grenade* is nothing less than miraculous when one reflects on the fact that this music was written by a foreigner guided almost entirely by his visionary genius. Here we are truly confronted with Andalusia: truth without authenticity, so to speak, for not a bar is directly borrowed from Spanish folklore yet the entire piece down to the smallest detail makes one feel the character of Spain.[35]

What does not apply is that Bizet borrows not just motives and bars, but entire phrases and underlying musical processes, from Spanish music: whether by way of "folkloric" music (which Bizet may have heard in various Paris cafés and, I argue, may also have "heard" from the pages of *Échos d'Espagne*) or by way of indigenous artistic compositions (such as those of García and Iradier) that were themselves profoundly indebted to vernacular, largely unwritten performing traditions.[36]

Of course, my proposal (based on Parakilas's) that Bizet's opera takes Spain's "inhabitants" seriously skirts an obvious question: which inhabitants of Spain are being described in these few minutes of D minor or A Andalusian/Phrygian orchestral music, played with the curtain down, before act 4? Carmen and her Gypsy companions? Don José and his Spanish countrymen? Are we hearing, more generally, the Spain of dark alleys and nighttime assignations, in contrast to the D major that follows immediately, with the chorus gaily mingling in the sunlit plaza in front of the stadium? Or, if we can momentarily merge the plot of *Carmen* with the story the hero of García's *El criado fingido* is telling in his aria—if Bizet knew that story, perhaps directly or indirectly from García's daughter Pauline Viardot—we might envision in this orchestral music an ill-starred, nearly deranged lover singing a serenade with

35. From an article by Falla in *La revue musicale* (December 1920), as translated in its entirety by Edward Lockspeiser in appendix B, "Manuel de Falla on Debussy," in Lockspeiser, *Debussy: His Life and Mind*, corrected ed. (Cambridge: Cambridge University Press, 1978), 2:257. Similar quotations are found in Carol A. Hess, *Manuel de Falla and Modernism in Spain, 1898–1936* (Chicago: University of Chicago Press, 2001), 176–77.

36. One wonders if Bizet heard the Spanish opera singer Lorenzo Pagans, who repeatedly sang Spanish songs in Parisian homes to his own guitar playing and is memorialized in two superb paintings by Degas that show the painter's father listening intently. One of these—*Degas's Father Listening to Lorenzo Pagans Playing the Guitar* (c. 1869–72)—is now in the Boston Museum of Fine Arts. On Spanish singers in the Paris salons of Spanish émigrés and others, see Montserrat Bergadà, "Musiciens espagnols à Paris entre 1820 et 1868: État de la question et perspectives d'études," in *La Musique entre France et Espagne: Interactions stylistiques, 1870–1939*, ed. Louis Jambou (Paris: Presses de l'Université de Paris-Sorbonne, 2003), 17–38.

mounting desperation, then finally resignation or sullen depression, up to a balcony that is suddenly . . . empty. Perhaps his adored beauty has just run off with a much-acclaimed toreador?

This and other interpretive options I must leave hanging in the air. Other observers may propose equally valid readings, perhaps colored by performances they have experienced of the entr'acte or of the opera as a whole. Still, these diverse answers will surely recognize that Bizet and his very skillful and perceptive librettists, Henri Meilhac and Ludovic Halévy, created what Parakilas aptly described as a "gripping musical drama" out of "pulp-fiction . . . [and] magazine-romance stereotypes," thereby putting "real 'soul' into the put-on Spain." [37]

And when we find ourselves sensing the presence of human soul—or *alma* or *âme*—in a work of art, are we not coming within hailing distance of the German *Geist* that, we are told, reveals itself in the greatest works of the Austro-German classicists?

Bizet's Séguedille: Indebted to Iradier?

The other Spanish song that is regularly linked with Bizet's *Carmen* is Iradier's "El arreglito." The matter here is more straightforward, in a way. There is only one surviving version of the song: the one that Bizet knew, presumably in one of the editions published in Paris by Heugel in the 1860s (see figs. 14.6 and 14.7). It is often said that Bizet heard the song sung and copied it down, but the closeness of the accompaniment to Iradier's surely proves that Bizet—however he first encountered the song—ended up working from its published music.

McClary repeatedly refers to the song as a "cabaret number" or even a "pop song" and states emphatically that it *may* have been in the repertoire of Céleste Mogador, who was what we might call a nightclub performer. But it is worth mentioning that the French edition of the song carries an "as sung by" dedication to "Mlle [Zélia] Trebelli" of the Théâtre-Italien, a singer notable for her performance of some of the standard mezzo and contralto roles, such as Rosina, Urbain, Azucena, and, a few years later, Preziosilla. (Azucena and Preziosilla are, of course, Spanish Gypsies; in time, Trebelli would become an exponent of a third such role, Carmen.)[38] The cover of the sheet music can be seen in figure 14.7. Indeed, as recent research is revealing, Spanish music was in no way as disreputable as McClary's presentation might lead one

37. Parakilas, "How Spain Found a Soul," 163–66. Parakilas is, of course, referring (by way of a remark from the mezzo-soprano Teresa Berganza) not to Mérimée's startlingly brutal novella, but to the day's more usual literary and light-opera portrayals of Spain.

38. Zélia Trebelli [Gloria Caroline Gillebert] was born in Paris in 1838 and died in Étretat on 18 August 1892. Her Italianate stage name evidently derives from her family name (minus the initial G), spelled backward. She can be seen as Amneris in an illustration of the end of act 3 of Verdi's *Aida* as staged at Her Majesty's Theatre, London (1879). See Nicholas John, ed., *Aida: Giuseppe Verdi*, English National Opera Guide 2 (New York: Riverrun Press, 1980), 82.

FIGURE 14.6. Short history of Sebastián Iradier, "El ar[r]eglito: La promesse de mariage" [*chanson havanaise*] (Paris: Heugel, c. 1865).

- First published by Enrique Abad in Madrid (1857, 1863) and in Paris (under the general title *Hom[m]age à sa Majesté la Reine d'Espagne* (c. 1857 [Alonso, *Cien años*, xv–xvi]). The date of 1840 that is sometimes given (e.g., Arno Fuchs, "Habanera," in *Die Musik in Geschichte und Gegenwart: Allgemeine Enzyclopädie der Musik*, ed. Friedrich Blume, 17 vols. (Kassel: Bärenreiter, 1949–86), 5:1186–90, is presumably erroneous.

- Published as "El ar[r]eglito" (Heugel et Cie., [1863]), pl. no. H. 2888, with French words by D. Tagliafico; survives in the British Library, the Biblioteca Nacional (Madrid), and the Kunitachi College of Music Library (Tokyo). A facsimile of the title page of this edition is reproduced in Draayer, *Canciones de España*, p. x, and in figure 14.7, showing the dedication to "Mlle [Zélia] Trebelli of the Théâtre-Italien."

- Distributed more widely (one assumes) in *Fleurs d'Espagne: Album 1864; [25] Chansons espagnoles . . . chantées par Mesdames Viardot . . . [et al.]; paroles françaises de [D.] Tagliafico & P[aul] Bernard* (Heugel, 1865). "El ar[r]eglito" is no. 3. One copy is at Oxford University.

- In the piano-vocal score of *Carmen*, prepared by Bizet himself in 1875, the Habanera contains the following footnote: "Imitée d'une chanson espagnole. Propriété des Editeurs du *Ménestrel* [i.e., Heugel]."

- The *Fleurs d'Espagne* edition was reprinted as *Chansons espagnoles del Maëstro Yradier (avec double texte Espagnole et Français)*, trans. Paul Bernard and D. Tagliafico (H. Heugel, 1882 [Harvard University]), 18–25 (pl. no. H. 5585). The song in question (no. 3) is dedicated to the mezzo Zélia Trebelli. The word "arreglito" is consistently spelled with one "r."

- The *Chansons espagnoles* version of the *Fleurs d'Espagne* collection presumably was reprinted over the years, as copies survive in a number of libraries. Bizet's wife (or daughter—accounts vary) recalled that the composer owned a copy, though Winton Dean plausibly supposes that she meant *Échos d'Espagne*.

- Celsa Alonso, ed., *Cien años de canción lírica española*, vol. 1, Música hispana, Serie C, Antologías 8 (Madrid: Instituto Complutense de Ciencias Musicales, 2001), 221–27. Alonso bases her edition on the Paris edition, with corrections derived from the Madrid edition. Alonso's volume also prints García's "El contrabandista," an anonymous song ("La neguita") that Édouard Lalo uses in the *Symphonie espagnole*, and other intriguing items.

- Suzanne Rhodes Draayer, ed., *Canciones de España: Songs of Nineteenth-Century Spain* (Lanham, MD: Scarecrow Press, 2003), 123–31. Corrects a note in m. 26. Based upon the separate Heugel publication of the song (see fig. 14.7).

- CD recording: A straightforward performance is included on the CD that accompanies Draayer, *Canciones de España* (Suzanne Rhodes Draayer, soprano, and Judy Stafslien, piano).

FIGURE 14.6.(*continued*)

> - CD recording: A performance done in more of a "café style" was released in 2000, with the text split (in a somewhat misleading manner) between a male and female singer and the piano accompaniment fleshed out for a small ensemble: Felipe Sánchez, dir., *En un salón de la Habana: Habañeras y contradanzas (1830–1855),* with Noemí Mazoy, soprano; César Carazo, tenor; and other members of Axivil Criollo, CD 64073 (RTVE Música, 2000).

to think.[39] This is not to deny that Galli-Marié's performance of the role of Carmen transgressed the boundaries of bourgeois propriety—a different point entirely, well supported by some of the newspaper and magazine reviews published by Lesley Wright.[40]

Bizet's alterations to Iradier's melody have been keenly, if briefly, noted by Edgar Istel, Raoul Laparra, Winton Dean, Susan McClary, James Parakilas, and others, and a closer analysis—like that provided above for the entr'acte—would prove revealing.[41] For my present purposes, I would like to stress merely that one might link the words of the Iradier song to the dramatic situation in a later number in Bizet's act 1, the Séguedille and duo. Or, to put it more cautiously, we might propose that Iradier's words were misunderstood in such a way as to suggest the plot carried out in the Séguedille.

I say "might propose" for a reason. Iradier's song—parts of whose text are given in figure 14.8—is a conversation between a rather ardent suitor and his somewhat proud but teasing girlfriend. Iradier neglected to state the two characters' names, but the woman calls the man Pepito, and he addresses her as "Chinita mía," which could mean either "my Chinita" or else "my little darling." (The word begins a line of verse, and thus the fact that it is capitalized does not help us distinguish. The French translation in the 1865 publication treats it as her name, ignoring that Pepito addresses her again, later in the song, with a parallel expression: "Vidita mía," "my precious life.") Furthermore, either Iradier or his publisher neglected to give much punctuation or to indicate which of the two characters sings which phrases. (The two characters never sing at the same time, and the vocal line is written on a single staff.) Thus, one might easily

39. See Bergadà, "Musiciens espagnols," 23–26, 30; the article includes chronological and alphabetical lists.

40. Wright, *"Carmen": Dossier de presse,* iv. The reviews collected in Wright's book offer objections to "the movements of [Galli-Marié's] lower body"), 23; "astonishing moves of her physiognomy" (des jeux de physionomie étonnants), 28; the need for more "sober" (*sobre*) movement of the shoulders, 28; and so on.

41. Istel, *Bizet et "Carmen,"* 111–22; Laparra, *Bizet et l'Espagne,* 18–21, 28–29; McClary, *Georges Bizet: Carmen,* 51–56, 74–77; Dean, *Bizet,* 229–30; Parakilas, "How Spain Got a Soul," 165.

FIGURE 14.7. Sebastián Iradier, "El ar[r]eglito," sheet music (Paris: Heugel, c. 1865), "as sung by Mlle Trebelli of the Théâtre-Italien." Courtesy Sibley Music Library, Eastman School of Music.

apportion the second stanza (lines 6–9, indented as in figure 14.8) in such a way as to create quite a little drama: he declaring that the two will be lovers ("y enamorados"—the measure is marked fortissimo), she responding only (in a piano dynamic) that she will join him on the dance floor ("una dancita vamos a bailar").

I am not claiming that this interpretation was intended as a valid option by Iradier. It is clearly wrong if one considers the entire text of the song. (Suzanne Rhodes Draayer, in her modern edition, gives a more reliable reading, in which these lines

FIGURE 14.8. Translation of text of Sebastián Iradier, "El arreglito" (based freely on Draayer, *Canciones de España*, 123–31).

Note: Presumed "he" lines are in roman font, "she" in italic.

Chinita mía, ven por aquí	You little darling, come here to me
Que tú ya sabes que muero per ti.	For you already know that I die for you.
No voy allí	*No, I won't go there*
Porque no tengo confianza en ti.	*Because I have no confidence in you.*
Qué, si? *Qué no, no, no [etc.].*	Yes? *No [I don't].*
Si tú me quieres dilo quedito	If you want me, say it softly
y en seguidita seré tu arreglito	And in a little while I will be your match.
y enamorados sin abusar	And, in love with each other, without imposing,
una dancita vamos a bailar.	Let us go do a little dance together.
[Or *she/he/she*:]	
Si tú me quieres dilo quedito	*If you want me, say it softly*
y en seguidita seré tu arreglito.	*And in a little while I will be your match.*
Y enamorados! *Sin abusar*	And [we'll be] full of love for each other! *[Well,] without imposing,*
una dancita vamos a bailar.	*We will [at least] do a little dance together.*
. . .	
. . . yo veo con gran pesar	*. . . I see with great regret*
Que todo es guasa, música celestial.	*That all [men's talk of love] is teasing and music of the spheres.*
. . .	
Si tú me juras serás constante	*[But] if you swear to me that you will be faithful*
. . . yo te lo juro que tu arreglito	*. . . I swear to you that in no case*
por ningún caso te faltará.	*Will your match fail you.*

Note: In the underlaid French text, reproduced below, the woman expresses her doubts even more sarcastically, but likewise yields in the end.

Chinita mia, danse avec moi,	My darling, dance with me,
Ne sais-tu pas que je me meurs pour toi?	Don't you know that I'm dying away for you?
Pepito mio, mourir pour moi!	*Pepito mio, dying because of me!*
Le beau discours, je n'en crois rien, ma foi!	*Such fancy talk, I don't believe a word of it!*
. . .	
Veux-tu, mon âme, dis, sans façon,	Do you want (oh my soul)—say it plainly!—
Être ma femme, oui? Pour tout de bon?	To be my wife? Yes? Seriously?
Chanson charmante, au doux refrain,	*What a lovely song, with a tender refrain,*
Pepito chante, jusqu'à demain. . . .	*Pepito sings, until tomorrow comes. . . .*
Je suis unie, à toi, Pepito, et pour jamais!	*I am united with you, Pepito, forever!*

in the song are entirely assigned to the man; see fig. 14.8).[42] Still, this very "he/she" division of the four lines, however erroneous, is one that a strong, intelligent singer from Ecuador who performed the song at my request in an undergraduate class immediately landed upon when typing up the words and translating them for distribution to the students. Perhaps she was influenced by the "natural" (i.e., long culturally inculcated) tendency in so much European music to associate a loud (forceful) dynamic with maleness and a soft (gentle, yielding) one with femaleness. Perhaps through the same gender logic, this treatment of the four lines as a bantering exchange between two singers was adopted a few years later in what was to my knowledge the song's first-ever commercial recording (details are given in fig. 14.6), by the freely historicist Spanish dance band Axivil Criollo. In the transcription of the four indented lines in fig. 14.8, I have put Chinita's/"darling's" supposed lines in italics, Pepito's supposed two words in roman. And I have provided the exclamation point that suits this reading of Pepito's two words. This (apparent) parrying of (he, loudly:) "Love?" / (she, softly:) "*No, dance!*" is, of course, precisely what happens at the crux of Bizet's Séguedille and duo (see fig. 14.9). Did Bizet and his librettists, early in the process of creating the opera's scenario, page through various Iradier songs, stumble upon this passage, and then—truly stumbling—read its Spanish text in the same way that my Ecuadoran singer and the musicians of Axivil Criollo did? Did they thus get the idea from Iradier of creating a number—there's nothing like it in the Mérimée novella—in which a badgering Don José tries to persuade Carmen to promise to love him and she merely replies with an agreement to go dancing ("Oui, nous danserons la séguedille . . . ")?[43]

I also wonder whether Bizet and his librettists were more generally intrigued by other lines of text in the song—either in the original Spanish or in the French singing text that the early editions of the song also provided—whose meaning, about men's untrustworthy promises, *is* crystal clear. One hears in them a voice that, to my mind, is very like that of Bizet's taunting heroine in the Séguedille and elsewhere in the opera.

If I am right about a possible influence of the words of Iradier's song (in Spanish or French) on the end of act 1 of *Carmen,* or even on the characterization of its teasing

42. Suzanne Rhodes Draayer, ed., *Canciones de España: Songs of Nineteenth-Century Spain* (Lanham, MD: Scarecrow Press, 2003), 123–31. On the CD accompanying the anthology, Draayer sings the entire song rather than splitting it between a male and a female performer as Axivil Criollo do.

43. On a related matter—what Carmen means by "Oui"—see Ralph P. Locke, "What Are These Women Doing in Opera?" in *En travesti: Women, Gender Subversion, Opera,* ed. Corinne Blackmer and Patricia Juliana Smith (New York: Columbia University Press, 1995), especially 69–74 and 86–87. Lesley Wright has kindly confirmed for me that, in the published piano-vocal score, prepared and proofread by Bizet himself, the composer put a comma after the "Oui," though the tail of the comma wore off in later printings.

FIGURE 14.9. Bizet, *Carmen*, Séguedille and duo (act 1), excerpt.

Don José:	
Si je cède, si je me livre,	If I give in, if I turn myself over [to you],
Ta promesse tu la tiendras . . .	You will keep your promise. . . .
Ah, si je t'aime, Carmen,	Ah, if I love you, Carmen,
Carmen, tu m'aimeras!	Carmen, you will love me!
Carmen:	
Oui, nous danserons la Séguedille	Yes, we will dance the seguidilla
En buvant du Manzanilla, ah!	While we drink manzanilla wine, ah!
Don José:	
Chez Lillas Pastia, tu le promets?	At Lillas Pastia's: you promise me?
Carmen . . . tu le promets! . . .	Carmen . . . you promise! . . .

heroine generally, then this connection would prove that Bizet knew Iradier's song months before he decided to use it as the basis for the version we know of Carmen's entrance song (whose words begin "L'amour est un oiseau rebelle"), the well-known version that is, musically, a habanera. This number was the last extended stretch of music composed for the opera when the performer of the role of Carmen rejected—wisely—the charming but relatively bland song that Bizet originally wrote for that spot, to many of the same words.[44]

Besides, whether one accepts that (tentative) conclusion or not, there is no doubt that Bizet knew Iradier's song. And its words, the sarcastic French ones (the woman: "*Le beau discours!*") almost more than the (possibly misunderstood) Spanish ones (the man: "y enamorados," misreadable as "Y enamorados!"), suggest that some crucial aspects of Carmen herself—such as her tendency to ridicule her lover and his claims of passionate devotion, especially in act 2, when he interrupts her dancing to go back to the bunkhouse—were not as unprecedented as one might think. Although such traits had not yet been put on the Parisian operatic stage, they were already "hiding in plain sight": in sheet music of 1863 that graced the piano racks of many middle- and upper-class music lovers, bearing a prominent dedication to, and portrait of, one of France's more prominent mezzos (see fig. 14.7), or in Iradier's *Fleurs d'Espagne* anthology, published a year later.

44. Bizet's first song for this spot (which begins with the familiar words "L'amour est enfant de Bohème") is emphatically not a habanera. It remains unpublished, though bits of it were visible in the appendix to Oeser's "new critical edition" of the opera. This number can be heard on Georges Bizet, *Carmen*, Orchestre du Capitole de Toulouse, cond. Michel Plasson, with Angela Gheorghiu and Roberto Alagna, CD 724355743428 (EMI Classics, 2003). It is discussed in rich detail in Hervé Lacombe, "La version primitive de l'air d'entrée de Carmen: Réflexion sur la dramaturgie et l'autorialité' d'un opéra," in *Aspects de l'opéra français de Meyerbeer à Honegger*, ed. Jean-Christophe Branger and Vincent Giroud (Lyon: Symétrie, 2009), 29–45.

In any case, whatever one thinks of my speculation about the Iradier song's possible link to the events that occur in the course of the Séguedille and duo, the various other connections that I have proposed here regarding the uses to which Bizet put García's "Cuerpo bueno" seem to me solid—and suggestive of wider implications worth pursuing. We shall be spilling more ink about the Spanish element in *Carmen* for some time to come, and—I hope—thereby coming closer to understanding the extent and multiple implications of cultural transfer within French lyric theater in the age of some of its greatest achievements.

La princesse paysanne du Midi

Steven Huebner

The stage door of an unnamed American opera house, a cold and blustery winter's night, a small bundle "carefully done up in a gray shawl" . . . and in it, a baby girl. So begins the novel *Signora* (1902) by the American music critic and operatic lexicographer Gustav Kobbé. An old chorister-turned-custodian named Yudels finds the infant, and the cast (it is a *Carmen* night) gathers quickly around. After a few moments of absorbed silence around the sleeping child, "the German mezzo asked Yudels this practical question: 'Vat are you going to geeve her to eat?'"[1] The little Italian baritone suggests a dish of macaroni. Implausibly, no one thinks of calling the authorities. No need to do so in Kobbé's tale, for Yudels instantly bonds with the baby and resolves to look after her, enshrining her anonymity in the title of the novel. He soon hoists Signora with a pulley up to his little room high above the Plaza del Toro of the last act.

Signora grows up in the opera house, a child of Yudels, but also of the choristers, set designers, costumiers, and opera stars with inflated egos. The real-life identities of the performers would not have been difficult for opera fans of the day to discern in Kobbé's roman à clef: Édouard and Jean are the de Reszke brothers, the German mezzo Mannheim-Weink is Ernestine Schumann-Heink, the handsome bass Planky is Pol-Henri Plançon, and the temperamental Carmen of that memorable winter's

1. Gustav Kobbé, *Signora* (New York: Thomas Y. Crowell, 1902), 34.

FIGURE 15.1. Portrait of Emma Calvé as Carmen. Emma
Calvé, *My Life*, trans. Rosamond Gilder (New York: D. Appleton, 1922), 101. Courtesy of the Music Library, University
of North Carolina at Chapel Hill.

evening, the French soprano Caravé, is Emma Calvé. Signora becomes particularly
attached to Caravé, the "greatest Carmen that ever lived."[2] As a baby and young girl,
Signora sits up in Caravé's dressing room to watch the prima donna prepare for her
favorite role: the makeup, the costume that Caravé herself bought from a secondhand
shop in Spain, the spontaneous swaying of her body to the rhythm of the Habanera
with "all the arch coquetry she knew so well how to put into the role."[3] And the
inevitable dropping of the mirror: if it did not break, the soprano declared that her
performance would go well. "Strange mixture of music, coquetry, and superstition!

2. Ibid., 67.
3. Ibid., 72.

Is it a wonder that no other singer could approach her as Carmen?"[4] As she grows up, in her absorption with Caravé Signora learns the role of Carmen by heart, at first imitating all of the prima donna's true-to-life gestures and then experimenting with her own in the same spirit.

Kobbé's narrator emphasizes that Caravé/Calvé is temperamentally suited to Bizet's protagonist and, by extension, that she brings rich realism to the character. Although Kobbé's novel can hardly lay claim to the rank of great literature, it is worth dwelling a bit longer on its refractions of realism in the inherently artificial genre of opera. Removing the veil of stage illusion, *Signora* offers a compelling look behind the scenes—the cannon balls dropped into a trough to make thunder, the wooden horses in *Die Walküre,* the little boy who climbs into the dragon in *Siegfried* in order to manipulate its limbs. That's the artificial part, and Signora herself participates from the wings. Yet there is also the matter of increasing realism on the stage, the denial of illusion—which brings us to the end of the novel. Signora is a young woman now, Planky has become enamored of her, Caravé has retired, and a new Carmen and Don José have been hired for Bizet's opera. The haughty tenor, one M. Varu, naturally assumes that Signora will reciprocate the attention he lavishes upon her. She will have none of it, preferring the warm friendship of Planky to the blandishments of the newcomer. Varu's jealousy percolates. Meanwhile, opening night does not go well for the new Carmen. In a fit of anxiety and desperation, she impulsively cancels her second performance just before the curtain. Nurtured in the part by Caravé, Signora is available—of course—to save the day. Planky beams as the audience greets her performance in the first two acts with wild enthusiasm. Fired by the coquetry of Signora's acting and seething with anger, Varu's Don José lunges at Planky's Escamillo in the third-act dagger fight. But artifice breaks down, and it requires all of Planky's manly force to escape real injury. Yet the show must go on: Caravé would not have had it any other way had she been there. Planky fears the worst for Signora in the concluding duet. He sees the savage look in Varu's eyes, the raised blade. And . . . in the nick of time—and (miraculously) unseen by the audience—Planky interposes his cloak between Varu's weapon and Signora's back. Carmen falls, the crowd streams out of the bullring, and Don José is led off. "Signora had been saved—and so had the scene."[5] Varu slinks away, right onto the next steamer bound for Europe, and the heroine falls into Planky's arms in her dressing room.

"La commedia è finita" sings Tonio after Canio brutally stabs Nedda on stage at the end of Leoncavallo's *I pagliacci,* in which the real-life Nedda-Canio-Silvio love triangle gets mapped onto the Columbina-Pagliaccio-Arlecchino commedia dell'arte stage business. (It will be recalled, however, that unlike Planky, Silvio cannot intervene in time to save his lover from her husband.) Taken on its own terms, Kobbé's conclusion inscribes the slice-of-life approach onto the imagined plot of the novel

4. Ibid., 74.
5. Ibid., 203.

(and the real plot of the opera) by representing an erasure of the boundary between fiction and reality. *Pagliacci* became a banner for verismo opera for the same reason. Whether intentionally or not, Kobbé's mutation of *Carmen* into a *Pagliacci*-like situation hints at the ancestry of veristic opera in Bizet's work, a venerable interpretative tradition alluded to several times by Andreas Giger in his excellent *Handwörterbuch* article on verismo.[6] Mosco Carner is particularly forceful on this point: "Don José's *crime passionel* in Act IV of *Carmen* was the point of departure for all those scenes of stabbing, strangling, execution, suicide and attempted rape that are found in realistic opera of the following period."[7]

My purpose in drawing attention to Kobbé's novel, however, lies not just with the well-articulated chiaroscuro between artifice and reality that emerges at the end, but mainly with the figure of Caravé/Calvé—the "greatest Carmen that ever lived"—as the symbol of a shift in operatic aesthetics. For in Kobbé's account, the conflation of singers and their roles occurs not only in the actions of a berserk tenor, but in the very identification of Caravé with the role of Carmen earlier in the story, that is, the slice of life enacted via the claims of a performer to authenticity.

It is worth recalling that verismo was notoriously difficult to define as an operatic phenomenon after it erupted from the blockbuster success of Pietro Mascagni's *Cavalleria rusticana* (1890), which influenced works by Leoncavallo, Giordano, Puccini, and, on the French side, Jules Massenet in *La Navarraise* and *Sapho*. Even the term's origins lie in tangled paradoxes: as Giger points out, Giovanni Verga never applied it himself to his own short stories and novellas, important components of veristic opera's literary substrate (he preferred the French-derived term "naturalism"). Furthermore, Verga developed an emotionally restrained style, with characters given to relatively terse utterances and narrative passages that reflect cool detachment. Such an impersonal aesthetic runs against the impassioned language of Italian opera, though of course the adroit critic will argue that standards of measurement need to be adjusted according to the premises of any genre. And in the wake of French *grand opéra* and Verdi's works, violent conclusions and shocking juxtapositions in themselves hardly seem well-profiled markers of a veristic category in opera, though reactions against previous idealizations of lower classes as well as attendant authentic detail in staging were perhaps more indicative. Musical style category, dramaturgical recipe, period marker in Italian opera: Giger unpacks verismo from these and other perspectives, and to his survey we might add the writing of Matteo Sansone, Adriana Guarnieri-Corazzol, Manfred Kelkel, and others, including myself, in a recent study of *La Navarraise*.[8]

6. Andreas Giger, "Verismo," in *Handwörterbuch der musikalischen Terminologie* (Wiesbaden: Steiner, 2004).

7. Mosco Carner, *Giacomo Puccini: Tosca* (Cambridge: Cambridge University Press, 1985), 8.

8. See Adriana Guarnieri Corazzol, "Opera and Verismo: Regressive Points of View and the Artifice of Alienation," trans. Roger Parker, *Cambridge Opera Journal* 5 (1993): 39–53; Manfred Kelkel, *Naturalisme, vérisme et réalisme dans l'opéra de 1890 à 1930* (Paris: Librairie philosophique

In all this critical work, however, period performers receive relatively short shrift for their contributions to the articulation of operatic realism, both Italian and French. Emma Calvé certainly exemplifies this new trend. What I suggest about her in the remainder of this essay cries out for more extended consideration in light of her contemporaries in the operatic firmament: Nellie Melba and Luisa Tetrazzini, and, in a more veristic vein, Gemma Bellincioni (the first Santuzza), Cesira Ferrani (the first Mimì), Rosina Storchio (the first Butterfly), and many others. In the present context of a collection of studies about French opera and its institutions, the example of Calvé will also serve as a reminder that performers played a role in the ineluctable process by which institutions shape genres and genres shape institutions. The Opéra-Comique in this period was not only *Manon, Pelléas et Mélisande,* and *Carmen,* but also the performers who brought stage characters to life, particularly in the case of those who seemed to "own" a role for a period of time, such as Sibyl Sanderson and Manon, Mary Garden and Mélisande, and Calvé and Carmen. This might almost go without saying were it not that Calvé was also something of a transitional figure on the road to a phenomenon more common in the twentieth century. For she was among the first opera singers who pursued a truly global career, one that included extended tours of the United States and Asia. As she put it in the title of her French-language memoirs, *Sous tous les ciels j'ai chanté.*[9] Such peripatetic inclinations among leading performers would contribute to a weakening of closely knit performing troupes—one sense that the expression "operatic institution" might have—at least at the major opera houses of the world.

J. Vrin, 1984); Jay Nicolaisen, *Italian Opera in Transition, 1871–1893* (Ann Arbor: UMI Research Press, 1977), 243–50; and Matteo Sansone, "Verismo," in *New Grove Dictionary of Music and Musicians,* ed. Stanley Sadie, 2nd ed. (London: Macmillan, 2001), 26:477–78; as well as Steven Huebner, "*La Navarraise* face au vérisme," in *Le naturalisme sur la scène lyrique,* ed. Jean-Christophe Branger (Saint Étienne: Publications de l'Université de Saint Étienne, 2004), 129–49.

9. Emma Calvé, *Sous tous les ciels j'ai chanté* (Paris: Plon, 1940). One sign of Calvé's international popularity is that she published her English-language memoirs first: Calvé, *My Life,* trans. Rosamond Gilder (n.p.: D. Appleton, 1922; reprint, New York: Arno Press, 1977). Although both books contain many of the same anecdotes and are concordant on major points, they are largely different accounts. The most extended biography of Calvé is Jean Contrucci, *Emma Calvé: La diva du siècle* (Paris: Albin Michel, 1989). Contrucci follows *Sous tous les ciels* quite closely and folds in period reviews from the French press. This is a novelistic account that makes for an enjoyable read but is also hampered by its avoidance of English-language sources (including *My Life* and *Signora*) as well as by vague documentation of its findings. Two earlier studies, more important for the primary documents they bring to light than for their pretensions to scholarly method are Georges Girard, *Emma Calvé: La cantatrice sous tous les ciels* (Millau: Ed. Grand Causse, 1983), and Girard, "Emma Calve étoile dans tous les cieux, cigale sous tous les ciels," *Les cahiers Rouergats* 5 (1971): 9–46. As president of the Société d'Études millavoises et des amis d'Emma Calvé, Girard has safeguarded many of her papers. He recently communicated a number of these papers to Jean-Christophe Branger, who used some of them in "Massenet et Emma Calvé, la 'Duse lyrique,'" *Sapho; La Navarraise,* vol. 17 of *L'avant-scène opéra* (2003): 50–53. Branger kindly made this material available to me.

Emma Calvé (Rosa-Emma Calvet) was born in the Cévennes in 1858, raised there except for a four-year period in Spain, and taken to Paris at age twenty to develop her obvious vocal gifts. Studies with Mathilde Marchesi, a debut at the Théâtre-Italien in 1884 opposite no less an artist than Victor Maurel in the premiere of Théodore Dubois's ephemeral *Aben-Hamet,* further work at the Opéra-Comique, and supportive comments from Charles Gounod followed in the mid-1880s. After hearing her Marguerite in Nice, the publisher Edoardo Sonzogno offered to smooth her way to engagements with the French repertoire in Italy.[10] Noticed by the French press—but not celebrated—she repaired south of the Alps to improve her fortunes.

In September 1886, soon after her arrival in Florence, she experienced a professional epiphany when she attended a performance of *La dame aux camélias* given by the theatrical company managed by the great actress Eleonora Duse. Said Calvé of Duse's Marguerite Gauthier: "What a revelation! This is the artistry to which one must aspire. I would have never thought it possible that a human being could give so much of herself."[11] Or, in her American memoirs: "Hers was the spark that set my fires alight. Her art, simple, human, passionately sincere, was a revelation to me. It broke down the false and conventional standard of lyric expression to which I had become accustomed."[12] Indeed, if Calvé's recollections are to be believed, during those early months in Italy she became something of a Duse groupie: reading biographies, attending many performances in succession, and standing by stage doors in vain attempts to meet the elusive actress who was just then rising to international prominence. Although Calvé herself had kind words for Sarah Bernhardt in her memoirs,[13] many of her contemporaries contrasted Duse's ostensible genuineness with the "false and conventional standard of lyric expression" of the French actress, as Helen Sheehy so aptly describes it in her recent biography of Duse.[14] For Edmond Rostand, Bernhardt was the "queen of posture," a paragon of beautiful intonation and sculptural elegance.[15] Whereas Bernhardt as Marguerite Gauthier would repeat the same striking gestures night after night, Duse cultivated a more spontaneous impression, changing details according to the emotional temperature and her state of mind. She often shunned stage makeup and elaborate costume, as Calvé noted: "She taught me

10. Calvé, *Sous tous les ciels,* 29.

11. "Quelle révélation! Voilà l'art auquel il faut aspirer. Je n'aurais jamais cru possible qu'un être pût donner autant de soi." Ibid., 41.

12. Calvé, *My Life,* 60.

13. Ibid., 171–74.

14. Helen Sheehy, *Eleonora Duse: A Biography* (New York: Alfred A. Knopf, 2003). See also William Weaver, *Duse: A Biography* (San Diego: Harcourt, Brace, Jovanovich, 1984).

15. As cited in Sheehy, *Eleonora Duse,* 47.

to appreciate sincerity in art, a sincerity which in her case went to the length of being unwilling to make up for the stage."[16] She communicated anger as effectively through understatement and chilling silence as through vocal eruption. So in tune with her body was Duse that she could blush or blanch at will. In short, her art was intense, shot through with attention to detail right down to small gestures of the body and face, and infused with empathy for her characters. As Duse herself put it: "Acting? That ugly word! If it were only *acting*. . . . Those poor women in my plays have so entered my heart and my head that while I do my utmost to make them understood to those who listen to me, almost as if I wanted to comfort them, it is they that have slowly wound up comforting me!"[17] While we must acknowledge that what it is to be "natural" is relative and changes from generation to generation, to read accounts of Duse on stage is to suspect that even today her performances would be deemed true to life.

Among the many roles that Calvé saw Duse perform was Santuzza in Giovanni Verga's adaptation for the stage of his famous story *Cavalleria rusticana*. In 1890, six years after the premiere of the play, Pietro Mascagni's operatic version had much greater success than it, and although the distinction of creating Santuzza went to Bellincioni, Calvé was soon performing the part to great acclaim in Italy. When Léon Carvalho returned to the directorship of the Opéra-Comique in 1891, *Chevalerie rustique* seemed a natural choice both to freshen the repertoire and to score large box-office returns (to judge by its spectacular success beyond the borders of Italy: over thirty productions in less than two years). Although Calvé had sung sporadically in Paris during the years she was primarily active in Italy, her rendition of Santuzza at the Opéra-Comique in January 1892 brought her much greater attention. She even managed to emerge unscathed from the massive critical assault the French press made on Mascagni's work.[18] According to Reynaldo Hahn, critics were greatly impressed by the transformation of the pale and timid performer they had seen in the mid-1880s into a compelling presence on the stage—so impressed that her Santuzza launched her into stardom at home.[19] In *My Life* Calvé writes about how her performance also astonished her Opéra-Comique colleagues: "My spontaneous and apparently unstudied gestures shocked them." And in *Sous tous les ciels* she recorded her impact on the benign pastoral world of traditional Opéra-Comique *paysannerie:* "In this somewhat traditional theater people are surprised by the sincerity that I bring to playing this role of the peasant woman, without mannerism, shabbily dressed: blouse of coarse mate-

16. Calvé, *My Life*, 60.

17. Sheehy, *Eleonora Duse*, 53.

18. For more on this see Steven Huebner, "*La Navarraise* face au vérisme,"134–35, as well as Fiamma Nicolodi, "Parigi e l'opera verista: Dibatti, riflessioni, polemiche," *Nuova rivista musicale italiana* 15 (1981): 577–623.

19. In a radio account from 1942 reproduced on the CD *Reynaldo Hahn*, CDRG 127 (Malibran Music, n.d.).

rial, wool skirt, battered sandals, and sleek hair looped back at the sides and almost without makeup."[20]

"Spontaneous," "unstudied," "almost without makeup"—all would serve as fair descriptions of Duse's art, whose approach to the role surely had some influence on Calvé. The critic Herman Klein made the link directly when he recalled Calvé's 1892 London debut as Santuzza:

> Emma Calvé had no difficulty in surpassing her rivals of the period in this particular role; for it fitted her to absolute perfection. . . . Calvé seemed to bring into the opera the Sicilian atmosphere of Verga's story, just as Duse had brought it into the drama. . . . Unforgettable, then, was the impression made on 16 May, by the first *real* Santuzza, when she emerged from a hot, dusty lane into the burning sunshine of the village market-square. Gliding covertly, restlessly, in search of her missing lover; glancing from side to side with anxious face; her fingers pulling at her Sicilian shawl, as ever and anon she slipped it off and replaced it on her shoulders—she looked a veritable picture of abject, hopeless misery. . . . [She fills] in the picture with a hundred little artistic touches that tell the story where the librettist and musician cannot.[21]

Likewise, Bernard Shaw characterized Calvé's Santuzza as "irresistibly moving and beautiful and fully capable of sustaining the inevitable comparison with Duse's impersonation of the same part."[22]

Calvé brought this approach to her other roles as well. Recalling her Marguerite, the New York critic Arthur Wisner, writing under the pseudonym A. Gallus, once reported that Calvé had told him that the character "was a little working girl so she must not be noticed by the crowd." Consequently, she should first emerge from the crowd at the end of act 2 in "dull, dark wool" instead of a white dress (supposedly) "worn only by princesses."[23] The diva clearly reacted against a Marguerite-as-prima-donna *entrée en scène,* an orientation in the spirit of Duse's revision of the tradition for Marguerite Gauthier's first entrance, as described by Sheehy: "Traditionally, actresses called attention to Marguerite's first appearance by crossing from up center to down center stage between two rows of carefully positioned party guests. Duse, instead, simply appeared among the party guests who were grouped naturally."[24] Gallus re-

20. "Dans ce théâtre, quelque peu traditionnaliste on est surpris de la sincérité que j'apporte à jouer ce rôle de paysanne, sans maniérisme, pauvrement vêtue: chemise de toile rude, jupe de laine, sandales usagés, et les cheveux lisses en simples bandeaux et presque sans maquillage." Calvé, *Sous tous les ciels,* 66.

21. Hermann Klein, *Great Women Singers of My Time* (London: Routledge, 1931), 149–50.

22. Bernard Shaw, *Shaw's Music,* ed. Dan H. Laurence (New York: Dodd, Mead, 1981), 3:227.

23. A. Gallus [Arthur Wisner], *Emma Calvé: Her Artistic Life* (New York: R. H. Russell, 1902), unpaginated.

24. Sheehy, *Eleonora Duse,* 121.

called that, pursuant to her expurgation of prima-donna behavior from Gounod's opera, Calvé did not carry the jewel box right in front of the prompter's box "as if she were saying 'I come here in order to make my voice carry further.' She left the case where it was, sang in the back of the stage, and—made a hit."

That Calvé also made a lasting impression as Ophélie in Ambroise Thomas's *Hamlet* is a reminder of her bel canto training with Marchesi and Rosine Laborde. (Although not well reflected in her legacy of recordings available today, mostly from late in her career,[25] contemporary reviewers often noted that Calvé had a beautiful voice—ringing, agile, and even on the top, and with a marvelous chest tone that had a contralto quality.) Yet despite the traditional vocal technique required in Ophélie's mad scene, Calvé had a naturalistic approach. During her first performance of the role at La Scala in 1888, it was her memory of a previous fiasco at that very house that broke down the barrier between art and life. So distraught did she become at the cool reception of the audience during the first three acts—believing another failure imminent—that she appeared on stage for the mad scene "too frantic to care how I looked," without makeup, her dress in disorder: "I must have seemed indeed half mad!"[26] More than ten years later, at her Opéra premiere of Ophélie, Calvé sought an earthy effect in the mad scene derived, as she told the journalist Jules Huret, from the bawdy verse that Shakespeare himself (but not the librettists, Jules Barbier and Michel Carré) allots his character at the beginning the scene.[27] "Without makeup" once again, she ripped the flowers from her disheveled hair while sailing up and down the coloratura passagework. She also told Huret that her understanding of the scene had been shaped by a visit she had made to an asylum in Milan before her La Scala performances, an anecdote she would often repeat. There she had observed a young, pale, fair woman who, just like Ophélie, went mad after a lover had abandoned her. Although the story carries a whiff of having been embellished for her fans, the important point remains that Calvé insisted she had done fieldwork for the role in order to underscore her concern for authenticity.

But what about the aesthetic of Thomas and his librettists? In his review of the Opéra production, Alfred Bruneau, true to his own naturalistic inclinations, applauded Calvé's "careful reflection and research," which allowed her to transcend what he felt to be the opera's fundamentally weak dramaturgy. In short, she had put a stamp of realism on a fundamentally unrealistic work.[28] The critic Gaston Carraud, however, found it more difficult to justify the perceived dissonance between Calvé's approach and Thomas's florid passage work, so much so that her stage movement seemed affected and artificial, just of the opposite of the effect at which she was aim-

25. For a discography of Calvé's recordings see W. R. Moran, "The Recordings of Emma Calvé," unpaginated appendix to the Arno Press reprint of *My Life*. A representative sample may be heard on the CD *Emma Calvé*, MR 533 (Malibran Music, n.d.).

26. *My Life*, 59.

27. Jules Huret, "Emma Calvé," *Le Figaro*, 29 May 1899.

28. Alfred Bruneau, "Emma Calvé dans *Hamlet*," *Le Figaro*, 30 May 1899.

ing.[29] *Le soleil*'s A. Goullet complained about Calvé's tendency to allow the sound of high notes to decay too quickly, ostensibly a naturalistic effect but really a violation of Thomas's musical style.[30] Whereas Bruneau saw Calvé rescue the putatively unstageworthy, Carraud and Goullet reacted against excessive eclecticism—in effect, inauthentic performance. The introduction of naturalistic acting and realistic, even histrionic vocal effects to the opera stage in the late nineteenth century created problems that continue to be familiar today.

Calvé made an especially impressive mark with her debut as Carmen at the Opéra-Comique on 15 December 1892. Comparisons with Duse followed her even in this role. "Note the face, the walk, the gestures," wrote Gallus a decade later. "It reminded me of nothing so much as Duse's *La femme de Claude*. A woman with a heap of pasts."[31] Before Calvé, the most noteworthy exponent of Carmen at the Opéra-Comique had been Célestine Galli-Marié, who premiered it there in 1875 and was coaxed out of retirement to sing the role one last time in 1890. In the words of one critic, Galli-Marié was much admired for "wild poetry, incandescent voice, provocative gestures [that] throw the smallest details into relief. It is impossible to be at once more realistic and more poetic."[32] The time was ripe for a worthy successor: Ernest Reyer greeted Calvé's performance by observing that, unlike all other Carmens, she had attained Galli-Marié's standard of passion and *vérité*.[33] Flattering as it was, Reyer's remark also highlights the real challenge that Calvé faced: to create a space for herself in the wake of a respected predecessor who had significantly undermined scenographic tradition with her own naturalistic—and for some, shocking—portrayal of the character. Calvé told one interviewer that she had never seen Galli-Marié in *Carmen* and that, at any rate, her own temperament and physique were so different that she inevitably had to develop her own approach—Galli-Marié was short and a little plump, Calvé, tall, dark, and statuesque.[34] "Therefore I just tried to be myself,"[35] she said, implicitly suggesting that naturalistic acting styles should not ossify into standardized practice (much the same attitude that Signora takes toward the role, it will be recalled).

29. Gaston Carraud, "A l'Opéra—Hamlet—Débuts de Mlle Emma Calvé," *La liberté*, 30 May 1899.
30. A. Goullet, *Le soleil*, 19 May 1899.
31. Gallus, *Emma Calvé*, unpaginated.
32. "La poésie sauvage, la voix chaude, les attitudes provoquantes [qui] mettent en relief les moindres détails avec une couleur admirable. Il est impossible d'être plus réaliste et plus poëte à la fois." As cited by Robert L. A. Clark in "South of North: *Carmen* and French Nationalisms," in *East of West*, ed. Claire Sponsler and Xiaomei Chen (New York: Palgrave, 2000), 204. Clark insightfully compares the Carmen interpretation of Galli-Marié and Calvé in one section of this article.
33. Cited in Calvé, *Sous tous les ciels*, 67.
34. Ponthiery, "Chez Mme. Emma Calvé," *La liberté*, 26 December 1904.
35. "J'ai donc taché d'être moi." Ibid.

More important—and consonant with her remarks about Ophélie—in her memoirs and interviews, Calvé repeatedly emphasized the almost "scientific" rigor of her preparations. On a fact-finding mission during the summer before her Opéra-Comique rendition, she toured Spain and even visited Gypsy camps.[36] The fortune-telling of an old woman Calvé saw there inspired her approach to the Card Aria.[37] She changed the costume from Galli-Marié's bolero and short skirt to the fringed shawl that is called in Spain the *manton di Manilla* (see fig. 15.1). "I often stood outside the cigarette factories and watched the girls coming to and going from their work," she told Gustav Kobbé, a remark that made its way into *Signora*.[38] Surreptitiously following a cigarette girl on one occasion, she observed how she flirted with her skirt. Mabel Wagnalls commented that her stage shoes for the role "were worn down and scuffed, as they must be if she was in the habit of running over the cobblestones of Seville."[39] Moreover, her hair was "carelessly pinned, and even tumbled quite down later on—a stroke of realism which was added to by the way she coiled it up and jabbed it into place again. . . . A strange performance to behold in a grand opera setting."[40]

In addition to the case she made for the ethnographic accuracy of her approach to Carmen, Calvé repeatedly suggested that her true feeling for the role came from reverberations with her own personality—this despite also claiming that "the character is, on the whole, antipathetic to me."[41] Her understanding of Bizet's protagonist came from her own Mediterranean blood, peripatetic lifestyle, and superstitious nature, even from the Gypsies with whom she had played as a little girl. She once noted that during concert tours in North America her childhood dream "to live in a gypsy van" became transmogrified into her own private rail car, in which she traveled from city to city.[42] Her interest in mystic religions and various occult fads did not go unnoticed by the press (nor by Kobbé in *Signora*), and neither did her volatility during rehearsals and performances. "They don't understand me here [in the United States]," she told Mabel Wagnalls. "In the Cévennes they wouldn't mind if I stormed about for a week at a time."[43] Calvé sustained the image of a moody outsider even in Paris. For the writer Léon Daudet she would remain forever *la princesse paysanne du Midi*: "The paragon of refinement, the enchantress that is Calvé, she retained throughout her career, and without a crack, the common sense, the solidity of a peasant woman . . . making olive paste and feeding the animals, all the while accompanying herself with

36. Calvé, *Sous tous les ciels*, 71–80.

37. Ibid., 80.

38. Gustave Kobbé, "Mme Calvé," in *Opera Singers: A Pictorial Souvenir* (Boston: Oliver Ditson, 1901), unpaginated. This passage is taken up in *Signora*, 73.

39. Mabel Wagnalls, "Calvé and Carmen," in *Stars of the Opera* (New York: Funk and Wagnalls, 1899), 107–8.

40. Ibid., 108.

41. *My Life*, 83.

42. Wagnalls, "Calvé and Carmen," 120.

43. Ibid., 112–13.

a refrain."[44] Calvé would cap performances of art music in the most elegant Parisian salons, and even at Queen Victoria's court, with renditions of *langue d'oc* folk songs, which she sang, in the words of the writer, librettist, and manager Pierre-Barthélémy Gheusi, "with that incomparable voice of miracle and dream which she is able to render distant, almost immaterial, as if it came from times erased from memory . . . the whole soul of her native soil, of castles, of streams, of pastures and fields."[45] And she never really settled in the capital, preferring to return to her roots in the Midi and eventually to purchase a chateau near Millau. All of this seems of a piece with Carmen the outsider, Carmen of the regal declaration "Libre elle est née et libre elle mourra" (Free she was born, and free she will die). For Calvé, then, an authentic performance was a conflation of research, life experience, and basic character. For all the study of milieu that an actress might bring to her task, certain roles simply did not fit—not necessarily for vocal reasons but for temperamental ones. She rejected the part of Charlotte in Massenet's *Werther* when it was offered to her in 1903 because the character was "too passive."[46]

The role of Anita in *La Navarraise,* written explicitly for Calvé by Massenet, has traces of both Santuzza and Carmen and once again solders a link between verismo and Bizet's opera via this artist. Premiered at Covent Garden in 1894, the next year it saw the boards at the Opéra-Comique. Whereas accounts both past and present have described *La Navarraise* as a pale imitation of *Cavalleria rusticana,* my own view is that Massenet thought his Italian precursor had not gone far enough in shock value.[47] Anita is even more marginalized than Santuzza (that is, closer to Carmen in this respect) and has a much more kinetic role than Mascagni's character; indeed, in the antecedent story, Jules Claretie's *La cigarette,* her analogue in the plot is actually a man. Set during the recent Carlist civil war in Spain, Claretie's story tells of a soldier who poisons an enemy captain in order to earn a reward that will enable him to rise to the social station of his beloved. In the opera, it is Anita who crosses enemy lines. She seduces the captain and then, Judith-like, treacherously knifes him in the back to gain a dowry. Thus, whereas in *Cavalleria rusticana* Santuzza merely triggers the murder of Turiddu by informing Alfio that he has been cuckolded, Massenet's Anita actually takes destiny into her own hands—only to have her tenor lover reject her as he lies dying of a bullet wound. She loses her mind over his corpse and breaks into hysterical laughter at the final curtain. From the smooth coloratura of Ophélie's mad scene to

44. "Cette raffinée, cette enchanteresse qu'est Calvé a gardé, à travers sa carrière, sans une fêlure, le bon sens, la solidité d'une paysanne . . . faisant les olivades et donnant à manger aux bêtes, en s'accompagnant d'un refrain." Léon Daudet, *Quand vivait mon père: Souvenirs inédits sur Alphonse Daudet* (Paris: Grasset, 1940), 212.

45. "De cette incomparable voix de miracle et de rêve qu'elle sait rendre lointaine, presque im-matérielle, comme venue des âges abolis . . . toute l'âme du sol natal, celle des bourgs, des ruisseaux, des pâturages et des plaines." P. B. Gheusi, *Midi* (Paris: Flammarion, n.d.), 95.

46. Emma Calvé, letter to Jules Massenet [c. 1905], Archives Calvé, Millau.

47. See Huebner, "*La Navarraise* face au vérisme."

the histrionics of Anita: that Calvé performed both roles with success is certainly a tribute to her vocal versatility. In giving his mad scene a more true-to-life ambience, at least in its vocal character, Massenet effectively erased the dissonance between the aesthetic world of Thomas's style and Calvé's naturalistic acting that some critics had censured in her performances of Ophélie.

Again, circumstances surrounding *La Navarraise* hint at Calvé's quest for authenticity and lived experience. Perhaps not coincidentally, it was soon after her initial Opéra-Comique success with *Carmen* (and her preparatory trip to Spain) that she began pressing Massenet to accept the libretto to *La Navarraise*, the work of her lover at the time, Henri Cain.[48] That Calvé may have had a decisive hand in the selection of *La Navarraise* has an echo in her American memoirs where she tells a story of how as a young girl she experienced the Carlist wars firsthand.[49] The tale is gripping, operatic in itself: a rebel fighter bursts into their house, with government troops in hot pursuit; her mother hides him under Calvé's bed and orders the child to feign sleep; the soldiers appear at the threshold; the ruse works, and the rebel is saved. Even if Calvé had embellished these childhood events, the act of fabrication would still suggest an attempt to persuade her audiences that her artistry was grounded in experience. The anecdote informs understanding of the large poster that advertised the first French production of *La Navarraise* (see fig. 15.2). It features an outsize image of Calvé in the role, almost certainly the first use of photography on a mass-produced French poster in this period: realistic technology for a realistic operatic genre. Calvé's gritty costume is especially noteworthy, but not as much as the question the poster prompts. Does it represent Anita, the character in Massenet's opera, or Emma Calvé, the opera star with a Mediterranean complexion presenting herself boldly in low, unidealized peasant dress—*la princesse paysanne du Midi*?

A performer such as Emma Calvé may be profitably folded into the story of veristic opera in other ways as well, and I conclude with two additional critical paths of a more speculative nature. The first concerns her approach to the musical score. Even a casual perusal of Calvé's recorded legacy reveals a singer who took great liberties with the notated text in all the music she sang. She often applied rubato with undisciplined abandon, substituted words, changed rhythms on the local level, and demonstrated scant feel for metrical accent (producing recordings where, despite the best intentions

48. A letter from Calvé to Massenet, probably written in February 1893, strongly encourages him to rise up to the veristic challenge of Italian composers such as Mascagni and Puccini with "the little lyric drama which I spoke about" (almost certainly *La Navarraise*). See Demar Irvine, *Jules Massenet: A Chronicle of His Life and Times* (Portland, OR: Amadeus Press, 1994), 185. On Cain and Calvé see Jean-Christophe Branger, "Henri Cain, artiste peintre et librettiste," *Sapho; La Navarraise*, vol. 217 of *L'avant-scène opéra* (2003): 40–43.

49. Calvé, *My Life*, 5–9.

FIGURE 15.2. Poster for the first performance of Jules Massenet's *La Navarraise*. The first French poster to include a photograph. The letters of the title and of the composer's name are in blue; the other letters are black. Photograph by Reutlinger. Private collection.

of conductors and pianists, downbeats between the voice and the accompaniment are often out of phase). Of course, these are general observations, and each of her recordings deserves study on its own musical merits. But if we accept the generalizations that I propose, we must ask: how typical was she of contemporary performers in this respect? That critics of the day wrote about her rhythmic and metrical inaccuracies suggests that on a continuum of fidelity to the notation she was relatively liberal. As I have already suggested, George Bernard Shaw much admired Calvé, for her sheer sex appeal as much as for her acting, acting that so effectively communicated Carmen's "superstitious, pleasure-loving good-for-nothing nature" that it actually divested her of beauty.[50] But in 1894 he vowed never to see her again in the role, for in it she "carried her abandonment to the point of being incapable of paying the smallest attention to the score. . . . She acted out of time the whole evening; and I do not see why artists should act out of time any more than sing out of time."[51] Back in Paris at the Opéra-Comique, Arthur Pougin, also favorably disposed to Calvé the actress, asked: "What has happened, with Emma Calvé, to Bizet's adorable music? What has happened to the tempos, what has happened to the rhythms? Everything has changed, everything is upended, and the orchestra is confused, it is no longer able to follow, and not only are traditions broken, but so too is logic, even musical sense no longer exists."[52] But not all contemporaries were unforgiving. A critic at the *New York Herald* gushed: "There was much of the panther in the woman's voice, too. To express her meaning, she frequently took all sorts of liberties with time and rhythm. No one but a metronome fiend, however, would think of taking Mlle. Calvé to task for her musical arbitrariness, the effects she obtained being so often positively tragical."[53] Reynaldo Hahn, who wrote the role of Louise de la Vallière in *La Carmélite* for her (and was surely aware of the liberties she would take with his score), declared once that she never betrayed "the spirit" of the music.[54] The British critic Vernon Blackburn remarked that Calvé was an "incomparable vocal actress. Her voice is in itself beautiful; but her method of using her voice may be described only by the single word 'dramatic.'"[55] By emphasizing her beauty of tone (a point Hahn made as well), Blackburn implicitly distinguished Calvé from other singers who cultivated effects of gasping and rasping seen in certain quarters as appropriate to

50. Shaw, *Shaw's Music,* 3:225.

51. Ibid., 226.

52. "Que devient, avec Mlle Calvé, la musique adorable de Bizet? Que deviennent les mouvements, que deviennent les rythmes? Tout est changé, tout est bouleversé, l'orchestre est dérouté, il ne sait plus comment la suivre, et non seulement toutes les traditions sont rompues, mais la logique, le sens musical même n'existent plus." Arthur Pougin, *Le ménestrel,* 18 December 1892.

53. As cited in Gallus, *Emma Calvé* (unpaginated).

54. Cited in Georges Girard, *Emma Calvé: La cantatrice,* 49.

55. Vernon Blackburn, *The Fringe of an Art: Appreciations in Music* (London: Unicorn Press, 1898), 67.

verismo.[56] In a passage that illuminates Calvé's approach to rhythm and meter, he added, more subtly:

> Calvé's movement is . . . finely attuned to the motion of the voice, swift with its swiftness, solemn with its majesty; and thus she effects an extraordinary unity of accomplishment. The voice distracts you from no preponderance of bodily activity; the weakness of action distracts you from no undue effort of the voice . . . as a vocally dramatic artist she stands where no modern operatic actress can approach her. Shut your eyes, and listen to her as she enters upon any dramatic circumstance of opera and you can picture her pose, her gesture, her facial expression.[57]

Voice as gesture, gesture as voice. For Blackburn, Calvé achieved an ideal fusion of the two, a kind of bodily control reminiscent of Eleonora Duse's discipline and craft. Although this binary relationship serves well as a critical perspective on other repertoires—Gilles de Van has pointed to its appositeness for melodrama, for example[58]—in Calvé's case, gestural language seems to break the fetters of notation and modestly suggests a challenge to the increasing hegemony of the "work-concept" in fin-de-siècle European musical culture, at least inasmuch as that concept relates to an ideal of compliance with the score. This is because for some of her supporters the immediacy of an electrifying and dramatic performance clearly could trump certain prescriptions of notation followed more rigorously by others. Of course, the dynamic interplay between written text and effective realization forms a substantial chapter in the history of Western music. And Calvé's performance liberties might well have been partially the result of unpremeditated carelessness. My point here, however, is that in the context of a musical culture with increasingly prescriptive musical scores, she presents a striking case of performance freedoms implicitly justified by at least some critics with an aesthetic of realism, a combined quest for authenticity and originality. In Blackburn's words, Calvé's fusion of gesture and voice was "a combination of powers that stir one with the sense of a personal life, of a story and an intelligence seated behind the voice, and prompting its utterances."[59] And we might add for Blackburn: if the notation suffers, so be it. Today we expect performers to be both believable and accurate (relatively speaking, of course), yet to increase the prescriptive character of the score is logically, in Calvé's terms, to decrease the room for exploration into authentic realization, where realism combines magically with temperament. If she were with us today, perhaps she might even say that one kind of conformity—that of her contemporaries to staid and artificial staging traditions at the Opéra-Comique—has

56. For a brief description see Rupert Christiansen, *Prima Donna: A History* (Harmondsworth, Middlesex: Penguin, 1984), 301–5.

57. Blackburn, *Fringe*, 68–69.

58. Gilles de Van, *Verdi's Theater: Creating Drama through Music*, trans. Gilda Roberts (Chicago: University of Chicago Press, 1998), 25–28.

59. Ibid., 69.

become replaced by another kind of conformity to the rhythms and tempos of the written score.

My second speculative concluding point centers on an example of how one might press Calvé's quest for authenticity into hermeneutic service. Her next veristic creation after *La Navarraise* was Massenet's *Sapho*, which was premiered at the Opéra-Comique in 1897.[60] He styled it a "pièce lyrique," in itself a strong generic marker for a realistic orientation. The plot tells of a courtesan "of a certain age"—Fanny Legrand, the model for a famous sculpture of the Greek poet Sappho—who seduces Jean, a young student from Provence. They live together; Jean becomes angered when he learns of her previous affairs; they separate; he returns to Provence; they become reconciled, but in the end she leaves him with regret, realizing that he will never get over his anxiety about her past. The opera, far more than Daudet's antecedent eponymous novel, plays up the contrast between the idyllic Provençal society from which Jean comes and a fin-de-siècle urban environment peopled by degenerate bohemians and prostitutes. In the first scene Jean meets Fanny/Sapho at a masked ball, with music sounding in an adjacent room. As elsewhere in this opera, *La traviata* stands as an obvious and important intertextual reference, in this instance the first meeting of the tenor and soprano against a foil of offstage music. But Massenet describes his *banda* as "un orchestre de faux Tziganes"—canned and commodified Gypsy music for urban pleasure seekers. Rather like Marguerite Gauthier's (and Violetta's) barely concealed quest for virtue, Fanny Legrand finds herself drawn to Jean as a way of rehabilitating herself. (The comparisons with Dumas and Verdi extend only so far, however: it is Jean's youth and innocence that attract Massenet's courtesan.) He teaches her a love song from his *pays*, the well-known "O Magali, ma tant amado."

Whereas the song does not figure in Daudet's novel (and the play based thereupon contains only a fleeting reference to it), "O Magali" occupies an important role in a love duet of reconciliation in the second act of Massenet's *Sapho*, as well as elsewhere in the opera. Here the heroine seems to recall the melody as if in a dream, an Eden that she wants to recreate with her lover. Emma Calvé frequently sang "O Magali" at her concerts, as Massenet doubtless knew; it was something of a signature piece for her, a way of reminding her listeners of her own Provençal culture. In the opera, therefore, one might hear it as a binary opposite to the "orchestre de faux Tziganes" that sets the tone for the initial meeting. "Magali" is also authentic because it is a real folk song, instead of the famous facsimile with the same text in Gounod's *Mireille*, performed regularly at the Opéra-Comique in this period. And it must have appeared all the more genuine to contemporary listeners as sung onstage by Emma Calvé.

60. On this work see most recently Gérard Condé, "Commentaire musical," *Sapho; La Navarraise*, vol. 217 of *L'avant scène opéra* (2003): 7–39; Brigitte Olivier, *J. Massenet: Itinéraire pour un théâtre musical* (Arles: Actes Sud, 1996), 163–75; Anne-Simone Dufief, "*Sapho*: Du roman au livret," in *Le livret d'opéra au temps de Massenet: Actes du colloque des 9–10 novembre 2001, Festival Massenet*, ed. Alban Ramaut and Jean-Christophe Branger (Saint-Étienne: Publications de l'Université de Saint-Étienne, 2002), 303–27.

Although the task of interpretation is muddied because the song does not "belong" to the character Fanny, inasmuch as she was not born in the Midi, this disjunction also suggests one hermeneutic strategy. For during the hectic course of Fanny's life, "O Magali" is heard in the opera as something she *wants* to own—an escape, as a talisman of contentment. Here one might think of the escape that Calvé, the self-styled *bohémienne*, cherished when she repeatedly returned to Millau to seek refuge from her urban and international existence as an opera star. That she poignantly brought her French memoirs to a close with a citation from the local poet François Fabié speaks volumes: "Si vous avez semé votre âge le plus beau / Sur les mille chemins où l'orgueil vous entraîne / Le pays vous fera la vieillesse sereine" (Although you have sowed your youth / On the thousand roads where pride leads you / Your native soil will provide you with serene old age).[61] At the end of the opera Fanny finds herself confronted with a continued peripatetic existence, just like Calvé at the opera's premiere in 1897. She was just then at the height of her career, with years of travel behind her and many more to come. When Massenet wrote to her upon completing the score that *Sapho* "c'est du théâtre vrai, vrai, vrai" (What real theater, real, real) perhaps he struck a personal chord that even he did not anticipate.[62]

"Air! air! I stifle!": in *Signora,* every evening Caravé bursts into her dressing room and commands that the windows be opened. In the final analysis, to contemplate the extent to which Calvé's nostalgia was awakened by enacting an unsettled character who sings "O Magali" is the point where the endeavor of the critic joins that of the novelist who created a character with "the mercurial temperament of Southern France."[63]

61. Calvé, *Sous tous les ciels,* 295.
62. Jules Massenet, letter to Emma Calvé, 10 August 1896, Archives Calvé, Millau.
63. Kobbé, *Signora,* 70.

A Documentary Overview of Musical Theaters in Paris, 1830–1900

Alicia C. Levin

When Napoleon Bonaparte turned his attention to the theater during the early part of the First Empire, he found that years of revolution had taken a significant toll on the theaters and theatrical arts in Paris. Revolutionary backlash against ancien régime traditions and the proliferation of new theaters (opened after the 1791 law permitted the free establishment of public theaters) had left Parisian theaters and theater troupes in financial and artistic crisis. Napoleon's response, the three imperial decrees of 1806 and 1807, securely harnessed French theaters under state authority.[1] Replacing the chaos of the 1790s with a strict licensing system, these laws established an institutional framework that shaped the development of theatrical arts in France during the nineteenth century. As the essays in this volume illustrate, navigating this framework was a fundamental part of producing opera; whether they worked with the grain or against it, composers, directors, and librettists could not avoid engaging with the legacy of Napoleon's reforms.

The 1807 laws reduced the number of licensed theaters to eight (four *grands théâtres* and four *théâtres secondaires*) and assigned each a specific repertoire. Among the four primary theaters were the Académie Impériale de Musique (hereafter "Opéra"; see table 16.1), the Théâtre de l'Opéra-Comique (table 16.2), and the Théâtre de l'Impératrice (hereafter "Théâtre-Italien," table 16.3); among the secondary institutions was the

---

1. Nicole Wild, *Dictionnaire des théâtres parisiens au XIXe siècle: Les théâtres et la musique* (Paris: Aux Amateurs de Livres, 1989), 13.

FIGURE 16.1. The theaters on the boulevard du Temple; engraving by A. Provost, *L'illustration*, 12 April 1862. Courtesy of Duke University Library.

Théâtre de la Gaîté (table 16.4).[2] To establish a new theater, it was necessary to apply to the state for a license, which stipulated the repertoire and, in some cases, the size of the troupe.[3] The practice of censorship, initially banned in 1791, was also reinstated to allow the state an official measure of influence over new productions.

Despite the stringent level of control implied by the 1807 laws, administrations of the July Monarchy and the Second Empire adopted a less rigorous position toward theater management than those of the First Empire or the Restoration. The number of theater licenses in Paris steadily increased after 1820, all of which delimited specific repertoires for the new companies. Official censors, however, were more concerned with the content than with the genre of new operas. Directors successfully expanded the repertoire of their theaters by gradually blurring the lines between genres. The emergence of *opéra bouffe* at the Théâtre des Bouffes-Parisiens, a theater initially licensed for works with fewer than five performers, is perhaps the clearest example of this trend. Companies such as the Opéra and the Opéra-Comique, whose long-standing monopolies were threatened by this development, responded to the state's leniency by policing repertoire violations themselves.[4] Several key opera troupes were

2. Ibid. The specific repertoire of each theater is discussed below.

3. Mark Everist, *Giacomo Meyerbeer and Music Drama in Nineteenth-Century Paris* (Burlington, VT: Ashgate, 2005), 4.

4. See Mark Everist's discussion of the role played by the Opéra and Opéra-Comique in the

founded in this atmosphere, including the Théâtre de l'Odéon in 1829 (table 16.5), the Théâtre de la Renaissance in 1838 (table 16.6), the Opéra-National in 1847 (table 16.7), and the Théâtre des Bouffes-Parisiens in 1855 (table 16.8).

In 1864 Napoleon III granted the *liberté des théâtres,* dissolving the license system and creating a body of works in the public domain from which any theater company could draw. He did not, however, repeal the censorship law, which remained in place until the end of the century.[5] The state also sustained its influence by continuing to contribute financially to the maintenance of most Parisian theaters.

The tables below provide a brief overview of eight major stages for opera in Paris from 1830 to 1900.[6] They are intended to contextualize the essays presented in this volume. Each table charts the history of a single theater company to avoid the inherently confusing overlap between company name and theater name that characterized the theatrical world of nineteenth-century Paris.[7]

The Théâtre de l'Opéra, founded in 1669 by the poet Pierre Perrin, stood as the dominant institution of French opera during the nineteenth century.[8] Although the temporary exile of the Parisian aristocracy after 1789, the proliferation of theaters after 1791, and a general resistance to ancien régime customs in the 1790s detracted from its popularity during the early years of the First Empire, the reforms of 1807 reasserted the Opéra as the center of operatic production in Paris.[9] Napoleon reserved for the Opéra company the exclusive right to perform through-composed French operas

---

development of the repertoire for the Théâtre de la Renaissance. Everist, "Theatres of Litigation: Stage Music at the Théâtre de la Renaissance, 1838–1840," *Cambridge Opera Journal* 16, no. 2 (2004): 133–61.

5. Official censorship of opera was lifted for brief periods following the revolutions of 1830 and 1848, only to be reinstated by the September laws of 1835 and the 1851 coronation of Napoleon III respectively. See Hervé Lacombe, *The Keys to French Opera in the Nineteenth Century,* trans. Edward Schneider (Berkeley and Los Angeles: University of California Press, 2001), 16; and Everist, *Giacomo Meyerbeer,* 7–9.

6. The data presented in these tables is drawn largely from Wild, *Dictionnaire,* and Rebecca Harris-Warrick, David Charlton, Janet Johnson, Richard Langham Smith, and Charles Pitt, "Paris," in *The New Grove Dictionary of Opera,* ed. Stanley Sadie (London: Macmillan, 1992), 3:855–82. Other sources were consulted for specific theaters and are noted accordingly.

7. In a franchised entrepreneurship, a state-appointed director managed the company for personal profit. I have adopted this term from Hervé Lacombe, "The 'Machine' and the State," in *The Cambridge Companion to Grand Opera,* ed. David Charlton (Cambridge: Cambridge University Press, 2003), 26–27.

8. As a Society of Artists, the stage performers managed the company themselves. See Lacombe, "The 'Machine' and the State," 28.

9. James Johnson, *Listening in Paris: A Cultural History,* Studies on the History of Society and Culture 21 (Berkeley and Los Angeles: University of California Press, 1995), 103–4.

TABLE 16.1. Chronology and administration of the Opéra company

Name	Location	Date	Director	Status
Théâtre de l'Opéra Académie Royale de Musique	Salle le Peletier	4 Aug. 1830	Emile Lubbert	Under administration of the Maison du Roi
		10 Aug. 1830		
		1 Mar. 1831	Louis Véron	Franchised entrepreneurship with state subvention[7]
		1 Sept. 1835	Edmond Duponchel; Léon Pillet	
		1 Dec. 1839	Duponchel; Édouard Monnais	
		1 June 1840	Pillet; Duponchel; Monnais	
		1 June 1842	Pillet	
		1 Aug. 1847	Duponchel; Pillet; Nestor Roqueplan	
		Nov. 1847	Duponchel; Roqueplan	
Théâtre de la Nation		26 Feb. 1848		
Opéra-Théâtre de la Nation		29 Mar. 1848		
		21 Nov. 1849	Roqueplan	
Académie Nationale de Musique		2 Sept. 1850		
Académie Impériale de Musique		2 Dec. 1852		
Théâtre Impérial de l'Opéra		1 July 1854		Under administration of the Maison de l'Empereur
		11 Nov. 1854	François-Louis Crosnier	
		1 July 1856	Alphonse Royer	
		20 Dec. 1862	Emile Perrin	
		1 May 1866		Franchised entrepreneurship with state subvention
Théâtre de l'Opéra		4 Sept. 1870		
Théâtre National de l'Opéra		17 Sept. 1870		
		1 Oct. 1870		Reverted to state administration
		28 Oct. 1870	Perrin (president)	Society of Artists with state subvention[8]
		9 May 1871	Eugène Garnier	
		3 July 1871	Perrin	
		9 July 1871	Hyacinthe Halanzier	

TABLE 16.1. (*continued*)

Name	Location	Date	Director	Status
Théatre National de l'Opéra	Salle le Peletier	1 Nov. 1871	Halanzier	Private entrepreneurship with state subvention
	Salle Ventadour	19 Jan. 1874		
	Salle Garnier	5 Jan. 1875		
		July 1879	Auguste Vaucorbeil	
		1884	Pierre Gailhard; Eugène Ritt	
		1892	Eugène Bertrand	
		Apr. 1893 (to Dec. 1898)	Gailhard; Bertrand	

SOURCES: Wild, *Dictionnaire*, 299–321; Harris-Warrick, Charlton, Johnson, Smith, and Pitt, "Paris," 3:866–68, 873–77.

(works in French with no spoken dialogue) and one- to five-act ballets-pantomimes. The imperial government took an active role in its administration, rehabilitating the company and mounting elaborate productions that displayed the glory of France.[10] The genre of *grand opéra* developed further under Bourbon rule (1814–30); audiences enjoyed the complete aesthetic effect of superior musical performances and innovative (and expensive) stage productions.[11]

In 1831 the Opéra's administration was turned over to Louis Véron, who assumed (with some help from the state) personal responsibility for the company's artistic and financial success. For the next twenty-three years the Opéra was governed by a series of *directeur-entrepreneurs,* with varying degrees of success.[12] Napoleon III placed the Opéra under the direction of the Ministry of the Interior after Nestor Roqueplan's disastrous financial management left the Opéra with a debt of nearly one million francs.[13] This move coincided with the rise of the Théâtre-Lyrique (see table 16.5), one of the Opéra's first major competitors for the French *grand opéra* repertoire. In 1866, the Opéra reverted again to a state-supported franchised entrepreneurship. With the

10. See the chapter entitled "Napoleon's Show" in Johnson, *Listening in Paris*, 165–81. The Opéra also charged the highest ticket prices in town. See also Anselm Gerhard, *The Urbanization of Opera: Music Theater in Paris in the Nineteenth Century,* trans. Mary Whittall (Chicago: University of Chicago Press, 1998), 35.

11. Johnson, *Listening in Paris,* 239–41.

12. I have adopted this term from Wild, *Dictionnaire,* and Lacombe, "The 'Machine' and the State." Lacombe employs it to describe the director of the franchised entrepreneurship.

13. Gerhard, *Urbanization,* 35.

FIGURE 16.2. The new theater for the Opéra in the Salle le Peletier, view from the rue de Provence, c. 1822; engraving by Rousseau. Bibliothèque musée de l'Opéra. Bibliothèque nationale de France.

---

brief exception of 1870–71 (during which time the performers managed the company themselves), it remained so for the rest of the century.

In addition to French *grand opéra*, the Opéra company regularly performed ballets and foreign works in translation. Among the latter were the 1841 version of Weber's *Der Freischütz* (with recitative composed by Berlioz), the infamously scandalous 1861 version of Wagner's *Tannhäuser* (as well as its 1891 antidote, *Lohengrin*), and a number of Verdi operas. The Opéra generally performed three times a week during its season, which lasted most of the year.

Below is a list of notable premieres by the Opéra company.[14]

Gioachino Rossini, *Guillaume Tell* (3 Aug. 1829)
Giacomo Meyerbeer, *Robert le diable* (21 Nov. 1831)
Daniel-François-Esprit Auber, *Gustave III, ou le bal masqué* (27 Feb. 1833)
Fromental Halévy, *La juive* (23 Feb. 1835)
Giacomo Meyerbeer, *Les huguenots* (29 Feb. 1836)
Hector Berlioz, *Benvenuto Cellini* (10 Sept. 1838)
Gaetano Donizetti, *La favorite* (2 December 1840)

14. Except where otherwise noted, I have consulted Stanley Sadie, ed., *The New Grove Dictionary of Opera*, 4 vols. (London: Macmillan, 1992), for the premiere dates listed in this essay.

Adolphe Adam, *Giselle* (28 June 1841)[15]

Gaetano Donizetti, *Dom Sébastien, roi de Portugal* (13 Nov. 1843)

Giuseppe Verdi, *Jérusalem* (26 November 1847)

Giacomo Meyerbeer, *Le prophète* (16 Apr. 1849)

Charles Gounod, *Sapho* (16 Apr. 1851)

Charles Gounod, *La nonne sanglante* (18 Oct. 1854)

Giuseppe Verdi, *Les vêpres siciliennes* (13 June 1855)

Charles Gounod, *La reine de Saba* (28 Feb. 1862)

Giacomo Meyerbeer, *L'Africaine* (28 Apr. 1865)

Giuseppe Verdi, *Don Carlos* (11 Mar. 1867)

Ambroise Thomas, *Hamlet* (9 Mar. 1868)

Léo Délibes, *Coppélia* (25 May 1870)[16]

Jules Massenet, *Le roi de Lahore* (27 April 1877)

Victorin Joncières, *La reine Berthe* (27 Dec. 1878)

Camille Saint-Saëns, *Henry VIII* (5 Mar. 1883)

Jules Massenet, *Le Cid* (30 Nov. 1885)

Camille Saint-Saëns, *Ascanio* (21 Mar. 1890)

Jules Massenet, *Thaïs* (16 Mar. 1894)

Augusta Holmès, *La montagne noire* (8 Feb. 1895)

Alfred Bruneau, *Messidor* (19 Feb. 1897)

The Théâtre Royal de l'Opéra-Comique of 1830 emerged from the 1801 union of the Comédie-Italienne with the Théâtre Feydeau.[17] Designated as one of the four *grands théâtres* in 1807, the Opéra-Comique stood second in prestige only to the Opéra throughout most of the nineteenth century. This did not, however, protect the company from financial crisis. Beginning in 1829 the Opéra-Comique experienced several disastrous years, resulting in the eventual transfer of the theater's financial burden from the state to an independent director.[18] Competition from the Théâtre de la Renaissance, the Théâtre-Lyrique, and the Théâtre des Bouffes-Parisiens, as well as several fires, prevented the Opéra-Comique from achieving a solid financial footing.

Like the Opéra, the Opéra-Comique's repertoire was constructed around French composers and performers. The company possessed the exclusive license for the per-

15. This date is listed in Joël-Marie Fauquet, ed., *Dictionnaire de la musique en France au XIXe siècle* (Paris: Fayard, 2003).

16. For this date, see ibid.

17. For a more detailed account of the early administration of the Opéra-Comique, see M. Elizabeth C. Bartlet, "Archival Sources for the Opéra-Comique and its Registres at the Bibliothèque de l'Opéra," *Nineteenth-Century Music* 7 (1983): 119–29.

18. Wild, *Dictionnaire*, 329–30.

TABLE 16.2. Chronology and administration of the Opéra-Comique company

Name	Location	Date	Director	Status
Théâtre Royale de l'Opéra-Comique	Salle Ventadour	20 Apr. 1829	Paul-Auguste Ducis	
		July 1830	Jean-François Boursault; Alexandre Huvé de Garel	Société des Propriétaires with state subvention
		5 Aug. 1830	Alexandre Singier	
		12 Aug. 1831		Closed
		1 Oct. 1831	Emile Lubbert (provisional director)	
		13 Dec. 1831		Closed
		14 Jan. 1832	Emile Laurent	
		Mar. 1832		Closed
		1 June 1832	Paul Dutreich	Limited partnership with state subvention
	Salle de la Bourse	24 Sept. 1832		
		May 1834	François-Louis Crosnier (director); Alphonse Cerfbeer (administrator)	
	Salle Favart (2nd salle)	16 May 1840		
		May 1845	Alexandre Basset	
Théâtre Impérial de l'Opéra-Comique		May 1848	Emile Perrin	
	Salle Ventadour	26 June 1853		
	Salle Favart (2nd salle)	4 July 1853		
		20 Nov. 1857	Nestor Roqueplan	
		19 June 1860	Alfred Beaumont	
		1 Feb. 1862	Perrin	
		20 Dec. 1862	Adolphe de Leuven; Eugène Ritt	
		July 1870	De Leuven; Camille du Locle	
		Jan. 1874	du Locle	
		Mar. 1876	Perrin (interim director)	
		Aug. 1876	Léon Carvalho	
		25 May 1887	Jules Barbier	
	Salle du Théâtre Lyrique (until 30 June 1898)	15 Oct. 1887		
		Jan. 1888	Paravey	
		1 Jan. 1891	Carvalho	
		16 Jan. 1898	Albert Carré	
	Salle Favart (3rd salle)	8 Dec. 1898		

SOURCES: Wild, *Dictionnaire,* 324–38; Harris-Warrick, Charlton, Johnson, Smith, and Pitt, "Paris," 3:868–70, 877–79.

FIGURE 16.3. Fire at the Opéra-Comique, view from the Place Boieldieu. *L'illustration*, 28 May 1887. Courtesy of Duke University Library.

formance of *opéra comique:* works consisting of musical numbers connected by spoken dialogue in French. In the first half of the nineteenth century, formulaic romantic plots including traditionally French sentimental *romances* and comic strophic songs dominated the conservative repertory of the Opéra-Comique. After 1848, Émile Perrin began to include works that resembled farcical *opéra bouffe,* in response to the growing popularity of Offenbach's Bouffes-Parisiens.

In the latter part of the century, the Opéra-Comique's repertoire and aesthetic vision underwent significant transformation. By the 1870s works featuring sung recitative had begun to appear on its stage. Under the directorship of Albert Carré, Opéra-Comique productions turned toward a realist aesthetic, preparing the stage for such dramatic works as Gustave Charpentier's *Louise* and Claude Debussy's *Pelléas et Mélisande*.[19]

Below is a list of notable premieres by the Opéra-Comique company.

Daniel-François-Esprit Auber, *Fra Diavolo, ou l'hôtellerie de Terracine* (28 Jan. 1830)

Ferdinand Hérold, *Zampa, ou la fiancée de marbre* (3 May 1831)

Ferdinand Hérold, *Le pré aux clercs* (15 Dec. 1832)

Adolphe Adam, *Le postillon de Lonjumeau* (13 Oct. 1836)

Gaetano Donizetti, *La fille du régiment* (11 Feb. 1840)

Ambroise Thomas, *Le caïd* (3 Jan. 1849)

Ambroise Thomas, *Le songe d'une nuit d'été* (20 Apr. 1850)

Giacomo Meyerbeer, *L'étoile du Nord* (16 Feb. 1854)

Daniel-François-Esprit Auber, *Manon Lescaut* (23 Feb. 1856)

Ambroise Thomas, *Mignon* (17 Nov. 1866)

Camille Saint-Saëns, *La princesse jaune* (12 June 1872)

Georges Bizet, *Carmen* (3 Mar. 1875)

Léo Délibes, *Jean de Nivelle* (8 Mar. 1880)

Jacques Offenbach, *Les contes d'Hoffmann* (10 Feb. 1881)

Léo Délibes, *Lakmé* (14 Apr. 1883)

Jules Massenet, *Manon* (19 Jan. 1884)

Emmanuel Chabrier, *Le roi malgré lui* (18 May 1887)

Edouard Lalo, *Le roi d'Ys* (7 May 1888)

Jules Massenet, *Esclarmonde* (15 May 1889)

Alfred Bruneau, *Le rêve* (18 June 1891)

Jules Massenet, *Cendrillon* (24 May 1899)

Gustave Charpentier, *Louise* (2 Feb. 1900)

Claude Debussy, *Pelléas et Mélisande* (30 Apr. 1902)

The "Bouffons" troupe, formed in 1801, was incorporated by the 1807 laws as part of the Théâtre de l'Impératrice. Now called Théâtre-Italien, the company was licensed to perform Italian opera (both serious and comic) in its original language. Rossini's arrival in Paris with the 1817 premiere of *L'Italiana in Algeri* marked the start of an exciting era during which the Théâtre-Italien functioned as a gateway for Italian opera composers into French operatic life.[20] Donizetti, Bellini, and later Verdi came to Paris to mount productions of their smash hits and stayed to compose operas specifically for Parisian audiences.

19. Harris-Warrick, Charlton, Johnson, Smith, and Pitt, "Paris," 3:878–79.

20. For a detailed study of the earlier history of the Théâtre-Italien, see Janet Johnson, "The Théâtre Italien and Opera and Theatrical Life in Restoration Paris, 1818–1827" (Ph.D. diss., University of Chicago, 1988).

TABLE 16.3. Chronology and administration of the Théâtre-Italien company

Name	Location	Date	Director	Status
Théâtre-Royal-Italien	Salle Favart	1 Oct. 1830	Édouard Robert; Carlo Severini	Franchised entrepreneurship with state subvention
		14 Jan. 1838	Robert	Closed due to fire
	Salle Ventadour	30 Jan. 1838 to 31 Mar. 1838		
	Théâtre de l'Odéon (until 31 Mar. 1841)	Oct. 1838		
		10 Nov. 1838	Louis Viardot (until 22 Feb. 1840)	
		27 Apr. 1840	Charles Dormoy	
	Salle Ventadour	2 Oct. 1841		
		6 May 1842	Joseph Janin	
		12 Dec. 1843	August-Eugène Vatel	
Théâtre-Italien		1848		
		1 Apr. 1848	Henri Dupin	
		3 Jan. 1849	Georges Ronconi	
		1 Oct. 1850	Benjamin Lumley	
Théâtre-Impérial-Italien		1852		
		7 Oct. 1852	Alexandre Corti (until 28 July 1853)	
		20 Oct. 1853	Colonel César Ragani	
		16 July 1855	Torribio Calzado	
		15 Feb. 1863	Andres Mico, provisional director	
		1 May 1863	Prosper Bagier	
Théâtre-Italien		1870		
		18 May 1870		Closed
		9 Mar. 1872	Amédée Verger	Reopened
		28 Dec. 1872		Closed due to bankruptcy
		1 Oct. 1873	Maurice Strakosch (until May 1874)	Reopened
		19 Jan. 1874		Shared Salle Ventadour with Opéra
Théâtre Ventadour		Oct. 1874	Bagier	
3e Théâtre-Lyrique		31 Aug. 1874		
Théâtre Ventadour		Jan. 1875		
Théâtre-Italien		Nov. 1875	Enrico (one performance only)	
		Apr. 1876	Léon Escudier	
		28 June 1878		Final performance

SOURCES: Wild, *Dictionnaire,* 194–209; Harris-Warrick, Charlton, Johnson, Smith, and Pitt, "Paris," 3:870–71.

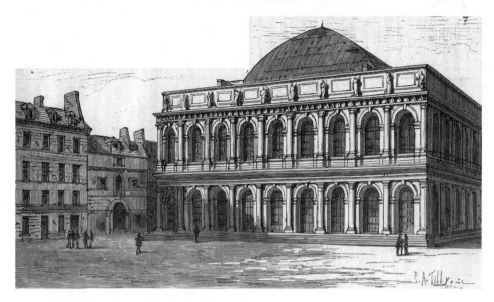

FIGURE 16.4. Théâtre-Italien at the Salle Ventadour. *L'illustration*, 15 December 1883. Courtesy of Duke University Library.

Despite the constant threat of bankruptcy, this theater boasted the best singers and orchestra in Europe. During the July Monarchy the Théâtre-Italien was sustained by performances of hit operas from the 1820s, particularly those of Donizetti and Rossini. The French premiere of Verdi's *Nabucco* was given in 1845; the first of fifteen operas by Verdi to be performed at the Théâtre-Italien, this production brought new life to the theater in the late 1840s and 1850s. Competition from the Opéra and Théâtre-Lyrique after the termination of the Théâtre-Italien's exclusive right to Italian-language operas eventually resulted in its permanent bankruptcy and closure in 1878.

Below is a list of notable premieres by the Théâtre-Italien company.[21]

Gioachino Rossini, *Il viaggio a Reims* (19 June 1825)
Vincenzo Bellini, *I Puritani* (24 Jan. 1835)
Gaetano Donizetti, *Marino Faliero* (12 Mar. 1835)
Gaetano Donizetti, *Don Pasquale* (3 Jan. 1843)

Established well before 1789, the Théâtre de la Gaîté was licensed as a *théâtre secondaire* in 1807. During the first half of the nineteenth century, the company performed a mix of pantomime, melodrama, and comic plays. The construction of a new

21. Most premieres given at the Théâtre-Italien introduced operas that had already received their first performances elsewhere. The four premieres listed here can thus be considered exceptional events.

TABLE 16.4. Chronology and administration of the Théâtre de la Gaîté company

Name	Location	Date	Director	Status
Théâtre de la Gaîté	68, Boulevard du Temple	5 July 1825	Charles Guilbert de Pixérécourt	Franchised entrepreneurship with state subvention
		1 Apr. 1835	Jean-Henri Bernard, *dit* Bernard Léon	
		6 Jul. 1837	Baron de Cès-Caupenne	
		2 Aug. 1837		Combined operation with Théâtre de l'Ambigu-Comique
		8 Oct. 1838	Horace Meyer; Adolphe Lemoine, *dit* Montigny	
		1844	Meyer	
		5 Mar. 1849	Hippolyte Hostein	
		After 3 Oct. 1849	Hostein; Achille Collin; Frédéric Soulié	
		1 May 1850	Collin	
		20 Feb. 1851	Hostein	
		1 May 1858	Alfred Harmant	
	Square des Arts et Métiers	3 Sept. 1862		
		1 June 1865	Louis-François Dumaine	
		1 Apr. 1868	Victor Koning	
		13 Mar. 1869	Maurice Boulet	
		1 June 1873	Jacques Offenbach	
		1 July 1875	Albert Vizentini	
Opéra-National-Lyrique		5 May 1876		
Théâtre de la Gaîté		2 Jan. 1878		
		11 Feb. 1878		Society of Composers and state subvention
		18 May 1878	Camille Weinschenk	Franchised entrepreneurship with state subvention
Opéra Populaire		27 Oct. 1879	Louis Martinet; Husson; Rival de Rouville	
Théâtre de la Gaîté		Feb. 1880		
		Mar. 1880	de Rouville	

SOURCES: Wild, *Dictionnaire*, 165–74; Harris-Warrick, Charlton, Johnson, Smith, and Pitt, "Paris," 3:872.

TABLE 16.5. Chronology and administration of the Théâtre de l'Odéon company

Name	Location	Date	Director	Status
Théâtre Royal de l'Odéon	Salle de l'Odéon	1 Sept. 1829	Charles-Jean Harel	Adm. Gér.
		Sept. 1832		Comédie-Française and Opéra-Comique in residence
		1 Dec. 1837	Alexandre Poulet *dit* Vedel and Valmore	Adm. Gér.
		1 Oct. 1838		Théâtre-Italien in residence
		1 Oct. 1841	Jean-Baptiste Violet d'Epagny	Adm. Gér.
		Feb. 1842	Auguste Lireux	
		1 June 1845	Pierre-François Tousez, *dit* Bocage	
		1 Mar. 1847	Augustin Vizentini	
		Mar. 1848	Eugène Lemaire	Conseil d'administration [board of directors]
		July 1848	Alexandre Mauzin	Société [company]
		1 Apr. 1849	Bocage	
		21 Aug. 1850	Michel Altaroche	
		1 Aug. 1853	Alphonse Royer	
		1 July 1856	Charles de La Rounat	
		1 June 1866	Charles de Chilly	
		11 June 1872	Félix Duquesnel	
		1 June 1880	de La Rounat	
		25 May 1882	de La Rounat; Paul Porel	
		26 Dec. 1884	Porel	
		31 May 1892		Porel handed it "back" to "the State"

SOURCES: Wild, *Dictionnaire*, 291–96; Harris-Warrick, Charlton, Johnson, Smith, and Pitt, "Paris," 3:872.

FIGURE 16.5. Théâtre de l'Odéon, view from the Place de l'Odéon; engraving by Le Campion. Estampes et photographie. Bibliothèque nationale de France.

building on the Square des Arts et Métiers in 1862 gave directors of the Théâtre de la Gaîté a suitable space in which to present full-scale operas. Both Offenbach and Albert Vizentini engaged troupes to perform a variety of opera (including *grand opéra, opéra comique,* and *opéra féerie*) and other musical entertainments in the 1870s. Offenbach's extravagant productions far exceeded his budget, and he left the theater after just two years. In Vizentini's hands (1875–78) the company returned to *opéra bouffe* and spoken drama. No major operatic premieres were mounted at this theater.

Reincarnated in 1819 as a second Théâtre-Français, the Théâtre Royal de l'Odéon functioned as a branch of the Comédie-Française. The two companies performed essentially the same theatrical repertoire until 1823, when the Odéon obtained permission to mount productions of public-domain *opéras comiques* or translated Italian and German operas with spoken dialogue. The Théâtre de l'Odéon maintained the opera troupe until 1828, when it was dissolved for financial reasons.[22]

As a result of the 20 March 1832 statute that placed the stage at the disposal of other theater companies, opera productions at the Salle l'Odéon after 1828 were scheduled mainly when other opera companies needed alternative accommodation. The Comédie-Française and Opéra-Comique troupes performed in the Salle l'Odéon between 1832 and 1838, and the Théâtre-Italien company performed there between

22. Everist, *Giacomo Meyerbeer,* 145–46.

1838 and 1841. In the latter part of the nineteenth century, the important musical premieres were not opera productions, but spoken dramas with incidental music by major French composers.[23]

Below is a list of notable premieres by the Théâtre de l'Odéon company.

Félix Mendelssohn, music for Sophocles' *Antigone* (21 May 1844)
Jules Massenet, music for Leconte de Lisle's *Les Érinnyes* (6 January 1873)
Georges Bizet, music for Daudet's *L'Arlésienne* (5 May 1885)
Charles Marie Widor, music for Dorchain's *Conte d'avril* (22 Sept. 1885)
Gabriel Fauré, music for Dumas's *Caligula* (8 November 1888)
Gabriel Fauré, music for Shakespeare/Haraucourt's *Shylock* (17 Dec. 1889)

After two years of negotiation, the first incarnation of the Théâtre de la Renaissance opened in 1838 with a license to perform both spoken and music drama. In order to avoid the potentially litigious wrath of the Opéra-Comique and Opéra companies, the Renaissance's founder and director, Anténor Joly, agreed to produce only *vaudevilles avec airs nouveaux* and *opéra de genre*—no *grand opéra* or *opéra comique*.[24] Although both genres technically fell within the letter of the laws that protected the other theaters' rights to particular repertoires, in reality they gave the Théâtre de la Renaissance the opportunity to challenge traditional generic boundaries.[25] The lack of state funding, however, led ultimately to the theater's closing in 1841. At this time the Théâtre-Italien took over the Salle Ventadour.

A second Théâtre de la Renaissance appeared briefly in 1868 under the direction of Léon Carvalho. Before resigning from the Théâtre-Lyrique, Carvalho produced lyric opera in the Salle Ventadour with the company from the Théâtre-Lyrique.[26] Bankruptcy forced him to give up both enterprises in May of 1868.

A third theater was established in March 1873. Though its repertoire consisted mainly of spoken dramas and comedies, the company also performed operetta, *opéra comique, opéra bouffe,* and, after 1893, *opéra lyrique.*[27]

Below is a list of notable premieres by the Théâtre de la Renaissance company.

Friedrich Flotow, *Lady Melvil* (15 Nov. 1838)
Friedrich Flotow, *L'eau merveilleuse* (30 Jan. 1839)
Jacques Offenbach, *La jolie parfumeuse* (29 Nov. 1873)

23. Harris-Warrick, Charlton, Johnson, Smith, and Pitt, "Paris," 3:872.
24. In *vaudevilles avec airs nouveaux,* musical numbers are connected by spoken dialogue while sung recitative appears in *opéras de genre.* Everist, "Theatres of Litigation," 140.
25. Ibid., 135–37.
26. Wild, *Dictionnaire,* 378.
27. Ibid., 281.

TABLE 16.6. Chronology and administration of the Théâtre de la Renaissance company

PHASE 1

Name	Location	Date	Director	Status
Théâtre de la Renaissance	Salle Ventadour	8 Nov. 1838	Anténor Joly	Private entrepreneurship with no state subvention
		2 May 1840		Closed due to financial problems
		26 Jan. 1841		Reopened to perform only spoken drama
		16 May 1841		Theater permanently occupied by Théâtre-Italien troupe

PHASE 2

Name	Location	Date	Director	Status
Théâtre de la Renaissance	Salle Ventadour	16 Mar. 1868	Léon Carvalho	Private entrepreneurship with no state subvention
		5 May 1868		Closed due to bankruptcy

PHASE 3

Name	Location	Date	Director	Status
Théâtre de la Renaissance	20, Boulevard Saint-Martin	8 Mar. 1873	Hippolyte Hostein	Private entrepreneurship with no state subvention
		1875	Victor Koning	
		1882	Gravière	
		1884	Hecquart	
		1884	Fernand Samuel	
		1888	Victor Silvestre	
		1889	Letombe	
		1891	Lerville	
Théâtre-Lyrique		Jan. 1893	Léonce Detroyat	
Théâtre de la Renaissance		Apr. 1893	Sarah Bernhardt; Maurice Grau	
Théâtre-Lyrique de la Renaissance		Mar. 1899 to Mar. 1900	Adolphe and Georges Milliaud	

SOURCE: Wild, *Dictionnaire*, 375–81.

FIGURE 16.6. Théâtre de la Renaissance, near the Porte Saint-Martin; lithograph by Ferdinand, drawing by L. Avenet. Iconographie sur le Théâtre de la Renaissance, Arts du spectacle. Bibliothèque nationale de France.

Charles Lecocq, *La petite mariée* (21 Dec. 1875)
Charles Lecocq, *La camargo* (20 Nov. 1878)
Charles Lecocq, *La petite mademoiselle* (12 Apr. 1879)
Jacques Offenbach, *Belle Lurette* (30 Oct. 1880)
Charles Lecocq, *Janot* (21 Jan. 1881)
Marguerite Olagnier, *Le saïs* (18 Dec. 1881)
Gaston Serpette, *Madame le diable* (5 Apr. 1882)
Raoul Pugno, *Ninetta* (26 Dec. 1882)
Edmond Audran, *Miette* (24 Sept. 1888)
Raoul Pugno, *La petite poucette* (7 Mar. 1891)
Paul Lacome, *Mademoiselle Asmodée* (24 Nov. 1891)
Gabriel Fauré, music for Clemenceau's *Le voile du bonheur* (4 Nov. 1901)

In the 1840s Hector Berlioz, Adolphe Adam, and Ambroise Thomas, among others, submitted the first of several petitions that would ultimately result in the foundation

TABLE 16.7. Chronology and administration of the Opéra-National/
Théâtre-Lyrique company

Name	Location	Date	Director	Status
Opéra-National	Converted Cirque Olympique building	15 Nov. 1847	Adolphe Adam	Private entrepreneurship
		29 Mar. 1848		Closed due to revolution
		1 May 1851	Sébastien *dit*	
	Théâtre-Historique	27 Sept. 1851	Edmond Seveste	Reopened
Théâtre-Lyrique		4 Mar. 1852	Jules Seveste	Private entrepreneurship
		12 Apr. 1852		
		26 July 1854	Émile Perrin	
		26 Sept. 1855	Pierre Pellegrin	
		15 Feb. 1856	Léon Carvalho	
		1 Apr. 1860	Charles Réty	
	Salle du Théâtre-Lyrique (Place du Châtelet)	7 Oct. 1862	Carvalho (until May 1868)	
		30 Oct. 1862		
		1864		Private entrepreneurship with state subvention
		22 Aug. 1868	Jules Pasdeloup	
		1 Feb. 1870	Charles Benou	Society of Artists
		1 July 1870	Louis Martinet	
		31 May 1871		Closed due to fire
Théâtre-Lyrique (Salle de l'Athénée)	Salle de l'Athénée	11 Sept. 1871		Private entrepreneurship with subvention
Théâtre-National-Lyrique		Mar. 1872		
		31 May–6 June 1872		Closed permanently due to bankruptcy

SOURCE: Wild, *Dictionnaire*, 237–44, 339–42.

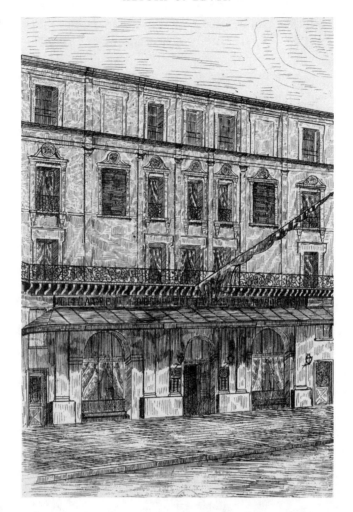

FIGURE 16.7. Théâtre-Lyrique; engraving by Georges-François
Guiaud. *L'illustration*, 15 December 1883. Courtesy of Duke University Library.

of the Théâtre-Lyrique. The Théâtre de la Renaissance had recently failed, once again
limiting the performance of French opera to the Opéra and the Opéra-Comique.
Establishing a third stage for new French works proved to be no easy task. The Opéra-
National finally opened its doors in November 1847, only to close them a few months
later amid the tumult of the 1848 Revolution. Eventually reopened in 1851 with a new
name, the Théâtre-Lyrique company challenged the dominance of the Opéra and
Opéra-Comique in French operatic life over the course of the next twenty years.[28] The

28. T. J. Walsh, *Second Empire Opera: The Théâtre Lyrique, Paris, 1851–1870* (London: John
Calder; New York: Riverrun Press, 1981), 1–2.

TABLE 16.8. Chronology and administration of the Théâtre des Bouffes-Parisiens company

Name	Location	Date	Director	Status
Théâtre des Bouffes-Parisiens	Champs-Élysées, Carré Marigny	5 July 1855	Jacques Offenbach; Charles Comte	Private entrepreneurship
	Salle Choiseul	29 Dec. 1855		
		5 Feb. 1862	Alphonse Varney	
		27 Sept. 1864	Eugène Hanappier; Armand Lapoint	
		17 Sept. 1866	François Varcollier	
		8 Jul. 1867	Julien-Joseph-Henry Dupontavisse and August Lefranc	
		Aug. 1868	Jules Noriac; Comte	
		1870		Closed
		16 Apr. 1871		Reopened
		1873	Comte	
		1879	Louis Cantin	
		1885		

SOURCE: Wild, *Dictionnaire*, 61–65.

Opéra-National was initially licensed to perform new *opéras comiques* and revivals of old *opéras comiques* and *grands opéras*. Legislation of 1851 required the production of new operas by unknown French composers (totaling at least fifteen acts per year). It also permitted the performance of up to two translations of Italian or German operas per year as well as older French lyric or comic operas by contemporary composers at least ten years after their premieres.

The diverse repertoire of the Théâtre-Lyrique "cracked the strict organization of the Parisian operatic world by breaking away from the principle that institution and genre were of one substance."[29] Without the limitations or established reputation under which the Opéra, Opéra-Comique, and Théâtre-Italien companies operated, composers and directors at the Théâtre-Lyrique could experiment within the bounds of the preexisting genres of *grand opéra* and *opéra comique*. The language of the initial subvention privileged young, untried composers; hence, it comes as no surprise that despite its short career, the Théâtre-Lyrique provided important opportunities for the generation of French composers that succeeded Rossini and Meyerbeer.

29. Lacombe, *Keys to French Opera*, 245.

FIGURE 16.8. Théâtre des Bouffes-Parisiennes, in P. Loiseau-Rousseau, *Les théâtres de Paris: Eaux-fortes* (Paris: Deviers, 1878), n.p. Estampes et Photographie. Bibliothèque nationale de France.

Although the company benefited from annual government subsidies after 1863, Louis Martinet, who assumed directorship in 1870, was unable to recover after the theater's home at the Place du Châtelet was destroyed in 1871. Bankruptcy was declared in 1872 and the company was disbanded permanently.

Below is a list of notable premieres by the Théâtre-Lyrique company.[30]

Félicien David, *La perle du Brésil* (22 Nov. 1851)
Adolphe Adam, *Si j'étais roi* (4 Sept. 1852)
Adolphe Adam, *Le roi des Halles* (11 Apr. 1853)
Charles Gounod, *Faust* (19 Mar. 1859)
Fromental Halévy, *Jaguarita l'indienne* (14 May 1855)
Georges Bizet, *Les pêcheurs de perles* (30 Sept. 1863)
Hector Berlioz, *Les Troyens à Carthage* (4 Nov. 1863)
Charles Gounod, *Roméo et Juliette* (27 Apr. 1867)

30. For a complete account of performances and premieres given by the Théâtre Lyrique, see Walsh, *Second Empire Opera*, 323–30. The list in fig. 16.7 was drawn largely from Walsh's text.

In February 1855 Jacques Offenbach requested permission to bring to Paris what he called a "new and original" genre of musical entertainment. These productions, he claimed, would appeal to the masses while providing another outlet for the talents of young composers.[31] The company, called the "Bouffes-Parisiens," gave its first performance in the Salle Lacaze (on the Carré Marigny) in July 1855, during the Exposition Universelle. Offenbach immediately moved ahead with his plans, successfully petitioning in October 1855 to merge his new company and the Théâtre Comte, which occupied the Salle Choiseul. A partnership ensued between Offenbach and Charles Comte, then director of the Salle Choiseul. For its first five years, the Bouffes-Parisiens had the use of the Salle Choiseul during the theater season, and the Salle Lacaze during the summer months.[32]

The repertoire of the Bouffes-Parisiens initially included comic and musical sketches with two or three characters; pantomimes; dances performed by five or more dancers; and *chansonettes*. Performances given during the summer of 1855 consisted mainly of satirical sketches that included some musical numbers. After merging with the Théâtre Comte, the license was modified to include one-act comedies (with or without music) with fewer than five characters, but to exclude the shorter and less formalized musical "sketches." A further stipulation requiring the performance of works by at least two additional composers other than Offenbach was also passed at this time.

In spite of the restrictions that dictated the size and scope of Bouffes-Parisiens productions, Offenbach expanded the theater's repertoire to include one- and two-act *opéras bouffes* as well as longer operettas. His own *Orphée aux enfers,* for example, was premiered there in 1858 even though it failed to conform to the restrictions of the Bouffes-Parisiens license. After Offenbach left the Bouffes-Parisiens in 1866, taking his works with him, the theater continued to perform light operas.

Below is a list of notable premieres by the Théâtre des Bouffes-Parisiens company.

Jacques Offenbach, *Ba-ta-clan* (29 Dec. 1855)
Léo Delibes, *Deux vieilles gardes* (8 Aug. 1856)
Charles Lecocq, *Le docteur miracle* (8 Apr. 1857)
Georges Bizet, *Le docteur miracle* (9 Apr. 1857)
Jacques Offenbach, *Orphée aux enfers* (21 Oct. 1858)
Léo Delibes, *L'omelette à la Follembuche* (8 June 1859)
Jacques Offenbach, *Geneviève de Brabant* (19 Nov. 1859)

---

31. Wild, *Dictionnaire,* 61.

32. Legislation passed in March 1861 prevented the company from occupying both theaters. See ibid., 62.

Jacques Offenbach, *Le carnaval des revues* (10 Feb. 1860)

Jacques Offenbach, *Barkouf* (24 Dec. 1860)

Delphine Ugalde, *Halte au moulin* (11 Jan. 1867)

Charles Lecocq, *Gandolfo* (16 Jan. 1869)

Charles Lecocq, *Le barbier de Trouville* (19 Nov. 1871)

Emmanuel Chabrier, *L'étoile* (28 Nov. 1877)

Louis Varney, *Les mousquetaires au couvent* (16 May 1880)

Victor Roger, *Joséphine vendue par ses sœurs* (20 Mar. 1886)

Raoul Pugno, *Le sosie* (8 Oct. 1887)

Raoul Pugno, *Le valet de cœur* (19 Apr. 1888)

Victor Roger, *Oscarine* (15 Oct. 1888)

Raoul Pugno, *Le retour d'Ulysse* (1 Feb. 1889)

André Messager, *Le mari de la reine* (18 Dec. 1889)

Paul Vidal, *Eros* (22 Apr. 1892)

Emile Pessard, *Mam'zelle Carabin* (3 Nov. 1893)

Charles Lecocq, *Ninette* (28 Feb. 1896)

André Messager, *Les p'tites Michu* (16 Nov. 1897)

BIBLIOGRAPHY

Sigla

F-Pan   France, Paris, Archives nationales
F-Pn   France, Paris, Bibliothèque nationale de France
F-Po   France, Paris, Bibliothèque-Musée de l'Opéra
F-Psc   France, Paris, Bibliothèque de la Société des Auteurs et des Compositeurs Dramatiques

Archival Sources

Académie Royale de Musique. Archives 1836. Dossier I, "Représentations/Correspondance général." *F-Pan*, AJ[13] 182.

———. *Cahier des charges,* 1831. *F-Pan*, AJ[13] 187.

———. *Cahier des charges,* 1835. *F-Pan*, AJ[13] 180.

Calvé, Emma, and Jules Massenet. Autograph letters. Archives Calvé, Millau.

Carvalho. Dossier d'artiste. *F-Po.*

Castil-Blaze [Blaze, François-Henri-Joseph]. *Histoire de l'opéra comique.* Manuscript [1856]. *F-Po*, MS Rés 660.

F-Pn, Département des arts du spectacle. Richelieu, coll. Rondel, Ro. 2088, Rt 1260.

Massenet, Jules. Dossier d'artiste. *F-Po.*

Offenbach, Jacques. Letter to Camille Doucet [director of the Administration des théâtres], 3 July 1854. *F-Pan*, F[21] 1120/2.

Opéra-Comique. Archives, including Contracts. *F-Pan*, AJ[13] 1051–60.

———. Arch. 19e. [79] 1883–84. *F-Po.*

———. Presse 1887 (May–June). *F-Po.*

———. Registres du travail 1876–77. *F-Po.*

Schneitzhoeffer, Jean Madeleine. *La sylphide.* Rehearsal score. Private collection of Alexander Bennett.

———. *La sylphide.* Rehearsal score. *F-Po*, Mat 19 [302(25)].

Scribe, Eugène. Papers. *Traités* I. *F-Pn* Ms., n.a.fr. 22839.

Société des Auteurs et Compositeurs Dramatiques. Minutes of the meetings, 1876–87. *F-Psc.*

Société du Théâtre National de l'Opéra Comique. Archives. *F-Pan*, AJ[13] 1135.

Théâtre des Bouffes Parisiens. Archival Documents. *F-Pan*, F[21] 1136.

Véron, Louis. Correspondence with the Commission de Surveillance of the Opéra, and the Ministry of the Interior, March–May 1834. *F-Pan,* AJ[13] 183 (D).

Newspapers and Periodicals

L'ami de la religion
L'art
L'art musical
L'artiste
Les annales du théâtre et de la musique
La causerie
Le charivari
Le clairon
Le constitutionnel
Le corsaire
Le corsaire-satan
Le coureur des spectacles
Le courrier des théâtres
Le courrier français
L'écho français
Le Figaro
La France musicale
La gazette de France
Le gaulois
Gil Blas
Le globe
Le guide musical
L'indépendance belge
La jeune France
Le journal de Francfort

Journal des débats
La liberté
Le ménestrel
Mercure de France
Le monde illustré
Le moniteur universel
Musica
La nation
Le national
L'opinion nationale
La patrie
Le pays
La petite presse
La presse
La quotidienne
Revue contemporaine
Revue de France
Revue des deux mondes
La revue et gazette musicale de Paris
La revue musicale
Le siècle
Le temps
Le théâtre
L'univers musical

Primary Sources

Adam, Adolphe. *Souvenirs d'un musicien.* Paris: Michel Lévy frères, 1857.

Aldini, Antonio. *Mémoires du comte Aldini, ministre secrétaire d'État pour le royaume d'Italie, résidant à Paris.* Paris: Allard, 1857.

Alonso, Celsa, ed. *Antología (siglo XIX): La canción andaluza.* Música hispana, Serie C Antologías 3. Madrid: Instituto Complutense de Ciencias Musicales, 1996.

———. *Canciones y caprichos liricos.* Música hispana, Serie C, Antologías 1. Madrid: Instituto Complutense de Ciencias Musicales, 1994.

———. *Cien años de canción lírica española.* Vol. 1. Música hispana, Serie C, Antologías 8. Madrid: Instituto Complutense de Ciencias Musicales, 2001.

Auber, Daniel-François-Esprit. *Gustave ou Le bal masqué*. Paris: Troupenas, [1833]; reprint, New York: Garland, 1980.

Auber, Daniel-François-Esprit, and Eugène Scribe. *Correspondance d'Eugène Scribe et Daniel-François-Esprit Auber*. Edited by Herbert Schneider. Liège: Éditions Mardaga, 1998.

Barboux, Henri. "Défense de M. Carvalho. Plaidoirie de Mr. Henri Barboux (1888)." *F-Pn*, 4⁰ Fr. 173 4635.

Berganza, Teresa. "Ma Carmen." In *Carmen*, vol. 26 of *L'avant-scène opéra* (1980): 117.

Berlioz, Hector. *Critique musicale*. Vol. 1. Edited by H. Robert Cohen and Yves Gérard. Paris: Buchet/Chastel, 1996.

———. *The Memoirs of Hector Berlioz*. Translated and edited by David Cairns. London: Victor Gollancz, 1969.

Bini, Annalisa, and Jeremy Commons, eds. *Le prime rappresentazioni delle opere di Donizetti nella stampa coeva*. Milan: Skira, 1997.

Bizet, Georges. *Carmen*. Orchestral score. Edited by Fritz Oeser. 2 vols. Kassel: Alkor Verlag, 1964.

———. *Carmen*. Orchestral score and parts. Edited by Richard Langham Smith. London: Peters.

———. *Carmen*. Piano-vocal score. Edited by Robert Didion. Mainz: Schott, 2000.

———. *Lettres (1850–1875)*. Edited by Claude Glayman. Paris: Calmann-Lévy, 1989.

———. *Lettres à un ami, 1865–1872*. With an introduction by Edmond Galabert. Paris: Calmann-Lévy, [1909?].

Blackburn, Vernon. *The Fringe of an Art: Appreciations in Music*. London: Unicorn Press, 1898.

Blondeau, [Pierre] Auguste L[ouis]. *Histoire de la musique moderne, depuis le premier siècle de l'ère chrétienne jusqu'à nos jours*. 2 vols. Paris: Tantenstein et Cordel, 1847.

Bouchard, Alfred. *La langue théâtrale*. Paris: Arnaud et Labat, 1878.

Brown, John. *The Northern Courts, Containing Original Memoirs of the Sovereigns of Sweden and Denmark since 1766*. 2 vols. Edinburgh: Constable; London: Fenner, 1818. Translated by Jean Cohen as *Les cours du Nord, ou Mémoires originaux sur les souverains de la Suède et du Danemarck depuis 1766*. 3 vols. Paris: A. Bertrand, 1820.

Bruneau, Alfred Bruneau. *À l'ombre d'un grand cœur*. Paris: Fasquelle, 1931.

Calvé, Emma. *My Life*. Translated by Rosamond Gilder. N.p.: D. Appleton, 1922; reprint, New York: Arno Press, 1977.

———. *Sous tous les ciels j'ai chanté*. Paris: Plon, 1940.

Castil-Blaze [François-Henri-Joseph-Castil Blaze]. *L'Académie Impériale de Musique: Histoire littéraire, musicale, chorégraphique, pittoresque, morale, critique, facétieuse, politique et galante de ce théâtre de 1645 à 1855*. 2 vols. Théâtres lyriques de Paris [1]. Paris: The author, 1855.

———. *L'Opéra-Italien de 1548 à 1856*. Théâtres lyriques de Paris [2]. Paris: The author, 1856.

Charbonnel, Raoul. *La danse*. Paris: Garnier frères, 1899.

Cohen, H. Robert, ed. *The Original Staging Manuals for Ten Parisian Operatic Premières, 1824–1843/Dix livrets de mise en scène lyrique datant des créations parisiennes, 1824–1843*. Stuyvesant, NY: Pendragon Press, 1998.

———. *The Original Staging Manuals for Twelve Parisian Operatic Premières/Douze livrets de mise en scène lyrique datant des créations parisiennes*. Stuyvesant, NY: Pendragon Press, 1991.

Coxe, William. *Travels in Poland, Russia, Sweden and Denmark. Interspersed with historical relations and political inquiries*. London: Cadell and Davies, 1784. Translated by P. H. Mallet as *Voyage en Pologne, Russie, Danemarck, etc.* Geneva: Barde, Manget et Cie, 1786.

Czerwinski, Albert. *Brevier der Tanzkunst: Die Tänze bei den Kulturvölkern von den ältesten Zeiten bis zur Gegenwart*. Leipzig: O. Spamer, 1879.

Daudet, Léon. *Quand vivait mon père: Souvenirs inédits sur Alphonse Daudet*. Paris: Grasset, 1940.

Davillier, Charles. *L'Espagne* [with 309 woodcuts by Gustave Doré]. Paris: Hachette, 1874.

———. *Spain*. Illustrated by Gustave Doré. Translated by J. Thomson. New York: Scribner, Welford and Armstrong, 1876.

———. *Le voyage en Espagne*. Paris: Stock, 1980.

Debussy, Claude. *Correspondance (1872–1918)*. Edited by François Lesure and Denis Herlin. Annotated by François Lesure, Denis Herlin, and Georges Liébert. Paris: Gallimard, 2005.

———. *Esquisses de "Pelléas et Mélisande" (1893–1895)*. Edited by François Lesure. Geneva: Minkoff, 1977.

Dechaux, J. B., ed. *Collection des écrits politiques, littéraires et dramatiques de Gustave III, roi de Suède, suivie de sa correspondance*. Stockholm: C. Delén, 1803–5.

Donizetti, Gaetano. *Théâtre de la Renaissance / Lucie de Lamermoor* [*sic*]. Piano-vocal score. Paris: Bernard Latte, [1839].

Draayer, Suzanne Rhodes, ed. *Canciones de España: Songs of Nineteenth-Century Spain*. Lanham, MD: Scarecrow Press, 2003.

"Drame lyrique." In *Grand dictionnaire universel du XIXe siècle*, edited by Pierre Larousse. 17 vols. Paris: Administration du Grand dictionnaire universel, 1870. 6:1188.

Droux, Léon. *L'Espagne à l'Exposition universelle de 1867*. Paris: Dentu, 1867.

Duverger, L[ouis]-V[ieillard]. *Mise en scène et décorations de "La juive": Grand opéra en cinq actes, paroles de M. Scribe, musique de M. Auber* [sic]; *Représenté à l'Académie Royale de Musique, le 23 Février 1835*. [Paris]: Bureau de Commission Théâtrale, [c. 1835].

Escudier, Marie, and Léon Escudier. *Dictionnaire de musique théorique et historique*. 5th ed. Paris: E. Dentu, 1872.

Fage, Juste-Adrien Lenoir de La. *Histoire générale de la musique et de la danse*. 2 vols and atlas. Paris: Comptoir des imprimeurs unis, 1844.

Fétis, François-Joseph. *Biographie universelle des musiciens*. 3 vols. Paris: Firmin-Didot, 1860–65.

————. *Biographie universelle des musiciens et bibliographie générale de la musique: Supplément et complément [à la 2. éd.]*, edited by Arthur Pougin. Paris: Firmin-Didot, 1878–80.

————. *Histoire générale de la musique depuis les temps les plus anciens jusqu'à nos jours.* 5 vols. Paris: Firmin-Didot, 1869–76.

Fokine, Mikhael. *Memoirs of a Ballet Master.* Edited by Anatole Chujoy. Translated by Vitale Fokine. Boston: Little, Brown, 1961.

Gallet, Louis. "Quatre directeurs de l'Opéra." *Revue internationale de musique* 4 (15 April 1898): 208–21.

Gautier, Théophile. *Gautier on Dance.* Translated and edited by Ivor Forbes Guest. London: Dance Books, 1986.

————. *Voyage en Espagne suivi de España.* Edited by Patrick Berthier. Paris: Éditions Gallimard, 1984.

Gautier, Théophile, and Paul Siraudin. *Un voyage en Espagne: Vaudeville en 3 actes.* Paris: Tresse, 1843.

Gazzaniga, Arrigo, ed. *Il signor Bruschino, ossia Il figlio per azzardo: farsa giocosa per musica in un atto di Giuseppe Foppa, musica di Gioachino Rossini.* Edizione critica delle opere di Gioachino Rossini 1:9. Pesaro: Fondazione Rossini, 1986.

Gheusi, P. B. *Midi.* Paris: Flammarion, n.d.

Giraud, Victor. *La vie tragique de Lamennais.* Paris: Presses Universitaires de France, 1933.

Grangé, Eugène, and Philippe Gilles. *Le carnaval des revues: Revue de carnaval en 2 actes et 9 tableaux; Les souper de mardi-gras, prologue, Paris, Bouffes-parisiens, le 10 février 1860 . . . Musique de Jacques Offenbach.* [Paris]: Michel Lévy frères, [1860].

Guimet, Émile. *L'Espagne, lettres familières, avec des post-scriptum en vers, par Henri de Riberolles.* Paris: L. Cajani, 1864.

Halévy, Fromental. *La juive.* Vol. 100 of *L'avant-scène opéra* (1987).

————. *La juive.* Vol. 36 of *Early Romantic Opera*, edited by Philip Gossett and Charles Rosen. New York: Garland, 1980.

————. *Lettres.* Edited by Marthe Galland. Heilbronn: Musik-Edition Lucie Galland, 1999.

Halévy, Léon. *F. Halévy: Sa vie et ses œuvres.* 2nd ed. Paris: Heugel, 1863.

Heylli, Georges d'. *Foyers et coulisses: Histoire anecdotique des théâtres de Paris; opéra comique.* Paris: Tresse et Stock, 1885.

Hostein, Hippolyte. *La liberté des théâtres.* Paris: Librairie des Amateurs, 1867.

Imbert, Hugues. *Portraits et études . . . : Lettres inédites de Bizet.* Paris: Fischbacher, 1894.

Indy, Vincent d'. *Ma vie.* Edited by Marie d'Indy. Paris: Séguier, 2001.

Jacobshagen, Arnold, ed. *Les contes d'Hoffmann: Dossier de presse parisienne (1881).* Heilbronn: Musik-Edition Lucie Galland, 1995.

Joliet, Charles. *Les pseudonymes du jour.* Paris: Achille Faure, 1867.

Joncières, Victorin [Félix Ludger Rossignol]. "La question du Théâtre-Lyrique." In *Les annales du théâtre et de la musique,* edited by Édouard Noël and Edmond Stoullig. Paris, 1881. 6:i–xviii.

Kobbé, Gustave. "Mme Calvé." In *Opera Singers: A Pictorial Souvenir*. Boston: Oliver Ditson, 1901, unpaginated.

———. *Signora*. New York: Thomas Y. Crowell, 1902.

Laget, Auguste. *Chollet, premier sujet du Théâtre de l'Opéra-Comique*. Toulouse: A. Chauvin et fils, 1880.

Lasalle, Albert de. *Histoire des Bouffes-Parisiens*. Paris: Bourdillat, 1860.

Lecomte, Louis-Henry. *Les Folies-Nouvelles*. Histoire des théâtres de Paris 4. Paris: Daragon, 1909.

Lefèvre, Maurice. "Georges Bizet, le musicien." *Musica* 11, no. 117 (June 1912): 102–3.

Leich-Galland, Karl, ed. *Fromental Halévy: "La juive": Dossier de presse parisienne (1835)*. Saarbrücken: L. Galland, 1987.

Lichtenthal, Pierre. *Dizionario e bibliografia della musica*. Milan, 1826. Translated and augmented by Dominique Mondo as *Dictionnaire de musique*. 2 vols. Paris: Troupenas, 1839.

Lucas, Charles. *L'Espagne à l'Exposition universelle de 1867, aperçu des nombreux et intéressants envois de la Direction générale des travaux publics de Madrid*. Paris: Chez l'auteur, 1867.

Manet, Édouard. *Voyage en Espagne*. Edited by Juliet Wilson-Bareau. Caen: L'Echoppe, 1988.

Martin, Henri. "Avertissement." In *L'histoire de France depuis les temps les plus reculés jusqu'en juillet 1830: Par les principaux historiens et d'après les plans de MM. Guizot, Augustin Thierry et de Barante*. 15 tomes en 8 vols. Paris: L. Mame, 1833–36.

Massenet, Jules. *Les Érinnyes*. Manuscript MS 4274. Département de la musique, Bibliothèque nationale de France.

———. *Les Érinnyes: Partition pour chant et piano*. Paris: G. Hartmann, 1876.

Ménil, Félicien de. *Histoire de la danse à travers les âges*. Paris: A. Piard et Kaan, 1905.

Meyerbeer, Giacomo. *Briefwechsel und Tagebücher*. Edited by Heinz Becker et al. 8 vols. Berlin: W. de Gruyter, 1959–2006.

———. *The Diaries of Giacomo Meyerbeer*. Vol. 1, *1791–1839*. Translated, edited, and annotated by Robert Ignatius Letellier. Madison, NJ: Fairleigh Dickinson University Press; London: Associated University Presses, 1999.

Michelet, Jules. *Histoire de France*. 17 vols. Paris: Hachette and Chamerot, 1833–67.

———. *Histoire de France*. In *Œuvres complètes*. 40 vols. Paris: Flammarion, 1893–98.

———. *Histoire de la révolution française*. 2 vols. Paris: Gallimard, 1952.

———. *Introduction à l'histoire universelle*. Paris: Hachette, 1831.

———. *Précis de l'histoire de France*. Paris: Hachette, 1833.

Monnais, Édouard. *F. Halévy: Souvenirs d'un ami pour joindre à ceux d'un frère*. Paris: Imprimerie Centrale des Chemins de Fer, 1863.

Nijinska, Bronislava. *Early Memoirs*. Translated and edited by Irina Nijinska and Jean Rawlinson. Durham, NC: Duke University Press, 1992.

Noël, Édouard, and Edmond Stoullig, eds. *Les annales du théâtre et de la musique* 1–26. Paris, 1876–1901.

Palianti, L[ouis], comp. *Collection de mises en scène, "La juive": Opéra en cinq actes de*

M. E. Scribe, musique de F. Halévy; Représenté pour la première fois à Paris, sur le Théâtre de l'Opéra, le 23 février 1835. [Paris]: The author, [c. 1868].

Pergolesi, Giovanni Battista. *La servante maitresse: Opéra comique en deux actes.* Paroles françaises de Baurans; musique de Pergolese [*sic*]. Partition réduite pour piano et chant par Soumis. Seule édition conforme aux représentations de l'Opéra-Comique et précédée d'un notice historique par Albert de Lasalle. . . . Paris: E. Girod, 1862.

Pougin, Arthur. "Drame lyrique." In *Dictionnaire historique et pittoresque du théâtre.* Paris: Firmin-Didot, 1885. 309.

———. *Figures d'Opéra-Comique: Madame Dugazon, Elleviou, les Gavaudan.* Paris: Tresse, 1875. Reprint, Geneva: Minkoff, 1973.

———. *Hérold: Biographie critique.* Paris: H. Laurens, 1906.

———. *Question de la liberté des théâtres: Rapport présenté à Monsieur le Ministre de l'Instruction publique et des Beaux-Arts par la Société des Compositeurs de Musique.* Paris: Société des Compositeurs de Musique, 1878.

Quicherat, Louis. *Adolphe Nourrit: Sa vie, son talent, son caractère, sa correspondance.* 3 vols. Paris: L. Hachette, 1867.

Rossini, Gioacchino. *Bruschino: Opéra bouffe en deux actes.* Poème de Mr A de Forges. Acct de piano par H Salomon. . . . Paris: Léon Escudier, [1857].

Saint-Saëns, Camille. "Histoire d'un opéra-comique." In *École buissonnière notes et souvenirs.* Paris: Pierre Laffitte, [1913]. 21–31.

Scribe, Eugène. *Gustave III, ou Le bal masqué.* Paris: Jonas, 1833.

———. *Gustave III, ou Le bal masqué.* Lyons: Boursy, n.d.

———. *Gustave III, ou Le bal masqué.* In *La France dramatique au dix-neuvième siècle, choix de pièces modernes.* Paris: Tresse, 1845.

———. *Théâtre complet.* 2nd ed. Vol. 14. Paris: A. André, 1835.

Servières, Georges. *Tannhæuser à l'Opéra en 1861.* Paris: Librairie Fischbacher, 1895.

Shaw, Bernard. *Shaw's Music.* Edited by Dan H. Laurence. 3 vols. New York: Dodd, Mead, 1981.

Soubies, Albert, and Charles Malherbe. *Histoire de l'Opéra-Comique: La seconde salle Favart.* Vol. 1, *1840–1860.* Paris: Librairie Marpon and Flammarion, 1892.

———. *Histoire de l'Opéra-Comique: La seconde salle Favart.* Vol. 2, *1860–1887.* Paris: Flammarion, 1893.

Strobel, Otto. *König Ludwig II. und Richard Wagner: Briefwechsel.* Karlsruhe: G. Braun, 1936.

Tamvaco, Jean-Louis, ed. *Les cancans de l'Opéra: Le journal d'une habilleuse, 1836–1848.* 2 vols. Paris: Éditions du CNRS, 2000.

Véron, Louis. *Mémoires d'un bourgeois de Paris.* 3 vols. Paris: G. de Gonet, 1853–55.

———. *Mémoires d'un bourgeois de Paris.* 3 vols. Paris: Librairie nouvelle, 1857.

Wagnalls, Mabel. "Calvé and Carmen." In *Stars of the Opera.* New York: Funk and Wagnalls, 1899. 107–8.

Wagner, Richard. *Mein Leben: 1813–1868.* Edited by Martin Gregor-Dellin. Munich: List Verlag, 1994.

———. *Prose Works.* Translated by William Ashton Ellis. Vol. 2, *Opera and Drama.* New York: Broude Brothers, 1966.

———. *Quatre poèmes d'opéras: Le vaisseau fantôme—Tannhæuser—Lohengrin—Tristan,* *précédés d'une "Lettre sur la musique."* New ed. with a preface by Gustave Samazeuilh. Paris: Mercure de France, 1941.

Woestyn, Eugène, and Eugène Moreau. *Les Folies-Nouvelles.* Paris: Martinon, [1855].

Wright, Lesley, ed. *Georges Bizet, "Carmen": Dossier de presse parisienne.* Weinsberg: Lucie Galland, 2001.

Secondary Sources

Abbate, Carolyn. "The Parisian 'Vénus' and the 'Paris' *Tannhäuser.*" *Journal of the American Musicological Society* 36 (1983): 73–123.

———. "The 'Parisian' Tannhäuser." Ph.D. diss., Princeton University, 1985.

Acocella, Joan, and Lynn Garafola, eds. *André Levinson on Dance: Writings from Paris in the Twenties.* Hanover: Wesleyan University Press, 1991.

Alonso, Celsa. "La réception de la chanson espagnole dans la musique française du XIXe siècle." In *Échanges musicaux franco-espagnols, XVIIe–XIXe siècles: Actes des rencontres de Villecroze,* edited by François Lesure. Paris: Klincksieck, 2000. 123–60.

———. "Las canciones de Manuel García." In booklet notes to *Manuel García: Yo que soy contrabandista y otras canciones.* Ernesto Palacio, tenor; and Juan José Chuquisengo, piano. DS 0114. Almaviva, 1995. 18–25.

Álvarez Cañibano, Antonio. "The Company of the Lefevre Family in Seville." In "The Origins of the Bolero School," edited by Javier Suárez-Pajares and Xoán M. Carreira. Special issue, *Studies in Dance History* 4, no.1 (1993): 21–37.

Amico, Federico d'. "*Il ballo in maschera* prima di Verdi." *Verdi: Bollettino dell'Istituto di studi verdiani* 1, no. 3 (1960): 1251–1328.

Anderson, Benedict. *Imagined Communities: Reflections on the Origin and Spread of Nationalism.* London and New York: Verso, 1991.

Ashbrook, William. *Donizetti and His Operas.* Cambridge: Cambridge University Press, 1982.

Baker, Evan. "Scene Designs for the First Performance of Bizet's *Carmen.*" *Nineteenth-Century Music* 13 (1990): 230–42.

Balanchine, George, and Francis Mason. *Balanchine's Complete Stories of the Great Ballets.* Revised and enlarged ed. Garden City, NY: Doubleday, 1977.

Balard, Françoise. *Geneviève Straus: Biographie et correspondance avec Ludovic Halévy, 1855–1908.* Paris: CNRS Éditions, 2002.

Bara, Olivier. "Influence des emplois sur la dramaturgie d'opéra-comique: Elleviou, Martin et l'âge d'or de la comédie." In *L'Opéra-comique à l'époque de Boieldieu (1775–1834),* edited by Patrick Taïeb. Paris: Éditions du CNRS, forthcoming.

———. *Le Théâtre de l'Opéra-Comique sous la Restauration: Enquête autour d'un genre moyen.* Hildesheim and New York: Georg Olms Verlag, 2001.

Barricelli, Jean-Pierre, and Leo Weinstein. *Ernest Chausson: The Composer's Life and Works.* Norman: University of Oklahoma Press, 1955.

Bartlet, M. Elizabeth C. "Archival Sources for the Opéra-Comique and its *Registres* at the Bibliothèque de l'Opéra." *Nineteenth-Century Music* 7 (1983): 119–29.

———. "From Rossini to Verdi." In *The Cambridge Companion to Grand Opera*, edited by David Charlton. Cambridge: Cambridge University Press, 2003. 258–90.

———. *Guillaume Tell di Gioachino Rossini: Fonti iconografiche*. Pesaro: Fondazione Rossini, 1996.

———. "Staging French Grand Opera: Rossini's *Guillaume Tell* (1829)." In *Gioachino Rossini, 1792–1992: Il testo e la scena; Convegno internazionale di studi, Pesaro, 24–28 giugno 1992*, edited by Paolo Fabbri. Pesaro: Fondazione Rossini, 1994. 623–48.

Bartoli, Jean-Pierre. "L'orientalisme dans la musique française du XIXe siècle: La ponctuation, la seconde augmentée, et l'apparition de la modalité dans les procédures exotiques." *Revue belge de musicologie* 51 (1997): 137–70.

Benjamin, Walter. *Das Passagenwerk*. Edited by Rolf Tiedemann. 2 vols. Frankfurt am Main: Edition Suhrkamp, 1983.

Bennett, Alexander. "The Ballet Called *La sylphide*." Unpublished manuscript.

Bergada, Montserrat. "Musiciens espagnols à Paris entre 1820 et 1868: État de la question et perspectives d'études." In *La musique entre France et Espagne: Interactions stylistiques (1870–1939)*, edited by Louis Jambou. Paris: Presses de l'Université de Paris-Sorbonne, 2003. 17–38.

———. "Les pianistes espagnols au Conservatoire de Paris au XIXe siècle." In *Échanges musicaux franco-espagnols, XVIIe–XIXe siècles: Actes des rencontres de Villecroze*, edited by François Lesure. Paris: Klincksieck, 2000. 195–234.

———. "Espagne." In *Dictionnaire de la musique en France au XIXe siècle*, edited by Joël-Marie Fauquet. Paris: Fayard, 2003. 434–38.

Blay, Philippe. "Albert Carré et la rénovation de l'Opéra-Comique." *Revue musicale de la Suisse Romande* 57, no. 1 (2004): 42–49.

———. "Un théâtre français, tout à fait français, ou Un débat fin-de-siècle sur l'Opéra-Comique." *Revue de musicologie* 87, no. 1 (2001): 105–44.

Fuchs, Arno. "Habanera." In *Die Musik in Geschichte und Gegenwart: Allgemeine Enzyclopädie der Musik*, edited by Friedrich Blume. 17 vols. Kassel: Bärenreiter, 1949–86. 5:1186–90.

Boigne, comtesse de. *Les mémoires de la comtesse de Boigne*. Vol. 2, *De 1820 à 1848*. Paris: Mercure de France, 1999.

Bonnaure, Jacques, ed. *Docteur Véron: L'Opéra de Paris, 1820–1835*. Originally published as *Mémoires d'un bourgeois*, 1853–55. Paris: Édition Michel de Maule, 1987.

Bould, Graham Howard. "The Lyric Theatre in Provincial France (1789–1914)." Ph.D. diss., University of Hull, 2005.

Branger, Jean-Christophe. "Henri Cain, artiste peintre et librettiste." In *Sapho; La Navarraise*, vol. 217 of *L'avant-scène opéra* (2003): 40–43.

———. *"Manon" de Jules Massenet, ou Le crépuscule de l'opéra-comique*. Metz: Éditions Serpenoise, 1999.

———. "Massenet et Emma Calvé, la 'Duse lyrique.'" In *Sapho; La Navarraise*, vol. 217 of *L'avant-scène opéra* (2003): 50–53.

Braunbehrens, Volkmar. *Mozart in Vienna, 1781–1791*. Translated by Timothy Bell. New York: Grove Weidenfeld, 1990.

Brissac, Anne de Cossé. *La comtesse Greffulhe*. Paris: Perrin, 1991.

Buckle, Richard. *Diaghilev*. New York: Atheneum, 1979.

Budden, Julian. *The Operas of Verdi*. 3 vols. New York: Oxford University Press, 1981.

Carbonneau, Suzanne. "Michel Fokine." In *International Encyclopedia of Dance,* edited by Selma Jeanne Cohen. 6 vols. New York: Oxford University Press, 1998. 3:14–28.

Cairns, David. *Berlioz*. Vol. 2, *Servitude and Greatness, 1832–1869*. London: Penguin, 1999.

Carner, Mosco. *Giacomo Puccini: Tosca*. Cambridge: Cambridge University Press, 1985.

Chaillou, David. *Napoléon et l'Opéra: La politique sur la scène, 1810–1815*. Paris: Fayard, 2004.

Charlton, David. "The *romance* and Its Cognates: Narrative, Irony and *vraisemblance* in Early Opéra Comique." In *Die Opéra Comique und ihr Einfluß auf das europäische Musiktheater im 19. Jahrhundert,* edited by Herbert Schneider and Nicole Wild. Musikwissenschaftliche Publikationen der Hochschule für Musik und Darstellende Kunst Frankfurt/Main 3. Hildesheim: Georg Olms Verlag, 1997. 43–92.

———, ed. *The Cambridge Companion to Grand Opera*. Cambridge: Cambridge University Press, 2003.

Chimènes, Myriam. *Mécènes et musiciens: Du salon au concert à Paris sous la IIIe République*. Paris: Fayard, 2004.

Christiansen, Rupert. *Prima Donna: A History*. Harmondsworth, Middlesex: Penguin, 1984.

Christoforidis, Michael. "Georges Bizet's *Carmen* and Spanish Nationalism." In *Romanticism and Nationalism in Music,* edited by Anastasia Siopsi. Corfu, forthcoming.

Clark, Maribeth. "The Role of *Gustave, ou Le bal masqué* in Restraining the Bourgeois Body of the July Monarchy." *Musical Quarterly* 88, no. 2 (2005): 204–31.

———. "Finding the Merit in the Masked Ball from *Gustave, ou Le bal masqué*." In "Understanding French Grand Opera through Dance." Ph.D. diss., University of Pennsylvania, 1998. 118–79.

Clark, Robert L. A. "South of North: *Carmen* and French Nationalisms." In *East of West: Cross-Cultural Performance and the Staging of Difference,* edited by Claire Sponsler and Xiaomei Chen. New York: Palgrave, 2000. 187–216.

Cohen, H. Robert. *Cent ans de mise en scène lyrique en France (environ 1830–1930): Catalogue descriptif des livrets de mise en scène, des libretti annotés et des partitions annotées dans la Bibl. de l'Association de la Régie Théâtrale (Paris)*. New York: Pendragon Press, 1986.

———. "La conservation de la tradition scénique sur la scène lyrique en France au XIXe siècle." *Revue de Musicologie* 64 (1978): 253–68.

———. *Les gravures musicales dans "L'illustration," 1843–1899*. 3 vols. Québec: Presses de l'Université Laval, 1983.

———. "On Preparing Critical Studies of the Original 'mise en scène' of Nineteenth-Century Operas." In *Opera & Libretto,* vol. 2, edited by Gianfranco Folena, Maria Teresa Muraro, and Giovanni Morelli. Florence: Olms, 1993. 215–24.

————. "On the Reconstruction of the Visual Elements of French Grand Opéra." In *International Musicological Society: Report of the Twelfth Congress, Berkeley, 1977*, edited by Daniel Heartz and Bonnie Wade. Kassel: Bärenreiter Verlag, 1981. 463–80.

Colmeiro, José F. "Exorcising Exoticism: *Carmen* and the Construction of Oriental Spain." *Comparative Literature* 2, no. 54 (Spring 2002): 127–44.

Condé, Gérard. "Commentaire musical." In *Sapho; La Navarraise*, vol. 217 of *L'avant scène opéra* (2003): 7–39.

Contrucci, Jean. *Emma Calvé: La diva du siècle*. Paris: Albin Michel, 1989.

Cooper, Barry. *Beethoven's Folksong Settings: Chronology, Sources, Style*. Oxford: Clarendon Press, 1994.

Copeland, Roger, and Marshall Cohen. *What Is Dance? Readings in Theory and Criticism*. New York: Oxford University Press, 1983.

Corazzol, Adriana Guarnieri. "Opera and Verismo: Regressive Points of View and the Artifice of Alienation." Translated by Roger Parker. *Cambridge Opera Journal* 5 (1993): 39–53.

Cortizo, Encina. "La zarzuela espagnole du XIXe siècle: Relations et divergences avec le théâtre français du XIXe siècle (1832–1866)." In *Échanges musicaux franco-espagnols, XVIIe–XIXe siècles: Actes des rencontres de Villecroze*, edited by François Lesure. Paris: Klincksieck, 2000. 62–122.

Crossley, Ceri. *French Historians and Romanticism: Thierry, Guizot, the Saint-Simonians, Quinet, Michelet*. London: Routledge, 1993.

Curtiss, Mina. *Bizet and His World*. New York: Alfred A. Knopf, 1958.

Dahlhaus, Carl. *Grundlagen der Musikgeschichte*. Cologne: Musikverlag Hans Gerig, 1977.

Dean, Winton. *Bizet*. 3rd ed. Revised reprint. London: J. M. Dent and Sons, 1975.

Denommé, Robert T. *The French Parnassian Poets*. Carbondale: Southern Illinois University Press, 1972.

————. *Leconte de Lisle*. New York: Twayne, 1973.

de Van, Gilles. *Verdi's Theater: Creating Drama through Music*. Translated by Gilda Roberts. Chicago: University of Chicago Press, 1998.

Drillon, Lilyane. "Carmen, regards croisés." In *Actes du colloque Carmen miradas cruzadas*. Seville: Institut Culturel Français de Seville, 2002. 14–17.

Drummond, John. *Speaking of Diaghilev*. London: Faber and Faber, 1997.

Drüner, Ulrich. "La version parisienne du *Tannhäuser* de Richard Wagner, ou L'introduction du psychologique dans le grand opéra." In *Le théâtre lyrique en France au XIXe siècle*, edited by Paul Prévost. Metz: Éditions Serpenoise, 1995. 163–80.

Drysdale, John D. *Louis Véron and the Finances of the Académie Royale de Musique*. Perspektiven der Opernforschung 9. Frankfurt am Main: Peter Lang, 2003.

Dufief, Anne-Simone. "*Sapho:* Du roman au livret." In *Le livret d'opéra au temps de Massenet: Actes du colloque des 9–10 novembre 2001, Festival Massenet*, edited by Alban Ramaut and Jean-Christophe Branger. Saint-Étienne: Publications de l'Université de Saint-Etienne, 2002. 303–27.

Duhamel, Raoul. *Lucien Fugère*. Paris: Bernard Grasset, 1929.

Dunn, Susan. "Michelet and Lamartine: Regicide, Passion, and Compassion." *History and Theory* 28, no. 3 (1989): 275–95.

Eckart-Bäcker, Ursula. *Frankreichs Musik zwischen Romantik und Moderne.* Regensburg: Bosse, 1965.

Ellis, Katharine. "Funding Grand Opera in Regional France: Ideologies of the Mid-Nineteenth Century." In *Art and Ideology in European Opera,* edited by Clive Brown, David Cooper, and Rachel Cowgill. Woodbridge: Boydell and Brewer, forthcoming.

———. *Interpreting the Musical Past: Early Music in Nineteenth-Century France.* Oxford: Oxford University Press, 2005.

———. *Music Criticism in Nineteenth-Century France. "La revue et gazette musicale de Paris," 1834–1880.* Cambridge: Cambridge University Press, 1995.

———. "Rewriting *Don Giovanni,* or 'The Thieving Magpies.'" *Journal of the Royal Musical Association* 119 (1994): 212–50.

———. "Wagnerism and Anti-Wagnerism in the Paris Periodical Press." In *Von Wagner zum Wagnérisme: Musik, Literatur, Kunst, Politik,* edited by Annegret Fauser and Manuela Schwartz. Deutsch-Französische Kulturbibliothek 12. Leipzig: Leipziger Universitätsverlag, 1999. 51–83.

"European Cultural Transfer in the Eighteenth-Century Cultures in Europe." Proceedings of the Eleventh Quadrennial Congress of the International Society of Eighteenth-Century Studies. University of California, Los Angeles, 3–10 August 2003.

Espagne, Michel. *Les transferts culturels franco-allemands.* Paris: Presses Universitaires de France, 1999.

Everist, Mark. "Enshrining Mozart: *Don Giovanni* and the Viardot Circle." *Nineteenth-Century Music* 25 (2001–2): 165–89.

———. *Giacomo Meyerbeer and Music Drama in Nineteenth-Century France.* Aldershot: Ashgate, 2005.

———. "Lindoro in Lyon: Rossini's *Le barbier de Séville.*" *Acta Musicologica* 63 (1992): 50–85.

——— "Mozart and *L'impresario.*" In *"L'esprit français" und die Musik Europas: Entstehung, Einfluß und Grenzen einer ästhetischen Doktrin,* edited by Rainer Schmusch and Michelle Biget-Mainfroy. Hildesheim and New York: Olms, 2007. 420–33.

———. *Music Drama at the Paris Odéon, 1824–1828.* Berkeley and Los Angeles: University of California Press, 2002.

———. "Theatres of Litigation: Stage Music at the Théâtre de la Renaissance, 1838–1840." *Cambridge Opera Journal* 16, no. 2 (2004): 133–61.

Fauquet, Joël-Marie, ed. *Dictionnaire de la musique en France au XIXe siècle.* Paris: Fayard, 2003.

Fauser, Annegret. *Musical Encounters in the 1889 Paris World Fair.* Rochester, NY: University of Rochester Press, 2005.

———. "Phantasmagorie im deutschen Wald? Zur *Freischütz*-Rezeption in London und Paris 1824." In *Deutsche Meister—Böse Geister? Nationale Selbstfindung in der Musik,* edited by Hermann Danuser and Herfried Münkler. Schliengen: Edition Argus, 2001. 245–73.

Fenlon, Iain. *Music and Patronage in Sixteenth-Century Mantua. Music and Patronage in Sixteenth-Century Mantua.* Vol. 1. Cambridge and New York: Cambridge University Press, 1980.

Février, Henry. *André Messager: Mon maître, mon ami.* Paris: Amiot-Dumont, 1948.

Fulcher, Jane F. *French Cultural Politics & Music: From the Dreyfus Affair to the First World War.* New York: Oxford University Press, 1999.

———. *The Nation's Image: French Grand Opera as Politics and Politicized Art.* Cambridge: Cambridge University Press, 1987.

Gallus, A. [Arthur Wisner.] *Emma Calvé: Her Artistic Life.* New York: R. H. Russell, 1902.

Garafola, Lynn, ed. *Rethinking the Sylph: New Perspectives on the Romantic Ballet.* Hanover, NH: University Press of New England, 1997.

Gerhard, Anselm. *The Urbanization of Opera: Music Theater in Paris in the Nineteenth Century.* Translated by Mary Whittall. Chicago: University of Chicago Press, 1998.

Giger, Andreas, "Verismo." In *Handwörterbuch der musikalischen Terminologie.* Wiesbaden: Steiner, 2004.

Gildea, Robert. *The Past in French History.* New Haven, CT: Yale University Press, 1996.

Girard, Georges. *Emma Calvé: La cantatrice sous tous les ciels.* Millau: Éd. Grand Causse, 1983.

———. "Emma Calvé étoile dans tous les cieux, cigale sous tous les ciels." *Les cahiers Rouergats* 5 (1971): 9–46.

Gooch, George Peabody. *History and Historians in the Nineteenth Century.* London: Longman, 1952.

Goodwin, Noël. "Sight and Sound: Fokine and Chopin." *Dance and Dancers* (November 1991): 15–17.

Gossman, Lionel. *Between Literature and History.* Cambridge, MA: Harvard University Press, 1990.

———. "The Go-Between: Jules Michelet, 1798–1894." *MLN* 89, no. 4 (1974): 503–41.

Goubault, Christian. "La décentralisation de l'art lyrique à Rouen (1830–1900)." In *Regards sur l'opéra: Du "Ballet comique de la reine" à l'Opéra de Pékin,* edited by Elisabeth Bernard. Paris: Presses Universitaires de France, 1976. 47–85.

Gourret, Jean. *Histoire de l'opéra-comique.* Paris: Éditions Albatros, 1983.

Grand-Carteret, John. *Les mœurs et la caricature en France.* Paris: À la Librairie Illustrée, 1888.

Grayson, David. "Debussy on Stage." In *The Cambridge Companion to Debussy,* edited by Simon Trezise. Cambridge: Cambridge University Press, 2003. 61–83.

———. *The Genesis of Debussy's "Pelléas et Mélisande."* Ann Arbor, MI: UMI Research Press, 1986.

Guest, Ivor Forbes. *Fanny Cerrito: The Life of a Romantic Ballerina.* 2nd, revised edition. London: Dance Books, 1974.

———. *Fanny Elssler.* Middletown, CT: Wesleyan University Press, 1970.

———. *Jules Perrot: Master of the Romantic Ballet.* London: Dance Books, 1984.

———. *The Romantic Ballet in Paris.* Middletown, CT.: Wesleyan University Press, [1966].

Hadlock, Heather. *Mad Loves: Women and Music in Offenbach's "Les contes d'Hoffmann."* Princeton, NJ: Princeton University Press, 2000.

Hallman, Diana R. *Opera, Liberalism, and Antisemitism in Nineteenth-Century France: The Politics of Halévy's "La Juive."* Cambridge: Cambridge University Press, 2002.

Harris-Warrick, Rebecca. "Historical Introduction." In Gaetano Donizetti, Alphonse Royer, Gustave Vaëz, and Eugène Scribe, *La favorite: Opéra en quatre actes,* edited by Rebecca Harris-Warrick. Critical ed. 2 vols. Milan: Ricordi, 1997. 1:xvii–xx.

Harris-Warrick, Rebecca, David Charlton, Janet Johnson, Richard Langham Smith, and Charles Pitt. "Paris." In *The New Grove Dictionary of Opera,* edited by Stanley Sadie. 4 vols. London: Macmillan, 1992. 3:855–82.

Heidlberger, Frank. *Carl Maria von Weber und Hector Berlioz.* Würzburger Musikhistorische Beiträge 14. Tutzing: Hans Schneider, 1994.

Hemmings, Frederick William John. *Theatre and State in France, 1760–1905.* Cambridge: Cambridge University Press, 1994.

Hess, Carol A. *Manuel de Falla and Modernism in Spain, 1898–1936.* Chicago: University of Chicago Press, 2001

Hibberd, Sarah. "'Dormez donc, mes chers amours': Hérold's *La somnambule* (1827) and Dream Phenomena on the Parisian Lyric Stage." *Cambridge Opera Journal* 16, no. 2 (2004): 107–32.

———. *French Grand Opera and the Historical Imagination.* Cambridge: Cambridge University Press, 2009.

———. "*La muette* and Her Context." In *The Cambridge Companion to Grand Opera,* edited by David Charlton. Cambridge: Cambridge University Press, 2003. 149–67.

Hoffmann, Léon-François. *Romantique Espagne: L'image de l'Espagne en France entre 1800 et 1850.* Paris: Presses Universitaires de France, 1961.

Huebner, Steven. *French Opera at the* fin de siècle*: Wagnerism, Nationalism, and Style.* Oxford: Oxford University Press, 1999.

———. "*La Navarraise* face au vérisme." In *Le naturalisme sur la scène lyrique,* edited by Jean-Christophe Branger. Saint Étienne: Publications de l'Université de Saint Étienne, 2004. 129–49.

———. "Opera Audiences in Paris, 1830–70." *Music & Letters* 70 (1989): 206–25.

———. *The Operas of Charles Gounod.* Oxford: Clarendon Press, 1990.

Hunt, Lynn. *Politics, Culture, and Class in the French Revolution.* New ed. Berkeley: University of California Press, 2004.

Irvine, Demar. *Jules Massenet: A Chronicle of His Life and Times.* Portland, OR: Amadeus Press, 1994.

Istel, Edgar. *Bizet und "Carmen": Der Künstler und sein Werk.* Stuttgart: J. Engelhorns Nachf., 1927.

Jacobshagen, Arnold. "Staging at the Opéra-Comique in Nineteenth-Century Paris: Auber's *Fra Diavolo* and the *livrets de mise en scène.*" *Cambridge Opera Journal* 13, no. 3 (2001): 239–60.

John, Nicholas, ed. *Aida: Giuseppe Verdi.* English National Opera Guide 2. New York: Riverrun Press, 1980.

Johnson, Douglas. "Historians." In *The French Romantics,* edited by Donald Geoffrey Charlton. Cambridge: Cambridge University Press, 1984. 2:274–307.

Johnson, James H. *Listening in Paris: A Cultural History.* Studies on the History of Society and Culture 21. Berkeley and Los Angeles: University of California Press, 1995.

Johnson, Janet L. "The Théâtre Italien and Opera and Theatrical Life in Restoration Paris, 1818–1827." Ph.D. diss., University of Chicago, 1988.

Join-Diéterle, Catherine. *Les décors de scène de l'Opéra de Paris à l'époque Romantique.* Paris: Picard, 1988.

———. "La monarchie, source d'inspiration de l'opéra, à l'époque romantique." *Revue d'histoire du theatre* 35, no. 4 (1983): 430–41.

Jost, Peter. "Zu den französischen Übersetzungen von Wagners Schriften zu Lebzeiten." In *"Schlagen Sie die Kraft der Reflexion nicht zu gering an": Beiträge zu Richard Wagners Denken, Werk und Wirken,* edited by Klaus Döge, Christa Jost, and Peter Jost. Mainz: Schott, 2002. 32–47.

Kahan, Sylvia. *Music's Modern Muse: A Life of Winnaretta Singer, Princesse de Polignac.* Rochester, NY: University of Rochester Press, 2003.

Kahane, Martine, and Nicole Wild, eds. *Wagner et la France.* Paris: Éditions Herscher, 1983. An exhibition catalog.

Kelkel, Manfred. *Naturalisme, vérisme et réalisme dans l'opéra de 1890 à 1930.* Paris: Librairie philosophique J. Vrin, 1984.

Kerman, Joseph. *Opera as Drama.* New and revised ed. Berkeley and Los Angeles: University of California Press, 1988.

Klein, Herman. *Great Women Singers of My Time.* London: Routledge, 1931.

Kracauer, Siegfried. *Jacques Offenbach und das Paris seiner Zeit.* Frankfurt am Main: Suhrkamp, 1994.

Krakovitch, Odile. *Hugo censuré: La liberté au théâtre au XIXe siècle.* Paris: Calmann-Lévy, 1985.

———. *Les pièces de théâtres soumises à la censure, 1800–1830: Inventaire.* Paris: Archives Nationales, 1982.

Kroen, Sheryl. *Politics and Theater: The Crisis of Legitimacy in Restoration France, 1815–1830.* Berkeley: University of California Press, 2000.

Küster, Konrad. *Beethoven.* Stuttgart: Deutsche Verlagsanstalt, 1994.

Lacombe, Hervé. "Définitions des genres lyriques dans les dictionnaires français du XIXème siècle." In *Le théâtre lyrique en France au XIXeme siècle,* edited by Paul Prevost. Metz: Serpenoise, 1995. 297–334.

———. "L'Espagne à l'Opéra-Comique avant *Carmen*: Du *Guitarrero* de Halévy (1841) à *Don César de Bazan* de Massenet (1872)." In *Échanges musicaux franco-espagnols, XVIIe–XIXe siècles: Actes des rencontres de Villecroze,* edited by François Lesure. Paris: Klincksieck, 2000. 161–93.

———. "L'Espagne à Paris au milieu du XIXe siècle (1847–1857): L'influence d'artistes espagnols sur l'imaginaire parisien et la construction d'une 'hispanicité.' " *Revue de musicologie* 88, no. 2 (2002): 389–431.

———. *Georges Bizet: Naissance d'une identité créatrice.* Paris: Fayard, 2000.

———. *The Keys to French Opera in the Nineteenth Century.* Translated by Edward Schneider. Berkeley and Los Angeles: University of California Press, 2001.

———. "The 'Machine' and the State." In *The Cambridge Companion to Grand Opera,* edited by David Charlton. Cambridge: Cambridge University Press, 2003. 21–42.

———. "La version primitive de l'air d'entrée de Carmen: Réflexion sur la dramaturgie et l''autorialité' d'un opéra." In *Aspects de l'opéra français de Meyerbeer à Honegger,* edited by Jean-Christophe Branger and Vincent Giroud. Lyon: Symétrie, 2009. 29–45.

———. "The Writing of Exoticism in the Libretti of the Opéra-Comique, 1825–1862." *Cambridge Opera Journal* 11, no. 2 (1999): 135–58.

Langer, Arne. *Der Regisseur und die Aufzeichnungspraxis in der Opernregie im 19. Jahrhundert.* Perspektiven der Opernforschung 4. Frankfurt am Main: Peter Lang, 1997.

Laparra, Raoul. *Bizet et l'Espagne.* Paris: Delagrave, 1935.

Las Cases, Emmanuel [comte de]. *Le mémorial de Sainte-Hélène.* Paris: Gallimard, 1963.

Ledout, Annie. "Le théâtre des Bouffes-Parisiens, historique et programmes, 1855–1880." Ph.D. diss., Université de Paris IV, 2001.

Legrand, Raphaëlle, and Nicole Wild. *Regards sur l'opéra-comique: Trois siècles de vie théâtrale.* Paris: Éditions du CNRS, 2002.

Leroy, Dominique. "Personnel artistique et formation du star system." In *Histoire des arts du spectacle en France.* Paris: Éditions L'Harmattan, 1990. 254–56.

Lesure, François. *Claude Debussy: Biographie critique.* Paris: Klincksieck, 1994.

———. "La longue attente de *Pelléas* (1895–1898)." *Cahiers Debussy* 15 (1991): 3–12.

———, ed. *Échanges musicaux franco-espagnols, XVIIe–XIXe siècles: Actes des rencontres de Villecroze.* Paris: Klincksieck, 2000.

Levin, David. "Reading a Staging/Staging a Reading." *Cambridge Opera Journal* 9, no. 1 (1997): 47–71.

Levinson, André. *Ballet Old and New.* Translated by Susan Cook Summer. New York: Dance Horizons, 1982.

———. *Marie Taglioni.* Edited by Louis Schneider. Paris: Librairie Félix Alcan, 1929.

Lipschutz, Ilse Hempel. *Spanish Painting and the French Romantics.* Cambridge, MA: Harvard University Press, 1972.

Locke, Ralph P. "A Broader View of Musical Exoticism." *Journal of Musicology* 24 (2007): 477–521.

———. *Musical Exoticism: Images and Reflections.* Cambridge: Cambridge University Press, 2009.

———. "Paris: A Centre of Intellectual Ferment." In *The Early Romantic Era: Between the Revolutions, 1789 and 1848,* edited by Alexander Ringer. Englewood Cliffs, NJ: Prentice Hall, 1990. 32–83.

———. "What Are These Women Doing in Opera?" In *En travesti: Women, Gender Subversion, Opera,* edited by Corinne Blackmer and Patricia Juliana Smith. New York: Columbia University Press, 1995. 59–98.

Lockspeiser, Edward. *Debussy: His Life and Mind.* Corrected ed. 2 vols. Cambridge: Cambridge University Press, 1978.

Lomax, Sandra. "Fokine's Manifesto and *Les sylphides.*" In *New Directions in Dance,* edited by D. T. Taplin. Toronto: Pergamon Press, 1979. 113–20.

Loubinoux, Gérard. "Le chercheur d'esprit, ou Offenbach et la mémoire du xviiie siècle." In *Retour au xviiie siècle,* edited by Roland Morier and Hervé Hasquin. Études sur le xviiie siècle 22. Brussels: Éditions de l'Université de Bruxelles, 1994. 63–76.

Macdonald, Hugh, ed. *Selected Letters of Berlioz.* Translated by Roger Nichols. New York: W.W. Norton, 1997.

Maingueneau, Dominique. *Carmen: Les racines d'un mythe.* Paris: Du Sorbier, 1985.

Mansel, Philip. *Paris between Empires, 1814–1852.* London: John Murray, 2001.

Manuel, Peter. "From Scarlatti to 'Guantanamera': Dual Tonicity in Spanish and Latin American Musics." *Journal of the American Musicological Society* 88 (2002): 311–36.

Martin-Fugier, Anne. *Comédienne: De Melle Mars à Sarah Bernhardt.* Paris: Éditions du Seuil, 2001.

Martinoty, Jean-Louis. "De la réalité au réalisme." In *Carmen,* vol. 26 of *L'avant-scène opéra* (1980): 100–106.

Martí y Perez, Josep i, et al. "Spain, II: Traditional and Popular Music." In *The New Grove Dictionary of Music and Musicians,* edited by Stanley Sadie. 2nd ed. 29 vols. London: Macmillan, 2001. 24:135–54.

Mattsson, Inger, ed. *Gustavian Opera: An Interdisciplinary Reader in Swedish Opera, Dance and Theatre, 1771–1809.* Stockholm: Royal Swedish Academy of Music, 1991.

McClary, Susan. *Conventional Wisdom: The Content of Musical Form.* Berkeley and Los Angeles: University of California Press, 2000.

———. *Georges Bizet: Carmen.* Cambridge: Cambridge University Press, 1992.

McCready, Anna. "Gilding the Lily: Music and Monarchy in Paris (1814–1833)." Ph.D. diss., King's College, University of London, 2003.

Menneret, Pierre. "La musique de scène en France de Napoléon III à Poincaré, 1852–1914." Ph.D. diss., Paris Conservatoire, 1973.

Mikkelsen, Carol, ed. *Spanish Theater Songs: Baroque and Classical Eras.* Van Nuys, CA: Alfred, 1998. 49–53.

Mitjana, Rafael. "La musique en Espagne." In *Encyclopédie de la musique et dictionnaire du Conservatoire,* edited by Albert Lavignac and Lionel de La Laurencie. 11 vols. Paris: C. Delagrave, 1913–31. Part 1, vol. 4 (1920), 2296–98.

Mongrédien, Jean. *French Music from the Enlightenment to Romanticism, 1789–1830.* Translated by Sylvain Frémaux. Edited by Reinhard G. Pauly. Portland, OR: Amadeus Press, 1996.

Murphy, Kerry. "Berlioz, Meyerbeer, and the Place of Jewishness in Criticism." In *Berlioz: Past, Present, Future; Bicentenary Essays,* edited by Peter Bloom. Rochester, NY: University of Rochester Press, 2003. 93–96.

Newcomb, Anthony. *The Madrigal at Ferrara, 1579–1597.* Princeton, NJ: Princeton University Press, 1978.

Newark, Cormac. "Ceremony, Celebration, and Spectacle in *La juive*." In *Reading Critics Reading*, edited by Roger Parker and Mary Ann Smart. Oxford: Oxford University Press, 2001. 155–87.

———. "Staging Grand Opéra: History and the Imagination in Nineteenth-Century Paris." Ph.D. diss., Oxford University, 1999.

Nicolaisen, Jay. *Italian Opera in Transition, 1871–1893*. Ann Arbor: UMI Research Press, 1977.

Nicolodi, Fiamma. "Parigi e l'opera verista: Dibatti, riflessioni, polemiche." *Nuova rivista musicale italiana* 15 (1981): 577–623.

Northup, George T. "The Influence of George Borrow upon Prosper Mérimée." *Modern Philology* 13, no. 3 (1915): 143–56.

Nuñez, Faustino. "Polo." In *Diccionario de la música española e hispanoamericana*, edited by Emilio Casares Rodicio, José López-Calo, Ismael Fernández de la Cuesta, and María Luz González Penña. 10 vols. [Madrid?]: Sociedad General de Autores y Editores, 1999–2002. 8:873–74.

Ogbor, John O., and Johnnie Williams. "The Cross-Cultural Transfer of Management Practices: The Case for Creative Synthesis." *Cross-Cultural Management: An International Journal* 10 (2003): 3–23.

Olin, Elinor Nichols. "Concerts de l'Opéra, 1895–97: New Music at the Monument Garnier." *Nineteenth-Century Music* 16 (1993): 253–66.

———. "*Le ton et la parole:* Melodrama in France, 1871–1913." Ph.D. diss., Northwestern University, 1991.

Olivier, Brigitte. *J. Massenet: Itinéraire pour un théâtre musical*. Arles: Actes Sud, 1996.

Orr, Linda. *Headless History: Nineteenth-Century French Historiography of the Revolution*. Ithaca, NY: Cornell University Press, 1990.

Ozouf, Mona. *La fête révolutionnaire, 1789–99*. Paris: Gallimard, 1976.

———. *L'homme régénéré: Essais sur la révolution française*. Paris: Gallimard, 1989.

Parakilas, James. "How Spain Got a Soul." In *The Exotic in Western Music*, edited by Jonathan Bellman. Boston: Northeastern University Press, 1998. 137–93.

Parker, Roger. "*Don Carlos*." In *Grove Music Online*, edited by L. Macy. http://www.grovemusic.com (accessed 6 November 2004).

———. "Reading the *livrets,* or The Chimera of 'Authentic' Staging." In *Leonora's Last Act: Essays in Verdian Discourse*. Princeton, NJ: Princeton University Press, 1997. 126–46.

Patureau, Frédérique. *Le Palais Garnier dans la société parisienne, 1875–1914*. Liège: Pierre Mardaga, 1991.

Pendle, Karin, and Stephen Wilkins. "Paradise Found: The Salle le Peletier and French Grand Opera." In *Opera in Context: Essays on Historical Staging from the Late Renaissance to the Time of Puccini,* edited by Mark A. Radice. Portland, OR: Amadeus Press, 1998. 171–207.

Perchellet, Jean-Pierre. *L'héritage classique: La tragédie entre 1680 et 1814*. Paris: Honoré Champion, 2004.

Pitt, Charles. Liner notes to Daniel-François-Esprit Auber, *Gustave III, ou Le bal masque*.

French Lyrique Orchestra. Michel Swierczewski. With Laurence Dale. ARN 368220. Paris: Arion, 1993.

Poriss, Hilary. "A Madwoman's Choice: Aria Substitution in *Lucia di Lammermoor.*" *Cambridge Opera Journal* 13, no. 1 (2001): 1–28.

Pottinger, Mark. "The Staging of History in France: Characterizations of Historical Figures in French Grand Opera During the Reign of Louis-Philippe (D. F. E. Auber, Louis Niedermeyer, F. Halévy, Giacomo Meyerbeer)." Ph.D. diss., City University of New York, 2005.

Prioron-Pinelli, Béatrice. *"Le Juif errant," paroles d'E. Scribe et d'H. V. de Saint-Georges, musique de F. Halévy: Un grand opéra français au début du Second Empire.* 2 vols. Weinsberg: Musik-Edition Lucie Galland, 2005.

Pugliese, Romana Margherita. "The Origins of *Lucia di Lammermoor*'s Cadenza." *Cambridge Opera Journal* 16, no. 1 (2004): 23–42.

Putter, Irving. *Leconte de Lisle and His Contemporaries.* Berkeley: University of California Press, 1951.

Radomski, James. *Manuel García, 1775–1832: Chronicle of the Life of a Bel Canto Tenor at the Dawn of Romanticism.* Oxford: Oxford University Press, 2000.

Rees, Brian. *Camille Saint-Saëns: A Life.* London: Chatto and Windus; Random House, 1999.

Reicher, Gil [Gilberte Guillaumie-Reicher]. *Gautier et l'Espagne.* Paris: Hachette, [1935?].

Revel, Jean François. "Théophile Gautier et le goût pour l'Espagne en France au XIXe siècle." Introduction to Théophile Gautier, *Voyage en Espagne.* Paris: Julliard, 1964. 9–24.

Reyna, Ferdinand. "Ballet, History of." In *Concise Encyclopedia of Ballet.* Paris: Librairie Larousse, 1967. Revised and translated by André Gâteau. Glasgow: Wm. Collins Sons, 1974. 19.

Robert, Grace. *The Borzoi Book of Ballets.* New York: A. A. Knopf, 1946.

Robichez, Jacques. *Le symbolisme au théâtre: Lugné-Poe et les débuts de l'Œuvre.* Paris: L'Arche, 1957.

Rogers, Paul Patrick. "Spanish Influence on the Literature of France." *Hispania* 9 (1926): 205–35.

Röschenthaler, Ute M. "Translocal Cultures: The Slave Trade and Cultural Transfer in the Cross River Reason." *Social Anthropology* 14 (2006): 71–91.

Rosow, Lois. "Performing a Choral Dialogue by Lully." *Early Music* 15 (1987): 325–35.

Ross, James. "Crisis and Transformation: French Opera, Politics and the Press, 1897–1903." D.Phil. diss., Oxford University, 1998.

Saby, Pierre. *Vocabulaire de l'opéra.* Paris: Éditions Minerve, 1999.

Sadie, Stanley, ed. *The New Grove Dictionary of Opera.* 4 vols. London: Macmillan, 1992.

Salès, Jules. *Théâtre Royal de la Monnaie, 1856–1970.* Nivelles: Éditions Havaux, [1971].

Samuels, Maurice. *The Spectacular Past: Popular History and the Novel in Nineteenth-Century France.* Ithaca, NY: Cornell University Press, 2004.

Sansone, Matteo. "Verismo." In *New Grove Dictionary of Music and Musicians,* edited by Stanley Sadie. 2nd ed. 29 vols. London: Macmillan, 2001. 26:477–78.

Schneider, Herbert. *Chronologisch-thematisches Verzeichnis sämtlicher Werke von Daniel François Esprit Auber (AWV).* 2 vols. Hildesheim: Olms, 1994.

———. *"Gustave III, ou Le bal masqué."* In *The New Grove Dictionary of Opera,* edited by Stanley Sadie. 4 vols. London: Macmillan, 1992. 2:583–84.

———. "Scribe and Auber: Constructing Grand Opera." In *The Cambridge Companion to Grand Opera,* edited by David Charlton. Cambridge: Cambridge University Press, 2003. 168–88.

Schwartz, Manuela. *Wagner-Rezeption und französische Oper des Fin de siècle.* Berliner Musik Studien 18. Sinzig: Studio Verlag Schewe, 1999.

Sheehy, Helen. *Eleonora Duse: A Biography.* New York: Alfred A. Knopf, 2003.

Scherer, Jacques. *La dramaturgie classique en France.* Paris: Librairie Nizet, n.d.

Slonimskii, Yuri. *'Sil'fida' balet* Leningrad: Academia, 1927.

Smart, Mary Ann. "The Silencing of Lucia." *Cambridge Opera Journal* 4, no. 2 (1992): 119–41.

Smith, Marian. *Ballet and Opera in the Age of "Giselle."* Princeton, NJ: Princeton University Press, 2000.

———. "The Disappearing Danseur." *Cambridge Opera Journal* 19, no. 1 (2007): 33–57.

Solliers, Jean de. "Zur Mendelssohn-Rezeption in Frankreich." *Beiträge zur Musikwissenschaft* 15 (1973): 209–12.

Soubies, Albert. *Histoire du Théâtre-Lyrique.* Paris: Librairie Fischbacher, 1899.

———. *Soixante-neuf ans de l'Opéra-Comique en deux pages: De la première de "La dame blanche" à la millième de "Mignon," 1825–1894.* Paris: Librairie Fischbacher, 1894.

———. *Soixante-sept ans de l'Opéra en une page: Du "Siège de Corinthe" à "La Walkyrie" (1826–1893).* Paris: Librairie Fischbacher, 1893.

———. *Le Théâtre-Italien de 1801 à 1913.* Paris: Librairie Fischbacher, 1913.

Speare, Mary Jane. "The Transformation of Opéra-Comique: 1850–1880." Ph.D. diss., Washington University, 1997.

Spies, André Michael. *Opera, State and Society in the Third Republic (1875–1914).* New York: Peter Lang, 1998.

Starobinski, Jean. *L'invention de la liberté, 1700–89.* Geneva: Skira, 1987.

Strasser, Michael. "The Société Nationale and Its Adversaries: The Musical Politics of *l'invasion germanique* in the 1870s." *Nineteenth-Century Music* 24 (2001): 225–51.

Svetlov, Valerien. *Le ballet contemporain.* Translated by Michel Calvocaressi. Paris: M. de Brunoff, 1912.

Taruskin, Richard. *Stravinsky and the Russian Traditions: A Biography of the Works through "Mavra."* Berkeley and Los Angeles: University of California Press, 1996.

Tavora, Salvador. "Carmen, regards croisés." In *Actes du colloque Carmen miradas cruzadas.* Seville: Institut Culturel Français de Seville, 2002. 76–82.

Témime, Émile. "Les Français en Espagne au milieu du XIXe siècle: Une migration privilégiée." In *Exil politique et migration économique: Espagnols et Français aux XIXe–*

XXe siècles, edited by CNRS, Groupement de Recherche (0030). Paris: Éditions du CNRS, 1991. 55–69.

Thiès, Renée de. *Des poètes parnassiens: Entretiens.* Paris: J. Grassin, 1995.

Tiersot, Julien. "Bizet and Spanish Music." Translated by Theodore Baker. *Musical Quarterly* 13 (1927): 566–81.

Treadwell, James. "Reading and Staging Again." *Cambridge Opera Journal* 10, no. 2 (1998): 205–20.

Turbow, Gerald D. "Art and Politics: Wagnerism in France." In *Wagnerism in European Culture and Politics,* edited by David C. Large and William Weber. Ithaca, NY: Cornell University Press, 1984. 134–66.

Van der Merwe, Peter. *Roots of the Classical: The Popular Origins of Western Music.* Oxford: Oxford University Press, 2004.

Vizentini, Albert. *My Recollections.* Translated by H. Villiers Barnett. Freeport, NY: Books for Libraries Press, 1970.

Walsh, T. J. *Second Empire Opera: The Théâtre Lyrique, Paris, 1851–1870.* London: John Calder; New York: Riverrun Press, 1981.

Weaver, William. *Duse: A Biography.* San Diego: Harcourt, Brace, Jovanovich, 1984.

Wenderoth, Valeria. "The Making of Exoticism in French Operas of the 1890s." Ph.D. diss., University of Hawaii, 2004.

Werner, Michael, and Michel Espagne, eds. *Transferts: Les relations interculturelles dans l'espace franco-allemand (XVIIIe et XIXe siècle).* Paris: Éditions Recherche sur les Civilisations, 1988.

White, Hayden. *Metahistory: The Historical Imagination in Nineteenth-Century Europe.* Baltimore: John Hopkins University Press, 1973.

Wilberg, Rebecca Susan. "The 'Mise en Scène' at the Paris Opéra, Salle Le Peletier (1821–1873) and the Staging of the First French 'Grand Opéra': Meyerbeer's *Robert le Diable.*" Ph.D. diss., Brigham Young University, 1990.

Wild, Nicole. *Dictionnaire des théâtres parisiens au XIXe siècle: Les théâtres et la musique.* Paris: Aux Amateurs de Livres, 1989.

———. "Musique et théâtres parisiens face au pouvoir (1807–1864) avec inventaire et historique des salles." 3 vols. Ph.D. diss., Université de Paris IV, 1987.

———. "Théâtre-Lyrique." In *Dictionnaire de la musique en France au XIXe siècle,* edited by Joël-Marie Fauquet. Paris: Fayard, 2003. 1209.

Wilson-Bareau, Juliet. "Manet and Spain." In *Manet/Velazquez. The French Taste for Spanish Painting,* edited by Gary Tinterow and Genevieve Lacambre. New York: Metropolitan Museum of Modern Art; New Haven, CT: Yale University Press, 2003. 203–57.

Wolff, Stéphane. *Un demi-siècle d'opéra-comique.* Paris: André Bonne, 1953.

Wright, Beth Segal. *Painting and History during the French Restoration: Abandoned by the Past.* Cambridge: Cambridge University Press, 1997.

Wright, Lesley A. "Berlioz in the *fin-de-siècle* Press." In *Berlioz: Past, Present, Future; Bicentenary Essays,* edited by Peter Bloom. Rochester, NY: University of Rochester Press, 2003. 160–66.

———. "A Musical Commentary." In *Carmen: Bizet,* edited by Nicholas John. English National Opera Guide 13. London: John Calder, 1982. 19–44.

———. "Une critique revisitée: L'accueil de *Carmen* à Paris en 1883." In *Musique, esthétique et société au XIXe siècle: Liber amicorum Joël-Marie Fauquet,* edited by Damien Colas, Florence Gétreau, and Malou Haine. Wavre: Mardaga, 2007. 187–97.

Yon, Jean-Claude. "La création du Théâtre des Bouffes-Parisiens (1855–1862), ou La difficile naissance de l'opérette." *Revue d'histoire moderne et contemporaine* 39 (1992): 575–600.

———. *Jacques Offenbach.* Paris: Éditions Gallimard, 2000.

Discography and Filmography

Auber, Daniel-François-Esprit. *Gustave III, ou Le bal masqué.* French Lyrique Orchestra. Michel Swierczewski. With Laurence Dale. ARN 368220. Paris: Arion, 1993.

Bizet, Georges. *Carmen.* Orchestre du Capitole de Toulouse. Michel Plasson. With Angela Gheorghiu and Roberto Alagna. CD 724355743428. EMI Classics, 2003.

Donizetti, Gaetano. *Lucie de Lammermoor.* Orchestre et Chœur de l'Opéra National de Lyon. Evelino Pidò. With Natalie Dessay and Roberto Alagna. 7243 5 45528 2 3. Virgin Classics, 2002.

———. *Lucie de Lammermoor.* Orchestra Internazionale d'Italia. Maruizio Benini. With Patrizia Ciofi and Alexandru Badea. CDS 204/1–2. Genova: Dynamic, 1998.

Emma Calvé. MR 533. Malibran Music, n.d.

Liszt, Franz. *"Rapsodie espagnole" and Other Pieces on Spanish Themes.* Leslie Howard, piano. CDA67145. London: Hyperion, 1997.

Manuel García: Yo que soy contrabandista y otras canciones. Ernesto Palacio, tenor; and Juan José Chuquisengo, piano. DS 0114. Almaviva, 1995.

Reynaldo Hahn. CDRG 127. Malibran Music, n.d.

Sánchez, Felipe, dir. *En un salón de la Habana: Habaneras y contradanzas (1830–1855).* With Noemí Mazoy, soprano; César Carazo, tenor; and other members of Axivil Criollo. CD 64073. RTVE Música, 2000.

Townsend, Robert, dir. *Carmen: A Hip Hopera.* DVD. New Line Home Video, 2001.

CONTRIBUTORS

OLIVIER BARA is *maître de conférences* in nineteenth-century French literature at the Université Lyon 2. He is also a member of the Unité Mixte de Recherches LIRE (CNRS-Université Lyon 2). A specialist on opera and music theater in nineteenth-century France, he has published *Le Théâtre de l'Opéra-Comique sous la Restauration: Enquête autour d'un genre moyen* (2001). He has also edited a special issue of *Orages* titled *Boulevard du crime: Le temps des spectacles oculaires* (2005). He is currently completing a study on George Sand and the theater, *George Sand et le théâtre: Esthétique dramatique et morale de la scène.*

KATHARINE ELLIS is professor of music at Royal Holloway, University of London, and director of the Institute of Musical Research, School of Advanced Study, University of London. Author of *Music Criticism in Nineteenth-Century France* (1995) and *Interpreting the Musical Past* (2005), and joint editor with David Charlton of *The Musical Voyager: Berlioz in Europe* (2007), she has also written numerous journal articles and essays on the cultural history of music. Current projects embrace Chopin's Paris and music in the French regions. She is a former editor of both *Music & Letters* and the *Journal of the Royal Musical Association.*

MARK EVERIST is professor of music at the University of Southampton. His research focuses on the music of the Late Middle Ages, nineteenth-century stage music and Mozart reception. Recent publications include *Music Drama at the Paris Odéon, 1824–1828* (2002), and *Giacomo Meyerbeer and Music Drama in Nineteenth-Century Paris* (2005).

ANNEGRET FAUSER is professor of music at the University of North Carolina at Chapel Hill. She has published on French song and opera, women composers, exoticism, nationalism, reception history, and cultural transfer. Her publications include *Der Orchestergesang in Frankreich, 1870–1920* (1994), *Musical Encounters at the 1889 World Fair in Paris* (2005), and an edition of reviews of the first performance of Jules Massenet's opera *Esclarmonde* (2001); she co-edited, with Manuela Schwartz, a major publication on Wagnerism in France (1999). Currently she is editing the correspondence between Nadia Boulanger and Aaron Copland and writing a monograph on music in the United States during World War II.

DAVID GRAYSON is professor of musicology at the University of Minnesota. The author of *The Genesis of Debussy's "Pelléas et Mélisande"* (1986), he has written about the music of Debussy for American and European journals, including *Nineteenth-Century Music, Music and Letters,* and *Cahiers Debussy,* on whose editorial board he serves. He has contributed to the Cambridge Opera Handbook on *Pelléas, "I consigli del vento che passa": Studi su Debussy,*

Debussy Studies, Debussy and His World, and *The Cambridge Companion to Debussy.* He is completing a critical edition of *Pelléas et Mélisande* for the *Œuvres complètes de Claude Debussy,* to be published by Durand, a project that has involved collaboration with Pierre Boulez and with Claudio Abbado at La Scala.

DIANA R. HALLMAN is associate professor of music at the University of Kentucky. She centers her research on nineteenth-century French opera and cultural history, with a particular focus on French grand opera. She is author of the book *Opera, Liberalism, and Antisemitism in Nineteenth-Century France: The Politics of Halévy's "La Juive"* (2002), as well as chapters and articles on the life and works of composer Fromental Halévy in *The Cambridge Companion to Grand Opera* (2003), *Die Musik in Geschichte und Gegenwart* (2003), and the forthcoming book *Le Prix de Rome de musique (1803–1968).*

REBECCA HARRIS-WARRICK is professor of music at Cornell University in Ithaca, New York. Her research concerns French opera and ballet from the seventeenth to the nineteenth centuries, and she has prepared critical editions of the *Ballet des Amours déguisés* by Jean-Baptiste Lully (2001) and of *La favorite* by Gaetano Donizetti (1997). She is co-author with Carol G. Marsh of *Musical Theatre at the Court of Louis XIV: "Le mariage de la grosse Cathos"* (1994) and co-editor with Bruce A. Brown of *The Grotesque Dancer on the Eighteenth-Century Stage: Gennaro Magri and his World* (2005). At present she is working on a book about the dramatic functions of dance in French opera from Lully to Rameau.

SARAH HIBBERD is lecturer in music at the University of Nottingham. She has published widely on aspects of French opera and other types of music theater (including melodrama and ballet) and recently completed a book for Cambridge University Press titled *French Grand Opera and the Historical Imagination* (2009).

STEVEN HUEBNER is James McGill Professor of Music at McGill University. He has written on French and Italian music of the nineteenth and early twentieth centuries, with a concentration on opera. His articles and reviews have appeared in such journals as *Nineteenth-Century Music, Journal of the American Musicological Society, Cambridge Opera Journal, Music and Letters,* and *Journal of the Royal Musical Association,* as well as in several collections of essays in English, French, and Italian. He is the author of *The Operas of Charles Gounod* (1990) and *French Opera at the* fin de siècle: *Wagnerism, Nationalism, and Style* (1999). He is currently editor of *Cambridge Opera Journal.*

ARNOLD JACOBSHAGEN is professor of musicology at the Hochschule für Musik Köln. His research explores, among other topics, musical theater of the nineteenth and twentieth centuries, especially that of France. Recent publications include *Opera semiseria: Gattungskonvergenz und Kuturtransfer in Musiktheater* (2005), *Strukturwandel der Orchesterlandschaft* (2000), and *Der Chor in der französischen Oper des späten Ancien Régime* (1997). He has also edited and co-edited numerous volumes on music and culture, including *Rebellische Musik: Gesellschaftlicher Protest und kultureller Wandel um 1968* (2007), *Meyerbeer und die Opéra comique* (2004), and *Hector Berlioz in Deutschland* (2002).

PETER LAMOTHE is assistant professor of musicology at Belmont University in Nashville. His research interests include aspects of genre in French music and reception history. His doctoral work was funded through a Pew Younger Fellowship and a Fulbright Fellowship to Paris.

ALICIA LEVIN is a doctoral candidate in musicology at the University of North Carolina at Chapel Hill. Her dissertation investigates the musical life of nineteenth-century Paris through the lens of pianistic virtuosity. She has given papers at conferences in the United States, Great Britain, the Netherlands, and Poland.

RALPH P. LOCKE is professor of musicology at the University of Rochester's Eastman School of Music, and senior editor of the University of Rochester Press's Eastman Studies in Music, a series that has produced over fifty titles. He is the author of *Music, Musicians, and the Saint-Simonians* (1986) and *Musical Exoticism: Images and Reflections* (2009), and a contributing co-editor of *Cultivating Music in America: Women Patrons and Activists since 1860* (1997). Six of his articles on music and society have received the ASCAP–Deems Taylor Award. His 2005 article in *Cambridge Opera Journal* on exoticism in Verdi's *Aida* received the H. Colin Slim Award from the American Musicological Society.

KERRY MURPHY is associate professor of Music at the University of Melbourne. Her book *Hector Berlioz and the Development of French Music Criticism* (1988) was published by UMI Studies in Musicology, and she has published widely on nineteenth-century French music criticism. She also works in the area of Australian music research and has published editions of early Australian opera and art song. She recently coordinated a project investigating amateur music making in Colonial Melbourne, the results of which were published in a special issue of the *Nineteenth-Century Music Review* (2005).

MARIAN SMITH teaches at the University of Oregon, where she received the Thomas Herman Award for Distinguished Teaching in 2007. She also taught at Carleton College as a Benedict Visiting Professor in the fall of 2004. Her articles, essays, and reviews have appeared in *Cambridge Opera Journal, Journal of the American Musicological Society, Dance Research, Dance Chronicle,* and the program books of La Scala and the Royal Ballet (Covent Garden). She is the author of *Ballet and Opera in the Age of Giselle* (2000) and is writing a book, *Hidden Balanchine,* with Lisa Arkin and Beth Genné.

LESLEY A. WRIGHT is professor of music at the University of Hawai'i at Manoa, where, having served an extended stint as chair of the music department, she is the chair of graduate studies. Her numerous publications focus on Bizet and his contemporaries; the music, institutions, and press in nineteenth-century France; the posthumous reception history of Berlioz; and the Exposition of 1900.

INDEX

Académie des Beaux-Arts, 136

Académie Impériale de Musique, 6, 73, 81, 84–86, 94, 97, 230, 379, 382

Académie Royale de Musique, 7, 29, 34, 82, 87, 97, 209, 212–13, 382

Adam, Adolphe, 24–26, 52–54, 58, 62, 75, 82–83, 198, 262, 297, 385, 396–97; *À Clichy,* 82; *La reine d'un jour,* 82; *Le chalet,* 105; *Le muletier de Tolède,* 82; *Le postillon de Lonjumeau,* 13, 15, 25, 388; *Le roi des Halles,* 400; *Le roi malgré lui,* 103; *Le sourd ou L'auberge pleine,* 55, 281; *Richard en Palestine,* 7; *Si j'étais roi,* 55, 400

Adenis, Jules, *La fiancée d'Abydos,* 138

aesthetics, 188, 242, 244, 248, 255, 364

Andalusia, 295, 300, 301, 305, 310, 314, 352

Andalusian songs, 298, 305, 336, 337

Ashton, Lucy, 196–98

Auber, Daniel-François-Esprit, 25, 27, 35–36, 42, 57, 80, 93–94, 182, 239, 249, 255; *Fra Diavolo,* 13, 24, 81, 105, 179, 388; *Gustave III, ou Le bal masqué,* 5, 7, 157–75, 384; *La fiancée,* 23; *La muette de Portici,* 4, 39, 75, 296; *Le cheval de bronze,* 15; *Le domino noir,* 15, 113, 311; *Le lac des fées,* 35, 42–43, 75; *Le philtre,* 39; *Le serment,* 257; *Lestocq,* 15; *Manon Lescaut,* 31, 388

Bach, J. S., 148, 245, 337; F Major Fugue, 262

Bagier, Prosper, 62, 144, 389

ballet, 29, 129–34, 136, 195, 210, 230, 238–39, 253, 256–68, 270–72, 279, 283, 285; ballet-opéra, 30–31; classical dance, 259–60; national dance, 260, 264, 300;

pantomime, 31, 40, 169, 211, 260, 296, 390; props, 58, 69, 260, 262

Balzac, Honoré de, *Gambara,* 1

Barbier, Jules, 112, 122, 131, 135, 139, 141, 144, 285, 369, 386

Barbier, Pierre, 116

Bardoux, Benjamin-Joseph-Agénor, 70

Barrhoilhet, Paul, 199, 213

Barthe, Adrien, 132, 138, 141

Baryton Martin, 22

Basset, Alexandre, 15, 386

Bataille, Henri, and d'Humières, Robert, *La Belle au bois dormant,* 153

Battu, Léon, 89

Baudelaire, Charles, 232, 235, 254

Baurans, Pierre, *La servante maîtresse,* 90

Bayard, Jean-François, 15

Beaumarchais, Pierre, *Le mariage de Figaro,* 290

Beer, Jules, 104, 111

Beethoven, Ludwig van, 3, 93, 148, 222, 230–31, 245, 351; *Die Ruinen von Athen,* 285; *Egmont,* 103, 285, 288, 290

Beinex, Jean-Jacques, *Diva,* 1

Belin, Charles, 193

Bellincioni, Gemma, 365, 367

Bellini, Vincenzo, 146, 200, 215, 249, 388; *I puritani,* 199, 216, 390; *Norma,* 65, 225

Benoist, François, 261; *L'apparition,* 33

Berlioz, Hector, 29, 31, 42–43, 45, 46, 52–53, 75, 82, 148, 211, 213, 222, 223, 234–35, 239, 246, 253, 285, 384, 396; *Béatrice et Bénédict,* 148, 384; *Benvenuto Cellini,* 29, 39, 42–43, 384; *L'enfance du Christ,* 75; *Les Troyens à Carthage,* 29, 52, 55–56, 61, 102, 148, 237, 400